D1202240

A HANDBOOK OF THE
MODERN GREEK LANGUAGE

A HANDBOOK OF THE MODERN GREEK LANGUAGE

Grammar, Texts, Glossary

BY

Albert Thumb

Late Professor of Comparative Philology in Strassburg University
Sometime Professor in the University of Marburg

TRANSLATED FROM THE SECOND IMPROVED AND
ENLARGED GERMAN EDITION BY

S. Angus

ARGONAUT, INC., PUBLISHERS
CHICAGO   MCMLXIV

Library of Congress Catalog Card Number: *64-23434*

FOREWORD TO THE ENGLISH EDITION.

I HAVE been repeatedly approached from the English side with regard to a translation of my *Modern Greek Handbook*. English-speaking scholars are of course sufficiently familiar with the German language to consult German works in the original. But as there is a large number of English-speaking students who cannot do this, and as, besides, it is easier to master a foreign language in a grammar written in one's mother-tongue, I have been very pleased to give my consent when Messrs. T. & T. Clark of Edinburgh desired to arrange for a translation of the second edition of my Handbook, which was recently published and considerably enlarged. The translation gives the text of the German original without alteration, except that a few slips have been removed— partly due to the translator's accuracy.

I desire to express my sincere thanks to Dr. S. Angus for the carefully executed translation; he has performed his task with great ability and with a perfect understanding of the subject.

My wish is that my book, which has gained friends in its German form, may secure new friends in its English dress and contribute to an increased and deepened knowledge of Modern Greek among English-speaking scholars and students.

A. THUMB.

STRASSBURG

TRANSLATOR'S NOTE.

PROFESSOR THUMB'S FOREWORDS render any further words from the Translator unnecessary. The need for such a book as the present has been growingly felt in the English-speaking world. The works on Modern Greek with which the English student is familiar deal either exclusively or for the most part with the καθαρεύουσα, the "Atticizing" learned language of the present day. No fair account is to hand of the modern *vernacular*, which reflects the chequered history of the Greek people, and is alone the true descendant of the ancient language. It is not too much to claim that this book is the first in English to supply the want, and as such must prove welcome to the teachers and students of the Greek language. Professor Thumb's aim is to be practical in two ways,—first, to present a satisfactory account of the latest phase of Greek to those Hellenists who are convinced that they must pass beyond the classical and the Hellenistic periods for the study of a living language with an unbroken history of three thousand years; and, secondly, to furnish a Textbook of the modern Greek vernacular for beginners, as evidenced by the division into Grammar, Texts, and Glossary.

Finally, the Translator has much pleasure in placing before English readers the Handbook which he used in Professor Thumb's own Modern Greek class in Marburg.

S. A.

EDINBURGH

FOREWORD TO THE FIRST GERMAN EDITION.

THE past century witnessed the publication of modern Greek grammars in large numbers. This output corresponds in a certain measure to the sympathy which, during the different decades of the century, Europe bestowed upon modern Greece. We shall find that the number of grammars, pocket-dictionaries, elementary text-books increased in those periods in which the Greeks to a special degree attracted the eyes of Europe, so that the mere statistics of publishing firms could furnish an exact index of the interest of the West in the people of Greece; and, if we are to trust our index, this interest appears to have grown more intense again during the past lustrum. But notwithstanding the enormous output in this field, only a small proportion is of practical service, not a single one of the existing helps being adequate to the requirements which science imposes even on a grammar which professes to serve only a practical purpose. Indeed, one sometimes receives even the unpleasant impression that the book in his hand is a work "made to order," owing its existence solely to the speculation of the bookselling trade. The peculiar literary conditions of Greece contribute partly to this lack of really serviceable helps. The term "modern Greek," as is well known, designates *two* forms of language—first, the living language spoken by the people and split up into numerous dialects or *patois*, which form alone properly deserves the name of modern Greek; and, secondly, the literary language, the καθαρεύουσα, *i.e.* "pure speech," which is a literary and learned revival of the more or less modernised ancient Greek common language, and is therefore a product of art by no means of recent date, but the result of the written usage of centuries reaching back beyond Byzantine days. The extent to which this stereotyped form of ancient Greek admitted and still admits modern elements borrowed from the popular language varied not only in different times, but still varies also according to author and locality. The majority of modern Greek grammars have this in common, that they present neither the one nor the other form of language exclusively, but select as a working basis either the learned language or the vernacular without confining themselves further strictly to the standard chosen. Those who prefer the literary language are in the majority : ordinarily this form is taught in such a way as if it were κατ᾿ ἐξοχήν "the Greek language of the present day." And yet this literary complexion is not exclusively the dominant one even in the province of artistic literature, while lyrical and epic poetry belong almost entirely to the vernacular, which continues also to gain ground in other departments (comedy and narrative).

A combined account of both forms of the language suffers from want of clearness, quite apart from the fact that in most cases the vernacular in this way is denied fair treatment. Mitsotakis [1] so far has best succeeded in treating both together; but he, like all the others, displays a lack of the training in philology necessary to do justice to the more rigorous scientific demands : he also lacks the necessary discrimination of the essential distinction between the popular and the literary language. The former is by no means satisfactorily treated, and in his grammar appears but too faintly as a pronounced independent form of language. The only elementary grammar of recent date which has essayed the task of presenting the popular language is that of Wied. [2] This little volume, the popularity of which is attested by the immediate appearance of a second edition, is to be highly commended to the beginner for a rapid introductory sketch of the modern Greek vernacular; but certainly those who try to gain from it a complete knowledge of the copious popular literature of modern Greece, or to become acquainted with

---

[1] Mitsotakis, *Praktische Grammatik der neugriechischen Schrift- und Umgangssprache.* Stuttgart and Berlin, 1891 (Spemann). xii and 260 pp. (12 Marks). *Cf.* my review in the *Deutsche Literaturzeitung*, 1893, col. 235 f.

[2] Wied, *Die Kunst, die neugriechische Volkssprache durch Selbstunterricht schnell und leicht zu lernen.* Vienna : Hartleben, in the series "Kunst der Polyglotten," pt. xi. (2 Marks).

the structure of the speech of the common people, will soon be disappointed. There exists no text-book that can supply reliable and to some extent ample information upon the facts of the modern Greek popular language. An adequate text-book should be expected not only to introduce every scholar to an understanding of the abundant treasures of the modern Greek national and vernacular literature, but also to make the linguist and the philologist familiar with the principle of the growth of the language. To fill this breach is the object of my *Handbook*.

I have already in a separate brochure [1] pointed out that the vernacular, and not the literary, language should be first learned, together with the reasons for this view. To repeat briefly: those who are familiar with ancient Greek and then learn the modern vernacular possess all that is essential to understand the modern Greek literary language; while those who do not know ancient Greek will never gain a clear grasp of the linguistic conditions of Greek literature of the present time. My Grammar is not intended for readers who are complete strangers to ancient Greek. Nevertheless, I have fully adopted the standpoint of modern Greek: for a descriptive grammar—and such mine professes primarily to be—must treat a language only in its own light. It is, on the other hand, a confusing anachronism in a grammar of modern Greek to lay down rules, *e.g.*, on the long and short vowels ε and η, ο and ω, or for the " diphthongs " αι, οι, ει, or for the spiritus asper, the circumflex and acute accents, which possess no longer any meaning for the language of the present day, enjoying only a conventional existence in writing. The grammars of modern Greek with which I am familiar are simply drawn up on the model of ancient Greek, because the authors for lack of proper scientific knowledge of the language were not aware of the wide gulf between the ancient Greek orthography and the form of the present language. It is in the department of " phonetics," or rather in that of " characters," that our grammars betray this unfortunate habit most glaringly and senselessly; but even morphology cannot escape being crushed into this Procrustean bed to such an extent that its harmony and

---

[1] *Die neugriechi·che Sprache und ihre Erlernung*: Beilage to *Allgemeine Zeitung*, Aug. 6, 1891.

symmetry are quite obscured. Thus, *e.g.*, declension is treated according to the scheme of ancient Greek types of declension, that which is specifically modern Greek being attached as an accidental patch. Descriptive grammar demands, on the contrary, "that homogeneous phenomena should be grouped. But the criterion of what is to be regarded as homogeneous must not be sought in antiquity or in etymology, but in the ever-living genius of the language."[1] My classification of modern Greek declension satisfies, I believe, this requirement by treating and bringing together under a uniform point of view those elements which, in the consciousness of those who speak the language, fall together into groups, and consequently formally react upon one another. Deffner's,[2] as also Psichari's,[3] proposed classification of the declension forms appears to me less lucid than that which I have adopted. I myself have, however, only carried into effect a suggestion put forward by W. Meyer-Lübke in his commentary on the grammar of Simon Portius (p. 125)—a suggestion which he himself did not either follow up or carry out in his own classification of modern Greek declensions (p. 118). On the classification of verbs there can exist no doubt since the appearance of Hatzidakis' fine article "über die Präsensbildung im Neugriechischen,"[4] in which the formation of the present stem and its relation to the aorist are clearly stated. For the benefit of those who like to play with the term "practical," and who, in no way troubled with exact knowledge, regard "scientific" and "unpractical" as almost synonymous ideas, let me remark that the classification of the contents of a language based upon its own inner laws facilitates the acquiring of a language more than a grammar that presents the language on some external model.

I need not specially emphasise that I have not attempted an exhaustive account of the treasures of modern Greek, as is clear from the concise compass of my Grammar. But, notwithstanding, it contains considerably more than other grammars of greater size, and is above all a grammar of the

---

[1] G. v. d. Gabelentz, *Die Sprachwissenschaft* (Leipzig, 1891), p. 92.

[2] In his review of Legrand's Grammar, *Jenaer Literaturzeitung*, 1879, p. 392.

[3] Psichari, *Essais de Grammaire historique néogrecque*, i. 88 (Paris, 1886).

[4] Kuhn's *Zeitschrift f. vergl. Sprachf.* xxvii. p. 69 ff., and *Einl. in die neugriech. Grammatik* (Leipzig, 1892), p. 390 ff.

vernacular Greek " Κοινή." The existence of a common and uniform type of the "popular speech" (*Volkssprache*) is, of course, denied by some, it being maintained rather that beside the affected archaic written language there exist only dialects. The latter assertion I dispute, and I maintain that we are justified in speaking of a modern Greek " Κοινή," the language of the folk-songs in the form in which they are usually published being no more a specific dialect than that type of language of such popular poets as Christopulos, Drosinis, Palamas, and many others, can be dubbed dialect. A perfect uniformity is admittedly not yet to be found, for just as sometimes on the one hand equally correct, *i.e.* equally wide-spread, forms occur side by side, so on the other many poets (as, *e.g.*, Vilaras) manifest a marked propensity for dialect elements; yet in spite of all this we may speak of *the* "vernacular" in contrast to the dialects. Many folk-songs in the course of extensive diffusion, passing from place to place, must have had their dialectic peculiarities reduced to a minimum, so that by a quite spontaneous process a certain average speech resulted. Quite recently Ροΐδης has also made a similar assertion, guided, however, more by instinct than by any scientific sense, and consequently he has overshot the mark in disputing absolutely the existence of dialects.[1] This average popular speech—which readily arises particularly in the larger centres—serves as a means of communication which is intelligible not only in Patras, Athens, and Constantinople, but also in the country.

The collection of Texts served me as a guide for the limitation of my material: the less common (or dialectic) phenomena are in general only treated so far as they occur in these texts. The student will therefore not expect to find, *e.g.*, the Greek dialects of Lower Italy or those of Pontus—to say nothing of Zaconian—given in any exhaustive manner. I have exceeded the dialect material contained in the Texts only when some linguistic phenomena of special interest on more general grounds (*e.g.* the history of the language) called for attention. Of course, such a selection remains always more or less subjective and influenced by the personal

---

[1] Ροΐδης, Τὰ Εἴδωλα. Γλωσσικὴ μελέτη (Athens, 1893), p. 180 ff. It was naturally an easy matter for Hatzidakis to refute the "scientific" grounds of Ροΐδης' thesis ; *cf.* Ἀθηνᾶ, vii. 224 ff.

equation. I considered it imperative to cite *patois* phenomena not only to produce an approximately correct conception of the diversity of *patois*, but also efficiently to facilitate the study of modern Greek popular literature. When, however, either in *Grammar* or *Glossary*, I mention a definite region (*e.g.* Naxos, Velvendos, Cyprus) as exhibiting certain philological points, it is not to be understood that these occur *only* in those regions : such particulars, given generally in connection with the texts, mean no more than that a form or usage is locally restricted.

In the explanatory notes on the history of the language I confined myself to a selection of material on the same principles on which I made a selection from the dialect material. The relations between the ancient Greek forms and those of modern Greek are referred to in their salient characteristics. My object was to sketch in general outline their inner connection as the established result of the investigation upon modern Greek of the present time, and to put the reader on the right track, rather than to explain in detail all the separate linguistic points. Those who possess a scientific knowledge of philology will, with the aid of my directions, experience no difficulty in explaining many a detail. I aimed especially at presenting a clear account of the preservation or the disappearance of ancient, as well as the rise of new, types. A further consideration was to safeguard those who approach the study of modern Greek against such misconceptions as have been really exploded for science through the indefatigable exertions of Hatzidakis, but which misconceptions unfortunately still haunt the brains of unscientific dilettanti. In order not to frustrate my main object—to produce a textbook of the modern Greek vernacular—I have avoided the citation of scientific apparatus (literature, discussions, etc.), and have restricted to the smallest possible compass the employment of philological terminology—except the most common grammatical terms. The beginner will do well on the first reading to omit the section on Phonetics together with the notes and to go through the conjugation of the verbs before paragraphs 140–164 [§§ 175–212 of the new edition]. The annotations on dialect peculiarities will sometimes be best impressed on his mind by the reading of the texts. Let me refer those who seek information on the aims, method, and tasks of investigation in modern Greek to my little book, *Die neugriechische Sprache* (Freiburg, 1892, 36 pp.), which will serve as an introduction to the present Grammar. The older as well as the more recent literature upon this subject will be found collected there and in my reviews in the *Anzeiger der Indogermanischen Forschungen*, as also in the first part of G. Meyer's *Neugriechische Studien.*[1]

It is almost superfluous to remark how much I have profited by the successful labours bestowed upon investigation in modern Greek philology during the past fifteen years. First in importance come the achievements of Hatzidakis, the fruits of which, as I hope, are apparent in this Grammar. Another work which I have frequently consulted with the greatest profit should also be gratefully acknowledged, viz. the commentary of W. Meyer (Lübke)[2] on the grammar of Simon Portius. This commentary is the solitary attempt to furnish a brief but comprehensive account of the results of modern Greek philology. Its association with Simon Portius was a happy thought. His grammar (although of the seventeenth century) not only compares favourably for a clear grasp of the material with the modern Greek grammars of the past century, but surpasses them in scientific spirit.

The Texts, the requirements of which were constantly kept in view in the Grammar, offer a selection of pieces of poetry and prose from the vernacular, and from that section of the artistic literature which is based upon the vernacular. That the latter is more or less affected by the literary language will appear from a rapid comparison between Part I. and Part II. of the Texts. In the Grammar or the Glossary I have drawn attention to those elements of the literary language which formally betray themselves as such (and which are not altogether wanting in Part I. of the Texts) in order to prevent any doubt as to what is genuinely vernacular. The Table of Contents gives the sources whence I have taken my texts. From my own collections I admitted three pieces

---

[1] G. Meyer, *Neugriechische Studien.* I. "Versuch einer Bibliographie der neugriech. Mundartenforschung" ; *Sitzungsberichte der Wiener Akademie der Wissenschaft. Phil.-hist. Kl.* cxxx. (1894).

[2] Simon Portius, *Grammatica linguae Graecae vulgaris.* Reproduction de l'édition de 1638, suivie d'un commentaire grammatical et historique par Wilhelm Meyer. With an Introduction by J. Psichari, Paris, 1889, Vieweg ; lvi and 256 pp.

b

together with a distich; of these I have already published
III. 4 elsewhere, while I. d. 7 and III. 13 (b) are *inedita*.
Unfortunately no specially superior or authentic editions
were at my command for the selections from some of the
poets, still no real disadvantage can have, I believe, resulted.
In general, I retained the texts in the form in which they
were found in the editions which I used, in some cases with
the alteration or addition of the headings. In purely orthographical matters which in no way affect the pronunciation
(so especially in regard to vowels) the orthography adopted
in the Grammar is systematically carried out. In the first
part I have taken the liberty to make some other alterations
i.e. corrections, thus, *e.g.*, in the case of final ν, in order to
present the normally correct popular form in harmony with
my Grammar. I have, however, in this respect practised
considerable caution (*e.g.* I. a. 21, where forms like συγχωρητά,
ἔστωσαν are borrowed from the ecclesiastical language). In
the Texts of the artistic literature the orthography of the
literary language is retained in cases like σθ instead of στ, κτ
for χτ, νδ for ντ, final ν, etc., if such were found in my copy;
the Grammar will be found to furnish adequate information
upon these deviations from the vernacular language and
orthography. In the text of Psichari (II. b. 1) the author's
orthography remains absolutely unaltered, so as to present at
the same time a sample of his proposals toward reform of
orthography. My selection of texts was determined not only
by the language itself, but also by having in consideration the
history of literature and culture; on these principles the
attempts toward the creation of a popular prose, or those
selections which reflect wide-spread literary tendencies in
modern Greek dress, are inserted; and, again, the admission
of Rangavis' song (II. a. 14) was determined by its affinity
with the ballad literature (*cf.* I. a. 4). The brief biographical
dates for the poets will prove useful to fix their place and
time; unfortunately I was not able to ascertain the dates
for Ἰ. Τυπάλδος and some of the writers still living. I
venture to hope that the Texts, in the absence of a similar
collection and in spite of their small bulk, are adapted to
introduce the reader into the world of thought and ideas of
the present-day Greek and especially the "Ρωμιός."

The final part of the Texts consists of Specimens of

Dialect which give a fairly good idea of the multiplicity and variety of modern Greek *patois*. Annotations are here subjoined in order to render the dialects more easily intelligible. Every one who is at all familiar with how far the alphabetic representations of dialect texts fall short of phonetic exactness will comprehend the reason why I did not group the pieces in the first part, to which are attached notices of the places of origin (*e.g.* Epirus, Chios, Naxos), under Specimens of Dialect: at best they are to be considered merely as reproductions of a common language with dialect colouring. But in the Specimens of Dialect the purpose was to portray with as much faithfulness as possible the local *patois*, which is more or less the case in the texts selected. That from Cyprus (III. 8) is unfortunately very imperfect: there exist but few really reliable texts of modern Greek dialects. The second specimen of Pontic (III. 13. b) is taken from my own collections which I made during a prolonged stay last year in Samsun, and which represent predominantly the dialect of a village situate east from Samsun (Tšerakmán). But in order to secure simplicity in the phonetic transcription a peculiarity of the pronunciation has been left unnoticed, viz. that an initial tenuis after a preceding nasal is sometimes pronounced as a *voiceless* media (or also fortis): this I must reserve for detailed investigation on some other occasion.

The Glossary is primarily prepared to suit the texts, but embraces also all those words cited or discussed in the Grammar; from it the beginnner may acquire a serviceable stock of words. It was absolutely necessary to attach such a vocabulary, because the only handy dictionary, that of Kind (Leipzig: Tauchnitz), is long since antiquated and no longer serviceable, and the modern Greek-French dictionary of Legrand (Paris: Garnier) would not cover my texts.

The principles which guided me in orthographical questions are briefly indicated in § 3 n. Generally speaking, I endeavoured, of course, to harmonise the spelling with the principle of the historical orthography, *i.e.* to spell according to the origin and nature of a form; but occasionally I also ventured to simplify as well as to effect a compromise ("συμβιβασμός") between the orthography demanded on scientific grounds and that at present most commonly in use. Where the present orthography fluctuates among

various spellings (*e.g.* in comparatives in -ύτερος) I adopted
without hesitation that demanded on the grounds of the
history of the language ; while again from among several
methods of spelling in vogue I selected that one philo-
logically best justified.   On the other hand, I avoided
unusual spellings, like τοὶς for τὶς, in such a case preferring
the neutral sign ι.   In the same way I could not admit
spellings, *e.g.*, like -πουλλο, πουλλί, etc. (which Hatzidakis [1]
rightly demands on philological grounds), from a desire not to
introduce into a *Handbook.* an orthographical system too much
at variance with the general usage.   I have frequently aimed
at simplification of orthography ; thus in carrying throughout
all forms the ει in αὐτεῖνος as required by its origin,[2] or in
writing ἔχω δεθεῖ (for -ῆ, ῇ) to correspond to ἔχω ἰδεῖ and
ἔχω δέσει.   In the question of accents my principle was to
restrict the employment of the circumflex as far as possible,
affixing it as a rule only where it would correspond *immediately* to the ancient Greek circumflex (γλῶσσα): when possible
I carried systematically the same accent throughout a paradigm (*e.g.* ναύτης—ναύτες, not ναῦτες), or at least the same
accent in homogeneous groups (παπᾶς παπᾶ — παπάδες
παπάδω ; ἐπατοῦσα in the singular, but ἐπατούσαμε, ἐπατούσετε, ἐπατούσαν).   I regard it as pedantic to accent specific
modern Greek forms (like δούλα, κυνήγι, ἐκοιμώνταν) or loan-
words (like βούλ[λ]α) according to the rules of ancient Greek,
frustrating, as it does, a much needed simplification of the
historic orthography.   Spellings, moreover, like γναῖκά τ (III.
11) or εἰπέν ἄτεν (III. 13. a) are rejected because they are
used by editors manifestly only on analogy of ancient Greek :
I at least am not aware that any distinction can be made
between ἡ μάννα μου and ἡ γυναῖκα μου.   In regard to the
spelling of consonants I was guided by the pronunciation,
thus, *e.g.*, νύχτα, ἐλεύτερος, γελάστηκα, σκίζω, or I have
expressly called attention to a conflict between pronunciation
and orthography, *e.g.*, σβήνω more correctly ζβήνω or σχίζω
for σκίζω, etc. ; this latter course was absolutely necessary
for the reason that some account must be given of the
relations obtaining between the spoken language and the

---

[1] *Cf.* Παρνασσός, xviii. (1895) 1 ff.

[2] Cf. *e.g.* B. J. Schmitt in the Δελτίον τῆς ἱστορικῆς καὶ ἐθνολογικῆς ἑταιρίας,
iv. (1893) p. 306.

orthography, and also because the texts in this respect, as remarked above, reflect more frequently the orthography of the literary language. If in spite of painstaking correction I have here or there committed an orthographical slip, I beg indulgence.

A List of Abbreviations is given on p. 314.

Finally, mention should be made of the name which graces the publication of my book. The dedication is not to be regarded merely as a token of my high appreciation of the pioneer work of Professor Hatzidakis in the department of modern Greek philology, but also as an expression of my gratitude for the repeated encouragement and benefit gained from a most friendly exchange of ideas both orally and by letter. I have also for the present *Handbook* had the advantage of Professor Hatzidakis' assistance, inasmuch as he was ever ready to communicate to me valuable information, and very kindly undertook to read through a portion of the proofs.

FREIBURG IN BADEN

FOREWORD TO THE SECOND
GERMAN EDITION.

ON the occasion of a revised edition of my book I ventured
to be guided by the same principles which appeared to me
expedient fifteen years ago, when I first offered to the public
my account of the modern Greek vernacular. The plan and
design of the book were on the whole received with general
approval, and may therefore be allowed to remain unaltered.
If one critic took exception to my classification of modern
Greek declensions, another as highly commended it, so that
I had no particular reason to yield to the carper. Some
inequalities, either pointed out by critics or which I myself
detected, have, of course, been removed. But the volume of the
book has also been enlarged by the accession of new material
such as will certainly be welcomed by those who use this
edition. A brief account of Syntax had from the beginning
formed part of my plan, and was precluded in the first
edition for purely external reasons. On the present
occasion I was persuaded to insert such an account, not only
from a desire to furnish a fairly complete view of the
structure of modern Greek, but also by the consideration that
a modern Greek syntax is at least as imperatively needed as
phonetics or morphology for the interest with which the
Koiné studies are being at present prosecuted. For I had
more than once observed that the acquaintance with modern
Greek on the part of those philologists who, in their Koiné
studies, were conscious of the necessity of casting a glance at
the later development of the language, was limited to the
material of my Handbook. Moreover, the abundant citation
of examples for the rules of syntax, which will serve the
beginner as exercises, is an advantage on practical grounds,
and will, as I hope, enhance the usefulness of the book.

These examples will, moreover, facilitate the understanding of the texts from which they are as a rule selected, being only exceptionally taken from other sources. In preparing the sections on syntax I was, of course, obliged to confine myself to the most important points, and only quite rarely drew upon dialect examples—for the simple reason that practically no work has been done on the problems of syntax. I am conscious that several of my statements can claim only provisional value : it will be quite obvious that in the almost complete absence of preliminary works, my remarks and rules cannot approach that degree of certainty that we may look for in the department of ancient Greek syntax, in which the work and experience of centuries may be utilised. But it afforded me a peculiar pleasure in many cases to be the first to formulate rules of syntax for the modern Greek vernacular, and, it may be, thereby to stimulate investigations along special lines, and set afoot comparisons between ancient and modern Greek syntax. It will easily appear that historic considerations weighed considerably with me in the arrangement of the material, so that students familiar with the ancient Greek will experience no difficulty in tracing the effects of a two thousand year development of the language. I am even convinced that, on the other hand, the chapter on the Order of Words in modern Greek will be serviceable for the historical understanding of Hellenistic texts, since we as yet know but very little about the arrangement of words in ancient Greek. I would also remark that my rules on the order of words have been drawn only from the prose texts of the vernacular literature.

The other additions to my book are largely due to the increased number of texts. In the course of the last few years our knowledge of modern Greek dialects has been so enriched by a number of excellent works, that it appeared to me as obviously necessary to enlarge the third part of the Texts with some excellent and interesting specimens of dialect. From my own copies I again contributed a few more pieces in order that my dialect collections from the islands, the Maina, and Asia Minor might not lie completely fallow (*cf.* III. 3. 5. 13. b. c. 14. a and another version of 15). Here let me thank Professor N. G. Politis of Athens for having most willingly and amply furnished me with the information asked for upon some texts, especially the two *mirologies* (elegies) from Maina. I considered it further desirable to increase the material in the first and second parts. Some characteristic samples of the popular literature are added ; the output of recent years must be taken into account, particularly as regards the progress which the struggle over the popular language has undoubtedly made since the beginning of the present century. The popular prose, having first asserted its claim to the field of narrative literature, is now ever more and more taking possession also of the literary essay (cultivated so excellently by writers like Palamas), and is experimenting even on the themes of abstract science. Psichari's example has been, and still continues, fruitful. The weekly paper "'Ο Νοῦμας" has already for a number of years done service to the propaganda of the popular language. Contrast this with earlier days when newspapers in the pure vernacular were obliged to suspend after a brief run. The reform movement visibly assumes ever larger proportions. It even seems to me as if Hatzidakis himself, the greatest adversary of the "language-heretics," has very recently altered his standpoint perceptibly in favour of a genuinely popular reform of the literary language. At least at the close of his *Lectures on the Linguistic Question* (*cf.* the Appendix on Bibliography) he gives expression to principles upon a seasonable reform of the literary language that must sound to the advocates of the vernacular as a concession to their own views. If a man like Hatzidakis were to lend his support to the reform movement, that were a consummation to be wished.

Unfortunately, I was obliged to leave unfulfilled some wishes which were expressed to me in the event of a new edition of my book, and especially that for the admission of Solomos' *Hymn to Liberty*. I could not consent to give only a few verses, as G. Meyer proposed, and considerations for the bulk of my book forbade me to give it in its entirety, as Krumbacher advised (by letter). Further, it did not fall in with the character of this book to give selections from the mediaeval literature or from the written language. I do not ignore the practical object of such proposals, but I believe that this object would be better served in special collections.

The Appendix on Bibliography is intended as a guide for

those who are interested in the problems and the history of modern Greek. Here everything is entered that appeared to me as specially characteristic for the purposes of introduction to modern Greek philology, as is also everything that could offer further help in bibliography, *i.e.* could present in outline the whole activity in the field of modern Greek philology. The entries from 1902 on are relatively more numerous because my reviews in the *Indogermanische Forschungen* extend only to that year. Such works on the Koiné are selected as take account of the modern Greek standpoint.

After my book has served the cause of modern Greek for fifteen years, I hope that in its revised form it will continue to prove serviceable to modern Greek and related studies.

It remains to thank Doctor E. Kieckers for the kind assistance which he rendered me in the correction of the proof-sheets.

ALBERT THUMB.

STRASSBURG, *July* 1910.

CONTENTS

THE VERB.

TEXTS.

I. FOLK-LITERATURE.

I

GRAMMAR.

PART FIRST.

PHONETICS.

§ 1. The Greeks use the ancient Greek characters and orthography as used by us in Greek printing. For purposes of writing, in addition to the forms which we customarily use, they employ others which approximate to the Latin running-character (see Modern Greek Writing Alphabet).

For the Greek dialects of Lower Italy (villages in the Terra d' Otranto and in Bova) as well as for the Zaconian (a dialect spoken on the east side of the Peloponnesus between St. Andreas and Lenidi), usually (especially in philological works) transcription in Latin characters is employed. These Latin (or phonetic) characters are only occasionally employed also in scientific works upon other dialects.

§ 2. The present pronunciation of the Greek characters with their phonetic transcription is as follows :—

a (*ą*) = *a* (as in father).

β = (French) *v*, i.e. a labial (more correctly labio-dental) voiced spirant: *βάλλω válo* "I place, lay," *βρέχω vréχo* "I moisten," *στραβός stravós* "wry, squinting."

γ (1) *before palatal (dental) vowels (e, i)* = *y*, i.e. a palatal voiced spirant (like German Jod): *γελῶ yeló* "I laugh," *γείτονας yitonas* "neighbour," *γῦρος yíros* "circle," *πηγαίνω piyéno* "I go," *μάγερας máyeras* "cook."

(2) *before guttural (velar) vowels (a, o, u)* and *before consonants* = *ȝ* (in grammars commonly represented by *gh*), i.e. a guttural sounding spirant (like *g* in *ich sage* of some

3

German dialects, *e.g.* that of the Palatinate): γάλα ʒála (*ghála*) " milk," γομάρι ʒomári "ass," γουρούνι ʒurúni "pig," ἀγαπῶ aʒapó "love," λέγω léʒo "say," ἐπῆγα epíʒa "I went," γλῶσσα ʒlósa "language," ἔγνοια éʒn'a "care."

(3) on γγ and γκ, *v.* § 15.

δ = đ (*dh*), a sonant interdental spirant like the English so-called soft *th*, as in *then*: ἐδώ edó "here," δόντι đóndi "tooth," δρόμος đrómos "way, street."

ε = (medial) *e*, as in g*e*t.

ζ = *z*, sounding sibilant, like Fr. *z*, or (North) German *s* between two vowels (*Rose*), or *z* in *z*enith: ζουλεύω zulévo "I envy," μαζί mazí "together, with."

η (η) = *i* (as *ee* in f*ee*t): μῆνας mínas "month," σηκώνω sikóno "I raise."

θ = þ (*th*) unvoiced interdental spirant, like the English "hard" *th*, as in *thin*: θαμμένος þaménos "buried" σπίθα spíþa "spark."

ι = *i*.

κ (1) *before guttural (velar) vowels* = *k*, i.e. like Fr. *c* or *qu* before guttural vowels, and almost like Germ. *k* in *Kanne* (only without breath): καλός kalós "good," εἰκόνα ikóna "images," ἀκούω akúo "I hear."

(2) *before e, i = k′* (*ky*), a palatal stop approximating the Germ. *k* in *Kind* (but more palatal *ky*): καί k′e "and," σκυλί sk′ilí "dog," κοιμοῦμαι k′imúme "I sleep," παιδάκι peđák′i "child."

λ = *l*
μ = *m* } or *mouillé, v.* § 30.
ν = *n*

ξ = *ks* (sometimes *gz, v.* § 15).

ο = (medial) *o*, as in n*o*t.

π = *p*.

ρ = *r*, with the point of the tongue, aspirate (or also pronounced *mouillé*, § 30).

σ = *s* (North Germ. *ss*), i.e. always "voiceless" or "sharp," even between two vowels (ἐσύ esí "thou"). For the pronunciation of σ as *z, v.* § 29.

τ = *t*.

υ = *i*.

φ = *f* (labio-dental).

χ (1) *before the guttural vowels a, o, u* = a guttural voice-

less spirant like *ch* in *loch*, or as in Germ. *ach, Joch*: χάνω
" I lose," ἔχω " I have," ἔχουν " they have."

(2) *before the palatal (dental) vowels* e, i = palatal voiceless
spirant χ′, soft as in Germ. *ich, stechen*: χαίρω χ′éro "I
rejoice," μαχαίρι maχ′éri " knife," χοῖρος χ′íros " pig," ὄχι óχ′i
" no, not."

In cases where χ before guttural vowels is to be pronounced
palatal it is written χι: *e.g.* ἄχιουρα = áχ′ura " straw."

ψ = ps (sometimes bz; *v.* § 15).
ω (ῳ) = o.
Compound signs:
ει, οι = i: ἔχεις ἔχ′is " thou hast," μοῖρα míra " fate."
αι = e (ε): βγαίνω vyéno " I go out."
ου = u: βούδι vúđi " ox."

αυ, ευ (ηυ) (1) before voiced sounds = av, ev (iv), i.e. like
αβ, εβ: παύω pávo " I cease," αὐγή avyí " dawn," αὔριο ávrio
" to-morrow," δουλεύω đulévo " I work," ζεύγω zévȝo " I yoke,"
ξεύρω ksévro " I know," ηὗρα ívra " I found."

(2) before voiceless sounds (π, κ, τ, φ, χ, θ, σ, ξ): = af, ef
(αφ, εφ): αὐτός aftós " this," ψεύτης pséftis " liar."

In the modern pronunciation the Spiritus asper ('),
Spiritus lenis ('), and Iota subscriptum have no signification:
ὁ o " the," οἱ i " the " (pl.), ἅγιος áyos " holy " (ἀγαπῶ aȝapó
" I love," ἔτος étos " year "), ᾆσμα ázma " song."

On the diphthongs and ̗, γι (γι̯), ̌, τσ, τζ, *v.* §§ 8, 9,
28 (17), 35.

§ 3. The modern Greek vernacular (apart from dialects)
therefore has the following phonetic system:

(a) Vowels: a (a, ą), e (ε, αι), i (ι, η, ῃ, υ, ει, οι), o (o, ω,
ῳ), u (ου).

(b) Diphthongs: aị (αϊ, αη, αει), eị (εϊ, εη, εει, αϊι), oị, (οϊ, οη,
ωει), uị (ουι, ουη); *v.* § 8.

(c) Liquids: r (ρ), l (λ), r′ (ρι̯), l′ (λι̯).

(d) Nasals: m (μ), n (ν), ꞑ (γγ, γκ, *v.* §§ 15, 33), mn′ (μνι̯),
n′ (νι̯).

(e) Stops (mutes):

k (κ)	k′ (κ, κι̯)	g	g′
t (τ)		d	
p (π)		b	

On the mediae g, d, b, *v.* § 15.

(*f*) Spirants:

χ	χ' (χ, $\chi\iota$)	$\check{3}$ (γ),	y (γ, $\gamma\iota$, ι)
þ (θ)		$\bar{d}$ (δ)	
f (ϕ)		v (β)	
s (σ)		z (ζ)	

(*g*) Double sounds:

ks (ξ)	gz ($\gamma\xi$, $\nu\xi$)
ts ($\tau\sigma$)	dz ($\nu\tau\zeta$, $\tau\zeta$).

1. Apart from these sounds, there exist in the various dialects other sounds, the most important of which will be mentioned in the following paragraphs.

2. The fact that the modern Greek popular speech, though written according to the principles of a. Gk. orthography, has experienced an independent phonetic development, makes it impossible in every case to force the m. Gk. form into the old Greek orthography; accordingly such transcriptions as παληός for παλιός = old Greek παλαιός, ἡ for οἱ (fem.), βασιλειάς for βασιλιάς, are due merely to the attempt to restore an external connection between the a. Gk. orthography and the m. Gk. form. Other orthographical transcriptions, like ταῖς ἡμέραις for τὲς ἡμέρες, εἶχα γράψῃ for γράψει, καταιβαίνω for κατεβαίνω, etc., have arisen through mistaken ideas as to the origin of the forms. On the whole, up to the present no uniform orthography obtains, and even in philological circles we find the most opposite views (cp. the orthography of Psichari, TEXTS II. b. 1). The principle that a m. Gk. form ought to be written according to its origin, presupposes a correct understanding of this origin, as, *e.g.*, Nom. Acc. pl. μέρες (*v.* § 81, n. 1) and comparatives like καλύτερος (*v.* § 117), etc. Of course, when the source is obscure or doubtful, uniformity of orthography can be secured only after conventional fashion. The same holds true for forms where the principle given permits two equally justifiable spellings, *e.g.* κάφτω or καύτω "I burn." In many cases (especially in writing dialect forms) the historic orthography utterly fails, which makes the use of auxiliary signs necessary (*e.g.* ι, $\breve{o}$).

§ 4. The syllable which bears the stress is marked with an accent, acute ´; this acute changes to grave ` on the last syllable within the sentence, or circumflex ˆ. These three signs have absolutely the same value in the present-day pronunciation, the employment of the one or of the other of them being determined solely by the rules of accentuation in ancient Greek.

At this point also the a. Gk. rules and m. Gk. forms often come into conflict, *e.g.* it may be disputed whether *itan(e)*, "he was," should be written ἦταν(ε), in accordance with the ancient form ἦτο, or ἤταν(ε) according to the ancient rules of accent.

PHONETIC CHANGE.

(a) VOWELS AND DIPHTHONGS.

§ 5. Modern Greek does *not* differentiate long and short vowels in the ancient Greek sense. The vowels are of equal length under equal conditions of stress : the stressed vowels (*i.e.* those which bear the accent of the word) are pronounced somewhat longer than the unstressed, that is, they correspond approximately to the stressed short vowels in German. νόμος " law " and νῶμος (ὦμος) " shoulder," ῥίφτω " I throw" and δείχνω " I show," λύκος " wolf " and μοῖρα " fate," λέγω " I say " and φταί(γ)ω " I am at fault "; also γνωρίζω " I know " and νομίζω " I believe," λιθάρι " stone " and μητέρα " mother," λυποῦμαι " I lament " and κοιμοῦμαι " I sleep," γερός " strong " and παιδί " boy," are exactly alike as far as their stressed and their unstressed vowels are concerned.

The a. Gk. distinction between long and short (ω, ο, η, ε) has thus disappeared and given place to another principle—that of giving prominence to the accented syllable by stronger enunciation. In North. Gk. the contrast between stressed and unstressed syllables is greater than elsewhere (*v.* § 7, n. 1).

§ 6. *Medial vowels.* Unstressed *i* before a ρ is rare, being mostly replaced by an ε: κερί " candle," ξερός " dry," θεριό " animal," σίδερο " iron," πλερώνω " I pay," χερότερος (χειρότερος) " worse," κερά (κυρία) " lady, Mrs." On the other hand, βούτυρο " butter," τυρί " cheese," συρτάρι " drawer."

1. Spellings like ξηρός, σκληρός, πληρώνω are not really vernacular so far as they do not present the change of unstressed *e* to *i* (discussed in § 7, n. 1).
2. In the Pontic dialect the a. Gk. η is for the most part represented by ε :—ἔρθα " I came "= ἦρθα, πεγάδ " fountain "= πηγάδι, ἐφέκα " I permitted " = ἀφῆκα, ἐτρύπεσα = ἐτρύπησα " I pierced."
3. Isolated change of *i* to ε; *e.g.* in Cyprian γεναῖκα = γυναῖκα " woman," and μέ(ν) = μή(ν) " not " (in prohibitions).

ε becomes ο in ψόμα beside ψέμα " lie," γιόμα beside γέμα " meal," γιοφύρι beside γεφύρι " bridge," γιομίζω beside γεμίζω " I fill "; also dialectically γιόμα for γαῖμα, αἷμα " blood."

ου occurs often in an unaccented syllable where we should expect *i* (η, ι, υ); as, μουστάκι (μύσταξ) " moustache," μουστρί (μυστρίον) "ladle," ξουρίζω and ξυρίζω "I shave," σουπιά (σηπιά) "cuttle-fish," στουππί (στυππίον) "tow, oakum," φουμίζω (φημίζω) "I praise," ζουλεύω (ζηλεύω) "I envy," χουσός (Texts III. 12) = χρυσός, ἔρχουμουν (ἐρχόμην) "I came."

4. In many dialects (chiefly in Zaconian, but also in Aegina, Megara, and Athens) the a. Gk. υ and οι are, as a rule, represented by ου: e.g. τσουμοῦμαι "I sleep," σοῦκο = σῦκο "fig," ὄτσούλος = σκύλος "dog," τσουλία = κοιλιά "belly."

In the neighbourhood of gutturals and labials unstressed (a. Gk.) ο (ω) often becomes ου; as, κονδούνι "bell," κουλλούρι "cracker, biscuit," κουπί "rudder," ζουμί "broth," πουλῶ "I sell," πουρνό and πωρνό "morning," σκουλήκι "worm"; also in Italian loan-words: τὸ κουμάντο "command," κουμπανιάρω "I accompany," φλουρί (and φλωρί) "florin."

5. The change of an ο (ω) to ου varies according to dialects. Even stressed ο sometimes becomes ου, as in the word οὖλος = ὅλος, especially frequent in the region of the Aegean. On -ου for -ω in the end of a word, v. § 213, n. 3.

6. In addition to the general Greek vowel system we find in the Pontic dialects also three modified vowels ä, ö, ü (= ä, ö, ü), which are for the most part a result of a fusion of ι + α, ο, υ: δάβα = διάβα "go," τὰ πεντικάρä = πεντικάρια "mice," λöνω = λυώνω "I melt," σπέλöν = σπήλιο(ν) "cave," ἀχύρä = *ἀχιούρια (ἄχιουρα) "straw." The vowel ə (Pontus and Cappadocia) occurs only in Turkish loan-words (e.g. καθəλώκ "answer").

§ 7. An unstressed vowel after nasals and liquids drops out if the same vowel precedes: e.g. παρκαλῶ (from παρακαλῶ) "I request," σκόρδο (from σκόροδο) "leek, garlic," ἀκλουθῶ (from ἀκουλουθῶ) "I follow." Also the disappearance of the ι in κορφή (from κορυφή) "summit," περπατῶ (from περιπατῶ) "I walk," περβόλι (from περιβόλι), "garden," πέρσι (from πέρυσι) "of last year," σημερνός (from σημερινός) "of the present day," etc., is apparently to be attributed to the same cause (if we posit older intermediate forms rising through assimilation *κοροφή, *περεπατῶ). Cp. also the imperative forms without ε, φέρτε, etc., § 217. To another category belong ἐκάτσα (beside ἐκάθισα) "I sat down," σκώνω (beside σηκώνω) "I raise," στάρι (beside σιτάρι) "grain, corn."

1. In the continental dialects (except in Attica and the Peloponnesus), e.g. in Epirus, Thessaly, Macedonia, and Thrace, as also in the northern islands of the Aegean Sea, the adjacent Asia Minor

coast, and in part of the Pontus region, *i.e.* in the so-called Northern Greek dialects, the vowel system has suffered a complete transformation, in the extremest form of which (*e.g.* Velvendos, Lesbos) every unstressed *e* and *o* has become *i* and *u* respectively, every unstressed *i* or *u* has either disappeared or been considerably reduced:

πιδί = παιδί "child," κόντιβιν = ἐκόντευε "he approached," πάϊνιν = ἐπάγαινε "he went," χαίριτι = χαίρεται "he rejoices," πιρνάει = περνᾷ "passes by," ἔπιρνι (ἔπαιρνε) "he took," σί = σέ (unstressed!) "in, into," τσί (= καί) "and."

κιρδιμένους = κερδεμένος "acquired," ἔδουκαν = ἔδωκαν "they gave," οὐρμήνις = ὁρμήνιες "advice," φύτρουσι = φύτρωσε "grew," ἀγουράζου "buy," τοὺ λόγου = τὸ λόγο "the word," πούς (unstressed!) = πῶς "how?"

ζῴτσιν = (ἐ)ζήτησεν "he sought, asked," ἄφκε = ἄφηκε "he allowed," ἔστλι = ἔστειλε "he sent," σκώνω = σηκώνω "I lift up," ἐφοβήθκα = ἐφοβήθηκα "I feared," νὰ φλάξ = φυλάξῃς "be on your guard," νύφι "bride," ἀκόμ = ἀκόμη "still, yet," λεοντάρ = λιοντάρι "lion," πγάδ = πηγάδι "fountain," τ = τὴ(ν), λαγκεύ = λαγκεύει "he jumps," νὰ πιθάν = πεθάνῃ "let him die."

ζμί = ζουμί "broth," κορτσόπλο = κοριτσόπουλο "maid," δλέβι = δουλεύει "he works," ἔκσα = ἤκουσα "I heard," στάσ = στάσου "stop!" πάν = πάνου "above," τοὺ τσιφάλ΄ τ (Lesbos) or τὸ κιφάλν ἀτ (Pontus) = τὸ κεφάλι του "his head."

The modification of a preceding consonant through the *i*-sound holds throughout: *e.g.* ἔχ΄ = ἔχει, ἔγ΄νε = ἔγινε, οὐλ΄ = ὅλη or ὅλοι, μιγάλ΄νι = (ἐ)μεγάληνε "became great," δζουβάν΄s (Lesbos) = τσοπάνης "shepherd."

Differences within a paradigm or stem arise through difference of accentuation: *e.g.* φουνάζ = φωνάζει "he calls," but φώναξι = ἐφώναξε aor.; τσιρατέλ΄ "a little horn," τσέρατου (κέρατον) "horn"; these differences may disappear by assimilation: *e.g.* πάγκανε for παγήκανε after pattern of πάγκα = πάγηκα, "they went," ζάλσαμ (Cappad.) for ζαλίσαμε "we wandered, missed our way," after ζάλσα = ἐζάλισα.

Owing to such transformation the North. Greek forms often appear strikingly unfamiliar, especially if the consonants which come together also suffer alteration (*v.* § 37 n.).

2. A phonetic phenomenon—the opposite of the dropping of vowels—*i.e.* the spontaneous development of a vowel between consonants, takes place in, *e.g.*, λαμπιρός beside λαμπρός "bright," Πάτινος = Πάτμος, γονδί, more rarely γδί "mortar," φουκαριστῶ (Crete) = φκαριστῶ "I thank." From Velvendos, *cf.* σʼπίτʼ = σπίτι, νὰ μὴ σʼπέρς = νὰ μὴ σπείρῃς, ἀσʼταίνουμι = αἰστάνομαι, οὐ γαμπρόζουμ from ὁ γαμπρός μου (but οὐ πόνους μ = ὁ πόνος μου); from Lesbos νὰ βαστάξιν from βαστάξν (*i.e.* βαστάξουν), but also γράφτῃ = γράφτουν, ἄσπῃ = ἄσπρη, etc., with syllabic ῃ, ῤ.

§ 8. *Diphthongs* arise in m. Gk. from the coalition of originally separate vowels: ἀηδόνι is to be pronounced ai̯ðóni "nightingale," καημένος kai̯ménos "unhappy," λεημοσύνη *leįmosíni* "alms," and similarly βόϊδι (beside βόδι, βούδι) "ox," ρολόϊ (ὡρολόγιον) "clock," ἁπλάϊ (πλάγι) "side." Here belong also the verbal forms treated in §§ 239 and 252 ρωτάεις, etc., λέει, πάει, τρώει, ἀκούει, etc. An *e*-sound combines with a preceding vowel to form a diphthong in ἀϊτός (= a. Gk. ἀετός) "eagle." The diphthongs are of secondary origin in γάϊδαρος (or γάδαρος) "ass," κελαϊδῶ (or κελαδῶ) "sing" (of birds), χαϊδεύω (or χαδεύω) "I caress." Finally, diphthongs are to be found in words of foreign origin : γαϊτάνι "string, cord," καϊκτσῆς "boatman," λεϊμόνι "lemon," μαϊμοῦ "monkey," τσάϊ "tea."

1. Also *o*- and *e*-sounds may form the consonantal part of a diphthong, *e.g.* in πάῳ "I go" (TEXTS III. 9 *p*ᵃ*ó*) or ἅᵉτς "so" (TEXTS III. 13. c).

2. A peculiar kind of diphthong is found in southern Maina (*cf.* TEXTS III. 3)—an *i*-sound generally consonantal (§ 9) being transferred (epenthesis) into the preceding syllable and combining with the vowel of that syllable : *e.g.* μάįτα = μάτια "eyes," βάįζει = βάζει "he puts," μωįρή = μωρή, πωįδά = ποδιά "apron," κουλλοῦįρα κουλλούρια "crackers," ἔįδάητσε = ἐδιάβηκε "he went," παįδά (*reįdá*) = παιδιά "children," ἔįννιά (*eįήá*) = ἐννιά "nine," and φίįδα = φίδια "snakes." This phonetic principle is operative also between closely connected words, as : νᾶį διορδώσου = νὰ διορθώσω "let me mend."

§ 9. Every *i*- or *e*-sound, which collides in the middle of a word with a succeeding velar sonant, loses its syllabic value and becomes consonantal (*i.e.* becomes a *y* = German *Jod*). The consonantal value of an *i* (ι, η, υ, ει, οι) may be denoted by a ˷ or ‿ printed beneath (ι, η, υ, ει, οι or į, η, y, εį, οį), or by γι, γυ etc. ; this, however, is not absolutely necessary, since the consonantal pronunciation is the rule in the pure vernacular : *e.g.* βραδυάζει (or βραδυάζει) *vraḏyázi* " the evening comes," ὁμοιάζω (ὁμοιάζω) *omyázo* "I am like," ὅποιος "whoever," σιάζομαι (σιάζομαι) "I prepare myself, get ready," φτειάνω (φτειάνω) "I make," φτώχεια "poverty," ἀσημένιος "of silver" (adj.), ἴσιος "equal," λιοντάρι (from λεοντάρι) "lion," γενιά (γενεά) "race," παλιός (from παλαιός) "ancient," πανώριος (ὡραῖος) "very beautiful." Such an *i* fuses with a preceding γ to *one* (*y*) sound : ἅγιος *áyos* "holy," βάγια *váya* "wet-nurse," πλαγιάζω *playázo* "I go to sleep," γιωργός (γεωργός) *yorȝós* "farmer."

In the initial syllable this *y* (Germ. *Jod*) is usually written γι, γι (or γυ) : Γιάννης = Ἰωάννης "John," γιατρός (ἰατρός) "physician," γυαλί (*ὑάλιον) "glass," γιός (υἱός) "son," γιορτή (ἑορτή) "feast." In some dialects also an *i-* (*e-*) sound, arising through the disappearance of a consonant, unites with the following vowel and becomes consonantal, *e.g.* πηαίνει (Ios) = πηγαίνει, *l*ᵉύη = λέγουν (Chios).

The *i* is not protected even by the stress, the accent being pushed back ; as, ἀτέλει̯ωτος "unceasing," θεμέλι̯ωσα "I built," πι̯άνω "I seize," ἔπι̯ασα, κοπι̯άζω "I try," ἐκόπι̯ασα, κουβεντιάζω "I talk, chat," ἐκουβέντι̯ασα, λι̯ώνω "I dissolve," ἔλι̯ωσα.

Forms like ἐπλησίασα, ἐσημείωσα, ἐτελείωσα are not really vernacular.

All words, in which an originally stressed *i* or *e* precedes the vowel forming the end-syllable, carry the accent regularly on the end-syllable : βαρει̯ά fem. of βαρύς "heavy," παιδι̯ά pl. of παιδί "child," χερι̯οῦ gen. of χέρι "hand," θὰ πι̯ῶ "I shall drink" (ἤπια) ; ἐκκλησι̯ά "church," καρδι̯ά "heart," ματι̯ά "a look," and numerous other fems. in -ι̯ά : σκολει̯ό "school," μαγερει̯ό "kitchen, cooking," χωρι̯ό "village," ποι̯ός "who ? which ? " ἐλι̯ά "olive-tree," μηλι̯ά "apple-tree," and other names of trees and plants originally ending in -έα : βασιλι̯άς (βασιλέας) "king," γρι̯ά (γραῖα) "old woman," νι̯ός (νέος), "young," Ὀβρι̯ός (Ἑβραῖος) "Jew," πλι̯ό, πι̯ό, (πλέον) "more."

The retreat of the accent in ἀρρώστια "sickness," ἀχάμνια "weakness," ὀρμήνεια "counsel," πραμάτεια "goods," φτώχια "poverty," etc., is to be attributed to the analogy of substantives like ἀλήθεια, βοήθεια.

§ 10. Words borrowed from the literary language or from Italian form an exception to the rule given in § 9 : *e.g.* ἀρμ νία "harmony," ἀνδρεῖος (in Rigas, but ἀντρειά TEXTS I. a. 1), βασιλεία "kingdom," βιβλίο "book," ἀστεῖος "witty," εὐκαιρία "opportunity," κωμῳδία "comedy," νοσοκομεῖο "hospital," φιλολογία "literature," φιλία "friendship" (Velvendos), βίος (beside βι̯ός) " property " (TEXTS III. 5) ; ἀρχαῖος "old, ancient," νέος "new" (νι̯ός "young), σημαία "banner," ὡραῖος " beautiful ";—Ital. loan-words : *e.g.* κουμανταρία Commendaria), μπιραρία It. *birraria* "beer-shop," σπετσαρία *speceria* "apothecary's shop," σκαμπαβία "a kind of boat," and many such.

1. The older forms in -ία, -έα, etc., have remained unchanged in many dialects (in the old city of Athens, Aegina, Cyme in Euboea,

Western Maina, Lower Italy, Gortynia in Pelopon., Zaconia, Pontus, Cappadocia), so παιδία, pl. of παιδί "child," παλατίου gen. of παλάτι "palace," καρδία "heart," σκοτεινία (Cappad.) "darkness," φωτία "light," ποῖος "who? which?" βασιλέας "king," ἀξιναρέα "cut with an axe," ἐλαία "olive-tree," μηλέα "apple-tree," πλέο "more," etc.

2. The _i_ (_e_) usually remains after a consonant + ρ, _e.g._ κρύος "cold," κρέας "flesh" (but τὸ κριάτο), τρία (beside τριά) "three"; θεός (beside θιός) comes from the ecclesiastical language.

3. In some North. Greek dialects -ιa and -εa (half vocalic ι̯ and ε̯, not _y_) are still differentiated in the pronunciation as φωτιά, but μηλξά.

4. In several dialects (_e.g._ in the region of the Aegean Sea and in Eastern Crete) ι disappears after an σ (ξ, ψ, ζ): ἄξα for ἄξια, fem. "worthy," γρόσα for γρόσια, pl. of γρόσι "piastre," νησά for νησιά, pl. of νησί "island," διακόσα for διακόσια "200," τρακόσες for τριακόσιες "300" (_f._), πλούσος = πλούσιος "rich." The loss of the ι and ε is universal in the following words : [1] σώπα (from σιώπα) "keep silence," σαγόνι (σιαγόνιον) "chin," σάλι (σιάλιον) "saliva," ψάθα (ψίαθος) "straw"; also κερά (κυρά) "lady, woman" (κυρία); θωρῶ (θεωρῶ) "I consider," χρωστῶ (χρεωστῶ) "I owe."

5. Spirantic Jod (Eng. _y_) has become χι or ̌σ (š) in some dialects : _e.g._ (Velvendos) ὄπχιος = ὄποιος, τὰ μάτι·χ·α = τὰ μάτια, (Crete), πŏός = ποιός. In several of the islands (_e.g._ Calymnos, Scyros, Nisyros) a σ or ̌σ [2] develops after voiceless consonants, and ζ or ̌ζ (ž) after voiced consonants respectively : _e.g._ ἀέρφσα = ἀδέρφια "brothers," πσός = ποιός, σέρζα = χέρια "hands," παιχνίδζα = παιχνίδια "sports," πŏάνω = πιάνω "I seize," καράβζα = καράβια "boats," αΰρζο = αΰριο. In Velvendos it becomes a hard κ̓ after φ, θ, σ: τέθκ̓ος = τέτοιος, χουράφκ̓α = κωράφια, etc. Note also from Chios (TEXTS III. 9) forms like p₁̌óttera = πειότερα "more," ippᵍ̣asen = ἔπιασεν "he seized," ďg̓o = δυό "two," μ̣ύ̣dǵa = βούδια "oxen." Finally, in the Cyprian dialect and kindred patois every ι (except after sibilants, where ι disappears) becomes κ or κι, i.e. k̓: Κυρκακός = Κυριακός, περιστέρκα = περιστέρια "doves," χωρκόν = χωριό, τρικά (and τρία), ἀλήθκεια = ἀλήθεια "truth," πκοιός = ποιός, χαρκιά from χαρτκιά = χαρτιά "cards."

§ 11. When an end-vowel and an initial vowel come together a contraction (crasis) takes place :

-_a_ + _a_-, or _o_-, _u_-, -_e_, _i_- becomes _a_

-_o_ + _o_-, _u_-, _e_-, _i_- becomes _o_

-_u_ + _u_-, _e_-, _i_- becomes _u_

-_e_ + _e_-, _i_- becomes _e_

-_i_ + _i_- becomes _i_ ;

or in reverse order, i.e. -_o_, -_u_, -_e_, -_i_ + _a_- become _a_, etc.

_a_ is therefore the strongest vowel and swallows up all

---

[1] For Pontic ä, ö from ιa, ιo, v. § 6, n. 6.   [2] Instead of _y_.

the rest; next in order comes *o*, then *u*, *e*, *i*: e.g. θ' ἀλλάξω = θὰ
ἀ. "I shall change," θά 'χω (ἔχω) "I shall have," ἀπ' (ἀπὸ)
αὐτό "from this," τ' ὄνομα (τὸ ὄ.) "the name," τό 'χτισαν (τὸ
ἔχτισαν) "they built it," ἐγώ 'μουνα (ἤμουνα) "I was," εἶν'
(εἶναι) ὄμορφη "she is beautiful," νὰ σοῦ 'πῶ (εἰπῶ) "let
me tell you," ποῦ 'σαι (εἶσαι) "where art thou?" τοῦ 'δωκα
(ἔδωκα) "I gave him," πέντ' ἔξι (πέντε) "five or six," ἦρθ'
ἔνας (ἦρθε) one came," λείπ' ἐκεῖνος (λείπει) "that one (he) is
absent," τί 'δες (τί εἶδες) "what did you see?"

1. In Northern Greek *e* is stronger than *u*, so π' ἔρχεται = ποῦ
ἔρχεται.

2. In many parts *i* is not swallowed up by *a* (or *o*, *u*), but combines with the preceding vowel into a diphthong: νὰ ἰδῶ ναῐδό "that
I may see," τὸ εἶδα τόῐδα "I saw it," ποῦ εἶσαι πύῐσε "where art thou?"
Further, in several regions *u* + *e* unite to *o*: ὀπόχει = ὀποῦ ἔχει "who
has," σόλεγα = σοῦ ἔλεγα. Before velar vowels καί retains the
palatal pronunciation of the κ: κι αὐτός "and he," and also loses
its vowel before a following *i*: κ' ὕστερα "and then." Moreover, the
short words μέ "me," σέ "thee," usually lose their *e* before *i*: μ'
εἶδες "thou sawest me"; while, on the contrary, the article ἡ οἱ retains
its vowel: ἦρθ' (ἦρθε) ἡ μάννα "the mother came."

3. Vowel contraction within a word takes place in general
according to the same laws as in case of liaison of separate words:
e.g. πᾷς (πᾷς) from πάγεις, τρώς from τρώγεις, ἄκου from ἄκουε, πάνε
from πά(γ)ουνε, λέτε from λέγετε, etc., πωρνό (πουρνό) "morning,"
from *πρωνό, *i.e.* πρωϊνόν. (Similarly Pontic ἄν = ἄγιον).

§ 12. The initial unstressed vowel is subject to various
mutations.

(a) The dropping (aphaeresis) of an *i* and *e*, more rarely
of an *o* or *a*: e.g. γούμενος (ἡγούμενος) "abbot," γειά (ὑγειά)
"health," μέρα (ἡμέρα) "day," μισός (a. Gk. ἥμισυς) "half,"
πάγω (a. Gk. ὑπάγω) "I go," ψηλός (a. Gk. ὑψηλός) "high,"
'γώ and ἐγώ "I," 'δώ and ἐδώ "here," βρίσκω (εὑρίσκω) "I
find," κεῖ and ἐκεῖ "there," κεῖνος and ἐκεῖνος "that," μπορῶ
(beside ἐμπορῶ and ἠμπορῶ) "I can, am able," ρωτῶ and ἐρωτῶ
"I ask," σπέρα (ἑσπέρα) "evening," φκαριστῶ (εὐχαριστῶ)
"I thank," γίδι (αἰγιδιον) "goat," ματώνω (αἷμα) "I make
bloody," δέν (from οὐδέν) "not," Pontic 'κί (from οὐκί) "not,"
λίγος (ὀλίγος) "little," μάτι (ὀμμάτι) "eye," μιλῶ (ὁμιλῶ) "I
speak," σπίτι (ὀσπίτι) "house," ψάρι (a. Gk. ὀψάριον) "fish,"
γαπῶ (usually ἀγαπῶ) "I love," πὸ μακρά (usually ἀπὸ μ.)
"from afar," πεθαίνω, ποθαίνω (ἀποθαίνω) "I die," τοῦ 'φτί
Velv. = the usual τὸ αὐτί "ear," λαχτόρι (Cappad.) = ἀλόχτερας
(Aegina) "cock."

2

Aphaeresis may even take place when the initial vowel is of secondary origin caused by the disappearance of a consonant: *e.g.* ναῖκα (Capp.) = γυναῖκα " woman " (*cf.* § 22).

(*b*) Prothesis, that is, the prefixing of an *a* in most cases, more rarely another vowel: νέφαλο and ἀνέφαλο " cloud," πλάγι and ἀπλά(γ)ι " side," στήθι and ἀστήθι " breast," χεῖλι and ἀχεῖλι " lip," ἀβδέλλα (βδέλλα) " leech," κρυφά and ἀκρυφά " secretly," καρτερῶ and ἀκαρτερῶ " I expect," περνῶ and ἀπερνῶ " I pass by," λησμονῶ and ἀλησμονῶ I forget" (*elimonízo* in the Terra d' Otranto), ἀθερρῶ (Pontus) = θαρρῶ " I believe," ἐσύ (σύ) " thou," τότες and ἐτότε(ς), Pontic ἀτότε " then, at that time," τοῦτος and ἐτοῦτος " this " (on βλέπω and ἐβλέπω, etc., *cf.* § 182, n. 2); ἴσκιος (in patois ἰσκιά and σκιά) " shadow."

(*c*) Exchange of the initial vowel for another vowel: *e, i* are liable to be displaced by *a* or *o*; *o* in most cases is displaced by *a*, while *a* seldom yields to any other vowel: ἄντερα (a. Gk. ἔντερα) " bowels," ἀλαφρός (ἐλαφρός) " light," ἀξάδερφος (ἐξάδερφος) " cousin," ἀπάνω (πάνω, ἐπάνω) " above," ἀκεῖ (Pontus) = ἐκεῖ " there," ἀρωτῶ (= ἐρωτῶ, ρωτῶ), in Pontus also ὀρωτῶ, ἀχνάρι, and χνάρι (a. Gk. ἴχνος) " track," ἀπομονή (ὑπομονή) " patience," ὄμορφος (also ἔμορφος) " beautiful," ὀχτρός (or ἐχτρός) " enemy," ὀρμήνεια (ἑρμηνεία) " counsel," ὀρπίδα (ἐρπίδα) " hope," ὀγώ = ἐγώ " I," ἐδικός = usually δικός (ἰδικός) " own," ἐπίσω (usually ὀπίσω or πίσω) " behind," ἀρφανός (ὀρφανός) " orphan," ἀχταπόδι (χταπόδι, from ὀκταπόδιον) " polypus," beside μάτι (see above) also ἀμμάτι; οὖλος, usually ὅλος " whole "; εὐτός (Chios, Naxos, Crete, Ionic Islands) = αὐτός " this."

In the forms of the initial vowel there exists the greatest diversity in the different dialects. These forms are mostly due to an incorrect analysis of the close *liaison* of words according to § 11, especially in the union of the article and noun or νὰ, θὰ + verb: *e.g.* τομμάτι is analysed into τὸ μάτι (instead of τὸ ὀμμάτι), νακαρτερῶ into ν' ἀκαρτερῶ (instead of νὰ καρτερῶ), τάντερα into τὰ ἄντερα (instead of τὰ ἔντερα).

(*b*) STOPS.

§ 13. The tenues π, κ, τ generally undergo no change. In some cases they have arisen from spirants (see § 18). On the other hand, two exceptionless phonetic laws have decreased the number of the tenues:

§ 14. (1) The combinations ππ and κτ have become φτ and χτ: (a. Gk.) ππ has become φτ: φταρμίζομαι (a. Gk. ππάρνυμαι), " sneeze," φτερό (πτερόν) " wing," φτωχός (πτωχός) " poor," ἀστράφτει (ἀστράπτει), " it lightens," ἐφτά (ἐπτά) " seven," κλέφτης (κλέπτης) " thief," πέφτω (πίπτω) " I fall."

(a. Gk.) κτ = χτ: χτίζω (κτίζω) " I build," χτυπῶ (κτυπῶ) " I strike," ἀνοιχτός (ἀνοικτός) " open," δάχτυλος (δάκτυλος) " finger," δείχτω (from δείκνυμι) " I show," δίχτυ (δίκτυον) " net," νύχτα (νύξ νυκτός) " night," ὀχτώ (ὀκτώ) " eight," σφιχτός (σφιγκτός) " fixed."

1. ππ, κτ therefore are no longer to be found in a modern Greek word. ἀπ' τό = ἀπὸ τό, etc., is a different matter; yet even in this case the pronunciation is often ἀφ' τό; so also, e.g., κόφ' το from kop(s) to, § 37.

Whenever the spelling ππ, κτ (καθρέππης instead of καθρέφτης "looking-glass," ἀκτῖνα instead of ἀχτῖνα "ray," etc.) occurs in vernacular texts it is merely a survival of the historic orthography of the literary language, pronunciation being φτ, χτ.

2. In the Greek of Lower Italy χτ and φτ have passed into φτ (Otranto) and στ (Bova) respectively: nífta νύχτα (but épetta = ἔπεφτα !) ; está = ἐπτά, nísta = νύχτα.

§ 15. (2) The tenues after nasals become mediae, i.e. μπ, ντ, γκ are pronounced like mb, nd, ŋg (ŋ = ng in German Engel): ἀγκαλιάζω aŋgal'ázo " I embrace," πρίγκιπας príŋgipas (Lat. princeps) " prince," λάμπω lámbo " I shine," ἀντάμα andáma " together." The same sounds arise when a nasal and (a. Gk.) β, γ, δ come together, so that μβ, γγ and νδ are pronounced like mb, ŋg, nd, preserving the ancient Greek mediae; but it is better, except in the case of γγ, to write μπ, ντ: κολυμπῶ (a. Gk. κολυμβῶ) " I swim," ἐγγίζω eŋgízo " I touch," ἔντεκα éndeka (ἔνδεκα) " eleven," δέντρο (δένδρον) déndro " tree."

1. Spellings like κολυμβῶ, δένδρον come from the literary language and are unintelligible.

When, owing to the dropping of a vowel, the groups μπ, γκ (γγ), ντ begin the word, they are pronounced almost exactly like pure voiced mediae, i.e. like North German or Romanic b, g, d (or, more correctly, ᵐb, ᵑg, ⁿd with reduced nasal): μπροστά (ἐμπρός) " forwards," μπαίνω (ἐμπαίνω) " I go in," γγόνι (ἐγγόνι) " grandson," γκρεμίζομαι " I hurl down, precipitate (*ἔγκρημ[ν]ον), ντροπή (ἐντροπή) " disgrace," ντύνομαι (from ἐνδύνομαι) " I dress.'

The change of tenues to mediae after a preceding nasal takes place also in the liaison of words, final -ν uniting with the initial π (ψ), κ (ξ), τ (τσ) of a following word to *mb* (*mbz*), *ng* (*ngz*), *nd* (*ndz*): τὸν πατέρα = *tombatéra* " the father," τὸν ψεύτη *tombzéfti* " the liar," τὴν τσέπη *tindzépi* (acc.) " the pocket," τὴν κουράζω *tingurázo* " I weary her," δὲν ξέρω *dengzéro* " I do not know," δὲν ψηφῶ *dembzifó* " I care not," ἂν τὸν πάρῃς *andombáris* " if you bring him." Note also from Chios (TEXTS III. 9) (δ)ὲν εἶ(δ)εν κανεῖ en *ien gani* "he saw nobody," (δ)ὲν ἤρκουτον π͜κ͜ά en *irkutom b͜ǧ͜a* " he came no more," ἤφυεν τσεῖνος (= κεῖνος) *ifien dzínos* " that (man) fled." On the other hand, initial β, γ, δ, and *y* always remain spirants : τὸ(ν) βασιλιά, τὸ(ν) γάμο, τὴ(ν) δόλια, τὴ(ν) γυναῖκα (*cf.* § 33, n. 3).

2. In many regions (*e.g.* several of the Cyclades, Lesbos, *cf.* also TEXTS III. 12) μπ, γκ, ντ, both when initial and when within a word, have become pure mediae : μπάμπω has become *bábo* "grandmother," (ἐ)μπορῶ "I can," (*e*)*boró*, φεγγάρι "moon," *fegári*, δόντι "tooth," *dódi*, κοντά "near," *kodá*, ἄντρας "man," *ádras*, ἀραβωνιάζ(ου)νται "they are betrothed," *arravoniázdai*. The same phonetic change extends even to loan-words (*cf. e.g.* from Ios κουβάνια, Ital. *compagnia* "company," ἀρμαμέδο, Lat. *armamentum* "fleet," πάδα, Ital. *banda* "side"), and to word-liaison, *cf.* from Ios τὸ *gafé* = τὸν καφέ "coffee," from Lesbos τ *gardiá* = τὴν καρδιά (acc.) "the heart," *d galamniá* = τὴν καλαμνιά, "the reed," σὰ *dòn* = σὰν τὸν (acc.) "as the"; from Saranda Klisiés μὴ *dúχ* = μὴν τύχῃ "may it not happen," τὴ *gséskisan* "they rent it."

3. The softening of the initial syllable by the nasal of the preceding final has sometimes resulted in the voiceless initial of a word becoming voiced, or a voiced initial becoming voiceless, *i.e.* there arose a ὁ μπιστικός from a τὸμ πιστικόν, a μπέμπω (Crete) from τὸν πέμπω, a *gourevó* "I shear" (Lesbos) from τὸν κουρεύω, etc., or from τὴ μπάντα a ἡ πάντα "side" (Ios).

4. The m. Gk. mediae are therefore inseparably connected with an originally preceding nasal, there being no other mediae except in loan-words. As the alphabet has no signs for *b*, *d*, *g*,[1] the corresponding sounds are represented in the numerous Turkish and Italian words by μπ, ντ, γκ respectively : μπέης, Turk. *bei* "Bey," μπάρκα "bark," ντερβένι, Turk. *derven* "defile, narrow pass," ντάμα "lady" (in cards), σεβντάς, Turk. *sevda* "love," ἀντίο, Ital. *adío* "adieu," γκιαούρις "Giaour," γκαλερία "gallery," μπάγκα "bank." So also Γκαίτε "Goethe," Μπέκ "Beck," and similar foreign names, although in such cases the educated Hellenise the form (Γοίθιος Goethe, Δάντης Dante, etc.).

---

[1] Sometimes (in Constantinople, especially in Turkish newspapers printed in Greek characters) the signs β, γ, δ with a period underneath are employed.

§ 16. In addition to the rules already stated, the tenues suffer phonetic transformation only in isolated cases and dialectically; thus κ has fallen out before χ in ζάχαρι (from ζάκχαρι) "sugar," and σιχαίνομαι (from σικχαίνομαι) "I dislike," κβ becomes βγ, and κδ becomes γδ: βγάλλω (ἐκβάλλω) "I take out," βγαίνω (ἐκβαίνω) "I go out," γδύνω (ἐκ-δύω) "I undress," γδέρνω (ἐκ-δέρω) "I flay." The combination φτι becomes φκι in φκυάρι (*πτυάριον) "shovel," and φκειάνω (beside φτειάνω) "I make."

1. The disappearance of tenues in Chios (Texts 9), e.g. in aopáno = ἀπὸ πάνω "from above," etúos = ἐτοῦτος "this," is due to dissimilation. The cause of the disappearance of the κ in the same region in aloái = ἀλογάκι "little horse," sendúi = σεντούκι "chest," cannot be determined with certainty.

2. The change of τ to κ (before i) is found in Zaconian and in Lesbos (also in Mesta on Chios): thus, (Zacon.) ka'kidzíe = κατοικία, po'kíχa = ἐπότιζα (cf. Texts III. 15, n. 9. 2), χarkí = χαρτί, similarly aféngi = ἀφέντης "Mr., Sir," before mediae; (Lesbos) κεῖχος = τεῖχος "wall," ἀφκί = ἀφτί "ear," μάκ' = μάτι "eye," μαγηλ' = μαιτήλι "handkerchief." In Zaconian also π before i passes into κ: e.g. kísu = πίσω "behind."

3. On Crete (and several other islands of the Aegean) τ before ι becomes a spirant: τὰ μάθια = τὰ μάτια, τέθοιος = τέτοιος, στραθιώτης = στρατιώτης. Similarly ντι becomes δι: ἀνάδιος = ἀνάιτιος "opposite," ἀρχοδιά = ἀρχοντιά "nobility, gentry." Cf. also máddia = μάτια, Terra d' Otranto.

4. In Pontus the initial group στ becomes σ(σ): σ(σ)ὸ = στὸ "in the, to the," σάχτη = στάχτη "ashes."

§ 17. The palatalising of a κ before e and i (y), i.e. the change of ke ki to če či, ce ci or če či (τσ or τǰ τǰ) is widely spread (but only in dialects).

This transition takes place in Pontus, Cappadocia, Cyprus, Crete, on many islands of the Aegean (e.g. Lesbos, Amorgos, Naxos, Syra, Calymnos, Chios), in the dialect of the city of Athens, in Megara, Aegina, Cyme in Euboea, in many regions of the Peloponnesus (also in Zaconia and in the Maina), in Locris, Aetolia, Lower Italy; thus, e.g., τσεφάλι = κεφάλι "head," τσαί (τǰαί) = καί "and," τσαιρός = καιρός "time," τσερί = κερί "candle," τσερά = κερά (κυρία) "woman," ἐτσεῖ (ἐτǰεῖ) = ἐκεῖ "there," τσείτομαι = κείτομαι "I lie," τσῦμα = κῦμα "wave," τǰυρατǰή (Maina) = κυριακή "Sunday," κότσινος (κότǰινος) = κόκκινος "red," κουτσί = κουκί "bean," ἄκουτσε (Aegina) 3 pers. sing. of ἄκουκα "I heard," στσίζω = σκίζω (σχίζω) "I split." In τǰουμῶμαι (Chios τσοιμοῦμαι) = κοιμοῦμαι "I sleep," τǰουλία = κοιλιά "belly," ὀτǰούβω = σκύβω "I bow," ὀτǰουλί = σκυλί "dog," and in other instances (e.g. on Aegina), the phonetic change before u is only apparent, because this u has arisen from an older i-sound. This στσ (ὄτὄ) may become even σσ (or ὄ), *cf. e.g.* βρίσσει "he finds" (Chios, Calymnos, and elsewhere); on ὄ, *v.* § 28 n.

The media *g* (γγ, γκ) undergoes the same change: ἄντζελος, *i.e.* *ándzelos* = ἄγγελος "angel," ἀντζίστρι = ἀγκίστρι "hook," συδζενής (Ios) = συγγενής "relative"; or *dž*, thus ἄνdžελος, etc. (in Cos also ἄνdγελος, etc.).

In Cappadocia (Pharasa) κ also becomes *dž*: e.g. ἀdžεῖνος = ἐκεῖνος.

(c) SPIRANTS.

§ 18. The spirants φ, χ, θ have a tendency to pass into tenues (π, κ, τ) after a preceding *s* (or after another voiceless spirant). This is most generally the case with θ, which becomes τ after every σ, φ, χ: αἰστάνομαι (from αἰσθάνομαι) "I perceive," ἐγελάστηκα aor. pass. "I was laughed at," ἐσβήστηκε "it was extinguished" (from ἐγελάσθηκα, ἐσβή-σθηκε, but, *e.g.*, ἐτιμήθηκα "I was honoured), φτάνω (from φθάνω) "I overtake," (ἐ)λεύτερος (from ἐλεύθερος) "free," ἐγράφτηκε "it was written," ἐχτρός (from ἐχθρός) "enemy," ἐφυλάχτηκα "I guarded."

1. The spelling with θ (ἐλεύθερος, ἐγελάσθηκα, etc.) is historical, that is, it has no value for the present pronunciation.

Similarly χ becomes κ after σ and regularly also after *f*: ἄσκημος (ἄσχημος) "ugly," μόσκος (μόσχος) "musk, perfume," σκίζω (σχίζω) "I split," σκοινί (σχοινί) "rope," σκολειό (σχολεῖον) "school"; εὐκαριστῶ (εὐχαριστῶ) "I thank," καυκοῦμαι (καυχοῦμαι) "I boast," εὐκοῦμαι (εὐχοῦμαι) "I pray," εὐκή (εὐχή) "prayer."

2. The same holds true for the spelling σχ (σχεδόν, σχολαστικός) as for σθ.

3. The change of ρθ into ρτ is fairly wide-spread, especially in Eastern Greek: frequently ἦρτα = ἦρθα, "I came," ὀρτός = ὀρθός "straight." Less frequently ρχ becomes ρκ (*e.g.* in Cyprus,[1] Rhodes, Calymnos, Samos, Chios): ἔρκουμαι = ἔρχομαι "I come," ἀρκή = ἀρχή "beginning."

φ after σ becomes π only in some dialects.

4. Thus in Pontus, Cyzicus, and Icarus: *e.g.* ἀσπαλίζω = σφαλνῶ "I lock," σπάζω = σφάζω "I kill," σπίγγω = σφίγγω "I press," σπιντόνα = σφενδονή "sling."

5. The variations (τρέφω, θρέψω, etc.) arising from the a. Gk. law of dissimilation of aspirates are not found in m. Gk., θρέφω ἔθρεψα, τρέχω ἔτρεξα, or survive only in some rare cases, like ἐτέθηκα (a. Gk.

[1] More correctly *rk*.

ἐτέθην) from θέτω " I place," ἐτάφηκα (a. Gk. ἐτάφην) from θάβω "I bury," ἐτράφηκα (a. Gk. ἐτράφην) from θρέφω " I bring up, educate." *Cf.* § 205, I. 3, n. 3, and § 207.

§ 19. The combination *fs* (frequently for *ŏs, vs*) changes uniformly to *ps* (ψ): ἐδούλευσα (aor. of δουλεύω " I work ") becomes ἐδούλεψα, ἔπαυσα (παύω " I cease ") ἔπαψα, ἔκλαυσα (κλαί(γ)ω " I weep ") ἔκλαψα, and so forth (*cf.* aorist-formation, § 201, I. 1). Similarly, Λεψῖνα = 'Ελευσίς, ἡ κάψι (καῦσις) " burning heat "; *cf.* also κάτσε = κάθ(ι)σε " sit down " (imperat.) and (Turk.) μπαξές from μπαχ(τ)σές " garden."

1. In Lower Italy (Terra d' Otranto) exactly the opposite has occurred, ψ becoming *fs*: *e.g.* afsiló = ἀψηλός " high," *na kláfso* = νὰ κλάψω (from κλαίω).

2. The form ἀτός (*v.* § 136, n. 3) has not arisen from the more usual αὐτός through the dropping of *f*, but corresponds to an a. Gk. form ἀτός.

§ 20. θ sometimes becomes χ: χλιβερός, χλιμμένος, " afflicted," χλῖψι " affliction " (beside θλιβερός, etc.), παχνί (from παθνί) " manger "; θ has become φ in ἀρίφνητος (= ἀν-αρίθμητος) " innumerable," στάφνη (from στάθμη) " rule (line)."

1. In the dialect of the Terra d' Otranto, initial θ becomes *t*, θ in the middle of a word between vowels becomes *s*: *télo* = θέλω "I wish," *tínato* = θάνατος " death," *lisári* = λιθάρι " stone," *pesaméno* = πεθαμμένος " dead." In Eastern Greek also τ stands for θ (*cf.* νὰ χατῶ for χαθῶ, TEXTS III. 13. c, and ἄτρωπος for ἄθρωπος, TEXTS III. 14. a). σ instead of θ is especially characteristic of Zaconian, *e.g.* σέρι = θέρος " summer," *silikó* = θηλυκός " female."

2. In isolated cases δά (Velvendos), χά (Pontus), ἄ (Chios) = the regular θά, further ἐννά (Cyprus) = θεν(ν)ά (particles to form future tense).

§ 21. In Zaconian, in Cyprus, South-Western Asia Minor, on several of the Aegean Islands (*e.g.* Crete, Amorgos, Cos, Calymnos, Astypalaea), in the Pontic (as also in the Cappadocian) dialects, χ before *e* and *i* becomes š (ǒ) or even ŝ (ǒ): σέρι = χέρι " hand," σειμῶνας = χειμῶνας " winter," ἔσεις = ἔχεις " thou hast," ἔσετε = ἔχετε " you have." Sometimes (*e.g.* in Calymnos) this ǒ passes into σ: σέρι, ἔσει, ὄσι = ὄχι " not," νύσα = νύχια " nails, claws." In Bova, χ before velar sonants is pronounced aspirated *k* (*kh·*), before palatal *h* (*h·*); *h* = χ is also found occasionally elsewhere.

§ 22. Among the voiced spirants (β, γ, δ), γ especially shows a widely spread tendency to disappear between vowels, and sometimes even in the initial syllable. This disappearance of intervocalic γ (ʒ and y) is found in the most diverse regions (in Epirus, Peloponnesus, Macedonia, in the islands from Cyprus to Asia Minor): *e.g.* λέω and λέγω " I speak," (imperf. ἔλεα and ἔλεγα), πα(γ)αίνω πη(γ)αίνω πά(γ)ω " I go," τρώ(γ)ω aor. ἔφα(γ)α "I eat," λο(γ)αρι̯άζω "I reckon," φυλά(γ)ω "I guard," ρολό(γ)ι "clock," σα(γ)ίτα "arrow," φα(γ)ητό "eating," συλλο(γ)οῦμαι "I consider," πέλα(γ)ο "sea," (ὀ)λί(γ)ος "few," με(γ)άλος "great," ἀ(γ)απῶ "I love," ἐ(γ)ώ " I "; ἔλοια = γέλοια (Naxos), ὑρίζω = γυρίζω " I seek," ὑναῖκα = γυναῖκα " woman." The γ is omitted most frequently in the first-mentioned verbs.

The combination γι̯ (γυ) has become one simple sound *y* (= γ before *e, i*). This sign is therefore employed to represent a *y* before velar sonants: γι̯ομίζω = γεμίζω "I fill," γι̯όμα = γέμα "repast," γι̯οφύρι = γεφύρι, γιαρᾶς, Turk *yara* "wound." *Cf.* also § 9.

The omission of β is usual in διάολος = διάβολος "devil."

The regular omission not only of the γ but also of the β and δ (rarely of θ) is a marked peculiarity of the South-Eastern Gk. dialects, *i.e.* of Cyprus, Rhodes, Calymnos, and the neighbouring islands, but is not confined to these dialects: φοοῦμαι = φοβοῦμαι "I fear," κάουρας = κάβουρας "crab," περι(β)όλι "garden," ἀερφός = ἀδερφός "brother," γά(δ)αρος "ass," οἱ (δ)ώ(δ)εκα "the twelve," ὀρπί(δ)α "hope," πα(δ)άρι = πο(δ)άρι "foot," νὰ ὤσω = νὰ δώσω "that I may (let me) give," ἔ(ν) = δέν "not." *Cf.* also ἄ and ἐννά, § 20, n. 2. In the Terra d' Otranto the dropping of intervocalic (and initial) consonants obtains to a still larger extent (e.g. τόα = τότε, ρόα = πότε; ο, *i* = τὸ, τὴ(ν); stéo = στέκω).

In Chios, side by side with the complete dropping of γ, β, δ we find also a mere reduction: *e.g.* νὰ ⁱελάσωμε from γελῶ "I laugh," ὁ ᵛασιλές "the king," (ᵘ)οὐδι "ox," καᵛαλλίνα "horse-manure," γάᵘαρος "ass," etc. Texts III. 9.

§ 23. On the other hand, γ has been inserted between vowels: *e.g.* ἀ(γ)έρας "air" (Chios ἀⁱέρας), θε(γ)ός "God," ἀκού(γ)ω "I hear," καί(γ)ω "I burn," κλαί(γ)ω "I weep," φταί(γ)ω "I am at fault"; ἀγώρι "boy" (from a. Gk. ἄωρος) is quite common.

This phenomenon is found on the whole mainland, the Ionic Islands, the Cyclades, Crete, Chios, and Lesbos. Moreover, almost in the entire region of the Aegean as well as in Crete and Cyprus a γ is inserted between *v* and a vowel: πιστεύγω = πιστεύω "I believe," χορεύγω "I dance," κόβγω "I cut," ράβγω "I sew," τρίβγω "I rub," παρασκευγή "Friday," βγαγγέλι̯ο "gospel." The verbs in

-εύω end, in the Terra d' Otranto, in -éo (pistéo " I believe "), in Bova in -éguo (platéguo "I speak"), in Zaconian in -έϑϑgu (ᵭuléϑϑgu " I work ").

In some dialects a γ is prefixed even to the initial vocalic syllable : γαῖμα = αἷμα " blood," γέρημος = ἔρημος "empty," γίδιος = ἴδιος "like, the same " ; cf. especially TEXTS III. 12 (γεῖπε = εἶπε, γύστερα = ὕστερα, γούλος = ὅλος, etc.). Often a γ develops before ν in the words σύγνεφο = σύννεφο " cloud," ἔγνοιᾳ = ἔννοιᾳ " care," ἀγνάντια = ἀνάντια " opposite," τυραγνῶ = τυραννῶ " I oppress."

§ 24. γ and ν (β, υ) regularly disappear before μ : μάλαμα (from μάλαγμα) " gold," σαμάρι (from σαγμάριον) " pack-saddle," πλεμένος (from πλεγμένος) of πλέκω " I twist, plait," πνιμένος from πνίγω " I drown," πρᾶμα (from πρᾶγμα) " thing," ἐρωτεμένος (from ἐρωτεύω) " beloved," θᾶμα " wonder," θαμάζω " I wonder " (from θαῦμα, θαυμάζω), καμένος (from καυμένος, καίω, κάβω) " burnt," μαγεμένος (μαγεύω) " bewitched," ρέμα (ρεῦμα) " brook."

1. Usually πρᾶμμα, καμμένος, etc., are written with μμ. In this case, however, those dialects which actually possess double consonants (§ 36 n.) recognise only one μ in the pronunciation (except with two μμ in Chios). Spellings πρᾶγμα, πλεγμένος, ρεῦμα, etc., come from the literary language, unless the -γμ- in the continental dialects.

2. ν disappears before ρ only in ξέρω beside ξεύρω " I know " ; otherwise the ν remains : ἀλεύρι " flour," εὑρίσκω (θὰ εὕρω) " I find," μαῦρος " black," etc. Before ν, ν has become μ ; cf. λάμνω (a. Gk. ἐλαύνω) " I row," μνοῦχος (εὐνοῦχος) " castrated, eunuch."

§ 25. δ has disappeared before y (ι) in γιά = διά " through, on account of " (γιατί " why ? " = διὰ τί) ; but διαλέγω " I choose," διαβάζω " I read," διαβαίνω " I pass over," δυό " two," δυόσμος " jasmine," etc.

§ 26. In the dialect of Cyprus we find δ and γ treated in a manner analogous to the deaspiration of θ (χ, φ) given in § 18, the groups ργ, ρδ becoming ρκ, ρτ, and βγ, βδ, γδ becoming βκ, βτ, γτ : ἀρκάτης = ἐργάτης " worker," ἀρκυρός = ἀργυρός " silver," περτίκιν = πέρδικα " partridge," αὐκόν = αὐγό " egg," βκαίννω = βγαίνω " I go out," ἐβτομάδα = (ἐ)βδομάδα " week," γτέρνω = γδέρνω " I flay." On Rhodes and the neighbouring islands only ργ, ρδ, and βγ undergo this change ; otherwise (e.g. in Chios and Calymnos) this phonetic movement has usually attacked only ρg and βg, though the second sound is also found partially or wholly voiceless ; cf. βgάλλει " he takes out," πιστεύgω " I believe," μαρg'όλλος = μαριόλος " sly," φεύ$_υ^{κ}$ει "he departs," αυγά and αυκά "eggs," Γιώργις and Γιώρκις= Γεώργιος, ἀργάτης and ἀρκάτης = ἀργάτης.

In Terra d' Otr. δ is pronounced as d (analogous to t for θ, § 20, n. 1); there and in Bova γ (ʒ) is pronounced g before the vowels e and i.

§ 27. The palatal γ (y) has become in the Maina dialect a ź, i.e. a voiced palatal sibilant: e.g. ζῆ = γῆ "earth," ζομάτος = γεμάτος (γιομάτος) "full," Παναζία = Παναγία, μαζεριτσή = μαγερική "kitchen." Even the secondary y in γιά from διά, Γιάννης from Ἰωάννης, etc. (cf. § 9), undergoes the same change (ζά, Ζάννης). For other changes to which the spirant y is liable, v. § 10, n. 5.

§ 28. In many parts the sibilants σ and ζ are pronounced with the front palate (ś) (that is, dorsal) instead of with the tongue-tip; often σ (ζ) becomes a kind of sh-sound (š, ž, ś, ź). This pronunciation is found over the whole Greek-speaking territory, most frequently before i (e.g. εἴκοσι "twenty") and before ι (μιση ὀκά = μιση ὀκά). The latter (ι) sometimes disappears (τρακόσα = τριακόσια "300," γρόσα = γρόσια "piastres," v. § 10, n. 4). š for s before consonants is very rare (e.g. šκύλος for σκύλος "dog" in Pontus, šτὸ šπίτι "in the house," κašτρο "fortress" in Maina, μόšκος = μόσχος "perfume" in Taygetos), while kš, pš, tš (for ξ, ψ, τσ) are found wherever σ is sounded š. Texts III. 3 and 15 (Maina and Ladá in Taygetos) afford characteristic examples of the extension of this pronunciation of the σ and ζ to all other combinations.

For š (ś) from χ, v. § 21. In some dialects in which κ is palatalised to č (§ 17), e.g. in Bova and Cyprus, sč becomes š, as ἄšημος from ἄσκημος "ugly," šύλος from σκύλος "dog," etc. In Karpathos and some of the neighbouring islands (also Chios) we find the transition from σσ or σι to τσ: e.g. γλῶτσα = γλῶσσα, νητσά = νησιά; the transition from ζ to dζ (e.g. παίδζω = παίζω) is more widely spread.

§ 29. Before a voiced consonant (β, γ, μ, ν) σ is pronounced like ζ (z), that is, voiced: σβήνω zvíno "I extinguish," προσμένω prozméno "await," σμίγω zmiʒo "I join, unite." Similarly with close liaison of words: ποιὸς μπαίνει pyoz béni, τοὺς μεγάλους tuz meʒálus, ἀς λέη az leι, ἀς δώση az δósi.

1. Otherwise the σ is subject to few mutations; sometimes it disappears between vowels if the next syllable contains a σ, as, e.g., in Velvendos (σ'χουρεῖς = συχωρέσης), Bova (ἐγράφσαι = ἐγράψασι), Chios (νὰ πλερώης = νὰ πλερώσης), Lesbos (δρόγισα = δρόσισα), Pontus (Θανᾶις = Ἀθανάσις). In Lower Italy (also in Zaconian) the dropping of the final -s is a common phonetic law: teό = θεός "God," mástora

= μάστορας "master," *yelái* = γελάεις "thou laughest." In ἄντρε[s]
ξυναῖσ̌ε[s] from the Maina (TEXTS III. 3) and ὁ βασιλὲν νὰ . . . = ὁ
βασιλὲς νὰ, ἕνα[s] φρένιμος, etc., from Chios (Texts III. 9) -s has disappeared before a following ž or semi-vowel. Final -s may disappear
also through dissimilation; *cf. e.g.* occasionally ὁ πατέρα[s] μας or
(Chios) λωλλὸ τσαὶ = λωλὸς τσαὶ (*i.e.* καὶ), νὰ τοῦ πάρῃ[s] τσαὶ . . .,
πολλοὺ[s] ξένους, (Ios) τσῇ δούλα[s] τσης. Otherwise the *s* is everywhere phonetically retained, apparent exceptions (as, *e.g.*, in ἡ πόλι =
a. Gk. πόλις) being explained as new forms of declension.

(d) LIQUIDS AND NASALS.

§ 30. ρ, λ, ν before a *y* (ι) become mouillé (*r′*, *l′*, *n′*):
γριά *ȝr′(y)á* "old woman," ἥλιος *il′(y)os* "sun," λιοντάρι
l′(y)ondári "lion," ἐννιά *eń(y)á* "nine," ἀσημένιος *asimén′os*
"of silver." In many dialects between μ and ι a ń is inserted, though very often not written: μνιά *mńá* = μιά "one,"
ὁμνοιάζω *omńázo* "I resemble," καλαμνιά "reed," ποτάμνια
"rivers."

§ 31. Before a consonant λ regularly becomes ρ: *e.g.*
ἀδερφός from ἀδελφός "brother," ἐρπίδα (= ἐλπίδα) "hope"
Ἀρβανίτης "Albanian," ἦρθα from ἦλθα "I came," χάρκωμα
(χαλκός) "metal pot," βαρμένος = βαλμένος, pass. ptcp. of
βάλλω "I put," στέρνω (usually στέλνω) "I send," βόρτα,
Ital. *volta* (also βόλιτα).

1. *r*- and *l*-sounds are very liable to metathesis, *i.e.* to change
their position within a word: ἄρθωπος from ἄθρωπος "man,"
κρουσεύω from κουρσεύω "I commit piracy, live by robbery," πρικός
and πικρός "bitter," πουρνάρι from πρινάρι "(holly) oak," πουρνό
from πρωνό "early," σερνικός from ἀρσενικός "male," ἀρμέγω from
ἀμέργω ἀμέλγω, "I milk," ἄδεφλε from ἄδελφε "brother" (voc.
Pontus), or ἀδρέφι for ἀδέρφι (Ionic Islands), σκόρφα and σκρόφα
"sow." Metathesis is rarer with other sounds. If two *r*-sounds
occur in a word, one of them usually converts to λ through dissimilation: ἀλέτρι (a. Gk. ἄροτρον) "plow," γλήγορα from γρήγορα
"quickly," κριθάρι and κλιθάρι "barley," παλεθύρι and παραθύρι
"window," περιστέρι and πελιστέρι "dove," πλώρη from πρώρα
"poop (deck)," φλεβάρις from *φρεβάρις, the latter again through
transposition from φεβράρις "February." We find disappearance
of λ through dissimilation in ὁλάκερος = a. Gk. ὁλόκληρος "entire,"
φανέλα = Ital. *flanella*. Noteworthy is the disappearance of the ρ in
the word χουσός = χρυσός, TEXTS III. 12.

2. In the dialect of the Sphaciotes, Cretan mountaineers, λ
before velar vowels becomes a peculiar kind of *r* (cerebral *ṛ*), which is
spoken with the front edge of the tongue in a curved position:
ἄρρος *áṛos* = ἄλλος, καρός *kaṛós* = καλός, φίρος *fíṛos* = φίλος, θάρασσα
þáṛasa = θάλασσα. A sibilant *r* = Czech. *ř* is found in Scyros

(written χέρζι = χέρι). In Lower Italy intervocalic λ has become a (cerebral) ḍḍ : áḍḍo = ἄλλος, poḍḍí = πολύ, ndicheḍḍa = *δικέλλα (= ἰδική).

§ 32. In πλιό, πλιά "more" λ is very frequently expelled : πιό, πιά.

In the dialect of Samothrace λ and ρ completely drop out : ἄογο = ἄλογο "horse," τυί = τυρί "cheese," τεῖς = τρεῖς "three," ἔχεται = ἔρχεται "comes," χωιό = χωριό "village." Before a, o, u, λ is dropped also in Zaconian, in Naxos and Cappadocia (Pharasa) : e.g. éa = ἔλα "come," kuiḍí = κλουδί, κλουβί "cage," θάασσα = θάλασσα "sea," ξύο = ξύλον "wood."

§ 33. Modern Greek has three nasals, μ, ν, and ℩ (= n in Germ. *Enkel*). The last occurs (as in German) only before k-sounds (k, g) and is written with γ (cf. also § 15).

The (a. Gk.) nasals have disappeared before the spirants φ, θ, χ : νύφη from νύμφη "bride," πεθερός from πενθερός "father-in-law," ἄθρωπος from ἄνθρωπος "man," ἀθός from ἄνθος "flower," συχωρῶ from συγχωρῶ "I pardon," σφιχτός from σφιγχτός, σφιγκτός "bound" "fastened."

1. Likewise before σ in Κωσταντῖνος, Κωστῆς, etc. (*Constantinus*), before ξ and ψ in ἔσφιξα, aor. of σφίγγω "I press," ἔπεψα from πέμπω "I send" (usually στέλνω).

2. Forms or spelling like ἄνθος, ἄνθρωπος, συγχωρῶ, σύγχρονος, σύμφωνος are due generally to the literary language, nevertheless νθ has remained unchanged dialectically (in the North), as ἄνθος, ἄνθρωπος.

3. Original μβ, γγ, νδ are treated differently, v. § 15. The nasal disappears before the voiced spirant only in words which have forced their way in from the literary language and also before initial β, γ (3, y) δ (§ 15) ; as σύβασι from σύμβασις "agreement," συγυρίζω from συγγυρίζω, "I arrange, prepare," συδέω (συνδέω) "I bind," κίδυνος (κίνδυνος) "danger" ; spellings like συμβαίνει belong to the literary language.

4. ν also is sometimes, like ρ, changed by dissimilation to λ (e.g. μελίγγι for μενίγγι = a. Gk. μῆνιγξ "temple (of head)," πλεμόνι = a. Gk. πνεύμων, "lung"), or, like σ, is completely suppressed (thus in Chios καένας or κανέας = κανένας "anybody," κάουν = κάνουν "they do," and similarly κάω, κάεις, etc.).

§ 34. Final -ν is usually only pronounced in such words as are closely connected with the following word, and only when the following word begins with a vowel or with κ, π, τ, ξ, ψ, τσ, and these sounds then (according to § 15) become g, b, d (gz, bz, dz) ; the ν itself becoming ℩ and m before g and b. The forms which retain the final -ν under these conditions are especially the definite and the indefinite

article, the conjunctive pronoun of the 3rd pers. (§ 136), the
particles δέν "not," ἄν "if," πρίν "before," σάν "as, like,"
ὅταν "when": e.g. τὸν ἄθρωπο "the man," but τὸ φίλο "the
friend," τὴν πίστι "the faith," but τὴ γυναῖκα "the woman,"
ἕναν ἐργάτη "one (or a) workman," ἕνα βασιλιά "a king,"
τὴν εἶδα "I saw her," τὴ βλέπω "I see her," δὲν ξέρω (in
Lesbos, however, and other North Greek dialects, δὲ ξέρω,
etc.) "I don't know," δὲ θέλω "I will not," ἂν ἔχῃς "if thou
hast," ἂ θέλῃς "if thou willest," πρὶν ἔρθῃ "before he comes,"
πρὶ φύγῃ "before he flees," σὰν πατέρας "like a father," σὰ
μάννα "like a mother." The pronouns αὐτός and τοῦτος
"this," and ἐκεῖνος "that," together with adjectives, rarely
retain their -ν in connection with a substantive, the adjectives
retaining it only when the substantive begins with a vowel:
τοῦτον τὸν ξένο or τούτη τὴ φορά, τὸν καλὸν ἄθρωπο or τὸν
καλὸ ἄθρωπο; but note πολὺν καιρό "long time," πόσον
καιρόν "how long?"

1. Even under other circumstances the final -ν is sometimes retained, especially if it is protected by rival forms in -νε (-να); cf.
λοιπόν "now, therefore," κάν(ε) or κάνα "at least, even if," ἕναν(ε)
"one, a," τόν(ε) τήν(ε) "him, her," ἐκεῖνον(α) "that (one)," ποιον(α)
"whom," ἄλλον(ε) "another," τῶ χρονῶν(ε) "of the years," and other
genitives; also the verbal forms φέρουν(ε), ἔφεραν and ἐφέρανε "they
brought," (ἐ)κάθονταν and (ἐ)καθότανε "he sat," ἤμουν(α) "I was,"
ἐρχόμουν(α) "I came," νὰ ἰδοῦν(ε) "that they may see" (beside ἔφερα,
ἐκάθοντα, ἔρχουμου, etc.). But before spirants one has a choice
between, e.g., τόνε (τήνε) βλέπω "I see him (her)," ἐφέρανε βιβλίο
"they brought a book," or τὴ βλέπω, ἔφερα βιβλίο.

2. Following the model of δέν and δέ "not," we may also use
μήν beside μή "not" (prohibitive) and νάν beside νά "in order
that": e.g. νὰ μὴν ἀκούσω "in order that I may not hear," νὰ μὴν
πάρῃς "do not take," νὰν τὸ φέρῃ "in order that he may bring it."

3. In consequence of mistaken separation of words the final -ν
was sometimes carried over to the following word, and thus many
words have received a "prothetic" ν; as, νοικοκύρις "master of
house" (fr. οἶκος), νήλιος = ἥλιος "sun," νύπνος = ὕπνος "sleep," νουρά
"tail," Νικαριά "Island of Icarus," νή—νή = ἤ—ἤ "either . . . or,"
νέλα (TEXTS III. 15, Ladá) = ἔλα "come." Cf. also § 15, n. 3.

4. In some dialects (Cyprus, Rhodes, Chios, Naxos, and other
islands of the Aegean, Pontus) the final -ν has throughout (and
especially in the absolute final syllable) maintained its place (or has
only been reduced without disappearing), and has often been carried
over to other forms where, properly speaking, it does not belong;
thus, e.g., not only acc. ἡμέραν, μάνναν, κόρην, ἀδερφόν, τοῦτον, χωριόν,
γυναῖκαν, βασιλιάν, βρύσιν, neuter φύλλον, σπίτιν, 1 and 3 pl. μπορούμεν,
μπορούσιν, 3rd sing. (ἐ)πῆρεν, ἔβαλεν, but also ὄνομαν = ὄνομα, πρᾶμαν =

πρᾶμα, στόμαν = στόμα, ἡ ὑναῖκαν του = ἡ γυναῖκα του, τὰ παιδιάν του
= τὰ παιδιά του, ἐξέβην "he went out" (a. Gk. ἐξέβη). When the
nasal is so conspicuous in the final syllable, it often affects, as might
be expected, the following initial syllable; cf. e.g. ἤφυεν δζεῖνος (i.e.
τσεῖνος, κεῖνος) "that one went away," (δ)ὲν ἤρκουτομ βᵒᵢά (i.e. πιά)
"he came no more," and so forth, TEXTS III. 9.

In Chios, Karpathos, and in kindred dialects, together with the
Cyprian,[1] the final -ν is assimilated to the following initial before all
sounds except vowels and π, τ, κ: cf. e.g. from TEXTS III. 6. 8. 9
μιὰφ φοράν = μιὰ(ν) φοράν, τὸφ φέρω = τὸ(ν) φέρω, ἔναχ χάρκωμα =
ἔναν χ., τὸβ βασιλιάν = τὸν β., ἦτοὶ ἱεμάτο = ἦτον γεμάτο, ἔσ σ᾽ ἔχει =
δὲν σ᾽ ἔχει, τὴν αὐλήμ μου = τὴν αὐλήν μου, ἤσουλ 'Ληνιτσά = ἤσουν
(ἐλ)ληνικειά. Assimilation to κ, π, τ may be found in Karpathos
(e.g. ἂτ τὸ κάμουν = ἂν τὸ κ.). In the dialects of Cyprus and Chios the
-ν disappears when the following word begins with ξ, ψ or with
another consonantal group the first part of which is not π, κ, τ.
The -ν disappears in Chios also in the absolute final syllable (i.e.
before a pause in the sentence) provided an -ε does not intrude (cf.
ἐκούνεν-ε "he moved," σεντούιν-ε "chest," TEXTS III. 9).

(e) COMPOUND AND DOUBLE CONSONANTS.

§ 35. The composite or compound consonants are ξ (ks), τσ,
ψ (ps), which under certain conditions (after nasals) become
voiced (gz, dz, bz), v. § 15. Corresponding to the pronunciation
of σ = š given in § 28, there are also the sounds kš, tš, pš.

1. ξ and ψ correspond to the a. Gk. sounds, while τσ and τζ (ντζ)
are of later origin. τσ, in addition to the τσ (dz) arising dialectically
from κ (γκ) (v. § 17), sometimes takes the place of an ancient τ (before
i), e.g. κληματσίδα "clematis," ρετσίνη "resin" (a. Gk. ῥητίνη), or a
σ(σ), e.g. κοτσύφι (κόσσυφος) "blackbird," τσωπάζω (usually σωπαίνω)
"I am silent"; cf. also § 28 note. The transition from the sound τι
to τσι occurs more frequently in the Pontic and Cappadocian dialect.
τσ (τζ) is the result also of the throwing together of τ and σ in
ἔκατσε = ἐκάθισε, τσῆ = τῆς (v. § 55, n. 1), τίποτσι (e.g. Crete) from
τίποτις. Many words with τσ (τš) or τζ (τž = dž) have come in
through borrowing (from Turkish or Italian); as, τσακίζω "I smash,"
τσιμπῶ "I prick," καρότσα "carriage," πετσί "leather," καφετζῆς
"keeper of a café," (ν)τζαμί "mosque," τšαναβάρ (Pontus) "animal,"
τσοπάνης (Lesbos) džουβάν's "shepherd."

τζ is often written for τσ, although pronounced τσ.

2. In the Terra d' Otranto ξ has become φσ (ψ): édifse = ἔδειξε "he
showed," fséro = ξέρω "I know" (cf. also TEXTS III. 2); in Bova ξ and
ψ have become dz: dzílo = ξύλο "wood," dzomí ψωμί "bread."

3. Other compound consonants occur only dialectically: Zaconian,
Cyprian, and the neighbouring South-Eastern dialects possess kʽ, pʽ, tʽ
respectively κχ, πφ, τθ, i.e. tenues followed by an aspirate or spirant,
as (Zac.) akhú ἀσκός "bag," thénu σταίνω "rise up," tho = 's τὸ, phíru

---

[1] Cf. also ἔναλ λεοντάρ, ἐσκῶννεμ με, TEXTS III. 13. a (Pontus).

σπείρω "I sow," (fr. Calymnos) λάκχος = λάκκος "pit," σαΐτθα = σαγίττα "arrow," κάπφα = κάππα, ἡ ἄτθησι (*i.e.* ἄνθησις) "flowering, bloom," (fr. Chios) κόκhαλα "bone," πίτha "pitch," κούπhα "cup."

§ 36. Double consonants (ττ, ββ, σσ, λλ, νν, ρρ, etc.) are merely orthographical in the ordinary language, *i.e.* they are (as also in English or German) simplified in the pronunciation and have only the value of the single consonants; thus κρεβ-βάτι = *kreváti*, γλῶσσα = ꝫ*lósa*, ἄλλος *álos*, θαρρῶ *þaró*, etc.

The original pronunciation of "lengthened" or double consonants (as in the German dialects of Switzerland) is found still in Lower Italy, in the South-Eastern Greek dialects (Cyprus, Rhodes, Karpathos, Icarus, and also Chios), and in the interior of Asia Minor (Cappadocia), and that not only in words with double consonants from the a. Gk. or taken over from another language, like κόκκινος "red," χάννω "I lose," ἄλλος "another," τέσσερα "four," καπέλλο = Ital. *capello* "hat," σαΐττα = Lat. *sagitta* "arrow," σακκούλλι "little bag," γλῶσσα "language," but also as the result of later assimilation : καμμένος = καυμένος "wretched," πέττε = πέντε, ξαθθός = ξα(ν)θός "fair" (colour), ἄθθρωπος = ἄ(ν)θρωπος "man," νύφφη = νύ(μ)φη "bride," συγχχωρῶ = συ(γ)χωρῶ "I forgive" (*cf.* also § 33), τὸφ φίλο (§ 34, n. 4), etc. Along with the preservation of ancient double consonants the South-Eastern Greek dialects afford examples of the spontaneous doubling of originally single consonants both in initial and middle syllables : *e.g.* (from Chios) πι̯όττερα, ἐττρώγανε "they ate," δg̓ὸ ττριά "two or three," ἀππίδι "pear," βρέχχει "it rains," πράσσινος "green," χαλάζζι "hail," τὸ ζζουμί "broth," πάλλι "again," ἀννοίγω "I open," μμέ "but." The conditions governing such doubling of consonants have not yet been explained. In part of the Greek-speaking territory the lengthened explosives are aspirated, *v.* § 35, n. 3.

§ 37. In modern Greek the general tendency is toward the simplification of original consonant combinations. Apart from the phenomena already given in the last paragraph and elsewhere (§§ 16, 24, 28 n., 32, 33), mention should be made here of the frequent expulsion of one consonant out of a three-consonant group : *e.g.* ἔζεψα (fr. ἔζευξα), κόφ' το (fr. κόψ[ε] το), ψεύτης (a. Gr. ψεύστης), βίσεχτος "leap-year, unlucky year" (Lat. *bisextus*), ζεῦλα (fr. ζεῦγλα). This expulsion, however, is arrested, especially when the third consonant is ρ (ἐχτρός, στρατιώτης.

A fresh massing of consonants is restricted to the North. Greek dialects as a result of extensive vowel syncope. See examples, § 7, note 1. The consonants which come together in this way often undergo a change facilitating the enunciation. In Velvendos a dental creeps in between *l*, *n*, and a following *s*, a *b* between μ and λ : γειτόντσσις = γειτόνισσες "neighbouring women," γένντσιν = γέννησεν "gave birth," θέλτς = θέλεις, μπλιά = μηλιά, or a consonant is thrown out : ἔσλιν = ἔστειλεν, παντρεύκιν = παντρεύτηκεν, κούσκε = ἀκούστηκε, κθάρ᾽ = κριθάρι, ἀπ᾽ ν = ἀπ᾽ τὴν, or there takes place a partial assimilation to one of the sounds : θκός = δικός, φκέντρ = βουκέντρι "prick for oxen," ἔφχε = ἔφυγε ; *cf.* also ἔκσεν = ἔχυσεν, and ψή = ψυχή (Pontus).

(*f*) ON ACCENT

§ 38. The accent usually stands over one of the last three syllables, examples like ἔπιασε, ἐβράδυασε, γάϊδαρος forming no exception, since ι (ν) counts as a consonant, and αϊ a diphthong. From the standpoint of modern Greek the exact position of the accent within the last three syllables cannot be reduced to fixed rules; it is, generally speaking, governed by the ancient Greek rules of accent, from which modern Greek varies only in particulars. The fourth last syllable can carry the accent only when a secondary element is attached to the end of the word, or where a syllable is accented after the model of analogous forms : ἤπαιζενε, ἔλεγενε (Naxos) beside ἤπαιζε(ν), ἔλεγε(ν), ἔλεγαν(ε) ; ἐγέλιομουν(α), ἔρχουμεστα (on analogy of ἔρχουμουν, ἔρχουσουν) ; ἔφαγαμε (analogy of ἔφαγα, etc.). As a rule, in such case a secondary accent is given : ἔλεγένε, ἔλεγάνε, ἔφαγάμε, ἔρχουμέστα, ἐρχούσαστόνε. On the accent signs, *cf.* § 4.

1. The a. Gk. three-syllable law is thus still operative in m. Gk., but the force of the long ultimate has been obliterated (the difference between long and short being no longer maintained). Consequently forms like ξύλινος gen. ξυλίνου acc. pl. ξυλίνους from ξύλινος may be uniformly accented ξύλινου ξύλινους, or πλούσιος fem. πλουσία as πλούσιος πλούσια, or ἐκάθετο "he sat" ἐκαθόμην or ἐκάθετο ἐκάθομουν. This tendency has made itself specially felt in inflexion : note ἀθρώποι for ἄθρωποι (and other substantives of similar formation) after the model of ἀθρώπω(ν) ἀθρώπους, ἐκάμαν (beside ἔκαμαν) after ἐκάμαμε ἐκάμετε, or *vice versa* κούλθσαμ (Cappad.) = ἀκλουθήσαμε, "we followed," after the sing. κcύλθσα = (ἀ)κλούθησα ; ἄφηκα, ἔπηρα (beside ἀφῆκα, ἐπῆρα) after ἔδωκα, ἔθηκα, ἔδεσα, ἔδειρα, ἔστειλα, etc. Even the accent of individual words has been changed after the model of others ; as, ἀθός a. Gr. ἄνθος "flower" after καρπός "fruit," μονός "single" after διπλός "double." Moreover, when adjectives are turned into substantives the accent is thrown back (after a. Gk. model Γλαῦκος —γλαυκός) as Λάμπρος (proper name) from λαμπρός "bright," Χαλέπα (place in Crete) from χαλεπός, στάχτη "ashes" = στακτή (*sc.* τέφρα), βράδυ "evening" from βραδύς. As far as phonetics are concerned,

the accent has suffered alteration only through the phenomena treated in § 9.

2. The modern Greek accent may generally be termed expiratory or stress, though the musical element is not quite absent.

§ 39. Some small words have no accent of their own (though written with accent in many cases), but lean for accent on the preceding or following words. Such enclitics and proclitics are the forms of the conjunctive pronoun (§§ 134–136), whether they stand before or after the word to which they refer, the forms of the article, the prepositions, the particles νά and θά, the conjunctions καί "and," μά "but." Words which carry an accent on the ultimate or penultimate receive the enclitic without any change, those accented on the third last take on with the enclitic a second accent on the ultimate, as τὰ παιδιά μου " my children," ἡ μάννα σου "thy mother," στεῖλε μου "send me," τὰ σπίτια του " his houses," τ' ἄρματά μας " our weapons," etc.

1. Here also the three-syllable law is valid with this modification, that the properispomena are treated as paroxytones; thus δοῦλος σας " your servant," εἶδα τὸνε "I saw him" (usually τὸν εἶδα). The proclitics, except ὁ, ἡ, οἱ (and εἰς), are generally written with an accent. Note also that the proclitic ἴντα "what" (§ 152, n. 2) moves its accent to the end in cases like ἰντά 'θελε νὰ κάμῃ "what is he to do?" ἰντά 'φταιε κείνη "what was she guilty of?"

2. The principle of enclitics is carried much further in the dialects. In Cyprus the verb becomes enclitic after the negative or after adverbs, the noun after its adjective and (in the voc.) after the exclamations ἔ, οὔ, ὤ, ἄ, βρέ: e.g. ἔμ παρπατει = δὲν περπατεῖ "he does not go," ἐψές ἤρταμεν "we came yesterday," καλός παπας "a good priest" (παπᾶς), ἔ ἀφεντη "ho, Mr.!" (ἀφέντης), βρέ Βδοκα "ho, Eudocia" (Βδοκιά).

3

PART SECOND.

MORPHOLOGY.

INFLEXION OF NOUNS.

USE OF THE FORMS.

§ 40. Modern Greek differentiates *three* genders (masculine, feminine, and neuter) and *two* numbers (singular and plural). No trace of the dual has survived. When the subject is a neuter plural the verb is not in the singular (as in a. Gk.) but in the plural. A construction κατὰ σύνεσιν is permitted : *e.g.* τό 'μαθαν ὁ κόσμος "the world (= people) learned it." In most cases the gender is clearly determined by the grammatical form (nom. sing.). The natural distinction of sex in animal life is expressed either through the use of different words or by the formation of a feminine from the masculine stem : *e.g.* βούδι "ox"—ἀγελάδα "cow," ἄλογο "horse"—φοράδα "mare," τράγος "he-goat"—γίδα "she-goat," or γάτος—γάτα "cat," σκύλος "dog"—σκύλα "bitch," πρόβατο "wether"—προβατίνα "ewe." For the male animal a neuter form is frequently used (which is also mostly the common designation of the species), as ταυρί "bull," βούδι "ox," ἄτι "stallion" (ἄλογο "horse"), κριάρι "ram" (*cf.* also ἀγώρι "boy").

1. Although παιδί "child" and κορίτσι "maiden" (beside κοπέλα f.) are neuter, the use of neuter diminutives (like *Mariechen* or a. Gk. Λεόντιον) is quite restricted, forms like ξα(ν)θούλα dim. of "fair," μαννούλα dim. of "mother," Ἐλενίτσα dim. of "Helen," Μαριγώ dim. of "Mary" being much more usual. Also the wife or daughter of a man is correctly designated either by the genitive or by a feminine form of the masculine : *e.g.* κυρὰ Παναγιώτη or Παναγιώταινα "Mrs. Panayotis," Παυλήδαινα "Mrs. Παυλῆς,"

Αγγελίνα (uncommon) " Mrs. Angelis." Note also ἡ παπαδιά (from παπᾶς) " clergyman's wife."

When some other female relationship—not a man's *wife*—is to be expressed with reference to the masculine the suffix -ισσα is usually employed : *e.g.* γειτόνισσα "neighbour woman" fr. γείτονας, μάγισσα " witch " from μάγος, νησιώτισσα " a woman from the islands " fr. νησιώτης, Μανιάτισσα " woman of Maina " (but Συριανή " woman from Syra " fr. Συριανός).

2. In Icarus the *plural* of geographical names is employed in a peculiar fashion to designate the particular parts or the neighbourhood of a locality, as ἠπῆγεν εἰς τὰς Ἀνατολάς " he went into the different regions of Asia Minor," πάμεν κατὰ τοὺς Εὐδήλους " we went into the vicinity of Εὔδηλος." *Cf.* also § 103.

§ 41. Modern Greek has only three cases, nominative, genitive, and accusative. These are, however, not always formally differentiated from one another, since the acc. (usually without -ν) and the nom. in the sing. and pl. of the fem. and neut. nouns are always phonetically alike, and in the pl. of mascs. (with the exception of *o*-stems) the acc. and nom. coincide ; also the gen. and acc. sing. of mascs. (again with the exception of *o*-stems) are the same. The masc. *o*-stems best maintain the different cases, furnishing a separate form also for the vocative, which is in all other stems identical in the sing. with the acc. without -ν, in the pl. with the nom.

1. The acc. sing. is clearly distinguished only where it retains its -ν, or where this is secured by a vocalic addition (*cf.* § 34). On the other hand, through the dropping of -ς (§ 29 n.) in the Greek of Lower Italy the decay of cases has advanced further than elsewhere. Even in masculines in -ος, partial decay of nom. and acc. is found (Pontus, Aeg. Sea).

2. The dative has entirely disappeared from the vernacular language; at the most it is found only in formal phrases taken from the literary or ecclesiastical language ; as θεῷ δόξα " thank God," ἐνενήντα τοῖς ἑκατό " 90 per cent.," τῷόντι (whence also τόντις) "really." On the syntactical substitution of gen. acc. or εἰς ('ς, σέ) for the dative case, *cf.* § 54.

3. The gen. pl. is not very frequently used—sometimes limited to statements of measure, dates, or particular expressions ; *cf.* also § 44, n. 2.

§ 41*a*. Modern Greek having largely retained the power of forming substantival compounds, we find several varieties of compounds in which substantival elements form part.

1. Substantival compounds :

(*a*) Dvandva-formations : *e.g.* μαχαιροπέρουνο "knife and fork," ἀντρόγυνο "man and wife, married couple," γυναικόπαιδα " wives and children."

(*b*) Where a substantive is more precisely determined by an adjective : *e.g.* γεροντοκόριτσο "old maid," καλόγρια "nun" (properly "a good aged woman"), κακοκαιριά "bad weather." Note especially the combinations with παλιο-, used in a bad sense : *e.g.* παλιά(ν)θρωπος "a good-for-nothing fellow," παλιογυναῖκα "a common woman," παλιόπαιδο "dirty rascal," παλιόσπιτο "wretched hut," and so forth.

(*c*) Where a substantive is more precisely determined by another substantive either in apposition or in any other casual connection ; as καμαροφρύδι "eyebrow" (properly "arch-brow"), *cf.* also ὁ κὺρ Θόδωρος, etc., §§ 63, 64 ; νοικο-κύρις or σπιτο-νοικοκύρις "master of the house," βασιλόπαιδο "royal child," ἡλιοβασίλεμα "sunset," κλεφτοπόλεμος "war with Klefts or bandits," πετρότοπος "stony place," ἀνεμόμυλος "windmill," κρεββατοκάμερα "sleeping-room." Formations are rare in which the last element is a verbal noun with no independent existence, *cf.* *e.g.* καντηλανάφτης "candle-lighter, sacristan" (fr. ἀνάφτω "I light").

(*d*) Where a verbal stem supplies, somewhat like a participle, the more precise determination of a substantive : *e.g.* φουσκοθαλασσιά "stormy sea" (fr. φουσκώνω "swell").

2. Adjectival compounds :

(*a*) Where the final adjective is more precisely determined by another adjective (numeral) or by a substantive ; as μαυροκόκκινος "dark red," ὁλάνοιχτος "quite open," εὐκολόπιαστος "easily caught," δεκάδιπλος "tenfold," ῥοδοκόκκινος "rose red," μαρμαροχτισμένος "built of marble," αἰθερόπλαστος "formed of air." Note also ἀξιαγάπητος "amiable," ἀξιοσπούδαστος "worthy to strive after."

(*b*) Where the final substantive is more precisely determined by an adjective (a numeral) or by another substantive ; as, καλόκαρδος "good-hearted," καλύτυχος "fortunate," βαρειόμοιρος "having bad luck, unfortunate," μαυρομάτης "black-eyed," τρικόμματος "consisting of three pieces," σιδερόκαρδος "hard-hearted." Such adjectives may again be made substantives : *e.g.* τριαντάφυλλο "thirty leaved flower," *i.e.* "rose."

(*c*) Where a verbal stem forms the first element (as in 1. d) : *e.g.* τρεμοχέρης "with trembling hand."

§ 42. The nominative, when placed at the beginning of a sentence, may be used to designate the psychological subject even when the construction of the sentence in itself requires another case form, thus usually in instances like ὁ κυνηγός, σὰν τ᾽ ἄκουσε, πολὺ τοῦ κακοφάνη "the huntsman, when he heard it, it vexed him much," τὸ παιδὶ τὸ καημένο στὸ δρόμο τοῦ ᾽ρθε στὸ νοῦ καὶ λέει "on the way it came to the poor child's mind and it speaks" ; but sometimes even ἕνας χωριάτης, ἐπέθανε τὸ παιδί του "a peasant's child died" (lit. "a peasant (nom.), his child died").

The predicative nom. is very common and is not confined merely to verbs of the copula class, like γίνομαι, στέκω, μένω, etc. ; *cf.* ἐγὼ Γραικὸς γεννήθηκα "a Greek I was born," κερδεμένος θὰ βγῶ "I will come off gaining (gain thereby)," ὁ πατριωτισμὸς δὲ φτάνει μόνος "patriotism alone suffices not," προβάλλει ἀναγνωρισμένα τὸ ἔργο "acknowledged is the work" (lit. "appears acknowledged"), ἐλεύθερος ὁ κλέφτης ζῆ κ' ἐλεύθερος πεθαίνει "free lives the Kleft and free he dies," ὁλοένα ζεστότερος φεγγοβολοῦσε ὁ ἥλιος "ever warmer shone the sun," τρέχει χρυσὸ φίδι τὸ νερό "as a golden serpent flows the water," σπουδάζει γιατρός "he studies medicine" (lit. "he studies a doctor").

§ 43. In its attributive use the nom. has considerably enlarged its scope by replacing, by way of apposition, an explanatory or partitive gen.: e.g. τὸ ὄνομα φιλολογία "the name philology," σπυρὶ σινάπι "a mustard seed," μιὰ ποδιὰ χῶμα "an apron (full of) earth," ἕνα ποτήρι νερό "a glass of water," ἕνα ζευγάρι παπούτσια "a pair of shoes," μιὰ ὀκὰ κρασί "one oka of wine," μεγάλο πλῆθος Τούρκοι "a great multitude of Turks," μιὰ δεκαριὰ χρόνια "ten (a decade of) years." This nom., of course, participates in the construction of the word to which it relates; cf. βλέπω χιλιάδες κόσμο "I see thousands of people."

The use of the nom. in comparisons with σάν (in Pontus ἄμον) "as" has been considerably reduced; the object compared regularly appears in the acc. if it is a personal pronoun or is accompanied by the definite article: e.g. τὸ πρόσωπό του ἔγινε σὰν τὴ φωτιά "his countenance became like fire," τὸ μαγουλάκι ἔλαμψε σὰν τὴν αὐγή "the cheek shone like the dawn," μαῦρα φοροῦσε τὸ φτωχὸ σὰν ἐμένα "the poor (child) wore a black garment, as did I," —but ντύνεται σὰ λόρδος "he dresses like a lord," πέφτει σὰν ἄψυχος "he falls as if dead," φκαριστημένος σὰν εὐτός "pleased as he."

§ 44. Although the use of the genitive on the one hand has been extended as a substitute for the ancient dat. (§ 54), on the other it has been reduced in favour of other means of expression. Its losses are chiefly in the adverbial and ablatival usage, for which the acc. (§§ 49, 50) or acc. plus preposition (§§ 161, 162) have been substituted. Moreover, the explanatory gen. and the gen. of content or measure have given place to apposition (§ 43), the partitive gen. (except in particular phrases like ποτέ μου "never"), the gen. of material, and the gen. of comparison have all been ousted by prepositions. It is for the gen. pl. that most frequently other methods of expression are employed (cf. § 41, n. 3). For survivals of the gen. with prepositions, v. § 158.

1. Ancient usages occur especially in Cyprus: e.g. adnominal γεναῖκα τῶν γεναικῶν "a queenly woman," σκλάβος τῆς σκλαβιᾶς

"a vile slave," ποὺ πόρτα τῆς πόρτας "from door to door," δκυὸ φορὲς τῆς ἡμερού "twice daily"; *adverbal* with verbs of motion : *e.g.* πααίνω τοῦ πόρου "I go (on) the journey" (and similarly καλλικέβκω τοῦ χτηνοῦ "I ride the mule," δκιαβαίνω τῆς πόρτας "I go through the door," μπαίνω τοῦ χωρκοῦ "I come up to (into) the village "); also to designate *cause* or *occasion* : e.g. ἐψόφησεν τῆς πείνας "he perished of hunger" (found also elsewhere), ἀζουλέβκει τῆς γυναῖκας του "he is jealous of his wife" (ζηλεύω with gen. also elsewhere), ἐλούθην τοῦ κλαμάτου "I bathed because of tears, in tears."

2. In North. Gk. dialects (*e.g.* Thessaly, Macedonia) the gen. has all but disappeared (*cf.* § 41, n. 3), *i.e.* the prep. ἀπό has largely ousted it (*v.* § 161, 6, n. 1).

§ 45. (1) The adnominal gen. may be employed as the equivalent of the ancient objective gen.: *e.g.* ἡ συλλογὴ τοῦ κόσμου "meditation on the world," ἡ σχέσι τοῦ βασιλέα (III. 4) "the relation to the king." It is the rule in statements of age, time, and measure, like κοπέλα δεκάξι χρίνων "a girl of sixteen years," ἕνας παράλυτος ὡς εἴκοσι χρόνων "a palsied man about twenty years of age," ἐφτὰ μερῶν ζωή "a life of seven days," σκοινὶ δέκα πηχῶ "a rope ten cubits long."

1. Note specially the pregnant construction in τὴν εἶχες δώδεκα χρονῶν (I. a. 11) "thou hadst her (the daughter) as twelve years old," *i.e.* "during twelve years" (while *adverbial* definitions of time stand in the acc.).

2. The expression τί λογῆς "of what sort?" "what kind of?" is quite stereotyped; as, τί λ. τραγούδι "what (what kind of a) song"?

3. Even the complement of an adj. stands in the gen. : *e.g.* ἀνήξ-ερος τοῦ κόσμου "ignorant of the world," ἄφοβος τοῦ θεοῦ "having no fear of God"; also (in Cyprus) ἄπραχτος τῆς ἀγάπης "inexperienced in love," ἄρρωστος τῆς πύρεξις "sick of fever."

This gen. is found dialectically (Cyprus) in quite ancient manner as the complement of a pass. participle : *e.g.* φαημένον τοῦ σκουλουκιοῦ "eaten by the worms," σκοτωμένος τῆς δουλειᾶς "killed by work."

4. A *gen. qualitatis* occurs in expressions like φόρεμα τῆς μόδας "a garment *à la mode*," χαρτὶ τοῦ γραψίματος "writing paper," σαρδέλλες τοῦ κοντιοῦ "canned sardines."

§ 46. (2) The possessive gen. is noteworthy in instances like στοῦ κουμπάρου "at the house of a godfather," ἐπῆγε στοῦ Γιάννη "he went to Yanni," τρέχει στῆς μάννας του "he hurries to his mother," thus corresponding to a. Gk. (ἐν Ἅιδου); also for saints' days; as, *e.g.*, τ᾽ ἁγιοῦ Βασιλειοῦ "on Saint B.'s Day," αὔριο εἶναι τοῦ Μιχαὴλ Ἀρχαγγέλου "to-morrow will be Michaelmas."

The possessive gen. may also be predicative; as, ποιανοῦ

εἶναι "to whom does it belong?" τὸ παιδὶ εἶναι τοῦ βασιλέα
'Ύπνου "the child belongs to King Sleep," τὸ βιβλίο εἶναι
τοῦ φίλου μου "the book is my friend's" (cf. § 143).

The predicative usage of (1) and (2) has extended beyond its
original bounds in particular (or dialectical) phrases : e.g. εἶναι τῆς
μόδας "it is the fashion," εἶναι τοῦ σκοινιοῦ καὶ τοῦ παλουκιοῦ "he
is a gallows-bird," εἶναι τοῦ σκοτωμοῦ "he is death's," εἶσαι τοῦ ὕπνου
(in Cyprus) "thou art deep in sleep," εἶμαι τῆς θέρμης "I am (still)
feverish," τὸ τραγούδι ἐν τοῦ κλαμάτου, τοῦ ἀναγελασμάτου "the song
makes one weep, laugh." This gen. is not confined only to the verb
εἶμαι : e.g. ντύνεται τῆς μόδας "he dresses in fashion," κατάντησε τῆς
μόδας "it became fashionable," τοῦ θανάτου πέφτει "he falls down
as dead," μεγάλη ἀρρώστια μ' ἔρριξε τοῦ θανάτου (I. a. 11) "severe
sickness brought me nigh to death," τὸν ἔκαμε τοῦ ἀλατιοῦ "he salted
him" = "he pommelled him thoroughly."

§ 47. (3) The a. Gk. gen. as the complement of a verb
survives only dialectically.

Cf. Texts III. 7 (Karpathos) ἄκουσέ μου "hear me," τῆς λυερῆς
θὰ τῆς 'πολησμονήσω "I will forget the maiden," τῆς κόρης δέ ξεχάννω
"I forget not the girl" beside τὴκ κόρη νὰ ξεχάσῃς "forget the girl."
In Cyprus this gen. accompanies various verbs : e.g. λησμονῶ "forget,"
ἀθθυμοῦμαι "remember," ἀκούω "hear," μυρίζομαι "smell (of)," ἐγγίζω
"touch," νώθω "understand," γελῶ "deride." Cf. also § 44, n. 1.

§ 48. (4) The gen. may be absolute and serve for adverbial
expressions : e.g. ὦ τοῦ θάματος "oh ! the miracle !" τοῦ χρόνου "next
year," τοῦ κάκου "in vain," μιᾶς κοπανιᾶς "with one blow," μονομιᾶς
"all at once," μονοχρονοῦ "in the same year," κοντολογῆς "in a
word."

§ 49. The accusative is (1) the object case in the widest
sense, replacing very frequently the a. Gk. gen. and dat.
Apart from § 54, note the acc. construction with the following verbs : ἀκλουθῶ "follow," ἀκούω "obey," ζυγώνω
"approach," βιγλίζω "keep watch," ἀπαντῶ, ἀνταμώνω,
ἀντικρύζω "meet," ξεχωρίζω (also mid.) "I separate (myself)
from" (ὁ ἔνας τὸν ἄλλο δὲν ἠξεχώριζε), ξεφεύγω "escape,"
προφτάνω "overtake," βοηθῶ "help," πολεμῶ "fight" (or with
μέ), πιστεύω "believe (somebody or something)," προσκυνῶ
"humble myself before," "do honour to," ἐλεῶ "give alms,"
σπλαχνίζομαι "pity," λυποῦμαι "deplore" ; συλλογειέμαι
(συλλογίζομαι) "think upon," εὔχομαι "pray," χαίρω "rejoice
over," "enjoy" (or with γιά), θαμάζομαι "wonder at" (or with
γιά and ἀπό) βαρειέμαι "am tired of," καταπιάνομαι "undertake." Note also that many verbs are used both as transitives
and as intransitives, v. § 176. A locality or place affected

by a verb of motion may stand in acc.: *e.g.* κατέβαινε τσοὺ κάμπους (I. a. 8) "he came down through the fields," γύρισε βουνὰ καὶ λαγκάδια "he wandered over mountain and valley," πέρασε λόγγους καὶ κάμπους "he marched through forest and field," τῆς θάλασσας τὰ κύματα τρέχω "over the billows of the sea I hasten"; *cf.* also § 51.

How an originally passive or reflexive verb may through a peculiar development in meaning take the acc. as object may be seen in στεφανώνομαι, lit. "I am garlanded" (a ceremony at the celebration of a wedding in the church, and consequently) = "I marry"; thus, *e.g.*, τὴν στεφανώνεται "he marries her."

§ 50. (2) A double accusative is very common—being carried sometimes beyond a. Gk. usage.

(*a*) Acc. of the object + predicative acc.: *e.g.* ἔχουνε στενὴ τὴ φαντασία "they have little power of imagination," νά 'χῃς τὸ θεὸ βοήθεια "have God as helper," δὲ σ' ἔχω πλιὸ μήτ' ἄνθρωπο μήτε καὶ παλληκάρι "I consider thee no longer either man or *pallicar*." ὅλα ρόδινα τὰ βλέπω "I see everything rosy," λὲν πρόστυχη τὴ γλῶσσα τοῦ λαοῦ "they call the language of the people ordinary," σὲ ξέρω τίμιο ἄθρωπο "I know you to be an honourable man," ψύλλους ἐνόμιζε τὶς τσεκουριές "he regarded the axe-blows as fleas," τὸν πιάνει φίλο "he makes him a friend," θέλει νὰ πάρῃ τὴ θυγατέρα τοῦ βασιλιὰ γυναῖκα "he wishes to secure the daughter of the king for wife," τὸν ἔβγαλαν (or ἐφανέρωσαν) ψεύτη "they proved him a liar," ἔφκειασε τὸ σπίτι του λαμπρό "he made his house magnificent," τὸν ἔκαμαν βασιλιά "they made him king," τὸ κάνει μάλαμα "he makes it into gold," or, "he makes gold out of it," ἴντα νὰ κάμῃ τόσα γρόσα "what will he do with so much money?" τὸ κάνω δουλειά "I make it my work (task)," "I apply myself to it," δένω δεμάτια τὸ στάρι "I bind the corn into sheaves," τριαντάφυλλα τὰ πλέκω κορώνες "I weave roses into garlands."

The prep. γιά is also used instead of the predicative acc.: *e.g.* ἔχω τοὺς βράχους γιὰ κρεββάτι "I have the rocks for a bed," beside ἔχω τοὺς λόγγους συντροφιά "I have the forests as comrades," τὴν ἐζήτησε γιὰ γυναῖκα "he sought her for wife," τὸν κλαίγω γιὰ πεθαμένο "I lament him as dead."

(*b*) Acc. of the whole + acc. of the part affected (rare); as, τὸν κέντρωσε τὸ δάχτυλο ἕν' ἀγκαθάκι "a small thorn pricked him in the finger."

(c) Acc. of the person (or the object) + acc. of the thing :
e.g. with the verbs μαθαίνω "teach, learn," ρωτῶ "inquire
about, ask for," ὑστερῶ, στερεύω " deprive of," γεμίζω (γιομίζω)
" fill with," φορτώνω "load with," ταγίζω " feed with," ποτίζω
" cause to drink," χορτάζω " satisfy one (or myself)," and even
σαγίτες μὲ βαρεῖς " thou hittest me with arrows "; note also τί
μὲ θέλεις " what do you want with me, of me ? "

1. When the verb is changed into a passive (which is rare, v.
§ 175), then the double accs. become in (a) double noms. and in (c)
nom. and acc.: e.g. πιάστηκαν φίλοι " they became (were made)
friends," but τὸν ὕπνο του στερεύεται " he is deprived of his sleep,"
ἡ ἄρκλα εἶναι γιομάτη ψωμί " the cupboard is filled with bread,"
φορτωμένος φλουριά " laden with florins."

2. In (c) the accusatives of the thing have to some extent taken
the place of the a. Gk. gen. or dat. ; also for the acc. the prep. ἀπό or
μέ offers an alternative ; as, γιόμωσεν (or γέμισεν) τὸ σπίτι ἀπὸ γυναῖκες
" the house was full of women," οἱ μοῖρες τὴν εἴχανε προικίσει μ' ὅλες
τὶς ὀμορφιές " the fates had endowed her with every charm."

§ 51. (3) An acc. of content occurs : e.g. in κοιμᾶται ὕπνο
βαθύ " he sleeps soundly (deep sleep)," τὰ φταίω " I am to
blame for it," τρέχουν βροχὴ τὰ δάκρυα " the tears flow in
streams," μέλι τρέχουν τὰ μάθια σου " thy eyes drop honey,"
στάζει τὸ χυμὸ τῆς ζωῆς " he distils the fluid of life " = " he is
in the prime of life," λιβανιὲς μυρίζεις " thou are fragrant with
incense," βγαίνω (βγάζω) περίπατο " I go out (take out) for a
walk, I go walking," κάθομαι σταυροπόδι " I sit with my legs
crossed," παίρνω ἀγκαλιά " I take to an embrace, embrace."
A local acc. has developed directly from such usages : e.g.
ἐπῆγαν κυνήγι " they went hunting (to the chase)," πάμε
σπίτι " we are going home," τὸ παίρνει σπίτ dou (TEXTS III.
12) " he takes it home "; analogous also εἶμαι σπίτι " I am at
home " (beside στὸ σπίτι). It is impossible to draw a hard
and fast distinction between the usage of (1) and that of (3).

Note also the following phrases :—γιαλὸ γιαλὸ πηγαίνουμε " we
are going along the beach," ἀρμενίζουμε ἄκρη ἄκρη " we are sailing
close along the coast,' περπατῶ τὸ βουνὸ βουνό " I wander over
mountain and valley," περπατῶ τὸν τοῖχο τοῖχο " I am walking along
the wall."

§ 52. (4) The adverbial use of the acc. (v. § 122 f.) is
not confined merely to stereotyped forms of the neut. sing. or
neut. pl.; it is used also freely in other constructions—to
designate *point of time* and *duration of time, extent and distance*

in space, price, measure, and sometimes *manner* : *e.g.* μιὰ μέρα
" one day," (ἐκείνη) τὴ νύχτα " in the (that) night," τὸ πουρνό
" early in the morning," μιὰ κυριακὴ πρωΐ " early one Sunday,"
τὸν παλιὸ καιρό " in the good old days," τὶς πρόαλλες (*sc.*
μέρες) " lately," " recently," τόσον καιρό " for such a long
time," τόσες φορές (βολές) ' so many times," δεκαπέντε μέρες
" during a fortnight," τρεῖς χρόνους " for three years " (note
τρ. χ. εἴχαμε νὰ γελάσουμε " we had *not* laughed for three
years," etc., *v.* p. 101), τὸ σανίδι εἶναι τρεῖς πήχες μακρύ " the
board is three cubits long " (also σανίδι τ. π. μ. " a board
three cubits long "), τὸ κάστρο εἶναι τρεῖς ὦρες (τρία μίλια)
μακρειὰ ἀπ' τὸ χωριό " the fort is distant three hours (miles)
from the village," δέκα φορὲς, χίλια μεράδια ὀμορφύτερη " ten
times, a thousand times more fair," τὸ βιβλίο κοστίζει (ἀξίζει)
τρεῖς δραχμές " the book costs (is worth) three drachmae,"
πόσο τὸ πουλεῖς " for how much do you sell it ? " τὸ παίρνω
δυὸ δραχμές " I take it for two drachmae," τὸ πλερώνω
πενήντα λεφτά " I (am willing to) pay 50 centimes for it,"
μιὰ (ἐ)μορφιά " in the nicest way," ραχάτ (III. 13. c) " in
peace, quietly," λόγο τὸ λόγο " word for word," *i.e.* " little by
little, gradually."

§ 53. (5) Note also the following isolated usages : τὸν καημένο
" the poor (fellow) ! " (exclamation of pity), τὸν κατεργάρι " the
scoundrel ! " τὸν κὺρ Θόδορο " behold Mr. Th. ! " καλῶς τον " a
welcome for him," ἀναθεμά τους, ἀνάθεμα ἐσένα " curse upon them,
upon thee ! " νά με or γιά με " here I am," νά τον(ε) (beside νά τος)
" here he is," νὰ τὴν Ἀρετή σου " there is thine A." (beside νὰ ὁ
Χάρος), νάτε (*v.* § 218, n. 2) ἔναν παρά " there take your one para."
Cf. also νανὰ νανὰ τὸ γιούδι μου in the cradle song, and μὰ τὸ θεό
" by God."

§ 54. Gen. and acc. compete for the function of the
indirect or *dat. object.*

(*a*) The gen. is most commonly used both of the noun and
the pronoun ; as, ἔδωκε τῆς μικρῆς τὸ γράμμα " he gave the
letter to the little (girl)," τοῦ Χάρου κακοφάνη " it vexed
Charon," ἡ χήρα δὲν τῆς πρέπει " widowhood becomes her
not," κακὸ ἔκαμες τοῦ παιδιοῦ " thou didst injury to the boy,"
τοῦ κάμαν τόσες τσιριμόνιες " they treated him so formally,"
σοῦ φώναξε λόγια κακά " he addressed bad words to you "
(but φωνάζω " I call to " takes acc.) ; εἶπε τῆς μάννας του
" he told his mother," μὄστειλε ὁ θιός " God commissioned

me," τοῦ κουντραστάρει "he resists him," τ᾽ ἀρσενικὸν τοῦ
θηλυκοῦ γυρίζει "the man turns to his wife," τοῦ ἀπλώνανε
τὰ χέρια "they stretched out their hands to him," τοῦ
χαμογελᾷ "he smiles at him." Note also the gen. for dat.,
particularly with ἀκλουθῶ "follow," κοντεύω "approach" (cf.
§ 49), θυμίζω "remind (one of something)"; also with
χαλεύω, γυρίζω, ζητῶ "beg, request," e.g. σοῦ ζητῶ τὴ χάρι
"I beseech your favour," αὐτὸ ποῦ μοῦ χάλεψες εἶναι πολὺ
μεγάλο (TEXTS I. d. 2) "what you requested of me is very
considerable" (also χαλεύω ἀπό).

1. The gen. may also represent an ancient *Dat. ethicus* or *Dat.
commodi (incommodi)*: e.g. ὁ ἥλιος δὲ σοῦ τὴν εἶδε (TEXTS I. a. 11)
"the sun saw her not *for thee*," νά σου κ᾽ ἔρχεται ὁ φίλος σου
"behold, there comes for you your friend," σοῦ θέλω ἀκόμα δέκα
δραχμές "I want 10 drachmae more from you" (properly "at your
expense").

2. The following examples will show how the gen. has succeeded
to the place of the dat.: πᾶρε τοὺν πλούσιων τὰ φλουριά (TEXTS I. a.
8) "take the money of the rich" (*i.e.* "from the rich"), τέτοια ρόδα
καὶ τοῦ Χάρου κάνουν ὄμορφα τὰ στήθια "such roses make fair even
Charon's breast" (breast to Charon), μου πιάνετ᾽ ἡ ἀναπνοή "my
breathing stops," γιά σου "thy health," = "health to thee" (and
analogously also ἀλλοί του "woe to him," χαρά σας "joy to you").

(*b*) The acc. is not capriciously used as the equivalent
of the gen., but forms a marked characteristic of the Northern
dialects and of Pontus, cf. III. 11 (Velvendos, Maced.): *e.g.*
αὐτὸν τοὺν ἔδουκαν ἄλλ᾽ μνιὰ γναῖκα "they gave him another
wife," τοὺ πααίν᾽ τὴ γναῖκα τ "he brings it to his wife," τὴ
γναῖκα σ κρυφὸ νὰ μὴν πῆς "tell thy wife no secret";[1] from
III. 12 (Thrace) μὲ γεῖπε "he said to me," III. 10 (Lesbos)
τὸν ἔκανε τιβίχ "he gave him command," III. 13 (Pontus):
e.g. εἶπεν τὸ λεοντὰρ τὸν πάρδον "said the lion to the cat,"
στρώνν ἄτον τὸ ξύλον "they give him a cudgelling."

The gen. therefore is to be regarded as the normal usage.
Neither are gen. and acc. commonly confused by the best writers
either in prose or in poetry. Thus in our texts the writers Βηλαράς,
Βαλαωρίτης, Παράσχος, Πολέμης, Δροσίνης, Μάνος, Παλαμᾶς,
Ἐφταλιώτης, Πάλλης use the gen.; while, on the other hand,
both Σοῦτσος (of Constantinople), the Thessalian Ρῆγας Φεραῖος,
Ζαλακώστας (of Epirus), and Ψυχάρης use the acc. In general these
writers appear to be guided by the usage of their home, still the
Epirote Ζαλακώστας—in contrast to the Epirotes Βηλαρᾶς and

---

[1] ἔκλιψαν ᾽ᾱ βασιλιὰ τοὺ πλί (III. 11) is therefore to be translated "they stole
the king's hen."

Βαλαωρίτης—uses the acc. in his tales from Epirus (TEXTS I. d. 1, 2, 3). On the other hand, writers from Northern Greece also employ the gen.—apparently because of the usage of the majority; *cf. e.g.* Σοῦτσος, TEXTS II. a. 9, μοῦ πιάνετ' ἡ ἀναπνοή "my (to me) breathing stops," beside ἡ γλῶσσα μου μὲ δένεται "my tongue is (to me) shackled."

(c) The prep. 'ς (σέ, εἰς) may be used in place of the datival gen. or acc.: thus the TEXTS I. a. 8, I. d. 1, 2, 3, 5, 6, in addition to the gen., give rarer examples also of 'ς : *e.g.* ἔδωκε τὴ βούλα στὸ παιδί "he gave the boy the signet-ring," εἶπε στὸν πατέρα του "he said to his father"; or even a mixture of construction, as νὰ μὴ χρουστᾶς σὲ πλούσιο, φτωχὸν νὰ μὴ δανείζῃς (I. b. 7) "be not debtor to a rich man, lend not to a poor man." Even the higher literature employs 'ς as well as gen. or acc.: *e.g.* τί ὠφελεῖ στὸ ξένο "what use is it to the foreigner?" (Paraschos), χαρίζετε τὰ βιβλία σας στοὺς ξένους "you give your books to foreigners" (Psichari), ἀλλοίμονο στὴ λυγερή "alas, for the maiden!" (Chadzopulos).

1. It is a noteworthy fact that the writers who employ the acc. of the pronoun for the dat. apparently avoid the acc. of a noun, *i.e.* they prefer 'ς. In the case of the pronoun, 'ς is used only with the fuller forms (§ 134 ff.): *e.g.* σ' αὐτὸν χρωστῶ (I. d. 2) "*to him* I am debtor," αὐτὸ δὲν εἶναι τίποτε σ' ἐμένα (I. d. 2) "that does not matter to me."

2. The verb (ὁ)μοιάζω "I am like, resemble," may be construed with the gen. or the acc., with the preps. 'ς or μέ, or with σάν (ἔμοιασε ἡ βασιλεία τῶν οὐρανῶν σὰν ἄνθρωπος (TEXTS II. b. 6) "the kingdom of heaven is like a man"). With the nom. this verb means "appear," *e.g.* μοιάζει τρελλός "he appears to be crazy."

ARTICLE.

§ 55. Forms of the Definite Article:

Singular.

Nom.	ὁ the		ἡ the		τὸ the
Gen.	τοῦ of the		τῆς of the		τοῦ of the
Acc.	τὸ(ν) the		τὴ(ν) the		τὸ the

Plural.

Nom.	οἱ the		οἱ (ἡ) the		τὰ the
Gen.			τῶ(ν) of the		
Acc.	τοὺς the		τὲς (ταὶς), τὶς (τὴς, τοὶς)		τὰ the

On final -ν, v. § 34; sometimes an ε is attached (τόνε, τήνε, τῶνε). The forms in brackets are only orthographically different; τὶς is now more common than τὲς. The dat. is replaced by gen. or acc. and also by the prepositional combinations, in sing. στὸ(ν) στὴ(ν) στὸ, in pl. στοὺς, στὲς (στὶς), στὰ (cf. § 54).

1. In the Ionic islands, in Epirus, Crete and other Aegean islands the following initial τσ- forms are to be found :—

	Sing.			Plur.		
	m.	f.	n.	m.	f.	n.
Nom.	—	—	—	τσὶ (τσοὶ)	τσὶ	—
Gen.	—	τσῆ (τζῆ)	—	—	—	—
Acc.	—	—	—	τσοὺ(ς), τσὶ (τσοὶ)	τσὶ (τσῆ)	—

The forms τσῆ = τῆς and τσὶ = τὶς are most common, the others being much rarer.

2. οὐ for ὁ, τοὺ(ν) for τὸν; τʹ dʹ and ν (fr. τʹν) = τὴ(ν); τ or dʹ and d = τοῦ; τς = τῆς, τοὺς (in Velvendos, Lesbos)—the forms being governed by the phonetic laws of the Northern Greek (§ 7, n. 1). Initial τ drops out in Lower Italy : ο = τό, i = τὴ(ν). In the Pontic dialect, στὸν, στὴ(ν), στὸ, etc., become σὸ, σὴ, etc.; cf. § 16, n. 4.

3. The a. Gk. form αι (e) is still found in Lower Italy (Otr.) for masc. as well as fem.: the acc. pl. f. τὰς (beside τὶς) still survives in Chios. The more important new dialectic formations in addition to those given in n. 1 and 2 are i = ὁ in Northern Gk., e.g. Velvendos, Saranda Klisiés, and Lesbos, τὶ = τοῦ in Saranda Klisiés, τὶ = τοῦ, τῆς, τῶν, τοὺς, τὶς in Pontus, τοῦν = τῶν in Cephalonia and the Maina, τὶς also for acc. pl. m. in Karpathos, Saranda Klisiés.

4. Some dialects have reduced the forms of the article to very small dimensions: thus (in Cappad. and also in Pontus) τὸ is used for nom. and acc. sing., τὰ for nom. and acc. pl. of *all* genders.

§ 56. The Indefinite Article is identical with the numeral "one," v. § 128.

Only in Cappadocia (or rather Pharasa) the indef. art. has a special form ἀ or (before vowels and explosives, v. Texts III. 14. b) ἀν for ἔνας "one." The origin of this form is obscure—possibly due to a transformation of ἕνα (*ἄνα).

§ 57. The Definite Article is placed before proper names of all kinds and before geographical names (countries, islands, cities, mountains, rivers), also before names of months and days : eg. ὁ Γιάννης "John" (pl. οἱ Γιάννιδες "people with the name 'John'"), ἡ Μαρία (pl. οἱ Μαρίες), ὁ Διάκος (well-known hero of Greek liberty), ὁ Δαρβῖνος, ὁ (κὺρ) Λάζαρος "(Mr.) L.," ὁ Ἀλῆ πασᾶς "Ali Pasha," ἡ Μελπομένη (the Muse), ὁ θιός "God," ὁ Χριστός; ἡ Εὐρώπη, ἡ Γερμανία, ὁ Μοριάς, οἱ Ἰνδίες, ἡ Κρήτη, ἡ Χίο, οἱ Ψαρές, ἡ Πόλι (Constantinople), ἡ Ἀθήνα, ὁ κάμπος τοῦ Μαραθῶνα "the plains of M.," τὸ γιοφύρι τῆς Ἄρτας "the bridge of A.," ὁ Ὄλυμπος, ὁ Εὐρώτας; ὁ Ἀπρίλις, ἡ παρασκευή "Friday," τὸ σάββατο "Saturday."

1. Indeclinable expressions may also receive the article : *e.g.* μὲ τὸ αὔριο "with to-morrow," τὸ ἀνέβα καὶ κατέβα (imperat., *v.* § 218, n. 2) "the going up and down," τὰ ὄξω "the outside." On subordinate clauses with the art., *v.* §§ 266, 1 n., and 269 n.

The art. is always repeated when an adjectival or substantival attribute follows a substantive with the def. art. ; it is also usually repeated (almost always before names) when the articulated attribute precedes the word to which it refers : *e.g.* ὁ Βοριὰς ὁ παγωμένος "the icy Boreas," ἡ ὥρα ἡ ὡρισμένη "the hour appointed," στὸ δεξὶ χέρι τὸ γυμνό "in the naked right hand," ὁ καημένος ὁ Γιάννης "poor J.," ἡ καημένη ἡ βοσκοπούλα "the wretched shepherdess," τὸ κακὸ τὸ μάτι "the evil look," τὰ μακρινὰ τ' ἄστρα "the distant stars," τὰ πολλὰ τὰ δάκρυα "the copious tears," τὸ ἄλλο τὸ πουλί "the other bird" (Texts I. d. 1 beside οἱ ἄλλοι γιατροί "the other physicians"), στὰ ἔρημα τὰ ξένα "in the desert foreign land," ἡ σκύλα ἡ κερά σου "the bitch, thy mother" (I. a. 16), ὁ βασιλέας (ὁ) Ὕπνος "King H." Note ἐγὼ ὁ καημένος "I wretched man," ἐσεῖς οἱ ἀντρειωμένοι "you braves," τὸ ποτήρι τὸ νερό "the glass of water," τὸ σακκούλι τὸ μαργαριτάρι "the little bag of pearls" (*cf.* § 43).

2. As a consequence of this rule the gen. never stands between the art. and substantive; for exx. *v.* § 294.

§ 58. The indef. art. is not employed with predicates, *e.g.* εἶμαι Γερμανίς "I am a German," δὲν εἶσαι χριστιανός "you are not a Christian," τὸ παιδὶ εἶναι δικό σου "the child is thine," Γραικὸς θανὰ πεθαίνω "a Greek I will die," σὲ ξέρω τίμιο ἄθρωπο "I esteem thee as an honorable man," τὸν ἔλεγαν Λάζαρο "they called him L.," τὸν ἔκαμαν βασιλιά "they made him king."

1. Rather unusual is εἶμαι ἕνας Λόρδος (Texts I. d. 5) "I am a lord"; but the *def.* art. may be employed with the predicate : *e.g.* εἶμαι ὁ θάνατος "I am death," εἶμαι ὁ Γιάννης "I am J."

2. It may be remarked that in general the indef. art. is used more sparingly than, *e.g.*, in German : compare the beginning of II. b. 4, or, *e.g.*, ἔχει ὡραῖο σπίτι "he has a beautiful house," ἔχει μεγάλη μύτη "he has a large nose," τῆς μαννούλας σου ἡ εὐχὴ νά 'ναι γιὰ

φυλαχτό σου "thy mother's blessing be a protection for thee," φτωχὸν
νὰ μὴ δανείζῃς "do not lend to a poor man," στὸ χέρι βαστᾷ
ἀστροπελέκι (II. a. 14) "in his hand he holds a lightning-flash," ὁ
Χριστὸς ἔφτειασε καλύτερο πρᾶμα (I. d. 6) "Christ made a better
thing," ἄλλη φορά "another time," ἄλλη φορεσιά (I. d. 1) "another
garment." In such cases, however, the indef. art. is not impossible.

SUBSTANTIVE.

§ 59. The most convenient method of classification of
the declension of substantives is according to their gender.
In this way similar forms may be best reduced to uniform
groups or declensions. All the masculines fall again into
two sub-groups according as the nom. (and acc.) pl. ends in
-οι (acc. -ους) or -ες. All the feminines have -ες in the nom.
(and acc.) pl. The neuters in the nom. (and acc.) pl. end in
-α (more rarely in -η). According as the sing. and pl. are
parisyllabic or non-parisyllabic there are further subdivisions.

In *all* the paradigms two case-endings have the same method of
formation, viz. the acc. sing. and the gen. pl.—the former being
identical with the vowel-stem ($\pm \nu$), the latter always ending in ·ω(ν).
On final -ν, cf. § 34 ; in the following paradigms this -ν is omitted in
the noun, as it occurs only dialectically in the two cases in question.
The gen. pl. on the mainland frequently ends in ωνε, especially if
the ω is accented (κλεφτῶνε).

§ 60. The following declensions are accordingly to be
differentiated:

I. Masculine Nouns.

a. in -ος, Nom. pl. -οι,
b. in -ας (-ᾶς), -is (-ης, -ῆς, -ις), -ες (-ές), -οῦς,
    parisyllabic: pl. -ες,
    non-parisyllabic: pl. -δες.

II. Feminine Nouns.

in -α, -i (-η, -ι), -ο (ω), -οῦ, -έ,
    parisyllabic: pl. -ες,
    non-parisyllabic: pl. -δες.

III. Neuters.

a. in -ο(ν), -ιό(ν) [-ίο(ν)], -ι (-ί),
    parisyllabic: pl. -α,
    (*non-parisyllabic*: pl. -ία, -τα).

b. in -*ος*,

> *parisyllabic* : pl. -*η* (*ια*),
> (*non-parisyllabic* : pl. -*τα*).

c. in -*ο* -*μο*(*ν*), -*ας*,

> *non-parisyllabic* : pl. -*τα*.

	Parisyllabic.	Non-parisyllabic.	Nom. Pl.
I. Masculine	-*os*	—	Nom. -*οι*
	-*as*, -*is*	-*ás*, -*ís*, -*ís*, -*es*, -*ús*	-*ες*, -*δες*
II. Feminine	-*a*, -*i*, (-*o*)	-*a*, -*i*, -*ú*, -*é*	
III. Neuter	-*o*, -*yó* (-*ío*), -*i*	(-*í*, -*o*)	-*a*, -*ια* (-*τα*)
	-*os*	(-*os*)	-*η* -*ια* (-*τα*)
	(-*mo*)	-*a*, -*mo*, -*as*	-*τα*

The forms in brackets are rarer than the others.

I. Masculine Nouns.

A. Nom. Pl. -*οι*.

§ 61. Endings.

Singular.		Plural.	
Nom.	-*ος*	-*οι*	
Gen.	-*ου*	-*ω*(*ν*)	
Acc.	-*ο*(*ν*)	-*ους*	
Voc.	-*ε*	-*οι*	

Nom.	φίλος "friend,"	ἐχτρός "enemy,"	φίλοι	ἐχτροί
Gen.	φίλου	ἐχτροῦ	φίλω(ν)	ἐχτρῶ(ν)
Acc.	φίλο	ἐχτρό	φίλους	ἐχτρούς
Voc.	φίλε	ἐχτρέ	φίλοι	ἐχτροί

Similarly are declined, *e.g.*, κάμπος " field," λόγγος " forest," μπαρόνος " baron," σκύλος " dog," ἀδερφός " brother," γιατρός " physician," κυνηγός "hunter," λαγίς " hare," οὐρανός " heaven"; also verbal substantives in -μός (γλυτωμός " deliverance "), diminutives in -άκος (ἀνθρωπάκος " *hommunculus*," " little man," also proper names like Πετράκος), patronymics in -πουλος [1] (Δημητρακόπουλος "Son of Dimi-tracis"), and augmentatives in -αρος (παίδαρος "bigger boy").

Proparoxytones like ἄγγελος "angel," ἄνεμος "wind," ἄθρωπος "man," ἀπίστολος "apostle," ἔμπορος "merchant," δάσκαλος "teacher," πόλεμος "war," σύντροφος "companion," undergo change of accent—in the sing. they are usually proparoxytone, in the pl. paroxytone; thus, ἄθρωπος ἄθρωπον ἄθρωπο—ἀθρώποι ἀθρώπω(ν) ἀθρώπους, δάσκαλος—δασκάλοι, ἄνεμος—ἀνέμοι, σύντροφος—συντρόφοι. This rule, however, is not quite general; sometimes in the gen. sing. the ancient accentuation (ἀνέμου) is retained, while in the pl. ἄ(ν)θρωποι may be found.

§ 62. Notes on the several cases. Instead of the voc. in -ε, some proper names or appellatives (Νῖκος, Πέτρος, Χρῆστος, Διάκος) used as such form a voc. in -ο : Νῖκο, Πέτρο, etc.; also λούστρο for λούστρος "shoeblack." Το θεός, θιός "God," voc. (θεέ and) θέ. In Pontic ἄδεφλε "O brother!" (usually ἀδερφέ).—χρόνος "year" gives gen. pl. χρονώ(νε) beside χρόνω; so also Texts III. 3, ἀθρωπῶνε from ἄθρωπος. On the plural-formation λόγος λόγια, etc., v. §§ 96, 100, n. 1.

1. In some dialects, especially in the Aegean region, in the North. Gk. dialects, and in Asia Minor the nom. pl. is employed also for the acc. : e.g. τσὶ φίλοι = τοὺς φίλους (Thera, Ios), τοὺς ἀθρώποι, and other exx. In Cappadocia the cases of the pl. have generally fallen into desuetude : e.g. (Texts III. 14. b) nom. οἱ λύτζοι "the wolves," gen. τοῦ λύτζοι, acc. τοὶ λύτζοι. Pontic has advanced farther on a way of its own ; cf. the following paradigms, in which those forms are bracketed that are required merely according to the North. Gk. vowel laws, or that correspond to the common Gk. forms :

S. Nom.	ἄθρωπος [2]	φίλος [2]	ἀδελφός [2]	ἀλεπός [2]
	ὁ ἄθρωπον, ἄθρωπον [3]	ὁ φίλον [3]	ὁ ἀδελφόν [3]	ὁ ἀλεπόν [3]
Gen.	τ' ἀθρωπί (τ' ἀθρώπ) [4]	τὶ φίλονος	τ' ἀδελφί (τ' ἀδελφοῦ)	(τ' ἀλεποῦ)
Acc.	(τὸν ἄθρωπον)	(τὸ φίλον)	(τὸν ἀδελφόν)	(τὸν ἀλεπόν)
Pl. Nom.	(οἱ ἀθρώπ, ἀθρώπ)	(οἱ φίλ)	τ' ἀδέλφε	τ' ἀλεπούδε (οἱ ἀλεποί)
Gen.	τ' ἀθρωπιῶν	τὶ φιλιῶν	τ' ἀδελφιῶν	
Acc.	(τ' ἀθρώπς)	(τὶ φίλτς)	τ' ἀδέλφε	τ' ἀλεπούδε (τ' ἀλεπούς)

[1] Literally "youth," "son" (= Lat. *pullus*), but treated as a suffix.
[2] Without the definite article.
[3] With the definite article.
[4] On the other hand, τὶ δέσκαλονὸς from ὁ δέσκαλον "teacher."

2. In Scyros the nom. sing. both of substantives and adjectives ends in -ες (acc. -ε): *e.g.* πλάτανες = πλάτανος " plane-tree," ἀνάλατες = ἀνάλατος " saltless, stale," βάτες = βάτος " bramble-bush," ἄσπρες " white," γαμπρές " son in-law," γραμμένες " written," καλές " good." But all appellatives in -ος do not take this transformation.

§ 63. Some nouns that according to their inflection should belong to this category are indeclinable when they precede a proper name as a title. Such are κύριος " Mr.," γέρος " old man," ἄγιος " saint," καπετάνιος " captain," " leader"; thus, ὁ κὺρ Λάζαρος, ὁ γέρο-Κολοκοτρώνης " the aged Κ.," ὁ ῍Α(γ)ι-Γιάννης, ὁ καπετὰν Νικήτας, etc.

1. The masculines in -ος correspond exactly to the same a. Gk. declension. Many of the ancient examples have indeed been replaced by diminutives in -ι (§ 97), some have also partially fallen into the following group (§ 66 n.); while, on the other hand, this declension in -ος (in addition to loan-words) has been somewhat enriched by words like γέρος, etc., § 65, n. 1.

2. Of the a. Gk. formations the contracted nouns, the so-called Attic declension, and the feminine *o*-stems have disappeared. A fragment of the contracted class (*v.* also adjectives) is still to hand in νοῦς " mind," " intellect," acc. νοῦ(ν), pl. νοῦδες : gen. sing. νοός and nom. pl. νόες are not really vernacular.[1] The other ancient contracted forms have been replaced by new words : *e.g.* πλοῦς by ταξίδι. λαγός " hare"= a. Gk. λαγώς, is inflected like any other masc.

The old feminines were supplanted in various ways :

(*a*) they became masc.: *e.g.* ὁ πλάτανος " plane-tree," ὁ τράφος " grave";

(*b*) they remained fem., but dropped the -ς and passed over into another declension : *e.g.* ἡ Σάμο " Samos" ; *v.* § 87 ;

(*c*) they became neut. in -ο(ν) (τὸ βάσανο " agony "), or -ος (τὸ δρόσος " dew "); *cf.* §§ 92, 99 f. ;

(*d*) they became fem. in -α (παρθένα " maiden," καμήλα " camel "), or were otherwise transformed by the addition of a fem. ending: ἡ πλατανιά " plane-tree," δροσιά " dew," ἀρκούδα " she-bear " ;

(*e*) or supplanted by the diminutive forms: ἀμπέλι " vine," νησί " island," ραβδί " staff"; or

(*f*) were replaced by other words: δρόμος for ὁδός " way," μονοπάτ " path " for ἡ ἀτραπός, ἀρρώστια " sickness " for ἡ νόσος.

All the other forms do *not* belong to the common tongue ; the old forms are still to be found sometimes, but only dialectically ; *v.* § 87, n. 1. The same word may occur in different modifications : πλάτανος, πλατανιά, πλατάνι.

B. Nom. Pl. -ες.

§ 64. The stem vowels are : *a*, *i* (ι, η), *e* (ε), *u* (ου), which unite with the terminations in the following manner :

---

[1] More commonly τὰ μυαλὰ " brain," τὸ κεφάλι " head."

Parisyllabic.   Non-parisyllabic.
                    Singular.

Nom. -a, -i-, -e-, -u- s
Gen. -a, -i, -e, -u
Acc. -a- -i-, -e-, -u- (n).

                    Plural.

Nom. -es ⎫ in place -a-, -i-, -e-, -u- des
Gen. -o(n) ⎬ of the   -a, -i, -e, -u- do(n)
Acc. -es ⎭ stem-vowel -a-, -i-, -e-, -u- des.

Analogous to the usage cited in § 63, there are indeclinable
forms of παπᾶς "priest," and χατζῆς "pilgrim": *e.g.* ὁ παπᾶ-
Δημήτρις "Priest (Father) D.," ὁ χατζῆ-Κώστας "Pilgrim K."

Parisyllabic.

§ 65. ὁ γέροντας "old man."

          Singular.   Plural.
Nom.   γέροντας   γέροντες
Gen.   γέροντα   γερόντω
Acc. (Voc.) γέροντα   γέροντες.

The following are similarly declined: ἀ(γ)έρας "air," "wind,"
αἰθέρας "ether," ἄρχοντας "ruler," "prince," γείτονας
"neighbour," ἔρωτας "love," κλητῆρας "constable," πατέρας
"father," φύλακας "watchman," χειμώνας "winter"—that is,
practically all barytones in -ας.

1. This class had its origin in the a. Gk. masc. consonant stems
(or so-called 3rd decl.). Out of the old acc. sing. γέροντα(ν) a new
nom. (γέροντας) and gen. (γέροντα) were formed corresponding to
κλέφτης κλέφτη (§ 68), etc. Quite mechanically stated, the rule for
this formation is:—the a. Gk. masculines of the 3rd decl. form
their nom. sing. by attaching a -ς to the acc. sing.; yet *all* the a. Gk.
nouns have not been re-modelled in this fashion, γέρος "old man"
and Χάρος "Charon" being found at least equally frequent alongside of γέροντας Χάροντας, ὁ ἄρχος "the leader" alongside ἄρχοντας,
and δράκος always for a. Gk. δράκων (a monster frequently met with
in fable). *Cf.* also ἴδρος "sweat" (ἱδρώς) beside ἱδρῶας, and ὁ
προεστός "president" (borrowed from the literary language).[1] The
inflexion is the same as for φίλος; but note voc. γέρο, Χάρο (beside
Χάρε), δράκο (beside δράκε). The consonantal decl. has been very
frequently ousted by the creation of diminutives in -ι (*v.* § 97),
which are often employed side by side with the other forms: ἀστέρι
(ἀστέρας) "star," θερί "animal," κουδούνι "bell," σκουλήκι (and

---

[1] The word ὁ παρώ(ν) "the one present"—also from the literary language—
remains indeclinable: ὁ, ἡ, τὸ παρώ.

σκώληκας) "worm," δόντι "tooth," παιδί "child," "boy," "fellow";
λιοντάρι "lion," ποδάρι "foot" beside the rarer πόδι and πόδας (as
in Otranto). Other words have been ousted by entirely new ones,
as a. Gk. κύων by σκυλί (or σκύλος) "dog."

2. The a. Gr. paradigm νεανίας, ταμίας, etc., has as such disappeared or is no longer distinguishable from κλητῆρας.

3. πένητων for πενήτων, TEXTS I. a. 7 (Cephalonia).

§ 66. The paradigm just given frequently shows a
transition in the gen. sing. and nom. and acc. pl. into the
decl. of masculines in -ος.

Sing.		Plur.
Nom.	γείτονας "neighbour'	γειτόνοι
Gen.	γειτόνου	γειτόνω
Acc.	γείτονα	γειτόνους.

Similarly : κόρακας, φύλακας, ἄρχοντας, and others.

Note the change of accent—especially in the gen. sing.

Many masculines in -ος have taken on in the nom. sing. the
ending -ας ; as, ἔγγονας "grandson" = ἔγγονος, ἔμπορας (and ἔμπορος)
"merchant," κάβουρας "crab" (a. Gr. κάβειρος), μάγερας "cook"
(a. Gr. μάγειρος). These are declined like γείτονας (nom. pl. also
accented thus : ἔμποροι, κάβουροι).

§ 67. Some irregularities : ἄντρας "man," μῆνας "month"
(pl. μῆνες and μῆνοι) have ἀντρῶ(ν), μηνῶ(ν) in the gen. pl.;
these nouns and πατέρας "father" have also occasionally in
the gen. sing. ἀντρός (and ἀντροῦ), μηνός (and μηνοῦ), πατρός
(alongside τοῦ ἄντρα, μῆνα, πατέρα).

On the other hand, fr. πατέρας, gen. pl. τῶν πατέρω(ν). On the
occasional transition into the non-parisyllabic class, v. § 73.

§ 68. ὁ κλέφτης "robber," "Kleft."

Sing.		Plur.
Nom.	κλέφτης	κλέφτες
Gen.	κλέφτη	κλεφτῶ(νε)
Acc.	κλέφτη	κλέφτες.

Similarly : διαβάτης "traveller," ἐργάτης "worker," καθρέφτης
"mirror," μαθητής "pupil," μουρτάτης "renegade," ναύτης
"sailor," πολίτης "citizen," προφήτης "prophet," ράφτης
"tailor," χτίστης "mason," ψεύτης "liar," and all the proper
names in -της denoting place of origin ; as, Μοριώτης, Σπετ-
σιώτης, Χιώτης, Μανιάτης, etc.

Many have secondary forms like the non-parisyllabics ; v.
§ 76.

1. This class represents the a. Gk. masculines in -ης of the 1st decl. (note gen. pl.), all of which, so far as they have at all survived, may be declined according to this paradigm.

2. Such occasional forms as a voc. in -α or a nom. pl. in -αι arise out of the literary or ecclesiastical language; thus, δέσποτα fr. δεσπότης "bishop," "priest" (TEXTS I. a. 19), or ἐρασιτέχναι "amateurs," "dilettanti" (TEXTS II. b. 7).

§ 69. A decl. corresponding to that of γείτονας (§ 66) is rather uncommon: μάστορης (beside μάστορας) "master" is thus declined:

Singular.	Plural.
Nom. μάστορης	μάστοροι, μαστόροι
	(and μάστορες)
Gen. μαστόρου (and μάστορου, μάστορα)	μαστόρω
Acc. μάστορη	μαστόρους.

Similarly, nom. acc. pl. κλέφτοι, TEXTS III. 14. b.

Non-parisyllabics.

§ 70. ὁ παπᾶς "priest."

	Singular.	Plural.
Nom.	παπᾶς	παπάδες
Gen.	παπᾶ	παπάδω
Acc. (Voc.)	παπᾶ	παπάδες.

Similarly, all words in -ᾶς with accent on the final: e.g. κεφαλᾶς "blockhead," κοσκινᾶς "sieve - maker," μυλωνᾶς "miller," φαγᾶς "eater," "gourmand," ψαρᾶς "fisher," ψωμᾶς "baker"; and especially numerous (Turkish) loan-words: ἀγᾶς "Aga," ἀμιρᾶς "commander-in-chief," "ameer," καυγᾶς "quarrel," μπουταλᾶς "thickhead," ὀντᾶς "room," παρᾶς "para" (coin), pl. also "money," πασᾶς "Pasha," σουγιᾶς "pen-knife."

1. The (a. Gk. especially Hellenistic) suffix -ᾶς is very productive, partly to express certain bodily peculiarities: κεφάλα "big-head," κεφαλᾶς "big-headed," χείλι "lip," χειλᾶς "thick-lipped"; and partly to designate a trade or calling: ἄμαξα "carriage," ἀμαξᾶς "driver," "cabman," γάλα "milk," γαλατᾶς "milkman," κόσκινο "sieve," κοσκινᾶς "sieve-maker," πάπλωμα "bedcover," παπλωματᾶς "manufacturer of or dealer in bedcovers."

2. There is also a plural παράδια "money," from παρᾶς, TEXTS III. 9.

§ 71. Nouns in (-ιάς -εάς) are generally declined according to the last paradigm: e.g. βασιλιάς "king," Βοριάς "north wind," φονιάς "murderer," χαλκιάς "blacksmith."

But instead of βασιλ*εᾱ́ς*, etc., some dialects show βασιλέας (gen. and acc. τοῦ, τὸ βασιλέα) and plural:

Nom. βασιλέϊδες
Gen. βασιλέϊδω(ν)
Acc. βασιλέϊδες.

1. Note that the form βασιλέας is not confined to the dialects mentioned in § 10, n. 1; it is found, *e.g.*, also in Ios, and is a favourite in the written vernacular (*e.g.* συγγραφέας in Palamas).

2. Nouns in -*ιᾱ́ς* (except Βορ*ιᾱ́ς*) have arisen from the a. Gk. nouns in -*εύς*, in the same way in which γέροντας has come from γέρων; -*έας* passing into -*ιᾱ́ς*, according to § 9. A gen. βασιλ*ιῶς* (= a. Gk. βασιλέως) for the usual βασιλ*ιᾱ́* (βασιλέα) is of rare occurrence. The pl. οἱ βασιλεῖς comes from the literary language.

3. In place of such -*έας* substantives, forms in -*ές* occur in Lesbos, Chios, in W. Crete, and other parts of the Aegean (*e.g.* Icarus), and also in Saranda Klisiés: *e.g.* βασιλές for βασιλέας, ὁ φονές for φονέας, gen. and acc. βασιλέ, etc.

§ 72. A transition into the o-decl., analogous to γείτονας γειτόνοι, is rather uncommon:

(γονέοι) γον(*ι*)οί "parents"
(γονέω) γον*ι*ῶ
(γονέους) γον*ι*ούς.

Here belongs the sing. γον*ι*ός "father" (a. Gk. γονεύς, γονεῖς).

Family names in -*ας* regularly form their pl. in -*αῖοι* (-*έοι*): Γρίβας—Γριβαῖοι "family of the Griva," Ἀνδρούτσας —Ἀνδρουτσαῖοι, Τζαβέλλας—Τζαβελλαῖοι.

§ 73. Sometimes even barytones in -*ας* form non-parisyllabic plurals in -*ιδες* or -*αδες*; thus, regularly, χάχας "laugher," χάχιδες and χάσκας "gaper," παπατρέχας "shallow fellow," "swaggerer"; rarely πατεράδες and πατέριδες, ἀέρας ἀέριδες, κάβουρας καβουράδες, ἄρχοντας ἀρχοντάδες, etc.

§ 74. ὁ χατζῆς "pilgrim," Ἀράπης "Arabian," "Moor," "negro."

	Singular.	Plural.
Nom.	χατζῆς Ἀράπης	χατζήδες Ἀράπηδες
Gen.	χατζῆ Ἀράπη	χατζήδω Ἀράπηδω
Acc.	χατζῆ Ἀράπη	χατζήδες Ἀράπηδες.

Similarly, Turkish and other loan-words in -ῆς (-ης): *e.g.* καφετζῆς "keeper of a coffee-house," μουστερῆς "customer," παπουτσῆς "cobbler," τενεκετζῆς "tinker," and other names of

MORPHOLOGY 51

occupations in -τζῆς; βεζίρης "Vizier," μανάβης "greengrocer," μπακάλης "shopkeeper," μπέης "Bey," τσοπάνης
"shepherd," χαμάλης "porter," μπαρμπιέρης (Ital.) "barber,"
βλάμης (Alban.), Vlamis "brother in a feud."

1. Note the North. Gk. forms nom. sing. βιρβέρς "barber," gen.
and acc. βιρβέρ, nom. pl. βιρβέρδες (Lesbos).

2. ντελῆ "brave" (Texts I. a. 9), a nom. without -ς, is the unaltered Turkish form deli; σιόρ "Mr.," "Sir" (Texts III. 5), the
unaltered Ital. sior(e), the Grecianised decl. being ὁ σιόρης (σιόρις),
τοῦ σιόρη.

§ 75. The nouns in -ις differ merely orthographically
(from the last in -ῆς): e.g. καραβοκύρις "owner of a ship,"
"captain."

Singular.	Plural.
Nom. καραβοκύρις	καραβοκύριδες
Gen. καραβοκύρι	καραβοκύριδω
Acc. καραβοκύρι	καραβοκύριδες.

Similarly, νοικοκύρις "master of a house" and the nomina
agentis in -άρις, like βαρκάρις "boatman," καβαλλάρις "horseman," κυνηγάρις "huntsman," μακελλάρις "butcher,"
περ(ι)βολάρις "gardener"; and also names of persons, like
Βασίλις "Basilius," Γιώργις "George," Γρηγόρις; diminutives
in -ούλις, like αντρούλις "little (poor) man"; family names
(diminutives) in -άκις, like Χατζιδάκις, Γιανναράκις, as well as
all other names of persons and of families in -is: Γιάννης,
"John," Μανόλης, "Emmanuel," Μιχάλης "Michael," Θοδωρῆς
"Theodore," Κωσταντῆς "Constantine," Περικλῆς, Στεφανῆς,
Τρικούπης, Δεληγιάννης, Δραγούμης; thus the plurals
Γιώργιδες, Γιάννηδες, Περικλῆδες, Τρικούπηδες. The comic
formation οἱ ποσοπαίρνιδες "the bribe-seekers," is a pl. from
the expression πόσο παίρνεις; "how much will you take?"

1. The spelling fluctuates between -ις and -ης; in the pl. -ιδες
(-ιδες) is sometimes uniformly written in all words (thus also
χατζίδες, Ἀράπιδες, etc.).

2. Words in -ις are transformations from the a. Gk. in -ιος
(κύρις = κύριος, Γιώργις = Γεώργιος), the number of which has been
considerably increased by the Lat. suffix -άρις (-arius). Cf. the
neuters in -ι, § 95; but while the latter (in -ι) have in all the cases
except nom. and acc. sing. been faithful to the o-decl., the masculines
in -ις have entirely deserted on the analogy of the other substantives
in -is. Genitives in -ου, like κύρις κυρού, Μάϊς (Μάης) "May," Μαΐου
or Μαϊοῦ, are rare—the names of the months Γεννάρις, Φλεβάρις,
Μάρτις, Ἀπρίλις, etc., usually follow the paradigm given. The words

in -άρις still preserve (beside -ιδες) also the old form in the pl. ; thus, καβαλλάροι (fr. -άριοι), and so καβαλλάρω, καβαλλάρους. The terminations -άρις and -άρος are interchangeable in κουρσάρις, pl. κουρσάριδες beside κουρσάρος, pl. κουρσάροι (= Ital. *corsaro* " pirate ").

§ 76. Many parisyllabic substantives belonging to the category of § 68 take *beside* the pl. in -ες also a pl. in -άδες or -ηδες :

A. βουλευτής " delegate "—βουλευτάδες
   δικαστής " judge "—δικαστάδες
   δουλευτής " worker "—δουλευτάδες
   θεριστής " reaper,"—θεριστάδες
   κριτής " judge "—κριτάδες
   μαθητής " pupil," " apprentice "—μαθητάδες
   ποιητής " poet "—ποιητάδες
   πουλητής " vendor "—πουλητάδες
   πραματευτής " merchant "—πραματευτάδες
   τραγουδιστής " singer," " poet "—τραγουδιστάδες
   χορευτής " dancer "—χορευτάδες.

B. ἀφέντης " Mr.," " father "—ἀφεντάδες ἀφέντηδες
   δεσπότης " bishop," " priest "—δεσποτάδες δεσπότηδες
   κλέφτης " kleft "—κλέφτηδες
   ράφτης " tailor "—ραφτάδες ράφτηδες
   ψάλτης " singer "—ψαλτάδες ψάλτηδες
   χτίστης " mason "—χτιστάδης χτίστηδες
   χωριάτης " peasant," " boor "—χωριάτηδες.

Many popular writers manifest a propensity for generalising this type (especially A), and so extend it even to new formations : *e.g.* ἀεροκοπανιστής, pl. -κοπανιστάδες " one who beats the air, swaggerer."

§ 77. καφές " coffee."

Singular.	Plural.
Nom. καφές	καφέδες
Gen. καφέ	καφέδω
Acc. καφέ	καφέδες.

So also (mostly Turkish) loan-words : κατιφές " velvet," καφενές " coffee-house," μαχμουτιές (Turk. coin), μενεξές " violet," μιναρές " minaret,' τενεκές " tin," φιδές *vermicelli.*"

On βασιλές, *v.* § 71, n. 3.

§ 78. κόντες " Count."

Singular.	Plural.
Nom. κόντες	κόντιδες
Gen. κόντε	κόντιδω
Acc. κόντε	κόντιδες.

Thus also Italian loan-words like κουμαντάντες "commander," λεβάντες "east wind," and πονέντες "west wind."

§ 79. παππούς "grandfather."

Singular.	Plural.
Nom. παππούς	παππούδες
Gen. παππού	παππούδω
Acc. παππού	παππούδες.

Apart from this word and νούς (with the pl. νούδες beside νόες, v. § 63, n. 2) the vernacular tongue supplies no other example.

Cf. however (the acc.) κομσού, Texts III. 14. a (Cappad.) = Turk. komšú "neighbour."

II. Feminine Nouns.

§ 80. The stem vowels are : a, i (η, ι, υ), e (ε), o (o, ω), u (ου); the declension, apart from the nom. and gen. sing., is identical with that of the masculines under I. b.

Parisyllabic.   Non-parisyllabic.
(-a, -i)   (-a, -i, -e, -u)

Singular.
Nom. -a,   -i,   -e,   -o,   -u
Gen. -a-, -i-, -e-, -o-, -u-‹ s
Acc. -a-, -i-, -e-, -o-, -u- (n).

Plural.

Nom. -es	⎫ in place	-a-, -e-, -u- đes
Gen. -o(n)	⎬ of the	-a-, -e-, -u- đo(n)
Acc. -es	⎭ stem vowel	-a-, -e-, -u- đes.

Parisyllabic.

§ 81. καρδιά "heart," μέρα "day," θάλασσα "sea."

Singular.

Nom. καρδιά	μέρα	θάλασσα
Gen. καρδιάς	μέρας	θάλασσας
Acc. καρδιά	μέρα	θάλασσα.

Plural.

Nom.	καρδιές	μέρες	θάλασσες
Gen.	καρδιῶ(νε)	μερῶ(νε)	θαλασσῶ(νε)
Acc.	καρδιές	μέρες	θάλασσες.

An extraordinary number of substantives follow this paradigm : *e.g.*—

(1) γριά "old woman," φορά "time" (in enumeration, Fr. *fois*), κερά "lady" (when used as a title indecl. § 63), γλῶσσα "tongue," "language," δόξα "glory," δούλα "maid-servant," μοῖρα "fate," "goddess of destiny," πέτρα "stone," "rock," σπίθα "spark," τρύπα "hole," ὥρα "hour," "time," "o'clock."

(2) Substantives with suffixes :

(*a*) Abstract nouns in -(ε)ια, and particularly in -ιά— the latter partly of ancient origin and partly modern derivatives from apellatives, mostly employed only to designate a property or sphere of activity ; also names of trees rarely feminines from the same stem as the masculine : *e.g.* ἀλήθεια "truth," ἀρρώστια "sickness," στενοχώρια "perplexity" (*cf.* § 9), ἁμαρτιά "sin," μαγιά "magic," ὀμορφιά "beauty," φωτιά "light," "fire," παραξενιά "peculiarity," ἀρχοντιά "rank," "nobility," βελονιά "stitch of a needle," κανονιά "cannon-shot," ματιά "glance," πετριά "stone-throw," κουταλιά "spoonful," νυχτιά "night-time," χρονιά "(course of) a year," πρωτομαγιά "1st May," "May-day," μηλιά "apple-tree," τριανταφυλλιά "rose-bush," παπαδιά "wife of the clergyman."

(*b*) *Nomina actionis* in -σιά ; as, περπατησιά "walking," "running," ἀφροντισιά "carelessness."

(*c*) Abstract nouns in -ίλα, -ούρα, -μάρα : *e.g.* μαυρίλα "black cloud," ξυνίλα "sour taste," σκοτούρα "bother," κουταμάρα "stupidity," στραβωμάρα "blindness," "blinding." For the numeral nouns in -αριά, *v.* § 133.

(*d*) Fem. nouns in -τρ(ι)α, -αινα, -ινα, -ισσα : *e.g.* ράφτρ(ι)α "woman tailor," χορεύτρ(ι)α "ballet-girl" ; *cf.*, further, § 40.

(*e*) Augmentatives in -άρα : *e.g.* μυτάρα "big nose."

(*f*) Diminutives in -άκα (rare), -ίτσα, -ούλα : *e.g.* μαμάκα "little mother," Ἑλενίτσα, πετρίτσα "small stone," σαϊτίτσα "little arrow," μαννούλα "little mother," βαρκούλα "small boat" ; on βοσκοπούλα "shepherdess," *cf.* § 61.

(3) Ital. (Lat.) and other loan-words: ἀράδα "row,"
βούλα "signet-ring," γάτα "cat," κάμαρα "room," καμπάνα
"bell," κάπα "cloak," κοπέλα "girl," κουβέντα "conversation," "talk," πόρτα "gate," "door," σαγίτα "arrow," σκάλα
"staircase," στράτα "street."

1. Most of the nouns named in 1 and 2 correspond to the a. Gk.
feminines of the 1st decl. and are inflected like them. In m. Gk.
those nouns ending in -α (in addition to those under 3) have been
often enriched, partly at the expense of those in -η (e.g. δούλα
"maid" for δούλη, τουλούπα = τολύπη "coil," "roll," χελώνα = χελώνη
"tortoise"), partly by the formation of new words or new suffixes,
cf. σκύλα "bitch," παρθένα (cf. § 63, n. 2), ἡ τρέλλα "madness" fr.
τρελλός "mad," ἡ νέκρα "rigid death" fr. νεκρός "dead," ἡ ξέρα
"mainland" fr. ξερός "dry," ἡ πίκρα "sorrow" fr. πικρός "bitter,"
ἡ γλύκα "sweetness" fr. γλυκός, ἡ κλάψα "weeping" fr. κλαίω; and,
lastly, by augmentatives like κεφάλα "big head," κουτάλα "soup-
spoon," and the substantives in -άρα, -ίτσα, -ούλα, etc. The nom.
and acc. pl. in -ες has been taken over from the old consonant decl.
(§ 83).

2. In the dialects mentioned in § 10, n. 1, the productive suffix
-ιά takes the form -ία or -έα. In all other cases -ία comes from the
literary language, as, ἁρμονία "harmony," δυσκολία "difficulty," φιλία
"friendship"; or also from the Ital., as κουμανταρία name of a fine
wine; v. § 10.

For -έ = -έα as in μηλέ = μηλέα (μηλιά), cf. § 71, n. 3.

3. In some dialects (Chios, Icarus, Pontus) the acc. pl. has still
preserved the ancient ending -ας; cf. μέρας, Texts I. a. 22; δύο φοράς,
Texts III. 13. a. When such an acc. occurs in the poets it is merely
an intruder from the literary language.

In North. Gk. (§ 7, n. 1) we find the ending -ις for -ες: e.g.
οὐρμήνις = ὁρμήνεες (Velv.).

§ 82. The accent of the nom. sing. is carried through all
the cases except the gen. pl., which usually bears the accent
on the final (as in a. Gk.); thus, γλῶσσα γλωσσῶ, πέτρα
πετρῶ, τρύπα τρυπῶ, ὥρα ὡρῶ, βασίλισσα βασιλισσῶ,
μέλισσα μελισσῶ, κάμαρα καμαρῶ, σαίτα σαιτῶ; but also
πάπια "duck" πάπιω, ἀλήθεια ἀλήθειω, γειτόνισσα γειτό-
νισσω, κάμαρα κάμαρω. Many genitive plurals have fallen
entirely into desuetude (cf. § 41, n. 3).

§ 83. ἡ ἐρπίδα "hope."

Singular.	Plural.
Nom. ἐρπίδα	ἐρπίδες
Gen. ἐρπίδας	ἐρπίδω
Acc. ἐρπίδα	ἐρπίδες.

So also: ἑβδομάδα "week," ἐφημερίδα "newspaper," θυγατέρα "daughter," μητέρα "mother," ὄρνιθα "hen," πατρίδα "fatherland," πέρδικα "partridge," σταφίδα "raisin," φροντίδα "care," φτερούγα "wing," etc. (mostly paroxytones), λαμπάδα "candlestick," and the abstract nouns in -άδα; as, λαμπράδα "brightness," νοστιμάδα "pleasant taste," πρασινάδα "green(ness)" (of fields, etc.), ἐξυπνάδα "wakefulness."

This group is descended from the a. Gk. feminine consonant stems (known as 3rd decl.). A new nom. and gen. have been formed from the acc. sing. on analogy of χώρα χώρας χώρα(ν), or—stated in other words—the acc. sing. *minus -ν* became a nom., which was then treated exactly as a noun of the α-decl.; *cf.* § 65, n. 1. The nom. (acc.) pl. -ες remained and was transferred also to the ancient α-decl., § 81. But even here *all* the nouns have not been remodelled in the same fashion: the a. Gk. abstract nouns in -της, -τητος, in addition to this new form (ἡ ἰδιότητα "likeness," ἡ ποιότητα "quality"), have also another more vernacular in -τη; thus, ἡ νιότη [1] "youth," θεότη "divinity," ἀνθρωπότη "humanity." Moreover, many fems. (especially those in -ών) have been replaced by diminutives in -ι; as, τὸ ἀηδόνι "nightingale," σεντόνι "linen-towel," χελιδόνι "swallow," χιόνι "snow," χέρι "hand," κλειδί "key." Other nouns have been completely ousted by new words: *e.g.* a. Gk. ῥῖς by μύτη "nose," κλῖμαξ by σκάλα "stair."

§ 84. Note the accent of the gen. pl., in which this paradigm differs from the preceding. Only a few dissyllabics and ἡ γυναῖκα "woman" (which on historical grounds belong here, not to § 81, *v.* preceding n.), give -ῶ(ν) in the gen. pl. These are ἡ νύχτα "night," πλάκα "plate," "slab," σφῆκα "wasp," φλέβα "vein," φλόγα "flame," χῆνα "goose," and so gen. pl. νυχτῶ(ν), γυναικῶ(ν), etc.

Cf. § 67. Here also an a. Gk. phenomenon has been preserved; even yet one may occasionally come upon the ancient gen. sing. in -ός: *e.g.* γυναικός, νυχτός (usually γυναῖκας, νύχτας). Sometimes the accentuation on the final extends its scope further than can be historically justified; as, ἑβδομαδῶ(νε) alongside ἑβδομάδω, fr. ἑβδομάδα "week."

Forms like ἡ ἐκλαμπρότης, πατρίς, πατρίδος, τὰς χεῖρας, etc., in the poets belong to the language of literature.

§ 85. νύφη "bride," ἀδερφή "sister."

	Singular.		Plural.	
Nom.	νύφη	ἀδερφή	νύφες	ἀδερφές
Gen.	νύφης	ἀδερφῆς	νυφῶ(νε)	ἀδερφῶ(νε)
Acc.	νύφη	ἀδερφή	νύφες .	ἀδερφές.

---

[1] Or even—quite commonly—τὰ νιάτα.

So also: γνώμη "opinion," ζέστη "warmth," κόρη "girl,"
μύτη "nose," στάχτη "ashes," ἀναπνοή "breath," αὐγή
"dawn," πληγή "wound," φωνή "voice," ψυχή "soul"; and
abstract nouns in -σύνη; as, γληγοροσύνη "swiftness," καλοσύνη
"goodness."

This class corresponds to the a. Gk. 1st decl. in -η. Note the
indeclinable ἡ γῆs "the earth," gen. τῆς γῆς, acc. τὴ γῆς (beside ἡ
γῆ, τῆς γῆς, τὴ γῆ). The transition of nouns in -α into the -η class
(as κάμαρη, TEXTS III. 15, Lada, or πλώρη for πρῴρα) is uncommon.

§ 86. ἡ βρύσι "fountain," θύμησι "remembrance."

	Singular.	Plural.
Nom.	βρύσι, θύμησι	βρύσες, θύμησες
Gen.	βρύσις, θύμησις	[βρυσῶ]
Acc.	βρύσι, θύμησι	βρύσες, θύμησες.

So also: γνῶσι "understanding," δύσι "sunset," ζέσι
"heat," κόψι "edge (of a knife)," κρίσι "judgment," ὄψι
"countenance," πίστι "faith," πόλι "city" (usually applied
to Constantinople), πρᾶξι "action," ράχι "back," "ridge (of a
mountain)," χάρι "charm," "grace," ἅλωσι "capture," ἄνοιξι
"spring," ἀπόφασι "decision," ζάχαρι "sugar," κάππαρι
"caper-bush," παρατήρησι "observation," "notice," συνείδησι
"conscience."

The gen. pl. of this paradigm is very little in use in
the language of the present day (cf. § 41, n. 3). Forms
of this kind (βρυσῶ, πραξῶ, etc.) are more common on the
S. Sporades. There is a gen. pl. κάππαρω fr. κάππαρι.

1. This paradigm is *formally* identical with the preceding, only
historically different. It embraces the ancient barytones in -ις
(πόλις, πόλεως), which have passed into the class of the 1st decl. feminines in -η, so that they may be also spelled ἡ πόλη, ἡ ἀπόφαση, etc.
Moreover, many of these appellatives come from the literary language.
τὸ πανηγύρι (also πανα[γ]ύρι) "ecclesiastical popular feast" = a. Gk. ἡ
πανήγυρις, has become neuter; τὸ φίδι "snake" = a. Gk. ὁ ὄφις, has
enlarged itself by a suffix.
Forms like ἡ φύσις or nom. acc. pl. λέξεις, found in the poets
and authors, have been taken from the literary language.
2. Even the a. Gk. nouns in -υς have been subjected to the same
remodelling; thus, ἡ πῆχυ "cubit," ἡ ράπυ "rape," "turnip."

πῆχυ	πῆχες
πῆχυς	πηχῶ (frequent)
πῆχυ	πῆχες.

A. Gk. ὁ στάχυς "ear" (of oats, etc.) became τὸ στάχυ (ἀστάχυ), ἡ
ὀφρῦς "eyebrow" τὸ φρύδι; ὁ δρῦς τοῦ δρῦ τὸ δρῦ "oak," is rare,

ἡ βελανιδιά being the word commonly in use. Similarly, words like μῦς, σῦς, βότρυς, ἰχθύς, πέλεκυς have been ousted by others (τὸ ποντίκι "mouse," χοῖρος "pig," τὸ σταφύλι "grapes," τὸ ψάρι "fish," τὸ τσικούρι [fr. Lat. *securis*] "axe," and so forth).

3. The a. Gk. diphthong stems γραῦς and ναῦς have disappeared, ἡ γριά (*i.e.* a. Gk. γραῖα) "the old woman," being used for the former, and τὸ καράβι "ship," for the latter. τὸ βούδι "ox" (ἀγελάδα "cow") for ὁ, ἡ βοῦς.

§ 87. ἡ Σάμο "Samos," Φρόσω, Μαριγώ, female names.

Singular.

Nom.	Σάμο	Φρόσω, Μαριγώ
Gen.	Σάμος	Φρόσως, Μαριγῶς
Acc.	Σάμο	Φρόσω, Μαριγώ.

So also many geographical names (esp. islands), female and pet names; as, Κόρθο "Corinth," Κύπρο, Μῆλο, Νιό "Ios," Πάτινο "Patmos," Ρόδο, Τῆνο, Χιό "Chios"; Ἀγαθώ, Ἀργυρώ, Ἐλέγκω, Κατίγκω, Χάϊδω, Χρυσώ, and a few appellatives: ἡ ἄβυσσο "abyss," ἡ ἄλυσο "chain," ἡ ἄμμο "sand," ἡ παράδεισο "paradise," ἡ μέθοδο "method." The pl. is rarely used, yet a pl. οἱ μέθοδες may be formed for the word ἡ μέθοδο taken from the literary language.

1. The paradigm is a transformation of the a. Gk. fem. *o*-stems, though the majority of the appellatives have been remodelled otherwise, *v.* § 63, n. 2; παράδεισος was originally masc. In some dialects (Rhodes, Chios, Scyros, Pontus) the old forms are still to be found (esp. in geographical names): ἡ Ἄμπελος, ἡ Ἐμοργός (= Ἀ.), ἡ Κύπρος, ἡ Σάμος; ἡ ἄμμος "sand," ἡ δρόσος "dew."

The names of some islands have been remodelled on the fashion of πλάτανος: πλατανιά; thus, Νικαριά "Icarus," Ἀξιά (also Ἄξα) "Naxos."

2. The a. Gk. forms ἡ ἠχώ, ἡ λεχώ, ἡ αἰδώς, ἡ ἠώς (ἕως), etc., have been replaced by new words: ἀντιλαλιά "echo," λεχοῦσα "pregnant woman," ντροπή "shame," αὐγή χαραυγή "dawn," etc.

Non-parisyllabics.

§ 88. ἡ ἀλεποῦ (ἀλωποῦ, ἀλουποῦ) "fox."

Singular.	Plural.
Nom. ἀλεποῦ	ἀλεπούδες
Gen. ἀλεποῦς	ἀλεπούδω
Acc. ἀλεποῦ	ἀλεπούδες.

Similarly: μαϊμοῦ "monkey," γλωσσοῦ "gossip," μυλωνοῦ "miller's wife," ὑπναροῦ "sleeper" (fem.), φαγοῦ "gourmand," ψαροῦ " fisherwoman," ψωμοῦ " baker's wife," and other fem. designations parallel to the masc. in -âς of § 70.

1. These feminines are rarely declined like the parisyllabics, *i.e.* in the pl. :

Nom. ἀλουπές (also ἀλούπες)
Gen. ἀλουπῶ(ν)
Acc. ἀλουπές.

2. The paradigm ἀλεποῦ has arisen from the a. Gk. (Ionic) suffix -ώ, which is especially prominent in abbreviated names, and already played an important part in Hellenistic Gk.

§ 89. νενέ " mother."

Singular.	Plural.
Nom. νενέ	νενέδες
Gen. νενές	νενέδω
Acc. νενέ	νενέδες.

Similarly, Turkish words like βαλιδέ " Sultan's mother," Ἐμινέ, Φατμέ. This paradigm is a special m. Gk. formation.

§ 90. As the nouns enumerated in § 76 have non-parisyllabic secondary plurals, so many feminine nouns in -α and -η have a pl. in -άδες (rarely -ήδες) :

κερά " wife," " Mrs."—κεράδες
μάννα " mother "—μαννάδες
χήρα " widow "—χηράδες
ἀδερφή " sister "—ἀδερφάδες
κορφή " summit "—κορφάδες
νύφη " bride "—νυφάδες
μαμμή " midwife "—μαμμήδες.

ἡ ὀκά (measure = *cir.* 1 quart) always ὀκάδες.

III. Neuter Nouns.

A. In -o(ν), -ιo(ν), -ι.

§ 91. Tabular view of the terminations :

Parisyllabics.	(Non-parisyllabics).
Singular.	
Nom. Acc. -o(n)	-i, -i-(n)
Gen. -u	-i-u = yú.

Plural.

Nom. Acc.	-α	-ι-α, -ι-α = -ya, -yá
Gen.	-o(n)	-ίο = -yó.

Some non-parisyllabics in -o with a pl. in -ata also belong here; v. § 94.

Parisyllabics.

§ 92. In -o(ν): ξύλο "wood," βουνό "mountain."

	Singular.		Plural.	
Nom. Acc.	ξύλο	βουνό	ξύλα	βουνά
Gen.	ξύλου	βουνοῦ	ξύλω	βουνῶ(ν).

Similarly: δέντρο "tree," καπέλο "hat," κουμάντο "command," μῆλο "apple," νερό "water," πάσσο "step," ροῦχο or pl. ροῦχα "clothes," φτερό "wing," "feather," φύλλο "leaf"; also the nouns in -ικο like μανάβικο "greengrocery," μπακάλικο "retail-shop" (fr. μανάβης, μπακάλης), and in -άδικο like παπουτσάδικο "cobbler's shop" (fr. παπουτσῆς), and other such (cf. § 114 n.). The accent of the gen. fluctuates in proparoxytones like ἄλογο "horse," βούτυρο "butter," κόκκαλο "bone," λούλουδο "flower," πρόσωπο "face," "person," etc.; thus, ἄλογου and ἀλόγου, βούτυρου and βουτύρου.

The compound neuters like ἀντρόγυνο "married couple," ἀρχοντόσπιτο "lordly house," "noble family," παλιόπαιδο "street-arab," and similar (v. § 41, a), also βασιλόπουλο "king's son," etc. (cf. § 61), usually maintain the accent of the nom. (thus gen. παλιόπαιδου).

1. Dialects which maintain the -ν *ephelkusticon* sometimes show this also in the pl. (τὰ μάγουλαν = τὰ μάγουλα "cheeks"); cf. § 34, n. 4.

2. Alongside τὸ ζῶο, etc., "animal," there is found the inflexion τὸ ζῶ, τοῦ ζοῦ, τὰ ζᾶ, τῶ ζῶ.

§ 93. The nouns in -'ιο, -ιό, and ιο are declined according to the preceding paradigms; such exx. belong here: βασίλειο "kingdom," σάλιο "saliva," καπηλειό "retail-store," σκολειό "school," στοιχειό "spirit," "ghost," χωριό "village," βιβλίο "book." Nouns like βιβλίο or νοσοκομεῖο "hospital," or such as εἰκονοστάσιο "shrine" ("place for images"), or συμβούλιο "counsel," and ἀτμόπλοιο "steamer," are *mots savants.*

Non-parisyllabics.[1]

§ 94. The neuters in -o(ν) beside the regular pl. in -α occasionally form their pl. after the model of the neuters given under *C*: ἀλόγατα for ἄλογα, ὀνείρατα for ὄνειρα, προσώπατα for πρόσωπα.

§ 95. In -΄ι or -ί: τὸ μάτι "eye," τὸ παιδί "child."

	Singular.		Plural.	
Nom. Acc.	μάτι	παιδί	μάτια	παιδιά
Gen.	ματιοῦ	παιδιοῦ	ματιῶ(νε)	παιδιῶ(νε).

The words coming under this paradigm are exceedingly numerous:

(*a*) In -΄ι.

(1) ἀδέρφι "brother," ἀσήμι "silver," γιοφύρι "bridge," καλοκαίρι "summer," καράβι "ship," κεράσι "cherry," κεφάλι "head," κορίτσι "maid," λουλούδι "flower," μαχαίρι "knife," παιγνίδι "game," παλληκάρι "*pallicar*, brave fellow," παραμύθι "tale," "myth," ποτάμι "river," ρολόγι (ὡρολόγιον) "clock," "watch," ταίρι "pair," "mate," τραγούδι "song," τραπέζι "table," ψάρι "fish."

(2) ἀηδόνι "nightingale," ἀστέρι "star," δόντι "tooth," κουδούνι "bell," ὀρνίθι "hen," σεντόνι "linen-napkin," χέρι "hand," χιόνι "snow."

(3) Nouns in -άδι, -άρι, -ίδι, diminutives in -άκι -ούδι, (rarely) -ούλι: λαγκάδι "valley," πηγάδι "fountain," "spring," λιοντάρι "lion," ποδάρι "foot," λιθάρι "stone," σιτάρι "wheat," ταξίδι (ταξείδι) "journey," φίδι "snake," παιδάκι "little child," χεράκι "little hand," ἀγγελούδι "little angel," γιούδι "little son," δεντρούλι "small tree."

Note also the Lesbian dim. suffix -ἐλ(ι), *e.g.* τσιρατέλ΄ "little horn."

(4) Many loan-words: παλάτι (Lat. *palatium*) "palace," σπίτι (Lat. *hospitium*) "house"; esp. Turkish: ἀσκέρι "army," λιμέρι "camp," ντεβλέτι "government," παπούτσι "shoe," σαράγι "castle," τουφέκι "musket," φέσι "Fez," χάνι "inn."

(5) δάκρυ "tear," δίχτυ "net" (now only orthographically different).

(*b*) In -ί.

(1) βουνί "mountain," γυαλί "glass," κλαδί "twig," κρασί "wine," μαλλί "hair," σκυλί "dog," σπαθί "sword," ψωμί "bread."

[1] *Cf.* § 95, n. 2.

5

(2) αὐτί "ear," θερί "animal," κλειδί "key."

(3) βρακί (Lat. *braca*) "trousers," πουλί (*pullus*) "bird," σκαμνί (*scamnum*) "footstool," φλουρί (Ital. *florino fiorino*) "florin," πουγγί "purse."

(4) φαγί "eating," "food," φιλί "kiss."

1. Those dialects which retain the final -ν, or extend it parasitically, have the termination -ιν: e.g. βούδιν "ox," κυνήγιν "chase," χέριν "hand," παιδίν; this -ν is present even in the pl., e.g. τὰ παιδιάν του "his children" (Naxos); cf. § 34, n. 4.

2. In those dialects which show the peculiarity mentioned in § 10, n. 1, the accent remains on the -ι-; thus, παλάτι παλατίου, παιδί παιδίου παιδία. And so the neuters in -ι are to be treated as nonparisyllabic,—a fact, however, disregarded in the common speech since ι has become ι̯.

Moreover, for the decl. of these neuters, all the other phonetic changes to which ι or ι̯ are subject must be taken into account; cf. γρόσα for γρόσια (γρόσι̯, Turk. coin), etc., § 10, n. 4; μάθια, § 16, n. 3; or μάτ'χ'α = μάτια, § 10, n. 5; περιστέρκα, etc. = περιστέρια, *ib.*, μάιτα, παιιδά = μάτια, παιδιά, etc., § 8, n. 2. In Pontic -ι̯α becomes -ä (*v.* § 6, n. 6); thus, τὰ πεντικάρä = πεντικάρια. In North. Gk. (§ 7, n. 1) ι drops out; thus λεοντάρ (Pontus) = λι̯οντάρι, σ'πίτ' (Maced.) = σπίτι, τσιφάλ' (Lesbos), or τὸ κιφάλν ἀτ (Pontus) = (τὸ) κεφάλι του; consequently Turkish loan-words in this region retain their original termination, as, τὸ χαϊβάν (pl. τὰ χαϊβάνä) "beast," "animal," τὸ πρίντς "rice," τὸ σείρ "condition" (Pontus).

3. In Pontic note the gen. sing. τὶ σακκί fr. τὸ σακκί, *i.e.* with the *i* maintained throughout, as in κλέφτης κλέφτη or βαθύ(ς) βαθύ, etc. (§ 110).

§ 96. A few masculines in -ος form their pl. in -ια, like the preceding neuters: λόγος "word," pl. λόγια, χρόνος "year," pl. χρόνια and χρόνοι; cf. also § 61, n. 1, and § 100, n. 1.

§ 97. 1. The forms discussed in the preceding paragraphs represent on the whole the a. Gk. neut. o-stems; the neuters in -ι came from the ancient type in -ιον through a process that was already completed in Hellenistic days. Both forms may still sometimes be found existing together; thus, θεριό and θερί, κατώφλι and κατέφλιο(ν) (Velv.) "threshold," σάλιο and (rather rare) σάλι "saliva." The neuters in -ι (-άρι, -άδι, -ίδι) have considerably extended their territory at the expense of other forms, and, having lost their original diminutive signification, they have largely supplanted the parent forms; cf. the exx. in A. 1 and B. 1 in place of the a. Gk. nouns like τράπεζα and ποταμός or κλάδος; A. 2 (and partly 3) and B. 2 in place of the old consonant stems. The words given under A. 5 and B. 4 have found their way into this category as a result of phonetic decay (φαγί and φιλί are really survivals of infinitives equivalent to a. Gk. φαγεῖν and φιλεῖν).

2. The contracted neuters (like the masc. § 63, n. 2) have disappeared, τὸ κόκκαλο " bone " being now employed for τὸ ὀστοῦν, and τὸ κανίστρι or τὸ καλάθι " basket " (or other words) for τὸ κανοῦν. There is also no trace of the Attic decl. of neuters; ἀνώγι "upper chamber" can trace its ancestry back to ἀνώγειον found in a. Gk.

B. In -ος.

§ 98. View of the terminations:

Parisyllabic.		(Non-parisyllabic.)
	Singular.	
Nom. Acc.	-os	
Gen.	-u(s)	
	Plural.	
Nom. Acc. -i (-ya)		(-ita)
Gen. -ó.		

Parisyllabics.

§ 99. τὸ λάθος " error."

Singular.	Plural.
Nom. λάθο(ς)	λάθη
Gen. λάθους	λαθῶ(ν)
Acc. λάθος	λάθη.

Similarly: βάθος " depth," δάσος " thicket," ἔθνος " nation," θάρρος " courage," κέρδος " gain," μέρος " part," " region," " locality," ὄρος " mountain," πλῆθος " multitude," τέλος " end."

§ 100. Together with the pl. in -η there is found quite frequently also one in -ι̯α (-ηα), as :

ἄνθος " flower "—ἄνθη, ἄνθια
βάθος " depth "—βάθη, βάθια
λάθος " error "—λάθη, λάθια
πάθος " suffering "—πάθη, πάθια
πάχος " fat "—πάχια
σκέλος " limb "—σκέλη, σκέλια
στῆθος " breast "—στήθη, στήθια
(χεῖλος " lip," usually pl.)—(ἀ)χείλη, ἀχείλια.

1. The decl. of the neuters in -ος is in general that of the corresponding a. Gk. paradigm; the termination -ου is found quite frequently beside -ους in the gen. sing. The nom. sing. also shows a similar fluctuation with the neut. o-stems (§ 92); thus, τὸ δάσο beside δάσος, τὸ κράτο beside τὸ κράτος, τὸ κρύο commoner than κρύος, τὸ λάθο beside λάθος. And contrariwise, neuters in -ο(ν) have often passed over into the decl. of those in -ος ; thus :

ἄστρο and ἄστρος "star," pl. ἄστρα, ἄστρη, and ἄστρια
διάφορο(ν) and διάφορος "gain"
κάστρο "fortress," κάστρα, κάστρη
μέτρο and μέτρος "measure,"
σκέδιο and σκέδιος, Texts I. d. 5.

Some mascs. (and fems., *v.* § 63, n. 2) in -ος have been transformed into neuters in -ος ; thus :

τὸ βιός for ὁ βίος "property," "means"
τὸ δρόσος for ἡ δρόσος "dew"
τὸ ἔπαινος for ὁ ἔπαινος "praise"
τὸ θρῆνος for ὁ θρῆνος "lamentation"
τὸ πλοῦτος for ὁ πλοῦτος (πλούτη, πλούτια) "wealth"
τὸ χρόνος for ὁ χρόνος "year."

The neuters in -ος have in this way been increased in numbers,
and have also taken into their ranks new formations like τὸ ψῆλος
"height" (fr. ψηλός "high"), τὸ ζῆλος "envy" (fr. ζηλῶ), τὸ κούρσος
τὰ κούρση "piracy" (fr. κουρσεύω), etc. But sometimes neuters in -ος
have deserted to the mascs., thus—in some dialects—ὁ ἀθός for τὸ
ἄνθος, with the accent shifted.

The blending of neuters in -ος, -ον, and masculines in -ος finally
resulted in some masculines like ὁ βάσανος "torment," ὁ βράχος
"rock," ὁ στέφανος "garland," λόγος "word," χρόνος "year," taking
neut. forms in the pl. (βάσανα, βράχια and βράχοι, στέφανα, λόγια,
χρόνια and χρόνοι).

2. Sometimes the pl. termination in -η has been treated as a
neut. *sing.* in -ι :

τὸ στῆθος—τὰ στήθη
τὸ στήθι—τὰ στήθια ;
(τό χεῖλος)—τὰ χείλη
τὸ (ἀ)χείλι—τὰ χείλια.

This misunderstanding may be said to have given rise to the pl.
in -ια.

(Non-parisyllabics.)

§ 101. Sometimes neuters in -ος form a non-parisyllabic pl. in
-ητα ; as, τὸ θάρρος "courage," pl. τὰ θάρρη and τὰ θάρρητα, κέρδος
"gain," pl. τὰ κέρδη and τὰ κέρδητα.

C. In -α -ιμο, -ας.

Non-parisyllabic.[1]

§ 102. The three paradigms of this class differ from one
another only in the nom. and acc. sing., agreeing in all other
cases. The gen. sing. shows the same number of syllables as
the pl.:

	Singular.	Plural.
Nom. Acc.	-α, im-o(n), -α-s	-ata
Gen.	(-atos) -átu	-áto.

[1] Excluding the type given in § 104 n.

§ 103. τὸ πρᾶμα "thing," ὄνομα "name."

	Singular.		Plural.	
Nom. Acc.	πρᾶμα	ὄνομα	πράματα	ὀνόματα
Gen.	πραμάτου	ὀνομάτου	πραμάτω	ὀνομάτω.

Like πρᾶμα are declined : αἷμα "blood," γέμα or γιόμα "repast," γράμμα "letter," δῶμα "apartment," "terrace," θάμα "wonder," κρῖμα "sin," κῦμα "billow," στόμα "mouth," στρῶμα "mattress," χῶμα "ground," ψέμα (ψόμα) "lie," and only in pl. ἄρματα "arms" (from Lat. arma).

Like ὄνομα: μάλαμα "gold," ναννάρισμα "lullaby," πάπλωμα "coverlet," πάτωμα "floor," "story," σκέπασμα "cover," στράτεμα "army," φόρεμα "garment," χάρισμα "gift"; also pure verbal nouns (nomina actionis) like βάσκαμα "bewitching," "evil eye," δάγκαμα "bite," μίλημα "proclamation," "conversation," πήδημα "leap," κάκιωμα "sickness," μπάλωμα "improvement," ψάρεμα "fishing," "fishery," σαπούνισμα "lathering."

Some abstract nouns have a preference for the pl.; as, κλάματα "weeping," χώματα "earth" (i.e. "piles of earth"), γεράματα "old age," περιγελάσματα "laughter," τζυρίγματα (TEXTS III. 14. b), "hissing," "whistling."

1. The neuters in -a- have pretty faithfully preserved the corresponding a. Gk. decl. and have not seriously lost in numbers. In the gen. sing. -άτου is more usual than -ατος (πράματος, ὀνόματος); in the gen. pl. the accent may also be proparoxytone, τῶ στρώματω, τῶν παπλώματω. Gen. sing. πραματιοῦ, pl. πραματιοῦν in some dialects (e.g. in Lesbos).

2. γάλα "milk" is declined like πρᾶμα; so also γόνα (or γόνατο = a. Gk. γόνυ) "knee," γονάτου γόνατα; δόρυ has been displaced by κοντάρι "spear," "lance."

3. Those dialects which maintain and tend to generalise the final -ν (v. § 34, n. 4) give the nom. and acc. sing. in -αν; thus, ὄνομαν, πρᾶμαν, σκίσμαν, στόμαν, etc.

4. The pl. οἱ νομάτοι fr. ὄνομα means "persons," "individuals."

§ 104. τὸ γράψιμο "writing," "handwriting."

	Singular.	Plural.
Nom. Acc.	γράψιμο	γραψίματα
Gen.	(γραψίματος) γραψιμάτου	γραψιμάτω.

So also the abstract verbal nouns (nomina actionis) in -σιμο, like βγάλσιμο "dislocation," δέσιμο "binding," δόσιμο "giving," θάψιμο "burial," τὸ κλείσιμο "locking," τὸ ντύσιμο "putting on (clothes), τὸ ξεγδύσιμο "putting off," ξύσιμο "scraping," ράψιμο "sewing," τάξιμο "vow," "promise," "command," τρέξιμο "running," φέρσιμο "behaviour," φκειάσιμο "making," "arranging," φταίξιμο "being at fault, guilt." These nouns often serve as a substitute for the obsolete infinitive.

A parisyllabic decl. (φέρσιμο, φέρσιμον) is occasionally to be found, while, *vice versa*, some ancient neuters in -o make up non-parisyllabic pl. in -ατα, *v.* § 94.

§ 105. τὸ κρέας "flesh" (more rarely τὸ κριάς).

	Singular.	Plural.
Nom. Acc.	κρέας	κρέατα (κριάτα)
Gen.	κρεάτου	κρεάτω(ν).

So also τὸ ἅλας "salt" (though τὸ ἁλάτι, τοῦ ἁλατιοῦ is more in use).

1. The two nouns just given are the only survivors of a class that even in a. Gk. was rather limited in number; σέβας is to be attributed to the literary language, while κέρας and τέρας have been displaced by κέρατο, sometimes also κριάτο, and τέρατο respectively. For τὸ γῆρας "old age," τὰ γεράματα or τὰ γερατειά.

2. The remaining a. Gk. neut. stems have been ousted partly by different words and partly by new formations, as, τὸ νερό "water" for ὕδωρ, ἡ ἄνοιξι "spring" for ἔαρ, τὸ συκώτι "liver" for ἧπαρ, τὸ πηγάδι "fountain" for φρέαρ, ἡ φωτιά "fire" for πῦρ, τὸ αὐτί "ear" for οὖς. τὸ μέλι "honey" is decl. like σπίτι (μελιοῦ, μέλια). On γόνα, *v.* § 103, n. 2. The forms τὸ φώσι, τοῦ φωσιοῦ, τὰ φώσια are found alongside τὸ φῶς "light."

ADJECTIVES.

§ 106. In m. Gk. the dividing line between adjective and substantive is hard to determine as in a. Gk. A. Gk. adjs. were converted into substantives and *vice versa* (*cf.* λυγερή "the young girl," literally "the slender (one)"),—a process which is still operative in the language spoken to-day: *e.g.* ἀγαπητικός "beloved" and "lover," νέος νιός "young" and "young man," ξένος "strange" and "the stranger," τὰ ξένα "the foreign country," φτωχός "poor" and "the poor man," ξα(ν)θός "blond" and ξα(ν)θή (ξανθούλα) "a blonde" ("little blond"), or *vice versa* γέρος "old man" and "aged," χωριάτης "peasant," "boor," and "boorish." But national names and the adjectives from the same are generally carefully distinguished from each other; as, Ρωμιός and ρωμαίικος, Τούρκος and τούρκικος "Turkish," "peculiar to the Turks," Φράγκος "a

European," and φράγκικος "European" (adj.), "in European fashion," 'Ιγγλέζος and ἰγγλέζικος "English," "peculiar to the English." Only it must be noted that in expressions like "(the) Turkish soldiers," "(the) English physicians," "(the) European scholars," m. Gk. employs the national name (*not* the adj.); thus, (οἱ) Τούρκοι στρατιῶτες, (οἱ) 'Ιγγλέζοι γιατροί, (οἱ) Φράγκοι λόγιοι.

For the position of adjs., *v.* § 293.

The adj., whether attributive or predicative, agrees in gender and in number with its noun. If the *attribute* belongs to several nouns of different genders, then the adj. accommodates itself to the nearest noun, but tends to be repeated with each; thus, καλὸ κρασὶ καὶ (καλὴ) μπίρα or κρασὶ (καλὸ) καὶ μπίρα καλή "good wine and good beer," ἀντρειωμένοι ἄντρες καὶ γυναῖκες "brave men and women." The adj., when *predicate*, is masc. when it goes with persons, neut. when it goes with things; thus, ἄντρες καὶ γυναῖκες καὶ παιδιὰ ἤτανε τριγυρισμένοι ἀπὸ τοὺς Τούρκους "men, women, and children were surrounded by the Turks," τὸ κρασὶ καὶ ἡ μπίρα εἶναι καλά "wine and beer are good." In longer enumerations of things the subject can be summed up with ὅλα; but, generally speaking, such a remedy is avoided by the repetition of the predicate; thus, καλὸ (εἶναι) τὸ κρασὶ καὶ καλὴ ἡ μπίρα. Expressions like "a mother's love is something noble" run τῆς μάννας ἡ ἀγάπη εἶναι κάτι(τι) λαμπρό or λαμπρὸ πρᾶμα. When the subject is a demonstrative pronoun it usually agrees with the predicate; as, αὐτὸς εἶναι (ὁ) φίλος μου "that (he) is my friend," αὐτὴ εἶναι ἀνοησία "that is nonsense," but one may also say αὐτὰ εἶναι ἀνοησίες.

§ 107. The declensions of the adjective correspond almost exactly with those of the substantive. For some pronominal forms, *v.* §§ 144, n. 1, 156. All adjectives have separate forms for masc. fem. and neut. Adjectives also, like substantives, fall into parisyllabic and non-parisyllabic.

Taking the masculine as the standard, we differentiate:

I. Adjectives in -*os*.
II. Adjectives in -*is*.
    a. Oxytones (-ύς).
    b. Barytones (-ις, -ης).

I. Adjectives in -*os*.

§ 108. καλός "good."

	Masc.	Fem.	Neut.
Sing. Nom.	καλός	καλή	καλό(ν)
Gen.	καλοῦ	καλῆς	καλοῦ
Acc.	καλό(ν)	καλή(ν)	καλό(ν)
Voc.	καλέ	καλή	καλό(ν).

	Masc.	Fem.	Neut.
Plur. Nom.	καλοί	καλές	καλά
Gen.	καλῶ(ν)	καλῶ(ν)	καλῶ(ν)
Acc.	καλούς	καλές	καλά
Voc.	καλοί	καλές	καλά.

The adjs. also, which are not accented on the final, retain in all cases the accent of the nom. sing. masc.; as, πρόστυχος "ordinary," "common," gen. πρόστυχου, fem. πρόστυχη, fem. pl. πρόστυχες, etc.

To this group belong: γερός "sound," "strong," ἐλαφρός "light," κακός "bad," μικρός "small," λαμπρός "bright," ξερός "dry," ξυνός "sharp," περισσός "very much," "enough," πικρός "bitter," ἄσπρος "white," μαῦρος "black," ἀφράτος "fresh," γεμάτος "full," μεγάλος "great," μονάχος and μοναχος "alone"; ἄδικος "unjust," ἄμοιρος "unlucky," ἀτέλειωτος "endless," ἄψυχος "lifeless," βάρβαρος "barbarian," ἐλεύτερος "free," ἥσυχος "quiet," κατάψηλος "very lofty," ὄμορφος "beautiful"; also adjs. in -ερός (e.g. βροχερός "rainy," λασπερός "dirty," μαυριδερός "blackish"), -ινος (denoting colour and material, e.g. κόκκινος "red," πέτρινος "stony"), -ινός (dates, e.g. σημερινός "of to-day," περσινός "of last year"), -ικος (-άτικος, § 212 n.), and -ικός (esp. of origin, e.g. τούρκικος, φράγκικος, νησιώτικος "from" or "belonging to the islands," κρητικός, ἀνατολικός "oriental"), -ωπός (to designate colours, e.g. κοκκινωπός "reddish"), diminutive adjs. in -ούτσικος and -ουλός (μικρούτσικος "quite small," τρελλούτσικος "rather crazy," παχουλός "somewhat fat"), and participial formations in -(ά)τος (§ 212 n.) and -μενος (§ 234, 2. 3). The feminine forms are: λαμπρή, μικρή, ἄσπρη, ἄδικη, ἄμοιρη, ἐλεύτερη, ἀτέλειωτη, ἥσυχη, φράγκικη, μικρούτσικη, etc.

1. Apart from the accent remaining uniform in *all* the forms, the adjs. deviate in two respects from the a. Gk:

a. The fem. termination -η has been made general, even after ρ (ἐλεύτερος—ἐλεύτερη).[1]

b. The conversion of all the adjs. of two terminations -ος, -ον into the class of those of three terminations (ἄδικος, fem. ἄδικη, κοντόμυαλος "limited," κοντόμυαλη).

For a further change *v.* § 111. In Pontic a new fem. form in -έσσα (or -ενα, Capp. -άσσα) has usurped the place of the old καλός καλέσσα καλόν, μικρός μικρέσσα μικρόν (γοτσαμάνος "old," fem.

---

[1] Exceptions are rare, *e.g.* ἄκρα (for ἄκρη) "extremity," "end," TEXTS II. a. 13, and λαμπρά (for λαμπρή), II. b. 2.

γοτσ̌αμάνενα). This suffix also serves as the feminine of substantives, e.g. ἀλεπέσ̌α "fox" (fem.) (TEXTS III. 13. c).

2. Note that μέγας has been replaced by μεγάλος; the neut. μέγα for μεγάλο, however, occasionally turns up.

3. The voc. of the masc. is sometimes used also for the fem.; as, καλὲ μάννα "good mother!" for καλὴ μάννα.

4. The nom. pl. masc. (as in the noun, § 62, n. 1) serves also for the acc.: e.g. TEXTS III. 5 (Ios) νά 'χῃς πολλοὶ τσοὶ χρόνοι, or III. 14. b (Capp.) μᾶς ἔβγαλ' ἀροί "he regarded us as sound." Note also ἕνα καλὸ ἄτρωπος, TEXTS III. 14. a (Pontus).

§ 109. πλούσιος "rich."

	Masc.	Fem.	Neut.
Sing.	πλούσιος	πλούσια	πλούσιο
	πλούσιου	πλούσιας	πλούσιου
	πλούσιο(ν)	πλούσια(ν)	πλούσιο.
Plur.	πλούσιοι	πλούσιες	πλούσια
	πλούσιω(ν)	πλούσιω(ν)	πλούσιω(ν)
	πλούσιους	πλούσιες	πλούσια.

Similarly, all adjectives with a vowel, usually ι (or y), before the termination; as, ἅγιος "holy," ἄγριος "wild," ἀκέριος "unhurt," "untouched," "pure," ἄξιος "worthy," "capable," γαλάζιος "blue," δίκιος (δίκαιος) "just," δόλιος "unlucky," καινούργιος "new," κρύος "cold," οὐράνιος "heavenly," τίμιος "honourable," τρύπιος "pierced," δεξιός "on right hand," νιός (νέος) "young," παλιός "old," χλιός "tepid"; the *mots savants*: ἀστεῖος "witty," ἀχρεῖος "bad," "common," ἀρχαῖος "ancient," τελευταῖος "last," ὡραῖος (beside ὤριος) "fair"; the adjs. in -ίσιος: e.g. βουνίσιος "mountainous," γυναικίσιος "womanish," ἀρνίσιος "like a lamb"; designations of material in -ένιος: e.g. ἀσημένιος "of silver," βελουδένιος "of velvet," μαρμαρένιος "of marble."

1. Except for the accent, the old fem. form has been retained, though even here the fem. formation in -η is found: e.g. βέβαιη fr. βέβαιος "sure," "certain."

2. In dialects in which ι after σ disappears (v. § 10, n. 4), note forms like ἄξα = ἄξια, πλούσος πλούσα = πλούσιος πλούσια, etc. On indeclinable ἅ(γ)ι = ἅγιος, v. § 63. ἅγιος "saint" has also the fem. ἀγιά (Ἁγιὰ Μαύρα = Leukada) and the masc. pl. οἱ ἁγιοί.

§ 109a. The ancient contracted adjs. (ἁπλοῦς) have disappeared or passed into the class in -ός; thus, ἁπλός "simple," διπλός "double," χρυσός "golden" (but χάλκινος "of brass," μπακιρένιος "of copper," or μπρούντζινος "of bronze," for χαλκοῦς). Most of the forms do not practically differ in pronunciation from the paradigm of καλός

($\chi\rho\upsilon\sigma\hat{\eta}$ like $\kappa\alpha\lambda\acute{\eta}$, $\chi\rho\upsilon\sigma\hat{a}$ like $\kappa\alpha\lambda\acute{a}$, etc.). Several of the exx. given above show that the adjs. in -os have been enriched to the detriment of others; *cf.* also § 110 n.

II. Adjectives in -*is*.

(*a*) Oxytones (-ύs).

§ 110. $\beta\alpha\theta\acute{\upsilon}s$ "deep."

	Masc.	Fem.	Neut.
Sing.	$\beta\alpha\theta\acute{\upsilon}s$	$\beta\alpha\theta\epsilon\iota\acute{a}$	$\beta\alpha\theta\acute{\upsilon}$
	$\beta\alpha\theta\epsilon\iota o\hat{\upsilon}$ ($\beta\alpha\theta\acute{\upsilon}$)	$\beta\alpha\theta\epsilon\iota\hat{a}s$	$\beta\alpha\theta\epsilon\iota o\hat{\upsilon}$ ($\beta\alpha\theta\acute{\upsilon}$)
	$\beta\alpha\theta\acute{\upsilon}$	$\beta\alpha\theta\epsilon\iota\acute{a}(\nu)$	$\beta\alpha\theta\acute{\upsilon}$
	$\beta\alpha\theta\acute{\upsilon}$	$\beta\alpha\theta\epsilon\iota\acute{a}$	$\beta\alpha\theta\acute{\upsilon}$.
Plur.	$\beta\alpha\theta\epsilon\iota o\acute{\iota}$	$\beta\alpha\theta\epsilon\iota\acute{\epsilon}s$	$\beta\alpha\theta\epsilon\iota\acute{a}$
	$\beta\alpha\theta\epsilon\iota\hat{\omega}(\nu\epsilon)$	$\beta\alpha\theta\epsilon\iota\hat{\omega}(\nu\epsilon)$	$\beta\alpha\theta\epsilon\iota\hat{\omega}(\nu\epsilon)$
	$\beta\alpha\theta\epsilon\iota o\acute{\upsilon}s$	$\beta\alpha\theta\epsilon\iota\acute{\epsilon}s$	$\beta\alpha\theta\epsilon\iota\acute{a}$
	$\beta\alpha\theta\epsilon\iota o\acute{\iota}$	$\beta\alpha\theta\epsilon\iota\acute{\epsilon}s$	$\beta\alpha\theta\epsilon\iota\acute{a}$.

Similarly: $\beta\alpha\rho\acute{\upsilon}s$ "heavy," $\gamma\lambda\upsilon\kappa\acute{\upsilon}s$ "sweet," $\mu\alpha\beta\acute{\upsilon}s$ "blue," $\mu\alpha\kappa\rho\acute{\upsilon}s$ "wide," "far," $\pi\lambda\alpha\tau\acute{\upsilon}s$ "broad," $\pi\alpha\chi\acute{\upsilon}s$ "thick," $\tau\rho\alpha\chi\acute{\upsilon}s$ "rough," $\phi\alpha\rho\delta\acute{\upsilon}s$ "wide," "broad."

The a. Gk. parent form is generally retained, *i.e.* most of the forms may be phonetically derived from the ancient; $\beta\alpha\theta\epsilon\iota o\hat{\upsilon}$, $\beta\alpha\theta\epsilon\iota o\acute{\iota}$, $\beta\alpha\theta\epsilon\iota o\acute{\upsilon}s$ are due to contamination with the adjs. in -os (esp. those in -ιός), brought about in the first instance chiefly by the fem. $\beta\alpha\theta\epsilon\iota\acute{a}$. The adjs. $\delta\epsilon\xi\acute{\iota}s$ ($\delta\epsilon\xi\acute{\upsilon}s$) = $\delta\epsilon\xi\iota\acute{o}s$ "on the right," and $\mathring{a}\rho\acute{\iota}s$ ($\mathring{a}\rho\acute{\upsilon}s$) = $\mathring{a}\rho\alpha\iota\acute{o}s$, $\mathring{a}\rho\iota\acute{o}s$ "thin," "rare," have gone the opposite way into the $\beta\alpha\theta\acute{\upsilon}s$ class. The neut. $\beta\alpha\theta\acute{\upsilon}$ is, moreover, declined like $\pi\alpha\iota\delta\acute{\iota}$. Analogous to the decl. of §§ 74, 75 we find also—but rarely—a gen. sing. masc. $\beta\alpha\theta\acute{\upsilon}$ and a nom. pl. in -δεs: $\beta\alpha\rho\acute{\upsilon}\delta\epsilon s$, $\pi\lambda\alpha\tau\acute{\upsilon}\delta\epsilon s$.

An almost wholesale transition of the adjs. in -ύs into the -ός or -ιός class is sometimes to be found; thus the decl. $\gamma\lambda\upsilon\kappa\acute{o}s$ ($\gamma\lambda\upsilon\kappa\epsilon\iota\acute{a}$) $\gamma\lambda\upsilon\kappa\acute{o}$ is quite as common as $\gamma\lambda\upsilon\kappa\acute{\upsilon}s$ $\gamma\lambda\upsilon\kappa\acute{\upsilon}$; $\mu\iota\sigma\acute{o}s$ (a. Gk. $\mathring{\eta}\mu\iota\sigma\upsilon s$) is invariably the rule (but $\pi\epsilon\nu\tau\acute{\epsilon}$ '$\mu\iota\sigma\upsilon$ = 5$\frac{1}{2}$, etc., *v.* § 131). Moreover, forms like $\pi\lambda\alpha\tau\epsilon\iota\acute{o}s$, $\gamma\lambda\upsilon\kappa\epsilon\iota\acute{o}s$, $\pi\alpha\chi\epsilon\iota o s$ are found, and in Lower Italy these are the usual forms; thus, *varío varía* (Bova), *varéo varéa* (Otr.), etc. = $\beta\alpha\rho\acute{\upsilon}s$ $\beta\alpha\rho\epsilon\iota\acute{a}$.

§ 111. Some adjectives (originally) in -ός have secondary forms in -ύs; thus, in addition to $\mu\alpha\kappa\rho\acute{\upsilon}s$ above: $\mathring{a}\delta\rho\acute{\upsilon}s$ "rough," $\mathring{\epsilon}\lambda\alpha\phi\rho\acute{\upsilon}s$ "light" beside $\mathring{\epsilon}\lambda\alpha\phi\rho\acute{o}s$, $\pi\rho\iota\kappa\acute{\upsilon}s$ "bitter," beside $\pi\iota\kappa\rho\acute{o}s$, $\pi\rho\iota\kappa\acute{o}s$, etc. *Cf.* also the comparatives in -ύτερος, § 117. The feminine formation—ειά—after the model of $\gamma\lambda\upsilon\kappa\acute{o}s$ $\gamma\lambda\upsilon\kappa\epsilon\iota\acute{a}$ occurs quite frequently with adjs.

in -ός, and especially with those in -ικός (mostly alongside the normal forms), *e.g.*:

κακός " bad," " vile "—κακειά (TEXTS III. 3 καϊτᣂά)
ἀγαπητικός " lover "—ἀγαπητικειά
ἀρρεβωνιαστικός " fiancé "—ἀρρεβωνιαστικειά
εὐγενικός " noble," " gallant "—εὐγενικειά
ἑλληνικός " Greek "—'ληνιτσά, TEXTS III. 6
παστρικός " clean "—παστρικειά
φυσικός " natural "—φυσικειά.

Even barytones have sometimes such a feminine:

κακόμοιρος " ill-fated "—κακομοιρειά (κακομοίρα " ill-fated woman ").

Many representatives of the popular literature are very fond of using this -ειά form.

§ 112. πολύς "many," "much."

	Masc.	Fem.	Neut.
Sing.	πολύς	πολλή	πολύ
	πολλοῦ	πολλῆς	πολλοῦ
	πολύ(ν)	πολλή(ν)	πολύ.
Plur.	πολλοί	πολλές	πολλά
	πολλῶ(ν)	πολλῶ(ν)	πολλῶ(ν)
	πολλούς	πολλές	πολλά.

Exactly corresponds to the a. Gk. decl.

(*b*) Barytones (-ις, -ης).

§ 113. ζουλιάρις " envious," " jealous."

	Masc.	Fem.	Neut.
Sing.	ζουλιάρις	ζουλιάρα	ζουλιάρικο
	ζουλιάρι	ζουλιάρας	ζουλιάρικου
	ζουλιάρι	ζουλιάρα	ζουλιάρικο
	ζουλιάρι	ζουλιάρα	ζουλιάρικο.
Plur.	ζουλιάριδες	ζουλιάριδες	ζουλιάρικα
	ζουλιάριδω	ζουλιάριδω	ζουλιάρικω
	ζουλιάριδες	ζουλιάριδες	ζουλιάρικα.

Similarly, *e.g.*: γρινιάρις " peevish," καυκησιάρις " boastful," σιχασιάρις " fastidious," τσιμπλιάρις " deep-eyed," χτικιάρις " consumptive," and also numerous compounds (denoting possession) like γαλανομάτης " blue-eyed," καστανομάτης

" chestnut-eyed," μαυροφρύδης " with dark eyebrows," σγουρομάλλης " curly-haired."

1. No value attaches to the spelling -ης (here and in the
following §) except in writing; *cf.* § 75, n. 1.

2. Diminutives like ἀσπρούλις "rather white," μακρούλις
" somewhat long," φτωχούλις " poor," give ἀσπρούλι, φτωχούλι, etc., in
the neut. (nom. pl. masc. and fem. ἀσπρούλιδες). The fem. pl. may
take also parisyllabic form: *e.g.* μαυρομάτες fr. μαυρομάτης " dark-
eyed."

§ 114. ἀκαμάτης "lazy."

	Masc.	Fem.	Neut.
Sing.	ἀκαμάτης	ἀκαμάτισσα	ἀκαμάτικο
	ἀκαμάτη	ἀκαμάτισσας	ἀκαμάτικου
	ἀκαμάτη	ἀκαμάτισσα	ἀκαμάτικο.
Plur.	ἀκαμάτηδες	ἀκαμάτισσες	ἀκαμάτικα
	ἀκαμάτηδω	ἀκαμάτισσω	ἀκαμάτικω
	ἀκαμάτηδες	ἀκαμάτισσες	ἀκαμάτικα.

Similarly: κανακάρις " darling," μακαρίτης " blessed," " late,"
μακρολαίμης " long-necked," etc.

The fem. form sometimes fluctuates between this paradigm
and the immediately preceding; thus the fem. of ζουλιάρις is
also ζουλιάρισσα; γρινιάρις " peevish " has two fems. γρινιάρα
and γρινιάρισσα, κοκκινομύτης " red-nosed " κοκκινομύτα and
-μύτισσα and even κοκκινομυτοῦ, σταυροπόδης " with crossed
legs " σταυροπόδα and σταυροπόδισσα.

ἀκαμάτης even forms a fem. ἀκαμάτρα, and ψεύτης " lying," ψεύτρα.
Note also κακούδης "ugly," κακουδιά, χρυσομάλλης χρυσομαλλοῦσα
" the golden-haired " *f.* Masc. substantives in -ᾶς have corresponding
fems. in -οῦ (§ 88) and neuts. in -άδικο: *e.g.* ψωμᾶς ψωμοῦ ψωμάδικο ;
those in -άδικο designating the place where a trade is carried on ; as,
ψωμάδικο " bakery," " bake-shop," ψαράδικο " fishmonger's shop."
For other suffixes of gender, *v.* §§ 40, 81 (2) d.

§ 115. Both the preceding paradigms are m. Gk. formations, their
decl. following that of the corresponding substantives. *The ancient
adjectives in -ής (εὐγενής) have disappeared from the real vernacular,*
being replaced either by *new adjectives* (ἀδιάντροπος "insolent" for
αὐθάδης, γερός = a. Gk. ὑγιηρός " healthy" for ὑγιής) or by *forms in*
-ος : ἀκριβός " dear," ἄμαθος " unlettered," διάφανος " transparent,"
δύστυχος (δυστυχισμένος) " unfortunate," πρεπός = εὐπρεπής " proper,"
" becoming," ἄπρεπος " unbecoming," ἰσόβαρος " of equal weight,"
τρίσβαθος " very deep," ἀληθινός " true," εὐγενικός " polite," ψεύτικος
" false," " falsified." Other types of the a. Gk. adj. have also disappeared ; thus, *e.g.*, θῆλυς and ἄρσην have been displaced by θηλυκός
" female," and ἀρσενικός (σερνικός) " male," πλήρης by γεμάτος " full,"
εὐώδης by μυρουδάτος " fragrant." Forms such as εὐγενεῖς, συγγενεῖς

(nom. and acc. pl. of εὐγενής "noble," and συγγενής "related"), or ἀκριβής "accurate," νευρώδης (gen. νευρώδους) "nervous," come from the literary language. But such adjectives from the literary language may be conformed to the vernacular paradigm: *e.g.* συγγενής, -ή, -ήδες, εὐλαβής, -ή, -ήδες, fem. συγγένισσα (rarely εὐλαβήδισσα), neut. συγγενικό.

Comparison of Adjectives.

§ 116. The adjectives in classes I. and II. a. form the comparative—so far as it is in use—by adding -τερος to the stem (what remains after cutting off -ς of the nom., *v.* n. 2), that is to -ο- or -υ-; thus:

<blockquote>
γερός " strong " γερώτερος
εὔκολος " easy " εὐκολώτερος
ζεστός " warm " ζεστότερος
λίγος " little " λιγώτερος
μικρός " small " μικρότερος
φρόνιμος " reasonable " φρονιμώτερος
φτωχός " poor " φτωχότερος
ψηλός " high " ψηλότερος
πλούσιος " rich " πλουσιώτερος
βαθύς " deep " βαθύτερος
βαρύς " heavy " βαρύτερος
γλυκύς " sweet " γλυκύτερος
μακρύς " long " μακρύτερος
παχύς " thick " παχύτερος.
</blockquote>

The superlative is formed by placing the article before the comparative; as, ὁ μικρότερος "the smallest," etc. The declension is the same as that of a corresponding adjective; thus, μικρότερος, μικρότερη, μικρότερο, etc., like, *e.g.*, ἐλεύτερος.

1. Note γεροντότερος fr. γέρος (a. Gk. γέρων) "old."

2. The distinction between εὐκολ-ώ-τερος and φτωχ-ό-τερος is merely orthographical, having no value for the living speech. But since in the majority of cases the comparative in -τερος is formed exactly like that of a. Gk., the present-day orthography maintains the a. Gk. rule of -ο- after a preceding long syllable and -ω- after a preceding short, although this rule has no meaning for genuine m. Gk. forms like λιγώτερος.

3. The a. Gk. superlative in -τατος is still to be found—only occasionally—in the so-called *elative* sense, *i.e.* to throw into prominence, translated by *very*: e.g. λαμπρότατος "very bright," καλώτατος "very good." These forms are somewhat freely employed in the vernacular literature in imitation of the usage in the written language. Still it is more customary to employ πολύ (also παρὰ πολύ) or πολλά

or other words signifying "*very*"; thus, πολὺ (πολλὰ) καλός "very good," etc. The doubling of the adj. serves the same purpose (ψηλὸ ψηλὸ βουνό "a very high mountain"), or compounding with κατα- or θεο-: *e.g.* κατακόκκινος "quite red," θεότρελλος "quite crazy." Finally, *cf.* § 281, 1, n. 2.

§ 117. A number of adjectives in -ος form their comparatives in -ύτερος; those most in use are:

   καλός "good" καλύτερος
   κακός "bad" κακύτερος and κακώτερος
   μεγάλος "great" μεγαλύτερος;
also: κοντός "near" κοντύτερος and κοντότερος
   μαῦρος "black" μαυρύτερος
   ὄμορφος "fair" ὀμορφύτερος and ὀμορφότερος
   πρῶτος "first" πρωτύτερος "earlier"
   τρανός "great" (*e.g.* in Maced.) τρανότερος and τρα-
      νύτερος
   χοντρός "thick" "coarse" χοντρύτερος and χοντρότερος.

The orthography fluctuates, the spelling usually being -ήτερος, -είτερος, or -ίτερος, even -ῆτερος, and so μεγαλύτερος may be spelled μεγαλήτερος, μεγαλείτερος, μεγαλίτερος, or μεγαλῆτερος,—καλύτερος also καλλίτερος (on account of a. Gk. καλλίων). The spelling -ύτερος corresponds to the origin of the form, comparatives in -ύτερος being formed on analogy of the adjs. in -ύς. The adjs. with double forms served as a model; *cf.* μακρός—μακρύς—μακρύτερος, γλυκός—γλυκύς —γλυκύτερος.

§ 118. Two adjectives employ different words for the comparatives:

   πολύς "much" περισσότερος and π(λ)εῐότερος.

1. *Cf.* also πλέτιρου in Velvendos; πολύτερος and πολλότερος are employed only in dialect.

   κακός "bad" χερότερος (χειρότερος) "worse" (beside
      κακύτερος, § 117).

2. Instances of double degrees of comparison occur in πλειότερος, χε(ι)ρότερος, the old comparatives πλείων, χείρων having been reinforced by the common m. Gk. compar. termination -τερος. The older language had still more exx. of this kind. The old formation in -ίων is retained intact in the neut. κάλλιο (occasionally used) (= a. Gk. κάλλιον) "better," in addition to which a κάλλιος (*m.*) and κάλλια (*f.*), or even (in Crete) a ὁ καλλιάς, ἡ καλλιά "the better" (*m.* and *f.*), and an adverb κάλλια or καλλιά (neut. pl.), were formed. In Bova, forms like *plen gália* (κάλλια) and *pleh·h·íru* (χεῖρον) have taken on the compar. particle *ple*(*n*) = πλέον.

§ 119. Beside the mode of comparison with -τερος, there is another equally common method which corresponds to that of the Romance languages :

καλός—πιὸ καλός " better "—ὁ πιὸ καλός " the best "
μικρός—πιὸ μικρός " smaller "—ὁ πιὸ μικρός " the smallest "
λίγος—πιὸ λίγος " less "—οἱ πιὸ λίγοι " the least."

1. The particle πιό (also πλιό, πιά) is the old πλέον (still used in the written language). It occurs as an independent adverb (πλιό[ν], πλιά, πιά, in the Terra d' Otranto *pléo*) in the signification " more," " now," " already," as δὲ μπορῶ πιά " I cannot any more," φτάνει πιά " it is enough now "; but note δὲν πίνω περισσότερο " I drink no *more* (than a definite quantity)."

This method is employed chiefly with adjective forms of modern (or foreign) origin, with compound and other adjectives belonging to II. b, with participles and generally with polysyllabic adjectives :

καινούργιος " new " πιὸ καινούργιος
τεμπέλης " lazy " πιὸ τεμπέλης
γεμάτος " full " πιὸ γεμάτος
ὄμορφος " fair " πιὸ ὄμορφος
ζηλιάρις " jealous " πιὸ ζηλιάρις
τιμημένος " honoured " πιὸ τιμημένος
ἁμαρτωλός " sinful " πιὸ ἁμαρτωλός.

2. One may occasionally say for emphasis πιὸ καλύτερος beside the simple καλύτερος or ὁ πλιὸ στερνότερος " the last," " latest " (*cf.* § 118, n. 2).

3. The periphrastic comparative has almost ousted the a. Gk. mode in Lower Italy. A different periphrastic method—borrowed from the Turkish—predominates in Pontus and elsewhere in the region of the Black Sea ; καλός—ἀκόμαν καλός " better," τσὶπ καλὸς " very good," " best "; similarly in Saranda Klisiés κὸμ (*i.e.* ἀκόμη) καλός " better," ὁ κὸμ καλός " the best." Finally, foreign influence has resulted in the complete loss of the compar. form ; *cf.* TEXTS III. 13. a, ἀς ἐσὲν μικρός " small from thee "=" smaller tl .n thou."

§ 120. In the comparison of nouns, " than " after the comparative is translated by ἀπό with acc., less frequently by παρά with nom. ; as, ὁ Γιώργις εἶναι μεγαλύτερος ἀπὸ τὸ Γιάννη " G. is taller than J.," καλύτερα μιᾶς ὥρας ἐλεύθερη ζωὴ παρὰ σαράντα χρόνων σκλαβιά " better one hour of liberty than forty years of slavery."

1. παρά (Velv. πέρι) is used especially for the comparison of adjectives, παρὰ νά or παρὰ ποῦ for comparison with a whole

sentence : *e.g.* ἡ φωνὴ ἦτο περισσότερο φοβέρα παρὰ ζητιανειά "the voice was more fearful than entreating," καλύτιρα νὰ τοὺν ἔπιρνις τοὺ κιφάλι περὶ τοῦ πλί (TEXTS III. 11) "better you had taken his head than the hen," κάλλιο νὰ σκάσω πρῶτα παρὰ νὰ μὴ σᾶς θυμηθῶ "better that I should perish sooner than forget thee," δὲν ὑπάρχει ἄλλο φοβερώτερο παρὰ ποῦ ἔπαθα "there is nothing more terrible than what I have suffered." Finally, παρά means "except" (Lat. *nisi*) : *e.g.* δὲν ἤξερε παρὰ τὰ παλιά μας "he knew nothing except our past history," δὲν κάνει παρὰ ὀνειρεύεται "he does nothing but dream."

2. The *genetivus comparationis* is occasionally to be found with the personal pronoun ; *cf.* μὶ τοὺν τρανύτιρό σ [*i.e.* σου] κουκκιὰ νὰ μὴ σ'πέρς (TEXTS III. 11) "sow no beans with him that is stronger than thou" ("have no business partnership"), δὲν ηὗρα ἀδερφὸ καλλιάν του (I. a. 15) "I did not find any brother better than he."

"The more . . . the more " ὅσο—(ἄλλο) τόσο.

" The best of all " runs τὸ καλύτερο ἀπ' ὅλα. The a. Gk. partitive gen. after comparative and superlative has been displaced by ἀπό ; thus, ὁ μεγαλύτερος ἀπ' τοὺς δῠό "the greater of the two."

" As . . . as " = τόσο—ὅσο or σὰν (καί) ; thus, εἶναι τόσο μέγαλος ὅσο (εἶμαι) ἐγώ or εἶναι μεγάλος σὰν καὶ μένα " he is as tall as I."

THE ADVERB.

§ 121. The adverb is not connected merely with verbs or adjectives (πολὺ καλός "very good"), but may be employed also attributively as in a. Gk.: *e.g.* ἡ μέσα κάμαρα " the middle room," ἡ κάτω γῆ " the lower world," τὸ ἀπάνω πάτωμα " the upper storey," τὰ καθαυτὸ ὀνόματα " the proper names " ; in some phrases it even becomes a quasi-substantive, as στὸ ἑξῆς " in the future," στὸ μεταξύ " in the meantime "; *cf.*, further, § 57 n.

§ 122. To form the adverb take the neut. pl.—only in exceptional cases the neut. sing.—of the corresponding adjective ; as, ἀκριβός " dear " ἀκριβά, ἀχόρταστος " insatiable " ἀχόρταστα, γλήγορος " speedy " γλήγορα, δυνατός " strong," " loud " δυνατά, ἴσιος " equal " ἴσια " even," " forthwith," καλός " good " καλά, κοντός " near " κοντά, κρυφός " secret " κρυφά, ρωμαίικος " Romaic," " modern Greek " ρωμαίικα, πρῶτος " first " πρῶτα, ψηλός " high " ψηλά ; βαρύς " heavy " βαρειά (and in dialects βαρύ), μακρός and μακρύς " wide " μακρειά, ζουλιάρις " jealous " ζουλιάρικα ; πολύς forms πολύ and πολλά, (ὀ)λίγος " little " (ὀ)λίγα, (ὀ)λίγο or λιγάκι.

§ 123. The comparative of adverbs is the neut. pl. of the adjective, though the neut. sing. is relatively more frequent than in the positive: καλύτερα " better," βαθύτερα " deeper," λιγώτερο " less," περισσότερα " more " (beside περισσότερο and πιότερο or πιότερα), χε(ι)ρότερα " worse," etc., or πιὸ καλά, πιὸ πολύ " to a higher degree," πιὸ βαθειά (or πιὸ καλύτερα, πιὸ βαθύτερα), etc.

Superlative τὸ π(λ)ιὸ καλύτερα and τὸ πιὸ καλύτερο, τὸ πιὸ βαθύτερα (-ο), τὸ πιὸ χειρότερα (-ο). Emphasis of comparison is secured by πολύ (πολλά) " very," and other such words, or by repeating the adverb; as, ἀγάλια ἀγάλια " very gradually," σιγά σιγά " very slowly," ἴσ(ι)α ἴσ(ι)α " just so," " even," κάτω κάτω " quite under," μιλᾷ καλὰ καλὰ ρωμαίικα " he speaks modern Greek most excellently."

1. Forms like φυσικώτατα " most naturally," ἑλληνικώτατα " in genuine Greek style," come from the literary language.

Adverbs with no corresponding adjective like ἀπάνω " above," πέρα " yonder," κάτω " under," form the comparative exclusively with πιό; thus, πιὸ 'πάνω, πιὸ κάτω, etc.

2. Note adv. ταχυτέρου " later " (Naxos) from ταχύς.

§ 124. Compared with this mode of forming adverbs the (old) adverbial forms in -ως have survived only in isolated cases in the popular speech; as, ἀμέσως " immediately," ἴσως " perhaps," καλῶς " well," in the expressions καλῶς ὡρίσατε, καλῶς ἦρθες " welcome," or καλῶς τον " long life to him," " a welcome to him," στανικῶς " unwillingly."

§ 125. Even substantival and prepositional expressions are sometimes stereotyped as adverbs: e.g. τοῦ κάκου " in vain," μιὰ φορά " once," πολλὲς φορές " often," μιὰ καὶ καλή " once for all," κάθε μέρα " daily," σὲ λίγο " soon," στὸν ἴδιο καιρό " simultaneously," " at once," στὰ τυφλά " at random," μὲ μιᾶς " suddenly," στὸ μεταξύ " in the meantime," etc. " Almost " is rendered by means of the verb κοντεύω " I am near " (or λιγό· λειψε " it wanted but little "), e.g. ἐκόντευα νὰ πέσω " I had almost fallen."

§ 126. Many adverbs have either never been accompanied by an appellative, or have lost all formal connection with such in the course of development of the Greek language.

6

Such are of various kinds. The most important are the following:

1. *Adverbs of Place.*

ποῦ " where ? " ἀπὸ ποῦ (also ποῦθε) " whither ? " κάπου " any-where," πουθενά (πούπετα, πούβετις) " anywhere," in negative sense " nowhere " (*cf.* the use of κανένας and τίποτε, § 153), ὅπου, ποῦ " where," relative

ἐδώ, δώ " here," " hither "

ἐκεῖ, 'κεῖ " there," " thither," " in that place," παρακεῖ " farther that way," " on that side "

αὐτοῦ (εὐτοῦ, αὐτουνοῦ) " there," " in that place "

ἀλλοῦ " elsewhere "

παντοῦ " everywhere "

ὁλοῦθε " everywhere," " on all sides "

ἀπάνω, πάνω (πάνου), ἀποπάνω " above "

κάτω (κάτου) " under," " underneath," παρακάτω " farther under," " lower down," ἀνωκάτω " up and down," " pell-mell "

χάμω (χάμου, more rarely χαμαί, χάμαι), also καταγῆς " on the ground "

ὄξω (ὄξου, ἔξω) " out," " outside "

μέσα (ἀπὸ μέσα) " inside," " within "

ὀμπρός (ἐμπρός, παρεμπρός), μπροστά " in front," " before," " forwards "

πίσω, ὀπίσω (πίσου) " behind," " back " (note πίσου πίσου in Lesbos " in the course of time ")

σιμά, κοντά " near "

δίπλα, ἀπὸ δίπλα " close by," " alongside "

πλάï πλάï " side by side," " alongside "

ἀντικρύ(ς) (ἀντίκρυ, ἀγνάτια) " opposite "

γύρω, τριγύρου, ὁλόγυρα " around "

πέρα (ἐκεῖθε) " beyond."

Cf. also combinations of two adverbs of place, like ἐκεῖ κάτω " there underneath," " below," ἐκεῖ πάνω (ἐκεάν Pontus) " there above," and especially (ἐ)κεῖ πέρα " yonder," ἐδὼ πέρα " here," " in this case."

2. *Adverbs of Time.*

πότε " when ? " πότε—πότε " sometimes—sometimes," " now —now " (also κάποτε καὶ πότε) " sometimes," ποτέ " ever," " never " (*cf.* πουθενά) ἄλλοτε " formerly," " once "

τότε(ς), ἐτότε(ς) " then," ἀπὸ τότες " since "

τώρα " now," " at present "

γλήγορα " soon "

κιόλας " already," " even "

μόλις " just now "

ἀκόμα " still," " yet "

ἀντάμα " at the same time," " together "

πάντα " always "

πάλι, πάλε " again "

ὅλο, ὁλοένα " continually," " incessantly "

εὐτύς, ἀμέσως, ὀχονοῦς (e.g. Chios) " immediately "

πρῶτα " first," πρωτύτερα " before " " previously "

ὕστερα (Chios ὕστερι, Ios ὑστερώτερα), ἔπειτα, κατόπι, ἀπέκει
    " afterwards," " later "

νωρίς (ἐνωρίς) " early," νωρίτερα " earlier "

ἀργά, ξώρας " late "

(τὸ) βράδυ (also βραδύς) " in the evening," (τὸ) ταχύ " in the
    morning "

(ἐ)χτές, (ἐ)ψές " yesterday," προχτές " day before yesterday "

σήμερα " to-day," ἀπόψε " this evening "

αὔριο " to-morrow," μεθαύριο " day after to-morrow "

ὁλημερίς " the whole day "

φέτος, ἐφέτος, (ἐ)φέτο " this year "

πέρυσι (πέρσι) " last year," προπέρυσι " two years ago " (τοῦ
    χρόνου " next year ").

Here also combinations like ἐχτὲς βραδύς or ἐχτὲς τὸ βράδυ
" yesterday evening," ἀργὰ τ' ἀποταχειά " late in the afternoon," etc.

3. Adverbs of Manner and Quantity.

πῶς " how ? " κάπως " somehow, anyhow," σάν " as " (in
    comparisons)

ἔτσι " thus "; ἔτσι κ' ἔτσι " so and so "

ἀλλιῶς, ἀλλιώτικα " otherwise," " else "

(ἀ)πάνω κάτω " about," " approximately," " nearly "

τόντις " really "

ἔξαφνα, ἄξαφνα, ξάφνω " suddenly," μονομιᾶς " all at once "

μαζί " together," " with "

χώρια (χωριστά, ξέχωρα) " apart," " separately "

μόνο (μόνε, μόνου), μοναχά " alone," " only "

ἀρκετά " enough "

λιγάκι " a little "
παραπολύ " too much "
τὸ πολὺ πολύ " at the most "
τὸ λίγο λίγο " at least."

NUMERALS.

(a) *Cardinal Numbers.*

§ 127.

1	ἔνας, μιά, ἔνα	30	τριάντα
2	δυό	31	τριάντα ἔνα, etc.
3	τρεῖς, τρία (τριά)	40	σαράντα
4	τέσσερις (τέσσεροι, τέσσερα, and τέσσαρα)	50	πενήντα
		60	ἑξήντα
5	πέντε	70	ἑβδομήντα
6	ἔξι, ἔξε	80	(ὀγδοήντα) ὀγδόντα
7	ἐφτά	90	ἐνενήντα
8	ὀχτώ		
9	ἐννιά	100	ἑκατό
10	δέκα	101	ἑκατὸ(ν) ἔνας, ἑκατὸ μιά
11	ἔντεκα	102	ἑκατὸ δυό
12	δώδεκα	111	ἑκατὸ ἔντεκα
13	δεκατρεῖς	121	ἑκατὸ εἰκοσιένα
14	δεκατέσσερις		
15	δεκαπέντε	200	διακόσιοι, διακόσιες, διακό-
16	δεκάξι (δεκαέξι)	220	διακόσια εἴκοσι [σια¹)
17	δεκαφτά	300	τρ(ι)ακόσιοι, -ιες, -ια
18	δεκοχτώ (δέκα ὀχτώ)	400	τετρακόσιοι, -ιες, -ια
19	δεκαννιά (δέκα ἐννιά)	500	πεντακόσιοι, -ιες, -ια
		600	ἑξακόσιοι, -ιες, -ια
20	εἴκοσι	700	ἐφτακόσιοι, -ιες, -ια
21	εἰκοσιένα	800	ὀχτακόσιοι, -ιες, -ια
22	εἴκοσι δυό, etc.	900	ἐννιακόσιοι, -ιες, -ια

1000	χίλιοι, χίλιες, χίλια
1894	χίλια ὀχτακόσια ἐνενήντα τέσσερα
2000	δυὸ χιλιάδες
3000	τρεῖς χιλιάδες, etc.
10,000	δέκα χιλιάδες
100,000	ἑκατὸ χιλιάδες
200,000	διακόσιες χιλιάδες

¹ The ι before the ending is always consonantal (= ι).

1,000,000 ἕνα μιλλιούνι (ἑκατομμύριον)
2,000,000 δυὸ μιλλιούνια (δυὸ ἑκατομμύρια)
(1,000,000,000 χιλιεκατομμύριον Milliard)
(1,000,000,000,000 δισεκατομμύριον Billion).

Of course the last two high numbers are no longer in evidence in the vernacular, since they lie outside the sphere of the usages and conceptions of the people.

§ 128. The numerals from 1 to 4 inclusive, and from 200 up, are declined; thus:

Masc.	Fem.	Neut.
1. ἕνας	μιά (μνιά)	ἕνα (ἕναν)
(ἑνός) ἐνοῦ, ἐνοῦς	μιᾶς, μιανῆς	(ἑνός) ἐνοῦ, ἐνοῦς
ἕνα(ν) (ἕνανε)	μιά(ν)	ἕνα (ἕναν).

After the analogy of μιανῆς there is even a gen. masc. μιανοῦ. In Pontic the nom. (masc. and fem.) εἷς, acc. εἴναν (m.), ἕναν (f.) are in use; in Saranda Klisiés the nom. sing. neut. τὸ ἕν "the one."

2. δυό nom. and acc. of all genders; gen. sometimes δυῶ(νε) and δυονῶ(νε).

κ' οἱ δυό (καὶ οἱ δυό) "both," καὶ οἱ δυό μας "both of us."

1. On μία, δύο, cf. § 10, n. 1; on neut. ἕναν (like στόμαν, etc.), § 34, n. 4.

μιανῆς, δυονῶν, ἕνανε have been affected by the pronominal declension.

2. μιὰν καὶ δυό like "one, two, three" = "immediately," "forthwith."

3. τρεῖς, masc. and fem.; τρία (or τριά) neut.; gen. τριῶ(ν).

4. Nom. and acc. masc. and fem. τέσσερις; neut. τέσσερα (τέσσαρα); gen. τεσσάρω(ν).

The following forms are also found: nom. m. τέσσαροι (τέσσεροι), acc. τέσσαρους or τεσσάρους, nom. and acc. f. πέσσαρες (τέσσερες).

5. The declension of the other numerals (διακόσιοι, etc.) is the same as that of corresponding adjectives.

On τρακόσα, τρακόσα, etc., v. § 10, n. 4.

§ 129. The examples given in the table show how the numerals are combined: the larger number precedes, the smaller follows without καί.

Numerals are combined with substantives as in German or in English, the numerals being always used as adjectives; thus, διακόσιες γυναῖκες, δυὸ χιλιάδες ἀθρώποι.

(b) Ordinals.

§ 130.   "the first" ὁ πρῶτος
"the second" ὁ δεύτερος
"the third" ὁ τρίτος
"the fourth" ὁ τέταρτος.

To express ordinal numbers higher than "the fourth" the cardinal numbers (in the neut.) are employed with the def. article placed before them; thus, ὁ πέντε "the 5th," ὁ ἕξε "the 6th," ὁ ἐφτά "the 7th," ὁ τριάντα "the 30th," ὁ ἑκατό "the 100th," ὁ διακόσια, ὁ χίλια, ὁ δυὸ χιλιάδες, ὁ ἕνα μιλλιοῦνι.

The ancient ordinal numbers have disappeared out of the present popular language. Those from 2 to 5 occur partially in older or modified forms in the names of some week-days: δευτέρα "Monday" (ἡ δεύτερη "the second"), τρίτη "Tuesday," τετράδη "Wednesday" (but ἡ τέταρτη "the fourth"), πέφτη (also πέμτη) "Thursday" (fr. a. Gk. πέμπτη). Note also τὸ δέκατο "the tenth," "tithe," ἡ σαρακοστή "Lent," ἡ πεντηκοστή "Whitsuntide."

(c) Derivatives and Special Usages of Numerals.

§ 131. *Fractions*: μισός, μισή, μισό "half," "half an hour" μισὴ ὥρα, "the half" τὸ μισό. When used in connection with other numbers it takes the form (ἥ)μισυ: e.g. ἐνά 'μισυ (μιά 'μισυ) 1½, δυό 'μισυ 2½, τρεῖς ἥμισυ 3½, πεντέ 'μισυ 5½, ἕξ ἥμισυ 6½, δεκά 'μισυ 10½.

If a substantive follows such numerical terms there are two usages: (1) e.g. μιά 'μισυ ὀκά "1½ oka," δυό 'μισυ χρόνια "2½ years," etc.; or (2) μιὰ ὀκὰ καὶ μισή, δυὸ χρόνια καὶ μισό.

(ἕνα) τρίτο "a third," ἕνα τέταρτο (also ἕνα κάρτο) "a fourth," "quarter," τρία τέταρτα "three-fourths," "three-quarters of an hour" = τρία τέταρτα τῆς ὥρας.

The larger fractions are expressed periphrastically: "one-fifth" = ἕνα ἀπὸ τὰ or στὰ πέντε (sc. κομμάτια); $\frac{2}{10}$ = δυὸ ἀπὸ τὰ (στὰ) δέκα (κομμάτια), or ἀπὸ (τὰ) δέκα (τὰ) δυό, etc.

1. *Per cent.*: e.g. 5 per cent. = πέντε (σ)τὰ ἑκατό (literary language, πέντε τοῖς ἑκατόν; cf. § 41, n. 2).

2. *Dates and o'clock.* The cardinal numbers are employed:—
"one o'clock" = μιὰ ὥρα, "five o'clock" = πέντε ὥρα, but more usually "one o'clock" = (στὴ) μιά, "three o'clock" = (στὶς) τρεῖς; "half-past one," "half-past three" = (στὴ) μιά 'μισυ, (στὶς) τρεῖς

ἥμισυ; "quarter past two" (στὶς) δυὸ καὶ τέταρτο; "a quarter to four" (στὶς) τέσσερες παρὰ τέταρτο; "twenty minutes past five," "twenty minutes to six" (στὶς) πέντε καὶ εἴκοσι, (στὶς) ἕξε παρὰ εἴκοσι; "it is one (two) o'clock" εἶναι μιὰ ὥρα, δυὸ ὥρες. "On the 1st, 10th, 25th April" (στὴν) πρώτη, or (στὶς) δέκα, εἰκοσιπέντε (τοῦ) Ἀπρίλι; "to-day is the 15th of the month" σήμερα εἶναι (ἔχομε) δεκαπέντε τοῦ μηνός; "the first of May" ("1st May") πρωτομαϊά, "1st Jan.," "New Year" πρωτοχρονιά; "in (the year) 1910" (στὰ) χίλια ἐννιακόσια δέκα; "Sunday, 13th Dec. 1909," κεριακὴ δεκατρεῖς (τοῦ) δεκέβρι χίλια ἐννιακόσια ἐννιά.

§ 132. *Distributive numbers* are formed (1) by placing ἀπό before the cardinal, or (2) by repeating the cardinal; thus, ἕνας ἕνας "one by one," "one at a time," ἀπὸ δυό or δυὸ δυό "two and two," ἀπὸ δέκα or δέκα δέκα "by tens."

"How many times (Fr. *fois*)" is expressed by φορά (occasionally also by βολά): μιὰ φορά "once," δυὸ, τρεῖς φορές "twice," "three times," πόσες φορές "how many times," πολλὲς φορές "many times," "often," ἀπὸ μιὰ δυὸ φορές "every once," "twice." Note also χίλια μεράδια ὀμορφύτερη "a thousand times fairer."

In multiplication φορά is omitted; as, τρεῖς (οἱ) δέκα κάνουν τριάντα "three times ten make thirty." The following are exx. of other arithmetical calculations: δυὸ καὶ τέσσερα (κάνουν) ἕξι "two and four make six," πέντε ἀπὸ δέκα (κάνουν) πέντε "five from ten leaves five," πέντε στὸ δέκα (κάνουν) δυό "five into ten gives two (goes twice)."

"For the first time, second time," πρώτη, δεύτερη φορά; "the tenth or twentieth time" δέκα, εἴκοσι φορές.

"Single" = μονός or ἁπλός, "double," "twofold" διπλός or ἄλλος τόσος, "three-, four-, five-, tenfold" τρεῖς, τέσσερες, πέντε, δέκα φορὲς τόσο, etc., or even τρίδιπλος, τετράδιπλος, πεντάδιπλος, etc.

§ 133. The *Numeral substantives* in -αριά denote a definite number of persons or things; δεκαριά "the number of ten," *e.g.* καμιὰ δεκαριὰ ἀθρώποι "some ten men," δωδεκαριά "twelve," "dozen" (also μιὰ ντουζίνα), εἰκοσαριά, εἰκοσιπενταριά, τριανταριά, διακοσαριά "a crowd of 20, 25, 30, 200." But "the number of one hundred" is ἑκατοστύ (fem.); "about fifty" πάνω κάτω πενήντα.

The suffix -άρα is especially employed for the names of coins the value of a definite number of units, of which the most common in use are πεντάρα "5 Lepta piece," δεκάρα

"10 Lepta piece," and analogously δυάρα, εἰκοσάρα, πενην-τάρα, etc.

1. Similarly the neuters δυάρι, πεντάρι, δεκάρι, ἑκατοστάρι, etc. (*e.g.* δεκάρι "tener in cards").

2. The abstract numbers in -άδα (a. Gk. -άς, -άδος) are rare, and employed only in specific senses : ἡ ῞Αγια Τριάδα "the holy Trinity," ἡ δωδεκάδα, lit. "the number twelve," then "retinue" (*e.g.* of a King).

3. An indefinitely large number is expressed by χίλια δυό ; in a similar sense ἑξήντα δυό.

The suffix -άρικο is employed in the same way to denote "containing a definite sum" : *e.g.* δεκάρικο, εἰκοσιπεντάρικο, πενηντάρικο, ἑκατοστάρικο "10, 25, 50, 100 drachma piece or bank note," χιλιάρικη μποτίλια "a bottle holding 1000 δράμια."[1]

The masculine suffix -άρις, fem. -άρα, denotes "of a particular age" ; as, τριαντάρις, ἑξηντάρις "thirty, sixty years of age" (fem. τριαντάρα). On the employment of the gen. for designating age, *v.* § 45.

Pronouns.

(a) *Personal.*

§ 134. First person ἐγώ "I."

	Absolute.	Conjunctive.
Sing. Nom.	ἐγώ "I"	—
Gen.	ἐμένα "of me"	μοῦ
Acc.	(ἐμέ) ἐμένα, μένα (ἐμένανε) "me"	μέ.
Plur. Nom.	ἐμεῖς "we"	—
Gen.	(ἐμᾶς)	μᾶς
Acc.	ἐμᾶς "us"	μᾶς.

1. The following forms are also found : nom. 'γώ and (in dialects) ὀγώ, ἐώ, also in Cyprus (ἐ)γιώ and ἐγιώνη, in Otranto ἐνό ; gen. sing. ἐμοῦ, ἐμενοῦ, ἐμουνοῦ, also ἐμέ (TEXTS I. a. 24. 41) ; acc. sing. ἐμόν and ἐμόνα ; the gen. pl. ἐμᾶς (formerly also ἐμῶν) is quite rare (*cf. e.g.* TEXTS I. a. 24. 23).

2. The forms ἐμεῖς, ἐμᾶς for a. Gk. ἡμεῖς, ἡμᾶς have been formed on model of the sing. ἐγώ. ἰμεῖς (in North. Gk., *e.g.* Velv.) bears only apparent resemblance to the a. Gk. ἡμεῖς, an unaccented ε becoming *i* everywhere (*cf.* § 7, n. 1), and so even ἰγώ = ἐγώ.

[1] δράμι is a unit of weight, nearly 2 drams avoirdupois (400 δράμια=1 ὀκά).

§ 135. Second person ἐσύ " thou."

	Absolute.	Conjunctive.
Sing. Nom.	ἐσύ, σύ	—
Gen.	ἐσένα	σοῦ
Acc.	(ἐσέ) ἐσένα, σένα (ἐσένανε)	σέ.
Plur. Nom.	ἐσεῖς, σεῖς	—
Gen.	(ἐσᾶς)	σᾶς
Acc.	ἐσᾶς, σᾶς	σᾶς.

1. Also: nom. esú (Bova), ἐσού and ἐσούνη (Cyprus); gen. sing. ἐσενοῦ, ἐσουνοῦ; acc. ἐσόν, ἐσόνα. Forms with initial ζ (ζέ, ζοῦ) occur in the Maina, TEXTS III. 3. Gen. pl. ἐσούν in the connection ἀποπές ἐσουν in Pontus, TEXTS III. 13. b.

2. ἐσύ after the model of ἐγώ; ἐσεῖς ἐσᾶς after ἐγώ ἐμᾶς. Between the a. Gk. ἐμέ and m. Gk. ἐμένα, and between σέ and (ἐ)σένα, come the intermediary forms ἐμέν and ἐσέν, which survive still in Pontic (and occasionally also elsewhere); cf. ἐσέν, TEXTS III. 13. a.

136. Third person αὐτός " he."

	Absolute.	Conjunctive.
Sing. Nom.	αὐτός, αὐτή, αὐτό	(τός, τή, τό)
Gen.	αὐτοῦ, αὐτῆς, αὐτοῦ	τοῦ, τῆς
Acc.	αὐτό(ν), αὐτή(ν), αὐτό	τό(ν), τή(ν), τό.
Plur. Nom.	αὐτοί, αὐτές, αὐτά	(τοί, τές, τά)
Gen.	αὐτῶ(ν), αὐτῶ(ν), αὐτῶ(ν)	τῶ(ν), τούς (m. f. n.)
Acc.	αὐτούς, αὐτές, αὐτά	τούς, τές, τά.

1. Instead of αὐτός, εὐτός also is found in the Ionic Islands and in the region of the Aegean (e.g. Crete, Naxos, Chios); sometimes (e.g. in Epirus and Pelop.) δαῦτος; in Bova ástos, according to § 14, n. 2.

2. The North. Gk. forms τ (= τοῦ or τή), τν (= τήν), τς (= τῆς, τούς) arise from the cause given in § 7, n. 1.

3. In Pontus (also elsewhere, e.g. Icarus) the pronoun appears as ἀτός (ἄτος), the forms of which are used both as absolute and conjunctive (exx. TEXTS III. 13). The regular forms of the conjunctive pronoun originated from the form ἀτο-. Further noteworthy forms of the pron. conj. are τσῆ (τσ') beside τῆς (Ionic Islands, Epirus, Aegean); the forms ending in -ν take on frequently ε (more rarely a); thus, τόνε (τόνα), τήνε, (gen. pl.) τῶνε, and even μᾶσε, σᾶσε; acc. (gen.) pl. τώς beside τούς. Gen. sing. ἀχτέ(ς) and neut. ἀ = τό in Pontic: e.g. τὸ παιδίν ἀχτε "his child," and ἔκσεν ἀ "he heard it."

§ 137. Use of the Personal pronouns. The nominative of the absolute form is employed only isolated or with the verb for emphasis; the verbal forms contain their subject in the termination. Accordingly we may say, *e.g.*, ἐγὼ λέγω, ἐσὺ ρωτᾷς, αὐτὸς ξέρει "*I* say," "*thou* askest," "*he* knows," only when it is intended to throw the subject into *prominence*; thus, *e.g.* σώπα ἐσύ "*thou*, keep still," ἔλα σὺ μόνος σου "*thou*, come *thou* alone," and especially in *contrast*: *e.g.* ἐγὼ ἔχω δουλειά, ἐσὺ περπατεῖς "*I* have work to do, *you* are taking a walk."

In the oblique cases likewise the absolute form stands only in isolation, or, if in the texture of a sentence, mostly in alliance with the conjunctive pronoun; but unless special emphasis is aimed at only the conjunctive pronoun is used in the sentence; thus, ποιὸν ἐρώτησες "whom didst thou ask?" σένα "*thee*," "thyself," μὲ ρωτᾷ "he asks me," σοῦ λέγω "I tell you," τὸ ξέρω "I know it," τόν(ε), τήν(ε), τοὺς γνωρίζεις "you know him, her, them." On the other hand, for the sake of emphasis, ἐμένα μὲ ξέρεις "*me* you know," ἐσένα πῶς σὲ φαίνεται "what do *you* think of it?" αὐτὸ θέλουν καὶ κεῖνοι "*that* is *what* they also wish," αὐτοὺς θέλω νὰ (τοὺς) ἰδῶ "I desire to see *them*," σ' ἐσᾶς τό 'πα "to *you* I said it" (or τό 'πα σ' ἐσᾶς "I said it to *you*").

1. The *pronomen conjunctum*, moreover, is quite frequently inserted pleonastically in instances like, *e.g.*, τό 'βρηκε τὸ μέρος "he found (it) the region," τ' ἄλλα τά 'βραν κυνηγοί "the hunters found (them) the others."

Note also the idioms τὴν ἔπαθα "I fell into it," πῶς τὰ πάτε (περνᾶτε) "how do you do?"

2. The nom. τός, τή, τοί appears in νά τος "there he is," νά τοι "there they are"; more rarely ποῦ εἶναι 'τος (ποῦ 'ν τος), ποῦ εἶναι 'τη "where is he, she?"

For other usages of the conj. pron, *v.* §§ 140–143.

§ 138. The *position* of the personal pronoun is clear from the examples given. The conjunctive pronoun *precedes* the verb, except with the 2nd. pers. imperative: δῶσε μου "give me," δές τονε "see him," πάρ(ε) το "take it," κυττάξετέ με "regard me," πέστε τους "tell them." When a verb is accompanied by a particle of negation, tense, or mood (θά, νά, ἄς) the pronoun stands between such particle and the verb; as, δὲν τὸν εἶδα "I did not see him," θὰ σοῦ δώσω "I will give you," νὰ σᾶς (εἰ)πῶ "let me tell you," ἂς τὴ(νε) φωνάξῃ "let him call her" (but: ἐμένα δὲ μὲ 'ρώτησε, αὐτὸν θὰ τὸν ἀκούσω). In combinations with the auxiliary ἔχω there is an option between, *e.g.*, τὸν εἶχα ἰδεῖ "I had seen him," δὲ μοῦ εἶχε εἰπεῖ "he had not told me," and εἶχα τοῦ εἰπεῖ, etc. θέλω when an auxiliary is treated like θά. With ἤθελα the usage fluctuates between σὲ ἤθελα παρακαλέσει and ἤθελα σὲ παρακαλέσει "I would request you." For the compound verbal forms, cf. § 223 ff.

1. In Cyprus, Rhodes, Crete, Chios, and other islands, and in Asia Minor (Pontus, Capp.), the rule for position is different, the pronoun being placed after the verb; as, παίρουμ με "they take me away," λέει μου, ἄκουσά τον, ἤμαθά το, ἐφώναξέν τον, ἐφορτώσαν τους; in Pontus, e.g., λέει ἀτον "he tells him," ἐβλέπ ἀτον "he sees him."

When two pronouns come together the indirect object always precedes the direct: e.g. σοῦ, σᾶς τό 'πα (τὸ εἶπα) "I said it to thee, you," νὰ τοὺς τὸ στείλῃς "see that you send it to them," δὲ θὰ μᾶς τὰ φέρετε; "will you not bring it to us?" and similarly with the imperat. δῶσ(ε) μου το "give me it," φέρτε του το "bring him it."

2. The conj. pron. is, properly speaking, unaccented (proclitic or enclitic, § 39); still, in the proclitic position it generally is written with an accent. On account of the fluctuating orthographical usage no hard and fast rule can be laid down.

§ 139. Besides the personal pronouns, the ordinary people use (especially in addressing a person) peculiar forms of courtesy: e.g. ἡ ἀφεντιά σου, ἡ εὐγενεία σου "your lordship." Instead of the pronouns "thou, he, you, they," periphrasis is very common with the aid of the stereotyped genitive τοῦ λόγου (which took its rise from a mutilation of the expression διὰ λόγου [σου] "at thy command"); thus:

τοῦ λόγου σου "thou"
τοῦ λόγου σας "you"
τοῦ λόγου του, της "he, she"
τοῦ λόγου τους "they."

These forms remain unchanged in all cases: τοῦ λόγου σου δὲν ἤσουνα στὸ σπίτι "you (Monsieur) were not at home," τοῦ λόγου τους τί κάνουν "how are their worships?" ἔχω καιρὸν νὰ ἰδῶ τοῦ λόγου της "it is a long time since I saw her," θὰ πάμε χωρὶς τοῦ λόγου σας "we will go without you."

When the expression is joined with the prepositions (εἰ)σέ, διά, ἀπό, or even with μέ, the art. is generally dropped: σὲ λόγου σας ἔρχομαι "I am coming to you," ζητῶ ἀπὸ λόγου σου "I request of you," ἐπερπατοῦσα μὲ (τοῦ) λόγου του "I went walking with him (with Monsieur)."

The first person τοῦ λόγου μου (μας) is used to express the reflexive: *e.g.* αἰστάνομαι τοῦ λόγου μου καλύτερα "I feel myself better."

For the pronoun "self," *v.* § 157.

1. In addressing a person the vernacular always employs the 2nd pers. *sing.*; the use of the 2nd pers. pl. is a foreign affectation and confined almost altogether to the educated and to city centres. Beside the forms already given, εὐτοῦ (= αὐτοῦ) is used as a form of courtesy for ἐσύ: *e.g.* εὐτοῦ νὰ τὸ κάμῃς "do it (thou)."

2. Note the following rules of concord: ἐγὼ καὶ σὺ θὰ πάμε τώρα "you and I will now go," ἐσὺ καὶ ὁ φίλος σου ἐφύγατε γλήγορα "you and your friend went away quickly."

(b) *Reflexive.*

§ 140.   1st Person.

(τοῦ ἐμαυτοῦ μου " of me "   τοῦ ἐμαυτοῦ μας "of us")
τὸν ἐμαυτό μου "me"   τὸν ἐμαυτό μας "us."

2nd Person.

τοῦ ἐμαυτοῦ σου " of thee,"   τοῦ ἐμαυτοῦ σας " of you "
τὸν ἐμαυτό σου " thee "   τὸν ἐμαυτό σας " you."

3rd Person.

(τοῦ ἐμαυτοῦ του " of him "   τοῦ ἐμαυτοῦ τους " of them ")
τὸν ἐμαυτό του, της " himself "   τὸν ἐμαυτό τους " themselves."

(ἑαυτοῦ) ἑαυτό is also employed instead of (ἐμαυτοῦ) ἐμαυτό, and in the same manner. To make emphatic, τὸν ἴδιον ἑαυτό μου or τὸν ἑαυτό μου τὸν ἴδιο, etc., is used.

1. These formations are merely stereotyped forms of the a. Gk. reflexive with the gen. of the pers. pron. following. In Crete a different expression is employed, τὸν ἀπατό μου (σου, etc.); for τοῦ λόγου μου, *cf.* § 139.

2. The reflexive is not much in use, often a middle voice taking its place, *v.* § 177, 2.

§ 141. The reciprocal pronoun "one another," "each other," is rendered (1) by combining ὁ ἕνας "the one" and ὁ ἄλλος "the other" (thus ὁ ἕνας τὸν ἄλλο, ἡ μιὰ τὴν ἄλλη, κοντὰ τὸ ἕνα μὲ τὸ ἄλλο τὰ πίθωσα "I placed them beside one another"); or (2) by (ἀνα-)μεταξύ, ἀνάμεσα (ἀνάμεσο) "between," "among," and the gen. pl. of the pers. pron. (ἀναμεταξύ μας, μεταξύ σας, μεταξύ τους, ἀνάμεσά τους); but frequently the middle voice expresses the reciprocal idea, *v.* § 177, 2.

In Capp. (Pharasa) an unchangeable (adverbial) πενεντά(β)ο is employed; as, δώκαμε πενέντ αο "we struck each other"—perhaps a remodelling of an expression ἀπ᾽ ἕν᾽α(ν) τ᾽ ἄλλο.

(c) *Possessive.*

§ 142. In m. Gk. there is no special adjectival pronoun denoting possession; it is supplied by the genitive of the conjunctive pronoun placed after the noun; thus, ὁ πατέρας μου "my father," ἡ μάννα σου "thy mother," τὸ σπίτι του, της "his, her house," τὰ παιδιά μας, σας, τω(ν) (τους) "my, thy, their children," ὁ πιστός μου φίλος "my dear friend," ἡ καλή σου ἀδερφή "thy good sister," ἡ δόλια του μαννούλα "his unhappy mother," ἡ ἐθνική σας γλῶσσα "your national tongue," μ᾽ ὅλη τοὺς τὴν καρδιά "with their whole heart." As the examples indicate, the pronominal form leans upon a preceding adjectival attribute (but τὰ μάτια της τὰ γλυκά "her sweet eyes," when the adj. is placed after the pronoun). It is less commonly attached to the second member (ἡ δόλια ἡ ᾽Αρετούλα μου "my unhappy A.," τὸ δύστυχο νησί τους "their unhappy island ").

The definite article is by no means absolutely necessary; it drops out in addresses and in indeterminate expressions; as, μάννα μου "(my) mother," γλυκειά μου ἀγάπη "my sweet love," καλή σου μέρα "good day to you," εἶναι φίλος μου "he is a friend of mine, my friend," ἕνας φίλος σου "a friend of yours," μὲ πόθο του (μου, etc.) "with longing for it (me)."

Instead of της also τσ(η) same as with art. and pron., Texts III. 5 (Ios) τσης (ἡ κόρη τσης). Instead of μου, σου (του): μ᾽, σ᾽ (τ᾽), especially in North. Gk. dialects (§ 7, n. 1); thus, ἡ μάννα μ᾽, ἡ ἀδερφή σ᾽, τοὺ τσιφάλ᾽ τ᾽, οὐ πόνος μ᾽, οὐ γαμπρόζουμ (§ 7, n. 2). Note also μα for μας, Texts III. 3 (Maina): e.g. τὸ βόδι μα. The final -ν of the noun is sometimes retained before the possessive gen. of the 3rd pers., cf. Texts I. d. 5; the resultant δου, δης, δους is occasionally generalised, cf. Texts III. 12. The Pontic ἀχτέ stands isolated, cf. τὸν κῶλον ἀχτὲ, Texts III. 13. b, beside του, ἀτου, and ἀτ: e.g. ἡ ψή ἀτου, τὸ σπίτιν ἀτ.

§ 143. If the possessive is used predicatively (or as a substantive, "mine," etc., or with emphasis "(my) own"), (ὁ) δικός (also ὁ ἐδικός) "own," is combined with the gen. of the personal pronoun:

ὁ δικός μου, ἡ δική μου, τὸ δικό μου " mine "
τοῦ δικοῦ μου, τῆς δικῆς μου, τοῦ δικοῦ μου

τὸ δικό μου, τὴ δική μου, τὸ δικό μου
οἱ δικοί μου, οἱ δικές μου, τὰ δικά μου
τῶ δικῶ μου, τῶ δικῶ μου, τῶ δικῶ μου
τοὺς δικούς μου, τὶς δικές μου, τὰ δικά μου.

Similarly: ὁ δικός σου "thine," ὁ δικός του, της "his, hers," ὁ δικός μας "ours," ὁ δικός σας "yours," ὁ δικός τω(ν) or τους "theirs"; e.g. αὐτὸ τὸ βιβλίο εἶναι δικό μου "this book is mine," τὸ δικό μου βιβλίο (more rarely τὸ βιβλίο τὸ δικό μου) "my own book," τὸ βιβλίο εἶναι τὸ δικό μου, ὄχι τὸ δικὸ σου "the book is *mine*, not yours," μὲ δύναμι δική του " with his own strength."

Note οἱ δυό μας "the two (both) of us," ὅλοι μας "we all," "all of us."

1. The poss. pron. is sometimes thrown into emphasis also by the method of § 137, cf. ἐμᾶς ἡ ἀγάπη μας (TEXTS I. a. 24. 23) "*our* love."

2. *i dichédda mu, su* (my, thy own daughter) TEXTS III. 2 (Terra d' Otr.) is equivalent to *ἡ δικέλλα μου, σου, i.e. δικός with (Ital.) diminutive suffix.

θκός (in Velv.) is a phonetic transformation of δικός (v. § 37 n.). The fem. ἡ δικειά (cf. § 111) means "my wife," "my beloved."

3. Modern Greek, compared with the ancient, has lost ground in the poss. pron. Only the Pontic and Cappadocian dialects retain the ancient possessive in various forms and modifications; thus, in the dialect of Trapezus, ἐμός or τ᾽ ἐμόν "mine," τ᾽ ἐσόν "thine," (ἐ)μέτερος "our," σέτερος "your," and even κεινέτερος "their," and ἀλλεινέτερος "belonging to others." Cf., further, TEXTS III. 14. a. τ᾽ ἀσὸν τὸ χάτσιμό σ "thy death."

(d) *Demonstrative.*

§ 144. The pronoun αὐτός (§ 136) is employed also as a demonstrative " this, that." Besides the declension already given the following additional forms occur:

	Masc.	Fem.	Neut.
Sing. N.	αὐτόνος (αὐτοῦνος), αὐτεῖνος	αὐτείνη (αὐτείνα)	αὐτόνο (αὐτοῦνο) αὐτεῖνο, αὐτεινό
G.	αὐτουνοῦ, αὐτεινοῦ	αὐτεινῆς	same as Masc.
Acc.	αὐτόνα (αὐτόνε)	αὐτείνη(ν)	same as Nom.
Plur. N.	αὐτεινοί (αὐτεῖνοι)	αὐτείνες	αὐτάνα, αὐτεῖνα
G.	αὐτονῶν, αὐτεινῶν	αὐτονῶν, αὐτεινῶν	same as Masc.
Acc.	αὐτούνους, αὐτεινούς	αὐτείνες	αὐτάνα, αὐτεῖνα.

1. Also ἀτουνοῦ, ἀτεινῆς (ἐτουνοῦ), whence τοῦνο = αὐτό, in Otranto gen. *tunú* and *túnu*, Bova *ettúno* = αὐτοῦνος, gen. (*et*) *tunú*,

etc.; *cf.* also Pontic ἀτεῖν' = αὐτεῖνοι. In North. Gk. αὐτουνοῦ, αὐτεινῆς, etc., becomes ἀφνοῦ, ἀφνῆς according to § 37 n. In Saranda Klisiés the acc. sing. masc. is αὐτόννα (neut. αὐτόνα). This pronominal termination is found also in the pronouns of the following paragraphs (κείνοννα, ποιόννα, and also κανείναννα, ἄλλοννα, ἔνναννα, fem. κείννα fr. κείνηνα, ποιάννα, τέτοιαννα, etc.), and has been extended even to oxytone adjectives (*e.g.* μικρόννα, μικρήννα, ἀδρύννα).

2. The voc. αὐτέ (ἀπαυτέ) is used when one is addressed whose name is unknown, or for the moment forgotten: ἄκουσε, αὐτέ "you there, hear!" For εὐτοῦ = ἐσύ, *v.* § 139, n. 1.

3. Instances like "George's house is larger than John's (*that* of John") are rendered τὸ σπίτι τοῦ Γιώργι εἶναι μεγαλύτερο ἀπὸ (τὸ σπίτι) τοῦ Γιάννη.

§ 145. τοῦτος, ἐτοῦτος "this."

	Masc.	Fem.	Neut.
Sing. Nom.	(ἐ)τοῦτος	(ἐ)τούτη	(ἐ)τοῦτο
Gen.	(ἐ)τούτου	(ἐ)τούτης	(ἐ)τούτου
Acc.	(ἐ)τοῦτο(ν)	(ἐ)τούτη(ν)	(ἐ)τοῦτο.
Plur. Nom.	(ἐ)τοῦτοι	(ἐ)τούτες	(ἐ)τοῦτα
Gen.	(ἐ)τούτω(ν)	(ἐ)τούτω(ν)	(ἐ)τούτω(ν)
Acc.	(ἐ)τούτους	(ἐ)τούτες	(ἐ)τοῦτα.

Forms with -ν(ο)- :

S. N.	—	—	
G.	τουτουνοῦ, τουτεινοῦ	τουτεινῆς	τουτουνοῦ, τουτεινοῦ
A.	τούτονε, τούτονα	τούτηνε, τούτηνα	—
Pl. N.	τουτεινοί	τουτεινές	—
G.	τουτονῶ(ν), τουτει-νῶ(ν)	τουτονῶ(ν), του-τεινῶ(ν)	τουτονῶ(ν), τουτει-νῶ(ν)
A.	τουτουνούς, τουτεινούς	τουτεινές	—

The pron. ἀοῦτος or ἀβοῦτος "this"—declined exactly like τοῦτος —is peculiar to Pontic; *cf.* nom. pl. ἀβουτείν', Texts III. 13. a. In Chios note τοῦος and ἐτοῦος with dissimilatory loss of the middle τ, in Bova the neut. forms are *túndo* = τοῦτο and *túnda* = τοῦτα.

§ 146. ἐκεῖνος and κεῖνος "that."

	Masc.	Fem.	Neut.
Sing. Nom.	ἐκεῖνος	ἐκείνη	ἐκεῖνο
Gen.	ἐκείνου, ἐκεινοῦ	ἐκείνης, ἐκεινῆς	ἐκείνου, ἐκεινοῦ
Acc.	ἐκεῖνο(ν), ἐκεί-νονα, ἐκείνονε	ἐκείνη(ν), ἐκεί-νηνα	ἐκεῖνο.
Plur. Nom.	ἐκεῖνοι, ἐκεινοί	ἐκείνες	ἐκεῖνα
Gen.	ἐκείνω(ν), ἐκεινῶν(ε)	= Masc.	= Masc.
Acc.	ἐκείνους, ἐκεινούς	ἐκείνες	ἐκεῖνα.

1. Sometimes (ἐ)κειός for ἐκεῖνος; in Pontic also ἐεῖνος.—(ἐ)τσεῖνος (τσεῖνος) in the dialects mentioned in § 17. In Chios τσείνοσε, Texts III. 9, shows the supplementary ε of the acc. also in the nom., only, however, in the absolute final, and in like position in Chios final -ς of any nom. is generally supplemented by -ε; as, λωλόσε = λωλός "crazed," and so forth.

2. The m. Gk. demonstratives correspond to the a. Gk., but they have suffered much by assimilation in their declension: in τοῦτος τ and ου are carried through (compared with a. Gk. οὗτος, ταύτην, etc.), τοῦτος and ἐκεῖνος produce ἐτοῦτος and κεῖνος. The accent of αὐτός gave rise to forms like ἐκεινοῦ (or τουτοῦ), just as, on the other hand, αῦτος (δαῦτος) is accented after model of τοῦτος; and, lastly, formations like αὐτεινοῦ, τουτεινοῦ, etc., have really been produced by the forms of ἐκεῖνος (ἐκεινοῦ), and have finally given rise to pronominal forms like τοῦνος, etc. Such remodelling on analogy has assumed huge dimensions; apart from μιανοῦ, μιανῆς (§ 128), cf. also the forms to be cited in the following paragraphs.

3. The neut. κεῖνο in Texts III. 12 means "that and that" = "such and such is the case."

§ 147. When one of the pronouns, αὐτός, τοῦτος, or ἐκεῖνος is connected with a substantive, the substantive is always preceded by the article; thus, αὐτὸς ὁ ἄντρας "this man," τούτη ἡ γυναῖκα "this woman," ἐκεῖνο τὸ παιδί, κειὸ τὸ παιδάκι "that child," or also ὁ ἄντρας αὐτός, ἡ γυναῖκα τούτη, τὸ βιβλίο μου ἐκεῖνο "that book of mine." The gen. of the pron. stands preferably before the word to which it refers, as ἐκεινῆς ὁ ἄντρας "the husband of that (woman)."

Moreover, αὐτός and ἐκεῖνος serve to point to a relative: e.g. αὐτὸ ποῦ or ἐκεῖνα ποῦ "that which," τὴν ὥρα αὐτὴ ποῦ "the hour in which."

The pronouns in this capacity may be strengthened by the particle δά: e.g. αὐτὸς δά, ἐκεῖνος δά "this one here," "that one there."

§ 148. τέτοιος "such a."

Sing.	τέτοιος	τέτοια	τέτοιο(ν)
	τέτοιου	τέτοιας	τέτοιου
	τέτοιο(νε)	τέτοια(ν)	τέτοιο(ν)
Plur.	τέτοιοι	τέτοιες	τέτοια
	τέτοιω(ν)	τέτοιω(ν)	τέτοιω(ν)
	τέτοιους	τέτοιες	τέτοια.

Thus: τέτοιος ἄνθρωπος "such a man," τέτοια ὄμοφη κόρη "such a fair girl."

1. τέθκιος in Velvendos (Texts III. 11) is a phonetic remodelling of τέτοιος, v. § 10, n. 5. The form ἀεῖκος "such a" is peculiar to Pontic.

2. The a. Gk. τοιοῦτος has been ousted by τέτοιος, really a re-modelling of an older τί-τοιο, i.e. "somewhat such."

3. Also τοσοῦτος has been thrust out by τόσος "so much, as much, as many, so great"; the neut. τόσο(ν) "so much," "so very," is quite common. Moreover, one may say, e.g., τριάντα μέρες καὶ ἄλλες τόσες νύχτες "thirty days and as many nights," τόσω χρονῶ ἄθρωπος "a man of so many years," τόσα καὶ τόσα "so many," i.e. "number-less." "So great" is rendered by τόσος in the sing. with the indef. article, in the pl. by κάτι; thus, ἕνα τόσο κομμάτι or ἕνα κομμάτι τόσο "so great a piece," pl. κάτι τόσα ξύλα "such great logs"; generally, however, τόσο μεγάλος "so great" is also employed.

(e) Relative.

§ 149. The most common relative is the relative adverb ποῦ (also ὅπου, ὁποῦ), lit. "where," which remains the same for all genders, numbers, and cases. To express the oblique cases the conjunctive pronoun is usually attached to the verb of the relative clause. Examples: ὁ ἄθρωπος (ὁ)ποῦ ἦρθε "the man who came," οἱ γυναῖκες ποῦ μ' ἐφώναξαν "the women who called me," ὁ γιατρὸς ποῦ τὸν ἔστειλα "the physician whom I sent," ἡ ἐφημερὶς ποῦ τὴν γράφει ὁ Σουρῆς "the news-paper which S. edits," τὸ βιβλίο ποῦ τὸ 'διάβασες "the book (that) you read," τὰ παιδιὰ ποῦ γνωρίζω τὴ μάννα τους, "the children whose mother I know," ὁ μαθητὴς ποῦ τοῦ (ἔ)δωκα τὸ βιβλίο "the pupil to whom I gave the book," τοὺ πλὶ ποῦ οὐ βασ'λιὰς χάνουνταν ἴάτι αὐτό "the hen which the king held so dear" (TEXTS III. 11).

The pronoun ὁ ὁποῖος "who," "which"—regularly declined—is of learned origin and little used by the common people.

§ 150. Relatives with a specific meaning:
ὅποιος, ὅποια, ὅποιο(ν) or ὅποιος κι ἄν "whoever, what-ever,"—declined like τέτοιος.

ὅσος "as great," "as much as" correlative to τόσος, especially in the forms ὅσο (ὅσο κι ἄν) "however much," "whatever,"[1] τόσο ὅσο "as much as," ὅσοι "all who," (ὅλα) ὅσα "all that, as many as," πῆρε πραμάτειες ὅσες ἤθελε "he took as many articles as he wished."

ὅτι (ὅτι κι ἄν) "that which," "whatever," "all that" (for which also ὅλα ὅτι); ὅτι λογῆς "of what(ever) kind," ὅτι ὥρα "whichever hour."

---

[1] Also a conjunction, v. § 275.

1. Other forms of the a. Gk. ὅστις are rare; a gen. sing. ὅτινος and gen. pl. ὅτινων are still met with. In Crete and S.-E. Gk. the article forms τόν, τήν, τό serve as relatives. Moreover, τά is also possible for ὅτι or ὅσα, as, τά 'βαλες στὸ νοῦ σου δὲν εἶν' ἀληθινά "what you have got into your head is not true." This τά is sometimes in dialects employed instead of the relative ποῦ. Note, finally, τοῦ for ποῦ in Cappadocia, Texts III. 14. b.

2. ὄγιος "qualis" (properly ὁ οἷος) is current in dialects: e.g. on the mainland and also in Syra.

Cf. § 263 ff. for the construction of the relative sentence.

(f) Interrogative.

§ 151. ποιός "who?" "which?"

	Masc.	Fem.	Neut.
S. N.	ποιός	ποιά	ποιό(ν)
G.	ποιοῦ, ποιανοῦ, ποιο(υ)νοῦ	(ποιᾶς) ποιανῆς	= Masc.
A.	ποιό(ν), ποιόνε, ποιόνα	ποιά(ν), ποιάνε, ποιάνα	ποιό(ν).
Pl. N.	ποιοί	ποιές	ποιά
G.	ποιῶν(ε), ποιονῶν, ποιουνῶν, ποιανῶν for all three genders		
A.	ποιούς, ποιονούς, ποιουννούς, ποιανούς	ποιές	ποιά

ποιός—ποιός "the one —the other" "this" "that" (indefinite).

Except as intruder from the literary language the form ποῖος for ποιός occurs only in the dialects mentioned in § 10, n. 1. On πχιός, πŏός, etc., v. § 10, n. 5.

§ 152. τίς "who?" τίνος "whose?" "of whom?" τίνα "whom?" are rare: e.g. τίνος εἶναι τοῦτο "whose is this?" The invariable τί "what," "which," is mostly employed: τί ἄ(ν)θρωπος "which man?" τί γυναῖκα "which woman?" τί λογῆς "of what kind?" as τί λογῆς ἀθρώποι "what kind of men?"[1] τί ὥρα εἶναι "what o'clock is it?" τί ἄντρες εἶν' αὐτοί "which men are these?" τί κάνεις "what are you doing?"

1. With τί belongs γιατί "why? wherefore?"—same meaning as the simple τί.

2. Instead of τί the word ἴντα (ἰντά) "what?" (γιάντα = γιὰ ἴντα "why?" ἴντα λοή "how? in what manner?") is used in the Aegean region (e.g. Crete, Naxos, Chios) and in Cyprus; in Lesbos τί(δ)α, in

---

[1] The stereotyped λογῆς in an expression like τὰ λογῆς λογῆς βιβλία means "books of all kinds," "the various books."

Aegina ντά, in Pontos ντό. These forms originated from τί εἰν(αι) τὰ (τὸ). Note also from Pontos τόσοιος = ποιός (TEXTS III. 13. a).

3. τούλγος, f. τούλγη "what?" "of what kind?" (TEXTS III. 12) is a new formation from τί λογῆς.

(g) Indefinite and quasi-pronominal Adjectives.

§ 153. κανείς, κανένας "any," "anybody" (adjective and substantive).

	Masc.	Fem.	Neut.
Sing. Nom.	κανείς, κανένας	καμ(μ)ιά	κανένα
Gen.	κανενός, κανενοῦ(ς)	κα(μ)μιᾶς	κανενός, κανενοῦ(ς)
Acc.	κανένα(νε)	κα(μ)μιά(ν)	κανένα.

With a negative or in a negative reply it means "no one," "nobody": κανένας ἄθρωπος δὲν τὸ εἶπε "no man said it," κανεὶς δὲν τὸ ξέρει "nobody knows it," δὲν εἶδα κανένα "I saw nobody," ἦρθε κανείς;—κανείς "did anybody come? Nobody." "Any one" may be rendered also by ἕνας.

1. κανείς does not appear in instances like δὲν ἔλαβα γράμμα "I received no letter," δὲν ἔχω παράδες μαζί μου "I have no money with me"; in the first instance κανείς may be inserted if no is emphatic.

"Anything," "something," when positive is κάτιτι or κάτι, when in a negative or quasi-negative sentence τίποτε; as, κάτιτι πρέπει νὰ γίνη "something must happen," ἃ σὲ ρωτῶ κάτιτι, πρέπει ν' ἀπαντᾶς "if I ask you anything you must answer"; but ἔχεις τίποτε γιὰ μένα; answer τίποτε "have you anything for me? Nothing." ἔφερες τίποτα πράματα; "did you fetch any articles?" κάτι (λίγα) βιβλία "some books."

"Nothing" in a sentence is rendered by τίποτε and the negative: δὲν ἦταν τίποτε "it was nothing," δὲν εἶδα τίποτε "I saw nothing."

"Some," "a little" (adj.) κάτι (indecl.): δῶσε μου κάτι ψωμί "give me a little bread"; κάτι with a plur. means "some" ("several"): κάτι στρατιῶτες "some soldiers," κάτι παιδιά "some children."

2. Beside κανένας sometimes καένας or κανέας (§ 33, n. 4), κάνας, κάνα (gen. κανοῦ), and καγκανένας καγκαμιά καγκανένα; also κατιντί for κάτιτι; τίποτε is quite plastic phonetically: e.g. τίποτες, τίποτα, τίποτας, τίποτις, τίβοτσι (Crete).

3. The a. Gk. indefinite τὶς has been lost except in the fragments in τί-ποτε, κά-τι(τι), κάθε-τις κάθε-τι (§ 155); the use of τινὰς =

τὶς is rare and not genuine vernacular. The word κανείς (also written κάνεὶς) that has supplanted τὶς is a combination of κἄν, *i.e.* καὶ ἄν, and εἶς; κἄν (κάν) "at least," "even" is also employed as an independent particle in a sentence: *e.g.* ἀ δὲν εἶναι ὅλο, ἀς εἶν' ἔνα μέρος κάν "if it is not all it is at least a part." The κα- taken from κανείς, κα(μ)μιά, etc., occurs again in κά-τι. Moreover, with this καν- or κα- the indefinite adjs. κάμποσος and κάποιος (§§ 154, 156) and the adverbs κάπως "somehow," κάπου "anywhere," κάποτες "sometimes," were formed.

4. κανείς is noteworthy as exhibiting a survival of the old nominative form (as in καθείς "every" beside καθένας and in the Pontic εἶς = ἔνας). Occasionally an acc. κανεί(ν) from κανείς is found.

§ 154. κάποιος "anybody," "somebody," pl. "some" (κάποιοι ποῦ "some who") is declined like τέτοιος; but note the additional forms of the gen. καποιουνοῦ, καποιανῆς, and acc. κάποιονε, gen. pl. καποιονῶ(ν).

§ 155. καθείς καθένας (also ὁ καθένας) as substantive "every one," "each."

	Masc.	Fem.	Neut.
Nom.	καθείς, καθένας	καθεμιά	καθένα
Gen.	καθένος, καθενοῦς	καθεμιᾶς, καθεμιανῆς	= Masc.
Acc.	καθένα(ν)	καθεμιά(ν)	καθένα.

Adjectival "each," "every" is κάθε (more rarely κάθα), indeclinable; thus, κάθε χρόνο "each year," κάθε φορά "every time," μὲ κάθε τρόπο "in every way," κάθε λογῆς "of every kind," κάθε τρεῖς μέρες "every three days." M. Gk. here employs the definite article where German employs the indefinite (*ein* jedes) and English no article: *e.g.* μάγευε τὴν κάθε καρδιά "she charmed each heart."

"Each, every (one, thing)" subst. is also κάθετις, neut. κάθετι, with or without the article: (τὸ) κάθετι ποῦ γένεται, γένεται ἀπὸ ἀνάγκη "everything that happens, happens of necessity."

1. Note in Pontic κάθα εἶς = καθένας. Beside κάθε or κάθα, πᾶσα is also found (properly fem. of a. Gk πᾶς) for all genders: πᾶσα ὥρα "each hour" (Velv.), πᾶσα βράδυ "every evening" (Naxos); similarly πασαένας "each one," gen. πασανός, etc. (*e.g.* in Crete and Cyprus).

2. καθένας originated from the a. Gk. καθ' ἔνα, which became stereotyped and passed for the acc. of a substantival pronoun.

§ 156. κάμποσος "good many," "pretty much," "considerable," "several" (κάμποσος κόσμος "good many people") or "fairly large" (κάμποση πόλι "a pretty (rather) large city"), pl. "some," "few," "several."

	Masc.	Fem.	Neut.
Sing.	κάμποσος	κάμποση	κάμποσο(ν)
	κάμποσου	κάμποσης	κάμποσου
	κάμποσο(ν)	κάμποση(ν)	κάμποσο(ν)
Plur.	κάμποσοι	κάμποσες	κάμποσα
	κάμποσω(ν)	κάμποσω(ν)	κάμποσω(ν)
	κάμποσους	κάμποσες	κάμποσα.

Plur. also καμπόσοι and sing. καμπόσος, etc.

"Some" may be rendered also by μερικοί or κάποιοι and (adj.) also by κάτι (§ 153); thus, κάμποσοι, κάποιοι, μερικοὶ, κάτι (ἀθρώποι) "some (men)."

ὅλος, in many parts οὖλος "whole," "all," pl. "all": ὅλος ὁ κόσμος "the whole world," μ' ὅλη μας τὴν καρδιά "with our whole heart"; if the subst. is indeterminate ὅλος takes no art., as, ὅλη μέρα "all day long," ὅλη νύχτα "all night." If used as a subst. ὅλος may take the article: ὅλα and τὰ ὅλα "all." Note specially ὅλοι μας, σας, τους "all of us (we all), you all, they all (all of them)."

1. "Whole," "complete" is ὁλάκερος: e.g. ὁλάκερο τὸ σπίτι "the whole house," or ἕνα ὁ. σπ. "a whole house."

ἄλλος or ἕνας ἄλλος "another, one more" (cf. ἄλλο [ἕνα] ψωμί "another [piece of] bread," ἄλλα ἑκατὸ γρόσια "a hundred piastres more"), ὁ ἄλλος "the other" (subst. and adj.); sometimes with the article repeated: e.g. οἱ ἄλλες οἱ γυναῖκες "the other women."

2. The word παϊκά "other" (TEXTS III. 14. a) is of Turkish origin.

ὅλος and ἄλλος are declined like an adj., but pronominal forms are also found, like gen. pl. ὁλονῶν, acc. ὁλουνούς, gen. sing. ἀλλουνοῦ, ἀλλεινῆς, acc. ἄλλονε, etc.

3. In Pontic (TEXTS III. 13. b) neut. pl. ὄλä (fr. *ὄλια) for ὅλα; in Saranda Klisiés (TEXTS III. 12) ἄλλ = ἄλλο: e.g. τ' ἀλλ' τὸ ποδάρι "the other foot" (cf. τὸ ἕν, § 128, 1 n.).

§ 157. ὁ ἴδιος "the same," "self," declined like πλούσιος (§ 109); ἐγὼ ὁ ἴδιος "I myself," σεῖς οἱ ἴδιοι "yourselves."

μόνος when meaning "self" is combined with the gen. of the personal pronoun: (ἐμὼ) μόνος μου "(I) myself," (αὐτὸς) μόνος του "himself," (ἐμεῖς) μόνοι μας "ourselves," etc. ; μοναχός (μονάχος) is similarly employed ; so also ὁ ἑαυτός μου or ἀτός μου (ἀτή μου) or ἀπατός μου (ἀπατή μου), etc., " myself."

ὁ (ἡ, τὸ) τάδε(ς) " the so and so," " certain," " the what-do-you-call-it," is usually indeclinable : gen. and acc. τοῦ, τὸν τάδε(ς), sometimes also gen. τοῦ ταδινοῦ, τῆς ταδινῆς. In the same sense also :

> Nom. ὁ δεῖνα(ς), ἡ, τὸ δεῖνα
> Gen. τοῦ, τῆς, τοῦ δεῖνος
> Acc. τὸ, τὴ, τὸ δεῖνα.

ὁ δεῖνας καὶ ὁ τάδες " the one as well as the other," " all together."

μόνος "alone" and μονός "single" are treated as regular adjectives.

PREPOSITIONS.

§ 158. The *proper* prepositions are regularly joined with the acc. ; the (old) gen. has maintained itself only in a few fixed formulae ; *v.* §§ 161, 6. n. 2, 162, 4. n. 2, 164 n. Prepositions may also govern an adverb (*e.g.* ἀπὸ μπροστά "from before," "in front," ἀπὸ τότες "since then," ὡς πότε " how long ? ") and sometimes even a nominative (*cf.* §§ 161, 1, 163, 2). The most commonly used prepositions are εἰς, ἀπό, μέ, γιά, less frequently κατά, παρά (*v.* n.), ἀντίς, χωρίς, δίχως, ὡς, and in dialects ὀχ, πρός. The *improper* prepositions arise from the union of an adverb with a proper preposition.

The proper preps. are inherited from the a. Gk. ; here m. Gk. has suffered considerable loss. Occasionally obsolete preps. turn up in the vernacular texts through borrowing from the literary language (thus πρό). Some a. Gk. preps.—apart from those used in compound verbs (§ 159)—survive only in an altered or a quite limited usage. Thus παρά appears with the comparative (§ 120), with dates (§ 131, n. 2), in expressions like παρὰ τρίχα "within a hairbreadth," παρὰ (ἕνα) γρόσι "a penny too little," and as a conjunction = *nisi* (§ 120, n. 1) or "but" (§ 260). Note παρακάτω *"farther under,"* "below," παραπάνω *"farther over,"* "higher up," etc., and also dialectically (in Cyprus) παρὰ γωνιᾶς "in a *queer fix.*" Other a. Gk. preps. survive only in adverbial expressions in which the meaning of the prep. is often more or less obscured ; cf. ἀναμεταξύ "between," "amongst," ἐπιπόνου in παίρνω ἐ. " I lay to heart," πίστομα "on the mouth," "prostrate," πρὸ κεφαλῆς (Cyprus) "at the head of the table" in dining, προχτές "day before yesterday," πρόμυτα "on the nose."

§ 159. In *compound verbs* the following prepositions are still in active use:

1. ἀπο-: *e.g.* ἀπολύνω "release," ἀποχαιρετίζω "take leave," "bid farewell"; especially to denote a completed act (*perfective*): *e.g.* ἀποτρώγω "finish eating," ἀποκοιμοῦμαι "fall asleep," ἀποδείχνω "prove," ἀποτελειώνω "complete." *Cf.* also τὸ ἀποφά(γ)ι "fragments left after dinner, broken meat."

μετα- or ματα- (*v.* μέ): μεταφιλῶ "kiss once more," ματαβγαίνω "come out again."

1. μάτα occasionally serves as an independent adverb, "again."

κατα- (κατε-): κατεβαίνω "descend," κατεβάζω "let down," καταπίνω "drink in one draught," κατασφάζω "butcher." *Cf.* also § 116, n. 3.

παρα-: παραβαίνω "transgress," παραδίδω "surrender," παρακάνω "exaggerate," παρακοιμοῦμαι "sleep in," παρατρώγω "overeat myself," παρακούω "I hear wrongly," "disobey." *Cf.* also παραγιός "adopted son," παραμάννα "foster-mother."

2. The preps. εἰς (σέ), διά and πρός are quite limited in their employment: *e.g.* σεβαίνω "enter" (usually μπαίνω), διαβαίνω "pass by," προσφέρω "offer."

2. ἀνα- (ἀνε-): ἀναβαίνω (ἀνεβαίνω) "go up," ἀναμένω "await," ἀνασέρνω "draw up," ἀναστενάζω "sigh aloud."

ξε- denotes separation, release, also overcoming, heightening or completion of an act or state, and is the most common verbal prefix: ξεβιδώνω "unscrew," ξεγλυτώνω "get free from," "escape," ξεκάνω "put aside," ξεφυτρώνω "grow up," ξεγράφω "erase," ξεδιψῶ "quench my thirst," ξεκουράζω "rest," "recreate," ξεπερνῶ "exceed," ξεφωνίζω "cry out," ξετρελλαίνω "drive quite mad," ξετελεύω "finish completely." *Cf.* also ξέσκεπος "uncovered."

1. For the origin of ξε-, *cf.* § 182, n. 2; the form ἐκ remains in βγαίνω, βγάλλω, γδέρνω, γλυτώνω, etc. = a. Gk. ἐκβαίνω, ἐκβάλλω, ἐκδείρω, ἐκ-λυτόω.

ξανα- (from ἐξ + ανα-) denotes repetition: ξανακάνω "do it once more," ξαναβλέπω "see again," ξαναλέγω "say again," "repeat."

2. ξανά serves also as an independent adverb "again."
3. Other a. Gk. prepositions are found only in certain verbs, and are for the most part entirely obscured; *cf. e.g.* (ἐ)μπαίνω "go in,"

"enter," μπάζω "bring in," (ἐ)ντρέπομαι "am ashamed," περ(ι)πατῶ "walk," προκόφτω "make progress," (ὑ)παντρεύω "marry," (ὑ)πάγω "go," συνάζω "collect."

Proper Prepositions.

§ 160. εἰς, before the article usually 'ς (v. § 55), otherwise σέ (εἰσέ) "in," "to," "at," "on," "into," "toward," "against," denotes:

1. Place or local relation in answer to the question *where*? *whither*? (either as goal or direction): *e.g.* εἶναι στὸ σπίτι "he is in the house, at home," ἔχει στὸ χέρι "he holds in his hand," μιὰ γωνιὰ στὸν ἥλιο "a nook in the sun," κάθεται στὸ παραθύρι "he is sitting at the window," κάθεται στὴν καρέκλα "he is sitting on the chair," πηγαίνω στὴν πόλι, στὴν ἐξοχή, στὸ βουνό, στὴν 'Αθήνα, στὸ λιμένα "I am going into (to) the city, into the country, to the mountain, to Athens, to the harbour," βάλλω στὸ τραπέζι "I lay on the table," καθίζω στὸ τραπέζι "I take a seat at the table," σηκώνω τὰ χέρια στὸν οὐρανόν "I raise my hands to (toward) heaven," στοὺς Φράγκους "among the Europeans," σ' αὐτὴ τὴ φτωχὴ κόρη (TEXTS III. 4) "with this poor maid," πῆγε στὸν πατέρα του "he went to his father," ἔλα σὲ μένα "come to me," ἔστειλε στὸ βασιλιά "he sent to the king," τὸ ἔχω στὸ νοῦ μου "I have it in my mind." For εἰς supplanting the dative, *v.* § 54, c; for the genitive construction after εἰς, *v.* § 46.

2. Point or duration of time in answer to *when*? *how long*? *e.g.* σὲ καιρό "at a (in) time," στὴν ἴδια ἐποχή "at the same epoch," στὴν ὥρα του "at the right time," στὰ χίλια ὀχτακόσια ἐνενήντα πέντε "in (the year) 1895," στὶς ἑπτὰ [ὧρες] "at seven o'clock," σὲ πέντε μέρες "in, within, five days," σὲ λίγο (καιρό) "in a short time, soon." For the accusative (without prep.) in the same function, *cf.* § 52.

3. A state or action during which something occurs, or which is regarded as the goal (or object): *e.g.* στὸ ταξίδι "on the journey," σὲ φτώχιας ἀνάγκη "in the grip of poverty," στ' ἄστρη "in (the light of) the stars," στὰ σκοτεινά "in the dark," βγαίνω στὸ σιργιάνι "I go for (on) a walk," πηγαίνω στὸ κυνήγι "I am going to the chase" (*cf.* § 51), κόφτω στὰ δυό "I cut in(to) two," καταγίνεται σὲ γράψιμο "he is engaged (at) writing," κάθισε στὸ φαγί "sit down to table (to eat)," περιορίζομαι σὲ τοῦτο "I confine myself to this," πάγαινε στὸ

καλό "go in peace," "success be with you" (ἐπῆγε στὸ καλό means also "he went away about his business").

Note also: προσέχω σέ "I care for," βλέπω στὰ μάτια μου "I see with my eyes" (usually μέ), τὸν περνῶ στὸ τρέξιμο "I surpass him in running," ὁρκίζομαι σέ "I swear by, upon," στὸ θεό (σου) "by (thy) God," στ' ἀλήθεια "in truth," "indeed."

For εἰς in the improper prepositions, v. § 170 f.

§ 161. ἀπό (also ἀπ', ἀφ' before the article; in dialects ἀπέ, πέ, and ἀπού) "of," "from," "out of," "ago," "by," denotes:

1. The point of departure in place or time: ἦρθε ἀπὸ τὴν πόλι "he came from (out of) the city," τὸ νερὸ τρέχει ἀπ' τὸ πηγάδι "the water runs from the fountain," φεύγει ἀπ' τὸ χωριό "he flees out of the village," ἀπ' ὀπίσω "from behind," ἀπὸ χείλι σὲ χείλι "from lip to lip," λέγω ἀπ' τὴν καρδιά μου "I say (it) from my heart," ἀπὸ τότε (also ἀ. τ. καὶ δῶθε) "from that time," "since then," ἀπὸ δέκα ὧρες "ten hours ago," ἀπὸ τὶς τρεῖς "since three o'clock," ἀπ' τὴν αὐγή "since dawn,"[1] ἀπὸ καιρὸ σὲ καιρό "from time to time";—with the nominative ἀπὸ παιδί or ἀπὸ μικρός "from childhood," ἀπὸ πλούσιος ἔγινε ζητιάνος "from being a rich man he became a beggar."

Notice the peculiar rendering in περνῶ ἀπὸ τὴν πόρτα σου "I go past your door," περάσανε ἀπὸ κάτω "they went by underneath," παίρνω ἀπὸ τὰ βουνά "I take the way over the mountains," θὰ περάσω ἀπὸ τὴ Σμύρνη "I will travel via S.," ἐβγῆκε ἀπ' ἄλλη πόρτα "he went out through another door," ἐπῆγε ἀπ' ἄλλο δρόμο "he went another way" (πῆγε ἀπὸ κακὸ σπαθί στὸ σεφέρι (TEXTS II. b. 5) "he went to the war to his undoing [lit. with an evil sword]"), πιάνω ἀπ(ὸ) τὸ χέρι "I grasp by the hand," δένω ἀπ(ὸ) τὸ δέντρο "I bind to the tree," ἀρχίζω ἀπὸ τὰ εὐκολώτερα "I begin with the easiest."

2. That (person or thing) from which one separates (by becoming free or differing, etc.), against which he defends himself, or which he fears: τοὺς χωρίζω τὸν ἕνα ἀπ' τὸν ἄλλο "I separate them from one another," ἀχώριστος ἀπό "in-

---

[1] The expression "not for a long time" is peculiarly rendered: ἔχω καιρὸ (μέρες, χρόνια) νὰ τὸν ἰδῶ (without a negative) "I have not seen him for a long time (for days, years)," πόσον καιρὸ ἔχεις νὰ πᾶς στὴν πατρίδα σου; "how long have you not been in your native land?" τρεῖς χρόνους εἴχαμε νὰ γελάσωμε (TEXTS III. 4) "we had not laughed for three years."

separable from," γλυτώνω ἀπὸ τὸ θάνατο "I rescue from death," ἐλευθερώθηκε ἀπὸ τοὺς δράκους "he freed himself from the monsters," φυλάγομαι ἀπ' τὸ κακό "I guard against evil," μιὰ σκέπη ἀπ' τὴ βροχή "a roof against the rain," ἐσκιάζονταν ἀπ' τοὺς δράκους "he was afraid of the draki" (but φοβοῦμαι "I fear" takes acc.).

3. Origin or author: εἶναι ἀπὸ τὴν Ἀθήνα, ἀπὸ μεγάλο σπίτι "he is from Athens, he is of a great house," γεμίζω τὴ στάμνα ἀπὸ τὴ βρύσι "I fill the pitcher from (at) the fountain," ἔλαβα ἕνα γράμμα ἀπὸ τὴ μάννα μου "I received a letter from my mother," ἔχω (ζητῶ) τὴν ἄδεια ἀπὸ τὸ βασιλιά "I have (seek) permission from the king," σκοτώθηκε ἀπ' τοὺς Τούρκους "he was slain by the Turks," φωτισμένο ἀπὸ τὸν ἥλιο "illuminated by the sun," ἐκόπηκε ἀπ' τὸ μαχαίρι "he cut himself with the knife."

4. Material: ἀπὸ μάρμαρο "of marble."

5. Cause or motive: γίνεται ἀπὸ ἀνάγκη "it happens of necessity," ἀρρώστησε ἀπ' τὰ γεράματα "he became sick through old age," ἀπέθανε ἀπὸ τὴ βλογιά "he died of the small-pox," τὸ κάνει ἀπὸ φόβο, ἀπὸ τὴ χαρά του "he does it through fear, for joy," ἀπ' αὐτὸ γνωρίζω "I perceive thereby (from that)."

After verbs like θαμάζομαι "I wonder at," ξυπάζομαι "I am astonished at," γιά and acc. may be employed equally with ἀπό.

6. Partitive sense: κανεὶς ἀπὸ τοὺς φίλους "none of the friends," ἕνας δράκος ἀπὸ αὐτούς "one of the monsters," πολλοὶ ἀπὸ τοὺς ἐχτρούς "many of the enemy," ὁ μεγαλύτερος ἀπ' ὅλους "the greatest of all," δειπνάω ἀπὸ χῶμα (TEXTS I. a. 10) "I eat (of) earth," δὲν ξέρει, δὲ νοιώθει ἀπὸ τοῦτο "he understands nothing of this."

For ἀπό in improper prepositions, v. §§ 170, 172; with the comparative, v. § 120; distributive usage, v. § 132, which is not absolutely confined to the presence of a numeral; cf. e.g. ἀπὸ βράδυ "every evening," ἀπὸ λίγο λίγο "little by little," "gradually."

1. The preposition ἀπό has partly taken the place of the a. Gk. preps. ἐξ, παρά, ὑπό, and partly the place of the a. Gk. gen. (cf. § 44); it also competes with the present usage of the gen.; cf. e.g. ἔχω ἀνάγκη ἀπ' ἀνάπαψι "I have need of rest," or ἤθελε νὰ πάρη σκέδιος ἀπὸ τὸ σπίτι (TEXTS I. d. 5) "he wished to make a plan of the house." In this way the gen. pl. can be avoided (cf. § 41, n. 3),

and in dialects (North. Gk.) the gen. has altogether been pushed into the background by ἀπό (*cf.* § 44, n. 2).

2. ἀπό with the gen. is found in some stereotyped formulae like ἀπὸ καρδιᾶς "from the heart" (TEXTS I. a. 6), ἀπ' ἀνέμου (Icarus) "away from the wind," *i.e.* "south (of the island)," ποὺ ῥίζας "from the ground" (Cyprus, where ἀπό with gen. is of more frequent occurrence).

§ 162. μέ (a. Gk. μετά) "with" denotes:

1. Accompaniment or presence and coincidence in time (*cf.* also μαζί, § 173): ἔκανα ταξίδι μὲ τὸ φίλο μου "I made a journey with my friend," παρὰ μὲ Τούρκους μὲ θεριὰ καλύτερα νὰ ζοῦμε "better to live with wild beasts than with Turks," ἔνα σπίτι μὲ τρεῖς πατωσιές "a house of three storeys," γέρος μὲ κάτασπρα γένεια "an old man with a very white beard," ἐφύλαε μὲ τὸ ντουφέκι "he lay in wait with the musket (in his hand)," χρόνο μὲ χρόνο "year after year," τὴν αὐγὴ μὲ τὴ δροσούλα "dawn at the time of (with) the early dew," (μιὰ νύχτα) μὲ τὸ φεγγάρι "(one night) by the moonlight" (*cf.* also 3).

Note in addition: πολεμῶ μέ "I fight with," κουμπανιάρει μέ "it suits," "agrees with" (TEXTS I. a. 24. 27), μοιάζω μέ "I resemble" (*cf.* § 54, c. n.), μιλῶ μέ "I speak with (to)," also with gen. and acc.; ἀντιλαλάει μὲ μένα "echo answers me," θυμώνω μέ "I am angry with," εἶπεν μὲ τὸ νοῦ του "he said to himself (in his mind)."

2. Means or instrument: τὸ ἐσκέπασε μὲ τὴν κάπα του "he covered it with his cloak," τὸ εἶδε μὲ τὰ μάτια του "he saw it with his own eyes" (*cf.* § 160, 2 n.), τὸ γύρεψε μὲ οὔλα τὰ μέσα "he sought it by all means," κρατῶ μὲ τὸ χέρι "I hold with (in) my hand," μὲ τὰ ποδάρια "on foot," ἔκοψα μὲ τὸ μαχαίρι "I cut with my knife," γιατρεύω μ' ἔνα γιατρικό "I cure with a cure," θέλω νὰ 'πῶ μ' αὐτό "I mean (wish to say thereby)"; μέ can also express material (*cf.* § 161, 4): καλύβα πλεγμένη μὲ φτέρες "a hut woven of ferns." *Cf.* also § 50, n. 2.

3. Accompanying circumstances: διαβάζω μὲ τὸ κερί "I read by candle-light," μὲ (μεγάλη) χάρα "with (great) joy," μὲ πόνο "with pain," μὲ θυμὸ καὶ μὲ φωνές, "with wrath and shouting," μὲ τὰ ματάκια χαμηλά "with downcast eyes," ἔφυγε μὲ καμένη τὴν καρδιά "he went away with a sad heart," μ' ὅλο τὸν πόθο "with, in spite of all the longing," μ' ὅλο τοῦτο "in spite of all this," ποῦ πᾶς μὲ τέτοια ψύχρα

"where are you going in such cold?" σηκωθηκαμε μὲ ἕνα δυνατὸ βοριά "we set out in a boisterous north wind."

4. Manner: μὲ τί τρόπο "in what way? how?" μὲ τὴν ἀράδα (also στὴν ἀράδα) "in order," ἐπερίμενε μὲ προσοχή "he waited attentively," μίλησε μὲ παραβολές "he spoke in parables," δανείζω μὲ σημάδι "I lend on security," νοικιάζω μὲ τὸ μῆνα "I rent by the month." Note also adverbial expressions like μὲ τὸ σωρό, μὲ τὲς φούχτες "in heaps," μὲ τὰ σωστά (μου, etc.) "in earnest," "really," μὲ λίγα λόγια "in a word," "to put it briefly," μὲ τὴ συφωνία "on the condition," μὲ τὸ παραπάνω (TEXTS III. 11) "still more"; τὸ καράβι μὲ τὴν πάντα (TEXTS I. b. 16) "the boat (rides) on the side."

1. The preposition μέ continues to perform the duties of the a. Gk. μετά only in a limited way. Thus the *temporal* usage "after" has disappeared from the vernacular, for expressions like μὲ τὸν καιρόν,[1] μὲ καιρούς "in time," μὲ χρόνους "with (after) the years" belong under the usages of 1 or 3. The form μετά is still found in dialects (*e.g.* in Pontus), and also in connection with the personal pronoun of the 1st and 2nd persons (μετὰ σένα, μετ' ἐσένα), and finally in a few stereotyped formulae (*v.* n. 2).

2. The construction with the gen. is found (partly, no doubt, from the influence of the literary language) in some expressions; as, μὲ μιᾶς "at once," μετὰ βίας "with effort" (TEXTS II. a. 2), μετὰ χαρᾶς "with joy" (TEXTS II. b. 6). In Cyprus μιτά takes the gen. of personal pronouns and proper names, *e.g.* μιτά μου "with me," ἐπῆεμ μιτὰ τοῦ Τροφῆ "he went with T."

§ 163. γιά (διά, *v.* § 25) "on account of," "for," "to," "as to," "because of," denotes:

1. Motion or extension in time to a goal or conclusion: ἔφυγε γιὰ τὴν Πόλι "he departed to (for) Constantinople," ἐβγῆκε γιὰ δυὸ ὧρες "he went out for two hours," γιὰ τρία χρόνια "for three years," γιὰ μιὰν ἄνοιξι "for (the duration of) one springtime," γιὰ πάντα "for ever," γιὰ ὕστερη φορά "for the last time."

2. An aim or purpose: πηγαίνω γιὰ νερό "I go for water (to bring water)," τὸν πὰν γιὰ κρέμασμα "they are leading him out for hanging (to the gallows)," ἐτοιμάστηκε γιὰ τὸ γάμο "he prepared for the wedding," εἶναι γιὰ χαρά "it is for joy," εἶναι γιὰ φυλαχτό σου "it serves thee for amulet," γιὰ (τὸ) καλό μου "for my good," δὲν εἶναι γιὰ τίποτε "he is (good) for nothing." With the nominative: ἦρθε γιὰ δοῦλος

[1] Also "at the stated time."

" he came as servant (to be a servant)," περνᾷ γιὰ σοφός " he passes as a sage."

For the competition of the double accusative in same sense, *v*. § 50, 2. a.

3. Proposed reason: γιὰ τοῦτο " therefore," γιατί " why," γιὰ σᾶς " for your sake," γιὰ ὄνομα τοῦ θεοῦ " for God's sake," εὐχαριστῶ γιὰ τὴν καλοσύνη σου " I thank you for your kindness," τὸ κάνω γιὰ τὸ καλό, ποῦ μου ἔκανες " I am doing it on account of the benefit which you did me," τόνε θαμάζω γιὰ τὶς γνώσες του " I admire him for his learning," χαίρομαι γιὰ τοῦτο " I rejoice on this account " (συχαίρω γιά " I congratulate on "), γιὰ μαῦρα μάτια χάνομαι " for the sake of black eyes am I perishing," *i.e.* " I am desperately in love with black eyes." Less commonly γιά gives the motive: *e.g.* τό 'καμε γιὰ ἔχτρα (usually ἀπὸ ἔχτρα, *v*. § 161, 5).

4. The advantage (protection) or disadvantage for that (person or thing) in regard to which a declaration is made: αὐτὸ εἶναι καλὸ γιὰ σένα " that is good for thee," ὅτι γιὰ μένα δὲν ζητῶ, γι' αὐτὸ (παιδί) γυρεύω " what I do not seek for myself I request for this (child)," πλερώνω γιὰ ὅλους " I pay for all," φροντίζω, φοβοῦμαι γιά " I care for, fear for," δὲ μὲ μέλει γιὰ τίποτις " I worry about nothing," εἶναι γιὰ μένα μυστήριο " it is for me a secret."

5. " Concerning," " in regard to," *e.g.* μιλήσαμε γιὰ σένα " we spoke of you," δυὸ λόγια γιὰ τοὺς Χιώτες " two words on the Chiotes "; ὅσο γιὰ means " as for," " in regard to " (Fr. *quant à*).

6. Price: γιὰ πέντε δραχμές " for, at 5 drachmae " (*cf.* § 52).

1. The preposition γιά—in addition to preserving the usage of the a. Gk. διά with acc.—has acquired the function partly of the old dative and partly those of ἐπί, περί, ὑπέρ, ἀντί. The local meaning of διά w. gen. has entirely disappeared (cf. μέσα, § 171).

2. In connection with pronouns (especially of the 1st or 2nd person) γιά often takes the form γιατά (like μετά beside μέ, § 162, n. 1): *e.g.* γιατὰ μένα; note also γιάτι αὐτό, TEXTS III. 11 (Velv.).

§ 164. κατά (rarely κά) denotes:

1. The direction toward, to, something (so far as the actual *reaching* of a goal does not come into consideration; cf. γιά): ἔρχεται κατὰ τὸ χωριό " he is coming towards the village," γυρνᾷ κατὰ τὸ γέρο " he turns to the old man,"

ἐπῆρε τὸ δρόμο κατὰ ποῦ τοῦ 'δειχνε " he took the way in the
direction he pointed him," κύττα ἐκειδὰ κατὰ τὸ μεγάλο τὸ
δρόμο "look there toward the highway."

2. "According to": κατὰ τὸ νόμο "according to the
law," κατὰ τὸν καιρό "according to the weather," ὀλίγο κατ'
ὀλίγο "little by little," "gradually"; κατὰ πῶς, κατὰ ποῦ,
v. § 281, 1.

The a. Gk. usage of κατά is consequently greatly reduced. We
miss above all the meanings "down" and "against"—for the expression κατὰ τῶν δυνατῶν, TEXTS II. b. 7, is taken from the *written*
language. It is found with the gen. in the adverbial expressions
καταγῆς "on the ground" (= χάμου), καταμεσῆς "in the midst,"
κατὰ θανατοῦ "fatally." The construction κατὰ διαβόλου " to the
devil," lit. "in the direction of the devil," must be taken like εἰς
w. gen. (§ 46).

§ 165. ἀντίς "instead of," also ἀντὶς γιά: *e.g.* νὰ πὰς
ἐσὺ ἀντὶς ἐμένα (ἀντὶς τὸν ἀδερφό μου) or ἀντὶς γιὰ μένα " go
you in my place (instead of my brother)," ἐκρέμασαν ἀντὶς
αὐτὸν τὸν παραγμό του "they hanged his adopted son in
place of him."

§ 166. ὡς "to," "up to," "till," of *place* and *time*: ὡς
τὴν πόρτα "(up) to the door," ὡς τὴν ὥρα "till this hour,"
"until now" (in Cyprus ὡς τῆς ὥρας), ὡς τὸ βράδυ "until
evening."

Also ὡς τὰ σήμερα "until to-day," ὡς τὰ χτές "until
yesterday."

§ 167. χωρίς, δίχως (also μὲ δίχως) "without": χωρὶς
κόπο "without trouble," χωρὶς ἄλλο "at all events," "without fail," δίχως βούλα "without signet-ring," δίχως (καμιὰ)
ἀφορμή "without (any) cause."

In Cyprus it takes the gen. of a pronoun χώρις σου, δίχως σου.

§ 168. The following are rarely used :

1. πρός "toward," of place and time, *e.g.* TEXTS I. d. 3; the
employment of πρός is in most cases due to the influence of the
literary language.

2. ὀχ w. acc. (= a. Gk. ἐκ): *e.g.* in Vilaras, Solomos, and in the
Ionic Islands, ὀχ or ἀχ in Pelopon., instead of ἀπό; *cf.* ὀχ τὸν κόπο
"in consequence of the effort," ὀχ τὸ νοῦ μου "out of my memory."
The genitive construction has persevered in ὀχονοῦς = ἐξ ἐνός ; ἐξ
οὐρανοῦ "from heaven," is ecclesiastical; in Icarus (ἐ)ξανέμου "from
the North, in the North," is used.

3. Pontic employs ἀς instead of (and along with) ἀπό: *e.g.* ἀς

ἐμέτερον τὴμ φυλὴν ἔν "he is from our tribe," ἐπιάστεν ἀσὸ (*i.e.* ἀς τὸ) σεῖλος "he was caught by the snout."

Improper Prepositions.

§ 169. The improper prepositions denote mostly spatial relations, rarely temporal or other relations. The component adverbs (otherwise used as independent adverbs) are converted into prepositions by a genitive coming after or by means of 'ς, ἀπό, or also μέ. The simple gen. is used *only* with the (enclitic) conjunctive pronoun.

1. The line between proper and improper prepositions is more pronounced than in a. Gk., for the reason that in m. Gk. the presence of a proper preposition is necessary in the improper. Still no hard and fast line can be drawn ; for, on the one hand, ἀντίς by the occasional addition of γιά (§ 165) approaches the improper prepositions, while, on the other hand, we find in dialects an approach between the improper and the proper through the former, like the latter, taking the simple accusative : *e.g.* ὀπίσω τὸλ λοῦρον "behind the rock" (Icarus). Neither can a hard and fast line be drawn between adverb and improper preposition ; thus expressions like μακρειά μου "far from me," πουθενά του "nowhere with him," ποτέ μου "never by me," παντοῦ μας "everywhere with us," or μακρειά ἀπό, πουθενὰ ἀπ' τὴ χώρα, παντοῦ ἀπ' ὅλους, are on the border between substantival and prepositional construction.

2. The improper prepositions, compared with the a. Gk., are quite new formations, although the adverbs employed therein come from the a. Gk. or are formed from a. Gk. material.

§ 170. The improper prepositions are divided as below according to the auxiliary prepositions 'ς, ἀπό, μέ : 'ς expresses a simple statement of proximity or approach, ἀπό a definite standpoint or point of departure, μέ distinct accompaniment or connection.

The adverb sometimes comes *after*; in addition to the exx. given *passim*, *cf.* also the Pontic and Cappadocian prepositions given in § 174.

§ 171. Exclusively or usually with 'ς :

κοντά 'ς "(near) at, by, to"; (1) of *place* : κοντὰ στὴν πόρτα "(near), at the door," κοντὰ στὴ λίμνη "by the sea," ὅλ' οἱ ἅγιοι κοντά σου "all the saints (be) with thee " ; ἦρθε κοντά του "he came up to him," πέρασε ἀπὸ κοντά του "he passed near him " ; (2) of *time,* "about, at, around " : [1] κοντὰ

---

[1] Also expressed by πάνω κάτω, *e.g.* π. κ. μεσάνυχτα "about midnight."

στὸ δειλινό "in the course of the afternoon," κοντὰ στὸ γιόμα γιόμα "exactly at meal time"; (3) "*in comparison with*": τὰ τριαντάφυλλα χάνονται κοντὰ σ' ἐσέ, στὰ κάλλη σου "the roses lose in comparison with thee, with thy fairness"; (4) κοντὰ στ' ἄλλα "besides, moreover."

1. σιμά 's is used like κοντά (but less commonly).

μέσα 's "within, inside, into, between, among"; (1) of *place*: μέσα στὸ σπίτι (or στὸ σπίτι μέσα) "inside the house," μέσα στὸν οὐρανό "in the midst of heaven," μέσα μου "within, with me," τὸν ἔμπασε μέσα σ' ἔναν ὀντᾶ "he led him into a room," μέσα στσοὶ πολλοὶ γιατροί (Ios) "among the many physicians."

2. Note Texts III. 12 μέσ' στὴ γιόλα μέσα "into the pool."

(2) Of *time and other relations*: μέσα στὴ ζέστη "in the (midst of the) heat," μέσα σὲ δυὸ βδομάδες "within two weeks" (*cf.* § 160, 2), εἶπε μέσα του "he said to himself," μέσα στ' ἄλλα "*inter alia.*"

3. The abbreviated form μέσ' 's is almost a proper prep., since 's cannot be distinguished in the pronunciation and may equally well be dropped: *e.g.* μέσ' (σ)τὸ πέλαγο "in the sea," μέσ' (σ)τὴ μέση τοῦ χωριοῦ "in the midst of the village," μέσ' (σ') ἕνα π(η)γάδ(ι) "into a fountain" (Lesbos), μέσ' (σ)τὸ καλοκαίρι "in the middle of summer." ἀνάμεσα "into, in the midst of" is used like μέσα, *e.g.* ἀνάμεσα στὸ σιτάρι "in (into) the corn."

4. τὸ εἰπωμένο μέσο τοῦ Προφήτη (Texts II. b. 6) "the word (spoken) in the prophet" is rather unusual.

(ἀπὸ) μέσ' ἀπό is used to render "from, from the midst of," or "through, through the midst of": τὸν ἔβγαλε μέσ' ἀπὸ τὸ κιβούρι "she brought him out of the grave," περνᾷ τὸ κορδόνι μέσ' ἀπὸ τὸ δαχτυλίδι "he draws the cord through the ring," ἐπέρασε ἀπὸ μέσα ἀπὸ τοὺς ἐχτρούς "he passed through the midst of the enemy."

δίπλα 's or πλά(γ)ι 's "beside, at": δίπλα στὸ σπίτι μου "beside my house."

μπροστά 's or (ἐ)μπρός 's, ὀμπρός 's (on the 's, *cf.* μέσ' 's) "before," "in front of," "in the presence of"; (1) of *space*: μπροστὰ 's τὴν πόρτα "before the door," ἔλα ἐμπρὸς ἐμπρὸς στὴ λίμνη "come quite near to the pond," μπροστά μου "before me, in my presence," κύτταζε μπροστά σου "look before you," φύγε ἀπὸ 'μπρός μου "get out of my sight";

also εἰς τὸν κόσμον ὀμπρός "before (the eyes of) the world";
(2) in *contrasts* or *comparisons*: τὰ βάσανα ποῦ εἶχε τραβήξει
ὡς τότε, ἤτανε τιπότενια μπρὸς στὰ σημερινά του "the
agonies which he had as yet endured were nothing compared
with his present," κανεὶς δὲ βγαίνει ὀμπρός του "none can
compare with him."

ἀντίκρυ 's or ἀγνάτια 's "opposite," "over against," of
space and in *comparison*: τὸ ξενοδοχεῖον εἶναι ἀντίκρυ στὸ
σταθμό "the hotel is opposite the station," ἀντίκρυ του
"opposite him."

5. Note ἔβγαν γνέντα μας (Texts III. 14. b) "they came to meet
us."

πέρα 's "over (across) to": ἐπήγαμε πέρα στὸν Ἀϊ-
Γιάννη "we went across to St. John's (chapel)."

χάμου 's or κάτω 's "down in," "below in": χάμου στὴ
ρούγα "below in the street."

(ἀ)πάνω 's (a. Gk. ἐπ' ἄνω) or (ἀ)πάνου (in dialects πὰ
's) "above, upon, on"; (1) of *place*: (ἀ)πάνω στὸ τραπέζι
"(above) upon the table" (also metaphorically "at the table,"
"at dinner"), ἀπάνω στὰ γόνατά μου "upon (before) my
knees," πάνω σὲ μία ψάθα "on a straw mat," ἔπεσε στ'
ἀγκάθια ἀπάνου "it fell upon the thorns," πέφτουν κατ'
ἀπάνω τους "they fall upon them," δὲν ἔχω παράδες ἀπάνω
μου "I have no money on my person," ἀπ' ἀπάνω του
"away from him"; (2) of *time*: ἦρθεν ἀπάνω στὴν ὥρα "he
came on the hour" (*i.e.* "punctually"), πάνω στὴν οὐσία "in
the prime of life"; (3) extended to different senses; *cf. e.g.*
ὄρκος ἐπάνω στὸν Σταυρόν "oath by the cross," τὸ παίρνω
πάνω μου "I take it upon me (make myself answerable),"
ἀπάνω σ' ὅλα "in addition to all, besides"; (4) seldom
"about, concerning": *e.g.* κρίσι ἀπάνω σ' ἕνα τραγούδι "criticism about a poem."

6. To render "over, above, beyond, out of" ἀπάνω is combined
with ἀπό: *e.g.* τὸ σπαθί του σκίστηκεν ἀπάν' ἀπὸ τὴ φούχτα "the sword
went to pieces in (over) his fist," παραπάνω ἀπό "beyond (a certain
measure)," ἀπὸ τό 'να καὶ πάνω "beyond, more than the one."

7. Note ἀπάνωθεν, Texts I. a. 2 = ἀπάνω.

γύρω 's, τριγύρω 's or τριγύρου 's, ὁλόγυρα 's (also with
ἀπό) "around, round, round about": *e.g.* (τρι)γύρω στὸ (ἀπ' τὸ)
βωμό "round the altar," (τρι)γύρω του "around him," τριγύρω
στὰ βουνά "round about on the mountains."

8

§ 172. Exclusively or usually with ἀπό:

μακρειὰ ἀπό " far from " : e.g. μακρειά μου " far from me."

ἔξω (ὄξω) ἀπό, ἀπέξω (ἀπόξω) ἀπό " outside, without, in front of " ; (1) of *place* : (ἀπ)έξω ἀπὸ τὸ σπίτι " outside (out of) the house," ὁ ἔξω ἀπ' ἐδώ = " the devil " ; (2) figuratively " beyond, except, besides " (*praeter*) : e.g. ἔξω ἀπὸ τὸ μέτρο " beyond the measure," ἔξω ἀπ' αὐτά " besides (this)," ἔξω ἀπὸ τοὺς φίλους " except my friends."

κάτω ἀπό, ἀποκάτω ἀπό (also παρακάτω ἀπό) " below, beneath, under, from under " : e.g. (ἀπο)κάτω ἀπὸ τὸ κάστρο " under the fortress," ἀποκάτω ἀπ' τὸ ποδάρι τοῦ ἀλόγου " underneath the horse's hoof," ἀπολάει ἀποκάτω ἀπὸ τὴν καπότα του " he brings out from under his cloak."

(ὁ)πίσω ἀπό, ἀποπίσω ἀπό " behind " : e.g. πίσω ἀπὸ τὴν πόρτα " behind the door," νὰ 'δῇς πίσω σου " look behind thee." More rarely (ὀ)πίσω 'ς : e.g. ἐγὼ πάνω πίσω σ' αὐτόν " I go behind him " (TEXTS I. d. 2).

Similarly ἔπεσε κατόπι του " he fell behind him," σέρνομε κατόπι μας " we drag after us."

ἀπ' ἐδὼ ἀπό or ἀπὸ—κ' ἐδώ " on this side " : e.g. ἀπ' ἐδὼ ἀπὸ τὸ ποτάμι or ἀπὸ τὸ ποτάμι κ' ἐδώ " on this side of the river."

ἀπὸ πέρα ἀπό or ἀπέκει (ἀπεκεῖ, παρέκει) ἀπό or ἀπὸ —καὶ πέρα " on that side, beyond": e.g. ἀποπέρα (ἀπέκει) ἀπὸ τὰ σύνορα or ἀπὸ τὰ σύνορα καὶ πέρα " beyond the border," ἀπὸ δὼ καὶ πέρα " from here, beyond." Similarly παραπέρα ἀπό " further than, beyond."

ὕστερα ἀπό " after," of time : ὕστερα ἀπὸ λίγο καιρό (ἀπὸ δυὸ μέρες) " after a little while (after two days)," ὕστερα ἀπὸ πολλὰ γυρέματα " after much searching." Note ὕστερα ἀπὸ μένα " after me."

πρωτύτερα ἀπό, πρὶν ἀπό " before," of time : ἔφτασα πρωτύτερα ἀπὸ σένα " I arrived before you," πρὶν ἀπὸ τὶς δεκαπέντε (τοῦ) 'Απρίλι " before the 15th April."

But *time past* (" *ago* ") is rendered by (ἀπ') ἐδὼ καὶ or τώρα καί: e.g. ἔγινε (ἀπ') ἐδὼ καὶ πέντε χρόνια " it happened five years ago," τώρα καὶ δέκα χρόνια ἤμουν στὴν Ἑλλάδα " I was in Greece ten years ago," or also εἶναι (τώρα) δέκα χρόνια ποῦ ἔγινε " it happened ten years ago."

κρυφὰ ἀπό " secretly, without the knowledge of " (Lat.

clam): *e.g.* κρυφὰ ἀπ' τὴ γυναῖκα του "without his wife's knowledge," κρυφά μου "without my knowledge."

§ 173. Usually with μέ:

μαζὶ μέ "(together) with": *e.g.* μαζὶ μὲ τοὺς φίλους "together with his friends," μαζί σου "with thee"; also "inclusive": *e.g.* τὸ γέμα μαζὶ μὲ τὸ κρασὶ κοστίζει τρεῖς δραχμές "the meal costs 3 drachmae inclusive of wine."

1. Similarly ἀντάμα μέ "together with."

ἴσ(ι)α μέ "till," "up to"; (1) of *place* or *time*: γεμάτο ἴσια μὲ τὰ χείλια "full to the lip," ἴσια μὲ τὴν κορφή τοῦ βουνοῦ "up to the top of the mountain," ἴσια μὲ τὸ μεσημέρι "till noon"; (2) in statements of *measure*: (μεγάλο) ἴσια μ' ἔνα φουντούκι "as (large) as a nut," ἴσα μὲ πέντε δραχμές "up to, about 5 drachmae"; (3) "*like as, just like*": τὸν ἀγαπῶ ἴσια μὲ παιδί μου "I love him as my own child," δὲν εἶναι ἴσια μὲ σένα "he is not like you."

2. Note ἴσια στὸ χωριό "up into the village," ἴσια κατὰ τὸν κάμπο "as far as the field."

σύ(μ)φωνα μέ "in accordance with," "after," σύ(μ)φωνα μὲ τοὺς νόμους "according to the laws."

§ 174. Other formations of similar kind are found in the dialects. The Pontic and Cappadocian dialect, which reveals a propensity for placing the adverb last, gives, *e.g.*, ἀπές (= ἀπ' ἔσω) or ποπές (= ἀπὸ ἀπέσω) "in, within," etc.; *cf.* ποῖος ἀποπέσ' ἔσουν (TEXTS III. 13. b) "who among you," στὰ πηγάδια ποπές (TEXTS III. 14. b) "into the fountain"; *cf.* also σὸ τρυπὶν κεικά (TEXTS III. 13. b) = στὸ τρυπὶν ἐκεῖ κατω "into the hole," ἀπὸ τρία μῆνες ὄμπρο (TEXTS III. 14. a) "three months ago."

THE VERB.

Preliminary Observations.

§ 175. In modern Greek the verb has two voices, an Active and a Passive: χτυπῶ "I strike," χτυπειοῦμαι "I am struck." The passive forms are, however, much less in vogue than in German or in English. The modern Greek passive serves not only as passive but is frequently employed (like the ancient middle) to express an action, or a condition, or even as a reflexive.

1. The a. Gk. middle has only formally disappeared, its original signification still survives. The special middle verbal forms (aorist)

have become obsolete, the passive forms maintaining the field and appropriating the meaning of the middle. Thus, generally speaking, the m. Gk. passive covers the usages also of the old middle, only that the delicate distinctions between the active and the so-called "dynamic," or the indirect reflexive middle, are lost.

2. A remarkable peculiarity of the m. Gk. verb is its faculty of forming compounds with a substantive or with another verb. The former (with a substantive) started with such a. Gk. formations as θαυματουργῶ, καρποφορῶ, etc. However, the combinations with an adjective outnumber those with a substantive ; cf. e.g. μοσκομυρίζω "I smell of musk," καλοπερνῶ "I live well," καλογνωρίζω "I perceive well," ἀργοσαλεύω "I move slowly," ἀκρανοίγω "I open a little," γλυκοφιλῶ "I kiss affectionately," κουτσοπίνω "I drink a little," χαμηλολογιάζω "I meditate with bowed head," βαρειακούω "I am hard of hearing, hear with difficulty," μισανοίγω "I open half-way." As we should expect, participial combinations are specially frequent, as πολυχρονεμένος "one worthy of many years," χαροτεντωμένος "stark in death," χιλιοπατημένος "trodden of thousands (i.e. oft)." Two verbs can unite to form a *dvandvac* construction ; as, ἀνοιγοσφαλίζω "I open and shut," ἀνεβοκατεβαίνω "I pace up and down," τρεμοσβήνω "I tremble and die away." Cf. § 41, a. 1. d and 2. c for the verb in compound substantives.

§ 176. The *Active* voice has—besides the transitive— also very frequently an intransitive, middle or reflexive meaning, and *vice versa* intransitive active verbs are often employed as transitive : *e.g.*

(a) ἀλλάζω "I change" trans. and intr., ἀνοίγω "I open" and "stand open," βόσκω "I feed" trans. and intr., (ξ)απλώνω "I spread out" trans. and intr., γεμίζω "I fill" and "am full," γλυτώνω "I rescue" and "escape," γυρίζω "I turn (round)" trans. and "return, turn back" intr., θεμελιώνω "I establish," "found" and "I have, obtain firm ground," καθαρίζω "I purify" and "am pure," κολλῶ "I glue to" (trans.) and "grow to," κουνῶ "I move" trans. and intr., λυώνω "I loose, dissolve" and "melt" intr., ξεχωρίζω "I separate (from)" trans. and intr., ξεσπάω "I break off" trans. and "break forth," προβάλλω "I hold forth (propose)" and "advance" intr., σκορπίζω "I scatter" and "am scattered," σταματῶ "I cause to stop, prevent" and "stop" intr. "remain," σέρνω or τραβῶ "I draw, drag" and "withdraw, go" intr., ταιριάζω "I associate, pair," and ταιριάζει "it is becoming," τρομάζω "I terrify" and "am terrified," χαλνῶ "I spoil" trans. and intr., χορταίνω "I satisfy" and "am satisfied," χτυπῶ "I strike," intr. of the clock (also "dash against," "am flung against ").

(b) ἀρρωστῶ "I am sick" and "I make one sick" (*e.g.* μὲ φωνές μου "by my screaming"), ἀστράφτει "it lightens" and ἀστράφτω "I thrash one," βαραίνω "I am heavy, weigh" and "I burden," βρέχει "it rains" and βρέχω "I cause to rain," βροντᾷ "it thunders" and βροντῶ "I beat down," γελῶ "I laugh" and "deceive," ζῶ "I live," and "I keep alive, preserve," καθίζω "I sit" and "place, seat," καταντῶ "I degenerate" and "reduce into a state," ξυπνῶ "I wake" and "rouse from sleep," περνῶ "I pass by" and "surpass," "exceed," πετῶ "I flee" and "throw away," πηγαίνω (πάγω, a. Gk. ὑπ-άγω) "I go" and "I bring," "lead," σιωπῶ "I am silent" and "keep secret," φτάνω "I arrive" (φτάνει "it suffices") and "I attain, reach." Note also a word of a different kind, μαθαίνω "I learn" and "I teach."

The causes of such numerous transitions between transitive and intransitive are to be sought partly in the a. Gk. itself; cf. a. Gk. ἄγω, ἐλαύνω, κινῶ, κλίνω, ἵημι, which by the ellipsis of an object became intrans., or καίω, κτυπῶ, σιωπῶ, ὕω, and ὕει, which even in antiquity served both as trans. and intrans. This usage persisted and occasionally reversed the a. Gk. status : *e.g.* πηγαίνω and πάγω "I go" (a. Gk. ὑπάγω) is to-day predominantly intransitive, κινῶ "I move, depart" is intransitive only (cf. κουνῶ). Moreover, the formal levelling of verbs in -άω, -έω, and -ίζω (*v.* § 204) has contributed to the levelling of their functions.

§ 177. The middle is found—

1. In the so-called *deponents*: like αἰστάνομαι "feel," ἀπελπίζομαι "doubt," ἀφικροῦμαι "hear," γίνομαι "become," διγοῦμαι "relate," ἔρχομαι "come," κάθομαι "sit," κοιμοῦμαι "sleep," σιχαίνομαι "feel an aversion," στοχάζομαι, συλλογίζομαι "think," φοβοῦμαι "fear," φταρμίζομαι "sneeze," χασμουρειοῦμαι "yawn," χαίρομαι "rejoice," χρειάζομαι "need," μέλλεται "is about to." In many instances the middle has developed as of secondary nature from an original passive or reflexive meaning: *e.g.* κουράζομαι "am tired" (κουράζω "make tired"), ξενιτεύομαι "go abroad," ξεραίνομαι "become dry" (ξεραίνω "dry" trans.), καμώνομαι "feign, pretend," βαστάζομαι "collect myself" (βαστάζω "I bear"), ὁρκίζομαι "swear" (ὁρκίζω "cause to swear"), παραξενεύομαι "wonder," περηφανεύομαι "am proud," πνίγομαι "drown" intr. (πνίγω "strangle, drown" trans.), σιάζομαι "set about, begin," σκιάζομαι "fear," φανερώνομαι "appear" (φανερώνω "reveal, disclose"), φαίνομαι "manifest myself, appear,"

χάνομαι " perish, am lost," also "am eager for, in love with "
(χάνω " I lose "). On στεφανώνομαι " wed," cf. § 49.

1. The majority of these cases represent the same or similar a. Gk
phenomenon. Sometimes modern Greek—following ancient models—
has increased its stock of deponents; cf. e.g. χαίρομαι for a. Gk.
χαίρω somewhat after λυποῦμαι " I regret," etc. Both are found
together in θαμάζω and θαμάζομαι (a. Gk. θαυμάζω) "admire" or
"wonder" (both with acc.), φαντάζω and φαντάζομαι "imagine."
Note, further, καί(γ)ομαι " I burn," intr. beside καίω trans. and intr.,
and στέκομαι " I stand," beside the more common στέκω, after model
of κάθομαι.

Conversely the active form has displaced the ancient middle:
e.g. in ἐξηγῶ "explain," θυμώνω "am enraged," παραιτῶ "abandon."

2. Only a few traces of the *dynamic* middle are left; thus, e.g.,
beside ἐξοδεύω " I spend (money)," "incur expenses," we find
ἐξοδεύομαι in the *intensive* sense.

2. As Reflexive:

(a) Direct reflexive: ντύνομαι "dress (myself)," λούζομαι
"bathe (myself)," ξουρίζομαι "shave (myself)," πλένομαι
"wash (myself)," χτενίζομαι "comb (my hair)," σηκώνομαι
"raise myself, rise," σιάζομαι "prepare (myself)," συγυρίζομαι
"adjust myself, prepare," σκοτώνομαι " kill myself," ταμπουρώ-
νονται "they entrench themselves," φανερώνομαι "allow
myself to perceive," φορτώνομαι "load (burden) myself with,"
φυλάγομαι "(protect myself), guard against."

The reflexive sense may be emphasised by the addition of the
pronoun "self" (§ 157): ξουρίζομαι μόνος (μοναχός) μου " *I* shave
myself," σκοτώθηκε ὁ ἴδιος or ἀτός του "*he* killed *himself*."

(b) Reciprocal reflexive: ἀγκαλιάζονται "they embrace
each other," ἀποχαιρετειοῦνται " they take leave of each other,"
γνωρίζουνται "they recognise one another," ἐρωτεύουνται
"they are in love with each other," καλημερίζουνται "they
bid good-day to each other," μαζώνονται "they assemble,"
παντρεύουνται "they intermarry," κυνηγειοῦνται "they chase
one another," πιάνονται "they take hold of each other (to
wrestle), come to close quarters," φιλειοῦνται "they kiss each
other."

The reciprocal idea may also be expressed by or strengthened by
ὁ ἕνας τὸν ἄλλο and by (ἀνα-) μεταξύ μας, etc. (v. § 141): e.g. μαλώνουν
or μαλώνουνται μεταξύ τους " they scold each other."

(c) Causative reflexive, generally with a negative: πιάνεται
" he allows himself to be caught," δὲ γελειέται " he does not

allow himself to be deceived," δὲ μιλειέται "he refuses to be interviewed," τὸ κρασὶ τοῦτο δὲν πίνεται "this wine cannot be drunk."

The active may likewise express the same meaning: *e.g.* ἔχτισα σπίτι "I got a house built," ἔκοψα τὰ μαλλιά μου "I caused my hair to be cut."

§ 178. Altogether there are eight *Tenses*, which are subdivided into two classes, simple and compound:

I. Simple.
    1. Present.
    2. Imperfect.
    3. Aorist.
II. Compound.
    4. Future present (*Fut. continuum*).
    5. Future aorist (*Fut. absolutum*).
    6. Perfect.
    7. Pluperfect.
    8. Future perfect

1. The tenses 6, 7, and 8 are much less in use than the others (*cf.* § 229).
2. Only the simple tense forms correspond to the a. Gk. formations; the compound tenses are m. Gk. formations to fill the places of the ancient forms that have disappeared.

§ 179. There are four *Moods*: three simple, Indicative, Subjunctive (Conjunctive), Imperative; and one compound, the Conditional or "Unreal." As far as terminations are concerned the Subjunctive is perfectly identical with the Indicative; it possesses a special form only in the aorist stem (active and passive). The subjunctive is employed always in dependence on conjunctions or particles (νά, θά, ἄς) (*cf.* § 193 f., and also the rules for subordinate clauses, § 264 ff.). There is a double imperative, representing both present and aorist mode of action (*Aktionsart*); but only the 2nd person sing. and pl. has distinct forms of its own, the 3rd person being supplemented from the subjunctive. The conditional has likewise two forms, for present and for past time.

Compared with the Moods of the ancient language m. Gk. shows an impoverishment—the optative having quite disappeared, and the subjunctive being considerably reduced. Indicative and subjunctive are only orthographically distinguished from each other in some of their forms in the a. Gk. fashion: (*na*) *gráfis* = γράφεις indic.,—*νὰ γράφῃς* subj., (*na*) *gráfome* γράφομε—*νὰ γράφωμε*; but in the spoken language both forms are absolutely identical.

§ 180. If modern Greek has suffered many losses compared with the parent language, it has not failed also to enrich its resources. It has not only preserved the distinction between present and aorist kind of action [1] (continuative or repeated action and a simplex [point] act) in the difference between imperfect and aorist, and in that between present and aorist imperative and subjunctive, but it has also developed further along the same lines in the analogous new creation of two futures, one of duration and one of simplex (point) act; thus:

		Duration and repetition.	Simplex act (Point action).
Tenses.	Present.	Present.	
	Past.	Imperfect.	Aorist.
	Future.	Future present (*continuum*).	Future aorist (*absolutum*).
Moods.	Timeless.	Present subjunctive.	Aorist subjunctive.
		Present imperative.	Aorist imperative.

For the usage of these forms, *v.* § 186 ff.

§ 181. The *verb infinite* is represented by only two *participles*, a present active and a perfect passive. For fragments of other participial formation, *v. seq.*

There is *no infinitive* in modern Greek. Its place is usually taken by *νὰ* with the subjunctive (*v.* § 262), or, less commonly, by abstract verbal nouns (*v.* especially § 104).

M. Gk. has lost heavily in the department of the participles and the infinitives. A very serious loss is the complete extinction of the infinitive through a process the germs of which are already apparent in the beginning of our era (in the language of the New Testament).

[1] [Ger.] *Aktionsart.*

It is a remarkable fact that other languages of the Balkan Peninsula (Bulgarian, Albanian, Roumanian) also share in this loss. The infinitive survives as a living form only in the Pontic dialects. Elsewhere it is preserved merely in stereotyped shape in certain compound verbal forms (for which *v.* § 227, n. 1) and in a few substantives (τὸ φαγί "eating, repast" = τὸ φαγεῖν, τὸ φιλί "the kiss" = τὸ φιλεῖν, *v.* § 97, 1).

§ 182. *Augment.* Verbs—whether simple or composite —beginning with a consonant regularly prefix an augment, *i.e.* the vowel ἐ-, to the historic tenses (imperfect and aorist) of the indicative : γράφω "write" aor. ἔγραψα "I wrote," γυρίζω "turn" aor. ἐγύρισα "I turned," πηγαίνω "go" imperf. ἐπήγαινα "I went," φοβοῦμαι "fear" aor. ἐφοβήθηκα "I feared," μαγερεύω "cook" imperf. ἐμαγέρευε "he cooked," ξεφυτρώνω "shoot forth" aor. ἐξεφύτρωσα "I shot forth," καθίζω "sit" aor. ἐκάθισα "I sat," καταλαβαίνω "understand" aor. ἐκατάλαβα "I understood," κατεβαίνω "descend" aor. ἐκατέβηκα "I descended," περιμένω "await" imperf. ἐπερίμενα "I was waiting," προσέχω "take heed" aor. ἐπρόσεξα "I took heed," κατέχω (in dialects) "know" imperf. ἐκάτεχα "I knew," καλοπερνῶ "live well" aor. ἐκαλοπέρασα "I lived well."

Usually the augment is employed when the accent would fall upon it; thus in cases like ἔγραψα fr. γράφω, ἔδωκα aor. fr. δίδω "give," ἔβαλα aor. fr. βάλλω "place, lay," ἔμαθα aor. fr. μαθαίνω "learn," ἔστειλα aor. fr. στέλνω "send," ἔφυγα aor. fr. φεύγω "flee, depart," etc. On the other hand (when the accent would not fall upon the augment if used) the augment may be omitted : γράψαμε "we wrote," βάλαμε "we laid," βαστοῦσα imperf. "I was carrying"; and in polysyllabic verbs : γύρισα, στενάσανε "they groaned," φοβήθηκα, φταρμίστηκα (aor. fr. φταρμίζομαι "sneeze"), ξέφυγα (ξεφεύγω "escape"), ξόρισα (ξορίζω "exile"), κατάλαβα, κατέβηκα, στραβοπάτησα (στραβοπατῶ "make a false step"), etc.

1. No uniform rule can be laid down, because the augment is treated differently in different regions. Southern Greek, *i.e.* the dialects which best represent the common vernacular, shows most regularity in prefixing the augment especially to words of two syllables. In many regions the augment is always employed, in others (in the North) it is avoided in verbs of more than two syllables. The augment is easier omitted the farther the accent is removed from it : *e.g.* σκοτώνω "kill" aor. ἐσκότωσα "I killed," σκοτωθήκανε 3rd pl. aor. pass. "they were killed."

2. The augment is not so essential a factor in m. Gk. as it was in the ancient language. Even in forms like ἔδωκα it disappears in *liaison*; *cf.* τό 'δωκα = τὸ ἔδωκα, τοῦ 'στειλα = τοῦ ἔστειλα : the e must disappear after preceding a, o, u, according to the laws of word *liaison* (§ 11). In Lesbos and elsewhere δῶκα = ἔδωκα (cf. also δέκεν, TEXTS II. 13. c) takes absolutely no augment.

The augment having thus become practically negligible as a sign of tense, augmented forms were often generalised, *i.e.*, for example, (τὸν) ἐκάνω could be used beside κάνω "I make," etc. κατεβαίνω and ἀνεβαίνω "I go down, go up," are quite common. Note, further, ἀνεζητῶ "I seek, inquire after" and (TEXTS II. b. 6) συνεπνίγω "choke." The very common verbal preposition ξε-, a. Gk. ξ-, has come from augmented forms : *e.g.* a. Gk. ἐκφεύγω—aor. ἐξέφυγον = m. Gk. ξεφεύγω—(ἐ)ξέφυγα. The augment has penetrated even into substantival derivatives : *e.g.* κατεβασιά "catarrh" (lit. "what runs down").

§ 183. Verbs beginning with a vowel as a rule undergo no change for augment : ἀκούω "hear" aor. ἄκουσα, ἀργῶ "delay" aor. ἄργησα, ἀφήνω "leave" aor. ἄφησα, ἀνεβαίνω "ascend" aor. ἀνέβηκα, ἐγγίζω "touch" aor. ἔγγιξα, ἐρπίζω "hope" aor. ἔρπισα, αἰστάνομαι "perceive" imperf. αἰστανόμουνα, ὀμώνω "swear" aor. ὄμοσα, ὀνομάζω "name" aor. ὀνόμασα (also spelled ὤμοσα, ὠνόμασα). Only a few verbs beginning with ἐ- give preterite forms with an i (written εἰ- or ἠ-) : ἔχω "have" εἶχα, ἔρχομαι "come" aor. ἦρθα, imperf. ἤρχουμουν and ἔρχουμουν, εὐρίσκω (βρίσκω) "find" aor. ηὗρα (but imperf. εὕρισκα). Here also the defective aorists εἶδα "I saw" and εἶπα "I spoke."

Also a few verbs beginning with a consonant augment with ἠ- instead of ἐ- ; thus, θέλω "wish, will" ἤθελα, ξέρω (ἠξέρω) "know" ἤξερα, πίνω "drink" ἤπια, and less frequently φέρνω "bear" ἤφερα.

1. Especially in the Aegean Islands the augment i (ἠ-), instead of ἐ-, after the model of the verbs just given, has become practically the rule : ἤφαγα "I ate," ἤκαμα "I made," ἤλαβα "I received," ἤπαιζα "I played," ἤπιασα "I took," ἤφυ(γ)α "I went away," ἤβγαλα "I took out," ἠκάθουμουν "I sat," ἠπρόσταξα "I commanded," etc., for the usual ἔφαγα, ἔκαμα, etc.

2. Verbs beginning with a- take likewise occasionally an augment in ἠ- (ἤκουσα = ἄκουσα, ἠγάπησα = ἀγάπησα, ἤνοιξα = ἄνοιξα, ἤφηκα = ἄφηκα "I discharged," etc.), or (in Asia Minor especially and in the islands on the coast of Asia Minor) instead of retaining the a- in the historic tenses they take an ἐ- like verbs beginning with a consonant (*cf.* ἔκσα = ἄκουσα, ἐπέντεσα = ἀπάντησα in Pontus, ἐρχίνισα = ἀρχίνισα in Ios). Finally, the proximity of i and e pro-

duced a form like ἔπε beside εἶπε and ἔδανε beside εἴδανε (Ios, v.
TEXTS III. 5).

§ 184. Reduplication entirely disappeared with the extinction of the old perfect: it is wanting also in the perfect
participle passive (§ 209 ff.).

§ 185. The modern Greek verb possesses for active and
passive separate personal endings which are attached to the
tense stem. All the terminations may be divided into two
groups, present and preterite: in addition to which there is
also a separate termination for the 2nd sing. imperative.
The present terminations are valid for the present and for all
moods, the preterite for the imperfect indicative and for all
aorists. For details on the terminations, *cf.* § 213 ff. on the
inflexion of the verb.

1. The m. Gk. endings correspond essentially to those of a. Gk.,
although they have undergone much modification in details. The
distinction between primary and secondary endings is maintained
(and as in a. Gk. many endings are alike in form). The uniform
declension of *all* aorists and imperfects (apart from dialect variations)
is especially remarkable.
2. The dual has entirely disappeared, as in the noun.

THE USE OF TENSE AND MOOD.

Present and Aorist Stem.

§ 186. The distinction between present and aorist action
(*Aktionsart*) has been carried further than in a. Gk. in the
formation of two futures (§ 180). Even the *present indicative*, at least in the verb πηγαίνω and πάγω " go,"
indicates the beginning of such a distinction, *i.e.* the creation
of a separate " *aorist present* " (πάγω); thus, πηγαίνομε " we
keep going, go again and again, go without resting," in
contrast to πάμε σπίτι " we are going (go) home " (single
act). Cf., further, ὁ βασιλέας παγαίνει κάθε νύχτα σ' αὐτῆς
τῆς φτωχῆς τὸ σπίτι (TEXTS III. 4) " the king *keeps going every*
night to the house of this poor girl," ποῦ παγαίνεις " whither
do you (continue to) go ? " but πάγει ἡ πέρδικα νὰ πιῇ (I. a.
16) " the partridge goes to drink " (this time, " point " action),
or στὸ σπίτι μου πηγαίνω, πάγω νὰ πάρω τὸ ψωμί (I. a. 9),
" I am on my way home, I am going to fetch bread." Or it
may be said of a dried up fountain τὸ νερὸ πάει " the water

is *gone* (goes, and does not come again)." Of course this distinction between πηγαίνω and πάγω is not consistently maintained; *cf. e.g.* πηγαίνει στὸν πατέρα της καὶ τοῦ λέει (I. d. 1) " she goes to her father and says to him." As a rule the present combines *cursive* (durative, continuous, etc.) and *aorist* action. The latter is specially prominent in the historic present, which stands in vivid narrative beside an aorist as an equivalent: *e.g.* τὸ παιδὶ μπῆκε μέσα, βρίσκει τὸν Ἀράπη " the child came in, (and) *finds* the Arab (Moor)," στὴ φωτιὰ χουμάει, ἔκοψε Τούρκους ἄπειρους " into the fire he *rushes*, (and) slew countless Turks." The association of καὶ λέει " and says " with a preceding aorist is very common (just as λέει " says he " in parenthesis).

1. The vivid effect in the course of a narrative secured by the interchange of historic present and aorist is seen, *e.g.*, in TEXTS I. a. 9, l. 16 ff. (φέρνει " brings out," ἀβροντάει " casts down "); but the present serves also for vivid description of a situation, the central event being related in the aorist; *cf.* TEXTS II. a. 14, strophe 9.

2. The present sometimes has a future meaning when the connection leaves no doubt as to the *time*, as in κάνε τὸ πρῶτα κ᾽ ὕστερα βλέπουμε " do it first and then we (shall) see," or αὔριο τὸ πρωὶ περνῶ ἀπ᾽ τὸ σπίτι σας " early to-morrow morning I (will) go past your house."

3. In Cappadocia (Silli) under the influence of Turkish the present continuous is expressed in a peculiar way by the addition of κὶ κάσουμι, *i.e.* καὶ κάθομαι: *e.g.* ἔρχουμι κὶ κάσουμι " I *am going.*"

§ 187. The *present stem* presents an action in progress without regard to its beginning or to the result (cursive action), and thus is well adapted to portray the circumstances, the duration or repetition of an action. The *aorist stem* denotes a single action complete in itself or conceived as complete and as a whole (" punctiliar " [1] action), and also the beginning (initial point) or the result (final point) of an action (terminative, or ingressive and effective action). The m. Gk. vernacular shows a decided preference—especially in the subjunctive (future) and imperative—for the aorist stem against the present.

In contrast to the classical Greek we find already in that of the New Testament a decided preference for both the indicative and subjunctive aorist, so that the process had already set in in the Hellenistic vernacular.

[1] The translator has borrowed this term from Moulton's *Gram. of N.T. Gk.*, vol. i. 3rd ed. p. 109 (T. & T. Clark), the word " punctual " having been already assigned its duties in English.

§ 188. The *Imperfect* is employed :

1. In a narrative to emphasise that an action (not in itself momentaneous) or an occurrence (of the same kind) was conceived as in progress, the result of the action being entirely left out of question : *e.g.* νά τον καὶ κατέβαινε τσοὺ κάμπους καβελλάρις "behold, there was coming a knight down over the fields" (TEXTS I. a. 8), ἐξεψυχοῦσε ἀπὸ ἀγάπη (II. b. 3) "he was pining away of love," τὴν τελευταία της πνοὴ ὁ Χάρος ἐροφοῦσε (II. a. 21) "Charon was about to sip her last breath," ἔδενε ὅλα τὰ δέντρα μὲ πέτσες (I. d. 3) "he was engaged binding all the trees with cords," ἡ δουλειὰ πάγαινε καλά "the work was progressing excellently," ἐζούσανε καλά "they were living well," ἀγαποῦσα ἕνα νέον καὶ τὸν ἀγαπῶ πολύ "I was in love with a youth and I love him dearly (still)," ἐσταμάτησε κ' ἐπερίμενε "he stopped and kept waiting," τρεῖς ὥρες ἐπολέμαε "he was struggling three hours."

The imperfect is therefore to be employed to represent an action as a situation which forms the background or consequence of an event : βροντοῦσε καὶ ἄστραφτε ἐχτὲς καὶ ὅμως περπατήσαμε πολλὴ ὥρα "there was thundering and lightning yesterday, but nevertheless we took a long walk," μιὰ μέρα ἔβγαινε πάλι ἡ βασιλοπούλα, etc. (II. b. 4) "one day the princess again came forth . . .," ἔφκειακαν ἕνα παλάτι καὶ ζοῦσαν μαζί "they built a palace and lived together"; and especially when a circumstance (or property) is narrated : *e.g.* δὲν ἤξευρα "I was not aware," μία φορὰ ἤτανε ἕνας βασιλέας "once there was a king," ἐκεῖ ἐκαθότανε οἱ δράκοι "there dwelt (were dwelling) the monsters," τὸν ἔλεγαν Λάζαρο "his name was (they called him) L.," ἀπολάει τὸ λαγό, ὁ ὁποῖος ἔτρεχε πολύ (TEXTS I. c. 6) "he lets go the hare which ran (had the property of running) well." From the nature of such instances the imperfect is relatively more common in accessory clauses.

Note, ἔλεγε in πῆγ' ἡ γάτα καὶ σγουροτρίβονταν καὶ μιαούριζε καὶ τοῦ ἔλεγε (TEXTS I. d. 2) is a kind of attraction to the preceding descriptive imperfects.

2. The Imperfect also calls attention (*a*) to the attempt at, or non-completion of, an action, and (*b*) the duration of an action : (*a*) τοῦ ἔδινε παράδες νὰ τὸν ἀφήσῃ μέσα "he tried (wished) to give him money to allow him inside," κανένας δὲν

ἀνέβαινε ποτὲ στὴν κορφὴ τοῦ βράχου (TEXTS II. b. 5) " nobody
ever attempted (succeeded) to climb to the summit of the
rock," δὲν ἐκινοῦσε τὸ καράβι " the boat would not move,"
δὲν ἀνεγνώριζε " he could not perceive," δὲν τὸν ἄφηνε νὰ 'μπῇ
μέσα (I. d. 5) " he refused to allow him to come in " (but he
came in all the same); (b) τοὺς ἔβριζε (I. a. 2) " he kept
scolding them," σ' ἐκύτταζα 'ναχόρταγα κ' ἐρώταγα (I. a. 19)
" I was gazing insatiably upon thee and kept asking," ἐγροίκουνα τὰ κάλλη σου (I. a. 24. 12) " I was (always) hearing of
thy fairness," πλούταινε " he kept growing richer."

This meaning of the imperf. can be strengthened by the repetition
of the verb : e.g. τὴν ἐπήγαινε τὴν ἐπήγαινε " he kept leading her still
farther" ("lead and lead"), δούλευε δούλευε "he kept working
without interruption."

3. Hence (from 2) arises the employment of the
imperfect to present that which was customary or the
repetition of an occurrence : μᾶς ἔβγαζε περίπατο, μᾶς
ἐμάθαινε (TEXTS II. b. 2) " he used to take us out for a walk
and used to instruct us," τῆς ἔλεαν ὅλοι " they all used to
tell her," τὸν ἐρώτα (I. a. 2) " he asked him again and again,"
δομέστικοι τὸν διώχνανε (II. b. 4) " the courtiers used to
chase him," στὰ σκοτεινὰ τὴν ἔλουζες (I. a. 11) " you used to
wash her in the dark." For the imperf. in temporal clauses,
cf. §§ 272–275.

Note TEXTS I. d. 1, σὰν ἔφτασε στὸ σπίτι του, τὸν ρώταγαν οἱ
τσιούπρες του "when he came home his daughters asked him (the
one after the other)."

§ 189. The *Aorist Indicative* is employed:

1. To portray simply an action or occurrence of the
past ; it is therefore the usual tense in progressive narrative,
numerous instances of which are supplied by every narrative.
The action is not necessarily a punctiliar or uniform act
(like, e.g., ἦρθε " he came," ἐπῆγε " he departed "), it may
extend over any length of time, and may even consist in a
repetition of occurrences : ἔμειν' ὁ Διάκος στὴ φωτιά " D.
remained in the fire," ἔζησαν ὅλη τὴ ζωή τους καλά " they
lived well their whole life," γιὰ μιὰν ἄνοιξι . . . ἐτραγούδησε
τ' ἀηδόνι (II. a. 12) " throughout a whole springtime sang
the nightingale." When a verb is colourless in regard to its
kind of action (*Aktionsart*) the aorist often lends it a

punctiliar (terminative) meaning, *i.e.* designates the initial or final point of the action : *e.g.* τὸ καράβι κίνησε " the boat began to move," ἀρρώστησα " I became sick," κολύμπησε στὸ νερό " he dived into the water," ἔφυγε " he went away," ἐπῆγε " he departed," ἔφερε " he brought," ἐπῆρε " he took away " or " fetched," ἔπεσαν τὰ λουλούδια " the flowers fell," ἐμαύρισε " it grew black."

2. The aorist indic. denotes an action just completed the effect of which still continues into the present. Here German employs the perfect or present, and English also the perfect or present, or more rarely the preterite : *e.g.* ἔμαθα " I (have) learned" and so " know," τὰ ἔφερα " I (have) brought them " and so " have them with me," ἔτσι θέλησε ὁ θεός "so God willed, so is it," τὸ καταφέραμε " we (have) attained it," ὁ 'Απρίλις ἔφτασε " April came " and so " is here," νύχτωσε " it became night, night is come," ἔπαψαν τὰ παγωτιά "the frost ceased, is past," πείνασα " I grew hungry," " am hungry still," χάθηκα " I am undone," ἄκουσες " did you hear ? do you hear ? " In cases like φέρνω " here I bring," ἀκούς " do you hear ? " the present may also be employed, but in other cases like παύουν τὰ παγωτιά the present would not properly express the idea of completion, since there is no " aorist " present.

1. The idea of completion and of the effect of an action is sometimes re-enforced by composition with ἀπο- : *e.g.* ἀπόφαγα " I (have) finished eating, ate up," τὸ εἶδε καὶ τὸ ἀπόειδε " he saw it, and saw it perfectly (only too well) " ; *cf.* § 159, 1.

2. Even completion in the immediate future (and so the function of an aorist present or a future perfect) may be expressed by the aorist, provided the connection leaves no ambiguity about the time intended (*cf.* § 186, n. 2) : *e.g.* κι ἂν μὲ σουβλίσετε, ἕνας Γραικὸς ἐχάθη (TEXTS I. a. 2) "even if you impale me only one Greek perishes (shall have perished)." Sometimes a πάει is placed immediately before such an aorist.

§ 190. In the present and aorist subjunctive or imperative, as well as in the two futures, this distinction of kind of action (*Aktionsart*) is similarly maintained ; examples for the imperative, *v.* § 196 ; for the futures, § 191.

1. The *Present Subjunctive* denotes a timeless action (occurrence, etc.) depicted in progress, either durative or repeated : δὲν εἶμ' ἄξιος κ' ἐγὼ τέτοιο ῥόδο νὰ φορῶ (TEXTS II. a. 12) " I am not worthy to bear such a rose," τῆς μαν-

νούλας σου ἡ εὐχὴ νά 'ναι γιὰ φυλαχτό σου, νὰ μὴ σὲ πιάνῃ βάσκαμα (I. a. 14), " thy mother's prayer be thy protection that witchcraft touch thee not," δὲ μοῦ δίδ' ὁ νοῦς μου πλιὸ νὰ φεύγω (I. a. 24. 12) " my reason allows me no longer to flee (think of flight)," τοῦ εἶπαν οἱ δράκοι νὰ πηγαίνουν μὲ τὴν ἀράδα γιὰ νερό " the *draki* said to him they should go for water by turns," δὲ μπορῶ κάθε μέρα νὰ ἔρχωμαι νὰ παίρνω νερό " I cannot come every day to fetch water."

νά with the pres. subj. is always used after ἀρχίζω (ἀρχινῶ, etc.) " begin " ; as, ἀρχίνισαν νὰ τὴν ρωτοῦν " they commenced to question her," ἀρχίζεις νὰ γίνεσαι σπλαχνική " thou beginnest to be merciful." If the paratactic construction with καί (§ 261) is preferred to νά, then the imperf. must follow ; as, ἀρχίρησε ὁ γιατρὸς κ' ἔλεγε τὸ παραμύθι " the doctor began to tell the fable." Note also the expressions νὰ τὰ κοντολο(γ)οῦμε, νὰ μὴν τὰ μακραίνουμε " in a word, to put it briefly."

2. The *Aorist Subjunctive* denotes a single action complete in itself or conceived as a whole, including, of course, the initial and the final point: λαχταρῶ νὰ τρέξω στὴν ἀγκάλη σου " I long to run into thy embrace," σὲ παρακαλῶ νὰ καθίσῃς " I beg you to take a seat," κάλλιο νὰ σκάσω παρὰ νὰ μὴ σᾶς θυμηθῶ " 'twere better that I perish than not think of thee (forget thee)," ξέρει νὰ ζήσῃ μὲ τιμή " he knows how to live honourably," τοῦ εἶπε νὰ περβατήσῃ τρεῖς ὥρες (TEXTS I. d. 1) " he told him to walk three hours," τὸ ζαλίκι . . . δὲν μπορούσα νὰ σηκώσω " I was not able to lift the burden," πρέπει νὰ φορέσῃς, νὰ βγάλῃς τὸ παλτό " you must put on, put off, your cloak." Note TEXTS II. b. 4, κατέβαινε στὴν Πόλι νὰ μοιράσῃ ἐλεημοσύνες " she used to go down to the city to distribute alms."

The usages under 1 and 2 may be brought out more clearly in some contrasted examples in which the present and the aorist stem may be viewed in proximity : ἃ δὲν ξέρεις κάτιτι, πρέπει νὰ ρωτᾷς ἄλλους " whenever (every time) you don't know anything you must ask others," and πρέπει νὰ ἐρωτήσῃς ἄλλονε γιὰ τὸ πρᾶμα αὐτό " you must ask (once) somebody about this (definite) matter " ; ἀπὸ τώρα θέλω νὰ τρώγω σ' ἄλλο ξενοδοχεῖο " henceforth I wish to eat (as often as I eat) in another hotel," and σὲ παρακαλῶ νὰ φᾶς αὔριο στὸ σπίτι μου " I request you to dine at my house to-morrow " ; τὸ ἄκουσε χωρὶς νὰ καταλαβαίνῃ " he heard it without being able to understand it," and χωρὶς νὰ καταλάβῃ " without grasping it " ; δὲ μπορῶ πλιὸ νὰ ἐλπίζω " I can no longer indulge in hopes," and δὲ μπορῶ πλιὸ νὰ ἐλπίσω " I can no longer hope at all " ; δὲ θέλω νὰ τόνε βλέπω " I don't want to see him (have him before my eyes)," and θέλω νὰ τόνε 'δῶ "I want to see him (catch one glimpse)," γένεσαι Τούρκος, τὴν πίστι σου ν' ἀλλάξῃς, νὰ προσκυνᾷς εἰς τὸ τζαμί; (I. a. 2) "are you turning Turk in order to change (once for all) your faith, and (henceforth) pray in the mosque?" παρακάλεσε τὸν πατέρα της νὰ τσ' δώσῃ κ' ἕναν Ἀράπη νὰ τὸν στέλνῃ ὅπου θέλει (I. d. 2) "she begged her father to give (single act) her a Moor whom she might (at any time) send wherever she wished." Cf., further, TEXTS II. a. 10 for the marked interchange of both kinds of action, or I. a. 17 for the two presents νὰ σκώνω τὰ ματάκια μου, νὰ ρίχν' ἀστροπελέκια (practically "I will play the coquette with my eyes") among pure aorists, all of which have "effective," or "terminative," value.

TEXTS I. a. 8. 14 f. (where νὰ χαροῦν and νὰ χαίρουνται are used in proximity and under like conditions) shows that sometimes it depends merely on the caprice of the speaker how he will formulate his ideas.

§ 191. The usage of the two *Futures* is already clear from the fundamental distinction of the aorist and the present stem discussed in the above paragraphs:

1. θανὰ σοῦ στέλνω μάλαμα (TEXTS I. a. 14) " I will (from time to time) send you gold," συχνὰ συχνὰ θὰ ροβολᾶν στοὺς κάμπους . . . νὰ πιάνουν Τούρκους "full oft will they descend to the plains (again and again) to seize the Turks."

The future continuous (fut. pres.) has sometimes potential value: *e.g.* ποιὸς θὰ εἶναι (τάχα); "who will (might) it (perhaps) be?" ποιὸς θὰ κτυπᾷ; (II. b. 3) "who can be knocking?" The aoristic future here would give no sense.

2. Γραικὸς θανὰ πεθάνω " a Greek will I die," θὰ φύγω, θὰ ξενιτευτῶ " I will depart, I will go abroad," ἡ ἀλήθεια θὰ μείνῃ ἀλήθεια (II. b. 1) " truth will remain truth (till the end of time)," πάντα θὰ σᾶς καταδικάσῃ ἡ ἐπιστήμη (II. b. 1) " always will science condemn you."

Cf., further, θὰ γυρίσουμε δυὸ τρεῖς χιλιάδες χρόνια πίσω καὶ θὰ περπατοῦμε στὴν ἀγορὰ νὰ ρωτοῦμε κτλ. (II. b. 2) "we shall turn back (one act) two or three thousand years and we shall pace over the agora (like our forefathers) in order to ask (in the usual way)," etc.; τὸ χειμῶνα θὰ πηγαίνω ταχτικὰ στὸ θέατρο "during winter I will go regularly to the theatre," but αὔριο θὰ πάω στὸ θέατρο "I will go to-morrow to the theatre."

§ 192. The relative stages of time are usually—as in a. Gk.—marked only by present, imperfect, or aorist and future, the new compound forms for pluperfect and future perfect (*fut. exactum*) are rather rarely employed; *cf.* § 229. In ordinary narrative the aor. indic. may have exactly the value of a pluperfect; cf. *e.g.* τί γιομάτισε (TEXTS II. a. 3)

9

"*had* dined." This usage of the *aorist* is almost general in
dependent clauses, and is the rule in temporal clauses, *v.*
§ 272, 1.

The Moods.

§ 193. The *Subjunctive* has its sphere principally in
secondary clauses, that is, dependent on conjunctions,
especially νά. Also in principal sentences it is usually distinguished by νά (neg. νὰ μή). The independent subjunctive
with νά has:

1. Deliberative (dubitative) force: τί νὰ γίνῃ; "what is
to happen? what must we do?" νὰ τὸ κάνω ἢ νὰ μὴν τὸ
κάνω; "shall I or shall I not do it?" τί νὰ σοῦ 'πῶ;
"what am I to say to thee?" τί νὰ τῆς εὐκηθοῦμε;
"what shall we wish her?" ὡς πότε, παλληκάρια, νὰ ζῶμεν
στὰ στενά; (TEXTS II. a. 1) "how long, boys, are we to live
in the passes?"

This subjunctive is closely akin to the potential (a. Gk. optative
with ἄν): *e.g.* ποιὸς νά 'ναι; "who might it be?" πῶς νὰ πάνω στὸν
ἀφέντη μου; "how can I go to my master?" τί νά 'χω; "what shall
I then have?" τί νὰ 'δῇς; "what can you possibly see?" γιατί νὰ μὲ
γελάσῃς; (I. a. 11. 22) "how can you laugh at me?" γιατί νὰ μὴν
ἐρθῆτε ἐχτές; "why then could you not come yesterday?" For
other forms of the potential, *cf.* §§ 191, 1 n., and 195.

2. Voluntative (in the 1st person): ν' ἀνοίξω
πραματευτάδικο "I wish to open a business," νὰ ἰδῶ (νὰ
ἰδοῦμε) "I (we) will (wish to) see." Very frequently it is
preceded by an encouraging γιά, ἔλα, σήκω, ἄϊντε, etc. "now
then!" "come!": *e.g.* γιὰ νὰ ἰδῶ "now then, I will see,"
ἔλα νὰ παίξωμε "come! let us play," γιά, ἔβγα νὰ παλέψωμε
"now come let us wrestle." ἄς is more frequently used
than νά; *v.* § 194, 2.

The conjunction is occasionally re-enforced by πά; as, ἐγὼ νὰ πὰ
σ' τὸ φέρω "I want to (will) bring it to you," νὰ πὰ πάρωμεν δά
(Chios) "we will fetch it"; this πά is a stereotyped 3rd sing. of
πά(γ)ω "I go."

3. Optative meaning: δόξα νά 'χῃ ὁ θεός "God be
praised (have the glory)," νὰ φυλάγεται κανεὶς ἀπ'
ἀνθρώπους ἀγενεῖς (II. a. 8), "may everybody be on his guard
against men of low birth," νὰ μὴ μᾶς πλακώσῃ τέτοιο κακό
"may such an evil not overtake us." It may be strengthened by the particles εἴθε, ἄμποτες, or μακάρι: *e.g.* εἴθε

(μακάρι) νὰ ζήσῃ χίλια χρόνια "may he live a thousand years."

A request (in the imperative) may be politely introduced by the optative expression (ἔτσι) νὰ ζήσῃς "may you live" = "be so kind," "kindly."

4. Imperative meaning, both in the 2nd and 3rd person : νὰ πᾶς χωρὶς ἄλλο "depart without fail," νὰ πάψῃς στὸ ἑξῆς "cease for the future," νὰ γράφετε τὴν ἐθνικὴ γλῶσσα "keep on writing your national language"; strengthened γιὰ (or σήκω, etc.) νὰ πῇς "come now, tell," ὁ νόμος νά 'ναι πρῶτος ὁδηγός "let the law be your first guide." In the 3rd sing. ἄς is more common; v. § 194, 2.

§ 194. The subjunctive without νά is used :

1. After μή(ν) as negative voluntative and as prohibitive (neg. imperat.) beside νὰ μή (§ 193) : e.g. μὴν τρέχουμε "we don't want to run," μὴ φοβᾶσαι "fear not," μὴν ἀφήνῃς τὸν Ἅγιο Βασίλι νὰ φύγῃ ἔτσι (TEXTS II. b. 3) "let not the holy B. so depart," μὴν κλαίς "weep not," μὴ λέγῃς "say not," μὴ φεύγῃς "go not away."

In cases like μὴ κλαίτε, μὴ σκοτώνετε (I. d. 2), μὴ φοβηθῆτε, μὴ πιστέψετε, etc., the imperat. and the subj. are identical in form. As a prohibitive the *aorist* subj. is on the whole less commonly used than the present.

2. With the particle ἄς (neg. ἄς μή) to denote the 1st person voluntative and the 3rd person imperative: ἄς 'διοῦμε "let us see," ἄς μὴν ἀπελπιζούμαστε "let us not doubt," ὁπόχει μάτια, ἄς βλέπῃ "who has eyes let him see," ἄς ἔρθῃ "let him, may he, come," ἄς ἰδοῦν "let them see." *Cf.* § 193. 2, 4.

This ἄς,—which corresponds to a. Gk. ἄφες (fr. ἀφίημι = ἀφήνω) "leave, allow," or to a. Gk. ἔασε—has sometimes purely *concessive* force : *e.g.* ἄς εἶναι "let it be (as far as I am concerned)," ἄς λένε "let them (have permission to) speak," and so is employed to form concessive clauses; v. § 278, 3.

3. In a few formal expressions like ὁ θεὸς φυλάξῃ "God forbid," and with the adverb ἴσως "perhaps"; as, ἴσως βροῦμε "perhaps we may find" beside ἴσως νὰ (also θὰ) βροῦμε (but ἴσως σοῦ εἶπε "perhaps he told you").

Note also ἔλα μὲ πλερώῃς (TEXTS III. 9) "now then, pay me," ἀργὰ ντυθῇ (I. a. 12) "let her dress slowly" (followed below in this connection by νά with subj.) and ἄμε τσαὶ μάννα γιὸ φιλήσῃ κτλ. (III. 5) "well, let the mother kiss her son," etc.

§ 195. The *Imperfect* has modal force in expressions like ἔπρεπε "it must (have)," "was fitting," ἤθελα (νὰ ξέρω) "I should like to (know)," ταίριαζε "it was proper, becoming," μ᾽ ἔφτανε "it sufficed me," ἔλεγες "you might have said," νόμιζες "you would think, have thought" (but λές "you might say, mean"). The imperfect is converted to conditional (v. § 230) by taking θά, etc.; for unreal conditional clauses, v. § 277, 4. An impossible (unreal) wish is expressed by (μακάρι or ἄμποτες) νά "O that," or by ἄς and the imperfect: e.g. (μακάρι) νὰ ἤμουν πλούσιος "oh that I were only rich," νὰ μπορούσα "if I only could," ἄς τό 'λεγες "had you but said so," νὰ μ᾽ ἄκουε "would that he could hear me," ἄς εἴχαμε παράδες "would that we had money," νὰ (ἄς) μᾶς ἔκαμναν τὴ χαρά "oh that they had given us joy," νὰ μὴν εἶχα γεννηθῇ "would I had not been born." Moreover, the *imperfect* or *aorist* may be converted by νά to past potentials in questions and exclamations: νὰ γελάστηκα; "could I have deceived myself?" νὰ μὴν ἦρθε ὁ Χάρος στὸ σπιτικό σας; "is it possible that Death entered not thy house?" νὰ μὴν ἤσουνα μεθυσμένος; "were you not (possibly) drunk?" πόσες μέρες νὰ ἤταν; "how many days might it be?" ποῦ νὰ πῆγε; "where can he have gone?" τί νά 'καναν; "what could they have done?" ποῦ νά 'γλιπις ἱκεῖ πούπουλου; (III. 11) "how could you see a multitude there?" Finally, the probability of an occurrence in the past is expressed by θά with the *aorist* indic.; thus, θὰ τό 'κανε "he will, of course, have done it."

Sometimes the last mentioned mode of expression is extended to an action completed in the future (cf. § 189, n. 2): e.g. τί θὰ συνέβη, πρῶτα νὰ στοχαστῆς (TEXTS I. b. 14) "consider first what will have happened."

§ 196. The usage of the aor. and pres. *Imperative* (2nd sing. and pl.) is apparent from the following examples:

1. πά(γ)αινε στὸ καλό "go to success" = "farewell," τοῦτο βλέπε "look (often) at this," σώπα "keep still," ξύπνα "keep awake," στέκα "keep standing."

Notice, however, that the imperatives in -α (τρέχα "run," φεύγα "get off," etc., v. § 218, n. 2), no doubt affected by ἔλα, take also aoristic force.

2. (γιὰ) ἰδές "just look," στάσου "stop," ἄφσε γειά "say good-bye," μεῖνε "stay," περβάτησε (I. a. 11) "get started." And even an action which in its nature is durative or repeated may be summed up into a whole by the aor. imperat.: χαρῆτε τούτην τὴ ζωή "enjoy this life," θυμήσου με "think of me (to the last)," μὲ τὸ δικό σου φάγε καὶ πιὲ καὶ πραγματειὰ μὴ κάμνῃς (I. b. 5) "with thy neighbour eat and drink together, but do no business (let the good fellowship cease in money matters)."

Compare, further, φύτεψε τρανταφυλλιά κτλ. καὶ πότιζέ τα ζάχαρι (I. a. 4) "plant a rose tree . . . and keep nourishing it with sugar"; γράφε μου ταχτικά "write me regularly," and γράψε μου, πότε θὰ 'ρθῇς "write me when you are coming"; πίνετε κρασί "drink wine (from time to time)," and πιέτε ἕνα κρασάκι "drink (now) a little glass of wine."

STEM FORMATION OF VERBS.

§ 197. Two stems of the verb must be taken into account in the formation of tense, the present and the aorist stem. The former is simply that part of the verb which is left when the -ω (or -ομαι in the middle) of the 1st pers. sing. pres. is stripped off; for the latter we strip off -σα or -α (1st pers. sing.) of the aorist.

From the present stem are formed the present and imperfect tenses with their moods and the future present (*continuum*); from the aorist stem are formed the aorist tense (active) in its different moods (subjunctive and imperative) and the future absolute (aor. future). For the compound tenses, *v.* § 223 ff.

The stem formation of the aor. pass. and the perfect participle pass. is in most cases identical with that of the aor. active; for details, *v.* §§ 205 ff., 209 ff.

§ 198. According to the varieties of the present and the aorist forms, verbs may be classified as follows:

	Present stem.	Aorist stem.	Aorist form.

I. Barytones (in -ω):

1. Labial.
   (*a*) simple labial: π, μπ, v (vз), φ
   (*b*) labial + -τω (-φτω) or -νω (-φνω)

labial + σ = ψ

Present stem.	Aorist stem.	Aorist form.
2. Guttural.		
(a) simple guttural: κ, γγ, γ, χ	guttural	+σ = ξ
(b) guttural + -τω or -νω (-χτω, -χνω)		
3. Dental.		
(a) simple dental: τ, δ, θ, σ, ζ (σσ)	dental or guttural	+σ = σ or ξ
(b) dental + -τω νω, (-στω, -ζνω)		
4. In -σκω	various	. . ±σ
5. Nasal or liquid.		
(a) radical μ, ν, λ, ρ + -(ν)ω	μ, ν, λ, ρ	non-sigmatic
(b) -αίνω	(a) minus -αίνω (β) -αν- or -ην-	
6. Vowel (a, e, i, o, u)+-νω . .	a, e, i, o, u	
II. Contracted verbs (in -ω̂):		+σ.
(a) in -ω̂	i, e, a	
(b) in -νω̂	a, i	
(c) semi-contracted	various	

The a. Gk. division of verbs into those in -ω and those in -μι holds no longer, as the latter class has disappeared in m. Gk., the verb εἶμαι "am" being the solitary survivor of the -μι verbs (v. § 224, 2). All the rest have passed over into one or other of the above present forms; thus, τίθημι became θέτω, ἵστημι became στήνω or στένω, ἵσταμαι became στέκω, δίδωμι became δίδω δίνω δώνω, κεῖμαι became κείτομαι,[1] κάθημαι became κάθομαι, κρέμαμαι became κρέμομαι. The verbs in -νυμι became verbs in -νω (but μίγνυμι became σμίγω, πήγνυμι became πήζω). Others have been lost or replaced by new verbs; thus, δύναμαι by (ἐ)μπορῶ (beside δύνομαι[2]), οἶδα by ξεύρω, φημί by λέγω or λαλῶ, πίμπλημι by γεμίζω, and so forth.

§ 199. Present Stems.

I. Barytones.

1. (a) In -πω (rare): βλέπω (also ἐβλέπω) "see," (ἐ)ντρέπομαι "am ashamed," πρέπει "it is becoming."

In -μπω (rare): λάμπω "shine."

In -φω: βάφω "dye," γράφω "write," ζίφω "press," θρέφω (τρέφω) "nourish," στρίφω "turn, twist," στρέφω "turn," καταστρέφω "destroy."

---

[1] κεῖται, TEXTS III. 13. c, is a solitary instance.

[2] δύναμαι, TEXTS I. a. 3, comes from the literary language.

In -βω : παύω " cease," κόβω " cut," νίβω " wasb," τρίβω " rub," κρύβω " hide," σκύβω " bow," γεύομαι " eat, try," ἀλείβω beside ἀλείφω " anoint."

Verbs in -εύω are very numerous : *e.g.* ἀρχινεύω "begin," βασιλεύω " set " (of sun), γυρεύω " seek," δουλεύω " work," κοντεύω " approach," μαζεύω " collect," πιστεύω " believe," σημαδεύω " mark," φιλεύω " greet, entertain," φυτεύω " plant," ψαρεύω " fish," τουρκεύω " turn (act) Turk," καβαλλικεύω " ride," κονεύω "stop, spend the night," μισεύω "start, depart on journey."

In the region of the Aegean with Crete (but not in Aegina) and in Cyprus these verbs end, not in -*vo* (-βω) but in *vʒo* (-βγω) ; thus, νίβγω, κόβγω, κρύβγω ; δουλεύγω, μαζεύγω, πιστεύγω, χορεύγω " dance," etc. (in Chios εύgω) ; ζεύγω " yoke " and φεύγω " flee " are formally identical with these, wherefore also ζεύω, φεύω, *e.g.* in Pontus.

These verbs appear in Bova in the form -*éguo* (*platéguo* " speak "), in Terra d' Otr. -*éo* (*pistéo*), in Zaconian -*éꝺgu* (*ꝺuléꝺgu*).

(*b*) -φτω : ἀνάφτω " light, kindle," ἀστράφτει " it lightens," κλέφτω " steal," πέφτω " fall " (irreg.), ράφτω " sew," σκάφτω " dig," σκέφτομαι " consider," χάφτω " am greedy for, gulp," σκοντάφτω and σκοντάφνω " stumble."

The partition between the forms of *a* and *b* is not consistently maintained ; many verbs take now the one and again the other mode of formation ; thus, γράφω and sometimes γράφτω, κάβ(γ)ω and καύτω (κάφτω) " burn," κλέβω, κλέφω and κλέφτω " steal," κόβ(γ)ω and κόφτω " cut," ράβγω and ράφτω " sew," σκάβ(γ)ω, σκάφω and σκάφτω " dig," etc.

2. (*a*) -κω : πλέκω " plait."

-γγω : σφίγγω " press together, squeeze," φέγγω " shine."

-γω : ἀνοίγω " open," ἀρμέγω " milk," λέγω " say," πνίγω " choke," σμίγω " blend, unite with," τυλίγω " envelop," φυλάγω " watch, beware."

-χω : βήχω " cough," βρέχω " moisten, make wet," δέχομαι " receive," ἔρχομαι " come," ἔχω " have," κατέχω (in dialects) " know, understand how," προσέχω " attend," τρέχω " run," ψάχω (by feeling) " search, feel."

(*b*) -χτω : δείχτω " show," διώχτω " pursue," ρίχτω " throw."

-χνω : ἀδράχνω " seize," δείχνω " show," διώχνω " pursue," ρίχνω = ρίχτω, σπρώχνω " push," ψάχνω = ψάχω.

1. On the interchange of -χτω and -χνω and of 2. a and b, *cf.* the note above ; -χνω is more common than -χτω. The form -κνω or -χνω

is specially wide-spread in Cappadocia: πλέκνω, δάκνω "bite," βήχνω, τρέχνω; there, too, φύγνω "flee."

2. Some verbs, which properly belong elsewhere, by the insertion of a γ (§ 23) fall into this class; thus, πλέ(γ)ω "sail," and φταί(γ)ω "am guilty" (for which also φταίχω).

3. (a) -τω: θέτω "place," κείτομαι "lie."

-θω: ἀλέθω "grind," ἀμπώθω "push," ἀναγνώθω "read," γνέθω "spin," κλώθω "spin," νοιώθω "notice, feel," πλάθω "form."

-δω: only in δίδω "give" (with its compounds), for which other forms are more common, v. 6.

-σω: ἀρέσω "please" (beside ἀρέζω and ἀρέγω, rarely ἀρέσκω; Texts I. d. 5, Syra).

-σσω: see following note.

-ζω: παίζω "play," σκούζω "shout," λούζω "bathe" (trans.), πήζω "become firm, curdle."

-άζω; these verbs are very numerous: βράζω "boil," διαβάζω "read," κράζω "cry," πράζω "do," σκάζω "explode," στάζω "drop," σφάζω "slay," τάζω "promise," προστάζω "command," φράζω "enclose," ἀγοράζω "buy," ἀλλάζω "exchange," ἀρπάζω "rob, seize," βαστάζω "endure, hold," διασκεδάζω "entertain," κυττάζω "behold," θαμάζω "admire," (ἐ)ξετάζω "prove," μοιράζω "divide," νυστάζω "fall asleep," πειράζω "tease," σκεπάζω "cover," σπουδάζω "study," στενάζω "sigh," τρομάζω "fear," φαντάζω "imagine," φωνάζω "cry, shout," ἀγκαλιάζω "embrace," βουλιάζω "sink" (trans. and intr.), βραδυάζω "it becomes evening," θυμιάζω "sprinkle with incense," κοπιάζω "try, take pains," λογιάζω "consider, meditate," ξελογιάζω "seduce," (ὁ)μοιάζω "resemble," πλαγιάζω "go to sleep," σιάζω "arrange," συννεφιάζω "becloud," φωλιάζω "dwell, nestle," χρειάζομαι "need," ὀρδινιάζω "command."

1. Many verbs in -ζω are transformations of a. Gk. verbs in -σσω (Att. -ττω); the latter present form occurs still in some regions, as in Crete and other Aegean Islands and in Cyprus; thus, πράσσω "do," τάσσω, ταράσσω, etc. Also κατανύσσομαι "am excited" belongs here.

-ίζω (-ύζω): καθίζω "sit," σκίζω "split," χτίζω "build, found," ἀντικρύζω "meet with," ἀξίζω "am worth, cost," ἀρμενίζω "vacillate, swing," ἀρχίζω "commence," γεμίζω "fill," γεματίζω "dine," γνωρίζω "know, recognise," γυρίζω "turn (back)," δακρύζω "weep," δανείζω "lend," ἐγγίζω

" touch," καλοτυχίζω " congratulate," κοκκινίζω " blush,"
νομίζω " think," ὁρίζω " command," πασκίζω " endeavour,"
σκορπίζω " scatter," σφυρίζω " hiss, whistle," τσακίζω " smash,"
(ὑ)βρίζω "insult," χαρίζω " bestow," ἀκουμπίζω " rely on,"
βιγλίζω " keep watch, lie in wait," κοστίζω " cost," σεργιανίζω
" go walking," ταμπακίζω " smoke tobacco."

2. -έζω (in dialects): ἀρέζω " please," εὐκαιρέζω "am at leisure,"
φορέζω " wear."

(b) rare: σκίζνω (Pontus) " split," βρίστω " find," βαρίστω
" strike " (cf. 4).

4. The present suffix -σκω is rare in the ordinary
language; besides the commonly used βρίσκω (εὑρίσκω, also
βρέσκω) " find," cf. also μνήσκω (also μνέσκω), ἀπομνήσκω =
(ἀπο)μένω " remain (behind)," ἀποθνήσκω " die " = ἀποθαίνω,
βόσκω "feed," πρήσκω " swell," βαρίσκω and βαρέσκω
" strike " (usually βαρῶ), χάσκω " gape." Cf. also ἀρέσκω, 3. a.

The usage is only locally further extended; thus, e.g., in Cyprus
the suffix -νίσκω is in vogue: πλυνίσκω = πλύνω, πλουτυνίσκω =
πλουτύνω, etc. In Pontus the suffix -σκω is commonly employed
to form the passive: e.g. ταγίζω "nourish," ταγίσκουμαι " am
nourished," but is also otherwise employed; as, λάσκουμαι (Texts III.
13. c) " I seek aimlessly."

5. (a) -μω: τρέμω " tremble," κρέμομαι " hang " (intr.).
-μνω: κάμνω (beside κάνω and κάμω) " make, do."
-νω: ἀπομένω " remain (over)," περιμένω or προσμένω
" expect, await," γίνομαι and γένομαι " become, take place,"
κρίνω and κρένω " speak " (also " judge "); -βαίνω " go,
march " in ἀνε-, κατε-, δια-, σε-βαίνω, βγαίνω " go out,"
μπαίνω " go in," γιαίνω " heal," ξαίνω and ξάνω " card wool,"
πεθαίνω (and ἀποθάνω) " die," φαίνομαι "appear " (" show myself ").

-λ(λ)ω: βάλλω " place, put, lay," βγάλλω " take out,"
προβάλλω " bring forward," ψάλλω " sing."

1. Instead of βάλλω, etc., we find also βάνω, βγάνω, καταβάνω
" cast down," and even βαίνω (Aegina), also βάζω, βγάζω. The latter
is really a different verb (a. Gk. βιβάζω), which has in meaning become
identical with βάλλω, βγάλλω (and from the same verb ἀνεβάζω "set
up," διαβάζω "read," [ἐ]μπάζω " bring in ").

-λνω: παραγγέλνω " order," στέλνω (also στέρνω according to § 31) " send," ψέλνω (= ψάλλω).

2. The ancient forms in -λλω are still to be found in those dialects that can enunciate double consonants; thus, *e.g.*, in Cyprus, Chios, Rhodes, and the surrounding islands, *v.* § 36.

-ρω: προφέρω "pronounce" (from the literary language), χαίρω and χαίρομαι "rejoice."

3. *Cf.* also ξεύρω, ξέρω "I know," and Italian loan-words like ἀρριβάρω (ριβάρω) "arrive," κουμπανιάρω "accompany," κουντραστάρω "go to meet," ξεμπαρκάρω "disembark," σερβίρω "serve," etc. But these verbs in the rest of their formation do not belong under this category.

-ρνω: δέρνω "whip," γδέρνω "flay," γέρνω "bow," ἀναγέρνω "search all over," παίρνω (in dialect also παίρω) "take, fetch," σέρνω (in Bova *sérro*) "draw," ἀνασέρνω "draw up," σπέρνω "sow," φέρνω "bring."

(*b*) Present suffix -αίνω: (*a*) with -αιν- vanishing in the aorist stem: λαβαίνω "obtain, get" (for which, however, παίρνω is more common), καταλαβαίνω "understand," ξαναλαβαίνω "acquire again," λαθαίνω "am concealed, escape notice," λαχαίνω "obtain by lot," μαθαίνω "learn, teach," πηγαίνω (and παγαίνω) "go," παθαίνω "suffer, endure," τυχαίνω "hit (get) by accident," ἀποτυχαίνω "have ill-luck," ἐπιτυχαίνω "am lucky."

Forms like καταλαμβάνω and μανθάνω belong to the literary language; only αἰστάνομαι has survived unaltered (but ἀσταίνουμι = *αἰσταίνομαι in Velv.).

(*β*) with -ν- also in the aorist stem: ἀνασαίνω "breathe," βαθουλαίνω "hollow, excavate," ζεσταίνω "make warm," μακραίνω "am prolix," μαραίνω "wither" (trans.), ξεθυμαίνω "give vent to (anger), subside," ξεραίνω "dry," πικραίνω "embitter," μεγαλαίνω "magnify," πλουταίνω "become rich," φτωχαίνω "become poor."

6. Vowel + νω.

πιάνω "seize, catch," φτάνω "arrive, attain," προφτάνω "overtake," φκειάνω φτειάνω "make," χάνω "lose," ἀμαρτάνω "commit sin," βυζάνω "suckle," δαγκάνω "bite."

δένω "bind," πλένω "wash," στένω (σταίνω) "place," κατασχένω "seize, appropriate," ἀβγαταίνω "multiply," ἀ(ὐ)ξαίνω "increase," (ξανα)βλασταίνω "shoot forth," κερδαίνω "gain," σωπαίνω "keep silent," χορταίνω "satisfy."

ἀφήνω "leave, allow," γδύνω "put off," ντύνω "put on," δίνω (also δίδω) "give," κλείνω "shut," λύνω "loose," πίνω "drink," ρύνω "pour in," σβήνω (spelled also σβύνω) " extinguish," χύνω "pour."

Verbs in -ώνω are quite numerous: ζώνω "gird," στρώνω "spread (out)," χώνω "penetrate," ὀμώνω "swear," ἁπλώνω "extend," γλυτώνω "release, rescue," διορθώνω "mend," "improve," κρυώνω "freeze," λυ̣ώνω "dissolve," μαλώνω "wrangle," πλερώνω "pay," σηκώνω "raise," σκοτώνω "slay," φορτώνω "burden, load," βουλώνω "seal, lock up."

1. Some verbs fluctuate between the present suffix -άνω, -αίνω (-ένω) and -ήνω (-ύνω); thus, βυζαίνω and βυζάνω "suckle," στήνω and στένω "put," ψήνω and ψένω "roast," ξύνω and ξένω "scrape," πλύνω and πλένω "wash." Occasionally also δώνω is employed for δίνω (in the region of the Aegean).

2. In the Cyprian dialect and wherever twin consonants are in vogue (§ 36) the suffix -νω becomes -ννω: πίννω "drink," πιάννω "seize," χάννω "lose," ξεχάννω "forget," πηαίννω (πααίννω) "go," σηκώννω "lift," φανερώννω "reveal."

3. The class in vowel + νω has supplanted many of the a. Gk. *verba pura* together with verbs in -μι (-νυμι) and the old contract verbs in -όω. The *verba pura* which have not taken this or another present suffix (like κλείνω, λούζω or λούνω, παλεύω = παλαίω "wrestle," φταίγω, etc.) have wholly or partly passed over into the conjugation of the contracted or semi-contracted verbs, *v.* II.

Interchange among various present forms for the same verb takes place not only within the same class but even between different classes; *cf. e.g.* the collateral forms συνάζω and συνάγω, πρήσκω and πρήζω, τινάζω and τινάγω, κερδαίνω, κερδεύω and κερδίζω, σιάνω and σιάζω, (ἐ)μπερδεύω "entangle" beside δένω "bind," νοιώνω beside νοιώθω, χορταίνω and χορτάζω, λούνω and λούζω, παγαίνω and πάνω, (ἐ)ξοδεύω and ξοδιάζω, μαζεύω and μαζώνω, ρίφτω and ρίχτω, θέτω, in Asia Minor θήκω θέχτω and τέκνω, βρίσκω βρίστω βρίχνω εὑρήκω, etc.

II. Contracted verbs: the stem vowel had already in ancient Greek mostly become blended with the present endings.

(*a*) In -ῶ: ἀγαπῶ "love," ἀπολῶ "let off," κυλῶ "roll," μεθῶ "am drunken," μηνῶ "announce," ρουφῶ "suck in," φιλῶ "kiss," βολεῖ "it is possible," παρηγορῶ "console," πονῶ "am grieved," παραπονοῦμαι "lament," φορῶ "wear (a garment)"; γελῶ "laugh," πετῶ "fly."

(*b*) In -νῶ: ἀπολνῶ "let off," γερνῶ "grow old," γυρνῶ "turn back," κερνῶ "pour in, give a drink," κρεμνῶ "hang," ξερνῶ "vomit," ξεχνῶ "forget," περνῶ "pass by," χαλνῶ "spoil," φυρνῶ (also φυρῶ) "lessen," σφαλνῶ "close, lock," καλνῶ "call."

(c) Half-contracted : ἀκούω "hear," καίω "burn," κλαίω "weep," κλείω "shut" (beside κλείνω), κρούω "knock, strike against," φταίω "am to blame," πλέω "sail."

For the peculiarities of the contracted verbs (e.g. the analytical forms in -άω for -ῶ) in the present system, see below, § 237 ff. Subdivision a contains the a. Gk. contract verbs in -άω, -έω ; b is a new formation (intermixture of verbs in -ῶ and -νω) ; c contains remains of the *verba pura*, for which also other forms (see above) are in use. Some of the *verba pura* have been converted completely into contracted verbs (of subdivision a) (cf. κυλῶ = a. Gk. κυλίω, ἀπολῶ = ἀπολύω, μηνῶ = μηνύω, μεθῶ = μεθύω) ; to the semi-contracted belong also some forms of the verbs λέ(γ)ω, πά(γ)ω, τρώ(γ)ω ; cf. § 251 f.

The contracted verbs have also quite frequently secondary forms like the barytones, just as *vice versa* the barytones take secondary forms similar to the contracted. The interchange is specially frequent between -άζω or -ίζω and -ῶ : e.g. βαστάζω and βαστῶ "stop," διψάζω and διψῶ "thirst," ξητῶ = ἐξετάζω, *elimonizo* (= ἀλησμονῶ) "forget" (Otranto), πεινάζω and πεινῶ "hunger," κρεμάζω, κρεμῶ and κρεμνῶ "hang," σκάζω and σκῶ "burst asunder," βογγίζω and βογγῶ "groan, roar," ξεσκίζω and ξεσκῶ "cleave," συλλογίζομαι and συλλογοῦμαι (συλλογειέμαι) "consider," χαιρετίζω and χαιρετῶ "greet," ψηφίζω and ψηφῶ "value, esteem," ἁρπάζω, ἁρπάχνω and ἁρπῶ "plunder" ; ξύνω (ξένω), ξύζω (Pontus) and ξῶ "scrape" ; ἀβγατῶ and ἀβγαταίνω "increase," ἀρχίζω (also ἀρχεύω), ἀρχινῶ, ἀρχινίζω (and ἀρχιρίζω) "begin" ; ξεχνῶ and ξεχάνω, θαρρῶ "think" and θαρρεύω "take courage," φιλῶ "kiss" and φιλεύω "welcome, regale," βαρίσκω, βαρῶ, βαραίνω "strike," βόσκω, βοσκίζω and βοσκάω "feed."

1. The verbs φωνάζω (ξεφωνίζω "cry out"), πειράζω "tease," ζωγραφίζω "paint," have generally supplanted the corresponding ancient contracted verbs. Similarly, in Asia Minor (Pontus and Cappadocia) μεθύζω = μεθῶ, σείζω = σείω "shake," ξύζω = ξύνω. In the Peloponnesus, on the other hand, verbs like φυλά(γ)ω have passed over into the conjugation of contracted verbs (v. also § 239).

2. *The interchange and variety of present systems assume much larger proportions in the different dialects than could be brought out in the above survey.*

The Aorist Stem.

(a) *Aorist Active.*

§ 200. The aorist active of a verb—so far as it is in use—is formed either with or without σ. Aorists are thus divided into sigmatic and non-sigmatic. The -σ- merges with the original stem ending into σ, ξ or ψ, so that all sigmatic aorist stems must end in one of these three sounds. The non-sigmatic aorist stems differ from the present stem (1) in the loss of the present formative suffix (παθ-αίνω : ἔπαθ-α, φέρ-νω : ἔφερ-α), or (2) by vowel change in the stem (φεύγω : ἔφυγα, μένω : ἔμεινα, ξεραίνω : ἐξέρανα), or (3) by the combination of both characteristics (στέλνω : ἔστειλα). Deponents have an aorist passive. For other less common formations, see below.

§ 201. The large majority of modern Greek verbs form their aorist with a σ. This holds, with few exceptions, of the present systems under I. 1, 2, 3, 4 (partly), 6, and II. The blending of the σ with the radical consonant produces the following aorist forms:

I. Barytones.

1. (*a* and *b*) -ψ- in place of the final radical of the present; thus, ἔλα(μ)ψα, ἄλειψα, ἔγραψα, ἔπαψα, ἔκοψα, ἔκρυψα, ἐπίστεψα, ἐτούρκεψα, ἐχόρεψα; ἄναψα, ἔσκαψα, etc.; ζεύγω gives ἔζεψα, and πρέπει irregularly ἐπρέπισε. The verbs βλέπω, πέφτω and φεύγω belong to a different aorist system; *v.* § 203, 2, 4, 5.

The spelling ἐδούλευσα for -ψα does not represent the real pronunciation, but arises from the literary language.

2. (*a* and *b*) -ξ- in place of the present final: ἔπλεξα, ἄνοιξα, ἐφύλαξα, ἔβρεξα, ἐπρόσεξα, ἔτρεξα, ἔψαξα; ἄδραξα, ἔδειξα, ἔρριξα, ἐδίωξα, etc. Notice especially ἔσφιξα from σφίγγω, ἔφεξα from φέγγω; for φεύγω, *v.* § 203, 2; for ζεύγω, *v.* 1. On ἔρχομαι, *v.* § 203, 5; ἔχω has no aorist, *v.* § 224, 1. On ὑπόσχομαι, *v.* § 205, I. 2.

3. (*a*) usually σ, though many verbs in -ζω give also ξ: ἔθεσα, ἄλεσα, ἔγνεσα, ἔνοιωσα, ἔπλασα, ἄρεσα (also ἄρεξα).

Verbs in -ζω : ἔπαιξα, ἔσκουξα, ἔπηξα, but ἔλουσα.

Verbs in -άζω (*a*) with aor. -σα : ἔβρασα, ἐδιάβασα

⟨ἀνέβασα, κατέβασα, ἔμπασα⟩, ἐξετάζω "prove," ἐξέτασα, καταδικάζω "condemn," καταδίκασα, ἔσκασα, ἀγόρασα, διασκέδασα, ἐθάμασα, ἐμοίρασα, ἐσκέπασα, ἀγκάλιασα, ἐκόπιασα and the majority in -ιάζω. (β) with aor. -ξα, the most commonly in use are: ἔκραξα, ἔταξα (ἐπρόσταξα), ἔφραξα, ἄλλαξα, ἅρπαξα, ἐβάσταξα, ἐβούλιαξα, ἐκύτταξα, ἐνύσταξα, ἐσπούδαξα, ἐπείραξα, ἐστέναξα, ἔσφαξα, ἐτρόμαξα, ἐφώναξα.

1. Many verbs show both forms; as, ἐξέταξα and ἐξέτασα, ἐκύτταξα and -σα, ἔμοιασα and ἔμοιαξα (μοιάζω "resemble").

Verbs in -ίζω (-ύζω) usually have -σα: ἔχτισα, ἔσκισα, ἐκάθισα or (usually) ἔκατσα, ἀντίκρυσα, ἄρχισα, ἐγνώρισα, ἐγύρισα, ἐδάκρυσα, ὅρισα (ὥρισα), ἐστόλισα, ἐτσάκισα, ἐχάρισα, ἐβίγλισα.

2. Here, too, some verbs take -ξα beside -σα: βρίζω "insult," ἔβριξα, ἀγγίζω "touch," ἄγγιξα, σφαλίζω "lock," ἐσφάλιξα, σφουγγίζω "dry off," ἐσφούγγιξα, σφυρίζω "whistle," ἐσφύριξα. Especially in dialect -αξα and -ιξα have been carried far beyond their original a. Gk. usage.

3. In North. Gk. dialects notice the expulsion of the unstressed ι; as, γύρσιν = ἐγύρισεν, γουνάτσιν = ἐγονάτισεν. In ἔκατσα = ἐκάθισα the expulsion of the ι is quite usual.

4. Verbs in -έζω give -εσα; as, φορέζω ἐφόρεσα; on ἀρέζω, see above.

3. (b) either like a (σκίζνω) or like the corresponding verbs of the following system.

4. Here belong πρήσκω ἔπρηξα, βαρίσκω (βαρέσκω) ἐβάρισα and ἐβάρεσα; ἐβόσκισα (pres. βόσκω and βοσκίζω) and ἐχάσκισα (from χάσκω) are irregular.

5. (a) Only the loan-words given in § 199, I. 5. a, n. 3 form sigmatic aorists: ἀρριβάρισα, ξεμπαρκάρισα, σερβίρισα, and the solitary θέλω "wish, will," ἠθέλησα.

(b) likewise belongs to a different aorist system (§ 203).

6. Vowel + σ; thus, -ασα, -εσα, -ισα, -ωσα, -ουσα:

ἔπιασα, ἔφτασα, ἔφκειασα, ἔχασα, ἐβύζασα, ἐδάγκασα, and ἀμάρτησα from ἁμαρτάνω.

ἔδεσα, ἔστεσα or ἔστησα, ἐκέρδεσα and ἐκέρδισα. Other verbs of this class in -αίνω (-ένω) give only -isa; as, ἔπλυσα, ἄ(υ)ξησα, (ξανα)βλάστησα; σωπαίνω and χορταίνω have also ἐσώπασα and ἐχόρτασα (in form aorists from σωπάζω and χορτάζω).

1. For the fluctuation among e, a, and i, cf. also that among -éno, -áno, -íno in the present system, § 199, I. 6, n. 1.

2. The verbs ἁμαρτάνω, αὐξαίνω, βλασταίνω, κερδαίνω belong in their origin properly to 5. b. Occasionally also πηγαίνω (παγαίνω) gives an aorist ἐπάγησα (in place of the more common ἐπῆγα, § 203, 1).

ἄφησα (see also § 202), ἔγδυσα, ἔκλεισα, ἔλυσα, ἔσβησα, ἔχυσα, ἔψησα; δίνω (δώνω): ἔδωσα or (in dialect) ἤδωσα (on which see also § 202). For πίνω, cf. § 199, 1.

ἔζωσα, ἔστρωσα, ἔχωσα, ἅπλωσα, ἐγλύτωσα, etc.

3. In the -νω system also -ξα forms are sometimes to be found beside the usual -σα; as, ἐβύζαξα, ἐμάζωξα (fr. μαζώνω), ἡμεγάλωξα (μεγαλώνω), ἔφταξα (φτάνω). μαζώνω—in addition to ἐμάζωξα—has also an aorist ἔμασα, a present to which (ὁ)μάζω occurs in dialect (Cappadocia).

II. Contracted verbs.

These have without exception sigmatic aorists; that is, *i-*, *e-*, *a + σ*.

(*a*) Usually in -*isa* (-ησα): ἀγάπησα, ἀπαντῶ "meet," ἀπάντησα, ἀποχτῶ "acquire," ἀπόχτησα, γλιστρῶ "slide," ἐγλίστρησα, ἐρωτῶ "ask," ἐρώτησα, ζῶ "live," ἔζησα; ζητῶ "seek," "ask," ἐζήτησα, περπατῶ "go walking," ἐπερπάτησα, φιλῶ ἐφίλησα, etc. Notice the spelling ἀπόλυσα, ἐμέθυσα because originally ἀπολύω, μεθύω; ἐμήνυσα, ἐκύλισα because originally μηνύω, κυλίω.

-*esa* is rare: βαρῶ "strike" ἐβάρεσα, βολεῖ "it is possible" ἐβόλεσε, μπορῶ "am able" ἐμπόρεσα, παινῶ "praise" (ἐ)παίνεσα, παρακαλῶ (περικαλῶ) "request" παρακάλεσα (also παρεκάλεσα), παρηγορῶ "console" παρηγόρεσα, πονῶ "am grieved" ἐπόνεσα, φορῶ ἐφόρεσα, πλανῶ "deceive" ἐπλάνεσα, συμπονῶ "sympathise" συμπόνεσα, συχωρῶ "forgive" συχώρεσα, φελῶ "am useful" φέλεσα, χωρῶ "hold (of space)" ἐχώρεσα.

-*asa* is likewise rare: γελῶ ἐγέλασα, διψῶ "thirst" ἐδίψασα, πεινῶ "am hungry" ἐπείνασα, πετῶ "flee away" ἐπέτασα (and ἐπέταξα).

1. For the Pontic ἐπέντεσα = ἀπάντησα, ἐτρύπεσα = ἐτρύπησα, cf. § 6, n. 2.

2. In North. Gk. unstressed ι drops out; thus, ἀγάπσιν = ἀγάπησε, γένντσιν = ἐγέννησε (γεννῶ "bear, give birth"), (Lesbos) ἠϑόρσα = ἠμπόρησα (for usual ἐμπόρεσα) etc. (*cf.* above). Through the accent of the sing. being generalised plural forms resulted like ζάλσαμ (Capp.) = (ἐ)ζάλισαμε for (ἐ)ζαλίσαμε.

(*b*) Commonly -*asa*: as περνῶ ἐπέρασα also ἐγέρασα,

ἐκέρασα, ἐκρέμασα, ἐξέρασα, ἐξέχασα, σκολνῶ (also σκολῶ) ἐσκόλασα, ἐφύρασα, ἐχάλασα.

-isa : ἀπόλυσα, ἐγύρισα, ἐσφάλισα.

-εσα : ἐκάλεσα.

(c) ἄκουσα, ἔκλεισα, ἔκρουσα ; φταί(γ)ω ἔφταισα and ἔφταιξα, πλέ(γ)ω ἔπλεξα. ἔκαψα (καίω, usually κάβω, etc.) and ἔκλαψα (κλαίγω) are quite irregular.

Analogous to the interchange between contracted verbs and other present systems, especially those in -ζω (-άζω, -ίζω), we find in the aorist also sometimes -αξα and -ηξα instead of -ασα and -ησα ; thus, apart from ἐπέταξα : e.g. ἀπαντῶ ἀπάντηξα, ἀρωτῶ "ask," ἀρώτηξα (TEXTS I. d. 5), βαστῶ "carry," ἐβάσταξα, βογγῶ "groan," ἐβούγγηξα, ρουφῶ "suck in," ἐρούφηξα, σκουντῶ "push against," ἐσκούνταξα, τραβῶ "draw," ἐτράβηξα, φυσῶ "blow," ἐφύσηξα, σφαλνῶ "close," ἐσφάλιξα, etc. The number of such forms may be easily enlarged from the different dialects.

§ 202. Three verbs form aorists in -κ- in addition to the σ- aorist forms: ἔδωκα (in dialect ἤδωκα) beside ἔδωσα from δίνω (δίδω, δώνω), ἔθεκα beside the more common ἔθεσα from θέτω, ἀφῆκα and ἄφηκα (North. Gk. ἄφ'κα) or ἤφηκα, rarely ἄφησα, from ἀφήνω.

1. The three κ-Aorists are a. Gk. In some dialects (Aegina, Athens, Cyme in Euboea, Scyros, Maina, Epirus, and elsewhere) the aorists in -κα- spread to such an extent as to supplant the -σα- form : ἐχτύπηκα, ἐγέλακα, ἄκουκα, ἔπιακα, ἐκάθικα, ἔφκειακα, (ἐ)γύρικα, (ἐ)ζύμωκα, etc. On εὑρῆκα, cf. § 208.

2. Notice Pontic ἐντῶκα "I struck" from (ἐ)ντούννω, (ἐ)ποῖκα "I made, did" from φτάω.

§ 203. The non-sigmatic aorists fall into three groups according to § 200, together with a few isolated formations. The non-sigmatic aorist formation is, with few exceptions, confined to the present system of barytones under class 5. τρέμω (I. 5) has no aorist.

1. The aorist stem differs from the present in the loss of the present suffix :

Loss of -ίσκω (I. 4): εὑρίσκω "find" : ηὗρα (beside εὑρῆκα, v. § 207 f.).

Loss of -νω (I. 5. a): κάμνω (κάμω, κάνω) "do, make" : ἔκαμα, φέρνω "bring" : ἔφερα. πίνω "drink" : ἤπια (ἔπια).

Loss of -αίνω (I. 5. b): λαβαίνω "receive," κατα-, ξανα-, περι-λαβαίνω : ἔλαβα, (ἐ)κατάλαβα, (ἐ)ξανάλαβα, (ἐ)περίλαβα. λαθαίνω "I am concealed, escape notice" : ἔλαθα.

λαχαίνω "obtain by lot": ἔλαχα.

μαθαίνω "learn": ἔμαθα (which serves also as aorist to ξεύρω " I know ").

παθαίνω " endure": ἔπαθα.

πηγαίνω "go": ἐπῆγα (accent !); cf. also ἐπάγησα, § 201, 6, n. 2, and ἐπάγηκα, § 207.

τυχαίνω " chance " (ἀπο-, ἐπι-τυχαίνω " am unlucky, am lucky "): ἔτυχα.

2. The aorist stem differs by radical vowel change:

(I. 2. a) φεύγω "flee": ἔφυγα.

(I. 5. a) μένω (or μνήσκω, μνέσκω, I. 4) " remain " (ἀπο-, περι-, προσ-μένω): ἔμεινα.

(ἀ)ποθαίνω, (ἀ)πεθαίνω " die ": ἀπόθανα, ἀπέθανα, ἐπέθανα.

ξαίνω " card-wool ": ἔξανα.

The vowel difference between aorist and present is not always clearly expressed if the present has two forms:

(I. 5. a) γένομαι and usually γίνομαι " become," ἔγινα and also ἔγενα (cf., further, § 207).

Note the Cappad. ἔννε (with both consonants pronounced) from ἔγινε.

κρίνω and κρένω " judge, speak," ἔκρινα.

(I. 6) πλένω and πλύνω " wash ": (in dialect, in Amorgos) ἔπλυνα, but commonly ἔπλυσα. Cf. also βραδύνει " it is growing evening ": (ἐ)βράδυνε.

Besides μένω: ἔμεινα there exists also a present μείνω.

Here belong also all verbs in -αίνω (I. 5. b) which have not been given already under 1. The e in some converts to a, in some to i.

-αίνω : -αν-α :

ἀνασαίνω " breathe ": ἀνάσανα.

βαθουλαίνω " hollow out ": (ἐ)βαθούλανα.

γιαίνω " heal ": ἔγιανα.

ζεσταίνω " heat ": ἐζέστανα.

μαραίνω " make to wither ": ἐμάρανα.

μοιραίνω " appoint one's destiny ": ἐμοίρανα.

ξεθυμαίνω " give vent to my rage, compose myself ": ἐξεθύμανα.

ξεραίνω " dry ": ἐξέρανα.

πικραίνω " embitter ": ἐπίκρανα.

τρελλαίνω " drive crazy ": ἐτρέλλανα.

ξαναφαίνω " I appear again " follows the model of these : ξανάφανα (but more usually ξαναφαίνομαι : ξαναφάνηκα).

-αίνω (-ένω) : -ην-α :

χοντραίνω " become thick " : ἐχόντρηνα.

μακραίνω " am diffuse " : ἐμάκρηνα.

πλουταίνω (πλουτένω) " become rich " : ἐπλούτηνα.

τραναίνω (τρανένω) " become great " : ἐτράνηνα (Pontus).

φτωχαίνω (φτωχένω) " become poor " : ἐφτώχηνα.

3. Where the aorist stem differs both in the dropping of the present suffix (-νω) and in radical vowel change (all in I. 5. a):

γέρνω " bow " : ἔγειρα ; ἀναγέρνω " search all over " : ἀνάγειρα.

δέρνω " whip, beat " : ἔδειρα.

γδέρνω " flay " : ἔγδειρα and ἔγδαρα.

παίρνω " take " : ἐπῆρα (accent !) and (less commonly) ἔπηρα.

παραγγέλνω " order " : παράγγειλα.

σέρνω " draw " : ἔσυρα.

σπέρνω " sow " : ἔσπειρα (pres. also σπείρω).

στέλνω (στέρνω) " send " : ἔστειλα.

ψέλνω " sing " : ἔψαλα (pres. also ψάλλω). Likewise βέλνω, though more commonly βάλλω (βγάλλω, προβάλλω): ἔβαλα (ἔβγαλα, for which also ἔβγανα).

Even in βάλλω ἔβαλα, ψάλλω ἔψαλα, σφάλλω "am mistaken" ἤσφαλα the aorist and the present stem become absolutely identical. The two forms are distinguished only in those dialects which pronounce double consonants (§ 36).

4. The aorist formation (I. 1. b) of ἔπεσα from πέφτω " fall " stands solitary ; it serves also as the aorist to κείτομαι.

5. A number of aorists that belong here take presents from a quite different root (defective verbs), viz. :

βλέπω " see " : εἶδα (ἔδια, TEXTS I. d. 5).

ἔρχομαι " come " : ἦρθα (ἦρτα, also in the Aegean ἦρχα, in Pontic ἔρθα, in Capp. ἦλτα).

λέγω " say, speak " : εἶπα.

But διαλέγω " choose " : διάλεξα.

τρώγω " eat " : ἔφαγα.

Note also in Pontic the aorists ἐσέγκα " I brought, led in," and ἐξέγκα " I took out " = a. Gk. εἰσ-, ἐξ-ήνεικα (-ήνεγκα) from -φέρω = m. Gk. φέρνω.

For the formally middle aorist active of -βαίνω, see below, § 207.

§ 204. *The historic relation of the aorist and the present stem.* The m. Gk. aorist active corresponds exactly to its a. Gk. predecessor. M. Gk. on the whole reflects the a. Gk. phenomena in the subdivision of the different aorist systems (sigmatic, aorist of liquid verbs, and strong aorist). Only in a few cases the sigmatic aorist has encroached upon the territory of the non-sigmatic ; thus, ἐκέρδεσα fr. κερδαίνω, ἐσύναξα fr. συνάγω (συνάζω), ἐπρόσεξα fr. προσέχω, ἁμάρτησα fr. ἁμαρτάνω (ἥμαρτο = a. Gk. ἥμαρτον has become stereotyped to mean "pardon, beg your pardon"). The two a. Gk. groups of the non-sigmatic aorist—the a. Gk. strong aorist and the aorist of liquid verbs—cannot any longer be sharply discriminated from the m. Gk. standpoint ; thus, ἀπέθανα fr. ἀποθαίνω is formally identical with ἐξέστανα fr. ζεσταίνω, although the former belongs historically to the "strong" aorists, the latter to the liquid aorists. Conversely, ψάλλω : ἔψαλα is formally identical with βάλλω ἔβαλα, although the former originally came under the type of ἔστειλα. Consequently further interchange of the two forms is not surprising : beside παραγγέλνω παράγγειλα one may also employ παράγγελα on the analogy of κάμνω ἔκαμα. The origin of the new creation φέρνω ἔφερα (for φέρω ἤνεγκα) is to be attributed to such models.

While in general the ancient aorist has maintained its place, the present stem has been quite frequently remodelled, and that on the basis of the aorist. Thus the type μένω ἔμεινα, στέλνω ἔστειλα set the model for κρένω (κρίνω) ἔκρινα, πλένω (πλύνω) ἔπλυνα, σπέρνω ἔσπειρα, σέρνω ἔσυρα, etc. The most numerous examples are found in verbs with a sigmatic aorist : the phonetic identity among ἔτριψα : ἐπίστεψα : ἔκοψα : ἄλειψα : ἔκαψα : ἔγραψα : ἔκλεψα gave rise to such analogous series as τρίβω : πιστεύω : κόβω (a. Gk. κόπτω) : ἀλείβω (a. Gk. ἀλείφω) : κάβω (a. Gk. καίω) or κόφτω : γράφτω : κάφτω or ἀλείφω : γράφω : κλέφω (a. Gk. κλέπτω). ἔκραξα : ἅρπαξα : ἔταξα : ἐτάραξα, etc., produced the series κράζω : ἁρπάζω : τάζω : ταράζω (for a. Gk. τάσσω, ταράσσω). As -isa may be aorist to verbs in -ίζω or verbs in -ῶ, so βογγίζω and βογγῶ or even ξεσκῶ for ξεσκίζω. ἐγέλασα from γελῶ, etc., set the analogy for ἔσκασα : σκῶ (beside σκάζω, a. Gk.).

Sometimes the present system was still further affected by the form of the aorist stem ; thus, παθαίνω for πάσχω from ἔπαθα on analogy of μαθαίνω : ἔμαθα. The a. Gk. ἐξεῦρον came to be regarded as an imperf. and a new present (ἐ)ξεύρω was formed (which then received ἔμαθα as complementary aorist). In several dialects (Aegean Sea and Pontus) from ἔστειλα, ἔμεινα there arose a στείλω, μείνω for στέλλω (στέλνω) μένω like σπείρω (σπέρνω) from ἔσπειρα.

The imperfects ὑπῆγα, ἐπῆγα (ὑπάγω) and ἔφερα were conceived as aorists (thus exactly the contrary of what took place with ἐξεῦρον) and took presents πηγαίνω and φέρνω according to existing models. Certain present suffixes (*e.g.* -νω, -αίνω, -ίζω, -[ι]άζω) are especially productive, as may be seen in the crop of new verbs.

The confusion reigning in the present sometimes affected also the aorist: τάζω (a. Gk. τάσσω): ἔταξα, ταράζω (ταράσσω): ἐτάραξά, etc., caused ἐξετάζω: ἐξέταξα, σπουδάζω: ἐσπούδαξα. Πήζω (πήγνυμι): ἔπηξα, etc., carried ἐγγίζω: ἔγγιξα, etc., along. And, finally, -ῶ and -ίζω, -άζω and -άνω being frequently interchangeable, there arose types like ρουφῶ ἐρούφηξα, ἀπαντῶ ἀπάντηξα, βυζάνω ἐβύζαξα, which here and there spread apace.

Thus the m. Gk. present and aorist systems are manifestly the evolution of older forms aided by the action of widely ramified analogies with the aorist as a fixed centre. Still greater variety obtains if all the different dialect forms were taken into account. It is enough to have discussed the principle in some examples, as with this principle there is no difficulty in the majority of cases in explaining the deviations of the modern forms from those of ancient Greek.

(b) *The Aorist Passive and kindred Formations.*

§ 205. The aorist passive (indicative) is regularly formed by attaching -θη-κα (1st pers. sing.) or less commonly -ηκα to the original verbal stem, that is, that stem which forms the basis of the σ-aorist. If a spirant (σ, φ, χ) precedes the -θηκα, then -θηκα converts into -τηκα (according to § 18), although the spelling with θ is often retained (§ 18, n. 1). The following examples show how from the several present systems the corresponding aorist passive in -θηκα is formed (for verbs with aorist in -ηκα, v. § 207):

I. 1. The final radical φ, and so -φτηκα:

ἐβάφτηκα, (ἐ)στρίφτηκα, ἐκαύτηκα, ἐκόφτηκα, ἐπαύτηκα, ἐκρύφτηκα (less commonly irreg. κρ[ο]υβήθηκα), ἐγεύτηκα, ἐπαντρεύτηκα (παντρεύω " marry "); ἐσκέφτηκα. On βλέπω, v. § 206; on γράφω, θάβω, θρέφω, κάβω, ντρέπομαι, στρέφω, τρίβω, v. § 207.

παντρεύκιν, in Velv., etc., is a phonetic transformation of παντρεύ-τ(η)κε according to § 7, n. 1, or § 37 n.

2. Final radical χ, and so -χτηκα:

ἐπλέχτηκα, ἐσφίχτηκα, ἀνοίχτηκα, ἐφυλάχτηκα, ἐδέχτηκα, ἐβρέχτηκα; ἐδείχτηκα, ἐδιώχτηκα, ἐρρίχτηκα (ἐρρίφτηκα).— ὑπόσχομαι (ὑπόσκομαι): ὑποσχέθηκα " promise " is irregular. On λέγω, cf. § 206; on βρέχω, πνίγω, § 207.

3. Final radical σ, and so -στηκα:

ἐκλώστηκα, ἐπλάστηκα, ἐλούστηκα, ἐβράστηκα, ἀγορά-στηκα, ἐξετάστηκα, σκεπάστηκα, (ἐ)τοιμάστηκα, στοχάστηκα, ἀγκαλιάστηκα, χρειάστηκα.

Verbs with aorist in -ξα form the aorist passive in -χτηκα:

ἐπαίχτηκα (παίζω), κράχτηκα, ἐτάχτηκα, ἐφράχτηκα, ἁρπάχτηκα, ἐβαστάχτηκα, ἐπειράχτηκα, ἐτρομάχτηκα ; ἐσκιάχτηκα beside ἐσκιάστηκα (σκιάζομαι " fear "). On σφάζω, v. § 207.

κατανύσσομαι : κατανύχτηκα.

ἐχτίστηκα, ἐσκίστηκα, ἐγνωρίστηκα, ἐσκορπίστηκα, ἐστολί-στηκα, ἐζαλίστηκα (ζαλίζομαι " become dizzy "), ὁρκίστηκα (ὁρκίζομαι " swear "), ἐφταρμίστηκα (φταρμίζομαι " sneeze ").

1. -ίχτηκα is rare ; as, ἐσφαλίχτηκα (σφαλίζω " lock ").
2. Without -σ- only in σαπίζω " putrefy " : ἐσαπήθηκα (beside the more usual ἐσάπισα with the same value).
3. θέτω takes aorist passive ἐτέθηκα (rare) ; δίδω : ἐδόθηκα.

4. βρίσκω (βρίστω) : εὑρέθηκα ; the form (ἐ)βαρέθηκα belongs formally to βαρίσκω, βαρέσκω, but according to its meaning to the middle βαρειέμαι " am weary of " ; πρήσκομαι : ἐπρήστηκα, βόσκω : ἐβοσκήθηκα.
5. When an aorist in -θηκα is found the forms are :
(a) (ἀ)ποκρίθηκα (ἀποκρίνομαι " answer "), ἐβάλθηκα (ἐβάρθηκα), ἐψάλθηκα (ἐψάρθηκα, ἐψάρτηκα), ἐσύρθηκι, ἐφέρθηκα.

1. ξεμπαρκαρίστηκα from ξεμπαρκάρω.

The vowel of the present (e) is changed to a in :
(ἐ)δάρθηκα, (ἐ)γδάρθηκα, ἐπάρθηκα (serves also to λαβ-αίνω), ἐσπάρθηκα, ἐστάλθηκα.

2. κάμνω " make " appropriates the aorist passive from φτειάνω (ἐφτειάστηκα). On North. Gk. πάρκα = πάρθηκα, cf. § 37 n.

(b) (a) αἰστάνομαι : αἰστάνθηκα (used as scarcely different from λαχήθηκα, or like μαθεύτηκα from μαθαίνω from a different present stem).
(β) ἐξεστάθηκα, ἐμαράθηκα, ἐξεράθηκα, ἐσιχάθηκα, ἐτρελλάθηκα.
6. Partly in -θηκα, partly -στηκα :
-θηκα (with vowel modification in some cases) : χάνω : ἐχάθηκα, δένω : ἐδέθηκα, πλένω (πλύνω) : ἐπλύθηκα, κερδαίνω : ἐκερδέθηκα, ἀξαίνω : ἀξήθηκα ; ἀφήνω : ἀφέθηκα and ἀφή-θηκα, γδύνω (ντύνω) : ἐγδύθηκα (ἐντύθηκα), δίνω (δώνω) : ἐδόθηκα, λύνω : ἐλύθηκα, χύνω : ἐχύθηκα, ψήνω (ψένω) : ἐψήθηκα, στήνω " place " : ἐστήθηκα (ἐστάθηκα, which be-longs to the same verb, serves as aorist to στέκω " stand "),

στρώνω: ἐστρώθηκα, σώνω "attain, finish": ἐσώθηκα, χώνω: ἐχώθηκα; also ἁπλώθηκα, μαζώθηκα, ἐπλερώθηκα, σκοτώθηκα, ἐφορτώθηκα, etc.

-στηκα: δαγκάνω: δαγκάστηκα, πιάνω: ἐπιάστηκα, φτειάνω: ἐφτειάστηκα, further ἐσωπάστηκα, χορτάστηκα; κλείνω: ἐκλείστηκα, ξύνω: ἐξύστηκα, σβήνω: ἐσβήστηκα, ζώνω: ἐζώστηκα.

-χτηκα rare: βυζάχτηκα from βυζάνω.

II. -θηκα (-στηκα) is attached to the radical vowel (there are here no -ηκα forms).

(a) -ή-θηκα: ἀγαπήθηκα, γεννήθηκα ("I was born"), ἐκοιμήθηκα (κοιμοῦμαι "sleep"), ἐζητήθηκα, ἐφιλήθηκα, εὐκή-θηκα (εὐκοῦμαι "bless"), ἐφοβήθηκα (φοβοῦμαι "fear").

-έ-θηκα: καταφρονέθηκα (καταφρονῶ "despise"), παινέ-θηκα, ἐπλανέθηκα, παραπονέθηκα, συμπονέθηκα, συχωρέθηκα, ἐφορέθεκα.

-στηκα is rare: ἐγελάστηκα, ἀρνήστηκα beside ἀρνήθηκα (ἀρνοῦμαι "I deny"), καυκήστηκα (καυκοῦμαι "I boast"), καταρήστηκα (καταρειέμαι "curse"), ἐκαλέστηκα (fr. καλῶ and καλνῶ), παρακαλέστηκα. πετῶ takes πετάχτηκα.

(b) Mostly -στηκα: ἐκεράστηκα, ἐκρεμάστηκα, ἐξεχάστηκα, ἐχαλάστηκα, ἐσφαλίστηκα, (ἐ)καλέστηκα (παρα-).

So also Pontic ἐπελύστα = ἀπολύθηκα.

(c) ἀκούστηκα, ἐκλείστηκα, ἐκρούστηκα, ἐκλαύτηκα.

The two forms -ήθηκα and -ήστηκα correspond to the double forms in -ῶ and -ζω. The aorist pass. -χτηκα from the -ξα form is less common; apart from the usual ἐπετάχτηκα notice also ἐμαζώχτηκα (beside ἐμαζώθηκα already cited, or also ἐμαζεύτηκα from μαζεύω) and τραβῶ "draw," ἐτραβήχτηκα.

§ 206. A separate stem increased by ω is employed as the basis of the aor. pass. in the following verbs:

βλέπω "see": ἰδώθηκα (διώθηκα).

λέγω "say": beside ἐλέχτηκα also εἰπώθηκα.

πίνω "drink": (ἐ)πιώθηκα.

τρώγω "eat" (aor.) ἔφαγα: (ἐ)φαγώθηκε.

§ 207. The aorist formed with -ηκα (without θ) is found in the following verbs:

(I. 1) γράφω "write": ἐγράφηκα, but usually ἐγράφτηκα.
θάβω "bury": ἐτάφηκα, but usually ἐθάφτηκα.

θρέφω "nourish": ἐτράφηκα, ἐθράφηκα.

κάβω (καύτω) "burn": ἐκάηκα (beside ἐκαύτηκα).

κλέφτω "steal": ἐκλάπηκα (and ἐκλέφτηκα).

κόβω (κόφτω) "cut": ἐκόπηκα.

ντρέπομαι "am ashamed": (ἐ)ντράπηκα.

στρέφω "turn": ἐστράφηκα (καταστρέφω "destroy":
    καταστράφηκα).

τρίβω "rub": ἐτρίβηκα (and ἐτρίφτηκα).

(II. 2) βρέχω "wet": ἐβράχηκα (and ἐβρέχτηκα).

πνίγω "drown" (trans.): ἐπνίγηκα (and ἐπνίχτηκα).

(II. 3) σφάζω "slay": ἐσφάγηκα (and ἐσφάχτηκα).

(II. 5) φαίνομαι "appear": ἐφάνηκα.

χαίρομαι (χαίρω) "rejoice": ἐχάρηκα.

γίνομαι "become": ἐγίνηκα (North. Gk. ἐγίν'κα) and
    ἐγένηκα (beside ἔγινα, see above).

The verb -βαίνω (only in compounds, see p. 133) forms
its aorist active with violent modification of the stem—likewise in -ηκα:

ἀνε-, κατε-, δια-βαίνω " I go up, down, past": ἀνέβηκα,
    κατέβηκα, διάβηκα (North. Gk. κατήβκα, διάβκα, v.
    TEXTS III. 12).

βγαίνω "go out": (ἐ)βγῆκα.

μπαίνω "go in": (ἐ)μπῆκα.

σεβαίνω (in dialect) "go in": (εἰ)σέβηκα.

On some other forms of -βαίνω, cf. § 208.

συνέβηκε "it happened" belongs to συμβαίνει (borrowed from the
literary language, instead of which the ordinary people use γίνεται).
The model of ἀνεβαίνω: ἀνέβηκα, etc., gave rise to a πάγηκα from
παγαίνω; cf. πάγ'κανε, i.e. ἐπάγηκαν, TEXTS III. 10.

The word in general use εὕρηκα or (ἐ)βρῆκα beside ηὗρα
from εὑρίσκω formally belongs under this category (cf. § 208).

§ 208. Historical note. The m. Gk. aorist passive (together with
ἀνέβηκα, etc.) corresponds to the a. Gk. aorist in -θην-ν or -η-ν, the stem
formation being based entirely on a. Gk. (cf. especially the vowel
system of ἐστάλθηκα, ἐγδάρθηκα). Innovations on analogy took place
only in a few cases: e.g. in the formation of ἐβάλθηκε for a. Gk. ἐβλήθη
after the model of the rest of the stem βαλ-. Moreover, the relation
between the formation in -θην and in -ην has altered only slightly in
favour of the former, cf. ἐστάλθηκα, ἐγδάρθηκα = a. Gk. ἐστάλην,
ἐδάρην; to which are to be added some new formations which lack
any corresponding a. Gk. form: e.g. ἐγίνηκα and the aorists in -ώθηκα
cited in § 206.

The enlargement of the -θη- by the addition of -κα (which is inflected exactly like a -σα- aorist) is practically but not absolutely universal. The unenlarged form is also found particularly in the 3rd sing.: *e.g.* εὑρέθη, ἀποκρίθη, ἠχάρη (Ios), τοῦ (κακο)φάνη, κατέβη, ἐδιάη beside ἐϳδιάητόϵ (Maina) = ἐδιάβηκϵ; the unenlarged form is usual in Pontus and Cappadocia; *cf.* in Texts III. 13, 14, ἐπελύστα "I was left behind, remained behind," ἐσκώθϵν "he rose," φοβήθαμ "we feared," ἐσκώθαν "they rose," ἐκλϵιδώθαν "they were locked in," ἐχάραν "they rejoiced," ἐξέβϵν "he went out," ἐδέβϵν "he went away" (similarly in Syra, Texts I. d. 5, ἤμπϵ; Chios, Texts III. 9, ἤμπϵν = ἐμπῆκϵ), ἔβγαμ(ϵν), ἔβγαν "we, they went out." Besides the formation in -θη-κα there is another -θη-να; thus in Aegina ἐλυπήθηνα, ἐδέθηνα, ϵὑκήθηνα beside -θηκα; *cf.* also the inflection of the aorist passive in § 221. Finally, an enlargement in -σα is found, *v.* Texts III. 2, n. 22.

The form ϵὕρηκα comes formally under the type of aorist in -ηκα; it is identical with the a. Gk. perfect active of the same form, and is therefore the *only certain remnant of the ancient perfect.*

(c) *The Perfect Participle Passive and kindred Forms.*

§ 209. Immediately connected with the aorist passive is the passive participle of the past tense, a form considerably more in use than the aorist passive. Besides the usual form in -μένος there is also a less used form in -τός (§ 212).

§ 210. The ending -μένος is regularly attached to the same root as -θηκα. The connection of this ending with the verb stem results in the following forms:

I. 1. -(μ)μένος:

βαμμένος, γραμμένος, στριμμένος, στρέμμένος; θαμμένος (θάβω "bury"), θλιμμένος "afflicted" (θλίβω), κομμένος, τριμμένος, κρυμμένος; μαζϵ(μ)μένος, ἐμπιστϵ(μ)μένος ("trusted"), ἐρωτϵ(μ)μένος "beloved," φυτϵ(μ)μένος, ἀναμμένος, κλϵμμένος, ραμμένος, etc.

κάβω has besides the normal participle κα(μ)μένος also another καημένος (from ἐκάηκα), used in the figurative sense "poor, unhappy"; but even κα(μ)μένος may take this sense.

πέφτω: πϵσμένος. On βλέπω, *v.* § 211.

2. -(γ)μένος:

πλϵ(γ)μένος, ἀνοι(γ)μένος, πνι(γ)μένος, τυλι(γ)μένος, βρϵ(γ)μένος; δϵιγμένος, διωγμένος; ρίχτω (ρίφτω): ριμμένος (like 1) or even ριχμένος, so also σπρώχνω: σπρωχμένος. On ἔρχομαι, λέγω, τρώγω, *v.* § 211.

The phonetic combination -γμ- is retained only in North. Gk., elsewhere γ before μ disappears (*cf.* § 24).

3. Usually -σμένος:

θεσμένος, ἀλεσμένος, κλωσμένος (ἀρεσμένος).

λούζω: λουσμένος, παίζω: παιγμένος or παισμένος.

βρασμένος, ἀγορασμένος, (ἐ)ξετασμένος, θαμασμένος, σκεπασμένος, σπουδασμένος, τρομασμένος, ἀγκαλιασμένος, ἀραχνιασμένος "filled with cobwebs," βουλιασμένος (in spite of ἐβούλιαξα).

Corresponding to the aorist forms in -ξα and -χτηκα some participles end in -(γ)μένος: πη(γ)μένος (from πήζω), τα(γ)μένος, φρα(γ)μένος, ἀραγμένος (ἀράζω "land," from a ship), ἁρπαγμένος, κατασπαραγμένος ("torn, rent," metaph.), πειραγμένος, ρημαγμένος "isolated" (beside ρημασμένος), also τρομαγμένος, βουλιαγμένος.

χτισμένος, σκισμένος, καθισμένος, γυρισμένος, δακρυσμένος, εὐ-, δυστυχισμένος "happy, unhappy," ζαλισμένος, ὁρισμένος, σκορπισμένος, τσακισμένος, ἀκουμπισμένος, etc.

σφαλιγμένος beside σφαλισμέν ς.

4. (ἐ)βρίσκω: βρεμένος and βρημένος, πρήσκω: πρησμένος. βόσκω: βοσκισμένος, βαρίσκω: βαρισμένος.

5. -μένος.

(a) κρίνω: κριμένος, γιαίνω: γιαμένος, ξαίνω: ξαμένος, πεθαίνω: (ἀ)πεθαμμένος, βάλλω: βαλμένος, ψάλλω: ψαλμένος.

ἀνε-, κατε-βάζω, ἐμπάζω: ἀνε-, κατε-βασμένος, (ἐ)μπασμένος.

στέλνω: σταλμένος.

ξεμπαρκάρω: ξεμπαρκαρισμένος, σερβίρω: σερβιρισμένος (πικαριϋμένος, Texts I. d. 5 = πικαρισμένος "embittered").

(γ)δέρνω: (γ)δάρμενος, παίρνω: παρμένος, γέρνω: γειρμένος (also γερμένος), σπέρνω: σπαρμένος, σέρνω: συρμένος, φέρνω: φερμένος. On γίνομαι, κάμνω, v. § 211.

(b) (a) λαθαίνω: λαθαιμένος, λαχαίνω: λαχαιμένος; μαθαίνω: μαθημένος, πηγαίνω: πηγαιμένος. On παθαίνω as also on πηγαίνω, v. § 211.

(β) ζεσταίνω: ζεσταμένος, similarly μαραμένος, ξεραμένος, πικραμένος, σιχαμένος.

6. -μένος and -σμένος.

-μένος: χαμένος; ἁμαρτημένος; δεμένος, πλυμένος, κερδεμένος (and κερδημένος, κερδισμένος), ἀξημένος, ἀφημένος, ντυμένος, δομένος, λυμένος, στημένος (and στεμένος), χυμένος, ψημένος; στρωμένος, χωμένος, ἁπλωμένος, κρυωμένος, μαζωμένος, πλερωμένος σκοτωμένος, etc.

σμένος : πιασμένος, φτασμένος, φτειασμένος ; βυζασμένος
(less commonly βυζαγμένος), δαγκασμένος (also δαγκαμένος) ;
χορτασμένος ; κλεισμένος, ξυσμένος (and ξυμένος), σβησμένος
(and σβημένος), ζωσμένος ; also δοσμένος beside δομένος (from
δίνω, δώνω).

II. (a) Usually -μένος :

-η-μένος : ἀγαπημένος, εὐκαριστημένος ("satisfied," from
εὐκαριστῶ), ἀρρωστημένος " sick," etc.

-ε-μένος : πονεμένος " troubled " (παρα-), συχωρεμένος,
φορεμένος.

-σμένος : καλεσμένος ; γελασμένος, διψασμένος, πεινασ-
μένος.

μεθῶ : μεθυσμένος, ψοφῶ " die " : ψοφισμένος.

πετῶ : πετα(γ)μένος.

Cf. also ἀκουμπισμένος fr. ἀκουμπῶ and ἀκουμπίζω and κοιμισμένος
"sleeping," from κοιμοῦμαι, together with other verbs in -ῶ=-άζω,
and -ίζω (cited p. 137 f.).

(b) Usually -σμένος :

κερασμένος, κρεμασμένος, ξερασμένος, ξεχα(σ)μένος (" for-
getful "), περασμένος, χαλασμένος ; γυρισμένος (cf. also
γυρίζω), σφαλισμένος (cf. also σφαλίζω) ; καλεσμένος.

But ἀπολυμένος (from λύνω).

(c) -σμένος and -μένος :

ἀκουσμένος, κρουσμένος, κλεισμένος (cf. κλείνω) ; κλαίω :
κλαμένος " bathed in tears" (cf. καίω, κάβω : καμένος).

§ 211. The following are the participles corresponding to
the aorist formation given in § 206 :

βλέπω : ἰδωμένος (δωμένος).
ἔρχομαι : ἐρχωμένος.
λέγω : εἰπωμένος (and λε[γ]μένος).
τρώγω : φαγωμένος.
πίνω : πιωμένος " drunken."
γίνομαι : γινωμένος.
κάμνω : καμωμένος.
παθαίνω : παθωμένος.
πηγαίνω : παγωμένος (usually πηγαιμένος).

1. καμώνομαι, καμώθηκα means "act as if, pretend." Similarly,
γεννημένος (fr. γεννῶ) represents the aor. pass. participle of γίνομαι.

2. ὑπόσχομαι : ὑποσχεμένος.

3. What has been said about the aorist passive [§ 208] applies
practically to the relation between the m. Gk. and the a. Gk. parti-

ciple formation. The passive participle is (with the same limitations
that apply to the aorist passive) the continuation of the same a.
Gk. form, *i.e.* the ancient perfect participle passive.

§ 212. The verbal adjectives in -τός belong by their
formation to the aorist passive and participle (-τος instead of
-θηκα or -μένος respectively). They are found, however, to
only a few verbs, and have become for the most part pure
adjectives. *Cf. e.g.* ἀνοιχτός "open," βολετός "possible,"
ζηλευτός "enviable," κλειστός "shut," πλουμιστός "adorned,"
σβηστός "extinguished," σκυφτός "bent," σφαλιχτός "en-
closed," σφιχτός "fixed," ἀγέλαστος "without laughter,"
ἀπάτητος "untrodden," ἀπρόσεχτος "inattentive," ἀτίμητος
"inestimable," ἀχώριστος "inseparable"; πρωτόβγαλτος
"brought out for the first time, *débutant.*"

From these forms inherited from the a. Gk. must be distinguished those (few) formations in -άτος (Lat. *-atus*) which are
used as adjectives or sometimes even in the function of a participle:
γεμάτος "filled, full," πεμπάτος "sent" (fr. πέμπω), τρεχάτος "running, precipitate," φευγάτος "flown" (φεύγω); the last three
verbs are defective in the participle in -μένος. (*Cf.* § 227, n. 2).
The suffix -άτος is appropriated also for derivatives from substantives:
e.g. ἀφράτος "fresh" (from ἀφρός "foam"), μυρουδάτος "perfumed,
fragrant" (from μυρουδιά "perfume"), χιονάτος "white as snow"
(from χιόνι "snow"). It has even produced another suffix in -άτικος,
the usage of which may be seen in examples like πρωτοχρονιάτικος
"relating to, of the New Year," χειμωνιάτικος "wintry."

CONJUGATION OF VERBS.

I. BARYTONES.

Paradigm: δένω "I bind."

SIMPLE TENSES.

ACTIVE.

§ 213.   *Present.*

Indicative.	Subjunctive.
δένω "I bind"	νὰ δένω "that I may bind"
δένεις "thou bindest"	νὰ δένῃς etc.
δένει etc.	νὰ δενῃ
δένομε, δένουμε	νὰ δένωμε, δένουμε
δένετε	νὰ δένετε
δένουν, δένουνε	νὰ δένουν(ε).

1. Indicative and subjunctive differ merely in historic orthography : both forms may be spelled quite alike.

2. In the North. Gk. territory the paradigm runs : δένου, δέν῾s, δέν᾿ or δέν῾, δένουμι, δένιτι, δέν᾿ν(ε) ; cf. e.g. the Pontic forms στρώνν = στρώνουν, θέλνε = θέλουν, etc., or also Velv. τσακών = τσακώνουν.

3. Sometimes also outside the North. Gk. territory (e.g. in the Peloponnesus) the 1st sing. ends in -ου instead of -ω.

4. The -s has dropped off in *pézzi* and so forth in Bova = παίζεις (v. § 29 n.).

5. In Cyprus, Crete, the Maina, Aegean and Lower Italy, the 3rd pl. takes also the forms δένουνι (Crete), δένουνα (cf. τρέχνα, πέφνα, Texts III. 12 = τρέχουνα, πέφτουνα), or according to the ancient way δένουσι, δένουσιν(ε).

§ 214.   *Imperfect.*

έδενα " I bound, was binding "
έδενες   etc.
έδενε
ἐδέναμε
ἐδένατε or ἐδένετε
έδεναν, ἐδέναν(ε).

Aorist.

Indicative.	Subjunctive.
έδεσα " I bound "	νὰ δέσω " that I might bind "
έδεσες	νὰ δέσῃς
έδεσε	νὰ δέσῃ
ἐδέσαμε	νὰ δέσωμε, δέσουμε
ἐδέσετε (also ἐδέσατε)	νὰ δέσετε
έδεσαν, ἐδέσανε	νὰ δέσουν(ε).

Similarly also the non-sigmatic aorist :

κατάλαβα " I understood "	νὰ καταλάβω
κατάλαβες	νὰ καταλάβῃς
κατάλαβε	νὰ καταλάβῃ
καταλάβαμε	νὰ καταλάβωμε (-ουμε)
καταλάβετε (also -ατε)	νὰ καταλάβετε
κατάλαβαν, καταλάβαν(ε)	νὰ καταλάβουν(ε).

So also έστειλα " I sent " νὰ στείλω, έφαγα " I ate " νὰ φάγω, etc.

1. On the augment, v. § 182 f.   The position of the accent is sometimes the same throughout ; that is, ἐκάμα, ἐφάγα, etc., may also be employed (but seldom) after analogy of ἐκάμαμε, ἐφάγαμε or (North. Gk.) ἐφαγάμε, etc., after έφαγα (cf. § 38 n.), which explains forms like ζάλσαμ (§ 201, II. a, n. 2).

2. The imperfect and both aorists have therefore taken identical inflection. The aor. subj. is inflected like the pres. indic.

3. The North. Gk. forms result from the phenomena given § 7, n. 1. *Cf. e.g.* from Velvendos: ἔπιρνις = ἔπαιρνες, δούλιβιν = ἐδούλευεν, γύρσιν = ἐγύρισε(ν), πάϊνιν = ἐπάγαινεν, δούλιψἀμι = ἐδουλέψαμε, τὸ 'φαγἀμι = τὸ ἐφάγαμε; νὰ φκιάσου = νὰ φκιάσω, νὰ πάρς = νὰ πάρῃς, νὰ δείξ = νὰ δείξῃς, νὰ πιθάν' = νὰ πεθάνῃ, νὰ πχιάσουμι = νὰ πιάσωμε, νὰ κριμάσν = νὰ κρεμάσουν. On νὰ σ'χουρέῃς = συχωρέσῃς νὰ πλερώῃς = πλερώσῃς, etc., with expulsion of the σ, *cf.* § 29 n.

4. In many dialects (*e.g.* Pontus, Macedonia, Naxos, Epirus) the 3rd sing. ends in -εν (thus ἔδενεν, ἔδεσεν) or in -ενε (*e.g.* in Naxos, Cythnos): ἤκουενε = ἄκουε, ἤπαιζενε = ἔπαιζε, ἠβούλωσενε = ἐβούλωσε. This -νε has occasionally (particularly in Naxos) been carried over also to other personal endings, *e.g.* to the 2nd pl.; *cf.* ἀκούτενε = ἀκούτε, θέτενε = θέτε (to θέλω). The 1st and 2nd pl. end also in -αμαν, -εταν (-αταν), the 3rd pl. in -ανι and -ασι(νε) (ἐδέναντι, ἐδέσασι), the last in the same dialects that give -ουσι. Note further ἐπεφτὰνα, TEXTS III. 12. In Cappodocia (TEXTS III. 14. b) the 1st pl. ends in -αμ or -αμτι: *e.g.* ἤλεγαμ, ζάλσαμ, πόρκαμ (n. 6), εἴπαμτι, and the 2nd pl. in -εστι: *e.g.* ἤλεγἐστι.

5. The -κα- aorist is inflected exactly like the -σα- aorist: ἄφηκα ἄφηκες, etc. ἐκάθιτσε, etc. (TEXTS III. 14) = ἐκάθικε; *cf.* § 17. The subjunctive of ἄφηκα, ἔδωκα is usually ν' ἀφήσω, νὰ δώσω, *i.e.* after the manner of the sigmatic aorist; likewise ἄκουκα — ν' ἀκούσω, ἐγέλακα — νὰ γελάσω, ἔφκειακα — νὰ φκειάσω, etc., though side by side with these are found also νὰ δώκω (Naxos, Epirus, Aegina, Cappadocia), ν' ἀφήκου (Velv.), ν' ἀφήκῃ (Naxos), νὰ φκειάκω, etc. (Epirus). Likewise (in Asia Minor) νὰ πκῶ, νὰ πκῇς (= ποικῶ for ποίκω) from (ἐ)ποῖκα (§ 202, n. 2) and νὰ εὑρήκω (3rd sing. νὰ εὑρήκ, TEXTS III. 13. c) from εὑρῆκα (or ηὗρα or εὗρα).

6. There are some peculiar imperfect forms in Cappadocia, thus in Pharasa imperfects in -(ι)γκά, or -κα: *e.g.* φέριγκα = ἔφερα, πνώγκα "I slept" from πνώνω, πόρκα "I was able" from μπορῶ, κατζέφκα "I conversed" from κατζεύω; in Sili in -ισκα, -ινόσκα, and -ινόνδζίσκα: *e.g.* ἤσιλ'ίσκα or σελ'ινόσκα = ἤθελα, παγαιννινόνδζίσκα = ἐπάγαινα.

§ 215. In some verbs the subjunctive of the non-sigmatic aorist differs from the indicative in the radical vowel (*cf.* § 203):

> ἐπῆρα " I took ": νὰ πάρω
> ἐπῆγα " I went ": νὰ πάγω
> ἦρθα " I came ": νὰ ἔρθω
> (ἔγινα " I became ": νὰ γένω, usually νὰ γίνω).

1. The reason for this—except in the case of ἔγινα—is the retention of the ancient augment (ὑπ-ῆγον, ἐπ-ῆρα) in the indicative.

A few dissyllabic aorists take final accent in the subjunctive:

εἶπα " I said ":

νὰ εἰπῶ	νὰ εἰποῦμε
νὰ εἰπῇς	νὰ εἰπῆτε
νὰ εἰπῇ	νὰ εἰποῦνε

or νὰ 'πῶ, etc. (beside νὰ εἴπω).

Likewise εἶδα " I saw ": νὰ ἰδῶ, νὰ 'δῶ and νὰ δ̲ῶ (δ̲ῆς, and so on), ξαναεῖδα (ξανά̲ε̲ιδα) " I saw again ": νὰ ξαναϊδῶ.

ἦρθα (ἦρχα) " I came ": νὰ 'ρθῶ, νὰ 'ρτῶ (νὰ ἐλθῶ) beside νὰ 'ρθω, νὰ ἔρθω (νὰ ἔλθω, νὰ ἔρχω, νὰ 'ρχω).

ηὗρα " I found ": νὰ βρῶ beside νὰ εὕρω.

ἤπια " I drank ": νὰ πι̲ῶ.

ἔγινα " I became": νὰ γενῶ beside νὰ γένω (and νὰ γίνω).

2. On νὰ ἐρθοῦ, νὰ 'ποῦ (Texts III. 3), cf. § 213, n. 3.

§ 216. Imperative.

Present.

(ἂς, νὰ δένω " let me bind ")
δένε " bind thou "

ἂς (or νὰ) δένῃ	etc.
ἂς (νὰ) δένωμε (δένουμε)	„
δένετε	„
ἂς (νὰ) δένουν(ε)	„

Aorist.

(ἂς, νὰ δέσω)	(ἂς, νὰ μείνω)	(ἂς, νὰ φάγω)
δέσε	μεῖνε	φάγε
ἂς δέσῃ	ἂς μείνῃ	ἂς φάγῃ
ἂς δέσωμε (δέσουμε)	ἂς μείνωμε	ἂς φάγωμε
δέσετε	μείνετε	φάγετε
ἂς δέσουν	ἂς μείνουν	ἂς φάγουν.

In polysyllabic words the accent of the 2nd sing. withdraws unto the third last syllable; as, πήγαινε " go thou," κάθισε (or κάτσε) " sit down."

Only the 2nd sing. and pl. correspond to the ancient forms, with this difference, however, that the terminations of the present (-ε, -ετε) have been carried over also to the aorist. The Pontic forms like γράψον, ποῖσον (ποίησον), and such forms from the Terra d' Otranto as krátiso (κράτησον), pístefso (πίστευσον), correspond exactly to an a. Gk. γράψον, etc. The other forms of the imperative are constructed with the aid of the particle ἂς (negative ἂς μή) or νά (νὰ μή) and the subjunctive, cf. § 193 f.

§ 217. The initial ε of the 2nd pl. termination is quite frequently dropped: ἀκούστε "hear," ἀφήστε (sometimes ἀφῆτε or ἄστε) "let, allow," γράψτε, κόψτε (and κόφτε), λύστε "loose," ὁρίστε "command," ῥίξτε, βάλτε "put," "lay," ῥωτήστε "ask," πάρτε "take" (παίρνω), σύρτε "draw," φέρτε "bring." Even the termination ε of the 2nd sing. is occasionally dropped, particularly if a conjunctive pronoun of the 3rd pers. follows: ἄφησ᾽ το (also ἄφ το from ἄφς το, cf. ἄφσε = ἄφησε, or ἄς το from ἄσε, TEXTS I. a. 9), κόψ᾽ το (κόφ᾽ το), φκειάσ᾽του (Velv.) "do it," βάλ᾽ το, φέρ᾽ τα. δός "give thou" (as in a. Gk.) is quite common (beside δῶσε) pl. δώστε, θές "put, place" pl. θέστε.

1. Occasionally δό μου for δός μου; δός and θές are, of course, the a. Gk. forms, but, as δῶσε, δώστε, and θέστε show, may be treated exactly like the above cited forms.

2. The employment of ἀκούστε and so forth for the subjunctive, i.e. νὰ (fut. θὰ) ἀκούστε for νὰ (θὰ) ἀκούσετε (cf. TEXTS II. b. 6), etc., is rare.

§ 218. The following imperative forms of the 2nd sing. and pl. belong with the aorists cited in § 215:

ἐπῆρα: πᾶρε, πάρτε.

ἐπῆγα: either νὰ πᾶς, νὰ πᾶτε (i.e. subj.) or ἄμε, ἄμετε.

ἦρθα: ἔλα (in dialect νέλα, TEXTS III. 15, Ladá), ἐλᾶτε (in dialect also ἐλᾶστε).

ἔγινα: γίνε, usually νὰ γίνῃς, νὰ γίνετε.

εἶπα: εἰπέ, ᾽πέ, πές, pl. εἰπέτε, πέτε, πέστε (and πῆτε).

εἶδα: ἰδέ, δέ, (ἰ)δές, pl. ἰδέτε, δέτε, (ἰ)δέστε.

ηὖρα: εὑρέ, βρέ, βρές, pl. βρέτε, βρῆτε.

ἤπια: πιέ(ς), pl. πιέτε.

1. The imperat. to ἔμαθα (μαθαίνω) is μάθε; μαθέ or μαθές is, however, used in a parenthetic way, "that is to say," "then" (cf. § 259).

2. On analogy of ἔλα ἐλᾶτε a few other imperatives in -α, -ᾶτε have been formed: στέκα στεκᾶτε (beside στέκου) from στέκομαι "stand" (aor. στάσου σταθῆτε, v. below), τρέχα τρεχᾶτε from τρέχω "run" (aor. τρέξε τρέξετε), φεύγα φευγᾶτε from φεύγω "flee, go away" (aor. φύγε φύγετε): the forms of the compounds of βαίνω (§ 207), which belong to another class of aorist, also come under this category: ἀνέβα ἀνεβᾶτε (less commonly ἀνεβᾶστε), ἔβγα ἐβγᾶτε, διάβα διαβᾶτε, ἔμπα ἐμπᾶτε (beside plurals ἀνεβῆτε, βγῆτε, διαβῆτε, etc.). Even the particle νά "there is (are), behold" takes, according to such models, a plural νάτε. A -ς has attached to the final of the sing. in the forms ἔμπας, φεύγας, TEXTS I. d. 5 (Syra), pl. φιβγᾶσ᾽τι, i.e. φευγᾶστε, TEXTS III. 11 (Velvendos).

3. The imperative ἄμε ἄμετε is properly a stereotyped form of ἄ(γω)με. So likewise πάμε "let us go, now then" takes a pl. πάμετε.

PASSIVE.[1]

§ 219. *Present.*

Indicative.

δένομαι (δένουμαι) " I am bound "
δένεσαι
δένεται
δενόμαστε (δενούμαστε, -μεστε)
δένεστε
δένουνται.

Subjunctive.

νὰ δένωμαι
etc.
like the indic.

The North. Gk. forms δένουμι, δένισί, etc., arise from § 7, n. 1. In Southern Gk. δένουμαι is less in use than δένομαι. In Saranda Klisiés γίν'ται, etc., occurs for γίνεται, TEXTS III. 12.

§ 220. *Imperfect.*

ἐδένουμου(ν), ἐδενόμουν(ε)
ἐδένουσου(ν), ἐδενόσουν(ε)
ἐδένουντα(ν), ἐδενότουν(ε), ἐδενόταν(ε)
ἐδενούμαστε (-μεστε, -μεστα), ἐδενόμαστε
ἐδενούσαστε, ἐδενόσαστε, ἐδενούστε
ἐδένουντα(ν), ἐδενούνταν(ε), ἐδενόντουσαν.

1. In addition to these forms there are also numerous further variations, *e.g.* :

1st sing. ἐδένομη (Karpathos), ἐδένομουν, ἐδενούμουν(ε), ἐδένουμοὖνε, ἐδενόμαν(ε).

2nd sing. ἐδένεσουν (Cyprus), ἐδενούσουν(ε), ἐδένουσοὖνε.

3rd sing. ἐδένετο(ν) (*e.g.* in Calymnos), ἐδένετουν, ἐδένοντα(ν), ἐδένου-τον, ἐδενούτανε, ἐδενούνταν(ε) (also ἐδένουντανε, Naxos).

Instead of the final ε sometimes also α is found (ἐδενόμουννα and so on).

1st pl. ἐδενούμαστεν, ἐδένουμέστανε, ἐδένουμᾶσταν, (ἐ)δένουμᾶστουν.

2nd pl. ἐδένεστε (*e.g.* in Calymnos), ἐδένουσταν, ἐδενούσαστεν, ἐδένου-σᾶσταν, ἐδένουσᾶστουν. (Spellings with σθ for στ, as in ἐδένουσθαν, are due to the literary language.)

3rd pl. ἐδένουντο (*e.g.* Calymnos) ἐδένονταν, ἐδενούντασιν. Notice also ἔνταν = ἐγίνουνταν (TEXTS III. 13. c) and θαμάζδανα (from -ζουν-τανα), TEXTS III. 12.

2. The various forms have arisen from the a. Gk. (the forms of which are stiil well maintained in dialect, *v.* n. 1) through the mutual action of the different persons on one another and by the action of the active upon the passive.

---

[1] So also the deponents like ἔρχομαι, etc., § 177, 1.

§ 221. *Aorist.*

Indicative.	Subjunctive.
ἐδέθηκα " I was bound "	νὰ δεθῶ
ἐδέθηκες	νὰ δεθῆς
ἐδέθηκε	νὰ δεθῇ
ἐδεθήκαμε	νὰ δεθοῦμε
ἐδεθήκετε	νὰ δεθῆτε
ἐδέθηκαν, ἐδεθήκαν(ε)	νὰ δεθοῦν, δεθοῦνε.

Similarly: ἐφάνηκα νὰ φανῶ, ἀνέ- κατέ-βηκα ν' ἀνεβῶ νὰ κατεβῶ, ἐμπῆκα νὰ 'μπῶ (less commonly νὰ ἔμπω, νά 'μπω), ἐβγῆκα νὰ 'βγῶ. The subjunctive endings take the place of -ηκα.

1. North. Gk. ἐδέθκα, ἐλευτερώθκα, παντρεύκα (=παντρεύτηκα), (ἀ)κούσκα (=ἀκούστηκα), φκήσκα (=εὐκή[σ]τηκα), etc.: in the plural the accent remains on the same syllable as in the singular; thus, e.g. χάθκαμι=χάθηκάμε for χαθήκαμε, χάθκιτι=χάθηκὲτε for χαθήκετε.
2. The 3rd sing. also in -εν : e.g. σκίστηκεν, παντρεύκιν (Velv.).— ἐδέθητσε for ἐδέθηκε, etc., according to § 17.—The 2nd plural occasionally runs also ἐδεθήκατε instead of -ετε (cf. the active), the 3rd pl. also -ασι (ἐδεθήκασι) instead of -αν, likewise as the active; cf. § 214, n. 4.
3. The subjunctive corresponds exactly to the a. Gk. form. On the addition of -κα in the indic., v. § 208 : it appears in dialect also in the subj. in νὰ βήκω (TEXTS III. 12)=νὰ μπῶ (fr. ἐμπῆκα, § 207) ; cf. on this point § 214, n. 5. The form ἐδέθηνα (Aegina) inflects like ἐδέθηκα. On unenlarged formations, cf. § 208.

§ 222. *Imperative.*

Present.

δένου " be thou bound "	
ἂς δένεται	etc.
ἂς δενώμαστε	„
δένεστε	„
ἂς δένουνται	„

Aorist.

δέσου	ντράψου " be ashamed "
ἂς δεθῇ	ἂς ντραπῇ
ἂς δεθοῦμε	ἂς ντραποῦμε
δεθῆτε	ντραπῆτε
ἂς δεθοῦν(ε)	ἂς ντραποῦνε.

Before -σου of the 2nd sing. aorist imperat. the same stem form is used as before -σ- of the aorist act. (γέψου from

11

γεύομαι, στοχάσου from στοχάζομαι). Final accent in the 2nd sing. with -ου instead of -σου occurs in: φαίνομαι ἐφάνηκα "appear," φανοῦ (beside φάνου), χαίρομαι ἐχάρηκα "rejoice," χαροῦ (beside χάρου). γίνομαι "become" takes γένου and γίνου (and even γίνε).

1. As in the imperat. active, νά may be used instead of ἄς. The imperat. passive is not common, apart from that of middle verbs like γεύομαι, συλλογίζομαι, χαίρομαι. The most commonly used imperative is στάσου (North. Gk. στάσ᾽), pl. σταθῆτε "stop" (fr. στέκομαι ἐστάθηκα).

2. On the 2nd sing. and pl. aor. imperat. of ἀνεβαίνω, etc., v. § 218, n. 2. The other persons (ἂς ἀνεβῇ, etc.), and ἀνεβῆτε, etc., beside ἀνεβᾶτε, formally come under this head.

3. σήκω or σήκου "rise (up)" beside σηκώσου σηκωθῆτε fr. σηκώνω is used almost like a particle.

4. In Cyprus (and kindred dialects) the 2nd sing. imperat. (while maintaining the tense characteristics) ends in -θου (-του); as, λυπήθου = λυπήσου "regret," στάθου = στάσου, στοχάστου = στοχάσου. Cf., further, Pontic χάτ (TEXTS III. 14. a), i.e. χάτου (subj. νὰ χατῶ) for χάσου (fr. ἐχάθηκα). In Saranda Klisiés (v. TEXTS III. 12) the imperat. ends in -τσε; as, λούθτσε, κοιμήθτσε (from *λούθησε, etc., in active sense).

Compound Tenses.

§ 223. The auxiliary verbs ἔχω "I have," εἶμαι "I am," θέλω "I will," and the particle θά (θενά, θανά, θελά) are employed to form the compound verbal forms (futures, perfect, pluperfect, future perfect, and conditional).

§ 224. *Conjugation of the Auxiliary Verbs.*

1. ἔχω is found only in the present, imperfect (εἶχα), future (θά 'χω = θὰ ἔχω), and first conditional (θὰ εἶχα). The conjugation is quite regular. Usually the circumlocution with νά is employed for the 2nd person imperative. The aorist is sometimes supplied by that of λαβαίνω (ἔλαβα).

2. εἶμαι "I am."

Present.

Indicative.	Subjunctive.
εἶμαι	νὰ εἶμαι (νά 'μαι)
εἶσαι	νὰ εἶσαι (νά 'σαι)
εἶναι (εἶνε)	νὰ εἶναι (νά 'ναι)
εἴμαστε, εἴμεστα	νὰ εἴμαστε, εἴμεστα (νά 'μαστε)
εἶστε	νὰ εἶστε (νά 'στε)
εἶν(αι)	νὰ εἶναι (νά 'ναι).

1. The subjunctive is also written *νὰ ἦμαι*, etc. (3rd sing. *νὰ ἦναι*).

2. The older forms of the 3rd pers. still survive in some dialects (*e.g.* Maina, Pontus, Cyprus). The intermediate step between *ἔνι* and *εἶναι*, namely *ἔναι*, is met with TEXTS III. 14. a. Moreover, *εἶν* and even *εἶ* (Chios) are found.

Imperfect.

> *ἤμουν(a)*
> *ἤσουν(a)*
> *ἤτον(ε), ἤταν(ε)*
> *ἤμαστε, ἤμεστα*
> *ἤσαστε, ἦστε*
> *ἤταν(ε), ἤσανε.*

3. The following additional forms occur: 1st sing. *ἤμουνε, ἤμουνι, ἤμαν(ε)*. 2nd sing. *ἤσουνε, ἤσουνι, ἤσανε*. 3rd sing. *ἤτο, ἤτουν, ἤτονι*, (Lesbos, Saranda Klisiés) *ἦδαν* 1st pl. *ἤμεθα, ἤμασταν, ἤμαστον*. 2nd pl. *ἤσταν, ἤσασταν, ἤσαστον*. 3rd pl. *ἤντουσαν, ἤντούσανε*. Forms like 1st sing. *ἤμ* or *ἤμνα*, 2nd sing. *ἤς* or *ἤσνα*, arise in North. Gk. dialects. The forms *ἤμην, ἦσο* belong to the literary language.

Imperative.

> *νὰ εἶσαι* (or *νά 'σαι*), also *εἶσου*
> *ἂς εἶναι*
> *ἂς εἴμαστε*
> *(νὰ) εἶστε*
> *ἂς εἶναι.*

4. *ἔστωσαν* (TEXTS I. a. 21) "let them be" is a word from the ecclesiastical language.

The future present and conditional are regularly *θὰ εἶμαι, θά 'μαι (θανά 'μαι)* and *θὰ ἤμουν(ε), ἤθελ' εἶμαι* respectively: on their formation, *v.* §§ 225 f., 230. The defective forms may be supplied by the corresponding forms of *στέκω* "stand" (aor. *ἐστάθηκα*, etc.).

3. *θέλω* "I will."

Present.

> *θέλω*
> *θέλεις, θές*
> *θέλει, θέ*
> *θέλο(υ)με, θέμε*
> *θέλετε, θέτε*
> *θέλουν(ε), θένε.*

1. The abbreviated forms are less in use than the full forms. Notice, further, *θί = θέλει(ς)* TEXTS III. 9 (Chios).

Imperfect.

ἤθελα
ἤθελες
ἤθελε
ἠθέλαμε
ἠθέλετε (ἠθέλατε)
ἤθελαν, (ἠ)θέλανε.

Aorist.

ἠθέλησα, etc.

Imperative.

The 2nd pers. is little in use, otherwise regularly (ἂς
θέλῃ, ἂς θελήσῃ). Also the other parts of this verb are
regularly formed so far as they are at all in use.

2. The particle θά and the forms closely akin with it (§ 225)
were phonetically evolved only partly out of θέλω and νά "that":
θέ(λει) νά to θενά (θελά), θανά, θά. On the forms δά, χά, ἄ, ἐννά, v.
§ 20, n. 2.

3. Sometimes other verbal forms (partly stereotyped and of the
nature of particles) are employed to express a definite modality; thus,
e.g. súzi (*sóni*) pl. *sózune* in Otranto to denote "can" (*sózi fonási* "he
could cry," *sózune yelási* "they could laugh") or πὰ (a stereotyped
πάει) νά "am about to, going to" (νὰ πὰ νὰ σοῦ τὴ φέρω "I am going
to fetch her to thee"), or λάχ in Pontus to denote a wish (λὰχ ἔχω =
a. Gk. ἔχοιμι).

ACTIVE.

§ 225. The *Future* is a combination of θά (or in dialect
δά, χά, ἄ), or dialectically or archaically θενά (less commonly
θανά, θελά, Cyprian ἐννά), with I. the present subjunctive or
II. aorist subjunctive. The first (I.) is the present future,
the second (II.) the aoristic future. On the usage of both
forms, *v.* § 191.

I.	II.
θὰ [1] δένω	θὰ [1] δέσω
θὰ δένῃς	θὰ δέσῃς
θὰ δένῃ	θὰ δέσῃ
θὰ δένωμε	θὰ δέσωμε
θὰ δένετε	θὰ δέσετε
θὰ δένουν(ε)	θὰ δέσουνε.

If the verb begins with a vowel the final -a of the particle blends

---

[1] Or one of the equivalent forms θενὰ, etc.

with the following initial, *v.* § 11. Analogous to ναν and νυ (§ 34, n. 2), sometimes also θαν is used beside θα.

§ 226. In addition to the forms given the following circumlocutions for the future also are found :

(1) θέλω γράφω (γράψω), θέλεις γράφῃς (γράψῃς), etc.

(2) θέλω γράφει (γράψει), θέλεις γράφει (γράψει), etc.

(3) θέλει γράφω (γράψω), θέλει γράφῃς (γράψῃς), etc., before a vowel θέλ᾽ ἔχω, and so on.

(4) νὰ (also θὰ) γράφω (γράψω) θέλω, νὰ γράφῃς (γράψῃς) θέλεις or θές, etc.

These forms, however, are not extensively in use.

Notice TEXTS III. 1 (Bova) the future formed with ἔχω : *éh·yi na érti* "he will come."

§ 227. The *Perfect* and *Pluperfect* are formed with the help of ἔχω and the passive participle, or with ἔχω and an (invariable) root form similar to the 3rd sing. aorist subjunctive :

Perfect.

ἔχω δεμένο " I have bound "	ἔχομε δεμένο
ἔχεις δεμένο	ἔχετε δεμένο
ἔχει δεμένο	ἔχουν δεμένο

Or : ἔχω δέσει (δέσῃ)
ἔχεις δέσει
ἔχει δέσει
ἔχομε δέσει
ἔχετε δέσει
ἔχουν δέσει.

Pluperfect.

εἶχα δεμένο " I had bound "
εἶχες δεμένο
εἶχε δεμένο
εἴχαμε δεμένο
εἴχετε δεμένο
εἶχαν(ε) δεμένο.

Or : εἶχα δέσει
εἶχες δέσει, etc.

The second method is limited in popular usage to localities, though a favourite with the authors and poets. The difference which exists in German between, *e.g.*, " ich *bin* gegangen " and " ich *habe* gebunden," or in French, " je *suis* arrivé " and " j'*ai* trouvé," applies in modern Greek only to the first but not to the second method; thus, εἶμαι φτασμένος " I am (have) arrived " (usually aorist ἔφτασα), μεσάνυχτα εἶναι περασμένα " midnight is past," etc.; but for other forms only ἔχω (εἶχα) πάγει " I have (had) gone," ἔχω φτάσει " I have arrived," etc.[1]

δεμένα is also used in place of the form δεμένο. If the accusative of a conjunctive pronoun precedes, the participle agrees with it in gender and number; thus, τὴν ἔχω ἰδωμένη " I have seen her," τοὺς ἔχω ἰδωμένους " I have seen them." Sometimes, however, the participle remains invariable; *cf.* τὴν ἔχω ἰδωμένα, TEXTS III. 4.

1. δέσει resembles only on the surface the 3rd sing. subj. This form conceals the remnant or the transformation of the ancient infinitive in -ειν (δέσειν for δέσαι after the present). The preterite sense of ἔχω with the infin. is of quite recent date, and was evolved out of the scheme εἶχα + infin. after the latter had taken on pluperfect meaning.

2. Occasionally (particularly in Zaconian) instead of the participle in -μένο the verbal adjective in -τός is employed : ἔχω ἀκουστά " I have heard," ἔχει σφαλιχτὴ τὴ γυναῖκαν του " he has closed in his wife " (" keeps his wife closed in ") (TEXTS I. d. 5). Sometimes even a real adjective serves in this function : ἔχω πεμπάτο " I have sent," εἶναι φευγάτος " he is fled " (*cf.* § 212).

§ 228. The *Future Perfect* is a combination of the future of ἔχω and the same form which serves also in the perfect and pluperfect:

θὰ ἔχω δεμένο or θὰ ἔχω δέσει " I shall have bound " : θὰ ἔχω is conjugated quite regularly.

In place of θὰ ἔχω the other future combinations are also possible.

§ 229. The tense forms given in § 227 f. are not frequently used, since the aorist can represent also perfect and pluperfect (and even future perfect), *v.* §§ 189, 192. The simple vernacular has little need for these forms, which define more accurately the temporal course of an action. The use of the perfect ἔχω δέσει is least common, the aor.

---

[1] [In English the auxiliary *have* is universally employed to form the perfect and pluperf., but the auxiliary *be* may be employed with some intransitive verbs (of motion), " I *am* come " or " I *have* come."]

indic. quite frequently having the force of our perfect
(§ 189, 2); *cf. e.g.* δὲν ἔχουμε πολυσυνηθίσει (TEXTS II. 7) "we
have (not yet) accustomed ourselves." The pluperfect εἶχα
δέσει is employed to throw into relief the completion of one
action in contrast to another past event, or when the
expression of the past idea is required to understand clearly
the connection: τὸν εἴχανε φέρει μιὰ μέρα, τὴν ὥρα ποῦ
ἔβγαινε ἡ βασιλοπούλα (II. b. 4) "they had brought him one
day at the hour when the princess used to go out," θυμήθηκε
κεῖνο ποῦ εἶχε τάξει (I. d. 1) "he remembered what he had
promised," οἱ μοῖρες τὴν εἴχανε προικίσει μ' ὅλες τὶς ὀμορφιές
(II. b. 4) "the fairies had endowed her with every beauty."
The pluperfect is, further, the correct usage when an action of
the previous *past* is to be depicted in its course (a function
for which the aorist is manifestly unsuitable); *e.g.* ὅλα τὰ
βάσανα ποῦ εἶχε τραβήξει ὡς τότε, ἤτανε τιποτένια μπρὸς
. . . (II. b. 4) "all the trials which he had *until then* endured
were as nothing compared with . . ."

The form ἔχω (εἶχα) δεμένο denotes only by way of
exception a simple action of the past, but emphasises rather
the circumstantial result of an action. Thus, while ἔχω
γράψει τὸ γράμμα is akin to ἔγραψα, the sense of τὸ ἔχω
γραμμένο τὸ γράμμα is something like "I have the letter
written; here it is." *Cf.*, further, τό 'χα μερωμένο (τὸ
πουλάκι) (III. 15) "I have (the bird) tamed," *i.e.* "I have
in it a tamed creature," τοὺ πλί σ ζῇ, τό 'χου κρυμμένου
(III. 11) "thy bird lives, I have it concealed (in a hiding-
place)," στὸν ὦμο εἶχε κρεμασμένο ἕνα σακκούλι (II, b. 3)
"on his shoulder he had a bag hung." In most cases the
participle is little more than an adjectival determination
(complement) of the object.

The same applies to the perfect passive εἶμαι δεμένος
and the pluperfect ἤμουν δεμένος (§ 232): *e.g.* ἤταν γραμμένα στὸ σπαθί "it was (could be read) written on the
sword."

§ 230. The various forms of the *Conditional* are formed
either (1) with θά and the imperfect (or pluperfect), or (2)
with the imperfect of θέλω and an (invariable) basal form in
-ει, like the 3rd sing. pres. or aor. subjunctive (the *time* in
question deciding whether present or aorist stem).

Present Conditional.

θὰ ἔδενα " I should bind "   θὰ ἐδέναμε
θὰ ἔδενες   θὰ ἐδένετε
θὰ ἔδενε   θὰ ἔδεναν.

Or :   ἤθελα δέσει (al. δένει) "I should bind."
        ἤθελες δέσει (δένει)
        ἤθελε δέσει (δένει)
        (ἠ)θέλαμε δέσει (δένει)
        (ἠ)θέλετε δέσει (δένει)
        (ἠ)θέλανε δέσει (δένει).

1. The following combinations are also possible :
   (1) ἤθελα δένω (δέσω), ἤθελες δένῃς (δέσῃς), and so on.
   (2) ἤθελε δένω (δέσω), ἤθελε δένῃς (δένῃς), and so on.
   (3) θὰ ἤθελα (νὰ) δένω (δέσω), θὰ ἤθελες (νὰ) δένῃς (δέσῃς),
and so on.
   (4) θὰ ἤθελα δένει (δέσει), θὰ ἤθελες δένει (δέσει), and so on.
   (5) θὰ ἤθελε (νὰ) δένω (δέσω), θὰ ἤθελε (νὰ) δένῃς (δέσῃς), and so on.
The schemes (3), (4), and (5) emphasise the idea of contingency.
   (6) ἤθελα ἔδενα, ἤθελες ἔδενες or θελὰ (ἔ)δενα, θελὰ (ἔ)δενες,
and so on.
   (7) ἤθελ' ἔδενα, ἤθελ' ἔδενα, and so on.
2. On the sense of θὰ ἔδεσα, θὰ ἔδεσες, *cf.* § 195.

Past Conditional.

θὰ ἔδενα, etc.

Or : θὰ[1] εἶχα δεμένο or δέσει " I should have bound "
     θὰ εἶχες δεμένο or δέσει
     θὰ εἶχε δεμένο or δέσει
     θὰ εἴχαμε δεμένο or δέσει
     θὰ εἴχετε δεμένο or δέσει
     θὰ εἴχανε δεμένο or δέσει.

3. Instead of θὰ εἶχα the various combinations of the present
conditional may be used, δεμένο or δέσει remaining : ἤθελα ἔχει δεμένο
(δέσει), ἤθελα ἔχω δεμένο (δέσει), etc.

On the usage of the Conditional, *cf.* § 277, 4.

PASSIVE.

§ 231. *Future.*

I.	II.
θὰ[1] δένωμαι	θὰ δεθῶ
θὰ δένεσαι	θὰ δεθῇς

[1] Or one of the equivalent forms θενὰ, etc., § 225.

θὰ δένεται   θὰ δεθῇ
θὰ δενώμαστε   θὰ δεθοῦμε
θὰ δένεστε   θὰ δεθῆτε
θὰ δένουνται   θὰ δεθοῦνε.

Corresponding to the future active schemes given in § 226 the following are possible for the passive:

(1) θέλω δένωμαι (δεθῶ), θέλεις δένεσαι (δεθῇς), etc.

(2) θέλω δεθεῖ, θέλεις δεθεῖ.

(3) θέλει δένωμαι (δεθῶ), θέλει δένεσαι (δεθῇς)

(4) νὰ δένωμαι (δεθῶ) θέλω.

§ 232. The *Perfect, Pluperfect*, and *Future Perfect* are formed (1) with εἶμαι and the passive participle (declined like an adjective), or (2) with ἔχω and a form like the 3rd sing. aor. passive subjunctive.

Perfect

εἶμαι δεμένος (δεμένη, δεμένο) " I am (have been) bound "
εἶσαι δεμένος
εἶναι δεμένος
εἴμαστε δεμένοι (δεμένες, δεμένα)
εἶστε δεμένοι
εἶναι δεμένοι.

Or: ἔχω δεθεῖ (δεθῇ)
ἔχεις δεθεῖ
ἔχει δεθεῖ
ἔχομε δεθεῖ
ἔχετε δεθεῖ
ἔχουν(ε) δεθεῖ.

Pluperfect.

ἤμουν(α) δεμένος " I was (had been) bound "
ἤσουν(α) δεμένος
ἤτανε δεμένος
ἤμαστε δεμένοι
ἤσαστε δεμένοι
ἤτανε δεμένοι.

Or: εἶχα δεθεῖ
εἶχες δεθεῖ, etc.

Future Perfect.

θὰ (or θενὰ, etc.) εἶμαι δεμένος "I shall have been bound."

θὰ εἶσαι δεμένος, etc.

Or: θὰ ἔχω δεθεῖ, θὰ ἔχῃς δεθεῖ, etc.

δεθεῖ is the transformation of the ancient infinitive δεθῆναι. This scheme is, like that of the active, limited to certain localities.

§ 233.   *Conditional Present.*

θὰ[1] ἐδένουμουν[2] "I should be bound"
θὰ ἐδένουσουν
θὰ ἐδένουνταν
θὰ ἐδενούμαστε
θὰ ἐδενούσαστε
θὰ ἐδένουνταν.

Or: ἤθελα δεθεῖ
ἤθελες δεθεῖ
ἤθελε δεθεῖ
(ἠ)θέλαμε δεθεῖ
(ἠ)θέλετε δεθεῖ
(ἠ)θέλανε δεθεῖ.

1. As in the active, the following additional combinations are possible :

(1) ἤθελα δένωμαι (δεθῶ), ἤθελες δένεσαι (δεθῇς), etc.
(2) ἤθελε δένωμαι (δεθῶ), ἤθελες δένεσαι (δεθῇς), etc.
(3) θὰ ἤθελα (νὰ) δένωμαι (δεθῶ), θὰ ἤθελες (νὰ) δένεσαι (δεθῶ), etc.
(4) θὰ ἤθελα δεθεῖ, θὰ ἤθελες δεθεῖ, etc.
(5) θὰ ἤθελε (νὰ) δένωμαι (δεθῶ), θὰ ἤθελε (νὰ) δένεσαι (δεθῇς), etc.
(6) ἤθελ' ἐδένουμουν, ἤθελ' ἐδένουσουν, etc., or θελὰ δένουμουν, θελὰ δένουσουν, etc.

2. On the meaning of θὰ ἐδέθηκα, cf. § 195.

Conditional Past.

θὰ ἐδένουμουν

Or: θὰ ἤμουν(α) δεμένος "I should be (have been) bound"
θὰ ἤσουν(α) δεμένος
θὰ ἤτανε δεμένος
θὰ ἤμαστε δεμένοι
θὰ ἤσαστε δεμένοι
θὰ ἤτανε δεμένοι.

Or: θὰ εἶχα δεθεῖ
θὰ εἶχες δεθεῖ, etc.

---

[1] Or one of the equivalent forms θενὰ, and so on, § 225.

[2] Or one of the other imperfect forms, § 220.

3. Once more the various other combinations may be inserted for θὰ ἤμουνα and θὰ εῖχα.

THE PARTICIPLES.

§ 234. Modern Greek has the following participle system :

(1) Active present participle in -οντας : δένοντας " binding " (indeclinable).

(2) Past participle passive in -μένος : δεμένος " bound," on the formation of which v. § 209 ff. Sometimes also in the same sense a participle in -τός, v. § 212.

This participle in the case of intransitive verbs has an *active* value; as, φτασμένος " arrived," ἀνθισμένος " flowering," and even φαγωμένος " having eaten, satisfied " (εἴμαστε φαγωμένοι " we have eaten, are satisfied ").

(3) A number of middle (or passive) present participles in -ούμενος or -άμενος, of which those more commonly used are :

A. καθούμενος " sitting " (κάθομαι)
 κειτούμενος " lying, bed-ridden " (κείτομαι)
 τὸ μελλούμενο " the future " (μέλλει)
 πετούμενος " flying " (πετῶ), neut. " bird "
 τὸ πρεπούμενο " what is proper " (πρέπει)
 τρεχούμενος " running, current " (τρέχω); τὰ τρεχούμενα " what has taken place, event " (a. Gk τὰ γεγονότα)
 χαρούμενος " joyful " (χαίρω)
 χρειαζούμενος " necessary," " needful " (χρειάζομαι).
B. γενάμενος " becoming " (γένομαι)
 ἐρχάμενος " coming " (ἔρχομαι)
 κειτάμενος beside κειτούμενος
 λεγάμενος " what is (being) referred to," " aforesaid " (λέγω)
 πετάμενος beside πετούμενος " flying "
 πηγαινάμενος " going " (πηγαίνω)
 στεκάμενος " standing, stagnant " (of water); τὰ στεκάμενα " chattels " (στέκω)
 τρεμάμενος " trembling " (τρέμω)
 τρεχάμενος " running, flowing," particularly n. " running water " beside τρεχούμενος
 χαιράμενος " enjoying (a husband)," i.e. not a widow.

1. The participles in -ούμενος were taken from the contracted verbs, those in -άμενος from ancient models like, (ἱ)στάμενος, δεξάμενος. Some a. Gk. participles in -ούμενος have completely lost their original meaning; as, ὁ ἡγούμενος "the abbot," τὰ λαλούμενα "the musical instruments."

2. There are only solitary occurrences of other participial formations ; thus the Greek of Lower Italy still retains a participle from the aor. active, the pres. λύννοντα (-ας) giving an aor. λύσοντα, γέρνοντα giving γείροντα. Others again are retained only as adjectives or as substantives : e.g. ἡ ἐλεοῦσα " the compassionate" (sc. Παναγία "mother of God"); ὁ παρώ(ν) "present" (indeclinable) is taken from the literary language.

§ 235. The participle constructions are very limited compared with ancient Greek. The most common is the participle in -μένος (2), which is employed as an adjective, and sometimes even takes the place of a (relative) dependent clause; cf. e.g. III. 8. 1.

1. An absolute construction occurs in TEXTS I. a. 8 : τὸν περικαλῶ τὰ χέρια σταυρωμένα "I beseech him with folded hands (the hands folded)."

The participle in -ούμενος or -άμενος (3) stands either attributive, as τὰ πετάμενα πουλιά "the flying birds," ὁ λεγάμενος Ψυχαρισμός "the so-called P.," or converts to a substantive (see above), or is confined to fixed expressions, like στὰ καλὰ καθούμενα " at random."

2. In the employment of the vernacular for literary purposes an effort is made to extend this principle or to introduce the literary form (in -όμενος) into the vernacular usage (e.g. τὰ γραφόμενά του " his writings," TEXTS II. b. 7, or λεγόμενος = λεγάμενος).

§ 236. The participle in -οντας (§ 234, 1) is never employed attributively, but serves (like the French en with pres. participle) as an absolute form, and mostly to complement, illustrate, or explain the verbal action : e.g. βλέποντας δὲν βλέπουν "seeing (with their eyes) they do not see," τοὺς εἶπε λέγοντας "he spoke to them saying," κλαίοντας λέει "weeping he says," ὁ Χάρος πετεχέται τὸ δρεπάνι κρατῶντας στὸ χέρι "Death hastes, holding the sickle in his hand "; notice θέλοντας μὴ θέλοντας "whether (he) will or not." Further, it may express the contemporaneous occurrence of two actions ; as, αὐτὸ ἀκούοντας ἔγινε ἄφαντος " hearing (as he heard) this he became invisible." Constructions like ὄντας δίχως ρίζα ξεράθηκαν (Pallis) "being without root they withered," are rare.

1. The participle does not of necessity relate to the subject; *cf.* κλαδεύοντας . . . τὸν κέντρωσε . . . ἐν ἀγκαθάκι "stripping (as he stripped) (the bushes) a thorn pricked him," καρτεροῦν τὴν ἄνοιξι . . . ν' ἀκούσουν τὰ Βλαχόπουλα λαλῶντας τὲς φλογέρες (TEXTS I. a. 5) "they waited for the spring in order to hear the shepherd children playing (when they played) the flute."

2. A nominative absolute construction is rare. The writer Ἐφταλιώτης, who throughout his historic prose (Ἱστορία τῆς Ρωμιοσύνης, 1901) manifests a certain propensity for participial constructions, and introduces into the vernacular after the model of the pres. participle in -οντας aorist forms like θαρέψαντας, μαθόντας (*cf.* § 234, n. 2), φοβηθέντας, writes also, *e.g.*, γίνεται μεγάλο συνέδριο στὸ παλάτι, παρόντας κι ὁ πατριάρχης κι ὅλοι οἱ προύχοντες "a great assembly is held in the palace, at which the patriarch and all the dignitaries were present."

II. CONTRACTED VERBS.

§ 237. To the contracted verbs belong all verbs in -ῶ, that is, all those which bear the accent on the final in the 1st. sing. pres. Also the "semi-contracted" verbs given under present system II. c follow the contracted verbs in some forms. The contracted verbs are divided into two classes, the characteristic of which is found in the 2nd sing. pres. (1) in -ῶ, -ᾷς, and (2) in -ῶ, -εῖς.

Both classes correspond to the a. Gk verbs in -άω and -έω. Some are new-comers: *e.g.* εὐκοῦμαι for εὔχομαι (εὐκήθηκα), together with such as σκῶ, ἀρπῶ for σκάζω, ἀρπάζω, etc., *v.* p. 136 f. The two classes of a. Gk. verbs in -άω and -έω merge in many points in their conjugation, the verbs in -άω having appropriated forms of the -έω conjugation (*cf.* ρωτοῦμε, ρωτοῦνε, ἐρωτοῦσα, ἐρώτουνα, etc.). The ancient -όω verbs have converted into barytones in -ώνω, *v.* § 199, I. 6, n. 3.

The first class in -ῶ, -ᾷς is considerably more common than the second, *v.* § 250.

Contracted verbs differ from the conjugation of barytones only in the present (including imperative and pres. participle) and the imperfect, all the other forms being identical with those of the barytones (taking into account the stem formation of the aorists act. and pass. and the passive participle given under § 201, II. and § 210, II.).

FIRST CLASS.

Paradigm: ρωτῶ "I ask."

ACTIVE.

§ 238.   *Present.*

Indicative.   Subjunctive.

ρωτῶ	νὰ ρωτῶ
ρωτᾷς	νὰ ρωτᾷς
ρωτᾷ	νὰ ρωτᾷ
ρωτοῦμε	νὰ ρωτοῦμε
ρωτᾶτε	νὰ ρωτᾶτε
ρωτοῦν(ε)	νὰ ρωτοῦν(ε).

ρωτοῦσι like δένουσι, § 213, n. 5.

Imperfect.

(ἐ)ρωτοῦσα
(ἐ)ρωτοῦσες
(ἐ)ρωτοῦσε
(ἐ)ρωτούσαμε
(ἐ)ρωτούσετε (ἐρωτούσατε)
(ἐ)ρωτούσαν(ε).

(ἐ)ρωτούσασι like ἐδένασι, § 214, n. 4.

§ 239. On the Greek mainland (*e.g.* in Epirus, Central Greece), in the Greek of Lower Italy and that of the Ionic Islands and in the Peloponnesus, the following scheme of conjugation is found:

Present.

ρωτάω	ρωτᾶμε
ρωτάεις	ρωτᾶτε
ρωτάει	ρωτᾶν(ε) ρωτᾶσι.

Imperfect.

ἐρώτα(γ)α	ἐρωτά(γ)αμε (ἐρωτᾶμε)
ἐρώτα(γ)ες	ἐρωτά(γ)ατε (ἐρωτᾶτε)
ἐρώτα(γ)ε	ἐρώτα(γ)αν (ἐρωτᾶνε).

The so-called "analysed" (called also incorrectly "uncontracted") forms are most in vogue in the Peloponnesus. They are new formations on the basis of the a. Gk. contracted forms which survive in the regular inflection of the present (apart from the

infection by the -έω-conjugation). The analytic forms arose through
the addition of -ει and -ε to the 3rd sing. pres. ἐρωτᾷ, and imperf.
ἐρώτα on analogy of the barytones (ρωτᾷ-ει, ἐρώτα-ε), and these forms
consequently reacted by analogy on the 1st and 2nd sing. The
characteristic vowel -α- was finally carried over also to the 1st and
3rd pl. The -γ- in ἐρώταγα is secondary (to avoid hiatus). Such -γ-
forms were then placed on a par with φυλάγω ἐφύλαγα, etc. The
regular imperf. ἐρωτοῦσα is also a new formation, suggested by the
3rd pl. of the έω verbs. A more faithful continuation of the a. Gk.
imperfect is found, e.g., in the Aegean, in the inflection of the sing. :

ἐρώτουν(α)	(ἐρωτούσαμε
ἐρώτας	ἐρωτούσετε
ἐρώτα(νε)	ἐρωτούσαν).

§ 240. *Imperative.*

ρώτα (ρώτα[γ]ε)
ἀς ρωτᾷ (ἀς ρωτάῃ)
ρωτᾶτε
ἀς ρωτοῦνε (ἀς ρωτᾶν).

PASSIVE.

§ 241. *Present.*

Indicative.	Subjunctive.
ρωτοῦμαι (also ρωτᾶμαι)	νὰ ρωτοῦμαι, etc.
ρωτᾶσαι	
ρωτᾶται	
ρωτούμεστα (ρωτάμεστα)	
ρωτᾶστε	
ρωτοῦνται (ρωτᾶνται).	

Imperfect.

(ἐ)ρωτούμουν(α)
(ἐ)ρωτούσουν(α)
(ἐ)ρωτούνταν(ε)
(ἐ)ρωτούμαστε, (ἐ)ρωτούμεστα(ν)
(ἐ)ρωτούσαστε, (ἐ)ρωτούστε
(ἐ)ρωτούνταν(ε).

Besides forms like the following :

ἐρωτώμανε	ἐρωτώμαστε, ἐρωτώμασταν(ε)
ἐρωτώσανε	ἐρωτᾶστε, ἐρωτώσαστε, ἐρωτούσταν
ἐρωτάτον(ε), ἐρωτώταν(ε), ἐρωτώνταν.	ἐρωτώντουσαν, ἐρωτώντησαν.

§ 242. Beside the conjugation given above, many verbs take also the following:

Present.

ἀγαπειοῦμαι (rarely ἀγαπειέμαι)
ἀγαπειέσαι
ἀγαπειέται
ἀγαπειούμεστα
ἀγαπειέστε
ἀγαπειοῦνται.

Imperfect.

ἀγαπειούμουν(α) (ἀγαπειώμουν[α])
ἀγαπειούσουν(α)
ἀγαπειέτον, ἀγαπειούντανε (ἀγαπειώ[ν]ταν[ε])
ἀγαπειούμεστα, ἀγαπειούμαστε (ἀγαπειώμαστε)
ἀγαπειέστε, ἀγαπειούσαστε, ἀγαπειούστε (ἀγαπειώστε)
ἀγαπειούνταν(ε) (ἀγαπειώντουσαν).

These forms are found (commonly along with the first scheme of conjugation) mostly in those verbs which have both active and passive forms; as, ἀγαπῶ "love," βουτῶ "dive," βαστῶ "hold," γελῶ "laugh," πουλῶ "sell," τιμῶ "honour," τραβῶ "draw," χαλῶ "destroy," etc. The deponent verbs show a preference for the first form (in -οῦμαι or -ᾶμαι); thus, θυμοῦμαι "remember," κοιμοῦμαι "sleep," λυποῦμαι "regret," φοβοῦμαι "fear"; though also γκρεμειέται "he collapses," καταρειέται "he curses," καυκειοῦμαι "I boast" beside καυκοῦμαι.

Both the first and also particularly the second scheme of conjugation have arisen from an intermixture of the ancient verbs in -άω with those in -έω, on which see below.

§ 243.   *Imperative.*

ῥωτοῦ (ἀγαπειοῦ)   ῥωτᾶστε (ἀγαπειέστε)
ἂς ῥωτᾶται   ἂς ῥωτοῦνται.

The passive or middle imperative forms are rare (*e.g.* κοιμοῦ "sleep"), being replaced by νά with the 2nd pers. of subjunctive.

§ 244. The other forms of contracted verbs not belonging to the present system have no peculiarities:

Aorist.

Act. ἐρώτησα, subj. νὰ ρωτήσω, imperat. ρώτησε.

Pass. ἐρωτήθηκα, νὰ ρωτηθῶ, ρωτήσου.

COMPOUND TENSES.

ACTIVE.

Future: (I) θὰ ρωτῶ, (II) θὰ ρωτήσω (or one of the other variations).

Perfect: ἔχω ρωτημένο, ἔχω ρωτήσει.

Pluperfect: εἶχα ρωτημένο or εἶχα ρωτήσει.

Future perfect: θὰ ἔχω ρωτημένο or θὰ ἔχω ρωτήσει.

Conditional: θὰ 'ρωτοῦσα, ἤθελα ρωτᾶ or ἤθελα ρωτήσει (or one of the other variations); θὰ εἶχα ρωτημένο or ρωτήσει.

PASSIVE.

Future: (I) θὰ ρωτοῦμαι, (II) θὰ ρωτηθῶ.

Perfect: εἶμαι ρωτημένος, ἔχω ρωτηθεῖ.

Pluperfect: ἤμουνα ρωτημένος, εἶχα ρωτηθεῖ.

Future perfect: θὰ εἶμαι ρωτημένος or θὰ ἔχω ρωτησεῖ.

Conditional: θὰ 'ρωτούμουν, ἤθελα ρωτηθεῖ (or one of the other variations); θὰ ἤμουν(α) ρωτημένος, θὰ εἶχα ρωτηθεῖ.

PARTICIPLES.

ρωτῶντας, ρωτημένος: *cf.* also § 234, **3.**

SECOND CLASS.

Paradigm: πατῶ " I walk."

ACTIVE.

§ 245.   *Present.*

Indicative.	Subjunctive.
πατῶ " I walk "	νὰ πατῶ
πατεῖς	νὰ πατῇς
πατεῖ	νὰ πατῇ
πατοῦμε	νὰ πατοῦμε
πατεῖτε	νὰ πατῆτε
πατοῦν(ε) (πατοῦσι)	νὰ πατοῦν(ε).

12

Imperfect.

ἐπατοῦσα
ἐπατοῦσες
ἐπατοῦσε
ἐπατούσαμε
ἐπατούσετε
ἐπατούσαν(ε) (ἐπατούσασι).

Besides this the following scheme of the imperf. is found (particularly on the islands of the Aegean, Crete, and Cyprus) :

ἐπάτεια (ἐπάτειουν)	ἐπατούσαμε(ν)
ἐπάτειες	ἐπατούσετε
ἐπάτειε	ἐπατούσαν (ἐπάτειαν).

1. Notice also (after ρ) ἠμπόριγα or (ἠ)μπόρεγα, ἐφόριγα, ἐθώριγα (ἐθώριγες ἐθώριγε) beside ἐθώρεια, ἐφόρεια, ἠμπόρεια, etc.

2. On forms like ἐπάθεια ἐπάθειες, cf. § 16, n. 3.

3. These forms originated in a manner similar to the "analysed" in -άω : the ending -ε attached to the 3rd sing. ἐπάτει following the model of the other verbs, and then created analogous forms for the 1st and 2nd persons. πουλειοῦσα (TEXTS III. 12) is a cross between the type ἐπατοῦσα and ἐπάτεια. The present reflects correctly the a. Gk. scheme. The corresponding a. Gk. inflection of the imperfect still survives in different places (*e.g.* in Cyprus and the Aegean), ἐπάτουν(α) ἐπάτεις ἐπάτει (ἐπάτεν or ἐπάτενε) ἐπατοῦμε ἐπατεῖτε ἐπατοῦσαν. The form ἐπάτουνα was transferred also to the first class (*cf.* § 239 n.).

§ 246. *Imperative.*

πάτει and πάτειε
ἂς πατῇ
πατεῖτε
ἂς πατοῦν(ε).

PASSIVE.

§ 247. *Present.*

Indicative.		Subjunctive.
πατοῦμαι	πατειοῦμαι (πατειέμαι)	νὰ πατοῦμαι
πατεῖσαι	πατειέσαι	etc.
πατεῖται	πατειέται	and so on like indic.
πατούμεστα	πατειούμεστα	
πατεῖστε	πατειέστε	
πατοῦνται	πατειοῦνται.	

Imperfect.

ἐπατούμουν(α)	ἐπατειούμουν(α)
ἐπατούσουν(α)	ἐπατειούσουν(α)
ἐπατούνταν(ε)	ἐπατειέτον, ἐπατειούνταν(ε)
ἐπατούμαστε	ἐπατειούμεστα
ἐπατούσαστε	ἐπατειέστε
ἐπατούνταν(ε)	ἐπατειούνταν(ε).

1. Also other variant endings as in the paradigm, § 220.

The second scheme of conjugation is more in use than the first, although the first is more nearly akin to a. Gk. Deponents have become mostly exactly identical in their inflection with that of the first class (§ 241); θυμοῦμαι, λυποῦμαι, φοβοῦμαι belong under the first class according to their origin, but follow the second in their inflection. On the other hand always βαθειοῦμαι or βαρειέμαι "I am weary."

2. *Cf.* also συλλογειέμαι, συλλογειέσαι (TEXTS I. a. 14, Velv. συλλονέσι) beside the 1st person συλλο(γ)οῦμαι "I think."

§ 248.   *Imperative.*

πατειοῦ (νὰ πατειέσαι)
ἂς πατῆται, ἂς πατειέται
πατειέστε (νὰ πατειέστε)
ἂς πατοῦνται, ἂς πατειοῦνται.

§ 249. All the other parts are formed according to the same rules as in Class I. (§ 244). Notice particularly the participle πατῶντας like ρωτῶντας.

§ 250. The list of verbs which follow Class I. or II. respectively cannot be definitely fixed, as the same verb frequently gives double forms for the same part. In general the second class of contracted verbs is much less prominent than the first; only ἀργῶ "am late," ἐμπορῶ "am able," θαρρῶ "believe" (but θαρρεύω "I am brave"), ζῶ (also ζιῶ) "live," φιλῶ "kiss" (but φιλεύω "greet kindly, regale"), are universally (or practically universally) conjugated like πατῶ.

1. From ζῶ note the spellings ζῆς, ζῆ, ζῆτε (further, regularly ζοῦμε, ζοῦν[ε], ἐζοῦσα). This verb has become identical with πατῶ in the pronunciation of its endings, only orthography still maintaining the a. Gk. peculiarity of the verb.

All the rest of the contracted verbs may be conjugated after Class I. This is quite usual in the Peloponnesus and in Northern Gk. (*cf.* § 7, n. 1), while in the Aegean region (except the Northern part) Class II. is more plentifully represented, though still less prominent than Class I. Thus in m. Gk., *e.g.*, the following a. Gk. verbs in -έω are regularly conjugated like Class I. (-ῶ, -ᾷς): ἀκλουθῶ "follow," ζητῶ "request," βοηθῶ "help," κεντῶ "prick," κυνηγῶ "hunt," μετρῶ "measure, number," πολεμῶ "make an effort, struggle," προσκυνῶ "greet respectfully," χαιρετῶ "greet," χτυπῶ "strike."

The following verbs usually (especially in the region of the Aegean) inflect after Class II. (-ῶ, -εῖς): βαρῶ "strike," θωρῶ "see, consider," καρτερῶ "await," κελαϊδῶ "warble," κρατῶ "hold," λαλῶ "speak," λησμονῶ "forget," μιλῶ "speak," παρηγορῶ "console," παρακαλῶ (περικαλῶ) "request," περπατῶ "go walking," πονεῖ "it pains," συχωρῶ "pardon," φορῶ "wear" (a garment), χρωστῶ "owe"; but also μιλῶ μιλᾷς, καρτερῶ καρτερᾷς, κρατῶ κρατᾷς, χρωστῶ χρωστᾷς, ἀλησμονάω, καταφρονάω, συχωράω, etc. Notice βαστεῖ, TEXTS III. 6 (Calymnos), for the regular βαστᾷ.

2. Also mostly all the verbs in original -έω, which are borrowed from the literary language, follow Class II.; as, κατοικῶ "dwell" (vernacular μένω, κάθομαι), προξενῶ "cause," προσκαλῶ "invite," ὑπηρετῶ "serve" (δουλεύω), and others.

3. The secondary contracted verbs ξῶ "I scrape" (beside the usual ξύνω), φτῶ (usually φτύνω) "expectorate," σβῶ (σβήνω) "extinguish," and similar verbs, p. 136, inflect like Class II.; but also ἀπολῶ (a. Gk. λύω): ἀπολάει, μεθῶ: μεθεῖς and μεθᾷς, μηνῶ: μηνᾷς.

Semi-contracted Verbs.

§ 251. A few verbs with a vocalic final in the stem blend this final in some cases with the ending:

(1)   ἀκούω "I hear" ἀκούμε (ἀκοῦμε)

ἀκούς (ἀκοῦς)   ἀκούτε

(ἀκούει)   ἀκούνε.

      Imperative ἄκου ἀκούτε.

      (Imperfect ἄκου[γ]α, etc.)

Similarly κρούω "beat."

(2)   κλαίω "I weep"   κλαίμε (κλαῖμε)

κλαίς (κλαῖς)   κλαίτε

κλαίει (less commonly κλαί) κλαίν(ε) (κλαίσι).

      (Imperfect ἔκλαι [γ]α, etc.)

Similarly φταίω "I am guilty."

These forms appear also uncontracted with a γ inserted (*cf.* § 23), ἀκούγω, κρούγω, κλαίγω, φταίγω.

§ 252. Through the dropping of a γ (§ 22) in some verbs, vowel sounds come together and are contracted:

(1) πάω usually instead of πάγω πάγεις, etc., " I go " (alongside πηγαίνω, to which it serves as aorist stem; *cf.* §§ 186, 204) with the following forms:

πά(γ)ω	—
πάεις	πάς (πᾶς)
πάει	πά (πᾶ)
	πάμε (πᾶμε)
	πάτε
	πάν(ε).

Subj. νὰ πάω νὰ πάς, and so forth, future θὰ πάω θὰ πάς, etc. On ἄμε, *v.* § 218, n. 3.

Likewise νὰ (θὰ) φάω beside φάγω, etc. (aor. subj. of τρώγω " I eat ") :

νὰ φάς (φᾶς)
νὰ φάῃ
νὰ φάμε (φᾶμε)
νὰ φάτε
νὰ φάν(ε).

The aor. indic. runs regularly ἔφα(γ)α ἔφα(γ)ες ἔφα(γ)ε ἐφά(γ)αμε ἐφάγετε ἔφα(γ)αν.

Also the Pontic verb φτάω " I make," φτάς, etc.

(2)   τρώ(γ)ω " I eat "
τρώεις τρώς (τρῶς)
τρώει (less commonly τρώ)
τρώ(γ)ομε τρώμε (τρῶμε)
τρώ(γ)ετε τρώτε
τρώ(γ)ουν(ε) τρώνε
(Imperfect ἔτρω[γ]α ἔτρω[γ]ες, and so forth).

(3)   λέ(γ)ω " I say "
λέεις λές
λέει (less commonly λέ)
λέ(γ)ομε λέμε

λέ(γ)ετε λέτε

λέ(γ)ουνε λέν(ε) (λέουσι λέσι)

(Imperfect ἔλε[γ]α or ἤλε[γ]α, ἔλε[γ]ες, etc.).

1. Also θέλω θές follows this model, § 224, 3, and even ξέρω ξές. Likewise ρέω "flow" sometimes gives a 3rd pl. ρένε.

2. *Cf.*, further, from Chios (Texts III. 9) the 3rd sing. λẽ and λῖ (in unaccented position) and 3rd pl. *l῾ún*.

PART THIRD.

SYNTAX.

PRINCIPAL SENTENCES.

(a) Form and Content.

§ 253. Sentences *without verbal predicate* are not uncommon; they either express a maxim with epigrammatic brevity or serve to portray an event or circumstance vividly and picturesquely. *Cf.* μιᾶς στιγμῆς ὑπομονὴ δέκα χρονῶν ρεχάτι "one moment's patience (means) ten years' rest," αὐτὴ κατσούφα (Texts III. 12) "she (continued) peevish," αὐτὸς οὐ λόγους ἀπὸ χείλ᾽ σὶ χείλ᾽ καὶ ζd βασ῾λιὰ τοῦ ᾽φτί (III. 11) "this word (passed) from lip to lip and (reached) the king's ear," παντοῦ τρομάρα καὶ σφαγή, ἐδὼ φυγή, ἐκεῖ πληγή "everywhere (raged) consternation and carnage, here flight and there wounds"; *cf.* also Texts I. a. 19. With imperative force κάτω φέσια καὶ καπέλα "down (with) fez and hat."

Even a single member of a sentence may form a sentence by itself: the greatest animation of expression is secured by a series of such simple sentences in asyndeton: ἄργανα, τούμπανα, χαρὲς μεγάλες "organs (played), timbals (sounded), great joy (prevailed)"; τὰ πολλὰ πολλὰ κουμάντα, τὸ καράβι μὲ τὴν πάντα "too many commands (make) the boat ride on one side"; μεροδούλι μεροφάγι "day's work, day's food," *i.e.* "living from hand to mouth." Notice also πρῶτο φιλί—᾽ναστέναξε, etc., Texts I. a. 14. Abbreviated sentences are, of course, specially liked in exclamations; *v.* § 256.

§ 254. Sentences *without a subject* or *impersonal* sentences like βρέχει "it rains," χιονίζει "it snows," κάνει ἄσκημο καιρό "il fait mauvais temps," call for no special remark. The indefinite subject "one," "they," "people" [Ger. *man*, French *on*] is expressed (1) by κανείς (κανένας) "one, some one," as τὸν εἶδε κανένας "somebody has (they have) seen him"; (2) by the 2nd pers. sing., as λές "you might say," etc. (*cf.* § 195); (3) by the 1st or 3rd pl., as γλήγορα λησμονοῦμε τοὺς πεθαμμένους "people soon forget the dead," λένε "they say," *on dit*, μοῦ εἶπαν "it has been (they have) told me," ἐσκότωσαν τὸν κλέφτη "they slew the Kleft"; (4) by the passive voice (rare), as οἱ πεθαμμένοι γλήγορα λησμονειοῦνται "the dead are soon forgotten."

§ 255. *Interrogative sentences.* A question to which the answer may be either *yes* or *no* (Lat. *ne*) is marked by the tone of the voice, and requires no special interrogative word, not even a special arrangement of the words, though that member of the sentence to which the question relates (and so mostly the predicate) *may* be thrown to either extremity of the sentence: ἦρθε ὁ φίλος σου; or ὁ φίλος σου ἦρθε; "has your friend arrived?" τὸ βλέπεις κεῖνο τὸ βουνό; "do you see yon mountain?" εἶν' ἡ θυγατέρα σου τέτοια ὄμορφη; or εἶναι τέτοια ὄμορφη ἡ τσιούπρα σου; (TEXTS I. d. 1) "is thy daughter so fair?" μεθυσμένος εἶσαι ἢ (also γιὰ) τρελλός; "are you drunk or crazy?" ἕνα (*sc.* φιλὶ) σοῦ 'δωκε ἢ μὴ σοῦ 'δωκε πολλά; (I. a. 21) "did he give you one (kiss) or several?"

1. On the other hand, through contact with Turkish in Cappadocia (Sili) and elsewhere (as in Adrianople), the Turkish interrogative particle *mi* is employed: *e.g.* χαστάζ μι ἦσου; "were you sick?"

A question expecting an affirmative answer (*cf.* Lat. *nonne*) is introduced by δέν; as, δὲν εἶν' ὄμορφο τὸ ρόδο; "is the rose not beautiful? the rose is beautiful, is it not?" Such questions have sometimes the force of a mild (polite) request, particularly in the idiom δὲ μοῦ λές; "you tell me, do you not?" *i.e.* "tell me, please."

2. The idea of doubt (and also of refusal) may be expressed by τάχα (τάχατις), ἴσως (ἀνίσως), μήν(α), μήπως, μήγαρι(ς), etc., ἀρά (ἄραγε[ς]), μὴν πὰ(ς) (*i.e.* πάγεις[ς]) καί, μὴν πὰ(ς) νά, μπανά; as, τάχα δὲν καταλαβαίνεις; "perhaps you don't understand?" μὴν ἔταξες τίποτε; "did you perhaps promise something?" μὴ δὲν τό 'ξερες; "and did you not know it then?" μήνα τὰ φαγιά μας δὲ σᾶς ἄρεσαν;

"can it be that our fare has not pleased you?" μήπως or μηγάρι(ς) σοῦ εἶπα; "have I perhaps told you?" *i.e.* "I have not, of course, told you," ἀρὰ δὲν τοὺν ἀλ'πᾶσι; (III. 11) "can it be that thou deplorest him not?" μπανὰ φίλησες τὴν κόρη; (III. 5) "then did you kiss the girl?"

On the *modus potentialis* in questions, *v.* §§ 191, 1 and 195.

Questions *why? what?* (supplementary questions) are introduced by interrogative pronouns (§ 151 f.) or interrogative adverbs (γιατί; "why?" ποῦ, πότε, etc., § 126, ποῦ τάχα; "where then?"); the particle σάν before the interrogative word has the force of "well, exactly"; as, σὰν τί μὲ θέλεις; "well, what do you wish of me?" σὰν πῶς τοὺ λέ' ἡ λόγους; (TEXTS III. 11) "how then runs the proverb?"

§ 256. *Exclamatory sentences* have a partiality for the form of *abbreviated* sentences of predication, command, or interrogation: γιατρός καλός! γιατρικὰ καλά! " good physician! good physic!" and other ordinary exclamations: τί καλά! "how fine!" τί ζωὴ χαρούμενη! "what an enjoyable life!" The exclamatory nature of the sentence may be emphasised by ποῦ; as, τώρα δὰ ποῦ ἔφυγε! "just this moment gone!" ἤσυχα ποῦ εἶναι τὰ βουνά, ἤσυχοι ποῦ εἶν' οἱ κάμποι! "how still are the mountains, how still the plains!" τί βάσανο ποῦ εἶναι! "what a sorrow it is!"

Cf. also salutations and benedictions: καλὴ μέρα "good-day," καλὴ νύχτα "good-night," καλὴ σπέρα "good evening," ὥρα καλή (σου) "welcome!" καλὴ ἀντάμωσι "au revoir," στὸ καλό "adieu," καλὸ ταξίδι, καλὸ κατευόδιο "bon voyage," γειά σου "(to your) health," καλὴ ὄρεξι "good appetite," περαστικά "speedy recovery," σκάσε "go to the deuce."

§ 257. Abbreviated exclamations, commands, and vocatives have occasionally converted to *interjections*; *cf.* ποῦ! "how!" (ἐ)μπρός! "forward!" πίσω! "back!" στάσου! "stop!" διάβολε![1] τί διάβολο! "the devil!" Θέ μου! "my God!" Παναγιά μου! "holy Mother of God!" προσοχή! "attention!" καρδιά! "courage!" ψέματα! "cheat!" ἀλήθεια! "truly!" σώπα! "quiet!"

Genuine (old) interjections are: (calling) ἔ! οὔ! ντέ! "forward!" (surprise) ἄ! οὔ! πώ, πώ! ὤ, ὤ! (doubt) μπά! (lament and pain) ἄχ! ὤχ! ἄϊ! ὤϊ! (ὠϊμένα "alas for me!") βάϊ, βάϊ! βάχ! (anger, refusal, horror) οὔ! φτοῦ! οὔφ! σούτ!

---

[1] Also in several mutilated forms like, *e.g.*, διάντρε, διάτανε.

(joy) ὤχ! (laughter) χά, χά, χά! Notice also the onomatopoeic forms κράκ! πούφ! πάφ! μπούμ! μπάμ!

From the standpoint of the m. Gk. vernacular also words like
ζήτω! εὐγε! ἐβίβα! "up!" μπράβο! (frequently employed as a sign
of consent, generally with a pronoun μπράβο σου, μπράβο σας) or
βάρδα! "attention!" are treated as pure interjections, because such
words—borrowed from the literary language or from the Italian—have
for the m. Gk. vernacular lost all sense of connection. The same may
be said of such interjections as owe their origin to the violent mutilation of words which had an independent meaning; as, ἀλλοί! ἀλλοίμονο! "alas!" μπρέ! "hallo!" beside μωρέ! (μωρή! sometimes used
to address a woman). Here also we may reckon the ironical expression σπολλάτη "much obliged"= εἰς πολλὰ ἔτη. The serious
expression of good wishes (congratulation on special occasions) is εἰς
ἔτη πολλά! "(may you live) many years."

(b) Connection of Sentences.

§ 258. Sentences may be connected without any kind
of connective word; in this way sometimes a special effect
(vividness, grandeur) is obtained; *cf. e.g.* Texts I. a. 11.
22–23 or νὰ μὴ δείξ πονθενά χάθκαμι (III. 11) "show it to
nobody, (if you do) we are lost." The repetition of a verb in
asyndeton heightens the pictorialness of the course of an action;
as, πίνει, πίνει "he drinks (and) drinks" (*cf.* also § 188, 2 n.).
The repetition of another member of the sentence produces
the same effect; as, μαῦρος ἤταν, κατάμαυρος, μαῦρο καὶ τ᾽
ἄλογό του (I. a. 8), "black was he, all black, black too (was)
his steed."

Occasionally in the progress of a vivid narrative a question or an exclamation does duty for a connective: *e.g.* οὐ
παραγιός, τί εἶπεν μὶ τοὺ νοῦ τ; (III. 11) = "the adopted son
said . . . ," similarly ἔ, τί εἶπιν κι αὐτός (*ib.*), or ποῦ αὐτός!
τοὺ πλὶ . . . κρύβ᾽ (*ib.*), "and he, he conceals the hen."
Hence γιατί and τί "why?" often have the force of "for,
then"; γιατί in this sense may precede even an interrogative
sentence; *cf.* γιατί εἶμαι ἄξα ᾽γώ; (III. 4) "*for* am I worthy?"

§ 259. If sentences thrown together in asyndeton stand
in close logical dependence on each other, one part of the
entire series may be reduced to an accessory sentence or
even to an adverbial qualification or take the force of a
particle: *e.g.* ἔχουνε δὲν ἔχουνε παράδες, τὸ ἴδιο τοὺς κάνει
"whether they have money or not is all the same to them,"

θὲς δὲ θές, θὰ μὲ πλερώσῃς " whether you will or not you
shall pay me," ἂς εἶναι, τὸ πλερώνω " let it be (as far as I
am concerned), I pay for it," ἤτανε ἔνας βασιλέας "Ὕπνος τ'
ὄνομά του " there was a king named Sleep," λοιπόν, εἶχε δὲν
εἶχε, εὐτός ἀνεβαίνει (TEXTS I. d. 5) " well, at all events, he
goes up," τρέχα ρώτα, τό 'μαθέ = " by running and asking he
learned it." Likewise ἄψε σβῆσε " light, extinguish " =
" without much ado, in a trice" (οἱ γαμπροὶ δὲ γίνουνται ἄ.
σβ. " sons-in-law do not come without much ado "), μαθέ(ς)
(§ 218, n. 1) " that is (to say), then " (μαθέ[ς], δὲ μὲ πιστεύεις
" that is to say, you don't believe me," δὲν ἤταν κὶ μικρὸς μαθέ
" he was, then, not young "), θέλεις — θέλεις (θέλτς — θέλτς,
Velv.) " whether . . . or."

On the expression ἄρουν ἄρουν = " with all haste," cf. TEXTS III.
11 footnote. The following examples show how completely an
independent sentence may be obscured (e.g. made into a substantive):
τὸ πρᾶμα δὲν εἶναι παῖξε γέλασε " the matter is not for amusement
and laughter," τό 'λαβε μὲ τὸ γράψε γράψε " he obtained it after much
writing," imperat. τὸ ἔμπα = " the entrance."

§ 260. Co-ordination of sentences is effected by the
following conjunctions:

(a) Copulative: καί (before vowels κι) " and, also," καί . . .
καί " both . . . and," " as well as "; cf. § 261.

καί is also the ordinary conjunction with which single words are
connected. Sometimes it simply throws into prominence a single
member of the sentence; cf. ξέρω κ' ἐγώ; " am I to know it?" τί
ἤλιγιν κι αὐτός; (TEXTS III. 11) " and what did he say?" πὰν κεῖ καὶ
βῆκα (III. 12) " there above (and) I entered," σὲ τί ἀράδα εἴμεστ'
ἐμεῖς, καὶ νὰ μᾶς δώσ' ὁ βασιλιὰς τὴ θυγατέρα του; (I. d. 2) " in what
position are we that the king should give us his daughter?" Cf.
also the expressions τώρα καὶ μισὴ ὥρα " half an hour ago" and καὶ
καλά " right now, exactly," " just" (also ironically); as, θέλει καὶ
καλὰ καὶ σώνει = " he will, come what may (just now), finish it " (lit.
" and finishes "), δὰ τοὺ 'βροῦν κὶ καλά! δὲν τό 'φαγάμι κὶ καλὰ ἰμεῖς
ἰψές; (III. 11) " they will find it indeed! did we not eat it only
just yesterday?"

οὔτε (μήτε, οὐδέ, μηδέ, or μουδέ),[1] οὔτε (and so forth)
κἀν " neither, nor, not even "; as, οὔτε (κὰν) ἐμίλησε " he did
not even speak," μηδὲ τὸν εἶδα " neither did I see him," μηδὲ
τίποτε " nor anything, nothing at all "; οὔτε—οὔτε (μήτε—
μήτε, οὐδέ — οὐδέ, μηδέ — μηδέ)[1]) " neither . . . nor," cf.
§ 285; πότε—πότε " now . . . then " " at one time . . . anon."

[1] Without any difference even in affirmative sentences.

(b) Disjunctive: ἤ (γή), also γιά "or," ἤ—ἤ (γιά—γιά) "either . . . or"; θέλεις—θέλεις, v. § 259.

The particle is dropped with numerals; as, πέντ' ἕξι "five (or) six."

(c) Adversative: μά (in dialect ἀμά or ἀμμά, ἀμή, ἀμέ, Chios μμέ, Lesbos ἄμ), or ἀλλά "but, yet, but yet," μόνε (μόν, in dialect also μό) "only, however," after neg. sentence (or neg. member of a sentence) "but"; παρά "but" after a negative, also "not . . . but": e.g. παρὰ ὁ Γιάννης, ἂς ἔρθῃ αὐτός "(not) J., but let him come himself" (cf., further, § 158 n.); ὅμως, ὡς τόσο "nevertheless, however," not first in a sentence: e.g. ἐδ' ὅμως ἄρματα λαλοῦν "here, however, arms talk," or κι ὅμως "and yet," κι ὡς τόσο "and yet, still."

(d) Causal: γιαυτό, γιὰ τοῦτο "therefore": on γιατί (τί), v. § 258.

(e) Inferential: λοιπόν (τὸ λοιπόν) "now, well, then," either at the beginning of or later in the sentence; ἀμέ "but, so, indeed," stands first; as, ἀμὲ τί θέλεις; "what, then, do you want?"

Of course, in addition to the above, adverbs are employed as connectives between sentences; as, τώρα "now," τότε(ς) "then," ἔπειτα, ὕστερα "thereupon," ἔτσι "so," "thus." In Pontic (TEXTS III. 13. c) note the enclitic particle πὰ which stands second, ἄ⁰τς πα ποῖκα "so then I did it."

§ 261. The modern Greek vernacular shows a decided preference for paratactic construction, so that principal sentences with ἂς (§ 278, 3) and ἔτσι (§ 273) serve practically the function of dependent sentences. Καί, by far the most common conjunction, serves to connect any kind of sentences into a series (even in combinations like καὶ τότε, καὶ πάλι, etc.); and it may, according to the logical sequence of the thought, carry the meaning of "but," "for," "or," "and so"; cf. ὀχτ' ἀδερφοὶ δὲ θέλουνε κι ὁ Κωσταντῖνος θέλει "eight brothers do not wish it, but K. wishes it," φοβοῦμαι σ', ἀδερφάκι μου, καὶ λιβανιὲς μυρίζεις "I fear thee, my brother, for (because) thou smellest of incense," ἄνοιξε, κ' ἐγώ 'μ' ὁ Κωσταντῆς "open, for I am K."

The additional thought given by καί is frequently, according to the sense, subordinated like an accessory sentence to the preceding. Very frequently an object clause with νά or ποῦ, *e.g.*, after verbs of *perceiving, hearing, seeing*, etc., is displaced by this favourite parataxis; as, ἀκούν πουλιὰ καὶ λένε "they hear birds saying (and they say)," ἤκουσα καὶ σὲ μάλωνε ἡ κερά σου "I heard how thy mother scolded thee," μὲ γεῖπε καὶ τὸ ὀσείρισα (III. 12) "he said to me to take the lice off him [and I did so]," βλέπει τὸ φτωχὸ κ' ἔρχεται "he sees the poor man coming," τὸν εἶδα κ' ἐπήγαινε "I saw him going," θωρῶ τὸ πρόσωπό σου κ' ἔγινε σὰν τὴ φωτιά "I see how thy face became like fire": *cf.*, further, βρίσκει τὴν κ' ἐχτενίζουνταν "he finds her as she was combing herself," νά τον καὶ κατέβαινε "behold how he descended," δὲ ξέρουν οἱ γιατροὶ κι ἀπὲ τὸ βασιλόπουλο γιατρεύεται (Texts I. d. 1) "the physicians do not know by what means the royal child is cured," τοὺς βάνει κάθε νύχτα καὶ ὀργώνουν τὰ χωράφια του (Texts I. c. 6) "he makes them every night till (and they till) his acres," τοὺς ἀφήνει καὶ τοὺς πιάνουν τὰ λαγωνικά (*ib.*) "he allows the hounds to catch them," γιαυτὸ ἐμπόρεσε κ' ἔφκειασε τόσα κάστρα "therefore he was able to build (and he built) so many castles."

1. The following show other kinds of subordination: ἔχω γυναῖκα παρανιὰ καὶ χήρα δὲν τῆς πρέπει "I have a very young wife (and) widowhood becomes her not," εἶναι τόσο κουτὸς καὶ δὲν τὸ καταλαβαίνει "he is so stupid that (and) he does not grasp it," ἠντάμωνε τὸ φίλον του καὶ δὲν τοῦ 'λεγε παρὰ μνιὰ "καλὴ μέρα" (Texts I. d. 5) "(when) he met his friend he said nothing but a 'good-day.'"

2. The preference for parataxis has occasionally caused an originally subordinate conjunction to be treated as paratactic and consequently to be pressed into co-ordinating service: *e.g.* ἐπειδή almost = "for," ὡς (Texts I. a. 21) "and thus," ὅτι (I. d. 6) "just now."

3. M. Gk. has lost the classical Gk. wealth of connective and other particles which lend nicety and precision of thought. Only καί (οὔτε, οὐδέ), ἤ, and the less commonly used conjunctions ἀλλά, πλήν, ὅμως have been retained. The loss of γάρ, ἄρα has been compensated by new formations; but the a. Gk. τέ, δέ, μέν—δέ, μέντοι, μήν, οὖν (γοῦν), ἔτι, δή, γέ, πέρ have left no successors.

SUBORDINATE SENTENCES.

Preliminary Remarks.

§ 262. The propensity for parataxis has considerably reduced the a. Gk. wealth of dependent constructions. Long and complicated periods are, of course, still possible from the resources of the language, but are, as we should expect, of rare occurrence in the texts of the vernacular. Examples of rather long periods are found in Texts I.

d. 1 (κι αὐτὴ τὰ πῆρε καὶ πῆγε καὶ κλείστηκε, etc., including also an indirect discourse of some length), II. b. 1 (Ἀν ἤξεραν . . ., etc., in paragraph before the last), II. b. 2 (Ὁ δάσκαλος ἀφῆκε . . . etc., in fourth paragraph from the end). The a. Gk. conjunctions ἐπεί, ὁπότε (ὁπόταν), ἄχρις and μέχρις, εἰ, ἐφ' ᾧ have entirely disappeared ; ὡς survives still only in σάν (§§ 263, n. 1. 272, 281) and in καθώς (§§ 273, 281). On ὅπως, cf. § 281 ; on ὅτι, §§ 267, n. 2. 270, 273 ; on διότι, § 276, n. 1 ; μολονότι, § 278, 2 : ὥστε serves an entirely different purpose from a. Gk. (§ 275). The a. Gk. ἵνα (m. Gk. νά) alone has extended far beyond its original proper territory, a fact to be attributed chiefly to the loss of the infinitive (cf. §§ 263, n. 3. 266 f., 277, 4, n. 1. 278, 1 n., 279 n.–282, 1). Moreover, the following have been maintained (partly with phonetic transformation) : ὅτε and ὅταν (§ 272), ἅμα, ἐνῷ ἐνόσῳ (§ 273), ἀφοῦ (§§ 273, 276), πρίν (§ 274), ἕως in ὡς ποῦ (§ 275), ἐπειδή (§ 276), ἐάν (§§ 277–278, 1), εἴτε—εἴτε (§ 277, 4, n. 2). The old distinction between ὅτε, ὅταν, etc., is abolished, or only transferred to the verb, or effected by νά. Excluding dialect forms the new formations are the employment of the relative particle (ὁ)ποῦ (§§ 267 f., 271, 278, 2. 279, 281, 1. 282, 2), and the conjunctions ὅσο (with ποῦ or νά, §§ 275, 281, 1, n. 2), etc., μ' ὅλο ποῦ (§ 278, 2), πριχοῦ, προτοῦ (§ 273), ἀγκαλὰ καί (§ 278, 1), γιὰ νά (§ 280). Finally, paratactic constructions are pressed into service to form dependent clauses ; cf. §§ 261, 273, 2. 277, 4, n. 3. 278, 3.

ATTRIBUTIVE AND SUBSTANTIVAL CLAUSES.

§ 263. Attributive relative sentences are regularly introduced by the indeclinable relative particle ποῦ (ὅπου, ὁποῦ) (v. § 149). The relative sentence may be closely dovetailed into the antecedent by an arrangement of the words like ὁ Γιώργις ποῦ ἀρρώστησε ὁ καημένος . . . "poor George who was sick . . ." The syntactic order antecedent plus relative sentence represents an object clause (or, a. Gk. acc. with participle) in instances like εἶδε τὴν ἀλωποῦ ὅπου ἔρχουνταν μαζὶ μὲ τὸ δράκο (TEXTS I. d. 3) " he saw the fox (which was) coming along with the monster " (cf. also §§ 261 and 266, 3).

The tense of the relative sentence is conditioned only by the nature of the action or occurrence in question ; as, ηὗρε κάτι παιδιά, ποῦ σκότωναν ἕνα σκυλί (I. d. 2) " he found some children who were about to kill a dog." Relative sentences of a consecutive or final character are formed with ποῦ νά ; as, ἄνθρωποι ποῦ νὰ προσέχωνται (II. b. 6) " men such as are to be watched," γλῶσσα ποῦ νὰ μοιάξῃ μὲ τὴν ἀρχαία (II. b. 1) " a language to resemble the ancient," κανένα θανατικὸ δὲν ἦλθε στὸν κόσμο, ποῦ νὰ μὴν ἀφῆκε καὶ μερικοὺς νὰ διηγηθοῦν (II. b. 2) " no such disaster ever came

to the world which did not leave some (survivors) to relate
what happened" (on the aor. indic. *cf.* § 195). For the
use of the subjunctive in cases like πρῶτο πουλάκι πού
διαβῆ πιάνεται τὸ καημένο (I. a. 24. 2), *v.* § 264.

1. A relative sentence of causal nature appears in the construction τὰ ἔρριξε ὅλα, σὰν ἀδιόρθωτα ὁπού ἦταν, κάτω (II. b. 2) " he
hurled all down, incorrect it was."

2. The relative sentence πού θὰ 'πῆ = " that is (to say)," is used
as apposition to a whole sentence.

3. An attributive complement may also be expressed by νά; as,
e.g., ἄλλον τρόπον νὰ ζήσῃ δὲν εἶχε " he had no other means of living,"
ἦρθεν ἡ ὥρα νὰ πεθάνῃ " the hour came to die," ὦ τοῦ θάματος νὰ
γίνουν ὅλα " oh, the miracle, that all happened ! "

§ 264. Relative substantival sentences are introduced
either (1) simply by (ὁ)πού, or αὐτὸς (ἐκεῖνος) πού " he who ";
or (2) by ὅσος, ὅποιος, ὅτι; as, πόχουν παιδιά, ἀς τὰ κρύψουνε
(TEXTS I. a. 8) " they who have children, let them conceal
them," ὁπού 'ναι καλορίζικος γεννᾷ καὶ ὁ κότος του " whoever is lucky, even his hen lays him eggs," τοῦ εἶπε ὅσα τσ'
εἶπε ὁ βασιλιάς " she told him all that the king had told
her" (notice tense !), ὅποιος πνίγεται καὶ τὰ μαλλιάν του
πιάνει " he who is drowning clutches even his own hair."
ὅσος and ὅποιος may also be assimilated to the *case* of the
principal sentence (*Relative attraction*): *e.g.* πῶς ἀγαπῶ ὅποιον
φορεῖ ἐνδύματα θλιμμένα (TEXTS II. a. 15) " how I love him
who wears the garments of sorrow," σ' ὅποιον ἔχει θὰ δοθῆ
" he who has, to him shall be given," ἀπ' ὅσουν κόσμουν ἦταν
ἰκεῖ, κανέναν δὲν τοὺν ἄφνιν ἡ καρδγά . . . (III. 11) " of all
the people who were there, no one's heart allowed him. . . ."

What has been said in § 263 on *tense* holds good. Thus,
e.g., the present or imperf. is employed for a cursive or
iterative action. On the other hand the aor. subj. is employed (1) in a clause of an iterative nature in itself timeless (a general statement) when the action of the secondary
sentence is completed compared with the principal sentence;
or (2) when the action refers to a single definite event of the
future : exx. for (1) are ὅποιος καῆ στὰ λάχανα, φυσάει καὶ
τὸ γιαούρτι " he who is once burned on vegetables, blows
even on whey cheese," ὅποιος σ' ἀγάπη μπερδευτῆ, κάλλιο του
νὰ πεθάνῃ " he who is overtaken in love, it is better for him
to die "; for (2) ὅτι βρῆς, εἶναι δικό σου " what you will
find is your own," ὅποιος μαρτυρήσῃ τὸν κλέφτη, θὰ πάρῃ

μεγάλο δῶρο "he who points out the thief will receive a great reward." The same holds good for ὅποιος κι ἄν "who(so)-ever," ὅσος κι ἄν "however great," ὅτι κι ἄν "whatever," ὅπου κι ἄν "wherever"—for which there are also alternative forms ὅποιος καὶ νά, etc.

Even ποιός occasionally takes the force of "he who"; as, ἀλλοί του ποιὸς νὰ ντέσῃ (TEXTS I. a. 24. 43) "alas for him who is entangled!"

§ 265. Complicated relative constructions are avoided by dismemberment into co-ordinated parts; as, πυρωμένο γυαλί, ποῦ τ' ἀγγίζεις καὶ σκάνει "a heated glass which goes to pieces when touched." Of rare occurrence are constructions like ἕνα λούλουδο, ὅπου ὅποιος τό 'βρισκε . . . ἐμπορούσε νὰ τὸ κάμῃ μάλαμα (TEXTS I. d. 7) "flos quem qui invenisset . . ., aurum facere posset," or τὰ δ ό σου μάτια, ποῦ ποιὸν κυττάξουν τὴν καρδιὰ τοῦ κάνουν δυὸ κομμάτια (I. a. 24. 28) "thy two eyes, which rend the heart of him on whom they gaze."

§ 266. A substantival sentence with νά and the pres. or aor. subj. is the principal representative of the various usages of the a. Gk. infinitive or acc. and infin. constructions, viz.:

(1) As subject: e.g. after γίνεται "it happens, is possible," καταντᾷ "it happens that . . .," πρέπει "it is becoming, necessary" (πρέπει νὰ δουλεύῃς "you must work"), and in similar usages; cf. e.g. τί κακὸ νὰ ζῇ κανεὶς μὲ ἀνθρώπους ἀγενεῖς (II. a. 8) "how evil for one to live with ignoble men."

The clause with νά may be formally converted into a substantive by placing the article before it; as, τὸ νὰ ἀγαπᾷς εἶναι πρᾶγμα φυσικό (TEXTS I. a. 21) "that you love (to love) is a natural thing." Such a νά clause may be dependent even on a preposition (μὲ τὸ νά . . . "in order thereby, because," ἀπὸ τὸ νά . . . "because of, owing to").

(2) Complement of an adjective; as, εἶμαι ἄξα νὰ δέχωμαι τὸ βασιλέα στὸ σπίτι μου; (III. 4) "am I worthy to receive the king into my house?"

(3) As object after all kinds of verbs: e.g. verbs of willing, desiring, asking, demanding, inviting, being able, attempting, striving, agreeing, allowing, letting, promising, swearing, remembering, forgetting, and so on; thus, θέλω νὰ γράψω "I wish to write," πιθυμῶ νὰ γράψῃς "I desire you to write," σὲ παρακαλῶ νὰ τὸ κάνῃς "I request you to do it," etc.; further, after verbs of seeing, hearing, finding, making, causing, and so forth; thus, κανεὶς δὲν τοὺς εἶδε ποτὲ νὰ κάνουν τὸ σταυρό "no one saw them ever making the cross," ποιὸς εἶδε κόρην

ὄμορφη νὰ σέρν' ὁ πεθαμμένος (I. a. 11) "who ever saw a
fair maid conducted by a dead person?"[1] ἄκουσα νὰ λένε "I
heard them say," ἄκουτσε νὰ λέῃ ἡ κόρη "she heard the
maiden say," or ἤκουσαν τ' ἀηδόνι νὰ λαλῇ "they heard the
nightingale sing," ἤκουσα ἄλλη ν' ἀγαπᾷς (I. a. 18) "I heard
that you love another," τά 'βραν κυνηοὶ νὰ πίνουν (III. 18)
"huntsmen found them drinking," ποτὲς δὲ θὰ κάμετε τὸν
κόσμον νὰ σᾶς πιστέψῃ "you will never make the world
believe you," σὲ κάμω νὰ πιαστῆς "I cause you to be arrested." For other possible constructions, cf. §§ 263, 267.

Notice *me kánni peþáni* beside *na peþáni me kánni*, in Bova
(III. 1), "you make me die."

§ 267. νά is commonly employed after *verbs of saying*, if
the dependent clause conveys a demand or the expression of
a wish; thus, ὁ βασιλιὰς τσ' εἶπε νὰ τοιμαστῇ γιὰ τὸ γάμο
"the king told her to prepare for the wedding," νὰ τοῦ 'πῇς
νὰ μοῦ δώσῃ τῆ θυγατέρα του γυναῖκα "tell him to give me
his daughter as wife," τοῦ εἶπαν οἱ δράκοι νὰ πηγαίνουν μὲ
τὴν ἀράδα "the monsters said to him that they should go in
succession," τὴν ἄλλη μέρα τοῦ εἶπαν, νὰ τοῦ δώσουν ἕνα
ταγάρι φλουριὰ καὶ νὰ πηγαίνῃ στὸ σπίτι του "another day
they said to him that they *wished to give* him a bag of florins,
and that he *must* go home."

Only after expressions like λές, ἔλεγες, νόμιζες (§ 195)
a predicate is introduced by νά: e.g. λὲς νὰ μὴ εἶναι τίποτε
"you might say that it was nothing," *i.e.* "it appears to be
nothing." Otherwise after verbs of *saying, thinking*, and so
forth predicate clauses are generally formed with πῶς or ποῦ:
e.g. λέγει (εἶπε), πῶς (ποῦ) θέλει "he says (said) that he wishes
(wished)," or λέγει (εἶπε), πῶς (ποῦ) ὁ φίλος του δὲν ἦρθε "he
says (said) that his friend did not come," ὁ Λάζαρος τοὺς
εἶπε, πῶς ἔχει εὐκαρίστησι, καὶ νὰ πάρῃ (I. d. 3) "L. told
them that it pleased him, and that he would take. . . ."

1. A clause with πῶς (or ποῦ) may also form the complement to
other verbs than those of saying either as subject or object, or even
represent an attribute: e.g. τί μὲ μέλει ποῦ θυμώνετε; "what do I
care that you are angry?" θαμάζω πῶς δὲν τὸ ξέρεις "I am astonished
that you don't know,"[2] χαίρομαι πῶς (ποῦ) ἦρθες "I am glad that

---

[1] Note at the same time how passive constructions are avoided.

[2] Or—anticipating the subject—θαμάζομαι τὸν οὐρανὸ πῶς στέκει χωρὶς στύλο
(I. a. 24. 18) "I wonder that heaven stands without a pillar."

you came," ἐθύμωνε πῶς δὲν ἦρθε "he was angry because he had not come," ἡ ἰδέα, πῶς θὰ γυρίσουμε δυὸ τρεῖς χιλιάδες χρόνια πίσω, ἐριζο-βόλησε βαθειά (Texts II. b. 2) "the idea that we are to return two or three thousand years backwards has become deeply rooted."

2. The employment of ὅτι instead of πῶς is due to the literary language.

§ 268. The subjunctive is, of course, the rule with νά, though an historic tense of the indicative is also employed when the relative time of the past is otherwise unexpressed: *e.g.* πρέπει νὰ πήραμε στραβὸ δρόμο "we must have taken a wrong way," μπορεῖ νὰ μ' ἀγάπησες "it is possible that you loved me," φαίνεται νὰ μὴν ἄκουσε "it seems he did not hear," δὲ θυμοῦμαι ν' ἀπάντησα "I do not remember meeting (to have met)." Further, the imperfect is permitted (but not the rule) in an "unreal" clause: *e.g.* ἂς εἶχα (γιὰ) νά 'δινα "had I only to give."

1. Rather unusual is κ' ἐπόρεσεν νὰ γλύτωνεν (Texts III. 13. c) "he could not escape."

In clauses with πῶς (ποῦ, ὅτι) that tense of the indic. is employed which is required independently by the predicate: λέγει (εἶπε) πῶς εἶδε "he says (said) that he saw" [direct "I saw"], εἶπε πῶς δὲν ἔχει (εἶχε) καιρό "he said that he has (had) no time" [direct "I have (had)"], πάντεχαν πῶς τὸν ἐσκότωσαν "they believed that they had killed him," μιὰ πέρδικα καυκήστηκε πῶς δὲν εὑρέθη κυνηγὸς νὰ τήνε κυνηγήσῃ (I. a. 16) "a partridge boasted that no hunter was found to hunt it," ἤτανε πικαριïμένος, πῶς δὲν τοῦ μιλεῖς (I. d. 5) "he was enraged that you do not speak to him," τὴν εἶχε 'δεῖ στὸν ὕπνο του πῶς θὰ τὴν πάρῃ γυναῖκα "he had seen (her) in the dream, that he should receive her as wife," ἔμαθαν πῶς θὰ ἔρθῃ "they discovered that he would come."

On indirect discourse, *v.* § 270.

2. Only in exceptional cases the tense is selected from the stand-point of the *narrator*: *e.g.* εἶχε βρεῖ πῶς σ' αὐτὸ τὸ μέρος ἐφύτρωνε τὸ φυτὸ ἐκεῖνο (I. d. 7) "he had found that that plant *grew* (grows) in this region," or (III. 3) τῆς ἔλεαν ὅτι ὁ βασιλέας ἐπήγαινε στὸ σπίτι της "they told her that the king *was going* to her house" beside τῆς εἶπε ὅτι ὁ βασιλέας πηγαίνει "that . . . is going."

3. After verbs of *fearing* both πῶς and μή(πως) or νὰ μή are used; as, φοβοῦμαι πῶς τὸ παρακάνει (παράκανε) "I fear that he exaggerates (exaggerated)," φοβοῦμαι πῶς δὲ θά 'ρθῃ or μὴ (δὲν) ἔρθῃ "I fear he will come (will not come)."

§ 269. Indirect questions are introduced by an interrogative pronoun or adverb, or by the interrogative particle
ἄν " whether, if." Mood and tense remain the same as in
the direct question : τὸν ρώτησε γιατί εἶναι ἔτσι συλλογισμένος " he asked him why he was (is) so pensive," τὸν
ἐρώτησε ἂν τό 'καμε " he asked him if he did it," δὲ θυμοῦμαι,
ἂ(ν) σοῦ εἶπα " I don't remember whether I told you," [1] δὲν
ἤξερε τί νὰ κάνῃ " he did not know what to do," ἡ δωδεκάδα
ἐπῆγε ν' ἀκούσῃ τί θὰ εἰπῇ ἡ κόρη " the attendants went to
hear what the maiden should say." Here, too, the standpoint
of the *narrator* may be selected (as in § 268, n. 2): *e.g.* τὸν
ἐρώτησε, τί εἶχεν, τί ἤθελε " he asked him what he had, what
he wanted."

Indirect questions may, of course, represent subject or attribute
equally well as object : *e.g.* τί καταλάβαμε μὲ τὴν ἀλλαγὴ τούτη, εἶναι
γιὰ μένα μυστήριο (Texts II. b. 2) " what we have gained by all this
change is a mystery to me," τὸ ζήτημα, ποιὰ γλῶσσα θὰ νικήσῃ, ἡ
καθαρεύουσα ἢ ἡ δημοτική, δὲν εἶναι ἀδιάφορο γιὰ τὴ νεοελληνικὴ
φιλολογία " the question which language will gain the upper hand,
the learned or the vernacular, is not a matter of indifference for the
modern Greek literature."

Occasionally an indirect interrogative clause (similarly to the νά
clause, § 266, 1 n.) is converted into a substantive by prefixing the
article : *e.g.* ἐρώταγα τὸ ποῦ νὰ εἶν' ἡ μάννα σου (I. a. 19) " I asked
where thy mother might be."

Even an exclamation in the form of a question remains
unaltered in a dependent clause ; as, ξέρεις, τί καλὴ καρδιὰ ποῦ
ἔχει " you know what a good heart he has."

§ 270. It is apparent from the preceding paragraphs that the
indirect discourse is distinguished from the direct only in the
necessary change of person and in the insertion of πῶς " that " or ἄν
" if, whether "; that the imperatives are replaced by the construction
with νά (or also πῶς νά)—that is, so far as this construction is not
already present in the direct discourse—; also that all kinds of
dependent clauses in indirect discourse undergo no alteration either
in tense or mood. But, on the whole, lengthy indirect discourses are
avoided by the vernacular; an example of greater length—in
addition to those already given in § 262—is found in Texts I. d. 1 :
κουβέντιασαν, πῶς νὰ τσ' κάνουν κακό, κ' εἶπαν ἀνάμεσό τους, πῶς
ἐκεῖ ποῦ θὰ πάγουν νὰ λουστοῦν, νὰ πάρ' ἡ μεγάλη ἕνα σακκούλι
μαργαριτάρι, etc., " they discussed how they might do her harm, and

---

[1] Notice also θυμοῦμαι ἀκόμα, σὰν ἦλθε ὁ πρῶτος δημοτικὸς διδάσκαλος στὸ
χωριό μας (II. b. 2) " I still remember how the first popular school-teacher came
to our village."

they said among themselves that, as they would go to bathe, the elder (sister) should bring a bag of pearls. . . ."

Pallis (TEXTS II. 6) employs πῶς like a. Gk. ὅτι to introduce also a direct discourse. In a similar manner ὅτὄι—a. Gk. ὅτι—is in use in the dialect of Sili (in Cappadocia).

ADVERBIAL CLAUSES.

§ 271. Adverbial clauses of place are formed with the relative adverbs of place: πῆγε κεῖ ποῦ ἤταν ἀραγμένα τὰ καράβια " he went (there) where the ships had landed," τὸ καράβι ἄφησε νὰ πηγαίνῃ ὅπου τὸ ρίξῃ ἡ τύχη "he let the boat go wherever chance would drive it." Clauses like ἐκεῖ ποῦ πάγαιναν "there where they went" i.e. "while they went," etc., approach the nature of temporal clauses.

§ 272. Temporal clauses. A simple designation of time is usually expressed by the conjunction σάν (fr. a. Gk. ὡς ἄν) or ὄντας (also ὅταν[ε], ὄντα, ὄντε, ὄντες).

(1) Past time (a) σάν or ὄντας with the aor. indic. specifies a point of time; as, ὁ βασιλιὰς σὰν ἄκουσ᾽ αὐτό, χάρηκε "the king rejoiced when he heard it," σὰν τά 'πηρεν ὁ φτωχός, ἠσυλλοοῦνταν ἴντα νὰ κάμη τόσα γρόσα (I. d. 4) "when the poor man received them, he began to ponder what he should do with so many coins," ὄντας κίνησε, τὸν περικάλεσαν οἱ θυγατέρες του "when he departed his daughters requested him."

(b) With the imperf. to specify a period or length of time, i.e. when the time in question implies a durative (not completed) occurrence, or again to designate repeated action: exx. (of the former) ὄντας γύριζε, ηὖρε κάτι παιδιά "while he was returning he found some children," σὰν ἤκουενε κάθε βράδυ τὰ γέλοια, ἠπαραξενευγούντανε "when he heard the laughter every evening, he wondered" (or repeated action); (of the latter) ὄντας ἔμπαινε, ἔλεγε "as often as she entered she would say."

(2) Present or future, (a) σάν or ὄντας, and so forth,[1] with the aor. subj. to specify a point of time; as, σὰν ἡ ἄνοιξι γυρίσῃ, τὴ φωλιά του ποῦ θὰ στήσῃ; "when the spring returns, where will he build his nest?" ὄντας ἰδῆτε τὸ δράκο, νὰ φωνάζετε "when you see the monster, keep shouting," ὄντας χρειαστῆς τίποτε, νὰ ζίφῃς τὴ βούλα (TEXTS I. d. 2) "as soon as you need anything, turn (every time) the signet-ring."

---

[1] In this case ὄντας, etc., seems to be preferred to σάν.

When the idea of the future is to be prominently brought out, ὄντας is used with the future tense; *cf.* Texts I. a. 5. 7.

(*b*) With the present to specify *duration* of time (*cf.* 1, b) or *repetition*; as, ὅταν σὲ συλλογίζωμαι, τρέμω κι ἀναστενάζω " when (as often as) I think of thee I tremble and sigh "; *cf.* also Texts I. a. 24. 4, 28, I. c. 8.

The future is also possible, as in *a*; *cf.* ὄντε θὰ ξεχωρίζωμε, ἴντα θὰ μοῦ χαρίσῃς; (I. a. 24. 26) " when we shall bid farewell, what will you give us ? "

§ 273. 1. Like σὰν or ὄντας the following are employed : καθώς (Ios ὡς καθώς) " when " (with aor. indic.), " while " (with imperf.), and, in dialect, *e.g.*, σίντα, φόντες (fr. ἀφ᾿ ὅτε), in Pontus ἄμον ντὸ and σιτά and even τά, in Capp. σάμο. The following express particular phases of time : ἀφοῦ (also ἀφοῦ καί) " after " with aor. indic. (*cf.* also § 276), ἅμα or ὅτι (also ὅτι ποῦ) " as soon as " with aor. indic. or (futuristic) aor. subj. ; ἀπ᾿ ὅτα " since " with aor. indic. ; ἐνῷ or ἐνόσῳ " while " with pres. or impf. indic. ; σιμά νά " about to, going to . . .," *e.g.* σιμὰ νὰ βγοῦν " in the act of departing . . ." or " as they were about to depart . . ." Though not *formally* temporal clauses, yet as such may be reckoned also (relative) clauses with κάθε φορὰ ποῦ (with imperf.) " everytime that," " as often as," ἐκεῖ ποῦ (with imperf.) " there where," *i.e.* " while, during."

2. Occasionally paratactic clauses carry temporal force ; *cf. e.g.* μόλις τύχῃ . . . συφορά " as soon as a misfortune occurs," θὰ θυμώσῃ, μιὰ καὶ νοιώσῃ " he will be angry as soon as he remarks it," ἐκείνη σκιάχτηκε, ἔτσι τὸν εἶδε ἄξαφνα " she was terrified when she suddenly saw him."

§ 274. The adverb of time " before " (" until ") is rendered by πρίν or by πρὶ νά (πριτά, προτοῦ, πριχοῦ with or without νά) and the aor. or pres. subj. :

(1) Past time : δὲν τὸν ἄφησε, προτοῦ νὰ τῆς ὁρκιστῇ " she did not let him off before he swore to her," πρὶν μπῇ στὴ Χαλκῆ, τοῦ ἔστελνε παρηγοριά (Texts II. b. 4) " before she came to Ch. she used to send him consolation."

(2) Present (or future): φεύγα, πριτὰ σοῦ σύρουν θυμιατό (I. a. 10) " flee before they scatter incense on thee," παίρνει λουτρό, πρὶν καθίζῃ στὸ φαγί του " he always takes a bath before he sits down to eat."

§ 275. The pronominal form ὅσο serves to introduce temporal clauses with the meaning " as long as " or " until." In the former case (strengthened to ὅσο ποῦ) the pres. or imperf. indic. is used ; as, δὲ θὰ δακρύσω, ὅσο ἐσὺ κοντά μου μένεις " I shall not weep so long as thou art with me " (but *cf.* also Texts II. a. 3. 28), ὅσο (ποῦ) ζοῦσε, ἐδούλευε " as long

as he lived, he worked." For the latter meaning " until," ὅσο
ποῦ (or also ἴσα μὲ ποῦ) is used with the aor. indic. when the
event in question is related as an actual occurrence deter-
mining the course of the action ; as, πέρασε λόγγους καὶ κάμπους, ὅσο ποῦ ἔφτασε στὰ ριζιὰ τοῦ βουνοῦ " he wandered
over forest and field until he *came* to the foot of the
mountain." On the other hand, if it is only an event to be
expected, or if the dependent clause has merely the function
of a definition of time, ὅσο νά (or ὡς ποῦ νά, ὥστε νά) is
used with the aor. subj.: *e.g.* μόνο ἐφτὰ μερῶν ζωὴ θέλω νὰ
μοῦ χαρίστε, ὅσο νὰ φτάσ' ὁ ᾿Οδυσσεύς " I wish you to grant
me only seven days life until O. arrive," ὅσο νὰ πάῃ ἡ μάννα
στὴν ἄρκλα, τὴν ηὗρε γιομάτη ψωμί " until (such time as)
the mother came (could come) to the chest she found it full
of bread," ὥστε νὰ βγῇ στὴν πόρτα της, ἐβγῆκεν ἡ ψυχή της
" before she came to the door her soul departed."

Note also ὅσο γλύτωσε, θὰ τὸν ἔτρωγαν (TEXTS I. d. 3) " until he
had freed himself they would have eaten him."

§ 276. A causal clause is introduced either by ἀφοῦ,
ἐπειδή(ς) with or without καί " since, as, because," or by
γιατί " because " (in Pontus τǒίγκι, τσούγκι), accompanied by
that tense of the indicative required by the occurrence.

1. διότι " because " from the literary language.
2. γιατί occasionally competes with νά, ποῦ, or πῶς for a place
after verbs of emotion (*cf.* § 267, n. 1): *e.g.* ζούλεψε γιατί ἡ προγονή
δης νὰ πάρ' τὶ βασιλὲ τὸ γιό (TEXTS III. 12) " she was envious that
(because) her step-daughter should win the king's son."

§ 277. Conditional clauses are regularly introduced by
ἄν (ἂν καί) " if," sometimes by ἀνίσως (καί), ἂν τυχόν, ἂν τύχῃ
καί, ἂν εἶναι καί " if perhaps, in case that."

(1) When the condition pertains to the *Past*, and the
consequence to the past or present, then aor. (imperf.) indic.
in the protasis and the aor. (imperf.) or pres. indic. in the
apodosis ; as, ἂν τό 'κανες, καλά 'κανες " if you did so you did
right," ἂν ἀποφάσισες, δὲ μπορεῖς ν' ἀλλάξῃς τὴ γνώμη σου
" if you have made up your mind you cannot change your
opinion."

(2) When both condition and consequence pertain to the
Present :

(*a*) When the condition holds good generally (may

happen any number of times) or is a durative occurrence (cursive action): present in both protasis and apodosis; as, μπορεῖς ἃ θέλῃς "you are able if you wish," ἃ δὲν πιστεύῃς, ἔλα κοντά μου νὰ ἰδῇς "if you don't believe, come to me and see."

(b) When the condition is a punctiliar occurrence or an occurrence completed as regards the consequence: aor. subj. in protasis, pres. indic. in apodosis; as, δὲ φεύγω, ἃ δὲ μοῦ δώκῃς τὰ 'κατὸ γρόσα (I. d. 5) "I go not away if you give me not the hundred piastres," ἃ δὲ βρεθῇ, δὲν πειράζει "if it is not found it does not matter."

(3) When both condition and consequence pertain to the *Future*:

(a) The condition is a repeated or durative action then pres. in protasis and future (or imperative expression) in apodosis, ἂν πεινᾶς, δὲ θὰ σ' ἀφήσω νηστική (II. a. 20) "if thou art (becomest) hungry I will not leave thee in want."

(b) The condition is a punctiliar occurrence, or one completed as regards the consequence: aor. subj. in the protasis, future (or an imperative expression) in the apodosis: ἂν τυχὸν . . . διψάσῃς, θὰ σοῦ φέρω . . . νερό (II. a. 20) "if thou chance to thirst I will fetch thee water," ἂν παραβῶ τὸν ὅρκον, ν' ἀστράψ' ὁ οὐρανὸς καὶ νὰ μὲ κατακάψῃ (II. a. 1) "if I shall break my oath, let heaven strike me with lightning, and burn me up," θὰ τὸ κάνω αὔριο, ἂν μπορέσω "I shall do it to-morrow if I am able" (more correctly, "if I am placed in a position to do it").

(4) Where the terms of the condition are *impossible* (*unreal*): in the protasis the imperfect, in the apodosis the conditional (§§ 230, 233), regardless whether it pertains to present or past; as, ἂν τὸ ἤξευρα, δὲ θὰ ρωτοῦσα "if I knew (had known) I should not ask (have asked)," ἃ δὲν πήγαινα ἐχτὲς στὸ θέατρο, θὰ εἶχα τὴ δουλειά μου τελειωμένη "if I had not gone yesterday to the theatre, I should have had my work finished."

1. Conditional clauses may be formed also with νά: e.g. μιλιὰ νὰ κάνανε τὰ παιδιά του, τὰ μάλωνενε (TEXTS I. d. 4) "if his children talked he always scolded them," or νὰ τόνε κάμῃ νὰ γελάσῃ, τὴν ἐμάλωνε (ib.) "if she made him laugh he would scold her," νὰ τὸν ἰδῇς, θὰ τόνε λυπηθῇς "if you see him you will pity him," μῆλου νά 'ριχνις, καταῆς δὲν ἔπιφτιν (III. 11, without θά) "if you had thrown an apple it would not have fallen to the ground." The origin of

this usage of νά is apparent from cases like ἡ καρδιά μου πονεῖ, νὰ σᾶς ἀκούω (II. b. 1) "my heart is grieved that (if) I listen to you."

2. Notice also ἐξὸν ἄν "unless," εἴτε(ς)—εἴτε(ς) "whether . . . or"; as, εἴτες ἔρθῃ, εἴτες δὲν ἔρθῃ, ἐγὼ θὰ πάω "whether he comes or not *I* will go."

3. Even a direct question sometimes approaches the nature of a conditional clause: e.g. θέλετε ξένη γλῶσσα; πάρτε τὴν καθαρεύουσα (II. b. 1) "do you want a foreign tongue? then take the *pure language*"; τὸν θύμωσες; φεύγα ἀπὸ κοντά του "did you provoke him, then get out of his way."

§ 278. Concessive clauses are formed:

(1) By κι ἄν, ἂν καί or ἀγκαλὰ (*i.e.* ἂν καλὰ) καί "although, even if"; the construction is similar to that of the conditional sentences; as, ἂν καὶ τὸ γύρεψε μὲ οὖλα τὰ μέσα, δὲν ἐμπόρεσε νὰ εὕρῃ "although he had sought it by all means, still he could not find it," κι ἂν τὰ ντερβένια τούρκεψαν, ὁ Στέργιος εἶναι ζωντανός "even if the passes have become Turkish, Stergios is still alive," τί σ' ὠφελεῖ, κι ἂν ζήσῃς, καὶ εἶσαι στὴ σκλαβιά; (TEXTS III. a. 1) "what advantage is it to thee, though thou livest, if thou art in slavery?"

(καὶ) νά may also take the place of ἄν (*cf.* § 277, 4, n. 1); as, καὶ γερὸς νὰ ἦταν, θ' ἀρρωστοῦσεν "although he (were) had been strong he would still have become sick," νὰ σκάσῃ, θὰ τὸ κάμω "although he (it) burst, I will do it." ἔστωντας (καὶ νά) "notwithstanding" is not common.

(2) By μ' ὅλο ποῦ (μ' ὅλον ὁποῦ, μολονότι) with the indic.; as, μ' ὅλο ποῦ ἦταν καλὸς καιρός, δὲν ἐκινοῦσε τὸ καράβι "though it was fine weather the ship did not move."

(3) By the co-ordination of a clause with (κι) ἄς, after which a preterite indic. is also possible (*cf.* § 195); as, τὰ ἄστρα . . . λάμπουν ὁλομόναχα, κι ἂς μὴν τὰ βλέπῃ κανένας (TEXTS II. b. 1) "the stars shine all alone though no one look upon them," [τὸ παιδὶ] μοσχοβολοῦσε ἀρχοντιά, κι ἂς ἦτον γυμνωμένο (II. a. 15) "(the child) betrayed noble ancestry even though it was naked."

1. Somewhat different constructions are: ἂς ἦδαν καὶ τυφλό, ἦδαν ἀμμὰ ὄμορφο (III. 12) "even if it was blind, it was beautiful," ἂς μὴν ἔλεγε ποιὸς τό 'κανε, μὰ ἂς ἔλεγε πῶς δὲ φταίει "though he refused to say who had committed it, yet he should have said that he was not guilty."

2. Notice further ὅσο κι ἄν or ὅσο καὶ νά with subj. "however much," and καί or ἔτσι with an adjective and ποῦ: e.g. φοβοῦντανε, ἔτσι (καὶ) μεγάλος ποῦ ἦτανε "he was afraid, great though he was."

§ 279. Consecutive clauses are formed with ποῦ (ὁποῦ, ὅπου) and the indic. when the meaning is that the consequence actually occurred : *e.g.* ἤτανε πολλὰ φίλοι, ποῦ ὁ ἕνας τὸν ἄλλο δὲν ἠξεχώριζε "they were so great friends that the one did not separate from the other," ἀρρώστια μ' ἔρριξε τοῦ θανάτου, ποῦ 'πέσαν τὰ ξανθὰ μαλλιά "sickness brought me so far down to death so that my fair hair fell out," μᾶς ἐκοίμισε τόσο βαθειά, ποῦ τίποτε πλιὰ δὲ μπορεῖ νὰ μᾶς ξυπνήσῃ "he put us into such a deep sleep that nothing more can wake us." ποῦ νά is employed if the consequence is only imaginary or expected ; as, δὲν εἶναι καὶ τόσο πρᾶμα ποῦ νὰ 'πῇς "it is not such an important matter that you need speak of it," μ' ἔρχεται νὰ φωνάξω δυνατά, ποῦ ὅλος ὁ κόσμος νὰ μ' ἀκούσῃ "it occurs to me to call so loud that the whole world could hear me." Notice further τόσο μικρὸς εἶναι, ποῦ λὲς πῶς εἶναι παιδί "he is so small that one might say (*cf.* § 195) he is a child," ἡ Εὐρώπη ἀπὸ τότες ὡς ἐσήμερα ἄλλαξε σ' ἕνα τέτοιο βαθμό, ποῦ καὶ ὁ Βύρωνας ἀκόμη νὰ ζοῦσε, θὰ μᾶς ἔγραφε διατριβὲς γιὰ τὲς θεωρίες τοῦ Δαρβίνου (II. b. 2) "Europe has altered from that time to the present to such a degree that even Byron, if he were alive, would write brochures on the theories of Darwin."

Even νά alone may carry consecutive force : *e.g.* εἶναι νὰ χάσῃ κανεὶς τὸ μυαλό του "that is for one to lose his reason." On consecutive καί, *v.* § 261.

§ 280. Final clauses with νά denote the goal or purpose of an action after verbs like *go, come, send, give, begin,* and so forth : ἦρτα νὰ ξεγορευτῶ "I came to confess," νὰ μοῦ δώσῃς κάτιτι νὰ φάω "give me something to eat." πηγαίνω νά in a figurative sense means "I am about to, am going to . . ."[1] The intention or the actuating motive is brought out more distinctly by γιὰ νά: *e.g.* ἔφυγε γιὰ νὰ μὴν ξαναγυρίσῃ πιά "he went away (with the intention) never to return again," τί λόγια νὰ βρῶ γιὰ νὰ μὲ πιστέψετε ; "what words can I find in order that you may believe me?" Negatively (γιὰ) νὰ μή or simply μή ; as, μὲ πονηριὰ περπάτει μὴ σὲ νοιώσουν οἱ γειτόνοι "go carefully in order that the neighbours may not notice you."

---

[1] Hence the stereotyped form of the 3rd sing. πά or 2nd sing. πάς is practically identical with the simple νά, etc., in formulae like πὰ νά, νὰ πὰ νά, etc. (*cf.* n. 2, and §§ 193, 2 n., 224, 3, n. 3. 255 n.).

1. The distinction between νά and γιὰ νά is faint; *cf.* ἔνα καλὸ δὲν κάνεις . . . σκάλα στὸν κάτω κόσμο, νὰ κατεβαίνουν οἱ ἀδερφές, etc. (Texts I. a. 8) "thou doest not one good deed, . . . a bridge to the underworld, that brethren may descend . . ." and νὰ μοῦ δώκῃς κ' ἔνα καράβι καλό, γιὰ νὰ πάνω στὰ ξένα "give me a good ship in order that I may go abroad," and further, εἶναι παραπολὺ κουτὸς γιὰ νὰ τὸ καταλάβῃ "he is so stupid that he cannot grasp it."

2. "That perhaps, forsooth" is rendered τάχατις (γιὰ) νά, "lest perhaps," by μήπως or μὴν πὰ(ς) καί, (γιὰ) νὰ μὴν τύχῃ (λάχῃ) καί . . ., or more concisely μὴ τύχῃ (λάχῃ) καί . . . or μὴ τυχό(ν).

3. The νά clause is sometimes so loosely connected with the principal sentence that it approaches the nature of a principal sentence itself; *cf.* ὅλη νύχτα δὲν ἠβούλωσενε μάτι στὴ συλλοή· τὴν ἄλλη μέρα μηδὲ σὲ μεροκάματο νὰ πάῃ, etc. (Texts I. d. 4) "the whole night long he did not close an eye, occupied in thought to go next day neither to his day's work . . .," *i.e.* "and on the next day he went neither . . ."

§ 281. Adverbial clauses of manner are formed :

(1) With καθώς, ὅπως, also σὰν ποῦ, κατὰ πῶς, κατὰ ποῦ "as, just as, according to" : *e.g.* ἔκαμε (κάνει) καθὼς (ὅπως, σὰν ποῦ) εἶπε (θέλει) "he did (does) as he said (wishes)," καθὼς βλέπετε, ἔχω δίκαιο "I am right, as you see," κατὰ ποῦ (καθὼς) λέει ὁ λόγος "as the saying runs," ἔλα κατὰ πῶς εἶσαι "come just as you are."

1. Pontic ἄμον ντό; as, ἄμον ντὸ θέλνε, ἐφτειάγνε (Texts III. 13. a) "do exactly as you like."

2. Notice further expressions like ὅσο μπορεῖς γληγορώτερα "as quickly as possible, with all speed," and ὅσο νὰ πῇς, to emphasise an adjective : *e.g.* μιὰ βοσκοπούλα ὄμορφη ὅσο νὰ πῇς "a shepherdess as fair as you could tell," *i.e.* "incomparably fair."

(2) With σὰ(ν) νά "as if, as though"; ὁ γέρος σὰν νὰ μὴν τ' ἄκουσε, γυρνᾷ "the old man turns round as if he did not hear," τοῦ φάνηκε σὰν νὰ κατρακυλοῦσε τὸ σπίτι "it appeared to him as if the house would collapse."

1. "Do (act) as if, pretend," is rendered by κάμνω πῶς, καμώνομαι πῶς with indic. : *e.g.* ἔκαμε πῶς γλίστρησε "she acted as if she had slidden," ἔκαμε πῶς κυνηγάει τὸ παιδί "he made as though he were chasing the child," καμώνεστε πῶς μηδὲ ξέρετε "you act as if you did not at all know."

2. In an independent clause σὰν νά has the meaning "to a certain extent, so to speak"; as, σὰν νὰ μετανοιώνω ποὺ τὸ εἶπα (Texts II. b. 2) "I regret to a certain extent that which I said."

3. On comparative clauses with παρά, *v.* § 120, n. 1.

§ 282. Finally, in addition to the various kinds of clauses given, the following are to be noted :

1. χωρὶς νά or δίχως νά "without": ἐπέρασε χωρὶς νὰ τόνε χαιρετίσῃ "he passed by without greeting him."

χώρια νά "except, unless": ἄλλον τρόπον νὰ ζήσῃ δὲν εἶχε χώρια ξύλα νὰ κόφτῃ (Texts II. a. 2) "he had no other means of livelihood except felling wood."

μακρειὰ νά, μόνο νά or φτάνει μόνο νά "except when, provided that, up to the point": ἦταν ἀγαθὸς ἄθρωπος, μακρειὰ νὰ μὴ τόνε θυμώσῃς "he was a good natured fellow until you enraged him."

2. ποῦ "while, since, in that," to determine more precisely the circumstances or the concurrence (identity) of different actions; as, καλά 'καμες ποῦ ἦρθες "you did well in coming (since you came)," ἦρθε ποῦ δὲν τοῦ εἶπα νὰ 'ρθῇ "he came without my having told him to come (though I did not tell him)."

μόνο ποῦ (πῶς) "apart from, only, excepting that": εἶναι ἔξυπνο παιδί, μόνο ποῦ δὲ δουλεύει καθὼς πρέπει "he is a clever lad, only he does not work as he ought."

AFFIRMATION AND NEGATION.

§ 283. ναί, stronger ναίσκε "yes," μάλιστα (also together ναί, μάλιστα) "yes, indeed."

ἴσως, τάχα, τάχατες, τάχατις "perhaps."

ἀλήθεια "truly," σωστά "right, quite so," σίγουρα (βέβαια) "certainly, of course."

ὄχι, stronger ὄχι δά, ὄχισκε, ὄσκε "no"; also to negative a noun; as, θέλεις κρασὶ ἢ μπίρα;—ὄχι κρασί, προτιμῶ μπίρα "will you take wine or beer? Not wine, I prefer beer." For μή "no," v. § 284.

καθόλου, διόλου (also ντίπ, in Pontus and elsewhere [Turk.] ḥίτṣ) "by no means," used in a reply; another strong negation is also ψέματα! "by no means, not at all" (lit. "lies!").

The exclamations μιλιά! λέξι! or τσιμουδιά! signify a prohibition "not a word," i.e. "quiet!"

Negation is often emphasised, or even expressed, by gesture, not, however, by shaking the head, but by throwing it slightly backwards (accompanied sometimes with a sound like a gentle click of the tongue).

§ 284. The particles δέ(ν) and prohibitive 'μή(ν) "not" serve to negative a clause (verb); they immediately precede

the verb, from which they may be divorced only by a conjunctive pronoun or by the particle θά (δὲν τὸ θέλω, δὲ θὰ
'ρθῶ, δὲ σοῦ τὸ εἶπα, δὲ θὰ σοῦ τὸ εἰπῶ).

Instead of δέν the negative in Pontus appears as κί (Old Ionic
οὐκί) and in Cappadocia (Pharasa) τζό.

The negative μή is employed:

(1) Independently as a prohibition: e.g. μή, κύρ Λάζαρε
(TEXTS I. d. 3) "(do it) not, Sir L."

(2) In principal sentences in the cases given in §§ 193
and 194.

(3) In secondary clauses always after νά, even when νά is
accompanied by the indic.: e.g. ἀπὸ τὸ νὰ μὴν εἶχε παράδες
"because he had no money." For μή with verbs of fearing,
v. § 268, n. 2; and in final clauses, § 280.

(4) With the present participle (cf. § 236); as, μὴν
ξέροντας "not knowing," θέλοντας καὶ μή "whether willing
or not."

§ 285. Negation may be emphasised by καθόλου, διόλου:
e.g. δὲν εἶπα καθόλου "by no means did I say it," "absolutely
did not say." The negative particles οὔτε, οὐδέ, μήτε, μηδέ
"not even," or, when repeated, "neither . . . nor," are used
indiscriminately. If the verb comes at the beginning only
the simple form of negation can precede it; as, δὲν ἔχω οὔτε
(μήτε) μιὰ πεντάρα "I have not even a sou," νὰ μὴ πάρῃς
μήτε γρόσια μήτε φλουριά "take neither pennies nor florins,"
—but οὔτε μιὰ πεντάρα ἔχω or μηδὲ λυράκι πιὰ ἤκουενε μηδὲ
ἔλοια (TEXTS I. d. 4) "neither lyre nor laughter heard he
any more."

1. Notice, further, the use of κιόλας: δὲν ἔφαγα κιόλας "I have
not eaten at all."

2. The negative may be inserted pleonastically (but is not necessarily present) in νά clauses after verbs of hindering: e.g. δὲ σ'
ἐμποδίζω νὰ μὴ μιλᾷς "I do not hinder you from speaking."

ORDER OF WORDS.

§ 286. The m. Gk. vernacular has, on the whole,
maintained the a. Gk. freedom in the order of words, i.e. all
kinds of combinations are possible in the sequence of the
composite parts of the clauses. It is only in dependent

clauses that the place of the verb is restricted (*v.* § 289). But, generally speaking, there is a recognised normal sequence of words, so that any deviation from the same lends a special emphasis to the irregular member.

The normal order of words in m. Gk. appears in its main features to be ancient, that is, it goes back at least to the period of the ancient Κοινή.

§ 287. In a statement consisting of two members the normal sequence of words is Subject and Predicate. Of themselves introductory particles (τώρα, τότες, etc.) cause no alteration. Inversion of predicate and subject is, however, facilitated by a preceding dependent clause: *e.g.* ὄντας ἐπλησίασ' ὁ δράκος, ἐφώναξαν τὰ παιδιά "when the monster approached, exclaimed the children."

But in other cases also by inversion the verb takes frequently the first position or immediately follows an introductory particle, if (1) either the verb is to be indicated as the result of a preceding action (and so particularly after καί), *e.g.* ἔξιψε τὴ βούλα, κ' ἦρθ' ὁ 'Αράπης "he rubbed the signet-ring and there came the Arab," or (2) if the idea of the subject constitutes the essential element of the narrative: *e.g.* ἦταν μιὰ φτωχὴ γυναῖκα κ' εἶχε ἕνα παιδί "there was a poor woman who (and she) had a (one) child," ἐκεῖ ἐκάθονταν οἱ δράκοι "there dwelt the monsters," τότες τσ' εἶπ' ὁ βασιλιάς "then said to her the *king*," ἦρθε κ' ἡ ἀράδα τοῦ Λάζαρου "there came also the *turn* of Lazarus."

Further, an adverb which is emphatic—and consequently occupying an extreme position—entices its verb to the beginning; as, καὶ πάλι τὸν ἐμάλωσ' ἡ μάννα του καθὼς καὶ πρῶτα (TEXTS I. d. 2) "and *once again* his mother scolded him as at first."

A pronominal subject betrays an inclination to follow the verb: *e.g.* ἦρθεν ἕνας "there came one," ἔφυγε κεῖνος "he fled," πηγαίνουμε 'μεῖς "we go (go we)," δὲν τό 'σφαξα ἐγώ, μόν' ἡ ἀδερφή μου (I. d. 1).

§ 288. In a sentence of several members—enlarged by objects and adverbial qualifications—the predominant order is the middle position for the verb, while the object or (and) adverbial qualification follow: *e.g.* κι ὁ βασιλιὰς ἐφώναξε τὴ θυγατέρα του or τὸ παιδὶ πῆγε στὴ μάννα του. Final position is uncommon, and is due to special reasons; *cf. e.g.*

κ᾽ εὐτὺς τὸ καράβι ἐκίνησε "and immediately the boat moved off" (where the emphatic adverb has taken the initial place without attracting the verb after it, because the verb too has to be given emphasis), τὸ πολὺ κυριελέησο κι ὁ παπᾶς βαρειέται το "even the priest becomes weary of much Kurieleison" (where the two main contrasted ideas are placed in proximity to the front), or ὁ λόος εἰς τὴν ὤρα του χίλια φλουριὰ ἀξίζει (where the position renders the object prominent).

Initial position for the verb (with inversion of subject and predicate) is found under the same conditions as in § 287: e.g. πῆγε πάλι ἡ μάννα του στὸ βασιλιά "again went his mother to the king," ἔχει ὁ τοῖχος αὐτιά "even the wall has ears." Moreover, inversion is common when an adverbial qualification or an object introduces the sentence and when no special emphasis is put on the verb; thus the normal middle position for the verb is secured: e.g. μιὰ φορὰ ἤτανε ἕνας βασιλιάς "once upon a time there was a king" (cf. also § 287), τὸ πρωὶ σκώθηκε τὸ παιδί "early as the boy rose," τέχνη θέλει τὸ πριόνι (I. b. 17) "art requires the saw."

§ 289. In dependent clauses without exception the verb follows immediately upon the introductory particle (νά, σάν, etc.), or is separated from it only by the negative or the conjunctive pronoun, and practically without exception the verb follows upon an interrogative word and a relative: στέκα νὰ 'δῶ κ᾽ ἐγὼ ψίχα τὴ βούλα "stay that I also may examine the signet-ring a little," σὰν ἔφυγ᾽ ἡ βασιλοπούλα μὲ τὸν Ἀράπη "when the king's daughter had escaped with the Moor," τὸν ἐρώτησε πόσο κοστίζει τὸ βιβλίο "he asked him how much the book cost," τοῦ εἶπε ὅσα τσ᾽ εἶπ᾽ ὁ βασιλιάς "she told him all that the king had said to her."

Exceptions occur only after ποῦ (to throw emphasis upon the verb), as, ἦρχε καιρός, ποῦ ὁ ἕνας ἠπαντρεύτηκε (TEXTS I. d. 5) "there came a time when one of them married," and in predicate clauses with πῶς, which prefer the order of the principal sentence, as, ἤξερε πῶς ἐκεινῆς ὁ ἄντρας ἤτανε στὴ δουλειά (I. d. 5) "he knew that her husband was at work."

§ 290. The direct and indirect object regularly follow immediately upon the verb—the direct preceding the indirect, provided there is not more emphasis on the latter (ἔδωκε καὶ τῆς μικρῆς τὸ γράμμα, TEXTS I. d. 1). If the

subject and the predicate are inverted (*v.* § 288) the object
in that case regularly takes the end: *e.g.* καὶ πῆρε ὁ δράκος τὸ
δέντρο, λέει τὸ σκυλὶ τῆς γάτας. Rhetorical reasons may
cause the object to be pushed forward; *cf.* μοῦ πῆρε τὴ βούλα
ὁ Ἀράπης καὶ τὴ γυναῖκα (I. d. 2) "the Arab took from me
the *signet-ring* as well as the woman." The most effective
means, however, of securing prominence for the object is a
position immediately *in front of* the verb—an arrangement
which readily admits the former to the beginning of the
clause: *e.g.* ὁ λόος εἰς τὴν ὥρα του χίλια φλουριὰ ἀξίζει or
τὰ γρόσια σου δὲν τὰ θέλω "thy money I seek not."

§ 291. Adverbs and adverbial qualifications regularly
follow upon the predicate—the adverb immediately, the
adverbial qualification after the object or after the adverb:
τότες ἔστειλε πάλι τὴ μάννα του στὸ βασιλιά "then sent he
again his mother to the king," τρέχει λοιπὸν εὐτὺς κάτω
στῆς μάννας του "he runs now immediately down to his
mother." The inversion of subject and predicate attracts the
adverb likewise toward the beginning, but *not* the adverbial
qualification: *e.g.* πῆγε πάλι ἡ μάννα στὸ βασιλιά "again
went the mother to the king," but πῆγαν οἱ δράκοι γιὰ ξύλα
"the monsters went for wood." An adverb or adverbial
qualification may be given a mild emphasis by placing the
former at the end of the sentence (after the other enlarge-
ments of the verb) or also before the verb, and the latter
immediately before the verb; as, ἔζησαν ὅλη τὴ ζωή τους καλά
"they lived their whole life well," ὁ Γιώργις πάλι ἔκανε τὸ
λάθος "again G. made the mistake," ὁ δράκος μὲ μεγάλη
τρόμαρα ἄφ᾽κε τὰ φλουριά "with great consternation the
monster abandoned the money," αὐτὴ ἔκανε κι ἄλλη φορὰ τὸ
ἴδιο "once more she did the same thing."

Of course even the adverbial qualification comes before the
object when the latter is enlarged by a relative clause; as, τότες ὁ
διάβολος ἀπολάει ἀπὸ τὴν καπότα τοῦ τὸ λαγό, ὁ ὁποῖος . . . (I. d. 6).

The strongest emphasis is secured by an initial position,
which occurs particularly when an adverb or an adverbial
definition forms the transition from one clause to the other,
or introduces a situation (and so especially in definitions of
time and place): *e.g.* γλήγορα νὰ φύγῃς "quickly flee," ἀπ᾽ τὰ
παιδιὰ τοῦ κὺρ Λάζαρου ἐσκιάχτηκες; (TEXTS I. d. 3) "was

it the children of Sir L. that you were afraid of?" σ' ὀχτὼ μέρες διορία τὸ γιατρεύω "within the space of eight days I cure it," πάλι αὐτὴ ἔβαλε τὸ δαχτυλίδι στὸ τάσι μέσα " again she laid the ring in the cup," τὴν ἄλλη μέρα ὁ Χριστὸς τοῦ λέει τοῦ διαβόλου " another day said Christ to the devil," μιὰ φορὰ ἤτανε δυὸ παλληκάρια " once upon a time there were two youths." *Cf.* also the beginning of I. d. 7 and I. b. 5.

§ 292. In secondary clauses the object and adverb (adverbial qualifications) are frequently separated from the verb, which, according to § 289, gravitates toward the beginning; as, νὰ μᾶς δώσ' ὁ βασιλιὰς τὴ θυγατέρα του " let the king give us his daughter," καθὼς πῆρε τὸ σκυλὶ τὴ βούλα " as soon as the dog got the signet-ring," νὰ 'δῶ κ' ἐγὼ ψίχα τὴ βούλα " that I may also look at the signet-ring a moment," ὅσο νὰ πάῃ ἡ μάννα του στὴν ἄρκλα " until his mother went to the chest." Only clauses with ποῦ (ὅπου), πῶς (ὅτι) (as in principal sentences, *v.* § 290 f.) admit of object and adverbial determination being placed in front of the verb and thereby emphasised; as, ποῦ ὁ ἕνας τὸν ἄλλο δὲν ἠξεχώριζε " so that the one did not part from the other," πῶς σ' αὐτὸ τὸ μέρος ἐφύτρωνε τὸ φυτὸ ἐκεῖνο " that that plant grew in this place." In clauses with νά and other conjunctions that member of the clause which is to be strongly emphasised must be placed *before* the introductory conjunction : *e.g.* ἄλλο δὲ χαλεύω . . ., μοναχὰ ἕνα ζιαφέτι νὰ μοῦ κάμῃς " I request nothing else, *only* that you prepare me a banquet," δὲ μπορῶ, κάθε μέρα νὰ ἔρχωμαι " I cannot *every day* come." This precedence of object or adverbial determination is, however, less common than is the case in principal sentences.

§ 293. Adjectives and participles as a rule precede the word which they qualify. They follow :

(1) When there is an emphasis on the adjective : *e.g.* γιατρὸς καλός " a *good* doctor," μιὰ φορεσιὰ σωστή " a *proper* garment."

Notice also the expressions of goodwill ὥρα· καλή and εἰς ἔτη πολλά (*cf.* §§ 256, 257 n.).

(2) If the attribute is the essential element, the essential expansion of the content of the context; as, ἔκαμαν ἕνα γάμο λαμπρό " they celebrated a wedding splendidly," μιὰ φορεσιὰ

φράγκικη "a garment of European style," μέσ' τὰ χρόνια
τὰ παλιά "in the days of old, antiquity."

(3) When the attribute itself is expanded; as, ἕνα σαράγι
μεγαλύτερο ἀπ' τοῦ βασιλιά "a castle more beautiful than
that of the king," ἕνα ζιαφέτι πολὺ μεγάλο "a banquet very
magnificent."

(4) When the adjective stands in the relation of a predicate to the substantive; as, ὁ Λάζαρος μὲ μεγάλη δυσκολία
πῆγε τὸ ἀσκὶ ἄδειο στὸ πηγάδι "L. with much difficulty
brought the bag empty to the well" ("the empty sack" must
be rendered τὸ ἀσκὶ τὸ ἄδειο, according to § 57).

§ 294. The attribute genitive is placed, as a rule, after its
noun; but, to secure a slight emphasis, before the noun and
even *before* the article, but after any preposition: μιᾶς
στιγμῆς ὑπομονὴ δέκα χρονῶν ρεχάτι "a moment's patience
means ten years' quiet," τῆς μικρότερης τὸ χρυσὸ βεργί "the
golden rod of the younger (daughter)," σ' αὐτῆς τῆς φτωχῆς
κόρης τὸ σπίτι "into this poor maiden's house."

1. Note the free position of the gen. in TEXTS I. d. 5, τὸ σκέδιο
θὰ πάρω τοῦ σπιτιοῦ, where the emphatic object is pushed to the
beginning while the attributive gen. which belongs to it is left.

2. In Pontus and Cappadocia the gen. regularly is accorded the
first place.

§ 295. Dependent clauses with νά (γιὰ νά), indirect
interrogative clauses, predicate clauses with πῶς (ποῦ), con-
sequential, and comparative clauses, as a rule, follow upon the
principal sentence, only clauses like νὰ τὰ κοντολοοῦμε "to
sum up briefly" constituting fixed exceptions. Temporal
clauses as regularly precede, in which case a single (emphatic)
member of the principal sentence, or a member common to
both, may be placed at the beginning; as, οἱ δράκοι σὰν
ἄργησε ὁ Λάζαρος, ἐφοβήθ'καν "as L. delayed the *Draki*
feared (the monsters, as L. delayed, feared)," ὁ βασιλιὰς σὰν
ἄκουσ' αὐτό, χάρηκε "when the king heard it he rejoiced."
A position after the principal sentence is less common (apart
from clauses with "*until, as long as, before*"); as, αὐτὸς φοβήθηκε σὰν τοῦ εἶπαν πῶς εἶναι τὸ βασ(ι)λόπουλο (TEXTS I. d. 1)
"he was afraid when they told him that he was the king's
son." Causal sentences may either precede or follow (those

14

with γιατί follow) the principal sentence, so likewise conditional sentences. Relative sentences connect closely with
their antecedent, and thus sometimes secure a place within
the principal sentence : τὸ παιδὶ τὸ σαράγι, ποῦ τὸ παράγγελες,
τό 'φκειασε (I. d. 2) " the child has made the castle which
you ordered " ; but by means of the καί construction in place
of the relative clause (§ 261) and by the rules for the
position of the principal sentence the language can escape
the necessity for such insertions : e.g. καὶ πέφτει ἡ βούλα ποῦ
τὴν εἶχε κρυμμένη "and the ring fell, which he had kept
concealed."

1. But even a relative clause may be separated from its antecedent: e.g. μονάχα τὴ βούλα θέλω ὅπ' ἔχεις στὸ χέρι σου (TEXTS I.
d. 2) "only the signet-ring I wish which you hold in your hand."
2. Relatival subject (also object) clauses with ὅποιος, ὅτι, (ὁ)ποῦ,
ὅσοι incline to come before the principal sentence, exx. v. § 264.

§ 296. Modern Greek, having only in a limited number
of instances strictly prescribed the position of words, admits
of all kinds of variations for artistic purposes. Poetry is in
this respect more absolute for the sake of the rhythm : poetic
deviations from the normal order of words occur rather
frequently where they are not essentially required by the
thought. In the following examples note the dislocation of
elements that properly belong together : ἀπ' τὴ μύτη του
ἰδέτε, ἡ εὐγένεια πῶς τρέχει (TEXTS II. a. 8) "from his
nose, see how nobility trickles," ποιᾶς μάγισσας θὰ τὰ
λυτρώσῃ χέρι; (II. a. 23) "which witch's hand will free
them?" τῆς πατρίδος ἕνας νὰ γένῃ ἀρχηγός (II. a. 1)
"let there be one leader of his country," μέσ' τ' οὐρανοῦ
ἀρμενίζει τὴν ἥσυχη ἐρημιά (II. a. 13) "floats in the vault
of heaven's tranquil solitude," μὲ μάτι βλέπω φλογερό
(II. a. 9) "I behold with flaming eye"—in which the
essential elements of the sentence surround the less important.
A favourite artistic device is chiasm : e.g. τὸ στράτεμά μου
σύναξε, μάσε τὰ παλληκάρια (I. a. 2) "my army collect,
assemble my warriors," παρακαλοῦν οἱ γέροντες, τ' ἀγώρια
γονατίζουν (I. a. 7) "the old beseech him, at his knees fall
the young," me kánni peþáni, na peþáni me kánni esú (III. 1)
"me thou permittest to die, to die thou permittest me," ποῦ
δὲν βλέπει μάτι ξένο, δὲν ἀκούει ξένο αὐτί (II. a. 20)

"where gazes no eye of stranger, and no ear of stranger hears."

The treatment of these things, however, does not properly belong to the sphere of grammar, but to that of style: grammar is concerned only with establishing the given facts and means of expression in the natural language.

TEXTS.

I. FOLK LITERATURE.

a. Folk Songs.

1. Ἡ ἅλωσι τῆς Κωνσταντινούπολις.

a.

Καλόγρια ἐμαγέρευε ψαράκια στὸ τηγάνι,
Καὶ μιὰ φωνή, ψηλὴ φωνὴ ἀπάνωθεν τῆς λέγει·
„Πάψε, γριά, τὸ μαγερειὸ κ' ἡ Πόλι θὰ τουρκέψῃ."
„Ὅταν τὰ ψάρια πεταχτοῦν καὶ βγοῦν καὶ ζωντανέψουν,
Τότες κι ὁ Τοῦρκος θενὰ μπῇ κ' ἡ Πόλι θὰ τουρκέψῃ." —
Τὰ ψάρια πεταχτήκανε, τὰ ψάρια ζωντανέψαν,
Κι ὁ ἀμιρᾶς εἰσέβηκεν ἀτός του καβαλλάρις.

b.

Πῆραν τὴν πόλι, πῆραν την, πῆραν τῇ Σαλονίκη,
Πῆραν καὶ τὴν Ἁγιὰ Σοφιά, τὸ μέγα μοναστήρι,
Ποῦ 'χε τριακόσια σήμαντρα κ' ἑξῆντα δυὸ καμπάνες·
Κάθε καμπάνα καὶ παπᾶς, κάθε παπᾶς καὶ διάκος.
Σιμὰ νὰ βγοῦν τὰ ἅγια κι ὁ βασιλιὰς τοῦ κόσμου,
Φωνὴ τοὺς ἦρτ' ἐξ οὐρανοῦ, ἀγγέλων ἀπ' τὸ στόμα·
„Ἀφῆτ' αὐτὴ τὴν ψαλμῳδιά, νὰ χαμηλώσουν τ' ἅγια·
Καὶ στείλτε λόγο στὴ Φραγκιά, νά 'ρτουνε νὰ τὰ πιάσουν,
Νὰ πάρουν τὸ χρυσὸ σταυρὸ καὶ τ' ἅγιο τὸ βαγγέλιο
Καὶ τὴν ἁγία τράπεζα, νὰ μὴ τὴν ἀμολύνουν."
Σὰν τ' ἄκουσεν ἡ δέσποινα, δακρύζουν οἱ εἰκόνες·
„Σώπασε, κυρὰ δέσποινα, μὴν κλαίγῃς, μὴ δακρύζῃς·
Πάλε μὲ χρόνους, μὲ καιρούς, πάλε δικά σας εἶναι."

2. Ὁ Διάκος.

Τρία πουλάκια κάθουνταν στοῦ Διάκου τὸ ταμπούρι.
Τό 'να τηράει τὴ Λιβαδιὰ καὶ τ' ἄλλο τὸ Ζητούνι,

Τὸ τρίτο τὸ καλύτερο μοιριολογᾷ καὶ λέγει·
Πολλὴ μαυρίλα πλάκωσε, μαύρη σὰν καλιακούδα·
Μὴν ὁ Καλύβας ἔρχεται, μὴν ὁ Λεβεντογιάννης;
Οὐδ' ὁ Καλύβας ἔρχεται, οὐδ' ὁ Λεβεντογιάννης·
Ὀμὲρ Βρυώνης πλάκωσε μὲ δεκοχτὼ χιλιάδες.

Ὁ Διάκος σὰν τ' ἀγροίκησε, πολὺ τοῦ κακοφάνη·
Ψηλὴ φωνὴν ἐσήκωσε, τὸν πρῶτο του φωνάζει·
„Τὸ στράτεμά μου σύναξε, μάσε τὰ παλληκάρια,
Δός τους μπαρούτη περισσὴ καὶ βόλια μὲ τὲς φούχτες.
Γλήγορα· καὶ νὰ πιάσωμε κάτω στὴν Ἀλαμάνα,
Ποῦ 'ναι ταμπούρια δυνατὰ κι ὄμορφα μετερίζια."
Παίρνουνε τὰ λαφρὰ σπαθιὰ καὶ τὰ βαρειὰ τουφέκια,
Στὴν Ἀλαμάνα φτάνουνε καὶ πιάνουν τὰ ταμπούρια·
„Καρδιά, παιδιά μου," φώναξε, „παιδιά, μὴ φοβηθῆτε.
Σταθῆτ' ἀντρειὰ σὰν Ἕλληνες καὶ σὰ Γραικοὶ σταθῆτε".
Ἐκεῖνοι φοβηθήκανε κ' ἐσκόρπισαν στοὺς λόγγους.
Ἔμειν' ὁ Διάκος στὴ φωτιὰ μὲ δεκοχτὼ λεβέντες,
Τρεῖς ὧρες ἐπολέμαε μὲ δεκοχτὼ χιλιάδες.
Σκίστηκε τὸ τουφέκι του κ' ἐγίνηκε κομμάτια,
Σέρνει καὶ τὸ λαφρὸ σπαθὶ καὶ στὴ φωτιὰ χουμάει,
Ἔκοψε Τούρκους ἄπειρους κ' ἐφτὰ μπουλουκμπασίδες.
Καὶ τὸ σπαθί του σκίστηκεν ἀπάν' ἀπὸ τὴ φούχτα,
Κ' ἔπεσ' ὁ Διάκος ζωντανὸς εἰς τῶν ἐχτρῶν τὰ χέρια.
Χίλιοι τὸν πῆραν ἀπὸ 'μπρὸς καὶ δυὸ χιλιάδες πίσω.
Κι Ὀμὲρ Βρυώνης μυστικὰ στὸ δρόμο τὸν ἐρώτα·
„Γένεσαι Τοῦρκος, Διάκο μου, τὴν πίστι σου ν' ἀλλάξῃς,
Νὰ προσκυνᾷς εἰς τὸ τζαμί, τὴν ἐκκλησιὰ ν' ἀφήσῃς;"
Κ' ἐκεῖνος τ' ἀπεκρίθηκε καὶ μὲ θυμὸ τοῦ λέγει·
„Πάτε κ' ἐσεῖς κ' ἡ πίστι σας, μουρτάτες, νὰ χαθῆτε.
Ἐγὼ Γραικὸς γεννήθηκα, Γραικὸς θανὰ πεθάνω.
Ἂν θέλετε χίλια φλωριὰ καὶ χίλιους μαχμουτιέδες,
Μόνον ἐφτὰ μερῶν ζωὴ θέλω νὰ μοῦ χαρίστε,
Ὅσο νὰ φτάσ' ὁ Ὀδυσσεὺς κι ὁ Βάγιας ὁ Θανάσις."
Σὰν τ' ἄκουσ' ὁ Χαλὶλ μπέης, ἀφρίζει καὶ φωνάζει·
„Χίλια πουγγιὰ σᾶς δίνω 'γὼ κι ἀκόμα πεντακόσια,
Τὸν Διάκο νὰ χαλάσετε, τὸν φοβερὸ τὸν κλέφτη·
Γιατί θὰ σβήσῃ τὴν Τουρκιὰ κι ὅλο μας τὸ ντεβλέτι."
Τὸν Διάκο τότε παίρνουνε καὶ στὸ σουβλὶ τὸν βάζουν,
Ὁλόρτο τὸν ἐστήσανε κι αὐτὸς χαμογελοῦσε.
Τοὺς ἔβριζε τὴν πίστι τους, τοὺς ἔλεγε μουρτάτες·

„Σκυλιά, κι ἂν μὲ σουβλίσετε, ἕνας Γραικὸς ἐχάθη·
Ἂς εἶν' ὁ Ὀδυσσεὺς καλὰ κι ὁ καπετὰν Νικήτας·
Αὐτοὶ θὰ φάνε τὴν Τουρκιάν, θὰ κάψουν τὸ ντεβλέτι."

3. Ὁ Στέργιος.

(Thessaly)

Κι ἂν τὰ ντερβένια τούρκεψαν, τὰ πῆραν Ἀρβανίτες,
Ὁ Στέργιος εἶναι ζωντανός, πασάδες δὲν ψηφάει.
Ὅσο χιονίζουνε βουνὰ καὶ λουλουδίζουν κάμποι
Κ' ἔχουν οἱ ράχες κρυὰ νερά, Τούρκους δὲν προσκυνοῦμε.
Πάμε νὰ λιμεριάσωμεν ὁποῦ φωλιάζουν λύκοι,
Σὲ κορφοβούνια, σὲ σπηλιές, σὲ ράχες καὶ ραχούλες.
Σκλάβοι στὲς χῶρες κατοικοῦν καὶ Τούρκους προσκυνοῦνε,
Κ' ἐμεῖς γιὰ χώραν ἔχομε ρημιὲς κι ἄγρια λαγκάδια.
Παρὰ μὲ Τούρκους, μὲ θεριὰ καλύτερα νὰ ζοῦμε.

The same runs in phonetic transcription (to illustrate the pronunciation, *cf.* § 2) thus:

ǩ an da derveńa túrǩepsan, ta píran Arvanítes,
o Stéryos íne zondanós, pasádes đembzifáĵ.
óso χ'onízune vuná ǩe luluđízun kámbi,
ǩ éχun i ráχ'es krá nerá, Túrkus dembroskinúme.
páme na limeŕásomen opú fol'ázun líǩi,
se korfovúńa, se spil'és, se ráχ'es ǩe raχúles.
sklávi stes χóres katikún ǩe Túrkus proskinúne,
ǩemís ja χóran éχome rimńés ǩ áʒŕa laᵚgádja.
pará me Túrkus, me þeŕá▸kalítera na zúme.

4. Ὁ ἀποχαιρετισμὸς τοῦ κλέφτη.

„Μάννα, σοῦ λέω, δὲν ἠμπορῶ τοὺς Τούρκους νὰ δουλεύω,
Δὲν ἠμπορῶ, δὲ δύναμαι, ἐμάλλιασ' ἡ καρδιά μου.
Θὰ πάρω τὸ τουφέκι μου, νὰ πάω νὰ γένω κλέφτης,
Νὰ κατοικήσω στὰ βουνὰ καὶ στὲς ψηλὲς ραχούλες,
Νά 'χω τοὺς λόγγους συντροφιά, μὲ τὰ θεριὰ κουβέντα,
Νά 'χω τὰ χιόνια γιὰ σκεπή, τοὺς βράχους γιὰ κρεββάτι,
Νά 'χω μὲ τὰ κλεφτόπουλα καθημερνὸ λιμέρι.
Θὰ φύγω, μάννα, καὶ μὴν κλαίς, μόν' δό μου τὴν εὐχή σου,
Κ' εὐχήσου μέ, μαννούλα μου, Τούρκους πολλοὺς νὰ σφάξω.
Καὶ φύτεψε τρανταφυλλιὰ καὶ μαῦρο καρυοφύλλι
Καὶ πότιζέ τα ζάχαρι καὶ πότιζέ τα μόσκο·
Κι ὅσο π' ἀνθίζουν, μάννα μου, καὶ βγάνουνε λουλούδια,
Ὁ γιός σου δὲν ἀπέθανε καὶ πολεμάει τοὺς Τούρκους·

Κι ἂν ἔρθη μέρα θλιβερή, μέρα φαρμακωμένη,
Καὶ μαραθοῦν τὰ δυὸ μαζὶ καὶ πέσουν τὰ λουλούδια,
Τότε κ' ἐγὼ θὰ λαβωθῶ, τὰ μαῦρα νὰ φορέσης." —
Δώδεκα χρόνοι πέρασαν καὶ δεκαπέντε μῆνες,
Π' ἀνθίζαν τὰ τραντάφυλλα κι ἀνθίζαν τὰ μπουμπούκια.
Καὶ μιὰν αὐγὴ 'νοιξάτικη, μιὰ πρώτη τοῦ Μαΐου,
Ποῦ κελαϊδούσαν τὰ πουλιὰ κι ὁ οὐρανὸς γελοῦσε,
Μὲ μιᾶς ἀστράφτει καὶ βροντᾷ καὶ γίνεται σκοτάδι·
Τὸ καρυοφύλλι στέναξε, τρανταφυλλιὰ δακρύζει,
Μὲ μιᾶς ξεράθηκαν τὰ δυὸ κ' ἐπέσαν τὰ λουλούδια·
Μαζὶ μ' αὐτὰ σωριάστηκε κ' ἡ δόλια του μαννούλα.

5. Οἱ Κλέφτες καὶ ἡ ἄνοιξι.

(Epirus)

Ἥσυχα ποῦ εἶναι τὰ βουνά, ἥσυχοι ποῦ εἶν' οἱ κάμποι!
Δὲν καρτεροῦνε θάνατο, γεράματα δὲν ἔχουν,
Μόν' καρτεροῦν τὴν ἄνοιξι, τὸ Μάϊ, τὸ καλοκαίρι,
Νὰ ἰδοῦν τοὺς Βλάχους στὰ βουνά, νὰ ἰδοῦν τὲς Βλαχοπούλες,
Ν' ἀκούσουν τὰ Βλαχόπουλα λαλῶντας τὲς φλογέρες,
Βόσκοντας τὰ κοπάδια τους μὲ τὰ χοντρὰ κουδούνια.
Ὅντας θὰ στήσουν τὰ μαντριά, τὴν ἀρτυσιὰ νὰ φτειάσουν,
Θὰ βγοῦν καὶ τὰ κλεφτόπουλα νὰ παίζουν, νὰ χορεύουν.
Συχνὰ συχνὰ θὰ ροβολᾶν στοὺς κάμπους τῶν Φερσάλων,
Νὰ πιάνουν Τούρκους ζωντανούς, νὰ γδύνουν σκοτωμένους,
Νὰ φέρνουν γρόσια καὶ φλωριὰ κ' ἐκεῖ νὰ τὰ μοιράζουν,
Καὶ νὰ χαρίζουν κάνα δυὸ στὲς ἄσπρες Βλαχοπούλες,
Κλέφτοντας καὶ κάνα φιλὶ καὶ γλυκοπαιγνιδάκι.

6. Χελιδόνισμα.

Χελιδόνι ἔρχεται,
Θάλασσαν ἀπέρασε,
Τὴ φωλιὰ θεμέλιωσε,
Κάθισε κ' ἐλάλησε·
Μάρτι, Μάρτι χιονερὲ
Καὶ Φλεβάρι βροχερέ.
Ὁ Ἀπρίλις ὁ γλυκὺς
Ἔφτασε, δὲν εἶν' μακρύς·
Τὰ πουλάκια κελαϊδοῦν,
Τὰ δεντράκια φυλλανθοῦν,

Τὰ ὀρνίθια νὰ γεννοῦν
Ἀρχινοῦν καὶ νὰ κλωσσοῦν.
Τὰ κοπάδια ξαρχινοῦν
Ν' ἀναβαίνουν στὰ βουνιά,
Τὰ κατσίκια νὰ πηδοῦν
Καὶ νὰ τρώγουν τὰ κλαδιά·
Ζῶα, ἄνθρωποι, πουλιὰ
Χαίρονται ἀπὸ καρδιᾶς·
Ἔπαψαν τὰ παγωτιὰ
Καὶ τὰ χιόνια κι ὁ βοριᾶς.
Μάρτι, μάρτι χιονερὲ
Καὶ Φλεβάρι λασπερέ.
Ἦρτ' Ἀπρίλις ὁ καλός,
Μάρτι πρίτς, Φλεβάρι πρίτς.

7. Ὁ Χάρος καὶ οἱ Ψυχές.

Γιατ' εἶναι μαῦρα τὰ βουνὰ καὶ στέκουν βουρκωμένα;
Μήν' ἄνεμος τὰ πολεμᾷ; μήνα βροχὴ τὰ δέρνει;
Κι οὐδ' ἄνεμος τὰ πολεμᾷ κι οὐδὲ βροχὴ τὰ δέρνει·
Μόνε διαβαίν' ὁ Χάροντας μὲ τοὺς ἀπεθαμμένους·
Σέρνει τοὺς νιοὺς ἀπὸ μπροστά, τοὺς γέροντες κατόπι,
Τὰ τρυφερὰ παιδόπουλα στὴ σέλλ' ἀραδιασμένα.
Παρακαλοῦν οἱ γέροντες, τ' ἀγώρια γονατίζουν·
„Χάρε μου, κόνεψ' εἰς χωριό, κόνεψ' εἰς κρύα βρύσι,
Νὰ πιοῦν οἱ γέροντες νερὸ κ' οἱ νιοὶ νὰ λιθαρίσουν,
Καὶ τὰ μικρὰ παιδόπουλα νὰ μάσουν λουλουδάκια."
„Κι οὐδ' εἰς χωριὸ κονεύω 'γὼ κι οὐδὲ εἰς κρύα βρύσι,
Ἔρχοντ' οἱ μάννες γιὰ νερό, γνωρίζουν τὰ παιδιά των·
Γνωρίζονται τ' ἀντρόγυνα καὶ χωρισμὸ δὲν ἔχουν."

8. Χάρος.

(Cephalonia)

Ἀκούστε τί διαλάλησε τοῦ πρικοῦ Χάρου ἡ μάννα·
„Πὄχουν παιδιά, ἂς τὰ κρύψουνε, κι ἀδέρφια, ἂς τὰ φυλάξουν,
Γυναῖκες τῶν καλῶν ἀντρῶν νὰ κρύψουνε τοὺς ἄντρες!
Κι ὁ Χάρος συγυρίζεται γιὰ νά 'βγῃ νὰ κρουσέψῃ."
Μὰ νά τον καὶ κατέβαινε τσοὺ κάμπους καβελλάρις.
Μαῦρος ἦταν, κατάμαυρος, μαῦρο καὶ τ' ἀλογό του,
Σέρνει στελέττα δίκοπα, σπαθιὰ ξεγυμνωμένα·

Στελέττα τά 'χει γιὰ καρδιές, σπαθιὰ γιὰ τὰ κεφάλια.

Στέκω καὶ τὸν περικαλῶ, τὰ χέρια σταυρωμένα·

„Χάρο, γιὰ δὲ πληρώνεσαι, γιατί δὲν παίρνεις ἄσπρα;

Πᾶρε τοῦν πλούσιων τὰ φλωριὰ καὶ τοῦ φτωχῶν τὰ τρόσια,

Καὶ πᾶρε καὶ τοῦν πένητων τ' ἀμπελοχώραφά τους!"

Κ' ἐκεῖνος μ' ἀποκρίθηκε σὰ σκύλος μανιαμένος·

„Νὰ χαροῦν οἱ πλούσιοι τὰ φλωριὰ καὶ οἱ φτωχοὶ τὰ γρόσια,

Νὰ χαίρουνται κ' οἱ πένητες τ' ἀμπελοχώραφά τους!

Κ' ἐγὼ παίρνω ὄμορφα κορμιά, τ' ἀγγελοκαμωμένα,

Νὰ τσηγαρίζω τσ' ἀδερφές, νὰ λαχταρίζω μάννες

Καὶ νὰ χωρίζω ἀντρόγυνα, τὰ πολυαγαπημένα."

Ὦ θὲ μεγαλοδύναμε, πολλὰ καλὰ ποῦ κάνεις,

Πολλὰ καλὰ μᾶς ἔκαμες, μὰ ἕνα καλὸ δὲν κάνεις·

Γιοφύρι μέσ' στὸ πέλαγο, σκάλα στὸν κάτω κόσμο,

Νὰ κατεβαίνουν οἱ ἀδερφές, νὰ κατεβαίνουν οἱ μάννες,

Ν' ἀνεβοκατεβαίνουνε καλῶν ἀντρῶν γυναῖκες.

9. Ὁ Χάρος καὶ ὁ τσοπάνης.

(Arachova)

Τὸ βλέπεις κεῖνο τὸ βουνὸ ποῦ 'ναι ψηλὸ καὶ μέγα,

Πόχ' ἀνταρούλα στὴν κορφὴ καὶ καταχνιὰ στὴ ρίζα;

Ἀπέκεινα κατέβαινε ἕνας ντελὴ λεβέντης,

Φέρνει τὸ φέσι του στραβὰ καὶ τὸν γαμπᾶ στριμμένο.

Κι ὁ Χάρος τὸν ἐβίγλισεν ἀπὸ ψηλή ραχούλα,

Βγῆκε καὶ τὸν ἀπάντησε σ' ἕνα στενὸ σοκάκι.

„Καλὴ μέρα σου, Χάρο μου." — „Καλῶς τον τὸν λεβέντη.

Λεβέντη, ποῦθεν ἔρχεσαι, λεβέντη, ποῦ παγαίνεις;"

„Γώ; 'πὸ τὰ πρόβατ' ἔρχομαι, στὸ σπίτι μου παγαίνω,

Πάγω νὰ πάρω τὸ ψωμὶ καὶ πίσω νὰ γυρίσω."

„Λεβέντη, μὅστειλε ὁ Θιὸς νὰ πάρω τὴν ψυχή σου."

„Δίχως ἀρρώστια κι ἀφορμὴ ψυχὴ δὲν παραδίδω.

Γιά· ἔβγα νὰ παλέψωμε σὲ μαρμαρένι' ἁλώνι,

Κι ἂν μὲ νικήσῃς, Χάρο μου, νὰ πάρῃς τὴν ψυχή μου,

Κι ἂν σὲ νικήσω, Χάρο μου, νὰ πάρω τὴν ψυχή σου."

Πιαστήκαν καὶ παλέψανε δυὸ νύχτες καὶ τρεῖς μέρες,

Κι αὐτοῦ τὴν τρίτη τὴν αὐγὴ κοντὰ στὸ γιόμα γιόμα

Φέρν' ὁ λεβέντης μιὰ βολά, τοῦ Χάρου κακοφάνη,

Ἀπ' τὰ μαλλιὰ τὸν ἄδραξε, στὴ γῆν τὸν ἀβρροντάει,

Ἀκοὺν τὸ νιὸν καὶ βόγγιζε καὶ βαρυαναστενάζει·

„Ἄσε με, Χάρο μ', ἄσε με τρεῖς μέρες καὶ τρεῖς νύχτες·

Τὲς δυὸ νὰ φάγω καὶ νὰ πιῶ, τὴ μιὰ νὰ σεργιανίσω,
Νὰ πάω, νὰ διῶ τοὺς φίλους μου, νὰ διῶ καὶ τοὺς δικούς μου,
Πόχω γυναῖκα παρανιά, καὶ χήρα δὲν τῆς πρέπει,
Πόχω καὶ δυὸ μικρούτσικα, κι ὀρφάνια δὲν τοὺς πρέπει,
Πόχω τὰ πρόβατ' ἄκουρα καὶ τὸ τυρὶ στὸ κάδι."
Κι αὐτοῦ κοντὰ στὸ δειλινὸ τὸν καταβάν' ὁ Χάρος.

10. Μοιρολόγι.

(Cephalonia)

„Εὐτοῦ ποῦ ἐκίνησες νὰ πᾶς στ' ἀγύρικο ταξίδι,
Στὸν θεὸν σ' ὁρκίζω νὰ μοῦ 'πῆς, πότε νὰ σὲ προσμένω,
Νὰ ρίξω ρόδα στὴν αὐλή, τραντάφυλλα στὴν πόρτα,
Νὰ φτειάσω γιόμα νὰ γευτῆς καὶ δεῖπνο νὰ δειπνήσης,
Νὰ στρώσω καὶ τὴν κλίνη σου, νὰ πέσης νὰ πλαγιάσης."
„Ἄ φτειάσης γιόμα, γέψου το, καὶ δεῖπνο, δείπνησέ το,
Κι ἂ στρώσης καὶ τὴν κλίνη μου, πέσε, κοιμήσου ἀπάνω!
Κ' ἐγὼ πάγω στὴ μαύρη γῆς, στ' ἀραχνιασμένο χῶμα,
Κ' ἔχω τὴ γῆς γιὰ πάπλωμα, τὸ χῶμα γιὰ σεντόνι,
Καὶ γεύομαι τὸν κουρνιαχτό, δειπνάω ἀπὸ τὸ χῶμα
Καὶ πίνω τ' ὠριοστάλαχτο τσῆ πλάκας τὸ φαρμάκι."
„Ἂν ἀπεφάσισες νὰ πάς, νὰ μὴ ματαγυρίσης,
Ἄνοιξε τὰ ματάκια σου κ' ἰδὲς μιὰ μπάντα κι ἄλλη
Κι ἄφσε ὑγειὰ στὸ σπίτι σου κ' ὑγειὰ στοὺς ἐδικούς σου
Καὶ σήκω πάρε μίσεψε, σηκώσου πάρε φεύγα,
Πριτὰ σοῦ σύρουν θυμιατό, σὲ ψάλλουν οἱ παπάδες,
Πριτὰ σὲ περιλάβουνε τσῆ γῆς οἱ κλερονόμοι."

11. Ὁ Βουρκόλακας.

Μάννα, μὲ τοὺς ἐννιά σου γιοὺς καὶ μὲ τὴ μιά σου κόρη,
Τὴ κόρη τὴ μονάκριβη τὴ πολυαγαπημένη,
Τὴν εἶχες δώδεκα χρονῶν κ' ἥλιος δὲ σοῦ τὴν εἶδε,
Στὰ σκοτεινὰ τὴν ἔλουζες, στ' ἄφεγγα τὴν ἐπλέκες,
Στ' ἄστρη καὶ στὸν αὐγερινὸ τσ' ἔφκειανες τὰ σγουρά της·
Ὁποῦ σοῦ φέρναν προξενιὰν ἀπὸ τὴ Βαβυλώνη,
Νὰ τὴν παντρέψης μακρειά, πολὺ μακρειὰ στὰ ξένα·
Ὀχτ' ἀδερφοὶ δὲ θέλουνε κι ὁ Κωσταντῖνος θέλει·
„Δός τηνε, μάννα, δός τηνε τὴν Ἀρετὴ στὰ ξένα,
Στὰ ξένα 'κεῖ ποῦ περβατῶ, στὰ ξένα ποῦ παγαίνω,
Νὰ 'χω κ' ἐγὼ παρηγοριά, νὰ 'χω κ' ἐγὼ κονάκι."

„Φρόνιμος εἶσαι, Κωσταντῆ, κι ἄσχημ' ἀπηλογήθης·
Κι ἂν μόρθῃ, γιέ μου, θάνατος, κι ἂν μόρθῃ, γιέ μ', ἀρρώστια,
Κι ἂν τύχῃ πίκρα γὴ χαρά, ποιὸς θὰ μοῦ τήνε φέρῃ;"
Τὸ Θιὸ τῆς ἔβαλ' ἐγγυτὴ καὶ τοὺς ἁγιοὺς μαρτύρους,
Ἂν τύχη κ' ἔρθη θάνατος, ἂν τύχη κ' ἔρθ' ἀρρώστια,
Κι ἂν τύχῃ πίκρα γὴ χαρά, νὰ πάῃ νὰ τήνε φέρῃ.
Καὶ σὰν τὴν ἐπαντρέψανε τὴν Ἀρετὴ στὰ ξένα,
Κ' ἐμπῆκε χρόνος δίσεφτος καὶ μῆνας ὀργισμένος
Κ' ἔπεσε τὸ θανατικὸ κ' οἱ ἐννιὰ 'δερφοὶ πεθάναν,
Βρέθηκ' ἡ μάννα μοναχὴ σὰν καλαμιὰ στὸν κάμπο·
Στ' ὀχτὼ μνήματα δέρνεται, στ' ὀχτὼ μοιριολογάει,
Στοῦ Κωσταντίνου τὸ θαφτὸ τὲς πλάκες ἀνασκώνει·
„Σήκου, Κωσταντινάκι μου, τὴν Ἀρετή μου θέλω·
Τὸ Θιὸ μοῦ 'βάλες ἐγγυτὴ καὶ τοὺς ἁγιοὺς μαρτύρους,
Ἂν τύχῃ πίκρα γὴ χαρά, νὰ πᾶς νὰ μοῦ τὴ φέρῃς."
Τ' ἀνάθεμα τὸν ἔβγαλε μέσ' ἀπὸ τὸ κιβούρι·
Κάνει τὸ σύγνεφ' ἄλογο καὶ τ' ἄστρο σαλιβάρι
Καὶ τὸ φεγγάρι συντροφιὰ καὶ πάει νὰ τήνε φέρῃ.
Παίρνει τὰ ὄρη πίσω του καὶ τὰ βουνὰ μπροστά του,
Βρίσκει την κ' ἐχτενίζουνταν ὄξου στὸ φεγγαράκι·
Ἀπὸ μακρειὰ τὴ χαιρετᾷ κι ἀπὸ μακρειὰ τῆς λέγει·
„Περβάτησ', Ἀρετούλα μου, κυράνα μας σὲ θέλει."
„Ἀλλοίμον' ἀδερφάκι μου, καὶ τ' εἶναι τούτ' ἡ ὥρα;
Ἀνίσως κ' εἶναι γιὰ χαρά, νὰ βάλω τὰ χρυσά μου,
Κι ἂν εἶναι πίκρα, πές μου τα, νά 'ρτω κατὰ πῶς εἶμαι."
„Περβάτησ', Ἀρετούλα μου, κ' ἔλα κατὰ πῶς εἶσαι."
Στὴ στράτα ποὺ διαβαίνανε, στὴ στράτα ποὺ παγαίναν,
Ἀκοὺν πουλιὰ καὶ κιλαδοῦν, ἀκοὺν πουλιὰ καὶ λένε·
„Ποιὸς εἶδε κόρην ὄμορφη νὰ σέρν' ὁ πεθαμμένος;"
„Ἄκουσες, Κωσταντάκι μου, τί λένε τὰ πουλάκια;
Ποιὸς εἶδε κόρην ὄμορφη νὰ σέρν' ὁ πεθαμμένος;"
„Λωλὰ πουλιὰ κι ἂς κιλαδοῦν, λωλὰ πουλιὰ κι ἂς λένε."
Καὶ παρακεῖ ποὺ πάγαιναν, κι ἄλλα πουλιὰ τοὺς λένε·
„Τί βλέπομε τὰ θλιβερά, τὰ παραπονεμένα,
Νὰ περβατοῦν οἱ ζωντανοὶ μὲ τοὺς ἀπεθαμμένους!"
„Ἄκουσες, Κωσταντάκι μου, τί λένε τὰ πουλάκια;
Πῶς περβατοῦν οἱ ζωντανοὶ μὲ τοὺς ἀπεθαμμένους."
„Πουλάκια 'ναι κι ἂς κιλαδοῦν, πουλάκια 'ναι κι ἂς λένε."
„Φοβοῦμαι σ', ἀδερφάκι μου, καὶ λιβανιὲς μυρίζεις."
„Ἐχτὲς βραδὺς ἐπήγαμε πέρα στὸν Ἅϊ-Γιάννη,

Κ' ἐθύμιασέ μας ὁ παπᾶς μὲ περισσὸ λιβάνι."
Καὶ παρεμπρὸς ποῦ πήγανε, κι ἄλλα πουλιὰ τοὺς λένε·
"Ὦ Θὲ μεγαλοδύναμε, μεγάλο θᾶμα κάνεις,
Τέτοιαν πανώρια λυγερὴ νὰ σέρνῃ πεθαμμένος."
Τ' ἄκουσε πάλ' ἡ Ἀρετὴ κ' ἐράγισ' ἡ καρδιά της.
"Ἄκουσες, Κωσταντάκι μου, τί λένε τὰ πουλάκια;
Πές μου, ποῦ 'ν' τὰ μαλλάκια σου, τὸ πιγωρὸ μουστάκι;"
"Μεγάλη ἀρρώστια μ' εὕρηκε, μ' ἔρριξε τοῦ θανάτου,
Ποῦ 'πέσαν τὰ ξανθὰ μαλλιά, τὸ πιγωρὸ μουστάκι."
Βρίσκουν τὸ σπίτι κλειδωτὸ κλειδομανταλωμένο,
Καὶ τὰ σπιτοπαράθυρα ποῦ 'ταν ἀραχνιασμένα.
"Ἄνοιξε, μάννα μ', ἄνοιξε καὶ νὰ τὴν Ἀρετή σου."
"Ἂν εἶσαι Χάρος, διάβαινε, κι ἄλλα παιδιὰ δὲν ἔχω·
Ἡ δόλια ἡ Ἀρετούλα μου λείπει μακρειὰ στὰ ξένα."
"Ἄνοιξε, μάννα μ', ἄνοιξε, κ' ἐγώ 'μ' ὁ Κωσταντῆς σου·
Ἐγγυτὴ σὄβαλα τὸ Θιὸ καὶ τοὺς ἁγιοὺς μαρτύρους,
Ἂν τύχῃ πίκρα γῆ χαρά, νὰ πὰ νὰ σοῦ τὴ φέρω."
Κι ὥστε νὰ 'βγῇ στὴν πόρτα της, ἐβγῆκεν ἡ ψυχή της.

12. Τὸ γιοφύρι τῆς Ἄρτας.

(Corfu)

Σαράντα πέντε μάστοροι κ' ἑξήντα μαθητάδες
Τρεῖς χρόνους ἐδουλεύανε τῆς Ἄρτας τὸ γιοφύρι·
Ὁλημερὶς ἐχτίζανε κι ἀπὸ βραδὺ γκρεμειέται.
Μοιριολογοῦν οἱ μάστορες καὶ κλαὶν οἱ μαθητάδες·
"Ἀλλοίμονο στοὺς κόπους μας, κρίμα στὲς δούλεψές μας,
Ὁλημερὶς νὰ χτίζωμε, τὸ βράδυ νὰ γκρεμειέται."
Καὶ τὸ στοιχειὸ ποκρίθηκεν ἀπ' τὴ δεξιὰ καμάρα·
"Ἂν δὲ στοιχειώσετ' ἄνθρωπο, τεῖχος δὲ θεμελιώνει·
Καὶ μὴ στοιχειώσετ' ὀρφανό, μὴ ξένο, μὴ διαβάτη,
Παρὰ τοῦ πρωτομάστορα τὴν ὥρια τὴ γυναῖκα,
Πὄρχετ' ἀργὰ τ' ἀποταχειά, πὄρχετ' ἀργὰ στὸ γιόμα."
Τ' ἄκουσ' ὁ πρωτομάστορας καὶ τοῦ θανάτου πέφτει,
Κάνει γραφὴ καὶ στέλνει την μὲ τὸ πουλὶ τ' ἀηδόνι·
"Ἀργὰ ντυθῇ, ἀργ' ἀλλαχτῇ, ἀργὰ νὰ πάῃ στὸ γιόμα,
Ἀργὰ νὰ πάῃ καὶ νὰ διαβῇ τῆς Ἄρτας τὸ γιοφύρι." —
Καὶ τὸ πουλὶ παράκουσε κι ἀλλιῶς ἐπῆγε κ' εἶπε·
"Γοργὰ ντύσου, γοργ' ἄλλαξε, γοργὰ νὰ πὰς τὸ γιόμα,
Γοργὰ νὰ πὰς καὶ νὰ διαβῇς τῆς Ἄρτας τὸ γιοφύρι."

Νά τηνε καὶ ξανάφανεν ἀπὸ τὴν ἄσπρη στράτα·
Τὴν εἶδ᾽ ὁ πρωτομάστορας, ραγίζετ᾽ ἡ καρδιά του.
᾽Απὸ μακρειὰ τοὺς χαιρετᾷ κι ἀπὸ μακρειὰ τοὺς λέγει·
„Γειά σας, χαρά σας, μάστορες, καὶ σεῖς οἱ μαθητάδες,
Μὰ τί ἔχει ὁ πρωτομάστορας κ᾽ εἶν᾽ ἔτσι χολιασμένος;"
„Τὸ δαχτυλίδι τὅπεσε στὴν πρώτη τὴ καμάρα,
Καὶ ποιὸς νὰ μπῇ καὶ ποιὸς νὰ βγῇ, τὸ δαχτυλίδι νά ᾽βρῃ;"
„Μάστορα, μὴν πικραίνεσαι κ᾽ ἐγὼ νὰ πὰ σ᾽ τὸ φέρω·
᾽Εγὼ νὰ μπῶ κ᾽ ἐγὼ νὰ βγῶ, τὸ δαχτυλίδι νά ᾽βρω."
Μηδὲ καλὰ κατέβηκε, μηδὲ στὴ μέσ᾽ ἐπῆγε·
„Τράβα, καλέ μ᾽, τὴν ἄλυσο, τράβα τὴν ἁλυσίδα,
Τί ὅλον τὸν κόσμ᾽ ἀνάγειρα καὶ τίποτες δὲν ηὗρα." —
῍Ενας πηχάει μὲ τὸ μυστρὶ κι ἄλλος μὲ τὸν ἀσβέστη,
Παίρνει κι ὁ πρωτομάστορας καὶ ρίχνει μέγα λίθο·
„᾽Αλλοίμονο στὴ μοῖρα μας, κρίμα στὸ ριζικό μας,
Τρεῖς ἀδερφάδες ἤμασταν κ᾽ οἱ τρεῖς κακογραμμένες,
῾Η μιά ᾽χτισε τὸ Δούναβι κ᾽ ἡ ἄλλη τὸν Αὐλῶνα,
Κ᾽ ἐγὼ ἡ πλιὸ στερνότερη τῆς ῎Αρτας τὸ γιοφύρι.
Καθὼς τρέμ᾽ ἡ καρδούλα μου, νὰ τρέμῃ τὸ γιοφύρι,
Κι ὡς πέφτουν τὰ μαλλάκια μου, νὰ πέφτουν οἱ διαβάτες."
„Κόρη, τὸν λόγον ἄλλαξε κι ἄλλη κατάρα δῶσε,
Πὅχεις μονάκριβ᾽ ἀδερφό, μὴ λάχῃ καὶ περάσῃ."
Κι αὐτὴ τὸν λόγον ἄλλαξε κι ἄλλη κατάρα δίνει·
„Σίδερον ἡ καρδούλα μου, σίδερο τὸ γιοφύρι,
Σίδερο τὰ μαλλάκια μου, σίδερο κ᾽ οἱ διαβάτες.
Τί ἔχω ᾽δερφὸ στὴν ξενιτειά, μὴ λάχῃ καὶ περάσῃ."

13. Ναννάρισμα.

(Cyprus)

Νανὰ νανὰ τὸ γιούδι μου
Καὶ τὸ παλληκαρούδι μου,
Κοιμήσου γιούδι μ᾽ ἀκριβό,
Κ᾽ ἔχω νὰ σοῦ χαρίσω·
Τὴν ᾽Αλεξάντρεια ζάχαρι
Καὶ τὸ Μισίρι ρύζι
Καὶ τὴν Κωσταντινούπολι
Τρεῖς χρόνους νὰ ὁρίζῃς·
Κι ἀκόμη ἄλλα τριὰ χωριά,
Τρία μοναστηράκια·

Στὲς χῶρες σου καὶ στὰ χωριὰ
Νὰ πᾶς νὰ σεργιανίσῃς,
Στὰ τρία μοναστήρια σου
Νὰ πᾶς νὰ προσκυνήσῃς.

14. Ἡ ξενιτειά.

„Σ' ἀφήνω γειά, μαννούλα μου, σ' ἀφήνω γειά, πατέρα,
Ἔχετε γειά, 'δερφάκια μου, καὶ σεῖς ξαδερφοπούλες.
Θὰ φύγω, θὰ ξενιτευτῶ, θὰ πάω μακρειὰ στὰ ξένα·
Θὰ φύγω, μάννα, καὶ θὰ 'ρτῶ καὶ μὴν πολυλυπειέσαι.
Ἀπὸ τὰ ξένα ποῦ βρεθῶ, μηνύματα σοῦ στέλνω
Μὲ τὴ δροσιὰ τῆς ἄνοιξις, τὴν πάχνη τοῦ χειμῶνα
Καὶ μὲ τ' ἀστέρια τ' οὐρανοῦ, τὰ ρόδα τοῦ Μαῖου.
Θανὰ σοῦ στέλνω μάλαμα, θανὰ σοῦ στέλν' ἀσήμι,
Θανὰ σοῦ στέλνω πράματα π' οὐδὲ τὰ συλλογειέσαι."
„Παιδί μου, πάαινε στὸ καλὸ κι ὅλ' οἱ ἅγιοι κοντά σου,
Καὶ τῆς μαννούλας σου ἡ εὐχὴ νά 'ναι γιὰ φυλαχτό σου,
Νὰ μὴ σὲ πιάνῃ βάσκαμα καὶ τὸ κακὸ τὸ μάτι.
Θυμήσου με, παιδάκι μου, κ' ἐμὲ καὶ τὰ παιδιά μου,
Μὴ σὲ πλανέσ' ἡ ξενιτειὰ καὶ μᾶς ἀλησμονήσῃς."
„Κάλλιο, μαννούλα μου γλυκειά, κάλλιο νὰ σκάσω πρῶτα,
Παρὰ νὰ μὴ σᾶς θυμηθῶ στὰ ἔρημα τὰ ξένα." —
Δώδεκα χρόν' ἀπέρασαν καὶ δεκαπέντε μῆνες,
Καράβια δὲν τὸν εἴδανε, ναῦτες δὲν τόνε ξέρουν.
Πρῶτο φιλί — 'ναστέναξε, δεύτερο — τὸν πλανάει,
Τρίτο φιλὶ φαρμακερό — τὴ μάνν' ἀλησμονάει.

15. Ὁ μπιστικὸς φίλος.
(Crete)

Οὗλον τὸν κόσμο γύρεψα, πονέντε καὶ λεβάντε,
Νὰ βρῶ 'να φίλο μπιστικὸ σὰν καὶ τὸν ἀπατό μου.
Δὲν ηὗρα φίλο μπιστικὸ μηδ' ἀδερφὸ καλλιάν του
Σὰν τὸ σπαθάκι μ' ἀδερφό, σὰν τὸ πουγγί μου φίλο.
Κι ὅπου καυγᾶς καὶ πόλεμος, πολέμα σὺ σπαθί μου,
Κι ὅπου 'ναι γάμος καὶ χαρά, ξόδιαζε σὺ πουγγί μου.

16. Ἡ πέρδικα.

Μιὰ πέρδικα καυκήστηκε σ' ἀνατολὴ σὲ δύσι,
Πῶς δὲν εὑρέθη κυνηγὸς νὰ τήνε κυνηγήσῃ.
Ὁ κυνηγὸς σὰν τ' ἄκουσε, πολὺ τοῦ κακοφάνη,

15

Ρίχνει τὰ βρόχια στὸ γιαλό, τὰ ξόβεργα στοὺς κάμπους,
Τὰ δίχτυα τὰ μεταξωτὰ στὴ βρύσι στὴ χιονάτη·
Πάγει ἡ πέρδικα νὰ πιῇ καὶ πιάνετ' ἀπ' τὴ μύτη.
„Ἀχαμνοπιάσ' με, κυνηγέ· τώρ' ἡ ψυχή μου βγαίνει."
Καὶ μὲ τ' ἀχαμνοπιάσματα κάνει φτερὰ καὶ φεύγει·
„Ὥρα νὰ σ' εὕρῃ, κυνηγέ, ἀχαμνοκυνηγάρι·
Ἀφῆκες τέτοια πέρδικα, νὰ σοῦ τὴν πάρουν ἄλλοι."

17. Ἡ χορεύτρια.

(Dancing Song, Epirus)

Σήμερα μέρα Πασχαλιά,
Σήμερα πανηγύρι,
Κι ὅλες οἱ κόρες σιάζονται
Εἰς τὸ χορὸ νὰ βγοῦνε.
Γιὰ φέρτε τὰ στολίδια μου,
Γιὰ φέρτε τὸ γυαλί μου,
Νὰ στολιστῶ, νὰ γυαλιστῶ,
Νὰ βγῶ σὰν περδικούλα,
Νὰ πάω νὰ στρώσω τὸ χορὸ
Κάτω στὸ μεσοχώρι,
Νὰ σκώνω τὰ ματάκια μου,
Νὰ ρίχν' ἀστροπελέκια,
Νὰ κάμω Τούρκους νὰ σφαγοῦν,
Ρωμιοὺς ν' ἀλλοπιστήσουν,
Νὰ κάμω τὸ Μεχμέταγα
Νὰ χάσῃ τὰ δεφτέρια,
Νὰ κάμω τὸν πρωτόπαπα
Νὰ χάσῃ τὰ πασχάλια.

18. Ἐρωτικὸν παράπονο.

(Thera)

Ἐχτὲς βραδὺ ἀπέρασα ἀπὸ τὴ γειτονιά σου,
Ἤκουσα καὶ σὲ 'μάλωνε ἡ σκύλα ἡ κερά σου.
Καὶ πάλι ξαναπέρασα, θέλω νὰ σ' ἀρωτήσω,
Γιὰ νὰ μοῦ 'πῇς τὴν πίκρα σου νὰ σὲ παρηγορήσω.
„Κρῖνε μου σὺ τὴν πίκρα μου, τὴν παραπόνεσί μου,
Ἤκουσα ἄλλη ν' ἀγαπᾷς καὶ χάνω τὴ ζωή μου."
„Ψόματα, κρυσταλλένια μου, ψόματα, χλιά μου βρύσι,
Ψόματα μοῦ τὰ 'βγάλανε, λιγνό μου κυπαρίσσι."

„Ἀφ' ἄλλη νιὰ δὲν ἀγαπᾷς, μόν' ἀγαπᾷς ἐμένα,
Ἐχτὲς βραδὺ ἀπέρασες, γιατί δὲ μὲ 'χαιρέτας;"
„Ἡ μάννα σου κι ἀφέντης σου, ὁ θειός σου κι ἀδερφός σου
Ἤτανε εἰς τ' ἀπλάϊ σου, τ' ἀπλάϊ τὸ δικό σου."
„Ἐσὺ νὰ κλίνῃς κεφαλὴ καὶ μάθια πρὸς ἐμένα,
Κ' ἐγὼ τὸ καταλάβαινα πῶς χαιρετᾷς ἐμένα."
„Νὰ κάμω θέλω δυὸ δουλειές, τὴ μιὰ θὰ ξετελέψω,
Νὰ πάρω καὶ τσοὶ φίλοι μου γιὰ νά 'ρθω νὰ σὲ κλέψω."
„Δὲ σ' ἔχω πλιὸ μήτ' ἄνθρωπο μήτε καὶ παλληκάρι,
Ἂ δὲ μὲ κλέψῃς μιὰ βραδειὰ νύχτα μὲ τὸ φεγγάρι".

19. Ἡ χαμένη εὐκαιρία.

(Epirus)

Δικό μ' ἦταν τὸ φταίξιμο,
Νὰ χάσω τόσο τρέξιμο.
Ἦρθα καὶ σ' ηὗρα μοναχὴ
Καὶ δὲ σ' ἐχόρτασα φιλί·
Σ' ἐκύτταζα 'ναχόρταγα
Κ' ἐκάθομουν κ' ἐρώταγα,
Τὸ ποῦ νὰ εἶν' ἡ μάννα σου
Κι ὁ ἄγριος ὁ πατέρας σου·
Ἡ μάννα σου στὴν ἐκκλησιά,
Κι ἀφέντης σου στὰ Γιάννενα,
Κ' ἐσὺ κοντὰ στὸν μπουταλᾶ,
Μὲ τὰ ματάκια χαμηλά.

20. Τὸ σταμνὶ τσακισμένο.

(Aegean)

Οὖλες οἱ βέργες εἶν' ἐδώ,
Καὶ μιὰ βεργούλα π' ἀγαπῶ,
Πάγει στὴ βρύσι γιὰ νερό,
Πάγω κ' ἐγὼ κάτω νὰ πιῶ,
Νὰ τῆς θολώσω τὸ νερό,
Νὰ τῆς τσακίσω τὸ σταμνί,
Νὰ πάη στὴ μάννα τσ' ἀδειανή·
„Μωρὴ ποῦ 'ν' εἶναι τὸ σταμνί;"
„Μάννα μου, στραβοπάτησα
Κ' ἔπεσα καὶ τὸ τσάκισα."
„Δὲν εἶν' στραβοπατήματα,
Μόν' εἶν ἀντρὸς φιλήματα."

21. Ὁ παπᾶς ἀγαπητικός.

(Constantinople)

Μιὰ ἔμορφη κοπέλα εἰς τὸ σπίτ' ἑνὸς παπᾶ,
Γιὰ νὰ τὴν ξομολογήσῃ, εἶχε πάγει μιὰ φορά·
Σὰν τὴν εἶδε τόσ' ὡραία, κατανύχτη ὁ παπᾶς
Καὶ τῆς λέει· „Καλῶς ὁρίστε, τ' εἶν' αὐτὸ ποὺ μὲ ξητᾷς;"
„Δέσποτά μου, νὰ σ' ὁρίσω, ἦρτα νὰ ξεγορευτῶ·
Γιὰ νὰ μοῦ τὰ συγχωρήσῃς τσ' ἁμαρτιὲς ποὺ θὰ σοῦ 'πῶ."
„Μὴ φοβᾶσαι, κορασιά μου, δὲν ἄσπλαγχνος εἶν' ὁ θεός,
Ὡς καὶ μένα συγχωράει ποὺ 'μαι πιὸ ἁμαρτωλός."
„Δέσποτά μου, νὰ σ' ὁρίσω τὴν ἀλήθεια τὴ σωστή,
Ἀγαποῦσα ἕνα νέον καὶ τὸν ἀγαπῶ πολύ."
„Τὸ νὰ ἀγαπᾷς, παιδί μου, εἶναι πρᾶγμα φυσικό,
Μὲ εὐλάβειαν μονάχα καὶ σ' τὸ συγχωρῶ κ' ἐγώ."
„Δέσποτά μου, μιὰν ἡμέρα, ποὺ καθόμαν μοναχή,
Πέρασε κι αὐτὸς ὁ νέος καὶ μοῦ δίδ' ἕνα φιλί."
„Ἕνα σοῦ 'δωκε, κυρά μου, ἢ μὴ σοῦ 'δωκε πολλά;
Ἂν ἀπὸ τό 'να καὶ πάνω, ἔστωσαν συγχωρητά."
„Ἕνα ἕνα, δέσποτά μου, ἕνα ἕνα μοναχά·
Πλὴν θωρῶ τὸ πρόσωπό σου κ' ἔγινε σὰν τὴ φωτιά."
„Ἔ, παιδί μου, εἶναι πρᾶγμα ποὺ τό 'χω ἀπο παιδί,
Ὡς κ' ἐγὼ θὰ σὲ φιλήσω, κι ὁ θεὸς μὲ συγχωρεῖ."

22. Ἐξομολόγησι.

(Chios)

Σαράντα μέρας μελετῶ
Νὰ πάγω στὸν πνευματικό·
Πάγω μιὰ κυριακὴ πρωὶ
Καὶ τὸν εὑρίσκω στὸ κελλί.
„Παπᾶ μου, ξεμολόγα με,
Τὰ κρίματά μου ρώτα με."
„Τὰ κρίματά σου 'ναι πολλά,
Ἀγάπη νὰ μὴν κάμῃς πιά."
„Ἂν ἀρνηστῆς ἐσύ, παπᾶ,
Τὴν κόρην καὶ τὴν παπαδιά,
Τότε κ' ἐγὼ θεν' ἀρνηστῶ
Τὴν κόρη σ' ὁποῦ ἀγαπῶ."

23. Ἡ ἄσχημη νύφη.

(Epirus)

Φίλοι, γιατί δὲν τρώτε καὶ δὲν πίνετε;
Μήνα καὶ τὸ ψωμί μας δὲ σᾶς ἄρεσε;
Στέλνουμε στοὺς γειτόνους καὶ τ' ἀλλάζουμε·
Μήνα καὶ τὸ κρασί μας δὲ σᾶς ἄρεσε;
Βαγένια ἔχουμε κι ἄλλα καὶ τ' ἀλλάζουμε·
Μήνα καὶ τὰ φαγιά μας δὲ σᾶς ἄρεσαν;
Μαγείρισσες εἶν' κι ἄλλες καὶ τσ' ἀλλάζουμε·
Μήνα ἡ καψονύφη δὲ σᾶς ἄρεσεν;
Ἡ νύφη ὅπως κι ἂν εἶναι δὲν ἀλλάζεται.

24. Distiches.

1.

Ἀγάπη θέλει φρόνησι, θέλει ταπεινοσύνη,
Θέλει λαγοῦ περπατησιά, ἀῖτοῦ γληγοροσύνη.

2.

Ἀνάμεσα στὸ στήθι σου δίχτυ χρυσοπλεμένο·
Πρῶτο πουλάκι ποὺ διαβῇ, πιάνεται τὸ καημένο.
Πρῶτο πουλὶ πόδιάβηκε, ἐγώ 'μουνα, κυρά μου·
Παρακαλῶ σ', ἀφέντρα μου, δός μου τὴ λευτεριά μου.

3.

Ἀπὸ τὴν πόρτα σου περνῶ, τ' ἀχνάρι σου γνωρίζω,
Σκύβω καὶ τὸ γλυκοφιλῶ καὶ δάκρυα τὸ γεμίζω.

4.

Αὐτὰ τὰ μαῦρα μάτια ὅταν τ' ἀνοιγοκλεῖς
Κι ὅταν τὰ χαμηλώνῃς, σαγίτες μὲ βαρεῖς.

5.

Αὐτὴν τὴ φλόγα ποὺ θωρεῖς, πρῶτ' ἤτανε τσιμπίδα,
Τώρ' εἶν' φωτιὰ καὶ καίομαι, δὲν ἔχω πλιὸν ἐλπίδα.

6.

Βάσανα, πίκρες καὶ καημοί, ἀφῆστε τὴν καρδιά μου,
Γιατί τὴ φλόγα δὲ βαστῶ, ποὺ καίει τὰ σωθικά μου.

7.

Γιὰ μαῦρα μάτια χάνομαι, γιὰ γαλανὰ πεθαίνω,
Γιὰ 'κειά τὰ καταγάλανα στὸν Ἅδη κατεβαίνω.

8.

Δὲν ἤξευρα πῶς ὁ σεβντᾶς χορτάρ' εἶν' καὶ φυτρώνει,
Κ' ἐφύτρωσέ μου στὴν καρδιὰ καὶ πλιὰ δὲν ξεριζώνει.

9.

Δὲν εἶναι μιά, δὲν εἶναι δυό, τρεῖς εἶν', ἀνάθεμά τες·
Πέτε μου ποιὰ ν' ἀπαρνηθῶ, ποῦ 'ν' ὅλες μαυρομάτες.

10.

Δὲ νοστιμίζουν τὰ βουνὰ μὲ δίχως πρασινάδα,
Κι ἀγάπη δίχως κάκιωμα δὲν ἔχει νοστιμάδα.

11.

Δυὸ ἀστέρια σ' λαμπιρὰ εἶναι τὰ δυό σου μάτια,
Ποῦ ποιὸν κυττάξουν, τὴν καρδιὰ τοῦ κάνουν δυὸ κομμάτια.

12.

Ἐγροίκουνα τὰ κάλλη σου κ' ἦλθα νὰ τὰ ξανοίξω,
Καὶ δὲ μοῦ δίδ' ὁ νοῦς μου πλιὸ νὰ φεύγω νὰ τ' ἀφήσω.

13.

Ἔρωτα πονηρὸ πουλί, γιατί νὰ μὲ γελάσῃς,
Νὰ πάρῃς τὴν καρδούλα μου ἐσὺ νὰ τὴν χτικιάσῃς;

14.

Ἔρωτα ποῦ μ' ἐλάβωσες, δός μου καὶ τὸ βοτάνι,
Γιατί δὲ βρίσκω γιατρικὸ στὸν κόσμο νὰ μὲ γιάνῃ.

15.

Ἐσύ 'σαι, κόρη μ', ὁ γιατρὸς κ' ἐγώ 'μ' ὁ λαβωμένος,
Δός μου το, κόρη, τὸ φιλί, νὰ γιατρευτῇ ὁ καημένος.

16.

Ἡ ἀγάπ', ἀνάθεμά την, στὴν ἀρχὴ εἶναι γλυκειά,
Καὶ στὴ μέση πιπερίζει καὶ στὸ τέλος εἶν' πρικειά.

17.

Ἡ Μοῖρα ποῦ μ' ἐμοίρανε, ἤτανε μεθυσμένη,
Μ' ἐμοίρανε γιὰ νὰ περνῶ ζωὴ δυστυχισμένη.

18.

Θαμάζομαι τὸν οὐρανὸ πῶς στέκει χωρὶς στύλο,
Θαμάζομαι, πουλάκι μου, πῶς δὲ μὲ κάνεις φίλο.

19.

Θαμάζομαι σὰν περπατεῖς, πῶς δὲν ἀνθοῦν οἱ ρούγες
Καὶ πῶς δὲ γένεσ' ἀετὸς μὲ τὲς χρυσὲς φτερούγες.

20.

Κόρη, στὸ παραθύρι σου γαρουφαλιὰ δὲν πρέπει,
Τί ἐσὺ εἶσαι τὸ γαρούφαλο, κι ὀπόχει μάτια, ἂς βλέπῃ.

21.

Μ' ἐφίλησες κι ἀρρώστησα, φίλει με γιὰ νὰ γιάνω,
Καὶ πάλι μεταφίλει με, μὴν πέσω κι ἀπεθάνω.

22.

Μὴ μὲ μαλώνῃς, μάννα μου, κ' ἐγὼ νὰ σοῦ τὸ 'πῶ,
Πόσες βολὲς μ' ἐφίλησε ὁ νιὸς ὁπ' ἀγαπῶ.

23.

Μιὰ σπίθα λαμπιρότατη στὴ στάχτ' εἶναι κρυμμένη·
Ἔτσι κ' ἐμᾶς ἡ ἀγάπη μας κρυφὴ κ' ἐμπιστεμένη.

24.

Νά 'τον τὸ στῆθος μου γυαλί, νὰ βλέπῃς τὴν καρδιά μου,
Νὰ διῇς πῶς τσιροφλίστηκαν μέσα τὰ σωτικά μου.
Μικρὴ φωτιά, τρανὸς φανὸς καίγεται στὴν καρδιά μου,
Κ' ἐγέλα στὸ κεφάλι μου καὶ μέσ' στὰ σωτικά μου.

25.

Νόστιμα ποῦ 'ν' τὰ χείλη σου, σὰν τ' ἀνοιγοσφαλίξῃς,
Μέλι τρέχουν τὰ μάθια σου, ὄντας θὰ μοῦ μιλήσῃς.

26.

Ὄντε θὰ ξεχωρίζωμε, ἴντα θὰ μοῦ χαρίσῃς;
— Ἕνα φιλὶ στὸ μάγουλο νὰ μὴ μ' ἀλησμονήσῃς.

27.

Ὁ ξένος εἰς τὴν ξενιτειὰ πρέπει νὰ βάφῃ μαῦρα,
Νὰ κουμπανιάρ' ἡ φορεσιὰ μὲ τῆς καρδιᾶς τὴ λαύρα.

28.

Ὅποιος σ' ἀγάπη μπερδευτῇ, κάλλιο του νὰ πεθάνῃ,
Τὸν ὕπνο του στερεύεται καὶ τὴ ζωή του χάνει.

29.

Ὅποιος τὰ λόγια σου γροικᾷ καὶ τσ' ὅρκους σου πιστεύγει,
Στὴ θάλασσα πιάνει λαγοὺς καὶ στὰ βουνὰ ψαρεύγει.

30.

Ὅσ' ἄστρα ἔχει ὁ οὐρανὸς τὴν νύχτα ἁπλωμένα,
Τόσες βολὲς σ' ἀνεζητῶ, πουλί μου, τὴν ἡμέρα.

31.

Ὅταν γελᾷς, γελοῦν βουνὰ καὶ κάμποι λουλουδίζουν,
Τὰ ξωτικὰ μαζώνονται καὶ σὲ καλοτυχίζουν.

32.

Οὕλος ὁ κόσμος εἶν' δεντρὶ κ' ἐμεῖς τὸ πωρικό του,
Ὁ Χάρος εἶν' ὁ τρυγητής· σέρνει τὸ μερτικό του.

33.

Περδικούλα πλουμισμένη ποῦ στὰ δάση περπατεῖς,
Βρόχια καὶ βεργιὰ θὰ στήσω, νὰ σὲ κάμω νὰ πιαστῇς.
Κι ἂν εἰς τὰ βεργιὰ μου πέσῃς, περδικούλα πλουμιστή,
Κάμαρα θενὰ σοῦ κάμω ὅλ' ἀπὸ χρυσὸ φλωρί.

34.

Ποῦ πάρῃ χίλια πήρπυρα καὶ κακουδιὰ γυναῖκα,
Τὰ χίλια πᾶν στ' ἀνάθεμα κ' ἡ κακουδιὰ 'πομένει.

35.

Σαγίτ' ἀπ' ἀρχοντόσπιτο μ' ἔχει σαγιτεμένο,
Ὅλ' οἱ γιατροὶ μ' ἐκύτταξαν καὶ μοῦ εἶπαν πῶς πεθαίνω.

36.

Σαράντα βρύσες μὲ νερὸ κ' ἐξήντα δυὸ πηγάδια
Δὲ μοῦ τὴ σβήνουν τὴ φωτιὰ πὅχω στὰ φυλλοκάρδια.

37.

Στέλλω σου χαιρετίσματα χιλιάδες τὴν ἡμέρα
Μὲ τὰ πετάμενα πουλιά, ποῦ στέκουν στὸν ἀγέρα.

38.

Στοὺς κρίνους, στὰ τριαντάφυλλα ζητῶ τὴν ἐμορφιά σου,
Μὰ χάνονται κοντὰ σ' ἐσέ, στὰ κάλλη τὰ δικά σου.

39.

Τὰ μάτια μου τὰ μάλωσα νὰ μὴ σὲ ξαναϊδοῦνε,
Κι αὐτεῖνα τὰ μαριόλικα ὅταν σὲ ἰδοῦν γελοῦνε.

40.

Τὰ μάτια σου μοῦ ρίξανε σαῖτες ἀσημένιες,
Καὶ στὴν καρδιά μ' ἐμπήκανε κ' ἐβγῆκαν ματωμένες.

41.

Τῆς θάλασσας τὰ κύματα τρέχω καὶ δὲν τρομάζω,
Κι ὅταν σὲ συλλογίζωμαι, τρέμω κι ἀναστενάζω.

42.

Τῆς κορασίδας τὰ μυαλὰ γυρίζουν σὰν τὸ μύλο·
Ἕναν ποῦ διώχνει σήμερα, αὔριο τὸν πιάνει φίλο.

43.

Τοῦ ἔρωτα τὸ δίχτυ εἶναι μεταξωτό,
Ἀλλοί του ποιὸς νὰ ντέσῃ· δὲ ματαβγαίνει πλιό.

44.

Τὸ κάστανο θέλει κρασὶ καὶ τὸ καρύδι μέλι,
Καὶ τὸ κορίτσι φίλημα πουρνὸ καὶ μεσημέρι.

45.

Τρέμει τὸ ψάρι, στὸν ψαρᾶ σίντα ἐβγάν' ἡ τράτα,
Τρέμει κ' ἐμ' ἡ καρδούλα μου, σίντα σὲ διῶ στὴ στράτα.

46.

Τρία καλὰ στὸν ἄνθρωπο, ἡ ὀμορφιά, ἡ γνῶσι,
Κ' ἐκεῖν' ὁπόχει στὴν καρδιὰ νὰ μὴ τὸ φανερώσῃ.

47.

Φωτιὰ τρώει τὸ σίδερο καὶ σάρακας τὸ ξύλο,
Καὶ σὺ μοῦ τρὼς τὰ νιάτα μου σὰν ἄρρωστος τὸ μῆλο.

48.

Χαρῆτε τούτην τὴ ζωή, γιατ' ὁ καιρὸς διαβαίνει,
Κι ὅποιος νὰ 'μπῆ στὴ μαύρη γῆς, αὐτὸς δὲ ματαβγαίνει.

49.

Χελιδονάκι θὰ γενῶ, στὰ χείλη σου νὰ κάτσω,
Νὰ σὲ φιλήσω μιὰ καὶ δυό, καὶ πάλε νὰ πετάξω.

50.

Ὥρα καλή σου, μάτια μου, καὶ νὰ καλοστρατίσῃς,
Στὴ στράτα νὰ μὲ θυμηθῇς καὶ πίσω νὰ γυρίσῃς.

b. Proverbs.

1.
Ἀκριβὸς θαρρεῖ κερδίζει, μὰ φυρᾷ καὶ δὲν τὸ νοιώθει.

2.
Ἀλήθεια χωρὶς ψέματα
φαγὶ χωρὶς ἁλάτι.

3.
Ἔχει ὁ τοῖχος αὐτιὰ κι ὁ λόγγος μάτια.

4.
Λέγε τὴν ἀλήθεια,
νά 'χῃς τὸ θεὸ βοήθεια.

5.
Μὲ τὸ δικό σου φάγε καὶ πιὲ καὶ πραγματιὰ μὴ κάμνῃς.

6.
Μιᾶς στιγμῆς ὑπομονὴ δέκα χρονῶν ρεχάτι.

7.
Νὰ μὴ χρουστᾷς σὲ πλούσιο, φτωχὸν νὰ μὴ δανείζῃς.

8.
Ὁ λόος εἰς τὴν ὥρα του χίλια φλουριὰ ἀξίζει.

9.
Οἱ πολλοὶ καραβοκύριδες πνίγουν τὸ καράβι.

10.
Ὅποιος καῇ στὰ λάχανα, φυσάει καὶ τὸ γιαούρτι.

11.
Ὅποιος πνίγεται καὶ τὰ μαλλιάν του πιάνει.

12.
Ὅπου ἀκοὺς πολλὰ κεράσια,
Βάστα καὶ μικρὰ καλάθια.

13.
Ὁποῦ 'ναι καλορίζικος, γεννᾷ καὶ ὁ κότσος του.

14.
Ὅτι θὰ κάμῃς κι ὅτι θὰ 'πῇς,
Τί θὰ συνέβη πρῶτα νὰ στοχαστῇς.

15.
Παπούτζι ἀπὸ τὸν τόπο σου κι ἂς εἶναι μπαλωμένο.

16.

Τὰ πολλὰ πολλὰ κουμάντα, τὸ καράβι μὲ τὴ μπάντα.

17.

Τέχνη θέλει τό πριόνι
Κι ὅποιος τὸ κρατεῖ νὰ 'δρώνῃ.

18.

Τὸ πολὺ κυριελέησο κι ὁ παπᾶς βαρειέται το.

19.

Τοῦ γιωργοῦ ἡ δουλειὰ στ' ἁλώνι φαίνεται.

20.

Ὑστερνοὶ συλλογισμοὶ
Ἔξε πάνε στὸ σολδί.

c. Riddles.

1.

Δώδεκα καλογεράκια
Κυνηγειοῦνται κυνηγειοῦνται
Καὶ ποτὲ δὲν πιάνουνται.　　(Ἀνεμόμυλος)

2.

Ψαλίδι χρυσοψάλιδο
Κόβει καὶ καλά
Κόβει καὶ κακά.　　　　　　(Γλῶσσα)

3.

Ἔχω 'γώ, ἔχεις καὶ 'σύ,
Ἄλλος ἕνα κι ἄλλος δυό,
Κι ἄλλος μηδὲ τίποτε.　　　(Γονιοί)

4.

Μέσα σ' ἕνα τετράγωνον φαντάσματα καθίζουν.
　　　　　　　　　　　　　　(Καθρέφτης)

5.

Μέσ' στὴ μέση τοῦ χωριοῦ μας
Κρέμετ' ἡ Μαργαριτοῦ μας
Καὶ τινάζει τὰ φτερά της
Καὶ συνάζει τὰ παιδιά της.　　(Καμπάνα)

6.

Βασιλέας δὲν εἶμαι,
Κορώνα φορῶ,
Ρολόϊ δὲν ἔχω,
Τὲς ὥρες μετρῶ. (Κόκορος)

7.

Μιὰ καλὴ νοικοκυρίτσα
Χώρ(ι)ς ἀλεύρι φκειάνει πηττίτσα.
(Μέλισσα)

8.

῞Οταν ἔχω νερό, πίνω κρασί· κι ὅταν δὲν ἔχω νερό, πίνω
νερό. (Μυλωνᾶς)

9.

῎Ενα πρᾶγμα πραγματάκι
Πάει κι ὀπίσω δὲν κυττάει. (Ρέμα)

10.

Χιλιοτρύπητό 'ναι τὸ λαγύνι
Καὶ σταλαματιὰ δὲν χύνει. (Σφουγγάρι)

d. Popular Tales and Legends.

1. Τὸ χρυσὸ βεργί.

(Epirus)

῏Ηταν ἕνας πραματευτής, ὁποῦ πραματεύονταν στὶς ᾿Ινδίες,
κ' εἶχε τρεῖς θυγατέρες. Κι ὄντας κίνησε μιὰ φορὰ νὰ πάῃ στὶς
᾿Ινδίες, τὸν περικάλεσαν οἱ θυγατέρες του, ἡ μιὰ νὰ τσ' φέρῃ ἕνα
φόρεμα ἰνδικό, ἡ ἄλλη ἕνα φακιόλι ἰνδικὸ κ' ἡ μικρότερη τὸ χρυσὸ
βεργί. Καὶ τὸν ἐκαταρειώνταν, ἂν δὲν τὰ φέρῃ, νὰ μὴ κινήσῃ τὸ
καράβι του. Κι ὄντας πῆγε στὶς ᾿Ινδίες, πῆρε πραμάτειες ὅσες
ἤθελε καὶ πῆρε καὶ τῶν δυὸ θυγατέρων του ἐκεῖνα ποῦ τοῦ ἐζή-
τησαν· μούνε τῆς μικρότερης τὸ χρυσὸ βεργὶ λησμόνησε νὰ τὸ
πάρῃ. Κι ὄντας κίνησε νὰ φύγῃ ἀπ' τὶς ᾿Ινδίες, μ' ὅλο ποῦ ἦταν
καλὸς καιρός, δὲν ἐκινοῦσε τὸ καράβι. Τότες κάθονταν καὶ συλ-
λογειώνταν, κ' ἕνας χωριάτης πέρασε ἀπὸ κοντά του καὶ τὸν ρώτησε, γιατί εἶναι ἔτσι συλλογισμένος. ῾Ο πραματευτὴς δὲν ἠθέλησε
νὰ τὸ μαρτυρήσῃ. Τότες τὸν περικάλεσε ὁ χωριάτης, νὰ τοῦ τὸ
μαρτυρήσῃ. ῾Ο χωριάτης λοιπὸν τοῦ εἶπε· „στοχάσου, μὴν ἔταξες τίποτε;" ῾Ο πραματευτὴς στοχάστηκε καὶ θυμήθηκε κεῖνο, ποῦ

εἶχε τάξει τῆς θυγατέρας του, καὶ 'ρώτησε τὸ χωριάτη, ποῦ βρί-
σκεται αὐτὸ τὸ χρυσὸ βεργί. Κι ὁ χωριάτης τοῦ ἔδειξε ἕνα δρόμο
καὶ τοῦ εἶπε, νὰ περβατήσῃ τρεῖς ὧρες κ' ἐκεῖ εἶναι τὸ χρυσὸ
βεργί. Κι ὁ πραματευτὴς ἔκαμε σὰν ποῦ τοῦ εἶπ' ὁ χωριάτης,
κ' ἐπερβάτησε τρεῖς ὧρες καὶ πῆγε σ' ἕναν τόπο κ' ἐκεῖ 'ρώτησε·
„ποῦ εἶναι τὸ χρυσὸ βεργί;" Καὶ τοῦ ἔδειξαν ἕνα παλάτι καὶ τοῦ
εἶπαν, πῶς αὐτοῦ μέσα εἶναι τὸ βεργὶ κι αὐτὸ εἶναι τὸ βασ'λόπουλο. Αὐτὸς φοβήθηκε, σὰν τοῦ εἶπαν, πῶς εἶναι τὸ βασ'λόπουλο. Ὕστερις ἐθάρρεψε καὶ πῆγε στὸ παλάτι καὶ 'ζήτησε τὴν
ἄδεια ἀπὸ τὸ βασιλιὰ νὰ μπῇ μέσα, κι ὁ βασιλιὰς τὴν ἔδωκε.
Καὶ σὰν τὸν ἐρώτησ' ὁ βασιλιάς, τί θέλει, τοῦ εἶπε, πῶς θέλει
νὰ μιλήσῃ μὲ τὸ βασ'λόπουλο. Ὁ βασιλιὰς τὸν πῆγε στὸν ὀντᾶ,
ποῦ κάθονταν τὸ βασ'λόπουλο, καὶ τὸν ρωτάει τὸ βασ'λόπουλο·
„τί μὲ θέλεις;" Καὶ κεῖνος τοῦ 'μολόγησε ὅλα ὅσα τοῦ εἶπ' ἡ
θυγατέρα του. Τότες τὸ βασ'λόπουλο τὸν πῆρε καὶ τὸν ἔμπασε
μέσα σ' ἕναν ὀντᾶ, ὅπου εἶχε πολλὲς κοκόνες ζωγραφισμένες, καὶ
τὸν ἠρώτησε· „εἶν' ἡ θυγατέρα σου τέτοια ὄμορφη σὰν τούτες;"
Καὶ κεῖνος τοῦ εἶπε· „ποῦ! εἶναι χίλια μεράδια ὀμορφύτερη." Τότες
τὸν ἔμπασε σ' ἕναν ἄλλον ὀντᾶ, ὅπου εἶχε μιὰ ζωγραφισμένη, καὶ
τὴν εἶχε 'δεῖ στὸν ὕπνο του, πῶς θὰ τὴν πάρῃ γυναῖκα, καὶ τὸν
ρωτάει· „εἶναι τέτοια ὄμορφη ἡ τσιούπρα σου;" Κι αὐτὸς τοῦ εἶπε·
„αὐτὴ ἡ ἴδια εἶναι!" Τότες τὸ βασ'λόπουλο τοῦ ἔδωκ' ἕνα γράμμα
κ' ἕνα τάσι κ' ἕνα δαχτυλίδι νὰ τὰ δώσῃ τῆς θυγατέρας του.
Τότες τὰ πῆρ' ὁ πραματευτὴς καὶ πῆγε στὸ καράβι του. Κ' εὐτὺς
τὸ καράβι ἐκίνησε, κ' ἔφυγε στὴν πατρίδα του. Σὰν ἔφτασε στὸ
σπίτι του, τὸν ρώταγαν οἱ τσιούπρες του· „ἔ, πατέρα, μᾶς ἔφερες
ἐκεῖνα ποῦ μᾶς ἔταξες;" „Τὰ ἔφερα," τὶς εἶπε κ' ἔβγαλε κ' ἔδωκε
κάθε μιανῆς τὸ τάξιμο. Ἔδωκε καὶ τῆς μικρῆς τὸ γράμμα, τὸ
τάσι καὶ τὸ δαχτυλίδι, τὰ ὁποῖα τοῦ εἶχε δώσ' τὸ βασ'λόπουλο.
Κι αὐτὴ τὰ πῆρε καὶ πῆγε καὶ κλείστηκε μέσα στὸν ὀντᾶ της,
κι ἄνοιξε τὸ γράμμα καὶ τὸ ἀνάγνωσε κ' εἶδε, ποῦ τῆς ἔγραφε,
ὄντας τὸν χρειάζεται νὰ βάνῃ μέσα στὸ τάσι νερό, καὶ νὰ βάνῃ
καὶ τὸ δαχτυλίδι μέσα στὸ νερό, καὶ νὰ λέῃ τρεῖς φορές· ἔλα,
ἔλα, ἔλα, χρυσό μου βεργί! καὶ τότες αὐτὸς θὰ ἔρχεται περ'στέρι,
καὶ νὰ νίβεται στὸ νερὸ καὶ θὰ γένεται ἄθρωπος, καὶ ν' ἀφήσῃ
μιὰν τρύπα στὸ νταβάνι νὰ μπαίνῃ μέσα. Τότες κι αὐτὴ ἔκαμε
καθὼς τῆς ἔγραφε, κ' ἦρθε τὸ περ'στέρι, κι ἀφοῦ ἐκολύμπησε
στὸ νερό, ἔγιν' ἄθρωπος· κι ἀφοῦ ἐκουβέντιασαν πολλὴν ὥρα,
κολύμπησε πάλι στὸ νερὸ κ' ἔγινε περ'στέρι κ' ἔφυγε. Καὶ φεύ-
γοντας τσ' ἄφησε μιὰ κάχτα καὶ τσ' εἶπε νὰ τὴν τσακίσῃ, κι ὅτι

εὕρῃ μέσα νὰ τὸ ντυθῇ. Καὶ σὰν ἔφυγ' αὐτός, τὴν τσάκισε κ' ἠῦρε μέσα μιὰ φορεσιὰ σωστή, ὁποὖ εἶχε ζωγραφισμένο τὸν οὐρανὸ μὲ τ' ἄστρια. Τὰ ντύθηκ' αὐτὴ καὶ βῆκ' ἔξω. Ἀφοῦ τὴν εἶδαν οἱ ἀδερφές της, θιάμασαν κι ἀρχίνισαν νὰ τὴν ρωτοῦν, καὶ τὴν ἐφτόνησαν. Αὐτὴ ἔκανε κι ἄλλη φορὰ τὸ ἴδιο, καὶ πάλι ἦρθε ὁ χρυσοβεργῆς, κι ὄντας ἔφυγε, τσ' ἄφησ' ἕνα λεφτόκαρο καὶ τσ' εἶπε, νὰ τὸ τσακίσῃ, κι ὅτι 'βρῇ μέσα νὰ τὸ ντυθῇ. Κι ἀφοῦ ἔφυγε τὸ περ'στέρι, τότες τσάκισε τὸ λεφτόκαρο κ' ηῦρε μιὰ φορεσιά, ποὺ εἶχε ζωγραφισμένη τὴ θάλασσα μὲ τὰ κύματα, καὶ ντύθηκε καὶ βῆκ' ἔξω. Πάλι θιάμασαν οἱ ἀδερφές της, σὰν τὴν εἶδαν, καὶ τὴν φτονοῦσαν ἀκόμα περσότερο. Πάλι αὐτὴ ἔβαλε τὸ δαχτυλίδι στὸ τάσι μέσα μὲ νερὸ κ' εἶπε τρεῖς φορές· „ἔλα, ἔλα, ἔλα, χρυσό μου βεργί!" Κ' ἦρθε, κολύμπησε στὸ νερὸ κ' ἔγιν' ἄθρωπος. Σὰν ἔφυγε, πάλι τῆς ἄφησ' ἕνα σῦκο καὶ τσ' εἶπε νὰ τὸ κόψῃ, κι ὅτι 'βρῇ μέσα νὰ τὸ ντυθῇ. Ἀφοῦ ἔφυγε, τό 'κοψε κ' ηῦρ' ἄλλη φορεσιά, ποὺ ἦταν ζωγραφισμένος ὁ Μάϊς μὲ τὰ λουλούδια. Τὴ ντύθηκε καὶ βῆκ' ἔξω. Τότες θιάμασαν ἀκόμα περσότερο οἱ ἀδερφές της καὶ κουβέντιασαν, πῶς νὰ τσ' κάνουν κακό, κ' εἶπαν ἀνάμεσό τους, πῶς ἐκεῖ ποὺ θὰ πάγουν νὰ λουστοῦν, νὰ πάρ' ἡ μεγάλη ἕνα σακκούλι μαργαριτάρι καὶ νὰ κάμῃ τάχα πῶς θὰ τὸ χύσῃ καὶ νὰ κάτσῃ πίσω ἀπὸ τσ' ἄλλες νὰ τὸ μαζώξῃ· κ' ἐκεῖ ποὺ θὰ πάγουν οἱ ἄλλες νὰ λουστοῦν, αὐτὴ τάχα νὰ μαζώνῃ τὸ μαργαριτάρι, νὰ πάγῃ στὸ σπίτι καὶ νὰ κάμῃ κεῖνο ποὺ ἔκαν' ἡ μικρότερη — γιατὶ τὴν εἶχαν παραμονέψει κ' εἶδαν, πῶς ἔκαμε —, νὰ καμωθῇ πῶς εἶν' ἡ ἄλλη ἡ μικρή, γιὰ νὰ τῆς δώσῃ κι αὐτῆς τίποτες. Καὶ τὸ πρωΐ, ὄντας πῆγαν νὰ λουστοῦν, πῆρε ἡ μεγάλη τὸ σακκούλι τὸ μαργαριτάρι, κ' ἐκεῖ ποὺ πήγαιναν στὸ δρόμο, ἔκαμε πῶς ἐγλίστρησε κ' ἔχυσε τὸ μαργαριτάρι κ' εἶπε στὶς ἄλλες· „σύρτε σεῖς μπροστά, κ' ἐγὼ θὰ μάσω τὸ μαργαριτάρι", καὶ καθὼς ξεμάκρυναν οἱ ἄλλες, αὐτὴ τὸ ἔμασε ὅλο μὲ τὰ σκούπρα καὶ τό 'βαλε μέσα στὸ σακκούλι καὶ πῆγε στὸ σπίτι καὶ πῆρε τὸ κλειδὶ ἀπ' τὸν ὀντᾶ τῆς μικρῆς καὶ μπῆκε μέσα (ἐπειδὴς τὴν εἶχε παραμονέψει, ποὺ τό 'βαλε τὸ κλειδί) κι ἄνοιξε καὶ τὸ ντουλάπι καὶ πῆρε τὸ τάσι καὶ τὸ γιόμισε νερὸ κ' ἔβαλε καὶ τὸ δαχτυλίδι μέσα. Μόν' ἡ ἄλλη ἡ μικρότερη εἶχ' ἕνα μαχαίρι καὶ λησμόνησε καὶ τὸ ἄφησε πάνω στὸ τάσι· κι ὄντας εἶπε „ἔλα, χρυσό μου βεργί," ἦρθε τὸ βασ'λόπουλο καὶ κολύμπησε, καὶ καθὼς ἔκαμε νὰ σκωθῇ, ἐκόπηκ' ἀπ' τὸ μαχαίρι καὶ σκώθηκε κ' ἔφυγε. Αὐτὴ ἀφοῦ εἶδε τὸ αἷμα μέσα στὸ νερό, ἐχόλιασε πολλά· ἄφησε τὸ τάσι μὲ τὸ αἷμα μέσα στὸ ντουλάπι κ' ἔφυγε

καὶ πῆγε κι ἀντάμωσε καὶ τσ' ἄλλες τὶς τσιούπρες. Κι ὄντας γύρ-
σαν πίσω, πῆγ' ἡ μικρὴ μέσα στὸν ὀντᾶ της, κι ὄντας ἔμπαινε,
ἔλεγε· „ἔλα, χρυσό μου βεργί, νὰ μὲ 'δῆς τώρα, ποῦ πῆγα καὶ
λούστηκα!" Καὶ καθὼς πῆγε νὰ πάρῃ τὸ τάσι, τὸ γλέπει γιομάτο
αἷμα. Κλαίει, σκούζει, φωνάζει· „λέλε μ', τί ἔπαθα!" Σὰν ἔκλαψε
πολύ, ἐβγῆκ' ὄξω. Μούν' ἐκάταλαβε, πῶς τὸ ἔκαμαν οἱ ἀδερφές
της, καὶ πηγαίνει στὸν πατέρα της καὶ τοῦ λέει· „ἀφέντη, νὰ μοῦ
κόψῃς μιὰ φορεσιὰ φράγκικη καλὴ καλή, καὶ νὰ μοῦ δώκῃς κ'
ἕνα καράβι καλό, γιὰ νὰ πάνω στὰ ξένα." Τότες ὁ πατέρας της
τσ' ἔκοψε τὰ φράγκικα, καὶ τὰ ντύθηκε καὶ μπῆκε στὸ καράβι,
νὰ πάῃ στὶς Ἰνδίες, γιὰ νὰ τὸν εὕρῃ. Κ' ἐκεῖ ποῦ πήγαινε στὸ
δρόμο, εἶδ' ἕνα πουλί, ποῦ πῆγε νὰ πιάσῃ ἕν' ἄλλο, καὶ κεῖνο τὸ
πουλί, ποῦ ἦταν καὶ περ'στέρι, τοῦ εἶπε· „δὲ χολιάζεις, ποῦ 'ναι
τὸ βασ'λόπουλο ἄρρωστο, κ' οἱ γιατροὶ τὸ ἀπεφάσισαν;" Καὶ τὸ
ἄλλο τὸ πουλὶ τοῦ εἶπε· „δὲ ξέρουν οἱ γιατροί, κι ἀπὲ τὸ βασ'-
λόπουλο γιατρεύεται." Τὸ ἄλλο τὸ πουλὶ τὸ 'ρώτησε· „μὲ τί γιατρικὸ γιατρεύεται;" Καὶ κεῖνο τοῦ εἶπε· „νὰ μᾶς σκοτώσουν ἐμᾶς
καὶ νὰ μᾶς πάρουν καὶ νὰ πάρουν κι ὀλίγο νερὸ ἀπὸ κείνην τὴ
βρύσι, ποῦ εἶν' ἀγνάντια, καὶ νὰ τὸ φκειάσουν ἀλοιφὴ καὶ ν'
ἀλείψουν τὸ λαιμό του, ποῦ εἶναι κομμένος, καὶ γιατρεύεται." Ἡ
τσιούπρα κείνη σὰν ἄκουσ' αὐτά, ἐπειδὴς ἤξερε τὴ γλῶσσα τῶν
περ'στεριῶν ἀπ' τὸ χρυσὸ βεργί, ἐκατάλαβε τί εἶπαν τὰ πουλιά.
Τότες ἔρριξ' ἕναν τουφέκι καὶ τὰ σκότωσε καὶ τὰ δυὸ καὶ τὰ πῆρε
καὶ πῆρε καὶ νερὸ ἀπὸ κείνην τὴ βρύσι κ' ἔφκειασε τὴν ἀλοιφὴ
καὶ πῆγε στὸ σαράγι τοῦ βασ'λόπουλου 'ποκάτω καὶ φώναζε·
„γιατρὸς καλός, γιατρὸς καλός, γιατρικὰ καλά!" Τὴν ἤκουσ' ὁ βασιλιὰς τότες καὶ τὴ φώναξ' ἀπάνω καὶ τσ' εἶπε· „μπορεῖς νὰ για-
τρέψῃς τὸ παιδί μου:" Καὶ κείνη τοῦ εἶπε· „νὰ τὸ ἰδῶ!" Καὶ
σὰν τὸ εἶδε, εἶπε τοῦ βασιλιά· „σ' ὀχτὼ μέρες διορία τὸ γιατρεύω,
καὶ νὰ τὸ βγάλω στὸ κυνήγι." Ὁ βασιλιὰς σὰν ἄκουσ' αὐτό,
χάρηκε. Οἱ ἄλλοι γιατροί, ὁποῦ τὸν ἄκουσαν, ποῦ εἶπε πῶς τὸ
γιατρεύει, εἶπαν στὸ βασιλιά· „ἂν τὸ γιατρέψῃ αὐτὸ καθὼς λέει,
ἐμᾶς νὰ μᾶς κόψῃς τὸ κεφάλι." Τότες ὁ γιατρὸς πῆγε στὸ βασ'-
λόπουλο καὶ τὸ ἄλειψε μὲ τὴν ἀλοιφή, καὶ γίνηκε καλύτερα, κ'
ὕστερα ἀπὸ δυὸ μέρες ἄρχισε νὰ κρένῃ, καὶ σὰν τοῦ ἔβαλε πολλὲς
φορὲς τὴν ἀλοιφή, σ' ὀχτὼ μέρες τὸ γιάτρεψε καὶ τὸν ἔβγαλε καὶ
στὸ κυνήγι. Σὰν τὸν εἶδ' ὁ πατέρας του, χάρηκε πολὺ κ' εἶπε
τοῦ γιατροῦ· „τί καλὸ θέλεις νὰ σοῦ κάμω γιὰ τὸ καλό, ποῦ μοῦ
ἔκαμες;" Κι ὁ γιατρὸς τοῦ εἶπε· „ἄλλο δὲ χαλεύω ἀπὸ τὴ βασιλεία σου, μοναχὰ ἕνα ζιαφέτι νὰ μοῦ κάμῃς καὶ νὰ φωνάξῃς

ὅλους τοὺς ἄρχοντες τσ' Ἰνδίας." Τότες ὁ βασιλιὰς τοῦ εἶπε·
„αὐτὸ ποῦ χαλεύεις δὲν εἶναι τίποτε σ' ἐμένα." Καὶ τότες ἀρχίρησε
κ' ἔκαμ' ἑτοιμασίες γιὰ τὸ Ζιαφέτι καὶ φώναξ' ὅλους τοὺς ἄρχοντες τσ' Ἰνδίας κ' ἔκαμ' ἕνα Ζιαφέτι πολὺ μεγάλο, κι ἀφοῦ ἔφαγαν
κ' ἔπιαν, εἶπ' ὁ γιατρὸς τοῦ βασιλιά· „πρόσταξε νὰ τσωπάσουν,
γιατί θὰ εἰπῶ ἕνα παραμύθι." Τότες ὁ βασιλιὰς ἐπρόσταξε, καὶ
τσώπασαν ὅλοι, κι ἀρχίρησε ὁ γιατρὸς κ' ἔλεγε τὸ παραμύθι,
τοῦτο καὶ τοῦτο καὶ τοῦτο· εἶπ' ὅλα ὅσα ἔπαθε, χωρὶς νὰ μαρτυρήσῃ ποῦ ἦταν αὐτός. Καὶ τότες σὰν εἶπε, πῶς ἡ τσιούπρα
αὐτὴ γίνηκε γιατρός, φανερώθηκε κ' εἶπε· „ἐγὼ εἶμαι αὐτὴ ἡ τσιούπρα κ' ἡ γυναῖκα τοῦ βασ'λόπουλου, καὶ τὸ βασ'λόπουλο δὲν
τό 'σφαξα 'γώ, μόν' ἡ ἀδερφή μου." Τότες τὸ βασ'λόπουλο σὰν
ἄκουσ' αὐτά, τὴν ἀγκάλιασε καὶ τσ' εἶπε· „ἐσύ 'σαι ἡ νύφη μου·"
κ' ἔκαμαν ἕνα γάμο λαμπρὸ καὶ τοὺς ἐστεφάνωσαν.

2. Τὸ φίδι, τὸ σκυλὶ καὶ ἡ γάτα.

(Epirus)

Ἦταν μιὰ φτωχὴ γυναῖκα κ' εἶχ' ἕνα παιδί, καὶ δὲν εἶχαν
ψωμὶ νὰ φάν. Τότες τὸ παιδὶ παίρνει καὶ φορτώνει ἀσφάκες·
καὶ πῆγε καὶ τσ' πούλησε καὶ πῆρε δυὸ παράδες. Καὶ καθὼς
γύριζε, ηὗρε κάτι παιδιά, ποὺ σκότωναν ἕνα φίδι, καὶ τοὺς λέει·
„νάτε ἕναν παρᾶ καὶ μὴ τὸ σκοτώνετε!" Τοὺς ἔδωκε τὸν παρᾶ,
καὶ δὲν τὸ σκότωσαν τὰ παιδιά, καὶ τὸ φίδι τὸν ἐκυνήγησε. Καὶ
καθὼς πῆγε στὸ σπίτι του, εἶπε τῆς μάννας του, ὅσα ἔκαμε. Κ'
ἡ μάννα του τὸν ἐμάλωσε καὶ τοῦ εἶπε· „ἐγὼ σὲ στέλνω νὰ πάρῃς παράδες νὰ φάμε, καὶ σὺ μοῦ φέρνεις φίδια!" Κι αὐτὸς τσ'
εἶπε· „ἄς εἶναι, μάννα, κάτι θὰ μᾶς φελέσῃ κι αὐτό." Τὸ παιδὶ
πῆρε πάλι ἀσφάκες καὶ τὶς πούλησε, καὶ καθὼς γύριζε, ηὗρε κάτι
παιδιά, ποὺ σκότωναν ἕνα σκυλί, καὶ τοὺς εἶπε· „νάτε ἕναν παρᾶ
καὶ μὴ τὸ σκοτώνετε!" Πῆραν τὰ παιδιὰ τὸν παρᾶ κι ἀφῆκαν
τὸ σκυλί. Τότες αὐτὸ τὸν ἐκυνήγησε πάλι. Τὸ παιδὶ πῆγε στὴ
μάννα του καὶ τσ' εἶπ' ὅσα ἔκαμε. Καὶ πάλι τὸν ἐμάλωσ' ἡ μάννα
του καθὼς καὶ πρῶτα. Πῆρε πάλι ἀσφάκες καὶ τὶς πούλησε, κι
ὄντας γύριζε, ηὗρε κάτι παιδιά, ποὺ σκότωναν μιὰ γάτα, καὶ τοὺς
εἶπε· „μὴ τὴν σκοτώνετε, νὰ σᾶς δώκω ἕναν παρᾶ!" Καὶ τοὺς
ἔδωκε τὸν παρᾶ, κι ἄφηκαν τὴ γάτα. Καὶ καθὼς πῆγε στὸ σπίτι
του, εἶπε τῆς μάννας του πάλι ὅσα ἔκαμε, κι αὐτὴ τὸν ἐμάλωσε
καὶ τοῦ εἶπε· „ἐγὼ σὲ στέλνω νὰ πάρῃς παράδες νὰ φάμε ψωμί,
κ' ἐσὺ φέρνεις σκυλιὰ καὶ γάτες καὶ φίδια!" Τότες αὐτὸς τσ' εἶπε·
„ἄς εἶναι, μάννα, κάτι θὰ μᾶς φελέσουν κι αὐτά!"

Ὕστερα τὸ φίδι τοῦ εἶπε· „νὰ μὲ πᾶς στὴ μάννα μου καὶ στὸν πατέρα μου καὶ νὰ μὴ πάρῃς μήτε γρόσια μήτε φλουριά, μονάχα μιὰ βούλα νὰ χαλέψῃς ὅπ' ἔχει ὁ πατέρας μου στὸ χέρι του, κι ἀπ' αὐτὴ θὰ ἰδῇς μεγάλο καλό." Τότες αὐτὸς πῆγε τὸ φίδι στὸν πατέρα του, καὶ τὸ φίδι εἶπε τοῦ πατέρα του· „τοῦτος μ' ἐγλύτωσ' ἀπὸ τὸ θάνατο." Κι ὁ πατέρας τοῦ φιδιοῦ εἶπε σ' αὐτὸν τὸν ἄθρωπο· „τί θέλεις νὰ σοῦ δώκω γιὰ αὐτὸ τὸ καλό, ποὺ ἤκαμες τοῦ παιδιοῦ μου; „Τότες τὸ παιδὶ εἶπε στὸν πατέρα τοῦ φιδιοῦ· „οὔτε γρόσια θέλω οὔτε φλουριά, μονάχα τὴ βούλα θέλω ὅπ' ἔχεις στὸ χέρι σου;" Τότες εἶπ' ὁ πατέρας τοῦ φιδιοῦ στὸ παιδί· „αὐτὸ ποὺ μοῦ χάλεψες εἶναι πολὺ μεγάλο, καὶ δὲ μπορῶ νὰ σοῦ τὸ δώκω." Τώρα τὸ φίδι ἔκαμε πῶς κυνηγάει τὸ παιδί, κ' εἶπε στὸν πατέρα του· „ἐπειδὴς δὲ θέλεις νὰ δώκῃς τὴ βούλα σ' αὐτόν, ποὺ μ' ἐγλύτωσ' ἀπὸ τὸ θάνατο, ἐγὼ πάνω πίσω σ' αὐτόν, γιατί σ' αὐτὸν χρωστῶ τὴ ζωή μου." Τότες ὁ πατέρας του ἔδωκε τὴ βούλα στὸ παιδὶ καὶ τοῦ εἶπε· „ὄντας χρειαστῇς τίποτα, νὰ ζίφῃς τὴ βούλα, καὶ θὰ ἔρχετ' ἕνας Ἀράπης, καὶ νὰ τὸν προστάζῃς ὅτι θέλεις νὰ σου κάνῃ, καὶ θὰ σοῦ τὸ κάνῃ."

Τότες ἔφυγε τὸ παιδὶ καὶ πῆγε στὸ σπίτι του. Καὶ τοῦ εἶπ' ἡ μάννα του· „τί θὰ φάμε, μάτια μου;" Κι αὐτὸ τσ' εἶπε· „σύρε μέσα στὴν ἄρκλα καὶ βρίσκεις ψωμί." Τότες ἡ μάννα του τοῦ εἶπε· „παιδί μου, ἐγὼ ξέρω, πῶς ἡ ἄρκλα δὲν ἔχει ψωμί, κ' ἐσὺ μοῦ λές, νὰ πάνω νὰ 'βρῶ ψωμί." Αὐτὸ τσ' εἶπε· „σύρε ποὺ σοῦ λέγω ἐγώ, καὶ βρίσκεις." Κι ὅσο νὰ πάῃ αὐτὴ στὴν ἄρκλα, ἔζιψε τὴ βούλα, κ' ἦρθ' ὁ Ἀράπης καὶ τοῦ εἶπε· „τί ὁρίζεις, ἀφέντη;" Τὸ παιδὶ τοῦ εἶπε· „θέλω νὰ γιομίσῃς τὴν ἄρκλα ψωμί." Κι ὅσο νὰ πάῃ ἡ μάννα του στὴν ἄρκλα, τὴν ηὗρε γιομάτη ψωμὶ καὶ πῆρε κ' ἔφαγε. Κ' ἔτσι λοιπὸν ἀπερνούσαν μ' αὐτὴν τὴ βούλα καλά. Μιὰ φορὰ εἶπε τὸ παιδὶ τῆς μάννας του· „μάννα, νὰ πᾶς στὸ βασιλιὰ καὶ νὰ τοῦ 'πῇς, νὰ μοῦ δώσῃ τὴ θυγατέρα του γυναῖκα." Ἡ μάννα του τοῦ εἶπε· „σὲ τί ἀράδα εἴμεστ' ἐμεῖς, μάτια μου, καὶ νὰ μᾶς δώσ' ὁ βασιλιὰς τὴ θυγατέρα του;" Κ' ἐκεῖνος τῆς εἶπε· „νὰ πᾶς χωρὶς ἄλλο!" Κίνησε κι αὐτὴ ἡ καημένη νὰ πάῃ στὸ βασιλιά. Καθὼς μπῆκε μέσα, εἶπε τοῦ βασιλιὰ· „τὸ παιδί μου θέλει νὰ πάρη τὴ θυγατέρα σου γυναῖκα." Τότες τσ' εἶπ' ὁ βασιλιάς· „τοῦ τὴ δίνω, ἂν εἶν' ἄξιο νὰ φκειάκ' ἕνα παλάτι μεγαλύτερ' ἀπ' τὸ δικό μου." Ἡ γριὰ σκώθηκε καὶ πῆγε στὸ παιδί της καὶ τοῦ εἶπε, ὅσα τσ' εἶπ' ὁ βασιλιάς. Καὶ κείνην τὴ νύχτα ἔζιψε τὴ βούλα, κ' ἴσια φανερώθηκ' ὁ Ἀράπης

καὶ τοῦ εἶπε· „τί ὁρίζεις, ἀφέντη;‟ Κ’ ἐκεῖνος τοῦ εἶπε· „νὰ
φκειάκῃς ἕνα σαράγι μεγαλύτερο ἀπ’ τοῦ βασιλιά.‟ Κ’ εὐτὺς εὑ-
ρέθηκε σ’ ἕνα μεγάλο παλάτι. Τότες ἔστειλε πάλι τὴ μάννα του
στὸ βασιλιά, καὶ τοῦ εἶπε· „τὸ παιδὶ τὸ σαράγι, ποῦ τὸ παράγγελες, τό ’φκειασε.‟ Ὁ βασιλιὰς τσ’ εἶπε· „ἂν εἶναι ἄξιο νὰ φκειάσῃ
τὴ στράτα ἀπ’ τὸ παλάτι του ὡς τὸ δικό μου μὲ φλουρί, ἔτσι
παίρνει τὴ θυγατέρα μου γυναῖκα.‟ Τότες ἡ γριὰ πῆγε στὸ παιδί
της καὶ τοῦ εἶπ’ ὅλα αὐτά, καὶ τὸ παιδὶ φώναξε τὸν Ἀράπη καὶ
τοῦ εἶπε, νὰ φκειάσῃ τὸ δρόμο ὅλο μὲ φλουρί. Τὸ πρωῒ σκώθηκε τὸ παιδὶ καὶ τὸν ηὗρε φλουρένιο καθὼς ἐπρόσταξ’ ὁ βασιλιάς. Πῆγε πάλι ἡ μάννα του στὸ βασιλιὰ καὶ τοῦ εἶπε· „τὸ
παιδί μου ἔκαμε ὅλα ὅσα τὸ πρόσταξες.‟ Τότες ὁ βασιλιὰς τσ’
εἶπε νὰ ’τοιμαστῇ γιὰ τὸ γάμο. Κ’ ἡ γριὰ ἔφυγε καὶ πῆγε κ’ εἶπε
τοῦ παιδιοῦ ὅσα τσ’ εἶπ’ ὁ βασιλιάς. Τὸ παιδὶ τότες ’τοιμάστηκε
γιὰ τὸ γάμο. Κι ὁ βασιλιὰς φώναξε τὴ θυγατέρα του καὶ τσ’ εἶπε
ὅλα ὅσα ἔγιναν καὶ νὰ ’τοιμαστῇ γιὰ τὸ γάμο. Ἡ θυγατέρα του
χάρηκε καὶ περικάλεσε τὸν πατέρα της, νὰ τσ’ δώσῃ κ’ ἕναν
Ἀράπη νὰ τὸν στέλνῃ ὅπου θέλει. Κι ὁ πατέρας της τσ’ ἔδωκε.
Ὄντας ἔκαμαν τὸ γάμο, πῆρ’ ὁ γαμπρὸς τὴ νύφη κ’ ἔζησαν πολὺν
καιρὸ καλά.

Ὕστερα ἡ βασ’λοπούλα ἀγάπησε τὸν Ἀράπη, καὶ τὴ νύχτα
καθὼς κοιμώνταν μὲ τὸν ἄντρα της, τοῦ πῆρε τὴ βούλα κ’ ἔφυγε
μὲ τὸν Ἀράπη· καὶ πῆγαν στὴ θάλασσα κ’ ἔφκειακαν ἕνα παλάτι
μὲ τὴ βούλα καὶ ’ζούσαν μαζὶ ’κεῖ κοντὰ στὴ θάλασσα. Σὰν
ἔφυγ’ ἡ βασ’λοπούλα μὲ τὸν Ἀράπη, πῆγ’ ἡ γάτα καὶ σγουροτρίβονταν καὶ μιαούριζε καὶ τοῦ ἔλεγε· „τί ἔχεις, ἀφέντη;‟ „Τί νά
’χω, γάτα μου;‟ τῆς λέει, „τοῦτο καὶ τοῦτο ἔπαθα· τὴ νύχτα ποὺ
κοιμώμουν, μοῦ πῆρε τὴ βούλα ὁ Ἀράπης καὶ τὴ γυναῖκα κ’
ἔφυγε.‟ „Τσώπα, ἀφέντη,‟ τοῦ λέει ἡ γάτα, „ἐγὼ θὰ σοῦ τὴ
φέρω· δός μου τὸ σκυλί, νὰ τὸ καβαλλικέψω καὶ νὰ πάνω νὰ
πάρω τὴ βούλα.‟ Τότες τῆς δίνει τὸ σκυλί, τὸ καβαλλικεύει ἡ
γάτα καὶ περνάει τὴ θάλασσα. Κ’ ἐκεῖ ’ποῦ πήγαινε στὸ δρόμο,
βρίσκ’ ἕνα ποντίκι καὶ τοῦ λέει· „ἂν θέλῃς νὰ σοῦ γλυτώσω τὴ
ζωή, νὰ χώσῃς τὴν οὐρά σου μέσα στὴ μύτη τοῦ Ἀράπη, ὄντας
κοιμᾶται.‟ Τὸ ποντίκι τὴν ἔχωσε, καὶ τότες ὁ Ἀράπης φταρμί-
στηκε, καὶ πέφτει ἡ βούλα, ποὺ τὴν εἶχε κρυμμένη στὴ γλώσσα
του. Τὴν ἁρπάζ’ ἡ γάτα καὶ καβαλλικεύει τὸ σκυλί· κ’ ἐκεῖ ποὺ
ἔπλεαν στὴ θάλασσα, λέει τὸ σκυλὶ τῆς γάτας· „ἔτσι νὰ ζήσῃς,
γάτα, στέκα νὰ ’δῶ κ’ ἐγὼ ψίχα τὴ βούλα!‟ „Τί νὰ τὴν ἰδῇς,
μωρέ!‟ Καὶ καθὼς πῆρε τὸ σκυλὶ τὴ βούλα, τοῦ πέφτει στὴ

θάλασσα, καὶ τὴν ἁρπάζει ἕνα ψάρι κ' ἔγινε χιλιοπλούμπιστο. Τότες ἡ γάτα λέει τοῦ σκυλιοῦ· „τί μόκαμες, λέλε μου! πῶς νὰ πάνω στὸν ἀφέντη μου δίχως βούλα; ἔλα τώρα νὰ σὲ καβαλλικέψω!" Καὶ τὸ καβαλλίκεψε πάλι καὶ πῆγε 'κεῖ ποὺ ἦταν ἀραγμένα τὰ καράβια. Καὶ σ' ἐκεῖνο τὸ καράβι ποὺ κόνεψαν, ὁ καραβοκύρις εἶχε πιάσει τὸ ἴδιο ψάρι. Ἡ γάτα ἐσγουροτρίβονταν καὶ μιαούριζε πάλι, κι ὁ καραβοκύρις εἶπε· „μωρέ, τί καλὴ γάτα ποὺ μᾶς ἦρθε· βράδυ θὰ πάνω στὸ σπίτι νὰ φκειάσω τοῦτο τὸ ψάρι, καὶ θὰ τῆς ρίξω τ' ἄντερα νὰ τὰ φάη." Ἐκεῖ ποὺ καθάριζε τὸ ψάρι καὶ τσ' ἔρριχνε τ' ἄντερα, πέφτ' ἡ βούλα καὶ τὴν ἁρπάζ' ἡ γάτα· καβαλλικεύει τὸ σκυλὶ καὶ πάει στὸν ἀφεντικό της. Σὰν πῆγ' ἡ γάτα κ' εἶδε τὸν ἀφεντικό της χολιασμένο, μιαούριζε· μάου, μάου. Κι ὁ ἀφέντης σὰν τὴν εἶδε, „τὴν ἔφερες, μωρ' γάτα," τῆς λέει, „τὴ βούλα;" „Τὴν ἔφερα, ἀφέντη," τοῦ λέει, „μόνε νὰ σκοτώσῃς τὸ σκυλί, γιατί τὴν ἔρριξε μέσα στὴ θάλασσα, κ' ἔπαθα τόσα κακά, ὅσο νὰ τὴν εὕρω πάλι," καὶ τοῦ διηγήθηκε ὅλα ὅσα ἔπαθε. Τότες αὐτὸς πῆρε τὸ τουφέκι νὰ τὸ σκοτώσῃ, μόν' ἡ γάτα πάλι τὸν ἐμπόδισε καὶ τοῦ εἶπε· „ἄφσε το τώρα, γιατ' ἐφάγαμε τόσον καιρὸ μαζὶ ψωμί." Καὶ τότες αὐτὸς τὸ ἄφησε. Ὕστερα πῆρε τὴ βούλα καὶ τὴν ἔζιψε, κ' ἔρχεται ὁ Ἀράπης καὶ τοῦ λέει· „τί προστάζεις, ἀφέντη;" „Τώρα νὰ φέρῃς τὸ σαράγι ποὺ 'ναι στὴ θάλασσα ἐδώ," τοῦ λέει. Ἀμέσως ὁ Ἀράπης τὸ ἔφερε. Τὸ παιδὶ μπῆκε μέσα, βρίσκει τὸν Ἀράπη, ποὺ κοιμώνταν μὲ τὴ βασ'λοπούλα, καὶ τὸν σκότωσε. Ὕστερα πῆρε τὴ γυναῖκα του, κ' ἔζησαν ὅλη τὴ ζωή τους καλά.

3. Ὁ κὺρ Λάζαρος κ' οἱ δράκοι.

(Epirus)

Ἦταν ἕνας μπαλωματὴς καὶ τὸν ἔλεγαν Λάζαρο. Καὶ μνιὰ μέρα ὅπου μπάλωνε, μαζώθηκαν πολλὲς μυῖγες, καὶ τράβησε ἕνα μπάτο καὶ σκότωσε σαράντα μυῖγες. Τότες πῆγε κ' ἔφκειακ' ἕνα σπαθὶ κ' ἔγραψε· „μὲ μνιὰ τραβησιὰ σκότωσα σαράντα ψυχές." Κι ἀφοῦ τὸ ἔφκειακε τὸ σπαθί, κίνησε καὶ πῆγε στὴ ξενιτειά· καὶ σὰν πῆγε δυὸ μέρες μακρειὰ ἀπὸ τὸν τόπον του, ηὗρ' ἕνα πηγάδι κ' ἔπεσε κ' ἐκοιμήθηκε. Ἐκεῖ ἐκάθονταν οἱ δράκοι. Τότες ἦρθεν ἕνας νὰ πάρη νερὸ κ' εἶδε τὸ Λάζαρο, ποὺ ἐκοιμώνταν· εἶδε καὶ κεῖνα ποὺ ἦταν γραμμένα στὸ σπαθί του, καὶ πῆγε καὶ εἶπε καὶ τῶν ἄλλων. Οἱ ἄλλοι τοῦ εἶπαν, νὰ τοῦ 'πῇ νὰ γένουν βλάμηδες. Πῆγεν ὁ δράκος καὶ τὸν ἐφώναξε καὶ τοῦ εἶπε, ἂν ἔχει εὐκαρίστησι νὰ γένουν βλάμηδες. Ὁ Λάζαρος τοῦ εἶπε,

πῶς θέλει, καὶ γίν'καν καὶ κάθονταν ἀντάμα. Καὶ τοῦ εἶπαν οἱ
δράκοι νὰ πηγαίνουν μὲ τὴν ἀράδα γιὰ νερὸ καθὼς καὶ γιὰ ξύλα.
Πῆγαν οἱ δράκοι γιὰ ξύλα καὶ γιὰ νερὸ. Ἦρθε κ' ἡ ἀράδα τοῦ
Λάζαρου νὰ πάνῃ νὰ φέρῃ νερό. Οἱ δράκοι εἶχαν ἕνα ἀσκί, ὅπου
ἔπαιρναν νερό, κ' ἔπαιρνε διακόσιες ὀκάδες νερό. Ὁ Λάζαρος
μὲ μεγάλη δυσκολία πῆγε τὸ ἀσκὶ ἄδειο στὸ πηγάδι, κ' ἐπειδὴ δὲ
μποροῦσε νὰ τὸ φέρῃ τὸ νερό, δὲν τὸ ἐγέμ'σε τὸ ἀσκί, μόν' ἔ-
σκαφτε 'λόγυρα τὸ πηγάδι. Οἱ δράκοι, σὰν ἄργησε ὁ Λάζαρος,
ἐφοβήθ'καν κ' ἔστειλαν ἕναν νὰ πάῃ νὰ ἰδῇ, τί γίν'κε. Ὁ δράκος πῆγε καὶ τοῦ εἶπε· „τί κάνεις αὐτοῦ, κὺρ Λάζαρε;" „Δὲ
μπορῶ," τοῦ λέει, „κάθε μέρα νὰ ἔρχωμαι νὰ παίρνω νερό· νὰ
φέρω μνιὰ φορὰ ὅλο τὸ πηγάδι, γιὰ νὰ ξεγλυτώσω!" „Γιὰ ὄνομα
τοῦ θεοῦ, κὺρ Λάζαρε," τοῦ λέει, „μή! γιατί ψοφοῦμε ἀπὸ τὴ
δίψα, πηγαίνουμε 'μεῖς στὴν ἀράδα σου."

Τοῦ ἦρθε ἡ ἀράδα τοῦ Λάζαρου νὰ φέρῃ καὶ ξύλα, κ'
ἐπειδὴ δὲ μποροῦσε νὰ φορτωθῇ ἕνα δέντρο καθὼς οἱ ἄλλοι
δράκοι, ἔδενε ὅλα τὰ δέντρα μὲ πέτσες. Καὶ σὰν ἄργησε ὡς τὸ
βράδυ, ἔστειλαν πάλι οἱ δράκοι ἕνα δράκο νὰ ἰδῇ, τί κάνει. „Τί
κάνεις αὐτοῦ, κὺρ Λάζαρε;" τοῦ εἶπε. „Θέλω νὰ φέρω ὅλο τὸ
ρουμάνι μνιὰ φορὰ γιὰ νὰ ξεγλυτώσω," τοῦ λέει. „Μή! κὺρ
Λάζαρε," τοῦ λέει, „γιατὶ θὰ ψοφήσουμε ἀπὸ τὸ κρύο· πηγαίνουμε 'μεῖς στὴν ἀράδα σου." Καὶ πῆρε ὁ δράκος τὸ δέντρο
καὶ τὸ πῆγε. Ὕστερ' ἀπὸ κάμποσον καιρὸ εἶπαν οἱ δράκοι νὰ
τὸν σκοτώσουν, κι ἀπεφάσισαν τὸ βράδυ νὰ τὸν χτυπήσουν ὅλοι
ἀπὸ μνιὰ τσεκουριά. Ὁ Λάζαρος τὰ ἤκουσ' αὐτὰ καὶ τὸ βράδυ
ἔβαλ' ἕνα κούτσουρο καὶ τὸ ἐσκέπασε μὲ τὴν κάπα του. Τὸ
βράδυ ἐχτύπησαν τὸ κούτσουρο ὅλοι ἀπὸ μνιὰ καὶ τὸ ἔκαναν
κομμάτια καὶ πάντεχαν, πῶς τὸν ἐσκότωσαν. Ἀφοῦ ἀποκοιμήθ'-
καν οἱ δράκοι, ὁ Λάζαρος πῆρε τὸ κούτσουρο καὶ τό 'ριξε ὄξω
καὶ πλάγιασε, καὶ πρὸς τὰ ξημερώματα ἐβούγγιξε, καὶ τὸν ἤκουσαν οἱ δράκοι καὶ τὸν ρώτησαν καὶ τοῦ εἶπαν· „τί ἔχεις;" Κι
αὐτὸς τοὺς εἶπε, ὅτι κάμποσοι ψύλλοι τὸν ἐτσίμπησαν. Οἱ δράκοι πάντεχαν, ὅτι ψύλλους ἐνόμιζε τὶς τσεκουριές, καὶ τὴν ἄλλη
μέρα τοῦ εἶπαν, ἂν ἔχῃ παιδιά, γυναῖκα, κι ἂν θέλῃ, νὰ τοῦ δώσουν ἕνα ταγάρι φλουριά, καὶ νὰ πηγαίνῃ στὸ σπίτι του. Ὁ Λάζαρος τοὺς εἶπε, πῶς ἔχει εὐκαρίστησῃ, καὶ νὰ πάρῃ κ' ἕνα δράκο
ἀπὸ αὐτούς, νὰ τοῦ τὰ φέρῃ τὰ φλουριὰ στὸ σπίτι του. Πῆρε
τὸ δράκο φορτωμένο τὸ φλουρὶ καὶ πῆγε στὸ σπίτι του. Στὸ
δρόμο ὅπου πήγαινε, τοῦ εἶπε τοῦ δράκου· „στάσου, νὰ πηγαίνω
νὰ δέσω τὰ παιδιά μου, νὰ μὴ σὲ φάν!" Πῆγε κ' ἔδεσε τὰ παι-

διά του μὲ κάτι σκοινιὰ παλιὰ καὶ τοὺς εἶπε· „ὄντας ἰδῆτε τὸ
δράκο, νὰ φωνάζετε· κρέας ἀπὸ δράκο." Κι ὄντας ἐπλησίασ' ὁ
δράκος, ἐφώναξαν τὰ παιδιά· „κρειάτο ἀπὸ δράκο!" Ὁ δράκος
μὲ μεγάλη τρομάρα ἄφ'κε τὰ φλουριὰ κ' ἔφυγε. Στὸ δρόμο ὅπου
πήγαινε ὁ δράκος, ηὗρε μνιὰ ἀλωποῦ, καὶ τὸν ρώτησε, γιατί εἶναι
τρομαρισμένος τόσο. Κι αὐτὸς τσ' εἶπε, πῶς ὅσο γλύτωσε, θὰ
τὸν ἔτρωγαν τὰ παιδιὰ τοῦ κὺρ Λάζαρου. „Ἀπ' τὰ παιδιὰ τοῦ κὺρ
Λάζαρου ἐσκιάχτηκες;" τοῦ εἶπε· „αὐτὸς εἶχε δυὸ κότες καὶ τὴ
μνιὰ τοῦ τὴν ἔφαγα ἐψές, καὶ τὴν ἄλλη θὰ πάνω νὰ τοῦ τὴν
φάω τώρα· κι ἂν δὲν πιστεύης, ἔλα κοντά μου νὰ ἰδῆς· δέσου
ἀπ' τὴν οὐρά μου." Ἐδέθ'κ' ὁ δράκος ἀπ' τὴν οὐρὰ τῆς ἀλωποῦς
καὶ πῆγε νὰ ἰδῇ. Ὅντας ἐπλησίασαν στὸ σπίτι τοῦ Λάζαρου, ὁ
Λάζαρος ἐφύλαε μὲ τὸ ντουφέκι, γιατί ἐσκιάζονταν ἀπ' τοὺς δράκους. Σὰν εἶδε τὴν ἀλωποῦ, ὁποῦ ἔρχουνταν μαζὶ μὲ τὸ δράκο,
τσ' εἶπε· „δὲ σοῦ εἶπα νὰ φέρης μόνον αὐτὸν τὸ δράκο, μούν'
νὰ τοὺς φέρης ὅλους." Αὐτὸ ἀκούοντας ὁ δράκος ἔγινε ἄφαντος·
κι ἀπὸ τὴ μεγάλη τὴ βία, ὁποῦ ἔπαιρνε τὴν ἀλωποῦ, ἐψόφησε.
Κι ἀφοῦ ἐλευτερώθ'κε ἀπὸ τοὺς δράκους ὁ κὺρ Λάζαρος, ἔφκειασε
τὸ σπίτι του λαμπρὸ κ' ἔζησε καλά.

4. Ὁ φτωχὸς καὶ ὁ πλούσιος.

(Naxos)

Ἦταν ἕνας φτωχὸς μὲ πολλὰ παιδιὰ κ' ἠδούλευγαν ὅλοι
μὲ τὴ γυναῖκαν του ὅλη μέρα· πᾶσα βράδυ ποῦ 'τανε κουρασ-
μένοι, ἤθελα νὰ φάνε τὸ ψωμάκι τωνε ἥσυχα κι ἀνεπαμένα· ἀπέκειο νὰ πιάσ' ὁ πατέρας νὰ παίζη τὸ λυράκι του νὰ χορεύγουνε
τὰ παιδιάν του καὶ νὰ περνοῦνε μιὰ ζωὴ ἀγγελική. Δίπλα ἠκά-
θουνταν ἕνας πλούσιος, καὶ σὰν ἤκουενε κάθε βράδυ τὰ γέλοια καὶ
τσὶ χαρὲς τοῦ φτωχοῦ, ἐπαραξενεύγουντανε· „πῶς ἐγὼ μαθὲς νὰ
μὴν εἶμαι τόσο φκαριστημένος κι ἀνεπαμένος σὰν εὐτός; ὅλη μέρ'
ἀξίνη καὶ τὸ βράδυ ζεύκι," λέει, „νὰ τῶνε δώκω θέλω γρόσα νὰ
'δῶ, ἴντα θὰ τὰ κάμουνε." Πάει, βρίσκει τὸ φτωχό, λέει· „ἐπειδὴ
σὲ ξέρω τίμιο ἄθρωπο, νὰ σοῦ δίνω χίλια γρόσα, ν' ἀνοίξης πρα-
μάτια ὅτι θές, κι ἂν καζαντίσης, μοῦ τὰ δίνεις, εἰδεμὴς σοῦ τὰ
χαρίζω." Ὅλη μέρα πιὰ σὰν τά 'πηρεν ὁ φτωχός, ἠσυλλοοῦνταν,
ἴντα νὰ κάμη τόσα γρόσα· τά 'φερνεν ἀπὸ 'δώ, τά 'φερνεν ἀπὸ
'κεῖ· „ν' ἀνοίξω πραματευτάδικο, νὰ τὰ βάλλω στὸν τόκο, νὰ πάρω
ἀμπελοχώραφα." Ἔρχεται τὸ βράδυ μηδὲ λυράκι πιὰ νὰ πιάση·
μιλιὰ τσὶχ νὰ κάνανε τὰ παιδιάν του, νὰ γελάσουνε, τὰ μάλωνενε·
ὅλη νύχτα δὲν ἠβούλωσενε μάτι στὴ συλλοή· τὴν ἄλλη μέρα μηδὲ

σὲ μεροκάματο νὰ πάῃ μηδὲ πούβετις ἔξω μοὺ στὴ συλλοή· τὸν
ἀρώταν ἡ ὑναῖκαν του ἰντά 'χει; νὰ τόνε κάμῃ νὰ γελάσῃ, εὐτὸς
τὴν ἐμάλωνενε νὰ τὸν ἀφήκῃ ἥσυχο· ἀφηκρᾶται ὁ πλούσιος,
περνᾷ μιὰν ἀγραϋνιά, περνᾷ ἄλλη, περνοῦνε τρεῖς μηδὲ λυράκι
πιὰ ἤκουενε μηδὲ ἔλοια μηδὲ χορὸ τῶν παιδιῶ· μιὰν ταχυτερνὴ
βλέπει τὸ φτωχὸ κ' ἔρχεται — „νά, χριστιανέ, τὰ γρόσα σου καὶ
μηδ' αὐτὰ θέλω μηδὲ τὴ σκοτούραν τωνε.“ Ἀποστότε πάλι πάει
χαρούμενος στὸ σπίτιν του ὁ φτωχός, ἤπαιζενε τὸ λυράκι, ἠχο-
ρεύγανε τὰ παιδιάν του σὰν καὶ πρῶτα καὶ ταχυτέρου στὴ δου-
λειάν του.

5. Οἱ φίλοι.

(Ancient Syra)

Μνιὰ φορὰ ἤτανε δυὸ παλληκάρια, μὰ ἤτανε πολλὰ φίλοι,
ποῦ ὁ ἕνας τὸν ἄλλο δὲν ἠξεχώριζε, μόνου τὸ καιρὸ ποῦ ἤθελε
νὰ κοιμηθοῦ. Μὰ ἦρχε καιρός, ποῦ ὁ ἕνας ἠπαντρεύτηκε, κι
ἀπὸ τότες ἄρχεψε τὴ Ζούλια κ' ἠντάμωνε τὸ φίλον του καὶ δὲν
τοῦ 'λεγε παρὰ μνιὰ „καλὴ μέρα,“ γιὰ νὰ μὴν τύχῃ καὶ τόνε
πάρῃ στὸ σπίτιν του καὶ τοῦ ξελογιάσῃ τὴ γυναῖκαν του. Ἰντά
'καμε λοιπὸν εὐτός; Πιάνει καὶ χτίζ' ἕνα σπίτι μὲ τρεῖς πατωσιὲς
καὶ βάζει τὴ νενέν του στὴν κάτω πατωσιά, τὴν πεθεριάν του στὴ
δεύτερη καὶ τὴ γυναῖκαν του στὴν ἀπάνω, κ' ἠπρόσταξε τὴ νενέν του, μὴν τύχῃ καὶ πάῃ ἀσερνικὸς κάτης κι ἀνοίξῃ κ' ἔμπῃ
μέσα. Τί τοῦ καταφέρνει λοιπὸν ὁ φίλος του; Πάει κι ἀλλάζει
τὴ φορεσιάν του καὶ ντύνεται σὰ λόρδος, καὶ σὰν ἤξερε, πῶς
ἐκεινῆς ὁ ἄντρας ἤτανε στὴ δουλειά, πάει καὶ χτυπᾷ στὸ σπίτι
εὐτό· καὶ βγαίνει ἡ νενὲ τοῦ φίλου του. „Ἔ, ὥρα καλή, κερά.“
„Καλῶς τὸ παλληκάρι.“ Τὸν ἀρωτᾷ λοιπόν· „τί θέλεις ἐδώ;“
„Ἐγώ,“ λέει, „κερά, εἶμ' ἕνας λόρδος· τὸ σπίτι αὐτὸ μ' ἀρέσκει
πολλά, καὶ θὰ μοῦ κάμῃς τὴ χάρι ν' ἀφήκῃς νά 'μπω μέσα νὰ
πάρω τὸ σκέδιο.“ „Ὁ Θεὸς φυλάξῃ, παιδάκι μου, δὲν ἔχω τὴν
ἄδεια ἀπὸ τὸ γιό μου ν' ἀφήσω μέσα καένα.“ „Σοῦ δίνω ἑκατὸ
γρόσια, κι ἄφησέ με νά 'μπω.“ Σὰν ἤκουσεν εὐτὴ ἡ κακομοίρα
τὰ ἑκατὸ γρόσια, τὰ πῆρε καὶ τοῦ 'πεν· „ἔμπας, μὰ γλήγορα νὰ
φύῃς, νὰ μὴ 'ριβάρῃ ὁ γιός μου.“ Λοιπόν, εἶχε δὲν εἶχε, εὐτὸς
ἀγεβαίνει καὶ στὴ δεύτερην πατωσιά, τόνε γλέπει ἡ πεθεριά· λέει
του· „τί θὲς ἐδώ;“ Λέει· „ἤρχα νὰ σκεδιάσω τὸ σπίτι.“ Εὐτὴ
ἐγύρεψε νὰ τοῦ κουντραστάρῃ, καὶ δὲν τὸν ἄφηνε νὰ μπῇ μέσα.
Βγάνει καὶ τῆς δίνει ἄλλα 'κατὸ γρόσια· ἠστοχάστηκε εὐτὴ νὰ τὰ
πάρῃ, κι ἀφοῦ τὸν ἄφηκε ἡ μάννα του, ἰντά 'φταιε κείνη; Νὰ τὰ

κοντολοοῦμε, ἀνεβαίνει καὶ στὴν ἀπάνω πατωσιά. Σὰν τὸν ἔδιε ἡ κοπέλα, ἠτρόμαξε καὶ τὸν ἀρώτηξε, τί ἤθελε· „τὸ σκέδιος θὰ πάρω τοῦ σπιτιοῦ." Τί ἤθελε νὰ κάμῃ; Τὸν ἄφηκε κ' ἤπῆρε τὸ σκέδιος· σὰν τὸ πῆρε, κατεβαίνει στὴ δεύτερην πατωσιὰ καὶ κάθεται. Τοῦ λέει ἡ πεθεριά· „φεύγας γλήγορα, μὴν ἔρχῃ ὁ γαμπρός μου." Λέει· „δὲ φεύγω, ἃ δὲ μοῦ δώκῃς τὰ 'κατὸ γρόσια!" Ἰντά 'θελε νὰ κάμῃ; ἠφοβούντανε μὴν ἔρχῃ ὁ γαμπρός της, τοῦ δίνει τὰ 'κατὸ γρόσια, καὶ σὰν τὰ πῆρε, κατεβαίνει στὴν κάτω πατωσιά, καὶ μὲ τὸν ὄμνοιο μόδος παίρνει κι ἀπὸ 'κεῖ τ' ἄλλα ἑκατὸ γρόσια καὶ φεύγει καὶ πάει καὶ σταματᾷ σ' ἕνα μέρος, ἀπ' ὅπου ἤξερε πῶς ἤθελε νὰ περάσῃ ὁ φίλος του, κι ἀκαρτέρει. Ὁ φίλος του ἠπέρασε ἀπὸ 'μπρός του, τὸν ἔδιε καὶ τοῦ λέει· „καλὴ μέρα!" „Τί εἶπες; Καλὴ μέρα; Καὶ δὲν ἤκουσες τὸν ὁρισμό, ποὺ 'βγαλεν ὁ βασιλές, νὰ μὴ λένε 'καλὴ μέρα,' μόνου 'καλὴ μέρα, κ' ἤμαθά το';" „Καλή σου μέρα κ' ἤμαθά το!" Καὶ φεύγει καὶ πάει στὸ σπίτιν του· λέει τῆς νενές του· „καλὴ μέρα κ' ἤμαθά το." Εὐτὴ δὲν ἠμίλησε, ἀνεβαίνει στὴ δεύτερην πατωσιά, βρίσκει τὴν πεθεριάν του, λέει· „καλὴ μέρα, πεθεριά, κ' ἤμαθά το." „Καὶ σὰν τό 'μαθες," λέει, „ἡ μάννα σου τὰ φταίει, γιατί τοῦ 'νοιξε κ' ἤμπε μέσα!" Τρέχει λοιπὸν εὐτὺς κάτω στῆς μάννας του, λέει· „ποιοῦ ἤνοιξες, κ' ἤμπε μέσα;" „Ἦτανε, παιδάκι μου, ἕνας λόρδος, κ' ἤθελε νὰ πάρη σκέδιος ἀπὸ τὸ σπίτι σου." Τρέχει ἀπάνω, βρίσκει τὴ γυναῖκαν του, τὴν ἀρωτᾷ. Λέει· „τί νὰ σοῦ 'πῶ; ὁ φίλος σου ἤτανε πικαριϊμένος, πῶς δὲν τοῦ μιλεῖς, καὶ δὲν ἤξερε, μὲ τί τρόπο νὰ σὲ διαοντρέψῃ." Τότες πιὰ ἤκαμε τὴν ἀπόφασι, πῶς, ὅσο κι ἂν ἔχῃ κανεὶς σφαλιχτὴ τὴ γυναῖκαν του, εἶναι μπόσικα· καὶ τσ' ἔδωκε τὴν ἐλευτεριά, καὶ σὰν ἠντάμωνε τὸ φίλον του, ἤτανε πιὸ καλὰ παρὰ πρῶτα.

6. Πῶς ἐφτειάστη ὁ λαγὸς καὶ τὸ λαγωνικό.

(Legend from Φελλόη)

Ὁ Χριστὸς καὶ ὁ διάβολος ἦσαν μαζί. Μιὰ ἡμέρα λέγει ὁ διάβολος εἰς τὸ Χριστό· „ὅτι ἔφτειασα ἕνα πρᾶμα ὅπου δὲν τὸ πιάνει τίποτε." — „Γιὰ νὰ ἰδῶ", τοῦ λέγει ὁ Χριστός, „τί ἔφτειασες." Τότες ὁ διάβολος ἀπολάει ἀπόκατω ἀπὸ τὴν καπότα του τὸ λαγό, ὁ ὁποῖος ἔτρεχε πολύ. Τὴν ἄλλην ἡμέρα ὁ Χριστὸς τοῦ λέει τοῦ διαβόλου· „γιὰ ἀπόλυσε ἐκεῖνο τὸ πρᾶμα ὅπου ἔφτειασες." Καὶ ὁ διάβολος ἅμα τὸ ἀπόλυσε, ἀπολάει καὶ ὁ Χριστὸς τὸ λαγωνικὸ καὶ τὸν ἔπιασε.

Ὁ διάβολος ἐλυπήθη, διότι ὁ Χριστὸς ἔφτειασε καλύτερο πρᾶμα ἀπὸ ἐκεῖνον καὶ ἐμάζωξε ὅλους τοὺς λαγοὺς καὶ τοὺς βάνει κάθε νύχτα καὶ ὀργώνουν τὰ χωράφια του, καὶ ὅσοι δὲν πάγουν, ἐκείνους τοὺς ἀφήνει καὶ τοὺς πιάνουν τὰ λαγωνικά.

7. Ἡ Λαμπηδόνα.

(Legend from Patras)

Στὴν Πελοπόννησον ἀπάνου στὸν Ὤλενον ἐφύτρωνε κάθε χρόνο κατὰ ὡρισμένην ὥρα καὶ μέρα στὲς δώδεκα τῆς νύχτας ἕνα λούλουδο, ὅπου ὅποιος τό 'βρισκε καὶ τὴ ρίζα του τὴν ἔλυωνε καὶ ἔρυνε ἀπ' αὐτὸ τὸ νερὸ μέσα σὲ χάλκωμα λυωμένο, ἐμπορ”οῦσε νὰ τὸ κάμη μάλαμα. Λοιπὸν ἕνας Βενετζάνος καπετάνιος, ὅπου εἶχε 'βρεῖ στὰ κατάστιχα τοῦ πατέρα του, πῶς σ' αὐτὸ τὸ μέρος ἐφύτρωνε τὸ φυτὸ ἐκεῖνο, ἔφυγε ἀπὸ τὴν πατρίδα του μὲ καμπόσους δικούς του γιὰ νά 'ρθη νὰν τό 'βρη. Ἅμα λοιπὸν ἔφτασε, ἐπῆρε τὸ δρόμο κατὰ ποῦ τοῦ 'δειχνε τὸ βιβλίο, καὶ ὕστερα ἀπὸ πολλὰ γυρέματα τό 'βρηκε τὸ μέρος. Ἐσταμάτησε ἐκεῖ κοντὰ κ' ἐπερίμενε μὲ προσοχή· ἅμα ἦρθε ἡ ὥρα ἡ ὡρισμένη, ἔλαμψε ἡ λαμπηδόνα καὶ ἀμέσως ἔσβησε. Ἀλλ' ἐκεῖνος ἂν καὶ τὸ γύρεψε μὲ οὖλα τὰ μέσα, δὲν ἐμπόρεσε νὰ εὕρη τὶς ρίζες του. Τὸν ἄλλο χρόνο ἦρθε πάλι καὶ ἐπλησίασε τόσο κοντά του, ὅπου ἅμα ἔλαμψε ἦτανε μακρειὰ ἕνα πάσσο. Ἀμέσως λοιπὸν ἐσημάδεψε τὸν τόπο, τὸ γύρεψε, ἔσκαψε καὶ τό 'βρε. Σύμφωνα μὲ τὸ βιβλίο ἔφκειασε τὶς ρίζες καὶ τὶς ἔλυωσε καὶ ἀπὸ κεῖνο ἔρυνε στὰ χαλκώματα καὶ τά 'κανε μάλαμα καὶ χρήματα. Γι' αὐτὸ ἐμπόρεσε κ' ἔφκειασε τόσα κάστρα τοῦ Μοριά.

8. Ὁ σωρὸς τοῦ Μαραθῶνα.

(Attica)

Στὸν κάμπο τοῦ Μαραθῶνα κατοικοῦσε τὸν παλαιὸ καιρὸ πολὺς λαός, καὶ τὸν ἐκυβερνοῦσαν τρία πριγκηπόπουλα, καὶ τὰ τρία ἀδέρφια γκαρδιακά. Ἦρθε ὥρα κακὴ καὶ τὸ ἕνα πριγκηπόπουλο ἀρρώστησε βαρειά. Οἱ γιατροὶ τίποτε δὲν ἐμπόρεσαν νὰ τοῦ κάμουν, ἐπέθανε καὶ τὸ ἔθαψαν ἐκεῖ ἀνάμεσα στὸν κάμπο, καὶ οἱ κάτοικοι ὅλοι τοῦ κάμπου ἀπ' ἄκρη σ' ἄκρη ἐσηκώθησαν θλιμμένοι, ἐπῆραν ἀπὸ μιὰ ποδιὰ χῶμα κ' ἐπῆγαν καὶ τὴν ἔρριξαν ἀπάνω στὸν τάφο του. Καὶ ἀπὸ τότε ὁ τάφος τοῦ πριγκηπόπουλου ἔγινε σωρὸς ψηλός.

9. Οἱ Μυλόρδοι.

(Delphi)

Οἱ Μυλόρδοι δὲν εἶναι χριστιανοί, γιατί κανεὶς δὲν τοὺς εἶδε ποτὲς νὰ κάνουν τὸ σταυρό τους. Ἡ γενιά τους εἶναι ἀπὸ τοὺς παλαιοὺς εἰδωλολάτρες Ἀδελφιῶτες, ποὺ φύλαγαν τὸ βιό τους εἰς ἕνα κάστρο καὶ τὸ ᾽λέγαν Ἀδελφούς, ἀπὸ τοὺς δύο ἀδελφοὺς τὰ βασιλόπουλα ποὺ τό ᾽χτισαν. Ὅταν ἡ Παναγία καὶ ὁ Χριστὸς ἦρθαν σ᾽ αὐτοὺς τοὺς τόπους καὶ ὅλοι οἱ ἄνθρωποι ὁλόγυρα γινήκαν χριστιανοί, οἱ Ἀδελφιῶτες ἐσκέφτηκαν, πῶς ἦταν καλύτερα γι᾽ αὐτοὺς νὰ φύγουν· κ᾽ ἔφυγα στὴ Φραγκιὰ καὶ πῆραν καὶ ὅλα τὰ πλούτη τους μαζί. Ἀπ᾽ αὐτοὺς εἶναι οἱ Μυλόρδοι, καὶ ἔρχονται τώρα ἐδὼ καὶ προσκυνοῦν αὐτὰ τὰ λιθάρια.

10. Οἱ κόρες τοῦ κάστρου[1]).

(Athens)

Ὅταν ὁ Μυλόρδος ἐπῆρε τὴ μιὰ ἀπὸ τὶς ἔξι κόρες τοῦ Κάστρου, ἄφησε παραγγελία στοὺς Τούρκους νὰ τοῦ κουβαλήσουν καὶ τὶς ἄλλες τὴ νύχτα. Ἀλλὰ ᾽κεῖ ποὺ πήγαιναν νὰ τὶς βγάλουν, τὶς ἀκοὺν νὰ σκούζουν λυπητερὰ καὶ νὰ φωνάζουν τὴν ἀδερφή τους. Οἱ Τοῦρκοι τρομασμένοι ἔφυγαν, καὶ μὲ κανένα λόγο δὲν ἤθελαν νὰ δοκιμάσουν νὰ τὶς βγάλουν. Καὶ ἄλλοι πολλοὶ κάτω ἀπὸ τὸ Κάστρο τὶς ἄκουγαν τὶς μαρμαρένιες κόρες νὰ κλαῖν τὴ νύχτα γιὰ τὴν ἀδερφή τους ποὺ τοὺς τὴν πῆραν.

[1]) The reference is to the Caryatides, one of which Lord Elgin took to England.

II. ARTISTIC LITERATURE.

a. Poetry.

1. Πολεμιστήριον.

(Ρήγας Φεραῖος, of Βελεστῖνος in Thessaly, 1754–1798)

Ὡς πότε παλληκάρια νὰ ζῶμεν στὰ στενά,
Μονάχοι, σὰν λιοντάρια στὲς ράχες, στὰ βουνά;
Σπηλιὲς νὰ κατοικοῦμεν, νὰ βλέπωμεν κλαδιά,
Νὰ φεύγωμ' ἀπ' τὸν κόσμον γιὰ τὴν πικρὴ σκλαβιά;
Νὰ χάνωμεν ἀδέλφια, πατρίδα καὶ γονεῖς,
Τοὺς φίλους, τὰ παιδιά μας κι ὅλους τοὺς συγγενεῖς;
Καλύτερα μιᾶς ὥρας ἐλεύθερη ζωή,
Παρὰ σαράντα χρόνων σκλαβιὰ καὶ φυλακή.
Τί σ' ὠφελεῖ κι ἂν ζήσῃς καὶ εἶσαι στὴ σκλαβιά;
Στοχάσου. πῶς σὲ ψένουν κάθ' ὥρα στὴ φωτιά.
Αὐθέντης, δραγουμάνος, βεζίρης ἂν σταθῆς,
Ὁ τύραννος σὲ κάμνει ἀδίκως νὰ χαθῆς.
Δουλεύεις ὅλ' ἡμέρα εἰς ὅτι κι ἂν σοῦ 'πῇ,
Κι αὐτὸς πασχίζει πάλιν, τὸ αἷμα νὰ σοῦ πιῇ.
Ἀνδρεῖοι καπετάνοι, παπάδες, λαϊκοὶ
Σκοτώθηκαν κι ἀγάδες ἀπ' ἄδικο σπαθί.
Κι ἀμέτρητ' ἄλλοι τόσοι καὶ Τοῦρκοι καὶ Γραικοὶ
Ζωὴν καὶ πλούτη χάνουν χωρὶς καμιὰ ἀφορμή.
Ὁ Σοῦτσος, ὁ Μουρούζης, Πετράκης, Σκαναβής,
Γκίκας καὶ Μαυρογένης καθρέπτης εἶν' νὰ ἰδῇς.
Σᾶς κράζει ἡ πατρίς σας, σᾶς θέλει, σᾶς πονεῖ,
Ζητεῖ τὴν συνδρομήν σας μὲ μητρικὴν φωνή.
Ἡ Ρούμελη σᾶς κράζει μ' ἀγκάλας ἀνοικτάς,
Σᾶς δίδει πλοῦτον, τόπον, ἀξίας καὶ τιμάς.
Ἐλᾶτε μ' ἕνα ζῆλον σ' ἐτοῦτον τὸν καιρόν,
Νὰ κάμωμεν τὸν ὅρκον ἐπάνω στὸν Σταυρόν,

Συμβούλους προκομμένους μὲ πατριωτισμὸν
Νὰ βάλωμεν, εἰς ὅλα νὰ δίδουν ὁρισμόν.
Ὁ νόμος νά 'ναι πρῶτος καὶ μόνος ὁδηγός,
Καὶ τῆς πατρίδος ἕνας νὰ γένῃ ἀρχηγός.
῎Οτι κ' ἡ ἀναρχία ὁμοιάζει τὴν σκλαβιά,
Νὰ ζῶμεν ὡς θηρία εἶν' πλιὸ σκληρὴ φωτιά·
Καὶ τότε μὲ τὰ χέρια ψηλὰ στὸν οὐρανὸν
῎Ας 'ποῦμ' ἀπ' τὴν καρδιά μας ἐτοῦτα στὸν Θεόν·
   „῏Ω βασιλεῦ τοῦ κόσμου! ὁρκίζομαι εἰς Σέ,
„Στὴν γνώμην τῶν τυράννων νὰ μὴν ἐλθῶ ποτέ,
„Μήτε νὰ τὸν δουλεύσω, μήτε νὰ πλανηθῶ,
„Εἰς τὰ ταξίματά του νὰ μὴ παραδοθῶ.
„Ἐνόσῳ ζῶ στὸν κόσμον, ὁ μόνος μου σκοπός,
„Γιὰ νὰ τὸν ἀφανίσω νὰ εἶναι σταθερός.
„Πιστὸς εἰς τὴν πατρίδα συντρίβω τὸ ζυγὸν
„Κι ἀχώριστος θὰ εἶμαι ἀπὸ τὸν ἀρχηγόν.
„Κι ἂν παραβῶ τὸν ὅρκον, ν' ἀστράψ' ὁ οὐρανός
„Καὶ νὰ μὲ κατακάψῃ, νὰ γένω ὡσὰν καπνός.“

2. Γέρος καὶ Θάνατος.

(Ἰωάννης Βηλαρᾶς, of Joannina in Epirus, 1771–1823)

῎Ενας γέρος σὲ φτώχειας ἀνάγκη
῎Αλλον τρόπο νὰ ζήσῃ δὲν εἶχε,
Χώρια ξύλα νὰ κόφτῃ στὸν λόγγο,
Μετὰ βιᾶς τὸ ψωμί του νὰ βγάζῃ.

Μιὰν ἡμέρα βαρειὰ φορτωμένος,
Περπατῶντας σ' ὀρθὸ μονοπάτι,
᾿Οχ τὸν κόπο καὶ κᾶμα τοῦ ἥλιου
Τὴν ἀνάσα νὰ πάρῃ δὲ φτάνει.

Σ' ἕναν ὄχτο τ' ἀνάσκελα πέφτει·
Καὶ στὸ μέγα πολὺ κούρασμά του
Τὴ ζωή του μισῶντας βαρειέται
Καὶ τὸ Χάρο μὲ πόθο του κράζει.

Νὰ ὁ Χάρος ὀμπρός του πετειέται
Τὸ δρεπάνι κρατῶντας στὸ χέρι,
Μ' ἄγριαν ὄψι καὶ σχῆμα τρομάρας,
„Γιά με, γέρο,“ τοῦ λέγει, „τί θέλεις;“

„Ἄχ!" ὁ γέρος εὐτὺς ἀποκρίθη,
„Τὸ ζαλίκι μου αὐτὸ δὲν μποροῦσα
Νὰ σηκώσω· σὲ φώναξα ὁ δόλιος,
Νὰ μοῦ δώκῃς ὀλίγη βοήθεια."

3. Φιλάργυρος.

(By the same)

Ὁ καημένος Χρυσολάτρης
Ξάπλα κείτεται, βογγάει,
Μὲ τὸ Χάρο πολεμάει·

Ἐλαιμάργησεν ὁ δόλιος,
Τί.γιομάτισε σὲ σπίτι
Κάποιου πλούσιου συμπολίτη.

Τοῦ ἐπρόβαλαν καμπόσοι
Μὲ καρδιᾶς κι ἀγάπης ζέσι
Τὸ γιατρὸ νὰ προσκαλέσῃ.

Τώρα αὐτὸς καὶ τὴν ἀρρώστια
Καὶ τὸν κίνδυνο λογιάζει,
Μόν' τὰ ἔξοδα τρομάζει!

Ἕνας φίλος του ἀστεῖος,
Μὲ σκοπὸ νὰ χωρατέψῃ,
Τοῦ εἶπε, μήπως ἐξοδέψῃ

Πλιὸ παράνω στὴ θανή του,
Ἄν ἀπόμνησκεν ἀκόμα
Ἔτσι ἀνήμπορος στὸ στρῶμα.

Τότε πλιὸ ἐκαταζαλίστη·
Παντοχὴ καὶ θάρρος χάνει
Καὶ φωνάζει· θὰ πεθάνῃ!

Καὶ οἱ πόνοι του ἀβγαταίνουν,
Καὶ γιατροῦ ζητάει τὴ χάρι,
Μὴ ὁ θάνατος τὸν πάρῃ·

Ἐξανάλαβε ὡς τόσο
Μὲ ὀλίγα τὴν ὑγειά του.
Μόν' γι' αὐτὴ τὴ συμφορά του

Ἔκαμε ὅρκον, ὅσο ζήσῃ,
Νὰ δειπνάῃ μόν' τὸ βράδυ
Μὲ νερὸ καὶ παξιμάδι.

4. Οἱ Χάρες καὶ ὁ Ἔρωτας.

Ἀθανάσιος Χριστόπουλος, of Castoria in Macedonia, 1772–1847)

Οἱ Χάρες μὲ τὸν Ἔρωτα
Ἐπῆγαν νὰ διαλέξουν
Στοὺς κήπους τριαντάφυλλα,
Κορώνες νὰ τὰ πλέξουν.
Κι ὁ Ἔρωτας χαρούμενος
Ἐδὼ κ' ἐκεῖ πετοῦσε
Καὶ μόνος του τὰ κλάδευε
Καὶ τὲς ὑπηρετοῦσε.
Κλαδεύοντας ἀπρόσεχτα,
Ὡσὰν λωλὸ παιδάκι,
Τὸν κέντρωσε τὸ δάχτυλο
Πικρὰ ἕν' ἀγκαθάκι.
Γίετάει τὰ τριαντάφυλλα,
Τὸ κλαδευτήρι ρίχνει,
Καὶ κλαίοντας στὲς Χάρες του
Τὸ δάχτυλό του δείχνει·
„Ὢχ! ὤχ!" τὲς λέγει, „γίνεται
Ἕν' ἀγκαθάκι μόνον
Νὰ προξενήσῃ, Χάρες μου,
Μεγάλον τόσον πόνον;"
„Δὲν εἶν'," τοῦ λέν, „παράξενο,
Δὲν εἶν'· γιατί κ' ἐκείνη
Ἡ τόση σαϊτίτσα σου
Μεγάλον πόνον δίνει."

5. Ὁ λόγιος.

(By the same)

Τί τοῦ κάκου κοπιάζεις
Καὶ ἀνόητα σπουδάζεις,
Γιὰ νὰ μάθῃς τεχνικά,
Τ' εἶναι τ' ἄλφα καὶ τὸ βῆτα
Καὶ τὰ γάμμα, δέλτα, ζῆτα,
Καὶ τὰ ἄλλα τὰ κακά;

Ἐρωτῶ σε, τί κερδαίνεις,
Ἂν γραμματισμένος γένῃς,
Ἂν φιλόσοφος βαθύς;
Τάχα δὲν καταλαμβάνεις,
Ὅτι πάλε θὰ πεθάνῃς
Σὰν ὁ πρῶτος ἀμαθής;
Ἄφσε τούτη σου τὴ τρέλλα
Καὶ κολλήσου στὴν βαρέλλα,
  Ποῦ σὲ κράζει μὲ χαρά·
Νὰ σὲ μάθῃ, γιὰ νὰ γίνῃς
Σπουδαιότερος νὰ πίνῃς
  Ἕνα μέτρον στὴν φορά.
Τοῦτο βλέπε νὰ σπουδάξῃς,
Τοῦτο πάσχιζε νὰ πράξῃς,
  Κι ὄχι τ᾽ ἄλλα τὰ τρελλά,
Θέματ᾽ ἄρρητα γραμμένα,
Καὶ νερὰ κοπανισμένα,
  Καὶ δασκάλου λά, λά, λά.

6. Ἡ Ψυχούλα.

(Διονύσιος Σολωμός, of Zante, 1798–1857)

Ὡσὰν γλυκόπνοο
Δροσάτ᾽ ἀεράκι
Μέσα σὲ ἀνθότοπο
Ἐκειὸ τὸ παιδάκι
Τὴν ὕστερη ἔβγαλε
Ἀναπνοή.

Καὶ ἡ ψυχούλα του
Εἰς τὸν ἀέρα
Γλήγορα ἀνέβαινε
Πρὸς τὸν αἰθέρα,
Σὰν λιανοτρέμουλη
Σπίθα μικρή.

Ὅλα τὴν ἔκραζαν,
Ὅλα τ᾽ ἀστέρια,
Κ᾽ ἐκείνη ἐξάπλωνε
Δειλὴ τὰ χέρια,
Γιατί δὲν ἤξευρε,
Σὲ ποῖο νὰ μπῇ.

Ἀλλὰ νά, τοῦ 'δωσε
Ἕνα ἀγγελάκι
Τὸ φιλὶ ἀθάνατο
Στὸ μαγουλάκι,
Ποῦ ἔξαφνα ἔλαμψε
Σὰν τὴν αὐγή.

7. Ἡ φαρμακωμένη.
(By the same)

Τὰ τραγούδια μοῦ τά 'λεγες ὅλα.
Τοῦτο μόνον δὲν θέλει τὸ 'πῆς,
Τοῦτο μόνον δὲν θέλει τ' ἀκούσης,
Ἄχ! τὴν πλάκα τοῦ τάφου κρατεῖς!

Ὦ παρθένα, ἂν ἠμπόρειαν οἱ κλάψες
Πεθαμμένου νὰ δώσουν ζωή,
Τόσες ἔκαμα κλάψες γιὰ σένα,
Ποῦ θέλ' ἔχῃς τὴν πρώτη πνοή.

Συφορά! σὲ θυμοῦμ' ἐκαθόσουν
Στὸ πλευρό μου μὲ πρόσωπο ἀχνό·
„Τί ἔχεις;“ σοῦ 'πα, καὶ σὺ μ' ἀποκρίθης·
„Θὰ πεθάνω, φαρμάκι θὰ πιῶ.“

Μὲ σκληρότατο χέρι τὸ πῆρες,
Ὡραία κόρη, κι αὐτὸ τὸ κορμί,
Ποῦ τοῦ ἔπρεπε φόρεμα γάμου,
Πικρὸ σάβανο τώρα φορεῖ.

Τὸ κορμί σου ἐκεῖ μέσα στὸν τάφο
Τὸ στολίζει σεμνὴ παρθενιά·
Τοῦ κακοῦ σ' ἀδικοῦσεν ὁ κόσμος,
Καὶ σοῦ φώναξε λόγια κακά.

Τέτοια λόγια ἂν ἠμπόρειες ν' ἀκούσης,
Ὀχ τὸ στόμα σου τ' ἤθελε βγῆ;
„Τὸ φαρμάκι, ποῦ πῆρα, καὶ οἱ πόνοι
Δὲν ἐστάθηκαν τόσο σκληροί.“

Κόσμε ψεύτη! τὲς κόρες τὲς μαύρες
Κατατρέχεις ὅσο εἶν' ζωντανές,
Σκληρὲ κόσμε, καὶ δὲν τοὺς λυπᾶσαι
Τὴν τιμήν, ὅταν εἶναι νεκρές.

Σώπα, σώπα! θυμήσου πῶς ἔχεις
Θυγατέρα, γυναῖκα, ἀδελφή·
Σώπα, ἡ μαύρη κοιμᾶται στὸ μνῆμα,
Καὶ κοιμᾶται παρθένα σεμνή.

Θὰ ξυπνήσῃ τὴν ὕστερη ἡμέρα,
Εἰς τὸν κόσμον ὀμπρὸς νὰ κριθῇ,
Καὶ στὸν Πλάστη κινῶντας μὲ σέβας
Τὰ λευκά της τὰ χέρια θὰ 'πῇ·

„Κύττα μέσα στὰ σπλάχνα μου, Πλάστη!
Τὰ φαρμάκωσα, ἀλήθεια, ἡ πικρή,
Καὶ μοῦ βγῆκε ὄχ τὸ νοῦ μου, πατέρα,
Ποῦ πλασμένα μοῦ τά 'χες ἐσύ·

Ὅμως κύττα στὰ σπλάχνα μου μέσα,
Ποῦ τὸ κρῖμα τους κλαίνε, καὶ πές,
Πὲς τοῦ κόσμου ποῦ φώναξε τόσα,
Ἐδὼ μέσα ἂν εἶν' ἄλλες πληγές.‟

Τέτοια, ὀμπρὸς εἰς τὸν Πλάστη κινῶντας
Τὰ λευκά της τὰ χέρια, θὰ πῇ.
Σώπα, κόσμε, κοιμᾶται στὸ μνῆμα,
Καὶ κοιμᾶται παρθένα σεμνή.

8. Ὁ εὐγενής.

(Ἀλέξανδρος Σοῦτσος, of Constantinople, 1803–1863)

Ξόρισε τοὺς τίτλους ὅλους ὁ Τροιζὴν ἀπ' τὴν Ἑλλάδα.
    Ποῖος ὅμως τοὺς ἀφήνει;
Καὶ ἁπλοῦς πολίτης ποῖος καταδέχεται νὰ μείνῃ;
Τὸ „πανέκλαμπρέ μου Πρίγκηψ‟ ἔχει τόσην νοστιμάδα!
Ἐκλαμπρότητες ἐδώ, ἐκλαμπρότητες ἐκεῖ·
Ὅπου πάς, μιὰ ἐκλαμπρότης μὲ τὸ τρύπιο τὸ βρακί.
    Ὅπου κι ἂν σταθῇ κανείς,
    Νά σου κ' ἕνας εὐγενής!

Κάτω φέσια καὶ καπέλα! ἕνας Πρίγκηπας περνᾷ·
    Τ' ἡγεμονικὸ ποῦ ἔχει!
Βλέπει ὅλους σὰν μυρμήγκια καὶ τὰ μάτια του σφαλνᾷ·
Ἀπ' τὴ μύτη του ἰδέτε ἡ εὐγένεια πῶς τρέχει·
    Στὸ μανδήλι του φυσᾷ,

Ταμπακίζει, ξεροβήχει καὶ τὰ λόγια του μασσᾷ,
   Ἡμπορεῖ νὰ 'πῇ κανείς,
   Πῶς δὲν εἶναι εὐγενής;

Ἄκουσε τὸν ἥρωά μας, ἄκουσέ τον πῶς λαλεῖ·
„Πῶς μισῶ τοὺς δημοκράτας! ἐξεπάρθηκαν πολύ·
Κὺρ ἐπάνω καὶ κὺρ κάτω ξεφωνίζουν εἰς τ' αὐτί σου
Κι ἀπ' ἐμπρός σου κι ἀπ' ὀπίσου·
Σὲ φιλεύουν μ' ἕνα κρύο δημοκράτικο ἐσύ·
Αὔριο θὰ σὲ κεράσουν καὶ στὸ καπηλειὸ κρασί.
   Τί κακὸ νὰ ζῇ κανεὶς
   Μὲ ἀνθρώπους ἀγενεῖς!“

Εἶχε δίκιο νὰ φωνάζῃ ὁ Μπαρόνος ὁ γαμβρός μου.
   Καὶ ὁ Πρίγκηψ ὁ υἱός μου,
Κι ὁ πατέρας μου ὁ Κόντες, καὶ ἡ μάννα μ' ἡ Κοντέσσα,
   Κ' ἡ γιαγιά μ' ἡ Πριγκηπέσσα·
„Μὲ χωριάτηδες ἀνθρώπους πρόσεχε καλὰ μὴν μπλέξῃς·
Ἀγενὴς καὶ ζῷο εἶναι, πρᾶγμα ἕνα σὲ δυὸ λέξεις.
   Νὰ φυλάγεται κανεὶς
   Ἀπ' ἀνθρώπους ἀγενεῖς!“

Ἔγινε, χάριτι θείᾳ, ἡ Ἑλλάς μας βασιλεία·
Μὲ τοὺς κὺρ αὐτόχθονάς μας θὰ τὰ εἴχαμεν ἀχρεῖα.
Τώρα θά 'χωμεν, ἐλπίζω, τὰ καλὰ τοῦ παραδείσου
   Καὶ τοὺς θησαυροὺς τοῦ Κροίσου·
Πρίγκηπας ἐγὼ θὰ εἶμαι, πρίγκηπας μὲ τρεῖς οὐρές,
Καὶ σύ, Πρίγκηπά μου φίλε, πρέσβυς ἑκατὸν φορές.
   Δὲν μπορεῖ νὰ 'πῇ κανείς,
   Πῶς δὲν εἴμασθ' εὐγενεῖς.

9. Βάσανος.

(Παναγιώτης Σοῦτσος, of Constantinople, 1803–1868)

   Σὰν δὲν σὲ βλέπω, τί καημός!
     Τί σκότος καταχθόνιο!
   Καὶ σὰν σὲ βλέπω, τί παλμός!
     Τί βάσανο αἰώνιο!

   Σὲ βλέπω, κ' εὐθὺς λαχταρῶ
     Νὰ τρέξω στὴν ἀγκάλην σου,
   Μὲ μάτι βλέπω φλογερὸ
     Τὰ στήθη σου, τὰ κάλλη σου.

Σὲ βλέπω, καίω καὶ ψυχρὸς
Ἰδρὼς μὲ περιχύνεται,
Σὰν φύλλο τρέμω, μνήσκ' ὠχρός,
Κ' ἡ ὅρασίς μου σβήνεται.

Μοῦ πιάνετ' ἡ ἀναπνοή,
Τὸ στόμα μοῦ ξηραίνεται,
Μοῦ χάνεται ἡ ἀκοή
Κ' ἡ γλῶσσα μου μὲ δένεται.

10. Θάλασσα.

(Ἠλίας Τανταλίδης, of Constantinople, 1818–1876)

Ἂν ἤσουν, θάλασσα, κρασί,
Ὦ! τότε τί δουλειὰ χρυσῆ!
  Κοντά σου θὰ πασχίσω
  Τὸ σπίτι μου νὰ κτίσω,
Καὶ νὰ μεθῶ καὶ νὰ μεθῶ,
Χωρὶς ποτὲ νὰ βαρεθῶ,
  Νὰ πίνω καὶ νὰ πίνω
  Τὸν ἀφρισμένον οἶνο.

Ἂν ἤσουν, θάλασσα, κρασί,
Τωόντι τί δουλειὰ χρυσῆ!
  Σὰν ἀλκυὼν δική σου
  Νὰ ψάλλω στὴν ἀκτή σου,
Νὰ μὲ κτυπᾷ κάθε βραδειὰ
Κομανταρίας μυρωδιά,
  Καὶ μέθη νὰ ἀρχίζῃ
  Νὰ μὲ ἀποκοιμίζῃ·

Ἂν ἤσουν, θάλασσα, κρασί,
Τί τύχη, τί δουλειὰ χρυσῆ!
  Ν' ἀκούω νὰ σφυρίζῃς
  Κι ἀφροὺς κρασιοῦ ν' ἀφρίζῃς,
Κ' ἐκεῖ νὰ τρώγω τὰ φαγιὰ
Μὲ τὴν κρασένια σου μαγιά,
  Καὶ τὸ νερὸ ποῦ πίνω
  Κρασὶ νὰ εἶν' κ' ἐκεῖνο.

Ἂν ἤσουν, θάλασσα, κρασί,
Θεέ μου, τί δουλειὰ χρυσῆ!

Εἰς τὸ κρασὶ ἐπάνω
Ταξίδια νὰ κάνω.
Νὰ κολυμβῶ καὶ νὰ βουτῶ
Καὶ νὰ σὲ πίνω ἐνταυτῷ,
Κ' ἢ νὰ σὲ πιῶ νὰ σκάσω,
Ἢ πιέ με νὰ χορτάσω.

11. Ρόδον καὶ χορτάρι.

(Γεώργιος Ζαλακώστας, of Syrracos in Epirus, 1805–1858)

Ἕνα λουλούδι, ὅπου κυρτὸ τὸν ἥλιο ἀκολουθοῦσε,
   (Ἥλιος ἐλέγουνταν κι αὐτό)
Εἰς ἕναν κῆπον φουντωτὸ
Τριανταφυλλιὰ ἀγαπούσε.

„Ἔλα νὰ γίνωμε τὰ δυὸ ζευγάρι ταιριασμένο,
   Ἔλα, τριανταφυλλιὰ χρυσῆ,
Γιατί εἶσαι μυρωδάτη ἐσὺ
Κ' ἐγὼ καμαρωμένο.“

„Σώπα, λουλούδι ἀμύριστο, λουλούδι χωρὶς χάρι,“
   Ἕνα ἀηδονάκι τοῦ μιλᾷ·
„Τὸ ρόδο ποῦ μοσχοβολᾷ,
Δὲν μοιάζει στὸ χορτάρι.“

12. Νεκρικὴ ᾠδή.

(Ἀριστοτέλης Βαλαωρίτης, of Leucas, 1824–1879)

Τὴν αὐγὴ μὲ τὴ δροσούλα ἐξεφύτρωσ' ἕνα ρόδο,
Τὴν αὐγὴ μὲ τὴ δροσούλα ἐμαράθηκε τὸ ρόδο!
Γιὰ μιὰν ἄνοιξι μονάχα στὰ περήφανα κλαριά του
Ἐτραγούδησε τ' ἀηδόνι, ἔκαμε καὶ τὴ φωλιά του ...
Σὰν ἡ ἄνοιξι γυρίσῃ καὶ τ' ἀηδόνι σὰ γυρίσῃ,
   Τὴ φωλιά του ποῦ θὰ στήσῃ; ..

Ὅταν ἔβγαινε ἡ σελήνη, ὅταν ἔβγαιναν τ' ἀστέρια,
Μὲ ἀγάπη τὸ ἐθωρούσαν, τοῦ ἁπλώνανε τὰ χέρια.
Σὰν νὰ ἠθέλαν ἐκεῖ ἐπάνω νὰ τὸ πάρουν τὸ καημένο,
Ἔλεγαν πῶς εἶν' ἀδέρφι, ἔλεγαν πῶς πλανημένο
Τ' οὐρανοῦ τὸ μονοπάτι τ' ὀρφανὸ θὰ εἶχε χάσει.
Ὤχ! ἀστέρια! ὤχ ἀστέρια! γρήγορα ποῦ θὰ σᾶς φθάσῃ!

Κάποιοι ποῦ ἤκουσαν τ' ἀηδόνι στὸ κλαρί του νὰ λαλῇ,
Εἶπαν δὲν εἶναι τραγούδι, μοιρολόγι εἶν' ἐκεῖ . . .
Κι ὅσοι εἶδαν τὰς ἀκτῖνας τῶν ἀστέρων τ' οὐρανοῦ
Νὰ γελοῦν νὰ παιγνιδίζουν μὲ τὰ φύλλα τοῦ ὀρφανοῦ,
Εἶπανε τὰ φῶτα ἐκεῖνα ἄχ! δὲν εἶναι τῆς χαρᾶς,
Εἶπαν ὅτι εἶναι τὰ φῶτα νεκρικῆς κεροδοσᾶς.

Τὴν αὐγὴ μὲ τὴ δροσούλα ἐξεφύτρωσ' ἕνα ρόδο,
Τὴν αὐγὴ μὲ τὴ δροσούλα ἐμαράθηκε τὸ ρόδο!

Μὴν ἐπέρασεν ἐκεῖθεν ὁ Βοριὰς ὁ παγωμένος
Καὶ σὰν εἶδε τέτοιο ρόδο ὁ σκληρὸς ἐρωτεμένος,
        Ἅρπαξε τὴ μυρωδιά του
        Καὶ τὴν πῆρε στὰ φτερά του; . . .

Τόσον εἶναι μαραμένο καὶ τὰ φύλλα του ἔχει ἀχνά,
Ὁποῦ λὲς ὅτι γιὰ χρόνους τῆς αὐγούλας ἡ δροσὰ
Δὲν τὸ ἐδρόσισε τὸ μαῦρο. Τόσον εἶναι πικραμένο,
Ὁποῦ λὲς ὅτι ἐπάνω σὲ κορμὶ σαβανωμένο
        Κάποιο χέρι τὸ εἶχε στήσει
        Νεκρικὰ νὰ τὸ στολίσῃ.

Τὴν αὐγὴ μὲ τὴ δροσούλα ἐξεφύτρωσ' ἕνα ρόδο
Τὴν αὐγὴ μὲ τὴ δροσούλα πῶς ἐχάθηκε τὸ ρόδο;

Δὲν τὸ ξεύρω! . . Κάποιος εἶπε, ὅτι ἐψὲς τὸ βράδυ βράδυ
Εἶδε κάποιονε νὰ φεύγη σὰν καπνὸς μὲ τὸν ἀγέρα.
Τ' ἄλογό του ἦτο μαῦρο σὰν τῆς νύχτας τὸ σκοτάδι
        Κ' ἐλαφρὸ σὰν τὸν αἰθέρα,
Εἰς τὸ χέρι του ἐβαστοῦσε ἀχαμνὸ ξεγυμνωμένο
        Ἕνα ρόδο μαραμένο.
Ὅταν ἔφευγε ἀκλουθῶντας τοῦ πελάου τὴν ἄκρη ἄκρη,
        Ἄχ! δὲν ἔχυν' ἕνα δάκρυ,
Μόνον ἔλεγε στὸ κῦμα, ποῦ τὸν βλέπει καὶ τραβειέται,
        „Κύματά μου, εἰπέτε, εἰπέτε,
Δὲν εἶν' ὄμορφο τὸ ρόδο;" Μόνον λέγει στὸ χορτάρι,
        Ποῦ ὑποκάτω ἀπ' τὸ ποδάρι
Τοῦ ἀλόγου του πεθαίνει· „Δὲν εἶμ' ἄξιος κ' ἐγὼ
        Τέτοιο ρόδο νὰ φορῶ;"
Τέτοια ρόδα καὶ τοῦ Χάρου κάνουν ὄμορφα τὰ στήθια.
        Εἶναι ἀλήθεια, εἶν' ἀλήθεια!

13. Ἡ βαρκούλα.

(Ἰούλιος Τυπάλδος, of Cephallenia, 1814–1883)

Ξύπνα γλυκειά μ' ἀγάπη,
    Κ' ἡ νύχτα εἶναι βαθειά.
Κοιμᾶται ὅλ' ἡ φύσις,
    Κ' εἶν' ὅλα σιωπηλά.

Μόνον τ' ἀχνὸ φεγγάρι,
    Ποῦ σὰν ἐμὲ ἀγρυπνᾷ,
Μέσ' στ' οὐρανοῦ ἀρμενίζει
    Τὴν ἥσυχη ἐρημιά.

Ἂν μᾶς χωρίζῃ τώρα
    Μιὰ θέλησι σκληρή,
Μιὰν ἄκραν γῆς θὰ 'βροῦμε
    Νὰ ζήσωμε μαζί.

Ξύπνα γλυκειά μου ἀγάπη,
    Κ' ἡ νύχτα εἶναι βαθειά.
Μᾶς καρτερᾷ ἡ βαρκούλα
    Στὴν ἀκροθαλασσιά.

Κ' ἐνῷ τὸ φεγγαράκι
    Τοὺς φέγγει εὐσπλαχνικό,
Μὲ μάτια δακρυσμένα
    Τὸ χαιρετοῦν κ' οἱ δυό.

14. Ὁ Κλέφτης.

(Ἀλέξανδρος Ρ. Ραγκαβῆς, of Constantinople, 1810–1892)

Μαύρ' εἶν' ἡ νύκτα στὰ βουνά,
    Στοὺς βράχους πέφτει χιόνι·
Στὰ ἄγρια, στὰ σκοτεινά,
Στὲς τραχὲς πέτρες, στὰ στενὰ
    Ὁ κλέφτης ξεσπαθώνει.

Στὸ δεξὶ χέρι τὸ γυμνὸ
    Βαστᾷ ἀστροπελέκι·
Παλάτι ἔχει τὸ βουνό,
Καὶ σκέπασμα τὸν οὐρανό,
    Κ' ἐλπίδα τὸ τουφέκι.

Φεύγουν οἱ τύραννοι χλωμοὶ
　Τὸ μαῦρο του μαχαίρι·
Μ' ἱδρῶτα βρέχει τὸ ψωμί,
Ξέρει νὰ ζήσῃ μὲ τιμή,
　Καὶ νὰ πεθάνῃ ξέρει.

Τὸν κόσμ' ὁ δόλος διοικεῖ,
　Κ' ἡ ἄδικ' εἱμαρμένη·
Τὰ πλούτη ἔχουν οἱ κακοί,
Κ' ἐδὼ στοὺς βράχους κατοικεῖ
　Ἡ ἀρετὴ κρυμμένη.

Μεγάλοι ἔμποροι πωλοῦν
　Τὰ ἔθνη σὰν κοπάδια·
Τὴν γῆν προδίδουν καὶ γελοῦν,
'Εδ' ὅμως ἄρματα λαλοῦν
　Στ' ἀπάτητα λαγκάδια.

Πήγαινε, φίλα τὴν ποδιὰ
　Ποῦ δοῦλοι προσκυνοῦνε·
'Εδὼ στὰ πράσινα κλαδιὰ
Μόν' τὸ σπαθί τους τὰ παιδιὰ
　Καὶ τὸν σταυρὸν φιλοῦνε.

Μητέρα, κλαίς! Ἀναχωρῶ·
　Νὰ μ' εὐχηθῇς γυρεύω·
῍Ενα παιδὶ σὲ ὑστερῶ,
῍Ομως νὰ ζήσω δὲν μπορῶ,
　Ἂν ζῶ γιὰ νὰ δουλεύω.

Μὴ κλαίτε, μάτια γαλανά,
　Φωστῆρες ποῦ ἀρέσω·
Τὸ δάκρυόν σας μὲ πλανᾷ.
'Ελεύθερος ζῶ στὰ βουνὰ
　Κ' ἐλεύθερος θὰ πέσω.

Βαρειὰ βαρειὰ βοΐζ' ἡ γῆ . . . . .
　῍Ενα τουφέκι πέφτει.
Παντοῦ τρομάρα καὶ σφαγή,
'Εδὼ φυγή, ἐκεῖ πληγή! . .
　'Εσκότωσαν τὸν κλέφτη.

Σύντροφοι ἄσκεποι, πεζοὶ
Τὸν φέρνουν λυπημένοι
Καὶ τραγουδοῦν ὅλοι μαζί·
„Ἐλεύθερος ὁ κλέφτης ζῆ,
Κ' ἐλεύθερος πεθαίνει."

15. Τὸ ὀρφανὸ τῆς Κρήτης[1]).

(Ἀχιλλεὺς Παράσχος, of Nauplia, 1833–1895)

Ἕνα παιδάκι ἐπροχθὲς σὰν κρίνο μαραμένο,
    Εἰς ἕνα δρόμο σκοτεινό,
    Ἐκύτταζε τὸν οὐρανὸ
    Μὲ μάτι δακρυσμένο.

Μαῦρα φοροῦσε τὸ πτωχὸ κ' ἐκεῖνο σὰν ἐμένα
    Κ' εἶχε τὴν ὄψι θλιβερή.
    Πῶς ἀγαπῶ ὅποιον φορεῖ
    Ἐνδύματα θλιμμένα!

Μοσχοβολοῦσε ἀρχοντιά, κι ἃς ἦτον γυμνωμένο.
    Ἀκόμα χθὲς μέσ' στὴ φωλιά,
    Στῆς μάννας του τὴν ἀγκαλιὰ
    Πετοῦσε τὸ καημένο.

Ὅμως τουφέκια βρόντησαν στὴν Κρήτην μιὰν ἡμέρα·
    -    Τοῦ πῆρ' ἀγέρι τὴ φωλιά,
    Τὴ μάννα Τούρκου πιστολιά,
    Κ' ἡ μάχη τὸν πατέρα.

Ἀμίλητο καὶ σκυθρωπὸ τὸ δάκρυ του κρατοῦσε
    Κι ἅπλωνε χέρι μ' ἐντροπή·
    Ὅμως δὲν ἤθελε νὰ πῇ,
    Τὸ μαῦρο, πῶς πεινοῦσε.

Ἄχ! ὅποιος δὲν ἐπείνασε, „πεινῶ" ποτὲ δὲν λέγει·
    Δὲν τὸν ἀφήνουν οἱ λυγμοί·
    Κυττάζει μόνον τὸ ψωμὶ
    Ἀπὸ μακρειὰ καὶ κλαίγει . . .

Στὴν ἀγκαλιά μου τὸ 'βαλα μὲ πόνο τὸ καημένο
    Καὶ τοῦ 'δωκα πικρὸ φιλί·
    Ὅμως αὐτὸ τί ὠφελεῖ
    Στὸ ἔρημο τὸ ξένο;

[1]) Composed on the occasion of the insurrection in Crete, 1867.

Γιὰ τοῦτο σήμερα κ' ἐγὼ τὰ χέρια μου σταυρώνω,
Κι ὅτι γιὰ μένα δὲν ζητῶ,
Γι' αὐτὸ γυρεύω καὶ γι' αὐτὸ
Πόνου φωνὴν ὑψώνω.

Μητέρες! ὅπου ἔχετε παιδιὰ εὐτυχισμένα
Καὶ καλοσύνη στὴν καρδιά·
Πεινοῦν τῆς Κρήτης τὰ παιδιὰ
Καὶ κρυώνουν τὰ καημένα!

16. Ὁ μανάβης.

(Δ. Κόκκος, of Andritsena, 1856–1891)

„Πάρτε σταφύλια ραζακιά, πάρτε γλυκὰ σταφύλια . . .“
— Ἔχω ροδίτες τραγανοὺς τὰ ρόδινά της χείλια!
„Πάρτε γλυκὰ ροδάκινα, μὲ βελουδένιο χνοῦδο . . .“
— Ἔχω τὰ δυό της μάγουλα ἀτίμητο βελοῦδο!
„Πάρτε περιβολάρικα καὶ μελωμένα σῦκα . . .“
— Μανάβη, ἡ ἀγάπη μου εἶναι γεμάτη γλύκα!

17. Ὁ χαροκαημένος.

(Γεράσιμος Μαρκορᾶς, of Cephallenia, b. 1826)

Ἕνας θλιμμένος ποιητὴς ἐκύτταζε μία μέρα
Μὲ βλέμμα κρύο τὴ θάλασσα, τὴ γῆ καὶ τὸν αἰθέρα·
Τ' ἄνθια, τὸ φῶς, τὰ κύματα χαμογελούσαν, δίχως
Ν' ἀνοίξη μέσα του ἡ ψυχὴ καὶ νὰ πετάξη ὁ στίχος·
Γιατί μία τόση ἀναισθησιὰ καὶ ξένη λαύρα τόση;
Στὰ φυλλοκάρδια ὁ θάνατος τὸν εἶχε φαρμακώσει.
Λόγο δὲν ἔβγανε· μὲ μιᾶς περίσσια κατεβαίνουν
Πουλάκια ὡραῖα τριγύρω του καὶ ἀδελφικὰ του κρένουν·
„Στὴ συφορὰ ποῦ σ' εὕρηκε, στὸν πόνο τῆς ψυχῆς σου,
Πετούμενο τοῦ Παρνασσοῦ, τ' ἄλλα πουλιὰ μιμήσου·
Ἀγκαλὰ πέφτει καὶ σ' ἐμᾶς πικρὸ θανάτου βόλι,
Κιλαϊδισμὸς ἀτέλειωτος εἶναι ἡ ζωή μας ὅλη.“

18. Ξενιτειά.

(Γιάννης Καμπύσης, of Corona in Messenia, 1872–1901)

Ὁ κόσμος ποῦ δὲν πλάστηκε συντρίβεται,
Κ' εἶν' ἔρμο τὸ μυαλό μου·
Γυρίζω ὁλοῦθε κι ἀνωφέλευτα γυρίζω,
Γιατί εἶμαι ἀπόξενο πουλὶ φερμένο ἀπὸ ἄλλον κόσμο.

Ψέλνω τραγούδι ἀγνώριστο,
Κάποια ὁλομόναχη ψυχὴ νὰ συγκινήσω,
Κι ἀντιλαλάει μὲ μένα ὁ πόθος τῆς ἀγάπης
Ἀπὸ τὴ γῆς ἀνάκουστος ἀπάνου στὰ φεγγάρια.

Εἶμαι τὸ ἀπόξενο πουλὶ κάποιου ἄλλου κόσμου,
Ποιὸς ξέρει· πῶς ἐδὼ ἀποπλανημένο.
Μὲ σφίγγει ὁλοῦθε ἡ ξενιτειά,
Κι ὅπου διαβῶ κι ὅπου σταθῶ, δὲ βρίσκω μιὰ πατρίδα.

19. Τραγουδάκι.

(Ἰωάννης Παπαδιαμαντόπουλος, known as a French poet under the pseudonym Jean Moréas, of Athens, 1856–1910)

Ὅπου σταθῶ, ὅπου γυρίσω,
Στὸν κόσμο ἢ στὴν ἐρημιά,
Παντοῦ καὶ πάντα θ' ἀντικρύσω
Τὴν ἐδική σου ζωγραφιά.

Βλέπω τὰ μαῦρα τὰ μαλλιά σου
Μέσ' στὸ σκοτάδι τὸ βαθύ,
Βλέπω τὴ φλογερὴ ματιά σου
Στοῦ ἥλιου τὴ φεγγοβολή·

Τὰ στήθια σου τὰ χιονισμένα
Στὴν ἀνθισμένη μυγδαλιά,
Στὰ ρόδα τὰ μισανοιγμένα
Τὰ χείλη σου τὰ δροσερά·

Βρίσκω τὴν ἄδολη πνοή σου
Εἰς τὸ θυμάρι τοῦ βουνοῦ,
Ἀκούω τὴ γλυκειὰ φωνή σου
Εἰς τὸ τραγούδι τοῦ ἀηδονιοῦ.

Ἄχ, καὶ στοῦ τάφου της τὸ χῶμα
Ἡ πονεμένη μου ψυχὴ
Θὰ ὀνειρεύεται ἀκόμα
Τὴν ὄψι σου τὴν τρυφερή.

20. Στὴ ρεματιά.

(Γεώργιος Δροσίνης, of Missolonghi, b. in Athens, 1859)

Ἔλα, πὰρ' τὸ μονοπάτι
Θαρρετά, γοργὰ καὶ μόνη
Καὶ μὲ πονηριὰ περπάτει,

Μὴ σὲ νοιώσουν οἱ γειτόνοι.
Μέσ' στὴ ρεματιά, ποὺ τρέχει
Χρυσὸ φίδι τὸ νερὸ
Καὶ χνουδάτους βράχους βρέχει,
Ἔλα καὶ σὲ καρτερῶ.

Κάτω ἐκεῖ ποὺ τὰ πλατάνια
Μὲ θεώρατα κλαριὰ
Συννεφιάζουν τὰ οὐράνια
Καὶ τοῦ ἥλιου τὴ θωριά,
Ποῦ καὶ μέσ' στὸ καλοκαίρι
Χόρτο ὁλόδροσο ἔχει βγεῖ
Καὶ φυσᾷ γλυκὰ τ' ἀγέρι,
Σὲ προσμένω ἀπ' τὴν αὐγή.

Ἔλ' ἀγάπη μου, ἐκεῖ πέρα
Μακρει' ἀπὸ τὸ χωριό μας,
Νὰ περάσωμε μιὰ μέρα
Ἀλησμόνητην οἱ δυό μας·
Ἔλα ἐκεῖ καὶ σὲ προσμένω
Σὲ μιὰν ἄκρη Ζηλευτή,
Ποῦ δὲν βλέπει μάτι ξένο,
Δὲν ἀκούει ξένο αὐτί.

Ὄχι, δὲ θὰ ξεστομίσω
Λόγι' ἀγάπης πονεμένης,
Ἔλα καὶ δὲ θὰ δακρύσω,
Ὅσο ἐσὺ κοντά μου μένεις.
Καθὼς θέλεις, ἐκεῖ πέρα
Θά 'μαι πάντα χαρωπός,
Ὅπου θὰ βραδυάσῃ ἡ μέρα,
Καὶ δὲ θὰ τὸ νοιώσῃς πῶς.

Ἄν πεινᾷς, δὲ θὰ σ' ἀφήσω
Νηστική, καστανομάτα.
Σὰν πουλὶ θὰ σὲ ταΐσω
Μαῦρα μοῦρ' ἀπὸ τὰ βάτα.
Κι ἂν τυχὸν πάλι διψάσῃς
Κ' ἔχεις στόμα φλογερό,
Θὰ σοῦ φέρω νὰ χορτάσῃς
Στὲς παλάμες μου νερό.

Κι ἂν νυστάξῃς, θὰ σοῦ στρώσω
Στρῶμα μαλακὸ στὴ φτέρη,
Κι ἅμα κοιμηθῆς, θ' ἁπλώσω
Στὸ κεφάλι σου τὸ χέρι,
Τῆς ἀγάπης τὸ στεφάνι
Νὰ σοῦ βάλω, ὑπναροῦ,
Ποῦ Νεράϊδες τό 'χουν κάνει
Ἀπὸ τ' ἄνθη τοῦ νεροῦ.

21. Ἡ ὑστερνὴ ματιά της.
(Κωστῆς Παλαμᾶς, of Missolonghi, b. 1859)

Ὅταν ἡ δόλια ἡ μάννα μου τὸν κόσμο παραιτοῦσε,
Μ' ἐπῆγαν κ' ἐγονάτισα, μικρὸ πουλί, μπροστά της,
Τὴν τελευταία της πνοὴ ὁ Χάρος ἐροφοῦσε,
Κ' ἔμενε μόνο θλιβερή, σὰν κάτι νὰ ζητοῦσε,
    Ἡ ὑστερνὴ ματιά της.

Νὰ σβήσῃ δὲν τὴν ἄφηνε σὰ φῶς ἀπὸ καντήλι,
Προτοῦ τῆς εὕρη μιὰ φωλιὰ νὰ μοιάζῃ τὴ φωλιά της.
Σ' ἄλλη καντήλα ἤθελε τὸ φῶς της νὰ τὸ στείλη,
Καὶ ἦρθε μέσ' στὰ μάτια μου καὶ πάλι ν' ἀνατείλη
    Ἡ ὑστερνὴ ματιά της.

Καὶ ἀπὸ τότε ὅτι θωρῶ καὶ σ' ὅτι σταματήσω
Τὸ κουρασμένο βῆμα μου, πικρῆς ζωῆς διαβάτης,
Σὰ μάννα θὰ τ' ἀγκαλιασθῶ καὶ θὰ τὸ ἀγαπήσω,
Γιατ' εἶναι μέσ' στὰ μάτια μου, ὅσο νὰ ξεψυχήσω,
    Ἡ ὑστερνὴ ματιά της.

22. Ἀθῆναι.[1]
(Ἰωάννης Πολέμης, of Andros, b. 1862)

Τὴν ὥρα ὅπου χρυσόφωτος ὁ ἥλιος βασιλεύει
    Καὶ χύνεται περήφανος στὴ δύσι,
Ἡ δόξα ἀπ' τὸν παράδεισο ἄνθη χλωρὰ μαζεύει,
    Τὸ μέτωπό σου, Ἀθήνα, νὰ στολίσῃ.

Καὶ τὰ σκορπίζει ὁλόγυρα στὸ οὐράνιο σου κεφάλι
    Καὶ πρὸς τὸν Παρθενῶνα κατεβαίνει
Καὶ βλέπει τὰ συντρίμμια σου κι ἀναγαλλιάζει πάλι,
    Πατρίδα μου, Ἀθήνα δοξασμένη!

[1] The literary form.

Κι ὁ κόσμος βλέπει τ' ἄνθη σου, μὰ ὁ νοῦς του δὲν τὰ φθάνει
Καὶ σύννεφα πῶς εἶναι τὰ νομίζει,
Καὶ δὲν πιστεύει πῶς θωρεῖ τ' ἀνθόπλεκτο στεφάνι,
Ποῦ ἡ Δόξα κάθε βράδυ σοῦ χαρίζει.

23. Στιγμαὶ [1]) ποιητικῆς ἀδυναμίας.

('Αριστομένης Προβελέγγιος, b. 1850 in Siphnos)

Ξεύρω ποτάμια ποῦ κυλοῦν περήφανα κι ἀφρίζουν
Καὶ μέσ' στὰ διάφανα νερά των,
Τὰ γαλανὰ οὐράνια, τὴν πλάσι καθρεφτίζουν,
Κι ὅθε περνοῦν, μαγεύουνε μὲ τὸ μουρμούρισμά των.

Μὰ ἔξαφνα τὸ ρεῦμα των γκρεμίζεται καὶ πάει
Κάτω σὲ χάλαρα βαθειὰ καὶ πιὰ στὸ φῶς δὲν βγαίνει.
Στὰ τάρταρα ἠχολογᾷ, βογγᾷ καὶ τραγουδάει,
Σὰν ἄλλου κόσμου μουσική. Ποῦ τάχα νὰ πηγαίνη;

Ἔτσι καὶ τὸ τραγούδι μου, ποῦ εἶχεν ἀναβρύσει
Ἀπ' τὴν καρδιά μου ὡσὰν βρύσι,
Ξάφνω καταχωνιάστηκε, ἀνέλπιστα ἐχάθη
Στοῦ στήθους μου τὰ τρίσβαθα, σκοτεινιασμένα βάθη.

Ἐκεῖ ἀκούω μουσική, ἐκεῖ τραγούδια νοιώθω
Γλυκά, οὐράνια, μαγεμένα,
Καὶ μ' ὅλο τὸν ἐγκάρδιο, τὸν φλογερό μου πόθο,
Ἄχ, νὰ ξεθάψω δὲν μπορῶ τραγούδι μου κανένα.

Ποιὰ δύναμις, ποιᾶς μάγισσας θὰ τὰ λυτρώσῃ χέρι
Ἀπ' τῆς καρδιᾶς μου τὰ σκοτάδια,
Νὰ γλυκομουρμουρίσουνε μὲ τ' οὐρανοῦ τ' ἀγέρι
Καὶ στῆς ζωῆς τὰ φωτερὰ νὰ τρέξουνε λαγκάδια;

Ἀγάπη, ποῦ σὰν Μωϋσῆς ἀνοίγεις βρύσι κρύα
Καὶ στ' ἄκαρπο λιθάρι ἀκόμα,
Ποῦ καὶ τὸ πιὸ κακόφωνο ἐσὺ μανθάνεις στόμα
Ἤχους νὰ βρίσκῃ τρυφερούς, νὰ πνέῃ ἁρμονία!

Ἀγάπη παντοδύναμι, σὺ τὴν καρδιά μου σεῖσε,
Τὰ πέτρινα πλευρά της σχίσε,
Ν' ἀνοίξουν ἄμετρες πηγὲς κ' ἐκεῖθε νὰ πηδήσῃ
Τοῦ τραγουδιοῦ μου ὁ ποταμὸς τὴν πλάσι νὰ φιλήσῃ.

---

[1]) Form of the literary language for στιγμές.

24. Ὄνειρο.

(Στυλιανὸς Χρυσομάλλης, of Argostoli in Cephallenia)

Εἶδα πουρνὸ σ' ἔν' ὄνειρο, σταλμένο
Ἀπὸ κάποια ψυχὴ ποῦ μ' ἀγαπάει,
Ἕναν ἄγγελ' ὡραῖο, χαριτωμένο,
Στὸ κρεββάτι μου ἀντίκρυ ν' ἀκουμπάῃ·

„Εἶμαι ὁ θάνατος“, μοῦ εἶπε, „καὶ προσμένω,
Ἀφοῦ τόσο ἡ καρδιά σου τὸ ζητάει,
Νὰ σὲ πάρω ἀπ' τὸν κόσμο τὸ θλιμμένο
Στ' ἀστέρια ὅπου ἡ χαρὰ ἠχολογάει.

Ναί, θὰ σοῦ δώσω ἕνα φιλὶ στὸ στόμα,
Τόσο γλυκό, ποῦ τέλεια μαγεμένη
Ἡ ψυχή σου θὰ φύγῃ ἀπὸ τὸ σῶμα.“

Ἔσκυψε, ἅμα εἶπε αὐτά, νὰ μὲ φιλήσῃ·
Ξύπνησα, ὦἴμέ! . . . Τώρα ὁ καημὸς μοῦ μένει,
Ποῦ ἀφίλητο τὸ στόμα μὅχει ἀφήσει.

25. Ματαιοδοξία.

(Ἕρμονας, pseudonym for Πέτρος Βλαστός, b. 1879 in India)

Μέσ' στὴν καρδιά μου κύτταξα καὶ Μέδουσα πανώρια
Ξαντίκρυσα, ποῦ μάγισσας ἀγέλαστα καὶ κρύα
Μάτια ἀργοσάλευε. Ἅλικα τὰ χείλια της γυαλίζαν
Κ' ὑγρά, σὰ δάγκαμα ἔρωτα νὰ τά 'χε ματωμένα.

Κι ὅτι καλὸ εἶχα μέσα μου, πρᾶξες ἁγνὲς κ' ἰδέες
Καὶ θύμησες παιδιάτικες κι ἀγάπες καὶ λατρεία
Τῆς ὀμορφιᾶς, τῆς τά 'δινα μ' ἀγγαρεμένα χέρια,
Τῆς τά 'δινα, καὶ τὸ θεριὸ τὰ ξέσκισε ρουφῶντας

Σὰν αἷμα θείας ἡδονῆς ἀπ' τ' ἀνοιχτά τους σπλάχνα.
Κι ἀφάγανη ὅσο σπάραζε, τόσο κ' ἡ ὀμορφιά της
Ἀβγάτιζε κι ἀκράνοιγε τὸ στόμα γαυριασμένη.

Καὶ σκλάβου μοῦ 'ρθε πιθυμιά, νὰ μπόρεγα νὰ πνίξω
Μέσ' στὴν καρδιά μου κεῖ βαθειὰ τὴν ἄπονη τὴ Στρίγλα,
Ποῦ τῆς ζωῆς μου τὸ χυμὸ τυραννικὰ στερεύει.

b. Prose.

1. Χαμένα λόγια[1]).

(Jean Psichari [Ψυχάρης], 1888.)

Κάποτες μ' ἔρχεται[2]) νὰ φωνάξω δυνατά, ποῦ[3]) ὅλος ὁ κόσμος νὰ μ' ἀκούσῃ· „Μή! μή! μή! μὴ χαλνᾶτε τὴ γλῶσσα[4])! καταστρέφετε τὴν ἀρχαία καὶ τὴ νέα μαζί. Θέλετε γλῶσσα ποῦ νὰ μοιάζῃ τόντις μὲ τὴν ἀρχαία, ποῦ νὰ εἶναι ἡ ἴδια γλῶσσα; Πάρτε τὴ γλῶσσα τοῦ λαοῦ. Θέλετε ξένη γλῶσσα; Πάρτε τὴν καθαρέβουσα· θὰ δείξῃ σ' ὅλο τὸν κόσμο, ποῦ[5]) τόντις χάθηκε ἡ ἀρχαία. Θέλετε νὰ παίξετε; θέλετε νοστιμάδες, χωρατάδες καὶ κωμῳδίες; Τότες νὰ γράφετε τὴν καθαρέβουσα! Θέλετε ἐπιστήμη, κόπο καὶ μάθηση; θέλετε νὰ πιάσετε σοβαρὴ δουλειά; Νὰ γρά-φετε τὴν ἐθνική σας γλῶσσα. Ἀπὸ τὴν ἀπόφασή σας, θὰ φανῇ ἂν εἶστε ἢ ἄντρες ἢ παιδιά.

Ἀφῆστε τὴν ψεφτομάθηση, τὴν ψεφτοσοφία, τοὺς συμβι-βασμοὺς καὶ τοὺς δασκάλους. Μὴν πιστέβετε ὅσα λέν[6]), ποῦ[5]) βαθμηδὸν[7]) ἡ γλῶσσα θὰ καλητερέψῃ καὶ ποῦ θὰ γράφουμε μιὰ μέρα σὰν τὸν Ξενοφῶντα. Μόνο ποῦ σᾶς λέει κανεὶς τέτοιο λόγο, σᾶς δείχτει ποῦ[5]) δὲν κατάλαβε ἀκόμη μήτε τί εἶναι Ξενο-φῶντας[8]) μήτε τί θὰ πῇ γλῶσσα. Βαθμηδὸν[7]) ξέρετε τί θὰ γίνη; Θὰ χαθῇ ἡ ἐθνική μας γλῶσσα καὶ θαφανίσετε τὴν ἀρχαία. Τί μὲ μέλει ποῦ θυμώνετε τώρα μ' ὅσους σᾶς μιλοῦν ἔτσι; Μιὰ μέρα θὰ καταλάβετε οἱ ἴδιοι τὸ κακὸ ποῦ μᾶς κάμετε[9]) ὅλους· θὰ κλαῖτε καὶ θὰ λυπᾶστε καὶ δὲ θὰ μπορῆτε πιὰ νὰ διορθώσετε τὸ λάθος σας[10]). Ἄχ! τί βάσανο ποῦ εἶναι νὰ βλέπῃ κανεὶς τὴν ἀλή-θεια καὶ νὰ μὴν μπορῇ νὰ τὴ δείξῃ στοὺς ἄλλους!

Μὴν τὰ θέλετε ὅλα μισά. Ἀμάθεια καὶ περηφάνεια σᾶς ἔφεραν[11]) τέτοιο κακό· περηφάνεια, γιατί[12]) θέλει ὁ καθένας νὰ φαντάξῃ καὶ νὰ μὴν εἶναι σὰν τὸ λαό· ἀμάθεια, γιατί καταντήσαμε νὰ μὴν ξέρουμε τὴ γλῶσσα τοῦ λαοῦ, γιατί τόλμησαν[13]) οἱ δασκάλοι νὰ βρίσουν[14]) ὅλο τὸ ἔθνος καὶ νὰ πούνε βάρβαρη μιὰ γλῶσσα,

---

[1]) In regard to the author's orthography (which has been retained, see the Foreword) it should be particularly noticed that he writes the diphthongs αυ, ευ according to the sound which follows, αφ εφ or αβ εβ. The alterations in the second edition (1905) are given in the following footnotes, the orthographical changes only in the first instance in which they are found.   [2]) μοῦ ἔρχεται.   [3]) ποῦ.   [4]) γλώσσα.   [5]) πῶς.   [6]) λένε.
[7]) βαθμηδό.   [8]) Ξενοφώντας.   [9]) κάματε.   [10]) τὸ κακό instead of τὸ λ. σ.
[11]) φέρανε.   [12]) γιατὶ.   [13]) τολμήσανε.   [14]) βρίσουνε.

ποῦ δὲν τὴ σπούδαξαν¹⁵) ἀκόμη. Ἀφτὴ ἡ γλῶσσα ὅμως ὑπάρχει·
μπορεῖτε νὰ τὴν κάμετε κομμάτια· κανεὶς δὲ θὰ μᾶς τὴ σηκώση.
Μὲ κανέναν τρόπο δὲ θὰ γυρίση πίσω ἡ ἀρχαία. Οἱ ἱστορικοὶ
νόμοι γιὰ σᾶς δὲ θἀλλάξουν¹⁶).· Τοῦ κάκου βρίζετε τὴν ἐθνική
μας γλῶσσα καὶ τὴ λέτε πρόστυχη, καὶ καμώνεστε πῶς μήτε ξέρετε
τί εἶναι, καὶ πολεμᾶτε νὰ μᾶς δείξετε, ποῦ⁵) μιλεῖτε τὴν ἀρχαία,
ποῦ⁵) ἡ ἀρχαία ἀκόμη ζῆ.

Ποτές, ὄχι! ποτὲς δὲ θὰ κάμετε τὸν κόσμο νὰ σᾶς πιστέψῃ.
Τοῦ κάκου γράφετε γραμματικὲς τῆς καθωμιλημένης καὶ βάζετε
μέσα ὅλη τὴν ἀρχαία γραμματική, περιττοσύλλαβα, ὑπερσυντελικοὺς
καὶ μετοχές, ὕστερα μάλιστα χαρίζετε τὰ βιβλία σας στοὺς ξένους,
τάχατις γιὰ νὰ σᾶς καμαρώσουν¹⁷). Πάντα θὰ σᾶς καταδικάσῃ ἡ
ἐπιστήμη κ' ἡ ὀρθὴ κρίση. Πάντα κάπου θὰ βρεθῆ ἕνας νὰ σᾶς
τὸ πῆ — κι¹⁸)· ἂν πάλε δὲ βρεθῆ, δὲν πειράζει! Ἡ ἀλήθεια θὰ
μείνη ἀλήθεια. Ἡ ἀλήθεια, γιὰ νὰ ὑπάρχη, δὲν ἔχει ἀνάγκη μήτε
νὰ τὴ διοῦμε¹⁹), μήτε μάλιστα νὰ ξέρουμε τὴν ὕπαρξή της. Ἡ ἀλή-
θεια²⁰) μοιάζει μὲ τὰ μακρινὰ τἄστρα²¹) ποῦ δὲ φαίνουνται μέσα
στὸν οὐρανό, κι²²) ὡς τόσο λάμπουν²³) ὁλομόναχα, κι ἂς μὴν τὰ
βλέπη κανένας!

Ἡ καρδιά μου πονεῖ νὰ σᾶς ἀκούω! Τὸ χαμό σας θέλετε·
τὸ κακό σας γυρέβετε μόνο. Ἂν ἤξεραν²⁴) οἱ δασκάλοι τὴν ἀρχαία
μὲ τὰ σωστά τους, δὲ θὰ πολεμοῦσαν²⁵) κάθε ὥρα νὰ μᾶς δείξουν²⁶)
πῶς τὴν ξέρουν²⁷) καὶ θἄγραφαν²⁸) τὴ δημοτική, ἀφοῦ κ' οἱ ἀρ-
χαῖοι οἱ ἴδιοι ἔγραφαν²⁹) τὴ δημοτική τους γλῶσσα. Μὲ τὴν ψεφτο-
γραμματικὴ δὲ φτειάνεται γλῶσσα, δὲ φτειάνεται φιλολογία. Τί
λόγια νὰ βρῶ γιὰ νὰ μὲ πιστέψετε; Χαλνᾶτε μιὰ γλῶσσα ποῦ
εἶναι θησαβρὸς γιὰ τὴν ἐπιστήμη, ποῦ θὰ σᾶς δοξάση στὸν κόσμο.
Χαλνᾶτε μιὰ γλῶσσα ποῦ μόνη της μπορεῖ νὰ σᾶς δώση μιὰ μέρα
ἐθνικὴ φιλολογία, ποίηση καὶ φήμη, μιὰ γλῶσσα ποῦ θὰ σᾶς κάμη
νὰ μοιάξετε ἴσως καὶ σεῖς τοὺς ἀρχαίους. Μή! Μή! Μή!"

Ἄχ! Νὰ εἴμουν³⁰) κάτι καὶ γώ! Νὰ μποροῦσε κανεὶς νὰ
μ' ἀκούσῃ! Ἀφτὸ τὸ κεφάλαιο νὰ μποροῦσαν³¹) ὅλοι νὰ τὸ δια-
βάσουν³²) — καὶ νὰ μὲ πιστέψουν³³)! Τί ζητοῦμε; τὸ καλό. Τί
πολεμοῦμε; νὰ προκόψῃ, νὰ μεγαλώση τὸ ἔθνος. Ἔπρεπε κ' οἱ
δασκάλοι νὰ εἶναι μαζί μας. Ἀφτὸ θέλουν³⁴) καὶ κεῖνοι· ἂς διοῦν³⁵)

---

¹⁵) σπουδάσανε.   ¹⁶) θἀλλάζουνε.   ¹⁷) καμαρώσουνε.   ¹⁸) κι.
¹⁹) βλέπουμε.   ²⁰) κάποτες added.   ²¹) μὲ τἀστέρια τὰ μακρινὰ.   ²²) κι.
²³) λάμπουνε.   ²⁴) ξέρανε.   ²⁵) πολεμούσανε.   ²⁶) δείξουνε.   ²⁷) ξέρουνε.
²⁸) θὰ γράφανε.   ²⁹) γράφανε.   ³⁰) εἴμουνε.   ³¹) μπορούσανε.   ³²) δια-
βάσουνε.   ³³) πιστέψουνε.   ³⁴) θέλουνε.   ³⁵) διοῦνε.

τὸ λοιπό, μὲ τί τρόπο θὰ τὸ κατορθώσουν³⁶). Ἂς πάρουν³⁷) καλήτερο δρόμο. Ἄχ! νὰ μᾶς ἔκαμαν³⁸) τουλάχιστο μιὰ παραχώρηση· νὰ μὴ λὲν³⁹) πρόστυχη τὴ γλῶσσα τοῦ λαοῦ, νὰ μάθουν⁴⁰) τέλος πάντα ποῦ⁴¹) ὁ λαὸς καὶ μόνος ὁ λαὸς ἔκαμε καὶ κάμνει⁴²) ὅλες τὶς γλῶσσες τοῦ κόσμου. Τόσο μ' ἔφτανε⁴³) κι ἄλλο δὲ θὰ ζητοῦσα. Τότες δὲ θὰ μ' ἔμελε γιὰ τίποτις πιὰ⁴⁴) καὶ θὰ πρόσμενα τὸ θάνατο μὲ χαρά.

2. Τὰ ὀνόματά μας.

(Ἀργύρης Ἐφταλιώτης, 1890.)

Οἱ σφαγὲς τῶν Ψαρῶν καὶ τῆς Χίος εἶναι μικροδουλειὲς ἐμπρὸς στὴν καταστροφὴν ποὺ ἔπεσε στὰ ὀνόματά μας, σὰν ἄρχισε τὸ ἔθνος νὰ τὸ αἰσθάνεται, πῶς ξαναγεννήθηκε. Ἡ ἰδέα, πῶς θὰ γυρίσουμε δυὸ τρεῖς χιλιάδες χρόνια πίσω καὶ θὰ περπατοῦμε μέσα στὴν ἀγορὰ νὰ ρωτοῦμε „λέγεταί τι καινόν;" ἐριζοβόλησε τόσο βαθειὰ στὴν καρδιά μας, ποὺ κατάντησε σήμερα νὰ χρειάζεται γιατρικὸ συμβούλιο γιὰ νὰ μᾶς γιατρέψῃ!

Ἦτανε μεγάλη καὶ ὅμορφη ἰδέα στὸν καιρό της, τότες ποὺ ἀγωνιζούμαστε καὶ σέρναμε ὅλον τὸν πολιτισμένο κόσμο κατόπι μας, γιατί αὐτὸς δὲν ἤξερε παρὰ τὰ παλιά μας, κ' ἐνθουσιαζούτανε νὰ βλέπῃ μιὰ τέτοια μεγάλη καὶ λαμπρὰ νεκρανάστασι. Οἱ ἰδέες ὅμως εἶναι σύννεφα καὶ περνοῦν, ἡ Εὐρώπη ἀπὸ τότες ὡς ἐσήμερα ἄλλαξε σ' ἕνα τέτοιο βαθμό, ποὺ καὶ ὁ Βύρωνας, ἀκόμη νὰ ζοῦσε, θὰ μᾶς ἔγραφε διατριβὲς γιὰ τὲς θεωρίες τοῦ Δαρβίνου, — κ' ἐμεῖς ἐπάθαμε τὸ νόστιμο τοῦ Νασρεδδὶν Χότζα μὲ τὸ νέφτι· ἔχουμε ἀκόμη πολὺ δρόμο νὰ πάρουμε!

Ἀρχίσαμε φυσικὰ ἀπὸ τὰ εὐκολώτερα· ἀπ' τὰ ὀνόματα, κι ἀπ' τὴ γλῶσσα. Στὰ ὀνόματα τὸ καταφέραμε, γιὰ τὴ γλῶσσα δὲν εἶναι δική μου δουλειὰ νὰ τὸ ἐξετάσω. Μὰ ἐκεῖνο ποὺ μὲ κάνει καμιὰ φορὰ νὰ χαμογελῶ, ὅσο χολιασμένος κι ἂν εἶμαι γιὰ τὴν καταστροφὴ ποὺ γένηκε, εἶναι ποὺ κανενός μας δὲν ἦλθε στὸ νοῦ του νὰ φορέσῃ κ' ἕνα τρίβωνα! Ἢ κἂν νὰ παίρνῃ κ' ἕνα λουτρὸ πρὶν καθίζῃ στὸ φαγί του! Τέλος πάντων νὰ γίνῃ μιὰν ἀρχὴ καὶ νὰ γυρίσουν ὅλα τὰ παλιά, εἰδεμὴ πῶς θὰ βασταχθῇ μιὰ ἀττικὴ γλῶσσα δίχως ἀττικὴ ζωή!

Σὰν νὰ μισομετανοιώνω ποὺ τὸ εἶπα, γιατί μπορεῖ νὰ τὸ καταπιαστῇ κανένας καὶ τοῦτο!

---

³⁶) κατορθώσουνε.   ³⁷) πάρουνε.   ³⁸) κάνανε.   ³⁹) λένε.
⁴⁰) μάθουνε.   ⁴¹) πώς.   ⁴²) κάνει.   ⁴³) μοῦ ἔφτανε.   ⁴⁴) μοῦ ἔμελε
πια γιὰ τίποτα.

Ἂς ἔλθουμε στὰ ὀνόματα.

Θυμοῦμαι ἀκόμα σὰν ἦλθε ὁ πρῶτος Δημοτικὸς Δάσκαλος στὸ χωριό μας. Ἦτανε καλὸς ὁ καημένος, καὶ μᾶς ἔφερε πολλὲς καλὲς ἰδέες. Μᾶς ἔκαμε Βιβλιοθήκη, μᾶς ἔβγαζε περίπατο, μᾶς ἐμάθαινε νὰ συλλογιζούμαστε μὲ τὲς ἐρωτήσεις του (θυμοῦμαι ἀκόμα σὰν μ' ἐρώτησε, ἂν ἤθελα νὰ εἶμαι Λεωνίδας ἢ Ἐφιάλτης, καὶ ἐπειδὴ τὸ δεύτερο μοῦ φάνηκε πλιὸ καινούργιο, τοῦ εἶπα „Ἐφιάλτης" — κι ἀκόμα κοκκινίζω σὰν τὸ συλλογοῦμαι!), μὰ εἶχε κι αὐτὸς μαζὶ μὲ ὅλην τὴν ἀναστημένη Ρωμιοσύνη τὴν πετριὰ τῶν ἑλληνικῶν ὀνομάτων. Καὶ τί τὰ θέτε, τὴν πρώτη μέρα ποὺ μᾶς μάζεψε στὴν παράδοσι, μᾶς κατέσφαξε ὅλους! Ὅσα φαμιλικὰ ὀνόματα μπορούσαν νὰ „ἐξελληνισθοῦν", ἐξελληνισθήκανε. Ὁ Κυριαζῆς ἔγινε Κυριακοῦ, ὁ Κωσταντάρας Κωνσταντίνου, κι ἂν ἤτανε καὶ κανένας Καπλάνογλους, θὰ γινούντανε κι αὐτὸς Λεοντίδης. Ὅσα πάλι δὲν μεταφραζούντανε, τὰ ἔρριξε ὅλα, σὰν ἀδιόρθωτα ὁπου ἦταν, κάτω στὸ Σπαρτιατικὸ βάραθρο, πῆρε τὰ βαφτιστικὰ τῶν πατέρων μας, ἔβγαλε ἀπὸ τὸ σακκί του μερικὲς φουχτιὲς -ίδης καὶ -άδης, μᾶς τὰ κόλλησε μιὰ 'μορφιά, καὶ μπολιασθήκαμε ὅλοι Ἕλληνες χωρὶς νὰ τὸ καταλάβουμε!

Αὐτὰ γενήκανε στὸν καιρό μου καὶ στὸ χωριό μου. Στὲς πολιτείες μέσα ἤτανε παλιὰ δουλειά! Ἀπὸ τὴν Ἐπανάστασι καὶ πρὶν ἀκόμα εἶχε ἀρχίσει τὸ φονικό. Χιλιάδες φαμιλικὰ ὀνόματα πῆγαν στὸ καλό, καὶ πολλοὶ ποὺ γυρεύανε νὰ δείξουν στὸν κόσμο, τί παλιὸ σκαρὶ εἶναι τὸ δικό μας, δὲν ἠθέλανε νὰ ξέρουνε τὸν παππού τους!

Ἀμὲ τὰ καθαυτό, τὰ βαφτιστικὰ ὀνόματα; ἐκεῖ δὰ γένηκε τὸ μεγάλο κακό! Ὁ Γιάννης, ὁ Γιῶργος, ὁ Κώστας, ὁ Δημήτρις καὶ τόσα ἄλλα ἀγαπημένα ὀνόματα ἐπῆραν τὰ βουνὰ κ' ἐφεύγανε σιγὰ σιγὰ τὰ καημένα, καὶ στὸν τόπο τους ἐρχούντανε σὰν μελίσσια οἱ Ἀλκιβιάδηδες, οἱ Περικλῆδες καὶ οἱ Μιστοκλῆδες. Καθὼς βλέπετε, γυρέψανε οἱ γέροι καὶ οἱ γριές μας νὰ τὰ ἀνθρωπίσουν λιγάκι, μὰ τοῦ κάκου! Ὁ δάσκαλος ἀφῆκε τοὺς γέρους νὰ προφέρουνε μὲ τὰ γλωσσικὰ ὄργανα ποὺ τοὺς ἔδωσε ὁ θεός, καὶ σὰν καλὸς δαμαστής, πῆρε στὰ χέρια του τὰ παιδιὰ καὶ γύμναζε γύμναζε, τοὺς μαλάκωσε τὴ γλῶσσα, ποὺ σὰν φωνάζουμε τώρα ἀπ' τὸ ἀπάνω πάτωμα τὴν Μελπομένη καὶ τὴν Τερψιχόρη, τρέχει τὸ μέλι τοῦ Ὑμηττοῦ ἀπ' τὸ στόμα μας.

Τί καταλάβαμε μὲ τὴν ἀλλαγὴ τούτη, εἶναι γιὰ μένα μυστήριο. Τί ἐχάσαμε, δὲν εἶναι καθόλου μυστήριο. Ἐχάσαμε ἄλλη μιὰ χάρι τῆς γλώσσας μας, ἐκόψαμε καὶ καταπατήσαμε ἄλλο ἕνα λου-

18

λούδι της. Ήθελα νὰ ξέρω, τί λογῆς τραγούδι θὰ τραγουδούσαμε σὲ κανέναν Ἐπαμεινώνδα, ἂν ἔκλεφτε καμιὰν Ἀρσινόη! Ἢ σὲ κανέναν Εὐθυβουλίδη, ἂν μᾶς ἔπαιρνε τὴν Πόλι!

Ἂς μὴν ἀπελπιζούμαστε ὅμως. Κανένα θανατικὸ δὲν ἦλθε στὸν κόσμο, ποῦ νὰ μὴν ἀφῆκε καὶ μερικοὺς νὰ διηγηθοῦν τί συνέβηκε. Ὡς καὶ ἀπ' τὸν κατακλυσμὸ ἐσώθηκε ἕνας Νῶε. Ἔτσι κι ἀπ' τὴν καταστροφὴ τούτη ἐγλυτώσανε καὶ ἀνθοῦν ἀκόμα πολλὲς οἰκογένειες μὲ τὰ γλυκὰ ὀνόματα τῶν παππούδων τους. Ἀπ' αὐτοὺς πρέπει νὰ ἐλπίζουμε σωτηρία, αὐτοὶ θὰ μᾶς φέρουν πίσω τοὺς Γιάννηδές μας καὶ τὲς Μαρίες μας.

Δυὸ λόγια γιὰ τοὺς Χιῶτες· τοὺς πρέπει ἕνας ἔπαινος ἐδὼ πέρα. Αὐτοὶ σὰν ἐφύγαν' ἀπ' τὸ δύστυχο νησί τους κ' ἐσκορπισθήκανε στὴν ξενιτειά, ἐπῆραν δυὸ πράματα μαζί τους· τὰ εἰκονοστάσια τους καὶ τὰ ὀνόματά τους. Ἀπὸ τὴ σφαγὴ τοῦ 1822 δὲν ἐγλυτώσανε, τὴ σφαγὴ ὅμως τῶν δασκάλων μας τὴ ξεφύγανε καὶ μέσ' στὰ σπιτικὰ τους μοσχομυρίζουν ἀκόμα τὰ νησιώτικα τους ὀνόματα μαζὶ μὲ τὸ λιβάνι τους. Δὲν λέγω πῶς δὲν εἴμαστε κ' ἐμεῖς χριστιανοί· μὰ αὐτοὶ ἔχουν καὶ χριστιανικὰ ὀνόματα.

3. Ἡ Φωτιὰ τῆς Χαρᾶς.

Παραμύθι τῆς Πρωτοχρονιᾶς.

(Γεώργιος Δροσίνης, 1891)

Στὴν κρύα καὶ σκοτεινὴ καλύβα της γυρνᾷ πίσω ἡ ἄμοιρη χήρα μὲ θλιβερὸ περπάτημα.

Αὐτὴ ἡ παραμονὴ τῆς πρωτοχρονιᾶς, τόσο χαρούμενη γιὰ ὅλον τὸν κόσμο, γι' αὐτὴν μόνον εἶναι γεμάτη λύπη καὶ στενοχώρια.

Πουθενὰ δὲν βρῆκε δουλειά, οὔτε παρηγοριὰ κάν, οὔτε ἐλπίδα. Ὅλοι τῆς λέγαν μ' ἕνα στόμα:

„Σὰν περάσῃ ὁ χειμῶνας.“

Σὰν περάσῃ ὁ χειμῶνας — ποῦ θὰ πῇ σὲ τρεῖς μῆνες. Καὶ τοὺς τρεῖς αὐτοὺς μαύρους μῆνας πῶς θὰ ζήσῃ ἡ δύστυχη χήρα, πῶς θὰ ζήσουν τὰ δυό της ὀρφανά!

Κι ὅταν ἐγύρισε καὶ κύτταξε πάλι τὰ δυὸ παιδιά της ἐμπρὸς στὴ σβησμένη γωνιά, κρυωμένα, νηστικά, χωρὶς κανένα πρωτοχρονιάτικο χάρισμα, δὲν ἐβάσταξε πλιὰ κι ἄρχισαν νὰ τρέχουν βροχὴ τὰ δάκρυα ἀπ' τὰ μάτια της.

Τὰκ! τάκ!

Δὲν εἶναι ἡ θύρα ποὺ κτυπᾷ; Ὄχι! Ποιὸς θὰ κτυπᾷ; Στὴν ἄκρη αὐτὴ τῆς ἐρημιᾶς, ποιὸς θὰ εἶναι τάχα, μπροστὰ στὴν θύρα

τῆς κακομοιριᾶς, τὴν ὥρ᾽ αὐτὴ ποῦ χαίρεται ὅλος ὁ κόσμος καὶ
ἔχουν πανηγύρι κ᾽ οἱ φτωχότεροι; Ποιὸς θὰ κτυπᾷ; Θὰ εἶναι,
καλέ, ὁ ἀέρας ἢ κανένα κακοσήμαδο νυχτοπούλι. Αὐτὸ θὰ εἶναι.

Τάκ! τάκ! τάκ!

Ξανακτυποῦν πάλι καὶ κτυποῦν τώρα δυνατά, τόσο δυνατά,
ποῦ μισοξυπνοῦν τὰ δυὸ ὀρφανὰ καὶ μισανοίγουν τὰ μάτια μουρ-
μουρίζοντας·

„Μάννα, μάννα!"

Καὶ μὲ μιᾶς ἀνοίγεται ἡ θύρα καὶ στὸ κατώφλι προβάλλει
ἕνας γέρος μεγαλόσωμος μὲ κάτασπρα γένεια κατεβασμένα στὰ
στήθη του.

Καὶ μὲ μιὰ φωνὴ χονδρὴ καὶ ἄγρια, ποῦ ἦτο περισσότερο
φοβέρα παρὰ ζητιανειά, λέει·

„Λεημοσύνη, χριστιανοί!"

Στὸ χέρι κρατᾷ ἕνα χονδρὸ ραβδί, στὸν ὦμο ἔχει κρεμασμένο ἕνα σακκούλι, τὰ ροῦχα του εἶναι κουρελιασμένα καὶ περι-
πατεῖ ξυπόλυτος.

„Κόπιασε, κακόμοιρε," τοῦ λέει ἡ χήρα. „Δὲν ἔχω τὴ δύναμι νὰ σ᾽ ἐλεήσω· μὰ ἐδὼ θὰ βρῇς τουλάχιστον λιγώτερο κρύο
παρὰ ἔξω, καὶ μπορεῖς νὰ καθίσῃς νὰ ξαποστάσῃς μιὰ στιγμή.
Κόπιασε!"

Ὁ γέρος ἐσφάλισε τὴ θύρα καὶ πῆγε καὶ κάθισε κοντὰ στὴ
σβηστὴ γωνιά.

„Δὲν εἶναι οὔτ᾽ ἐδὼ ζέστη, οὔτε φέγγει καλά. Δὲν μπορεῖς
ν᾽ ἀνάψῃς ἕνα δαυλί;"

„Δὲν ἔχω!" ἀποκρίνεται ἡ χήρα.

Ὁ γέρος κτυπᾷ τὸ χῶμα μὲ τὸ χονδρὸ ραβδὶ καὶ καταρειέ-
ται· τὰ δυὸ παιδιὰ ξυπνοῦν κι ἀνατινάζονται μ᾽ ὀρθάνοιχτα μάτια.

„Νά!" φωνάζει τὸ ἀγωράκι, „εἶναι ὁ Ἅγιος Βασίλις."

Καὶ τὸ κοριτσάκι ἁπλώνει τὰ χέρια του κατὰ τὸν γέρο καὶ
τοῦ χαμογελᾷ φωνάζοντας·

„Καλησπέρα, Ἅγιε Βασίλι!"

Καὶ τὰ δυὸ μ᾽ ἕνα στόμα ξαναλένε·

„Τί χαρίσματα μᾶς φέρνεις, Ἅγιε Βασίλι;"

Ὁ γέρος σὰν νὰ μὴν τ᾽ ἄκουσε γυρνᾷ καὶ λέει τῆς χήρας·

„Δὲν θὰ μοῦ δώσῃς τίποτε νὰ φάω καὶ νὰ πιῶ;"

„Τὰ παιδιά μου ἔφαγαν σήμερα τὴν τελευταία γωνιὰ τοῦ
ψωμιοῦ, κ᾽ ἐγὼ εἶμαι νηστικὴ ἀπὸ χθές."

„Ποῦ θὰ πῇ δὲν ἔχεις ἐδὼ οὔτε ψωμί, οὔτε φωτιά, οὔτε τίποτε;"

„Τίποτε," ἀποκρίνεται ἡ ἄμοιρη γυναῖκα.

Ὁ γέρος σηκώνεται, ρίχνει τὸ σακκούλι στὸν ὦμο καὶ τραβᾷ κατὰ τὴ θύρα κτυπῶντας κάτω μὲ θυμὸ τὸ ραβδί του.

„Μάννα," φωνάζει τὸ κοριτσάκι, „γιατί εἶναι θυμωμένος ὁ Ἅγιος Βασίλις ; "

„Μάννα," φωνάζει τὸ ἀγωράκι, „μὴν ἀφήνῃς τὸν Ἅγιο Βασίλι νὰ φύγῃ ἔτσι."

Καὶ τὰ δυὸ μ' ἕνα στόμα ξαναλένε·

„Γιὰ ἰδές, δὲν μᾶς χάρισε τίποτε !"

Καὶ τὰ δυὸ παιδιὰ κλαίνε κ' ἡ δύστυχη μάννα τὰ φιλεῖ καὶ κλαίει μαζί.

„Γειά σου !" βροντοφωνᾷ ὁ γέρος στὸ κατώφλι τῆς θύρας.

„Μὴ φεύγῃς, Ἅγιε Βασίλι, μὴ φεύγῃς," φωνάζουν τὰ δυὸ παιδιά. „Ἐμεῖς εἴμαστε τόσο φρόνιμα."

„Ἀλήθεια," λέει καὶ ἡ χήρα, „εἶναι τόσο φρόνιμα !"

Ἔπειτα γυρνῶντας κατὰ τὸ γέρο παρακλητικά·

„Μεῖνε," τοῦ λέει σιγαλά, „μεῖνε λιγάκι, μόνον ὡς ποῦ νὰ ξανακοιμηθοῦν εὐχαριστημένα, καὶ νὰ ἰδοῦν στ' ὄνειρό τους τὸν Ἅγιο Βασίλι. Σὰν δὲν τοὺς χαρίζεις τίποτε ἄλλο, χάρισέ τους τὸ γλυκὸ αὐτὸ ὄνειρο.

Ἐκεῖνος ἐκοντοστάθηκε·

„Μεῖνε," τοῦ λέει πάλι ἡ χήρα, „μεῖνε, κι ἅμα κοιμηθοῦν, θὰ σ' ἀνάψω λίγη φωτιὰ νὰ ζεσταθῇς."

„Καλὰ λοιπόν !" ἀποκρίνεται ὁ γέρος. „Τώρα ποῦ ἀρχίζεις νὰ γίνεσαι σπλαχνική, μένω."

Λέγοντας τὰ λόγια αὐτὰ ἀνασέρνει ἀπ' τὸν κόρφο του ἕνα μικρὸ σταμνάκι καὶ κοντοζυγώνει στὰ παιδιά·

„Πιέτε το αὐτὸ μὲ μιᾶς. Εἶναι ἄγριο καὶ θὰ σᾶς τρυπήσῃ τὸ στομάχι. Μὰ ὕστερα θὰ κοιμηθῆτε γλυκὰ καὶ θὰ ἰδῆτε καλὰ ὄνειρα."

Τὰ παιδιὰ ἤπιαν, ἤπιαν ἀχόρταστα κ' ἔπεσαν κάτω σὰν ἄψυχα μὲ γλυκὸ χαμόγελο στὰ χείλη·

„Τ' εἶν' αὐτό ; " ἐρωτᾷ ἡ χήρα.

„Πιὲ καὶ σύ," ἀποκρίνεται ὁ γέρος· „εἶναι ρακί."

Πίνει, πίνει καὶ ἡ ἄμοιρη γυναῖκα καὶ πέφτει κ' ἐκείνη κάτω σὰν ἄψυχη, μὲ γλυκὸ χαμόγελο στὰ χείλη.

Κ' ἔξαφνα θαρρεῖ, πῶς ὁ γέρος ζητιάνος εἶναι στ' ἀληθινὰ ὁ Ἅγιος Βασίλις καὶ πῶς τῆς λέει·

„Ἀφοῦ καὶ σύ, ποὺ δὲν ἔχεις τίποτε, ἤθελες νὰ μ' ἐλεήσῃς, θὰ σ' ἐλεήσω κ' ἐγὼ τώρα. Κύτταξε πῶς θὰ ζούσαν τὰ παιδιά σου, ἂν δὲν ἐρχόμουν ἐδώ, κύτταξε καὶ τὴ ζωή, ποὺ θὰ περάσουν τώρα."

Καὶ ἡ ζωή, ποὺ θὰ περνούσαν τὰ παιδιά της, ἦτον φτωχικὴ κι ἀπελπισμένη. Τὸ ἀγώρι ἐγινότανε ταπεινὸς δουλευτής· ἐκέρδιζε τὸ ψωμί του μὲ τὸν ἱδρῶτα του, καὶ κατασπαραγμένος ἀπὸ τὴν ἀρρώστια, ποὺ τὸν ἐσαράκωσεν ἀπὸ τὰ παιδιάτικα χρόνια του, ἐξεψυχοῦσε στὸ νοσοκομεῖο. Καὶ τὸ κοριτσάκι, χειρότερα ἀκόμα, καταντοῦσε πλάσμα χαμένο, καὶ μάννα καὶ χήρα κι αὐτὴ μὲ ὀρφανὰ παιδιά, ποὺ θὰ προσμέναν᾽ κ᾽ ἐκεῖνα νηστικὰ καὶ ξεπαγιασμένα τὸν Ἅγιο Βασίλι. Καὶ αὐτὰ πάλι θὰ γεννούσαν ἄλλα παιδιὰ δυστυχισμένα, κι ἄλλα κι ἄλλα· κι ὁ κόσμος ὅλος θὰ γέμιζεν ἀπὸ καλύβες φτωχικὲς καὶ χήρες μάννες, ποὺ θὰ περνούσαν τὴ νύχτα τῆς Παραμονῆς καθὼς αὐτή.

Μὰ ἡ ζωὴ ποὺ θὰ περάσουν τὰ δυὸ ὀρφανὰ τώρα μὲ τὴ χάρι τοῦ Ἁγίου Βασίλι, τί ζωὴ χαρούμενη! Παντοῦ ξαστεριά, παντοῦ χρυσάφι, παντοῦ παιγνίδια καὶ πανηγύρια, παντοῦ τραγούδια καὶ γέλοια! Κι ὅλ᾽ αὐτὰ μέσα σὲ μι᾽ ἀτέλειωτη τοῦ ἥλιου λαμπράδα.

Ὢ! τί γλυκός, τί ζεστός, τί χαρούμενος, τί ἔμορφος ἥλιος! Πῶς ἄνοιγεν ὁλόφωτος μὲ μιᾶς ψηλὰ στὸν οὐρανὸ σὰν κανένα θεώρατο λουλούδι.

Γιὰ μιὰ στιγμὴ ἡ ἄμοιρη χήρα μισάνοιξε τὰ μάτια της καὶ εἶδε τὸν γέρο Ζητιάνο ποὺ ἔρριχνε κάτι κι ἄναφτε τὴ σβησμένη γωνιά.

Καὶ τώρα αὐτὴ ἡ φωτιὰ ἦτον ποὺ λαμπάδιαζεν ὁλόφωτη μὲ μιᾶς σὰν κανένα θεώρατο λουλούδι.

Ὁλοένα μεγαλύτερος, χαρωπότερος, ζεστότερος φεγγοβολοῦσεν ὁ ἥλιος.

Καὶ μές᾽ στὸν γαλανὸν οὐρανό, χρυσοφωτισμένον ἀπὸ τὸν ἥλιο, ἀνάμεσα στὰ παιγνίδια, στὰ πανηγύρια, στὰ γέλοια καὶ στὰ τραγούδια, τὰ δυὸ ὀρφανὰ ἐξεφτερούγιαζαν μὲ ὀρθάνοιχτα φτερά, φτερὰ χρυσᾶ, φτερὰ κόκκινα, φτερὰ ποὺ καθὼς ἐξεσπάθωναν στὸν ἀέρα, γλυκολαλοῦσαν οὐράνια ψαλμῳδία, ψαλμῳδία τοῦ Ὡσαννά!

Δοξασμένος ὁ Ἅγιος Βασίλις! κελαδοῦσεν ἡ μουσικὴ ἐκείνη. Δοξασμένος αὐτὸς ποὺ μᾶς ἔκαμε τὴν καλύτερη ἐλεημοσύνη, αὐτὸς ποὺ μᾶς ἔσωσεν ἀπὸ ὅλες τὲς δυστυχίες, αὐτὸς ποὺ μᾶς ἄνοιξε τὸν παράδεισο, αὐτὸς ποὺ μᾶς ἐκοίμισε γιὰ πάντα μές᾽ στ᾽ ὁλόμορφο ὄνειρό μας, καὶ μᾶς ἐκοίμισε τόσο βαθειά, ποὺ τίποτε πλιὰ δὲν μπορεῖ νὰ μᾶς ξυπνήση.

Καὶ ἡ ἄμοιρη χήρα ἄνοιξε πάλι τὰ μάτια της γιὰ ὕστερη φορά, κ᾽ ἐκεῖ ποὺ ἔννοιωθε, πῶς ξεψυχᾷ καὶ πεθαίνει κι αὐτή,

εἶδε τὰ δυὸ παιδιά της πεθαμμένα ἐμπρός της καὶ λαμπροφωτισμένα
ἀπὸ τὸν ὁλόφλογον ἥλιο, ποῦ ἄναψεν ὁ σπλαχνικὸς Ζητιάνος ἐκεῖ
στὴ γωνιά, φωτιὰ τῆς χαρᾶς γεννημένη ἀπὸ τὴν τόση δυστυχία.

4. Ἡ Βασιλοπούλα κι ὁ παράλυτος.

(Κωνσταντῖνος Μάνος, 1893)

Πορφυρογέννητη βασιλοπούλα, κοπέλα δεκάξι χρόνων, ἡ
Ζωή, ἡ κόρη τοῦ Καλογιάννη, ἤτανε τὸ ρόδο τοῦ Παλατιοῦ. Οἱ
μοῖρες τὴν εἴχανε προικίσει μ' ὅλες τὶς ὀμορφιὲς καὶ μ' ὅλες τὶς
καλοσύνες. Γαλανομάτα καὶ χρυσομαλλοῦσα, δαχτυλιδόμεση καὶ
βεργολυγερή, ἁγνὴ καὶ σοβαρή καὶ καταδεχτική, μάγευε τὴν κάθε
καρδιά.

Τριγυρισμένη ἀπὸ τὶς δούλες της καὶ τὶς βάγιες της καὶ
τὶς ἀναδεξιμιές της καὶ τοὺς ἀνθηφόρους της, ἄφηνε συχνὰ τὰ
περήφανα δώματα τῆς Πορφύρας, ἔμπαινε στὴ σέδια της καὶ κατέβαινε στὴν Πόλι νὰ μοιράση ἐλεημοσύνες. Κ' οἱ φτωχοὶ τὴν
προσκυνούσανε σὰν ἄγγελο, σὰν οὐράνια παρθένα.

Καὶ μπρὸς στὴ Χαλκή, στὴν Πόρτα τοῦ παλατιοῦ κάθουνταν ἕνας παράλυτος, ὡς εἴκοσι χρόνων. Τὸν εἴχανε φέρει μιὰ
μέρα, τὴν ὥρα ποῦ ἔβγαινε ἡ βασιλοπούλα. Οἱ δομέστικοι τὸν
διώχνανε μὲ θυμὸ καὶ μὲ φωνές. Μὰ ἡ βασιλοπούλα τὸν εἶδε
καὶ τόνε σπλαχνίστηκε ·

„Χαρίστε τοῦ φτωχοῦ μιὰ γωνιὰ στὸν ἥλιο καὶ μιὰ σκέπη
ἀπ' τὴ βροχὴ κι ἀπ' τὰ χιόνια."

Κι ἀπὸ τότε τὸν ἄφηναν ἐκεῖ. Κάθε φορὰ ποῦ ἔβγαινε ἡ
βασιλοπούλα αὐτὸν πρῶτον ἐλεοῦσε. Κι ὅτανε γύριζε στὸ παλάτι,
πρὶν μπῆ στὴ Χαλκή, τοῦ ἔστελνε μὲ τὸ βασιλικὸ χαμόγελό της
παρηγοριὰ κ' ἐλπίδα.

Ἐλπίδα; Καὶ τί μπορεῖ νὰ ἐλπίση τὸ σκουλήκι τῆς γῆς;

Κι ὅμως! Αὐτὸς, ὁ φτωχὸς παράλυτος, ὁ κουρελιασμένος,
ὁ ρυπαρός, αὐτός, τὸ σκουλήκι τῆς γῆς, ἀγάπησε μ' ὅλο τὸν
ἔρωτα τῆς ψυχῆς του τὴν αἰθέρια πεταλούδα, τὴν πορφυρογέννητη βασιλοπούλα. Κι ὅλα τὰ βάσανα, ποῦ εἶχε τραβήξει ὥς τότε,
ἡ φτώχεια κ' ἡ κακομοιριὰ κ' ἡ ἀρρώστια κ' ἡ βρώμα κ' ἡ
κατηφρόνια, ἤτανε τιποτένια μπρὸς στὰ σημερινά του. Τέτοια
λαύρα καὶ πίκρα καὶ καημός!

Καὶ κάθε φορὰ ποῦ τὴν ἔβλεπε, ἔχανε κ' ἕνα κομμάτι τῆς
ζωῆς του. Καὶ ξεψυχοῦσε ἀπὸ ἀγάπη.

Μιὰ μέρα ἔβγαινε πάλι ἡ βασιλοπούλα. Κ' ἦρθε κοντά του
γιὰ νὰ τὸν ἐλεήση. Κι ὁ παράλυτος τῆς εἶπε ·

„Ἐλέησέ με, βασιλοπούλα μου, καὶ δός μου τὸ φιλί σου, ποὺ μόνο μπορεῖ νὰ μὲ γιατρέψῃ."

Κ' ἡ πορφυρογέννητη βασιλοπούλα ἔσκυψε καὶ φίλησε στὸ μέτωπο τὸν παράλυτο. Καὶ τὴν ἴδια στιγμὴ ὁ φτωχὸς ξεψύχησε. Καὶ γιατρεμένη κ' ἐλεύθερη ἡ ψυχή του ἀνέβηκε στὸ γαλανὸν αἰθέρα.

5. Ἡ Βρύσι τῆς Κόρης.

(Μήτσος Χατζόπουλος, 1893)

Μέσ' στὰ χρόνια τὰ παλιά, τὰ χρόνια τὰ εὐτυχισμένα τὸ βασιλόπουλο τῆς χώρας βγῆκε στὸ κυνήγι μὲ τ' ἀσκέρι του. Γύρισε βουνὰ καὶ λαγκάδια, πέρασε λόγγους καὶ κάμπους, ὅσο ποὺ ἔφτασ' ἕνα φλογερὸ μεσημέρι στὰ ριζιὰ τ' ἀψηλοῦ βράχου μὲ τὴν ὀρθὴ καὶ κατάψηλη λεύκα στὴν κορφή. Ἐκεῖ λιμέριασε μὲ τ' ἀσκέρι του. Σὰν δρόσισε λιγάκι, τὸ βασιλόπουλο ἀνέβηκε ἀψηλὰ στὴν κορφή, στὸ ξάγναντο, καταμόναχο. Κανένας δὲν ἀνέβαινε ποτὲ στὴν κορφὴ τοῦ βράχου. Ἐκεῖ πάνω ἦταν μιὰ καλύβα πλεγμένη μ' ἀμαλαγιὲς καὶ φτέρες τοῦ βουνοῦ. Μέσα στὴν καλύβα κάθουνταν μιὰ βοσκοπούλα ὄμορφη, ὅσο νὰ πῇς. Σὰν τὴν εἶδε τὸ βασιλόπουλο, πῆγε νὰ χάσῃ τὰ λογικά του, σὰν τὸ εἶδε ἡ βοσκοπούλα τὸ βασιλόπουλο, ἔχασε τὸ νοῦ της. Ἐκεῖ στὴ φτωχικὴ καλυβούλα ἔστησε τὴ φωλιά του τ' ἀγαπημένο ζευγάρι, ἐκεῖ στὸ ἐρημικὸ καλύβι ἔπλεξε μὲ χρυσῆ κλωστὴ τὶς καρδιές τους ὁ ἔρωτας. Πέρασαν μέρες, μῆνες, χρόνος, καὶ τ' ἀσκέρι τοῦ κάκου γύρευε νὰ μάθῃ, τί λογῆς ἀφορμὴ εἶχε τὸ βασιλόπουλο νὰ κάθεται τόσον καιρὸ σ' ἐκείνη τὴν ἐρημιά.

Ἔτσι μιὰ μέρα ἔρχεται μίλημα στὸ βασιλόπουλο νὰ πάῃ στὸ σεφέρι. Κακὸ κι ἀπελπισμὸς στ' ἀγαπημένο ταίρι! ... Ἡ καημένη ἡ βοσκοπούλα ἔπεσε μέσα στὴν ἀγκαλιὰ τοῦ καλοῦ της, τὸν ἔσφιξε σφιχτὰ σφιχτὰ μὲ τὰ χεράκια της, καὶ τὸν κράτησε ὅλη τὴ νύχτα ἀπάνω στὰ στηθάκια της καὶ δὲν τὸν ἄφησε νὰ φύγῃ, προτοῦ νὰ τῆς ὁρκιστῇ στὰ μάτια της τὰ γλυκά, πῶς γρήγορα θὰ ξαναγύριζε στὸ καλυβάκι τὸ ἐρημικό. Καὶ τὸ πρωῒ τὸ βασιλόπουλο ἔφυγε μὲ καμένη τὴν καρδιά. Ἔφυγε γιὰ νὰ μὴν ξαναγυρίσῃ πιά. Πῆγε ἀπὸ κακὸ σπαθὶ στὸ σεφέρι. Κ' ἡ βοσκοπούλα ἡ καημένη κάθουνταν μερόνυχτα στὴν κορφὴ τοῦ βράχου, μὲ γυρισμένα τὰ μάτια πέρα κατὰ τὸν κάμπο, κ' ἔκλαιε, ἔκλαιε ὁλοένα. Τὰ πολλὰ τὰ δάκρυα σὰν ἔπεφταν καφτερά, βαθούλαιναν τὸν ξερόβραχο καὶ πήγαιναν βαθειὰ στὰ σπλάχνα του. Πέρασε καιρὸς κ' ἡ βοσκοπούλα ἔκλαιε, ἔκλαιε, ὅσο ποὺ ἀπόμεινεν ἕνας ἴσκιος μονάχα. Ἀπ' τὴν πολλή της θλῖψι τὴν συμπόνεσε τότες κι ὁ ξερόβραχος· ἄνοιξε μιὰ νύχτα τὴν πέτρινη ἀγκαλιά του καὶ τὴν ἔκλεισε μέσα στὰ σπλάχνα του. Μὰ καὶ μέσα στὸ βυθὸ τοῦ βράχου κλαίει, κλαίει ἀκόμα ἡ βοσκοπούλα, καὶ τὰ δάκρυα της κατασταλάζουν ἀπὸ τὸν ξερόβραχο μὲ θλιβερὸ παράπονο, γυρεύοντας τὸ δυστυχισμένο βασιλόπουλο, ποῦ πῆγε ἀπὸ κακὸ σπαθὶ στὸ σεφέρι. Μὰ δὲν τὸ βρίσκουν πουθενά, καὶ γίνουνται φαρμάκι καὶ πικρὴ χολὴ ὁλοένα τὰ πολλά της δάκρυα, κι ἀλλοιὰ κι ἀλλοίμονο στὴ λυγερὴ τοῦ χωριοῦ, ποῦ θὰ θελήσῃ νὰ γεμίσῃ τὴ στάμνα της ἀπὸ τὴ Βρύσι τῆς Κόρης.

6. Ἡ Νέα Διαθήκη, κατὰ τὸ Ματθαῖο κ. 13.

(Ἀλέξανδρος Πάλλης, 1902)

Ἐκείνη τὴν ἡμέρα βγῆκε ἀπὸ τὸ σπίτι ὁ Ἰησοῦς καὶ κάθουνταν κοντὰ στὴ λίμνη, καὶ μαζεύτηκαν κοντά του πλήθη πολλά, τόσο ποῦ μπῆκε σὲ καράβι καὶ καθότανε, καὶ τὸ πλῆθος ἔστεκε ὅλο στὴν ἀκρογιαλιά. Καὶ τοὺς μίλησε πολλὰ μὲ παραβολὲς κ' εἶπε· „Νά, βγῆκε ὁ σπάρτης νὰ σπείρῃ. Καὶ καθὼς ἔσπερνε, ἄλλα πέσανε σιμὰ στὸ δρόμο, κ' ἦρθαν τὰ πουλιὰ καὶ τά 'φαγαν. Κι ἄλλα ἔπεσαν ἀπάνου σὲ πετρότοπους ὅπου δὲν εἶχε χῶμα πολύ, κι ἀμέσως βγήκανε μὲ τὸ νὰ μὴν εἶχε βάθος γῆς, καὶ σὰ βγῆκε ὁ ἥλιος, κάηκαν, κι ὄντας δίχως ρίζα ξεράθηκαν. Κι ἄλλα πέσανε στ' ἀγκάθια ἀπάνου, καὶ μεγάλωσαν τ' ἀγκάθια καὶ τὰ συνεπνίξανε. Κι ἄλλα πέσανε στὸ χῶμα τὸ καλὸ κ' ἔδιναν καρπό, ἄλλο ἑκατὸ κι ἄλλο ἑξήντα κι ἄλλο τριάντα. Ὅποιος ἔχει αὐτιά, ἂς ἀκούῃ.‟

Καὶ πῆγαν οἱ μαθητάδες του καὶ τοῦ 'πανε· „Γιατί τοὺς μιλᾷς μὲ παραβολές;‟ Κ' ἐκεῖνος ἀποκρίθη καὶ τοὺς εἶπε πῶς· „Ἐσᾶς σᾶς δόθηκε νὰ μάθετε τὰ μυστικὰ τῆς βασιλείας τῶν οὐρανῶν, μὰ σ' ἐκείνους δὲ δόθηκε. Γιατί σ' ὅποιον ἔχει θὰ δόθῇ καὶ περισσέψῃ· κι ὅποιος δὲν ἔχει θὰν τοῦ πάρουν κι ὅτι ἔχει. Γιὰ τοῦτο τοὺς μιλῶ μὲ παραβολές, γιατί βλέποντας δὲ βλέπουν κι ἀκώντας δὲν ἀκούνε μήτε νοιώθουν. Καὶ τοὺς γίνεται ἡ προφητεία τοῦ Ἡσαΐα, ποῦ λέει· Μὲ τὴν ἀκουὴ θ' ἀκούστε καὶ δὲ θὰ νοιώστε, καὶ βλέποντας θὰ βλέψτε καὶ δὲ θὰ δῆτε· γιατί χόντρηνε τούτου τοῦ λαοῦ ἡ καρδιά, καὶ μὲ τ' αὐτιὰ βαρειάκουσαν καὶ τὰ μάτια τους σφάλισαν, μὴν τυχόνε δοῦνε μὲ τὰ μάτια κι ἀγροικήσουν μὲ τ' αὐτιὰ καὶ μὲ τὴν καρδιά τους νοιώσουν, καὶ γυρίσουνε καὶ τοὺς γιατρέψω.' Ὅμως ἐσᾶς καλότυχα τὰ μάτια γιατί βλέπουν, καὶ τ' αὐτιά σας γιατί ἀκούν· τί ἀληθινὰ σᾶς λέω, πῶς πολλοὶ προφῆτες κι ἅγιοι ἀποθύμησαν νὰ δοῦν τὰ ὅσα

βλέπετε καὶ δὲν εἶδαν, καὶ ν' ἀκούσουν ὅσα ἀκούτε καὶ δὲν ἄκουσαν. Ἐσεῖς λοιπὸν ἀκούστε τὴν παραβολὴ τοῦ σπάρτη. Καθενὸς
π' ἀκούει τῆς βασιλείας τὸ λόγο καὶ δὲ νοιώθει, ἔρχεται ὁ Κακὸς
κι ἁρπάζει τὸ σπαρμένο μέσα στὴν καρδιά του· αὐτὸς εἶναι ποὺ
σπάρθηκε σιμὰ στὸ δρόμο. Κι ὁ σπαρμένος στοὺς πετρότοπους,
αὐτὸς εἶναι π' ἀκούει τὸ λόγο καὶ ποὺ εὐτὺς μετὰ χαρᾶς τόνε
δέχεται, μὰ δὲν ἔχει ρίζα μέσα του, μόνε εἶναι πρόσκαιρος, καὶ
μόλις τύχῃ ἀπὸ τὸ λόγο συφορὰ ἢ καταδρομή, εὐτὺς σκουντάφτει.
Κι ὁ σπαρμένος μέσα στ' ἀγκάθια, αὐτὸς εἶναι π' ἀκούει τὸ λόγο,
κ' ἡ συλλογὴ τοῦ κόσμου κ' ἡ ἀπάτη τοῦ πλούτου συνεπνίγει τὸ
λόγο καὶ γίνεται ἄκαρπος. Κι ὁ σπαρμένος στὸ καλὸ τὸ χῶμα ἀπάνου,
αὐτὸς εἶναι π' ἀκούει τὸ λόγο καὶ ποὺ νοιώθει, ποὺ δὰ καρποφορᾷ
καὶ κάνει ἄλλος ἑκατὸ κι ἄλλος ἑξῆντα κι ἄλλος τριάντα."

Καὶ μιὰ ἄλλη ἀκόμα παραβολὴ τοὺς εἶπε λέγοντας· „Ἔμοιασε
ἡ βασιλεία τῶν οὐρανῶν σὰν ἄνθρωπος ποὺ 'σπειρε καλὸ σπόρο
στὸ χωράφι του. Κ' ἐνῷ ἐκοιμούνταν οἱ ἀνθρώποι, ἦρθε ὁ ἐχτρός του κ' ἔσπειρε κατόπι ἀνάμεσα στὸ στάρι ἦρες κ' ἔφυγε.
Κι ὅτα βλάστησε τὸ χόρτο κ' ἔκανε καρπό, τότες φάνηκαν κ' οἱ
ἦρες. Καὶ πὰν τοῦ νοικοκύρι οἱ σκλάβοι καὶ τοῦ λέν· Ἀφέντη,
δὲν ἔσπειρες καλὸ σπόρο στὸ χωράφι σου; πῶς λοιπὸν ἔχει
ἦρες;' Κ' ἐκεῖνος τοὺς εἶπε· Ἐχτρὸς ἄνθρωπος τό 'κανε αὐτός.'
Κ' ἐκεῖνοι τοῦ λένε· Θέλεις λοιπὸν νὰ πάμε καὶ νὰν τὶς μαζέψουμε;'
Κ' ἐκεῖνος λέει· Ὄχι, μήπως μαζεύοντας τὶς ἦρες ξεριζώστε μαζὶ
τους τὸ στάρι. Ἀφήστε τα μαζὶ νὰ μεγαλώσουν καὶ τὰ δυὸ ὡς
στὸ θέρος· καὶ τὸν καιρὸ τοῦ θέρου θὰ 'πῶ στοὺς θεριστάδες·
μαζέψτε πρῶτα τὶς ἦρες καὶ δέστε τες δεμάτια νὰν τὶς κάψουμε,
καὶ τὸ στάρι συνάξτε το στὴν ἀποθήκη μου'."

Καὶ μιὰ ἄλλη ἀκόμα παραβολὴ τοὺς εἶπε λέγοντας· „Μοιάζει
ἡ βασιλεία τῶν οὐρανῶν σπυρὶ σινάπι ποὺ τὸ πῆρε κ' ἔσπειρε
ἕνας ἄνθρωπος στὸ χωράφι του· ποὺ 'ναι πιὸ μικρὸς ἀπ' ὅλους
τοὺς σπόρους, μὰ σὰ μεγαλώσῃ, ξεπερνᾷ τὰ χόρτα καὶ γίνεται
δέντρο, τόσο ποὺ πὰν τὰ πετούμενα τ' οὐρανοῦ καὶ φωλιάζουνε
στὰ κλαδιά του." Ἄλλη παραβολὴ τοὺς εἶπε· „Μοιάζει ἡ βασιλεία
τ' οὐρανοῦ προζύμι, ποὺ τὸ πῆρε μιὰ γυναῖκα κ' ἔχωσε μέσα σὲ
τρία σάτα στάρι, ὅσο ποὺ ἀνέβηκε ὅλο."

Ὅλα αὐτὰ τὰ μίλησε ὁ Ἰησοῦς μὲ παραβολὲς στὰ πλήθη,
καὶ χωρὶς παραβολὴ δὲν τοὺς μίλησε τίποτα, γιὰ ν' ἀληθέψῃ
τὸ εἰπωμένο μέσο τοῦ Προφήτη ποὺ λέει· Θ' ἀνοίξω μὲ παραβολὲς τὸ στόμα μου, θὰ βγάλω τὰ κρυμμένα ἀπ' ὅτα θεμελιώθη
ὁ κόσμος.'

7. Ἡ φιλολογία μας.

(Κωστῆς Παλαμᾶς, 1902)

Φίλε κύριε, ρωτᾶτε· ὑπάρχει σήμερα φιλολογία στὴν Ἑλλάδα; Ἄνθρωποι δηλονότι ποῦ νὰ παράγουν ἔργα λογοτεχνικά, τὰ ὡραῖα παιδιὰ τῆς Φαντασίας, καὶ ποῦ νὰ προσέχωνται καὶ ποῦ νὰ θαυμάζονται. Αὐτὸ τὸ ὄνομα φιλολογία κοινὸ σ' ἐμᾶς ἐδώ, ὅπως δὲ συμβαίνει ἀλλοῦ, καὶ γιὰ κείνους ποῦ σπουδάζουν κ' ἑρμηνεύουν τοὺς κλασσικούς, καὶ γιὰ κείνους ποῦ σπουδάζουν ἢ ἑρμηνεύουν τὸν κόσμο γύρω τους καὶ τὰ βάθη τῆς ψυχῆς, δείχνει, πῶς ἡ φαντασία δὲν ἔχει σ' ἐμᾶς ἐδὼ τὸν τόπο της ξεχωριστὸ καὶ ἀναγνωρισμένο καὶ πυργοφύλαχτο καθὼς ἀλλοῦ. Ὅμως παντοῦ ἡ φαντασία ὑπάρχει — „Τὸ Πνεῦμα ὅπου θέλει πνεῖ" — καὶ καμιὰ φορὰ θαματουργεῖ. Εἶναι φυτὰ ποῦ ἀνθίζουνε σὲ ὅλα τὰ κλίματα· ὅμως ἐδὼ ἀρρωστημένα καὶ κακόμοιρα, κ' ἐκεῖ μεστὰ καὶ ἀκόλαστα. Τὸ εὐγενικώτατο φυτὸ ποῦ ποιητὴς ὀνομάζεται (καὶ ποιητὴ ἂς τὸν εἰποῦμε κάθε λαμπροφάνταστο πλάστη κάποιας καλλονῆς μὲ τὸ λόγο, μὲ τὸν ἦχο, μὲ τὸ χρῶμα, μὲ τὸ σχῆμα, μὲ τὸ ἔργο), τὸ φυτὸ αὐτὸ δὲν ἔχει στὴ χώρα μας μήτε τὴν ἀχάμνια, ποῦ θὰ εἶχε ἄλλοτε ἢ ποῦ θὰ εἶχε ἀλλοῦ, μήτε τὸ μέστωμα, ποῦ δείχνει σὲ ἄλλους τόπους καὶ ποῦ ταίριαζε κ' ἐδὼ νὰ δείχνῃ. Τοῦ ὡραίου μας αὐτοῦ φυτοῦ δὲν τοῦ φταίει τὸ χῶμα· τοῦ λείπει τὸ πλούσιο πότισμα καὶ τὸ χέρι τὸ φροντιστικό, γιὰ νὰ τοῦ κρατῇ πάντα γυαλιστερὴ τὴν πρασινάδα καὶ τ' ἄνθια δροσόπνοα.

Κ' ἔτσι καλά, φίλε κύριε. Ἔχουμε ἀνθρώπους διαλεχτοὺς τῆς Φαντασίας καὶ τῆς Τέχνης ἄξιους. Ποιὸς μὲ κάποια σκέψι φωτεινὴ καὶ μὲ κάποια γνώμη ἀνεπηρέαστη θὰ μποροῦσε νὰ εἰπῇ, πῶς φιλολογία δὲν ὑπάρχει στὸν τόπο μας; Αὐτὸς ὁ τόπος εἶναι βέβαια καλότυχος, γιατί μὲ τὸ σωρὸ τοὺς βγάζει τοὺς ἐμετικοὺς ἀεροκοπανιστάδες τῶν πεζῶν καὶ τῶν ἔμμετρων φλυαριῶν καὶ τοὺς ἄλλους ἐκείνους τοὺς ἀνήθικους, ποῦ ἐπειδὴ δὲν ἔχουν ὅπλα ἰσόβαρα γιὰ νὰ χτυπήσουν τὰ ἔργα ποῦ τοὺς κάθονται στὸ στομάχι, παίρνουν ἅγιες καὶ ἱερὲς ἰδέες καὶ πίσω ἀπ' αὐτὲς ταμπουριώνονται καὶ κλεφτοπόλεμο στένουν κατὰ τῶν δυνατῶν καὶ λυσσαλέα μετατοπίζουν τὰ ζητήματα καὶ μοιάζουν ἐκείνους, ποῦ σκεπάζουνε μὲ τὴν ἐθνικὴ σημαία τὰ πιὸ χυδαῖα τους γλεντοκοπήματα, τὰ πάθη τους τὰ πλέον ἀνίδεα. Ὅμως αὐτὸς ὁ ἴδιος τόπος ἔχει τὸ ἀτύχημα μέσα του νὰ κρατῇ καὶ κάποια ὀνόματα, ποῦ κάπως δείχνουν, πῶς ἀγάλια ἀγάλια σαλεύουνε κ' ἐδὼ καὶ περπατοῦν καὶ ὑψώνονται τὰ φιλολογικά μας, καὶ ἴσως γενναιότερα καὶ ὡραιό-

τερα ἀπὸ ἄλλοτε. Περιορίζομαι σὲ μερικὰ ἀπὸ τὰ ὀνόματα, ποὺ
ἀναφέρατε τὶς προάλλες μέσα στὴν „Ἀκρόπολίν" [1]) σας, φίλε κύριε.
Ὁ Βερναδάκης, ὁ Δροσίνης, ὁ Καρκαβίτσας, ὁ Παπαδιαμάντης,
ὁ Μητσάκης, ὁ Μαλακάσης, ὁ Μποέμ. Γνωρίζω, πῶς τὰ περισσότερα ἀπὸ τὰ ὀνόματα αὐτὰ θὰ νοιώσουν κάποιαν ἀνατριχίλα ἀπο-
στροφῆς, ποὺ ἔτσι ἀσυλλόγιστα κοντὰ τὸ ἕνα μὲ τὸ ἄλλο τὰ 'πίθωσα. Τί νὰ γίνῃ! Ἐσεῖς φταῖτε, κύριε, ποὺ δώσατε τὴν ἀφορμή.
Ἂν κάποια περιφρόνησι πρὸς τοὺς ἄλλους καὶ πολὺ περισσότερο πρὸς τοὺς γείτονες ταιριάζει στὸν ποιητὴ καὶ τοῦ δυνα-
μώνει τὸ ἔργο, καθὼς τονώνουν τὸ κορμὶ κάποια πολὺ πικρὰ
φάρμακα, φοβοῦμαι, πῶς τοῦ εἴδους αὐτοῦ ἡ περηφάνεια τὸ παρακάνει ἐδὼ πέρα. Ἂς εἶναι. Ἂν μὲ ρωτᾶτε, ἐγὼ πολλὰ ὀνόματα
τιμῶ μὲ τὴν τιμή, ποὺ καθενὸς τοῦ πρέπει. Στὴν πατρίδα τῆς
πολυθεῖας τέτοια λατρεία δὲν εἶναι ἄπρεπη. Ἄπρεπη εἶναι ἡ σταυροφορία τοῦ εὐνούχου σχολαστικοῦ κατὰ τοῦ τολμηροῦ τεχνίτη,
ποὺ νέους δρόμους ψάχνει ν' ἀνοίξῃ, τοῦ πεζοῦ ἀερολόγου, ποὺ
φαντάζεται νὰ δασκαλέψῃ τὸν ποιητή, ποιὰ ἰδέα πρέπει νὰ τὸν
συγκινῇ καὶ ποιὰ γλῶσσα πρέπει νὰ μεταχειρίζεται!
Ἄλλο τὸ ζήτημα, ἂν προσέχει ὁ κόσμος στὸν ποιητή. Ἡ
προσοχὴ ἢ ἀπροσεξία τοῦ κόσμου δὲν ἔχει τίποτε νὰ κάμῃ μὲ
τὴν ἀξία τοῦ ποιητή, καὶ δὲν εἶναι ἱκανὴ νὰ τοῦ σταματήσῃ τὸ
ἔργο. Ἴσως ἀνάγκη νὰ ξεχαστῇ λιγάκι καὶ νὰ καταφρονεθῇ γιὰ
καιρὸ ὁ ποιητής, γιὰ νὰ μείνῃ πιὸ ἐλεύτερος νὰ δημιουργήσῃ μέσα
στὴν εὐεργετικὴ ἀγκαλιὰ τῆς μητέρας Μοναξιᾶς. Εἶναι βαθὺς ὁ
στίχος, ποὺ τελειώνει ἕνα του ποίημα ὁ Σίλλερ [2]) καὶ μπορεῖ κ'
ἐδὼ νὰ ταιριαστῇ: „Ὅτι γραμμένο εἶναι νὰ ζήσῃ στὸ τραγούδι,
πρέπει νὰ λείψῃ στὴ ζωή." Ὅταν ὅμως ἡ ἀδιαφορία γύρω παρα-
τεντώνεται, κίντυνος εἶναι νὰ δυσκολέψῃ τὰ βήματα τοῦ ποιητή.
Ὁ Βερναδάκης δὲν ἐμποδίζεται νὰ γράψῃ τὸ „Νικηφόρο Φωκᾶ"·
μόνο πῶς ἀκόμα δὲν ἐστάθη δυνατὸ νὰ τὸν ἀνεβάσῃ στὸ θέατρο
ποὺ θ' ἄξιζε. Ὁ Δροσίνης, μέσα στὶς ἄλλες του φροντίδες, νομίζω
πῶς ζηλότυπα φυλάει στὸ συρτάρι του τὰ πλέον ἄψογα καλλι-
τεχνήματα. Ὁ Καρκαβίτσας, ἐξόριστος στὰ χιόνια τῶν συνόρων
τῶν θεσσαλικῶν, εἶμαι βέβαιος, πῶς δὲν ἐμποδίζεται ἀπὸ τοῦτο,
νὰ πλάθῃ ἀγάλια ἀγάλια μεγαλόπνοο τὸν „Ἀρματωλό" του. Μὰ
ὁ ἄνθρωπος δὲ θὰ μπορῇ πλέον ἀπὸ δικά του κομποδέματα νὰ
τυπώνῃ τὰ βιβλία του, καὶ ὡς στὴν ὥρα ἡ τόλμη τῶν φιλολογικῶν
ἐκδοτῶν δὲν ἀπλώθηκ' ἐδὼ παραπέρα ἀπὸ τὸν „Περιπλανώμενο

---

[1]) An Athenian newspaper, to which the essay is addressed as a letter.
[2]) Schiller.

Ἰουδαῖο" καὶ ἀπὸ τὰ λογῆς λογῆς Ἀναγνωσματάρια. Ὁ Παπα-διαμάντης ὅταν ἡ ζήτησις τῶν περιοδικῶν καὶ τῶν ἐφημερίδων θυμᾶται κι αὐτόν, προσφέρει κανένα του διηγηματάκι· μὰ εἶναι μοναδικὸ φαινόμενο πνευματικῆς κακομοιριᾶς, ὅτι βιβλίο δὲν ἀπό-χτησε ἀκόμα ἕνας ἀπὸ τοὺς πιὸ ποιητικοὺς ἀντιπρόσωπους τῆς νεοβυζαντινῆς τέχνης. Καὶ τοῦ Μητσάκη τὰ πεζογραφήματα, ποὺ φέρνουν ζωηρότατη τὴ βούλα μιᾶς ἐποχῆς ὀργασμοῦ φυσιο-κρατικοῦ σημαντικῆς κ' ἑνὸς ἀναρχικοῦ ἀτομισμοῦ στὴ γλῶσσα μας ἀξιοσπούδαστου, εἶν' ἐλπίδα νὰ τὰ ξεθάψῃ ποτὲ κανεὶς ἀπὸ κεῖ ποὺ βρίσκονται, σχεδὸν ἀγνώριστα; Δόξα νά 'χουν τὰ „Παν-αθήναια"[1]), βλέπουμε κάποτε καὶ πότ' ἐκεῖ κομματιαστοὺς κάποιους ὡραίους στίχους τοῦ Μαλακάση. Ὅσο γιὰ τὸ Μποέμ, ἀπὸ τότε ποὺ καβαλλίκεψε ἀλὰ Νίτσε[2]) τὴ Μοῖρα του, καταφρονεῖ, ὡς ταπεινὰ βέβαια καὶ ὡς πρόστυχα, κάθετι ποὺ θὰ τοῦ θυμίζῃ καὶ τὴ λέξι ἀκόμα ἠθογραφία, πολὺ δὲ περισσότερο τὴ χοντροκοπιὰ τῆς Ρούμελης.

Κατάρες καὶ περιγελάσματα γιὰ τὸ „Ρωμαῖικο θέατρο" τοῦ Ψυχάρη δὲν ἔλειψαν, καθὼς πάντα. Καὶ τί μ' αὐτό; Μέσα στὶς τρακόσες του σελίδες ἡ ἐθνικὴ ψυχὴ μιλεῖ παλληκαρίσια καὶ μεγαλό-στομα, καὶ δὲν ἔχουμε πολυσυνηθίσει σὲ τέτοιο μίλημα (τ' ὡμολό-γησε κ' ἕνας ἀπὸ τοὺς πλέον τυφλούς, ἀλλὰ καὶ ἀπὸ τοὺς πλέον καλοπροαίρετους πολέμιους τοῦ λεγομένου Ψυχαρισμοῦ, ὁ φίλος μου συντάχτης τοῦ „Ἀγῶνος")[3])· δὲν εἶναι λίγα τὰ μέρη, ποὺ ἀντι-φέγγει μέσα στὸ βιβλίο αὐτὸ δραματικὰ κ' ἑλληνικώτατα ἡ γυναικο-λάτρισσα φιλοσοφία τοῦ Βινύ, ποὺ ξεσπάει κάτι ἀπὸ τὸ σκληρὸ περιγέλασμα τοῦ Ἀριστοφάνη, ποὺ γλυκοκελαϊδάει κάτιτι, ποὺ δὲν ξέρω γιατί μου θυμίζει „τ' Ὄνειρο τῆς καλοκαιρινῆς νυχτιᾶς" τοῦ Σαίξπηρ. Μέσα σὲ ὅλη τὴν παραζάλη τῆς δημοσιογραφικῆς καὶ τῆς κοινωνικῆς ἐργασίας της μία γυναῖκα, ἡ Καλλιρρόη Παρρέν, μπορεῖ καὶ καταγίνεται στὸ γράψιμο τῆς γενναίας μυθιστορικῆς τριλογίας της· τὸ δεύτερο νεοτυπωμένο μέρος της, „ἡ Μάγισσα", φανερώνει τὴν κ. Παρρὲν συγγραφέα μὲ δύναμι δική της, ποὺ φιλοδοξεῖ νὰ ξανανιώσῃ τὴν ἑλληνίδα μέσα στὸ εὐλογημένο βάφ-τίσμα κάποιου ἀγγλοσαξονικοῦ ἰδανικοῦ μὲ τόλμη καὶ μὲ τέχνη, γιὰ νὰ τὴ ζηλέψουν πολλοὶ ἀπὸ τοὺς ὁμοφύλους μας, κ' ἐδὼ καὶ ἀλλοῦ.

Ὁ „Ἐσταυρωμένος Ἔρως" τοῦ κ. Ξενοπούλου μὲ συγκίνησε ἄλλοτε σὰν κάτι τόσο ὡραῖο, ὥστε νὰ τοῦ ψάλω ἕνα· τραγούδι.

---

[1]) A learned periodical. [2]) Nietzsche.
[3]) Name of a newspaper.

Σὲ καιρὸ ποὺ ἡ βδέλλα ρουτίνα βυζαίνει τὸ θέατρο πιὸ ἀνήμερ'
ἀπὸ κάθε ἄλλο εἶδος φιλολογικῆς παραγωγῆς, καὶ ποὺ καὶ μέσα
σ' αὐτὸ τὸ πλούσια καταρτισμένο Βασιλικὸ Θέατρο τώρα μόλις
μέλλεται νὰ δοθῇ ἕνα πρωτόβγαλτο ἔργο, „Οἱ ἐρασιτέχναι τῆς
ζωῆς" τοῦ κ. Πώπ, ὁ ποιητὴς Χρηστομάνος μὲ τὴ „Νέα Σκηνή"
του ἀξίζει νὰ συγκινήσῃ ὅλους ἐκείνους, ποὺ φροντίζουνε γιὰ τὸ
ξανάνθισμα τῆς τόσο ξεπεσμένης δραματικῆς τέχνης. Εἶδα τὴν
„Ἄλκηστι" τριγύρω σὲ ἀδειανὰ σκαμνιὰ νὰ παίζεται ξαναζωντα-
νέμενη σὲ μιὰ γλῶσσα, ποὺ στάζει τὸ χυμὸ τῆς ζωῆς. Μὲ τὶς
ὑψηλότερες σκηνὲς τοῦ „Κράτους τοῦ Ζόφου" χαμογελούσανε
μερικοί. Καὶ τί μ' αὐτό; Τὸ „Κράτος τοῦ Ζόφου" αἰσχύλειο εἶναι
ἀριστούργημα, καὶ πόση χάρι πρέπει νὰ χρωστᾷ ἡ φιλολογία μας
ἐκείνων, ποὺ τὰ μεγάλα τῶν ἀρχαίων καὶ τῶν ξένων ποιήματα,
ὄχι δασκαλικά, ἀλλὰ ποιητικὰ μᾶς τὰ παρουσιάζουνε στὴ γλῶσσα
μας, καθὼς ὁ μεταφραστὴς τῆς „Ἰλιάδας"[1]), καθὼς ὁ κ. Καλο-
στοῦρος μὲ τὸν „Προμηθέα" στὸ „Διόνυσο", καθὼς ὁ τρισχαριτωμένος ποιητὴς τῆς „Χρυσόφρυδης" μὲ τὸν „Ἀγαμέμνονα" τοῦ
Αἰσχύλου, ποὺ μᾶς ἑτοιμάζει.

Ἐκεῖ ποὺ τέτοια ἔργα φαίνονται, ὅσα δειλὰ καὶ ἀραιὰ καὶ
ἀπομονωμένα καὶ ἀπαρατήρητα, ὑπάρχει φιλολογία. Ὑπάρχει ἐκεῖ
ποὺ ὁ Βλαχογιάννης στὰ „Προπύλαια" μᾶς δίνει δείγματα ἐξαίσια
ποιητικῆς καὶ πραγματικῆς διηγηματογραφίας σκαλισμένα στὸ πιὸ
καθάριο μάρμαρο τῆς δημοτικῆς, μᾶς δίνει δείγματα πεζοῦ ἱστορικοῦ
λόγου φτερωτοῦ. Ὑπάρχει ἐκεῖ ποὺ ὁ Ἐφταλιώτης, λογογράφος
μὲ φλέβα Μεριμέ, βγαλμένος ἀπὸ τὴν ψυχὴ τῶν παραμυθιῶν μας,
μᾶς φέρνει τὶς „Νησιώτικες ἱστορίες" καὶ τὴν „Ἱστορία τῆς Ρωμιοσύνης". Ὑπάρχει ἐκεῖ ποὺ ὁ Βασιλικὸς καὶ ὁ Πορφύρας — ὁ
πρῶτος μεφιστοφελικός, ὁ δεύτερος κάτι σὰν ἀντίλαλος τοῦ Ἄριελ —
δὲν ἐσύντριψαν ἀκόμη τὶς μουσικόλαλες αἰθερόπλαστες φλογέρες
τους. Ὑπάρχει ἐκεῖ ποὺ ὁλοένα ὁ ποιητὴς τῶν „Πολεμικῶν τρα-
γουδιῶν" καὶ πιὸ γλυκοὺς ἤχους γεννάει σκυφτὸς ἀπάνω στὸ
μαντολίνο του· ἐκεῖ ποὺ νέοι, στὸ „Περιοδικόν" τοῦ νευρικοῦ καὶ
νευρώδους Βώκου πρωτοφανέρωτοι, ὅμως ἀγνιύριστοι ἀκόμα καὶ
ἀτύπωτοι, νέοι πεζογράφοι σὰν τὸ Βουτυρᾶ καὶ σὰν τὸ Μακρῆ,
στιχοπλέχτες σὰν τὸ Δελμοῦζο, καὶ σὰν τὸν Καμπάνη καὶ σὰν τὸ
Δημητριάδη — γιὰ νὰ σημειώσω τοὺς πιὸ γνωστούς μου — μὲ
ξαφνίζουν πολλὲς φορὲς μὲ τὸ ὁρμητικὸ περπάτημα τοῦ στίχου
τους, μὲ τὴν προσπάθεια νὰ μείνουν μακρειὰ ἀπὸ τὰ χιλιοπατημένα.

[1]) Ἀλέξανδρος Πάλλης (see p. 276).

Ὑπάρχει φιλολογία ἐκεῖ ποὺ ὁ Προβελέγγιος, σὰ νὰ στενο-
χωρειέται καὶ σὰ νὰ πονῇ ποὺ βρέθηκε βουλευτής, κι ἄλλο δὲν κάνει
παρὰ νὰ ὀνειρεύεται τὰ μισοτελειωμένα του δράματα καὶ περη-
φανεύεται, ποὺ ἀπομένει ποιητὴς Λαμαρτινικός, καὶ en attendant
μᾶς προσφέρει τὸ „Λαοκόοντα" τοῦ Λέσσιγγ ἀκαδημαϊκώτατα.
Ὑπάρχει ἐκεῖ ποὺ ὑπάρχουν „Παραμύθια" ὁλόχυτα ἀπὸ τὴν ἀκέρια
καλλιτεχνικὴ ψυχὴ τοῦ πολύτροπου Νιρβάνα, ἐκεῖ ποὺ ἀπὸ καιρὸ
σὲ καιρὸ πλουμίζουν τὸ φιλολογικό μας οὐρανὸ πλάσματα μιᾶς
ἀριστοκρατικῆς χάρις ἐξωτικῆς, σὰν τὸ „Ἄσμα τῶν Ἀσμάτων"
καὶ σὰν τὸ „Βασιλέα Κομφετοά". Ὑπάρχει ἐκεῖ ποὺ ὑπάρχουν
τόσοι ἀκόμα τεχνίτες τοῦ πεζοῦ καὶ τοῦ στιχηροῦ λόγου, ποὺ ἂν
δὲν ἔχω τόπο νὰ τοὺς ἀναφέρω ἐδὼ μαζί, δὲν τοὺς προσέχω
γιὰ τοῦτο λιγώτερο.

Ποιὸς ξέρει! ὕστερ' ἀπὸ λίγο ἢ πολὺν καιρό, ὕστερ' ἀπὸ
καμιὰ δεκαριὰ χρόνια σεῖς ὁ ἴδιος, φίλε κύριε, ἢ κανένας ἄλλος
νεώτερος ὁμότεχνός σας, θὰ γράφῃ· „Μπᾶ, ἐδὼ καὶ δέκα χρόνια
εἴχαμε ποίησι, δράμα, διήγημα, μὲ τεχνίτες καὶ μὲ τραγουδιστάδες
ποὺ δούλευαν καὶ ἀκούγονταν κ' ἐντύπωσι ἄφηναν, μὲ κόσμο ποὺ
τοὺς γύρευε καὶ ποὺ τοὺς μελετοῦσε! Τώρα, ἀδιαφορία καὶ νέκρα!"
Καὶ πιθανώτατα, ὕστερ' ἀπὸ δέκα χρόνια ὅσοι θὰ λειτουργοῦνε
γύρω στὸ βωμὸ τῆς τέχνης, θὰ εἶναι γερώτεροι ἀπὸ μᾶς καὶ
καλύτεροι. Ἕνα μονάχα ὄνομα ξεχωρίζετε μέσα στὴ γενικὴ ἀφρον-
τισιὰ καὶ στὴν ἐρήμωσι, καθὼς θέλετε. Τὸ ὄνομα τοῦ Σολωμοῦ.

Ἀλλ' ἴσα ἴσα ὁ Σολωμὸς δείχνει φῶς φανερά, ὅτι χρειάζεται
καιρὸς καὶ κόπος — δικά του εἶναι τὰ λόγια — γιὰ νὰ χτυπήσ'
ἡ δόξα τοῦ ποιητὴ στὰ μάτια τοῦ ἔθνους του. Ἑκατὸ χρόνια
ἔπρεπε νὰ διαβοῦνε, γιὰ νὰ προβάλῃ ἀναγνωρισμένο, καθὼς τοῦ
πρέπει, ἀπὸ τὴν ἐθνικὴ συνείδησι τὸ ἔργο του, γιὰ νὰ γίνῃ κάποια
θερμὴ ἐνέργεια πρὸς ἀγαλμάτων του ὑψωμοὺς καὶ βιβλίων του
τυπώματα, γιὰ νὰ σωπαίνῃ γύρω στ' ὄνομά του κάθε φιλονεικία
φιλολογικὴ καὶ κάθε ἀμφιβολία, γιὰ νὰ τὸν τιμήσουν καὶ αὐτοῦ τοῦ
Κράτους οἱ πλέον ἐπίσημοι ἀντιπρόσωποι σὰν ἕνα μεγάλον ἄνθρω-
πον. Μὰ σκύψε πιὸ σιμὰ καὶ ψάξε τα ὅλ' αὐτὰ στοχαστικώτερα·
βλέπεις πῶς ὁ κόσμος ἕναν ἴσκιο ἀσύστατο τοῦ μεγάλου ποιητή,
ἔτσι στὰ τυφλά, προσκυνάει, καὶ πῶς μὲ τὸν ἀληθινὸ καὶ μὲ τὸν
ἀκέριο Σολωμό, καθὼς τοῦ ἀξίζει νὰ γνωριστῇ, ἀκόμα δὲν καλο-
γνωρίστηκε. Ἀπὸ τὰ 97 πολεμᾶμε νὰ τοῦ πανηγυρίσουμε τὰ ἑκατὸ
χρόνια του, κι ὅλο γιὰ κεῖνον ἐπιτροπὲς κ' ἐπιτροπὲς ζητιανεύουν,
κι ἀκόμα δὲν τὸ κατορθώσαμε, ἕνα ἔθνος ὁλόκληρο, γιὰ τὸν
ἀσύγκριτο ποιητή του. Ὑπάρχουν ἄνθρωποι — καὶ δὲν εἶναι οἱ

πιὸ λίγοι — ποῦ τὸν ξέρουν μονάχ' ἀπὸ τὴν „Ξανθούλα" καὶ
ἀπὸ τὰ δύο πρῶτα τετράστιχα τοῦ Ὕμνου καὶ δὲ γυρεύουν τίποτε
παραπάνω· ἀκούνε, πῶς μεγάλος εἶναι ποιητής, δὲν ἀκούνε νὰ τὸν
περιγελοῦν καὶ νὰ τὸν ἀναθεματίζουν ὅπως ἄλλους — πιστεύουν
ἀγαθώτατα, πῶς κάτι βέβαια ξεχωριστὸ θὰ εἶναι, πείθουν τὸν
ἑαυτό τους, πῶς ἔτσι θὰ εἶναι, χασμουρειοῦνται, ἀνακλαδίζονται,
καὶ πέφτουν εὐχαριστημένοι νὰ κοιμηθοῦν. Ὑπάρχουν ἄλλοι σο-
φολογιώτατοι, ὄχι τόσον συμβιβαστικοί, καὶ λογικώτεροι, ποῦ,
φυσικώτατα, εἶναι ἀνήμποροι νὰ χωνέψουν τὴν τέχνη καὶ τὴ
φήμη τοῦ ψάλτη τῶν „Ἐλεύθερων Πολιορκημένων"· μόνο ποῦ δὲν
ἔχουν ἀκόμη τὸ θάρρος καὶ τὴ δύναμι, νὰ εἰποῦνε καὶ γιὰ κεῖνον
ἄφοβα καὶ μεγαλόφωνα καὶ ξέγνοιαστα ὅσα κοπανίζουν γιὰ ἄλλους,
ποῦ μέσα τους κάποιο αἷμα βράζει Σολωμικό, μὰ ποῦ δὲν τοὺς
λαμπρύνει καὶ τοῦ Σολωμοῦ ἡ δόξα. Κάποια ἀναποδιὰ ἱλαρο-
τραγικὴ ἐδῶ πέρα φανερὴ γίνεται στὸ νοῦ στὸ στοχαστικό. Ὁ
Σολωμὸς βέβαια δὲ δοξάζεται ἔτσι ξεχωριστά, γιὰ τὴν ἀγάπη του
πρὸς τὴν πατρίδα· ὁ πατριωτισμός, χρέος ἱερὸ τοῦ ἀνθρώπου,
δὲ φτάνει μόνος νὰ φορέσῃ τοῦ ποιητὴ τὸ στέφανο τῆς ἀθανα-
σίας· στὰ ἔργα τῆς Τέχνης τ' ἀγαθὰ αἰσθήματα δὲν ἐξετάζονται.
Ὕμνους πρὸς τὴν ἐλευθερία καὶ πρὸς τὸν ἀγῶνα μας ἔγραψαν
μὲ ἀνάλογη ὁρμὴ φιλοπατρίας, σύγχρονοι τοῦ Σολωμοῦ, στὴν ἴδια
ἐποχὴν ἀπάνω κάτω, ὁ Ρίζος Νερουλός, ὁ Παναγιώτης Σοῦτσος
καὶ ἄλλοι. Καὶ πῶς ἐκεῖνοι δὲ λογαριάζονται γιὰ τοῦτο, καὶ πῶς
τοὺς στίχους ἐκείνων τοὺς θάψαμε βαθειὰ στὰ χώματα τῆς λήθης,
πῶς δὲν ἀγωνιζόμαστε κ' ἐκείνων τ' ἀγάλματα νὰ στήσουμε; Γιατί
ἐκεῖνοι, ὅσο κι ἂν δείχνουν πλούσια τὴν ἀγάπη τῆς πατρίδας,
ἔχουνε στενὴ τὴ φαντασία καὶ μικρὴ τὴν τέχνη, ἀγνάντια στὸ
μεγαλοφάνταστο καὶ στὸ μεγαλότεχνο τραγουδιστὴ τοῦ Ὕμνου.
Γιατί δὲ δοξάζομε τὸν ἄνθρωπο μὲ τὴν καρδιάν, ἀλλὰ τὸν ποιητὴ
μὲ τὸ νοῦ, τὴ φαντασία καὶ τὴ θεία πνοή, τὴν ἰδέα καὶ τὴ μορφή,
τὸ στίχο καὶ τὸ ρυθμό, τὴ γλῶσσα καὶ τὸ λόγο τοῦ Σολωμοῦ
ἀχώριστα. Κ' ἐδῶ εἶναι ἡ ἀναποδιά. Ὁ Σολωμὸς ψηλὰ ν' ἀνα-
στυλώνεται καὶ νὰ καμαρώνεται ἀπὸ λαὸν ὁλόκληρο, καὶ ὅσοι
βλέπουν πρὸς ἐκεῖνον, καὶ ὁμόφυλοί του εἶναι καὶ ὁμόθρησκοι καὶ μ'
ἕνα τρόπο ξεχωριστὸν ὁ καθένας, ὅμως ἐκείνου σὰ νὰ φιλοδοξοῦνε
νὰ συμπληρώσουν τὸ ἔργο, μόνο πῶς δὲν κομματιάζονται ἀπὸ κάποιους πολυθόρυβους καὶ ξαφνισμένους, ποῦ πέφτουν καταπάνου
τους κράζοντας καὶ θυμίζοντας τοὺς κοράκες τῆς Πινδαρικῆς ᾠδῆς.
    Ὑπάρχει μάλιστα φιλολογία. Δὲ θὰ εἰπῇ μ' αὐτό, πῶς ὅλα
ρόδινα τὰ βλέπω, καὶ πῶς κάθε στίχο καὶ πῶς κάθε γραμμὴ τὸ

ρουφῶ σὰ γάλα. Ὑπάρχει, ὅμως μποροῦσε καλύτερα καὶ πλουσιώ-
τερα νὰ ὑπάρχῃ· μὰ ἡ ἀφορμὴ, ποὺ κρατεῖ κάπως ἀστενικὴ καὶ
κάπως δεμένη τὴ φιλολογία μας, εἶναι πιὸ πολὺ ἐξωτερικὴ, δὲν
εἶναι τόσο ἐσωτερικὴ· δὲ φταίει τόσο ὁ νοῦς, ὅσον ὁ ἀέρας γύρω
του. Ἔκαμα στὴν ἀρχὴ τὴν παρατήρησι, πῶς τὰ ἔργα τῆς φαντασίας δὲν ἔχουν ὄνομα ξεχωριστὸ στὸν τόπο μας. Εἶναι καὶ
κάτι ἄλλο, ποὺ δὲ συμβαίνει μοναχὰ σ' ἐμᾶς ἐδώ. Ἡ πέννα εἶναι
τὸ κοινὸν ὄργανο, ποὺ σημειώνει τὴ γνώμη του καὶ ὁ ποιητής
καὶ κάθε μελανωτὴς τοῦ χαρτιοῦ. Καὶ λοιπὸν ὁ μελανωτὴς φαν-
τάστηκε, πῶς συγγενεύει μὲ τὸν ποιητή, καὶ πῶς ἔχει δικαίωμα
ν' ἀκουστῇ καὶ νὰ τιμηθῇ σὰν ἐκεῖνον καὶ νὰ τὸν ἐπικρίνη καὶ
νὰ τὸν σφυρίξῃ! Καὶ λοιπὸν σταυροφορία κατὰ τοῦ ποιητή, σὰν
τὸν πόλεμο, ποὺ θὰ κήρυτταν στεῖρες γυναῖκες καὶ γεροντοκόριτσα
κατὰ μητέρων, ποὺ καὶ πρότυπα ὀμορφιᾶς ἂν δὲν εἶναι τὰ παιδιά
τους, πάλι βαραίνουν πιὸ πολὺ ἀπὸ τοὺς ἄγονους σταυροφόρους.

Κ' ἐπειδὴ στὴν Ἑλλάδα ὁ μελανωτὴς, ἐνενηνταεννέα τοῖς ἑκατό,
πιστεύει, πῶς μὲ ὅσο ἀρχαϊκώτερα λόγια καὶ τύπους μπαλώσῃ
τὰ γραφόμενά του, τόσο ἑλληνικώτερα στοχάζεται καὶ τόσο μοιάζει
τοῦ Θουκυδίδη καὶ τοῦ Σοφοκλῆ, καταφρονεῖ τὸν ποιητή· γιατί ὁ
ποιητὴς πάλι, κατὰ ἐνενηνταεννέα τοῖς ἑκατό, πιστεύει, πῶς ὅσο
συμφωνότερα τὰ λόγια του ὅλα τὰ ρυθμίσῃ μὲ τὰ δημοτικὰ τραγούδια μας καὶ μὲ τὴν ἐγκάρδια γλώσσα τῆς ζωντανῆς τριγύρω
του ὁλάνοιχτης ζωῆς, ἄλλο τόσο ἀξίζει νὰ εὐλογηθῇ ἀπὸ τοὺς
Ὁμήρους καὶ ἀπὸ τοὺς Πλάτωνες. Κ' ἔτσι ὁ ποιητὴς ἔγινε μαλλιαρός. Μὲ τ' ὄνομα τοῦτο βάφτισε — θὰ εἰπῇ μιὰ μέρα ἡ
Ἱστορία — πρόστυχος καιρὸς ἀντιποιητικώτατος κάθετι ποὺ εἶχε
ἢ ποὺ ἤθελε νὰ κάμῃ φτερά.

III. SPECIMENS OF DIALECT.

1. From Bova.

(Lower Italy, near Reggio)

In this and the following selection the transcription (*cf.* § 1 n.) employed by the editors *Morosi* and *Comparetti* has been retained. A few signs have been borrowed from the Italian orthography; thus, *cchi* = κ *k´*, *z* = (ν)τζ *dz* (but *źź* = ζ *z*), *gn* = νι *n´* ; *ć* stands for τσ̌ *č* (§ 17), *h·* = German *h* (*spiritus asper*), *ṅ* = ʋ. On *ḍḍ*, *v.* § 31, n. 2.

Mágni[1]) *kazzéḍḍa*[2]), *me kanni*[3]) *peþáni*[4]),
Na peþáni me kánni esú, kazzéḍḍa.
Sa mme túnda[5]) *lucchiáćia*[6]) *kanunái,*
Mu sérri tiṅ gardía me tiṅ gordéḍḍa.
Sa mmu platégui[7]), *péźźi će jeláï,*
To jóco[8]) *mu kánni ti alupuḍéḍḍa.*
Ma ćíni iméra kalí éh·ji na érti,
Na su síro to éma sa mmía avdéḍḍa.

Translation into the ordinary language :

Ὄμορφο κορίτσι, μὲ κάνεις νὰ πεθάνω,
Νὰ πεθάνω μὲ κάνεις ἐσύ, κορίτσι ·
Σὰ(ν) μὲ 'τοῦνα[5]) ματάκια (μὲ) θωρεῖς,
Μοῦ σέρνεις τὴν καρδιὰ μὲ τὴν κορδέλλα.
Σὰ(ν) μὲ μιλάεις, παίζεις καὶ γελάεις,
Τὸ παιγνίδι μου κάνεις τῆς ἀλωποῦς.
Μὰ κείνη μέρα καλὴ ἔχει νὰ ἔρθη,
Νὰ σου σύρω τὸ αἷμα σὰ(ν) μιὰ ἀβδέλλα.

[1]) *magno,* "beautiful."   [2]) "maiden."   [3]) *v.* § 29 n.   [4]) Fragment of the infinitive, *cf.* § 277, n. 1. In the next line the same form is treated as a stereotyped subjunctive (3rd pers. sing. instead of 1st). [5]) *Cf.* § 144.   [6]) Ital. word with a Gk. suffix (-άκι).   [7]) § 23 n.   [8]) Ital. word.

2. From Calimera in the Terra d' Otranto.

(Lower Italy, near Lecce)

On the transcription, see the note to No. 1. $c=κ$ before a, o, u; $ch=κ$ before e, i; $c=τσ$; gh before e, $i=γ(ι)$; $z=ζ$; $dd=ḍḍ$ in No. 1; $ψ$ has the value of fs, v. § 35, n. 2.

Calédda[1]) ψιχίμμυ.

Epóa[2]) a máddia dicúma ecanonistisasi[3]), i cardia mu en m'écame pléo[4]) na plóso[5]), ce pánda penséi[6]) se séna ce téli[7]) na cúsi na milisune ghi'eséna, ce mu váddi pu éssu[8]), ce sénza[9]) na ψéro[10]), evotó[11]) túrtea sto spítissu; ce póa cúo i foní ndichéddasu[12]), χánno o mílimma, a máddia mu scuriázune, o músomu[13]) o sózi fonási[14]) pesamméno[15]), a pódia ettélune pléo na pradisune ambró, ce épetta[16]) ecí mésa, an evó en pensone[17]) ca[18]) mu sózune jelási[14]) ecíni pu en eψérune ti έχο sti cardíamu ce possi lúmera[19]) esú móvale cíttin[20]) eméra pu ca[21]) ecanonistísomma[22]).

Pistéo ca ettéli ádda lója — súpa posso se gapó — ghizi árte se séna na mu píi pósso me gapá. Elimonízi[23]) na mu mbiéψi[24]) in agápissu? Cámeto présta[25]), ca evó stéo[26]) me éna póda cimésa ce me táddo séna nimma.

Stásu calí ce pénsa[27]) pánda se ména.

Translation into the ordinary vernacular:

Καλὴ ψυχή μου.

῞Οταν τὰ μάτια τὰ δικά μας ἀνταμωθήκανε, ἡ καρδιά μου δὲ μ' ἔκαμε πιὸ νὰ κοιμηθῶ καὶ πάντα συλλογίζεται σ' ἐσένα, καὶ θέλει ν' ἀκούσῃ νὰ μιλήσουνε γιὰ σένα καὶ μὲ βάλλει ἀπὸ μέσα, καὶ χωρὶς νὰ ξέρω, ἔρχομαι ἐδῶ πέρα στὸ σπίτι σου· καὶ ὅταν ἀκούω τὴ φωνὴ τὴ δική σου, χάνω τὸ μίλημα, τὰ μάτια μου θαμπώνονται, τὸ πρόσωπό μου μπορεῖς νὰ τὸ

---

[1]) -edda, i.e. -ella, an Ital. diminutive suffix.   [2]) epóa=ὁπόταν, on the loss of the τ, v. § 22 n.; initial τ has also dropped off in the article (o=τὸ, i=τὴν).   [3]) Cf. n. 22; for the termination, v. § 214, n. 4.   [4]) pléo, v. § 10, n. 1.   [5]) plónno "sleep."   [6]) § 199, I. 1. a. n. The stem of the word is Ital. (pensare).   [7]) v. § 20, n. 1.   [8]) "it drives me out" (pu éssu=ἀπὸ ἔσω).   [9]) Ital.   [10]) § 35, n. 2.   [11]) "I approach."   [12]) § 143, n. 2.   [13]) muso, Ital.   [14]) § 224, 3. n. 3.   [15]) § 20, n. 1.   [16]) § 14, n. 2.   [17]) Ital. form.   [18]) Ital. ca=che "that."   [19]) Ital.   [20]) =κειὴν τὴν (cf. ettélune from en télune); κειός, § 146, n. 1.   [21]) Cf. n. 18; ca is pleonastic here.   [22]) The aorist pass. is here enlarged by -sa- instead of -κα- or -να- (cf. § 208).   [23]) v. p. 136.   [24]) mbiévo, Ital. verb with a Greek present formation (-εύω).   [25]) Ital.   [26]) § 22 n.   [27]) Ital. form—imperative to pensare.

φωνάσης πεθαμμένο, τὰ πόδια δὲ(ν) θέλουνε πιὸ νὰ περπατήσουνε ἐμπρός, καὶ (θὰ) ἔπεφτα ἐκεῖ μέσα, ἂν ἐγὼ δὲ συλλογιζόμουνα, πῶς ἤθελα μὲ γελάσει ἐκεῖνοι ποὺ δὲν ἠξέρουνε, τί ἔχω στὴν καρδιά μου καὶ πόση φωτιὰ ἐσὺ μόβαλες ἐκείνη τὴν ἡμέρα ποὺ ἀνταμωθήκαμε.

Πιστεύω πῶς δὲ θέλεις ἄλλα λόγια — σοῦ 'πα πόσο σ' ἀγαπῶ — πρέπει τώρα σ' ἐσένα νὰ μοῦ πῆς πόσο μ' ἀγαπᾷς. Λησμονᾷς νὰ μοῦ δώσης τὴν ἀγάπη σου; Κάμε το γλήγορα, γιατί στέκω μὲ ἕνα πόδι ἐκεῖ μέσα καὶ μὲ τ' ἄλλο σ' ἕνα μνῆμα.

Στάσου καλὴ καὶ συλλογίζου πάντα σ' ἐμένα.

3. Maina.

For the pronunciation of σ and ζ, *cf.* § 28 : I have, however, sometimes heard distinctly a pure σ on listening attentively. As for the occasional dropping off of the -s, it was sometimes faintly audible. On τσ̌=κ, *cf.* § 17.

For the better understanding of the contents of both the elegies, which I wrote down in the year 1894 at the dictation of my Maniatic *Agoyat*, I here add (in somewhat abbreviated form) the information for which I have to thank the distinguished connoisseur of the m. Gk. popular art, Professor N. G. Politis of Athens : "Both elegies belong among the most popular in Maina. Both have reference to events of the fourth decade of the past (nineteenth) century. The first (a) is an elegy upon the death of Παρασκευή (Παρασ̌τή), the daughter of a certain Γρηγόρις or Δηγόρις (Δηγορίτσα). The mourner charges her to convey to her departed kin in the underworld tidings of a severe calamity which has overtaken the family, namely, that the fortified dwelling ('citadel') of the family is besieged by the enemy. The besieged leader of the family is Γιῶργος Σκυλακογιάννης, who participated in the year 1834 in the insurrection of the Maniates against the regency of King Otto. The beleaguering party are Maniates allied with the Bavarian troops under General Feder. Διακονοδιτσ̌αίακας is a Maniate of the name Δικαῖος (see n. 4). The 'bastard' (μοῦλος) of Κατσ̌εβαρδοῦ, or, more correctly, the bastards of K. were cowardly and stupid sons of a wealthy widow ; the 'conies' of Διοῦ are the cowardly sons of the wife of a certain 'Ηλίας, named contemptuously after their mother. The besieged (Σκυλακογιάννης) was taken captive, and died in prison at Tripolitza.

"The elegy (b) is also well known on account of the subject, a Maniatic vendetta which developed in a peculiar fashion. The husband of Δηγοροῦ, namely, Δηγόρις Βέτουλας, had been slain by Πέτρος Διόπουλος, who belonged to the same family, but after the murder came into conflict with his own relatives, on whom rested the obligation of avenging the murdered man. But because of the tie of kinship with the murderer they neglected to perform this obligation. The murdered man's wife (Δηγοροῦ) once went to Álika, a village in the department of Messa, on a visit to her relatives ; on the way thither she came through the village Σπηλιωτάνικα (near the village of Μπολαριοί). In the former she saw the near relatives of the murderer, and even the murderer himself. She greeted, and her kin returned the greeting, except the murderer, who not only refused to greet, but even derided her by punning upon the name of her late husband Βέτουλας (βετούλι a 'kid'). The murderer Λιόπουλος ironically proposes to pay blood-money for her husbaud, calculating the amount at highest at 9 piastres, *i.e.* about the price of a good kid. The widow, indignant over the insult, reveals her great perturbation when she came to her kin by not greeting them. Her brother-in-law Yannis, observing that it is something serious, approaches her and hears the words of the murderer. In other versions Λητορού reproaches him for leaving his brother unavenged. Yannis in wrath seizes his gun, and, with the devil's assistance, kills Λιόπουλος at his house from an ambush. He then flees and escapes to the house of the Σκυλακογιάννης, to whom elegy (a) refers."

a. Μοιρολόγι from Kitta.

Ἔ, Λητορίτσα Παρασͅτͅσή,
　　Ἄν ἒν τͅσαὶ πὰ$ στὴν κάτου ζͅῆ¹),
Νὰ πͅῆ$ τοῦν ἀθρωπͅῶνε²) μα³),
　　Ὅτι τὸ κάσͅτρο κρούͅιεται·
Τὸ κρούͅιει ὁ Βαβουλόλϊας
　　Τͅσͅαὶ ὁ Διακονοδιτͅσͅαίακα$⁴)
Τͅσͅαὶ ὁ μοῦλος τῆς Κατͅσͅεβαρδοῦ$
　　Τͅσͅαὶ τὰ κουνέλια τῆς Λιοῦ$.
Ἔλα νὰ σͅυφωνήσͅωμε
　　Ἄντρε⁵) ζͅυναῖτͅσͅε⁵) σͅυντετά
Ζͅέροντες¹) τͅσͅαὶ μικρὰ πᾳιδά⁶),
　　Νὰ τὴν ἐβγάλωμ' ἀπὸ 'πά
Τͅή ζͅειτονία τὴν κᾳϊτͅσͅά⁷),
　　Γιατί ζͅωὴ δὲν ἔχομε.

b. Μοιρολόγι from Μπολαρͅιοί.

Μͅιὰ σͅκόλη τͅσͅαὶ μͅιὰ τͅσͅυρατͅσͅὴ
　　Τͅσͅαὶ μͅιὰ δευτέρα τͅῆ⁵) Λαμπρͅῆ$
Ὄντ' ἀρδινͅιάσͅτ' ἡ Λητορού
　　Νὰ πὰ σͅτοῦν ἀθρωπͅῶνε τͅῆ$,
Βᾴιζͅει⁶) κουλλούͅιρα⁶) σͅτὴμ ποϊδά,
　　Κότͅσͅιν' αὐγὰ σͅτὴ ζͅουναρͅιά,

---

¹) § 27.　²) § 62.　³)=μᾶς.　⁴) The name Δικαῖος is turned into contempt with διακονο- (διακονιάρις) "beggar" and the pejorative suffix -ακας (Politis).　⁵) § 29 n.　⁶) § 8, n. 2.　⁷) § 111.

Πέραϊ' ἀπὸ τοὺς Μπουλαϊροὺϊ
    Τόϊ ἀπὸ τὰ Σπηλιωτάϊνικα.
Χάμου ϊτὴ ρούγα κάθουντα⁸),
    Τόϊ ὅλουϊ τοὺϊ ἐϊαιρέτιϊε⁹),
Κανένα¹⁰) δὲν ἐμίληϊε,
    Μ' ὁ¹¹) Πέτρος ὁ Λϊόπουλος
Εἶπε· „Καλῶϊ τὴ Ληγορού,
    Καλῶϊ τη, καλῶϊ ὥριϊες,
Μωϊρή⁶), ἆμ πὰς ϊτοῦν ἀθρωπῶνε σου,
    Πέϊ τουϊ νὰ κάμουμε καλά,
Τϊ' ἐμεῖϊ τοὺϊ τὸ πλερώνομε
    Τϊεῖνο τὸ παλιοβέτουλο¹²)
Νὴ ἔϊι γρόϊα νὴ τϊ' ἐφτά,
    "Ε, ϊτὴν ἀκρίβεια ἆϊ πάει τϊ' ἐϊννιά".
'Ετϊείνη ρεϊτενίϊτητϊε
    Τϊ' ἐδιάη¹³) ϊτοῦν ἀθρωπῶνε της,
Χάμου ϊτὴ ρούγα πέραϊε
    Τϊαὶ δὲν τοὺϊ ἐϊαιρέτιϊε.
Ζάννηϊ¹) ϊοφὸς τϊαὶ γνωστικὸς
    Σηκώθητϊε τϊαὶ τὴν ἔφταϊε·
„Μωϊρή, καλῶϊ τὴ Ληγορού,
    Καλῶϊ τη, καλῶϊ ὥριϊες,
Μωϊρή, τί 'ναι ἡ πίκρα ϊου,
    Τί 'ναι τὸ μαράϊι ϊου;" —
„Τί νὰ Ϊὲ¹⁴) 'ποῦ, ἀφεντάτϊι μου,
    Πέραϊ' ἀπὸ τοὺ Μπουλαϊροὺς
Τόϊ ἀπὸ τὰ Σπηλιωτάϊνικα.
    Χάμου ϊτὴ ρούγα κάθουντα,
Τόϊ ὅλουϊ τοὺϊ ἐϊαιρέϊτιϊα,
    Κανένα¹⁰) δὲ μοῦ μίληϊε,
Μ' ὁ Πέτροϊ ὁ Λϊόπουλοϊ
    Εἶπε· 'Καλῶϊ τὴ Ληγορού,
"Αν πὰϊ ϊτοῦν ἀθρωπῶνε ϊου,
    Πέϊ τους νὰ κάμουμε καλά,
Τϊ' ἐμεῖϊ τοὺϊ τὸ πλερώνομε
    Τϊεῖνο τὸ παλιοβέτουλο¹²)

⁸) 3rd plur.   ⁹) § 21.   ¹⁰) = κανένας.   ¹¹) = μόνο ὁ.   ¹²) See
the introductory note and § 41a, 1. b.   ¹³) § 208.   ¹⁴) § 135, n. 1.

Νὴ ἕξι γρόσα νὴ τσ' ἐφτά,
Ἐ, σ'τὴν ἀκρίβεια ἀ̱ξ πά̱ει τσ' ἐ̈ιννιά'."
Ζάννη̱ς ἐρεῐτενίσ'τητσ̑ε,
Στὸ σ̑πίτι του ἐ̈ι̱δάητσ̑ε ¹⁵)·
„Γιὰ δό ¹⁶) μου, νύφη, τὸ σ̑αλμᾶ,
Νὰ πά̱ω ζ̑ὰ¹) τὸ βόδι μα³),
Τσ̑ι̱ ἃ δὲν ἐρθοῦ ¹⁷) ὡ̱ξ τὸ πρωΐ,
Ρίξετε τὸ χαλίτσ̑ι μου ¹⁸)
Τσ̑' ἐμένα μὲ τοῦ Βέτουλα".
Στὸ δρόμο ποῦι̱ ¹⁹) ἐπά̈ιζαινε ²⁰),
Ἕνα βετούλι βέλαξε·
„Ἔλα κοντά μου, σ̑αῐτανά,
Νὰ̈ι ⁶) διορδώσ̑ου τὴ δουλειά".

4. Aegina.

Ὁ βασιλέας Ὕπνος.

Μία¹) φορὰ τσ'²) ἕνα τσαιρὸ²) ἥτανε ἕνας βασιλέας¹), Ὕ-
πνος τ' ὄνομά του. Δίπλα εἰς τὸ παλάτι ἐκαθότανε μία φτωχὴ
κόρη τσαὶ ξενοδούλευε τσαὶ 'ζοῦσε. Ἐνυχτόρευε τσαὶ ὄντες τῆς
ἐρχότανε ὁ ὕπνος νὰ τσ̑ουμηθῆ³), ἔπαιρνε κουτσία τσ' ἔτρωε τσ'
ἔλεε· „ἦρθες, ὕπνε, καλῶς ἦρθες, φάε κουτσία τσαὶ φύγε." Ἀπ'
ὄξω ἥτανε ἡ δωδεκάδα τοῦ βασιλέα τσ' ἄκουτσε⁴) νὰ λέη ἡ κόρη·
»,ἦρθες, ὕπνε, καλῶς ἦρθες, φάε κουτσία τσαὶ φύγε." Εἴπανε· „σ'
αὐτὴ τὴ φτωχὴ κόρη εἶναι ὁ βασιλέας μας μέσα." Τὴν ἄλλη
νύχτα πῆγε ἡ δωδεκάδα τοῦ βασιλέα ν' ἀκούσῃ τί θὰ εἰπῇ. Ἐ-
τσείνη νυχτόρευε, τσ' ὄντες τῆς ἐρχότανε ὁ ὕπνος, ἔλεε· „ἦρθες,
ὕπνε, καλῶς ἦρθες, πᾶρε τὸ σκαμνὶ τσαὶ κάτσε." Αὐτοὶ ἐλέανε·
„ὁ βασιλέας μας εἶναι μέσα." Τὴν ἄλλη νύχτα πάλι ἡ δωδεκάδα
ἐπῆγε ν' ἀκούσῃ, τί θὰ εἰπῇ ἡ κόρη, τσ' ἄκουτσε τὰ ἴδια λόγια.
Τότες ἐπῆγε ἡ δωδεκάδα στὴ μάννα τοῦ βασιλέα τσαὶ τῆς εἰπε,
ὅτι ὁ βασιλέας παγαίνει κάθε νύχτα σ' αὐτῆς τῆς φτωχῆς κόρης
τὸ σπίτι. Ὄντες τ' ἄκουτσε ἡ μάννα του, τὸν ἐφώναξε τσαὶ τοῦ

---

¹⁵) § 208.   ¹⁶) =δῶσε (δός).   ¹⁷) § 213, n. 3.   ¹⁸) The sense
is: "consider me also like Βέτουλας as dead." In Greece the custom of
piling up stones on the spot where a murder took place is wide-spread.
¹⁹) =ποῦ.   ²⁰) =ἐπάγαινε.
¹) v. § 10, n. 1.   ²) § 17.   ³) § 6, n. 4, and § 17 n.
⁴) § 202, n. 1.

εἶπε· „πῶς καταφρονάεις τὸν ἑαυτό σου, βασιλέας ἐσὺ καταδέχεσαι νὰ παγαίνῃς κάθε νύχτα σ' αὐτῆς τῆς φτωχῆς κόρης τὸ σπίτι;" — „Ἐγὼ οὔτε κἂν τὴν ἔχω ἰδωμένα στὰ μάτια μου." — „Νὰ πάψῃς στὸ ἑξῆς, παιδί μου, νὰ πηγαίνῃς. Γιατί; διότι δὲ σοῦ κάμει τιμή."

Ἐφώναξε τσ' αὐτὴ τὴ φτωχὴ κόρη τσαὶ τῆς εἶπε· „στὸ ἑξῆς νὰ μὴν ἔχῃς τὴ σχέσι τοῦ βασιλέα, νὰ μὴν τὸν δέχεσαι στὸ σπίτι σου, γιατί τί ἔχεις νὰ περάσῃς!" — Τῆς εἶπε· „ποτὲ δὲν ἔγινε τοῦτο· γιατί εἶμαι ἄξα⁵) 'γὼ μία φτωχὴ κόρη νὰ δέχωμαι τὸ βασιλέα στὸ σπίτι μου;" Ἀλλὰ τὸ 'πῆρε πολὺ ἐπιπόνου ἡ κόρη, δὲν ἤξερε τί νὰ κάνῃ. Τῆς ἔλεαν ὅλοι, ὅτι ὁ βασιλέας ἐπήγαινε στὸ σπίτι της. Πιάνει λοιπὸν τσαὶ βάνει πανιὰ στὴ τσ́ουλία³) της τσαὶ κάνει τὸ ψευτογγαστρωμένο, βγαίνει ὄξω στὴν αὐλή, κάθεται πάνω σὲ μία ψάθα τσαὶ δένει στὴν ἄκρη της ἕνα ἀλόχτερα τσαὶ τραβοῦσε τὴ ψάθα σὰ καρότσα. Ἐπεράκανε⁴) τρεῖς μοῖρες, τὴν εἴδανε τσ' ἐγελάκανε μ' ὅλη τους τὴν καρδία τσαὶ εἶπανε· „τρεῖς χρόνους εἴχαμε νὰ γελάσωμε τσ' αὐτὴ μᾶς ἔκανε νὰ γελάσωμε μ' ὅλη μας τὴν καρδία· τί νὰ τῆς εὐκηθοῦμε; νὰ τῆς εὐκηθοῦμε τὸ ψευτογγάστρωμά της νὰ γίνῃ ἀληθινό, νὰ βρεθῇ στὰ χέρια της ἕνα παιδὶ ἴδιος ὁ βασιλέας Ὕπνος· ἡ ψάθα νὰ γίνῃ μία ἅμαξα χρυσῆ, ὁ ἀλόχτερας νὰ γίνῃ ἕνα ἄτι χρυσό, τσ' αὐτὴ νὰ κάθεται στὴ μέση τῆς καρότσας τσαὶ νὰ βρεθῇ στοῦ παλατίου τὴν πόρτα, τσαὶ νὰ ζητήσουνε ὅλοι γιὰ βασίλισσα τσαὶ νὰ πάρῃ τὸ βασιλέα τὸν Ὕπνο νὰ γίνῃ βασίλισσα."

Ὦ τοῦ θάματος νὰ γίνουν ὅλα ὅπως τῆς εὐκηθῆναν'⁶) οἱ μοῖρες, νὰ τὴ δεχτοῦνε ὅλοι μὲ μεγάλη εὐκαρίστησι, τὸ παιδὶ νὰ εἶναι ἴδιος ὁ βασιλέας ὁ Ὕπνος, νὰ εἰποῦνε ὅλοι· „τὸ παιδὶ εἶναι τοῦ βασιλέα Ὕπνου, τσαὶ πρέπει νὰ τὴ στεφανωθῇ." Τοῦ λέει ἡ μάννα του· „τί κάθεσαι; Τὸ παιδὶ εἶναι δικό σου τσαὶ πρέπει νὰ τὴ στεφανωθῇς." Τότες τσ' ὁ βασιλέας τὸ πίστεψε τσ' αὐτὸς τσ' ἀποφάσιτσε νὰ τὴ στεφανωθῇ. Ἄργανα, τούμπανα, χαρὲς μεγάλες· τὴ στεφανώθητσε ὁ βασιλέας τσ' ἔγινε βασίλισσα, ἐκάθιτσε στὸ θρόνο τσ' ἐζούσανε ἐτσεῖνοι καλὰ ἐτσεῖ, τσ' ἐμεῖς ἐδὼ πιὸ καλύτερα.

5. Ios.

This story was told me by a very aged woman from the ranks of the common folk. The intermixture with forms not genuinely dialectical is striking. Palatalised κ (§ 17) was pronounced mostly as τσ, but often approached a τσ́ (τσ́).

⁵) § 10, n. 4.   ⁶) § 208 and § 221, n. 3.

Ὁ Φιορεδῖνος.

Ἥτον ἕνας βασιλέας τσαὶ εἶχε κακουσὰ στὸ τσεφάλι·
βασιλέας τσαὶ μὲ τὴ κακουσὰ μποροῦσε νὰ παρισιαστῆ. Τὸ
μεταχειρίζουδα πολλοὶ γιατροί, νὰ γιάνῃ ἡ λέπρα, ποῦ εἶχε στὸ
τσεφάλι του. Μέσα στσοὶ πολλοὶ γιατροὶ[1]) εὑρέθη ἕνας ἄλλος
γιατρός. Τοῦ λέει ὁ γιατρός· „βασιλέα μου, δὲ γιαίνεις μὲ για-
τρικά, ἃ δὲν εὕρῃς ἕνα βασιλόπαιδο νὰ τὸ σφάξῃς, νὰ τριφτῆ
τὸ γαῖμα του νὰ γένῃ καλά". Ἀφοῦ τοῦ τό ᾿πε ὁ γιατρός, ἐρ-
χίνισε ν᾿ ἀναστενάζῃ· „ποῦ θά ᾿βρω τέτοιο παιδὶ νὰ τὸ σφάξω;"
Ἡ κόρη του ἡ πρώτη τοῦ λέει. „Γιάδα[2]) ἀναστενάζεις;" — „Γιατί
δὲν ἔχω ἀγώρι νὰ μοῦ φέρῃ αὐτὸ τὸ παιδί". Τοῦ λέει ἡ κόρη
του· „μὴ πικραίνεσαι τσαὶ κάμε ἕν᾿ ἀρμαμέδο[2]) βασιλικό, νὰ γίνω
καπετάνιος, ἡ μιά σου κόρη νὰ ἔμπῃ καμαριέρα, ἡ ἄλλη λοστρόμος·
νὰ βάλῃς ὅλη τὴ κουβάνια μέσα τσαὶ τοὺς μαρινέρους".

Ἔπειτα ἤφυε τὸ πλοῖο τσαὶ πάει στὴν Εὐρώπη, ὅπου ἤξεραν,
ὅτι εἶναι ἕνας βασιλέας τσ᾿ εἶχε μόνον ἕνα παιδὶ σερνικό. Ὡς
καθὼς τὸ βλέπει ὁ βασιλέας τὸ πλοῖο, λέει τσῆ βασίλισσας·
„σήκω, βασίλισσα, νὰ συγυριστῆς· τσαὶ αὐτὸ τὸ πλοῖο ποῦ
᾿ρχεται εἶναι βασιλικό, τσαὶ κανένας βασιλέας μᾶς τὸ κάνει πεστσέσι". Τότε φεύγει ὁ βασιλέας τσ᾿ ἡ βασίλισσα τσαὶ τὸ παιδὶ
τωνε ὁ Φιορεδῖνος[2]) τσ᾿ ἐπῆαν στὸ πλοῖο τὸ βασιλικό. Ὡς καθὼς
τὸ εἶδαν τὸ παιδί, τοῦ ᾿κάμαν τόσες τσιριμόνιες τσαὶ κοβλιμέντα·
τότε ἤβγαλαν τὰ φαητὰ τσαὶ κάθισα νὰ φάνε. Μετὰ τὸ δεῖπνο
σερβίρανε τσοὶ καφέδες, στοῦ παιδιοῦ τὸ γαφὲ[2]) εἶχαν ὕπνο·
ἐτσοιμήθη τὸ παιδί. Λέει ἡ βασίλισσα στὸ βασιλέα· „βασιλέα μου
πολυχρονεμένε μου, νὰ φύωμε, γιατί ἐπέρασε ἡ ὥρα". Ἐτσείνες
οἱ κόρες στσέπασαν τὸ παιδὶ τσαὶ τοῦ ᾿δωσαν τσαὶ ἄλλο ὕπνο,
τσαὶ πῆε τὸ παιδὶ στὸν ἄλλο κόσμο[3]). Ἡ βασίλισσα ἐπῆε τσαὶ
τοῦ λέει· „σήκω, παιδί μου, νὰ πηαίνουμε". Τότε παρισιαστήκανε
ἐμπρός της ἐτσείνες οἱ κόρες τοῦ ἀλλουνοῦ βασιλέα τσ᾿ εἶπαν·
„γιατί θὰ πάρῃς τὸ παιδί σου νὰ κρυώσῃ, ποῦ εἶναι νύχτα; Μήπως
τσ᾿ εἴμαστε κουρσάριδες τσαὶ φοβεῖσαι; Ἐμεῖς εἴμαστε βασιλικὸ
ἀρμαμέδο. Τὸ πρωὶ θὰ τὸ σηκώσωμε, νὰ τὸ φέρωμε ἀπάνω στὸ
βασίλειο σου". Τσ᾿ ἔπειτα τσῆ λέει ὁ βασιλέας· „δὲ βειράζει[2]), ἂς
ἀφήσωμε τὸ παιδὶ νὰ μὴ κρυώσῃ". Ἔφυε ὁ βασιλέας μὲ τὴ
βασίλισσα τσαὶ πῆαν στὸ παλάτι τωνε. Ὡς καθὼς φεύγει ὁ
βασιλέας, ἐσηκωθήκανε, ἐσαρπάρανε τὴν ἄγκουρα πολὺ σιγὰ τσαὶ

[1]) § 62, n. 1.   [2]) § 15, n. 2.   [3]) An exaggerated expression for
" sank into deep slumber."

φύανε. Ἐφτάξανε στὸ ϑατέρα τωνε. Τὸ παιδὶ ἴντα ἤκαμε; ἤκλαιε
τὸ παιδί. Σὰν ἐφτάξανε, ἠχάρη ὁ βασιλέας, ὅπου τοῦ φέρανε
παιδί, τσαὶ ἤπαιξε κανονιὲς ἀπὸ τὴ χαρά του. Τὸ πῆραν τὸ παιδί
τσαὶ τὸ πήανε ἀπάνω στὸ ϑατέρα τωνε. Αὐτὸς ἀπὸ τὴ χαρά του
ἐμήνυσε τοῦ γιατροῦ νὰ πάη στὸ παλάτι, γιατί ηὗρε παιδὶ νὰ τὸ
σφάξουνε. Τότε τοῦ λέει ὁ γιατρός· „βασιλέα μου, ἠθέλαμε βασιλικὸ παιδί, γιὰ νά ᾽ναι τὸ γαῖμα του καθαρό. Τώρα ἂ τὸ σφάξης,
περισσότερο κακὸ θὰ κάνης παρὰ καλό· ἐπειδὴ ἀπὸ τὰ κλάματα
τὰ πολλά, ὅπου ἤκαμε τὸ παιδί, εἶναι τὸ γαῖμα του ἀνακατωμένο
μὲ τὴ χολή. Μόνο νὰ τὸ πᾶς στὸ περιβόλι σου μὲ μιὰ σου κόρη,
νὰ κάνουνε σαράντα μέρες, νὰ τρώνε, νὰ γλεδίζουνε, νὰ καθαρίση
τὸ γαῖμα [4]) του".

Ἐφτάξανε οἱ σαράντα μέρες νὰ τὸ σφάξουνε τὸ πρωΐ.
Τότε τοῦ λέει ἡ κόρη· „Φιορεδῖνε μου, πέσ᾽ ἀπάνω μου στὰ
γόνατά μου νὰ σὲ ψειρίσω". Τὸ Φιορεδῖνο τὸν ἐπῆρε ὁ ὕπνος.
Ἤρχισε νὰ κλαίη ἡ κόρη. Τὰ δάκρυά τσης ἠπέφτανε ἀπάνω του.
Τότε ξύπνησε μὲ τὰ δάκρυά τσης, τσαὶ τοῦ ᾽λέε ἡ κόρη· „πῶς
θὰ τὸ ᾽δῶ νὰ σὲ σφάξουνε;" — „Τσαὶ νὰ μὲ σφάξουνε;" — Τότε
λέει ἡ κόρη· „θὰ σὲ σφάξουνε, γιατί ἔχει ὁ πατέρας μου κακουσὰ
τσαὶ θέλει τὸ γαῖμα σου, νὰ τοῦ περάση". Τότε τση ἀποκρίνεται·
„τσ᾽ ἀφοῦ μὲ λυπᾶσαι, δὲ φεύγομε;" — „Φεύγομε, λικοδήσου
κομμάτι". Ἐπῆε στὸ παλάτι τοῦ πατέρα τσης τσ᾽ ἐπῆρε πολλὰ
χρήματα, τσαὶ σηκωθήκανε τσαὶ φύανε. Τὸ πωρνὸ ἐπήανε νὰ
᾽βροῦνε τὸ Φιορεδῖνο νὰ τόνε σφάξουνε. Ἤτανε ὁ Φιορεδῖνος
φευγάτος τσ᾽ ἡ κόρη τοῦ βασιλέα. Τότες λέει ἡ βασίλισσα τοῦ
βασιλέα· „πήαινε νὰ τσοὶ προφτάξης". Ἐπήαινε· λέει τότε ἡ
κόρη τοῦ βασιλέα τοῦ Φιορεδίνου· „γύρισε νὰ ᾽δῆς πίσω σου, τί
ἀνέφαλο ἔρχεται". Τσῆ λέει· „ἔρχεται κότσινο ἀνέφαλο". —
„Νὰ σοῦ δώσω μιὰ πατσά, νὰ σὲ κάμω ἐκκλησὰ [5]) τσ᾽ ἕνα καλοεράτσι [6]) νὰ σημαίνης τὴ gαϑάνα. Τσ᾽ ἐγὼ θὰ γενῶ μιὰ γάστρα
βασιλικό".

Ἔπειτα ἤφταξε ὁ πατέρας τσης· „καλοεράτσι, δὲν εἶδες
κανέν᾽ ἄδρα τσαὶ μιὰ γυναῖκα νὰ περάσουν ἀπὸ ᾽δώ;" — „Τὴ
gαϑάνα μου σημαίνω, τὴ gαϑάνα μου γυρεύγω". Ὁ βασιλέας
ἠστράφητσε πίσω στὸ παλάτι. Τοῦ λέει ἡ βασίλισσα· „δὲ τσ᾽ εὑ-
ρήτσες;" Λέει· „ὄχι, μιὰ γάστρα εἴδαμε μὲ βασιλικὸ τσ᾽ ἕνα
καλοεράτσι". Λέει· „αὐτοί ᾽τανε· γιὰ νὰ πάω ᾽γώ", τσαὶ πηαίνει.
Ρωτᾶ ἡ κόρη· „τί ἀνέφαλο ἔρχεται;" — „Ἔρχεται μαῦρο ἀνέφαλο".

[4]) § 23.   [5]) § 10, n. 4.   [6]) § 22.

Λέει· „μάννα μου είναι. Τώρα νὰ σοῦ δώσω μιὰ πατσά, νὰ σὲ κάμω λίμνη, τσ' ἐγὼ μιὰ πάπια νὰ σοῦ σεργιανίσω μέσα. Τσ' ἐτσείνη θὰ μοῦ λέει· ὦ τυατέρα[7]), πάρε τονε τσ' ἔλα, δὲν ἠξέρεις τὴ δυστυχία μας". Ἀφοῦ δὲν ἐπήαινε, τσῆ λέει ἡ βασίλισσα· „ἔλα σὺ μόνη τσ' ἄφησε αὐτόνε". Ἐτσείνη ἡ κόρη τσης, γιὰ νὰ τὴν εὐκαριστήσῃ, ἐπήαινε ἐμπρὸς ἐμπρὸς στὴ λίμνη, ἀλλὰ τὸ τσῦμα τὴν ἔπαιρνε πάλι μέσα. Ἐβαρίστισε ἡ μάννα τσαὶ τσῆ καταρήστη τσαὶ τσ' εἶπε· „Ἄμε, κόρη μου, τσαὶ μάννα γιὸ φιλήσῃ τσαὶ σένα λησμονήσῃ"[8]).

Ἡφύανε τσαὶ πήανε στὴν πατρίδα τοῦ παιδιοῦ. Τσαὶ τσῆ λέει τὸ παιδί· „κάθισε παδά, νὰ πάω νὰ φέρω μουσιτσές, συdζενεῖς μου, νὰ σὲ κατεβάσομε μὲ μουσιτσή". Τσ' ἔπειτα πῆε αὐτὸς στὸ σπίτι τωνε τσ' ἡ μητέρα του ἤθελε νὰ τόνε φιλήσῃ. „Ὄχι, νὰ μὴ μὲ φιλήσῃς, μακρειά! Μόνο θέλω νὰ 'τοιμαστῇ ἡ μουσιτσὴ τσ' οἱ συdζενεῖς, νὰ πάμε νὰ κατεβάσομε τὴ γυναῖκα μου". Βασιλικὸς ὁρισμός, ἑτοιμαστήκανε ἀμέσως ὅλα. Τὸ Φιορεdῖνο τὸν πῆρε ὁ ὕπνος. Πηαίνει[9]) ἡ μητέρα του τσαὶ τσοιμισμένο τὸ φιλεῖ. Τσ' ἔπειτα τοῦ λέει ἡ μητέρα· „σήκω, παιδί μου, οἱ συdζενεῖς ἤρχανε[10]), οἱ μουσιτσὲς ἕτοιμες, νὰ πᾶς νὰ φέρῃς τὴ γυναῖκα σου". — „Ἐγὼ δὲν ἔχω γυναῖκα". Ἡ βασίλισσα εἶπε· „νὰ φύουνε τὰ παιχνίδια τσ' οἱ συdζενεῖς, τσαὶ τὸ παιδί μου δὲν ἔχει γυναῖκα· μόνον ἤτον ἀπὸ τὸ δρόμο ζαλισμένος τσαὶ τό 'πε". Ἐτσείνη τί νὰ κάνη; τὸ κατάλαβε. Ἐπῆρε τὸ δρόμο τσαὶ κατέβη στὴ χώρα. Τότε λέει· „ἕνα σπίτι δὲν εἶν' ἐδὼ νὰ τὸ νοιτσάσω; Τσαὶ νὰ μοῦ 'βρουνε μιὰ δούλα".

Ὁ Φιορεdῖνος εἶχε ἕν' ἀξάδερφο, τσ' οἱ δυὸ φίλοι ἠβγαίνανε περίπατο. Ἤτανε μέρος ὅπου περνοῦσε τὸ σπίτι ποῦ ἤπιασε ἡ γυναῖκα του. Ἤτονε τὸ σοκάτσι ὅπου 'πέρνα αὐτός. Ὁ ἀξάδερφός του ὁ σιὸρ Στέφανος τσ' οἱ δυό του φίλοι τὴν εἴδανε τσ' εἶπανε· „τί ὡραία νέα!" Ὁ Φιορεdῖνος εἶπε· „αὐτὴ σᾶς ἀρέσει ἡ παλιογυναῖκα;" Τότε ὁ σιὸρ Στέφανος τσῆ δούλα τσης[11]) τσ' εἶπε· „γιὰ πὲ τσῆ κοκόνα σου[12]) νὰ τσῆ δώσω χίλια πεdακόσα γρόσα, νά 'ρχω τὸ βράδυ". Πάει τσαὶ τσῆ τὸ λέει· „ἄμε νὰ σοῦ τὰ δώσῃ τσαὶ νά 'ρχη". Ὑστερώτερα πάει ἡ δούλα τσαὶ τὰ παίρνει, τσ' ἐτσεῖνος ρωτᾶ, τί ὥρα νά 'ρχη. „Πέdε ὥρα". Ἐπῆε αὐτὸς τὴν ὥρα τσαὶ χτυπᾷ· τοῦ λέει· „ποιὸς εἶσαι;" — „Ἐγὼ ποῦ ἤδωσα τὰ χίλια πεdακόσα γρόσα". — „Τί ὥρα ἔχεις;" — „Πέdε". — „Νὰ

---

[7]) = θυγατέρα.   [8]) The subjunctive without νά is rare.   [9]) § 9 n.
[10]) § 203, 5.   [11]) § 29 n.   [12]) = τῆς κοκόνας σου.

χαθῆς ἀπὸ 'δώ, τσ' ἐγὼ ἔχω ἔξε". Τσ' ἔπειτα ὁ φίλος ἤθελε νὰ πάῃ τσ' ἐτσεῖνος τσαὶ λέει στὴ δούλα· „γιὰ πὲ τσῆ κοκόνα σου, νὰ 'ρχω τὸ βράδυ, νὰ τσῆ δώσω διακόσα γρόσα". Πάει τσαὶ τσῆ τὸ λέει. „Ἄμε νὰ σοῦ δώσῃ τσαὶ νά 'ρχῃ. — „Τσαὶ τί ὥρα νὰ 'ρχω;" — „Στὶς ἔξε". — Πάει, χτυπᾷ κτλ. ... Ὁ τρίτος πάλι λέει νὰ δώσῃ ἑκατὸ γρόσα.

Ἐβγήκανε στὸ σιργιάνι μὲ τὸ Φιορεσῖνο οἱ φίλοι τσαὶ περάσανε ἀπὸ κάτω τσαὶ στενάσανε. Τότε λέει ὁ Φιορεσῖνος στὸ σιὸρ Στέφανο·

„Τ' ἔχεις, σιόρι Στέφανε, τσαὶ χαμηλολογιάζεις;
Σὰν νά 'χασες τὸ βίο σου, στέτσεις τσαὶ λοαριάζεις".

Ἀποκρίνεται ὁ σιὸρ Στέφανος·

„Ὅτι τσὰν εἶχα, τά 'χασα, σιόρι Φιορεσῖνο,
Ποῦ τά 'χα, εἰς τὸ γάμο σου ὅλα νὰ τὰ σερβίρω".

Ὁ Φιορεσῖνος τοῦ λέει· „τί ἔχεις;" — „Δὲν ἤδωσα χίλια πεσακόσα γρόσα σ' αὐτὴ τὴ τσουρία ἀπάνω τσαὶ μοῦ 'πε, στὶς πέσε νὰ πάω, τσαὶ μοῦ 'πε πῶς εἶναι ἔξε τσαὶ μ' ἔσιωξε". Λέει ὁ Φιορεσῖνος· „δὲ τήνε φέρνετε στὸ βατέρα, νὰ ξεσερδέψετε; Νὰ τήνε πάμε στὸ βατέρα μου". Σὰν ἐπῆαν αὐτοὶ οἱ νέοι στὸ βασιλέα, εἶχε ἕνα δοῦλο ὁ βασιλέας τσαὶ τοῦ εἴπανε· „πήαινε νὰ 'πῇς τσῆ τσουρίας νά 'ρχῃ στὸ παλάτι". Ἔφταξε ὁ δοῦλος τσαὶ τσ' εἶπε·

„Κοπιάστε, ποῦ σ' ὁρίζουνε τσῆ χώρας οἱ βαρόνοι.
Τσερά μου, σὲ παρακαλῶ νά 'χης πολλοὶ τσοὶ χρόνοι."

Τσαὶ βαίνει[3]) στὴ μέσα κάμαρα, τσερνᾷ τὸν καστελάνο·

„Γιά, σύρε, Κώστα μου, νὰ πῇς, πῶς τώρα θενὰ πάω".
Βάζει τὸν ἥλιο πρόσωπο τσαὶ τὸ φεσάρι στῆθος
Τσαὶ τοῦ κοράκου τὸ φτερὸ βάζει καμαροφρύδι.

„Ἔλα, Χριστέ, στὴ πάσα μου, τσαὶ Παναγιά, κοσά μου,
Σήμερα νὰ φανερωθῇ τσ' ἐμὲ τὸ δίτσεμά μου".

Ἐπῆαινε. Ὡς καθὼς τὴν ἔσανε[13]) οἱ σαβατζήσες, εἴπανε·

„Νά τηνε ὅπου ἔρχεται τσαὶ τὸ θεὸ φοβοῦμαι,
Μὴ τὴν ἰσῇ ὁ βασιλιάς, τίποτα νὰ μὴ 'σοῦμε."

Τότε τσῆ λέει ὁ Φιορεσῖνος· „δὲν ἠσρέπουσοῦνε νὰ φᾶς τοῦ 'νοῦς τὰ ἑκατὸ τσαὶ τ' ἄλλουνοῦ σιακόσα τσαὶ τοῦ σιόρι Στέφανου τὰ χίλια πεσακόσα;" —

(Κόρη) „Σώπα ἐσύ, μὴν ἠπετάχτης σὰ τσαινούριος ἀβοκάτος;
Τσαὶ στὴ ράτσα μου θὰ πέσης τσ' ὕστερα θὰ μετανοιώσης."

(Φ.) „Σώπασε, μὴ ὃολλομιλῆς, ἔχει τὰ λόγια λία,
Τσαὶ τοῦτο ποῦ θωρεῖς ἐδώ, εἶναι παιδὶ τοῦ ρήγα."

(Κ.) „Θ' ἀρχίσω θέλω πειότερα ὅσο νὰ μὲ γνωρίσης,
Γιατ' ἀφορμὴ ἐγύρεψα νά 'ρθω τσ' ἐγὼ στὴ κρίσι."

(The Queen to the King.)

„Θυμᾶσαι, βασιλέα μου, ἴδα μᾶς ἔπ'[13]) ὁ γιός μας;
Θαρρῶ, πῶς εἶν' ἡ νύφη μας, θαρρῶ πῶς εἶμ[14]) παιδί μας."

(Φ.) „Ἀλλοῦ σὲ πέψα τσ' ἤσφαλες, νὰ 'βρῆς τὸ ριζικό σου
Τσαὶ σὺ θαρρεῖς, βαρειόμοιρη, πῶς εἶμ' ἐγὼ δικός σου;"

(Κ.) „Θυμᾶσαι, Φιορεδῖνο μου, τσαὶ γιάδα δὲ θυμᾶσαι,
Ποῦ ἥπαιρνα τὰ ποκάμισα τσ' ἥρχουμου τσ' ἥλλαξά σε;
Θυμᾶσαι, δὲ σ' ἐπιάσανε δεμένο οἱ γρουσάροι,
Στοῦ βασιλιὰ σὲ πήανε μὲ μιὰ τιμὴ μεγάλη;"

(Φ.) „Θυμοῦμαι ποῦ μὲ πιάσανε δεμένο οἱ γρουσάροι,
Στὸ βασιλιὰ μὲ πήανε μὲ μιὰ τιμὴ μεγάλη."

(Κ.) „Θυμᾶσαι, Φιορεδῖνο μου, ἂν εἶχε τυατέρα;"

(Φ.) „Θυμοῦμαι, πῶς τὴν εἴχανε, μά 'γου[15]) δὲν τὴν εἶδα."

(Κ.) „Ὦ δίγνωμε τοῦ δίγνωμου[16]), ἐπίσω μου γυρίζεις,
Ποῦ μὲ τὰ δάκρυα σ' ἔλουα, τώρα δὲ μὲ γνωρίζεις;

(To the Queen.) Τσερά μου, ὃάνα φίλησες τοῦ λόου σου τὸ γιό σου;"

(Queen.) „Ἐγὼ τσαὶ τὸν ἐφίλησα τσαὶ σὺ ἐκάτεχές το;"

(Κ.) „Γιὰ ξαναφίλησέ τονε νά 'ρχη στὰ λοϊκά του."

Στσύβγει ἡ μάννα τσαὶ τόνε ξαναφιλεῖ, τσ' ἔρχεται αὐτὸς στὰ λοϊκά του τσαὶ λέει στὴ ὃόρη·

„Καλῶς την τὴ ρουζέτα μου, καλῶς την τὴ ψυχή μου,
Καλῶς την, ποῦ μοῦ χάρισε ἐμένα τὴ ζωή μου".

6. Calymnos.

Μοιρολόγι.

Στῆς νιότης σου τὴν ἄτθησι[1]) τσαὶ πάνω στὴν οὐσία᾽
Πῆρε σ' ὁ Χάρος, πῆρε σε τσαὶ σὲ (δ)ίχως ὀρπί(δ)α[2])·
Κόρη μου χα(δ)εμένη μου, τῆς μάννας σου καμάρι,
Πῶς ἥφητσες[3]) τσ' ἐπρόσταξεν ὁ Χάρος νὰ σὲ πάρη;
Οἱ τετρακόσσοι[4]) ἄννδζελοι[5]) τσ' οἱ (δ)ώ(δ)εκ' Ἀπόστολοι
Σοῦ πῆραν τὴ ψυχούλα σου στὸ Ἄζιο περι(β)όλι.

---

[14]) = εἶν(αι). [15]) = μὰ ἐγώ. [16]) This turn strengthens the expression δίγνωμος, cf. § 44, n. 1.

[1]) § 35, n. 3. [2]) § 22 n. [3]) §§ 17 and 202. [4]) = τετρακόσιοι.

[5]) = ἄγγελοι, cf. § 17.

Παντέρα ἤσουλ⁶) 'ληνιτσὰ μὲ τὸ σταυρὸ στὴμ μέση,
Τσαὶ ἤχασά σ' ἡ μάννα σου, κόρην της πλιὸ ἐς⁶) σ' ἔσει⁷).
Τοῦ οὐρανοῦ τὰ νέφαλα τσαὶ πσὸς⁸) τὰ μποζιατίζει⁹)!
Τ' ἀγαπημένα ἀντρό(γ)υνα, ἄχ! πσὸς τὰ 'ποχωρίζει!
Ὁ τθάνατός¹⁰) σου μοῦ 'καψε τὰ σωτθικά¹¹) μου, κόρη,
Τσ' ὁ νοῦς μου μὲ (δ)ερνοχτυπᾷ νὰ κουτουλλῶ τὰ ὄρη.
Χριστὸς βαστεῖ τὰ στέφανα, τσ' ἀννdζέλοι τὰ τσερζά⁸) σου,
Ξεσταύρωσε τὰ σέρζα¹²) σου, τίναξε τὰ λουλλούdζα⁸),
Νὰ φέρουσι τ' ἀέρφσα⁸) σου τοῦ γάμου τὰ παιχνίdζα.
Γιὰ λύσε τὰ παάρζα¹³) σου, τὰ χαροτεντωμένα,
Τσαὶ 'νοῖξε τὰ σειλάτσα¹⁴) σου τ' ἀποτθανατωμένα.

7. Karpathos¹).

(Southern Sporades)

„Πῆτε μου, πῆτε μου, ἄρκοντες²), πῆτε μου τί νὰ γένω;
Ὁπ' ἀαπῶ μιὰλ³) λυερή, ππῶς⁴) νὰ τὴλ λησμονήσω;"
„Νὰ σ' ἀρμηνέψω, νιώττερε⁵), κι ἂθ θέληςː ἄκουσέ μου·
Ἄμμε, Γιαννῆ, πά'⁶) στὸ οὐνό⁷), νὰ κουαλῆς⁸) λιθάρια,
Νὰ κουαλῆς τὰ μάρμαρα 'πὸ τὸ μαρμαροούνι·
Νὰ κουαλῆς νὰ κουραστῆς, τὴκ³) κόρη νὰ ξεχάσης."
„Κ' ἰὼ⁹) κι ἂν ἔβγω στὸ οὐνό, κι ἂκ κουαλῶ λιθάρια,
Κι ἂκ κουαλῶ τὰ μάρμαρα 'πού τὸ μαρμαροούνι,
Κι ἂκ κουαλῶ κι ἂκ κουραστῶ, τῆς κόρης δὲ ξεχάννω.
Εἰμὴ κι ἂβ³) βάλω σίερα¹⁰) καὶ δέσουμ μὲ στὸβ βάτο,
Νὰ μὲ ἀροῦτ¹¹) τὰ σίερα, νὰ μὲ κεντᾷ τὸ βάτος,
Τότε κ' ἰὼ τῆς λυερῆς θὰ τῆς 'πολησμονήσω."

8. Cyprus.

Δύο περιστέρκα¹) κάτασπρα στὰ αὐκά²) τους καθισμένα
Κάθουνταν καὶ μοιρολοοῦν, κλαίσιν, παραπονοῦνται,
Τ' ἀρσενικὸν τοῦ θηλυκοῦ γυρίζει καὶ λαλεῖ του·

---

⁶) § 34, n. 4.   ⁷) § 21.   ⁸) § 10, n. 5.   ⁹) =μπογιατιζει, on
which cf. § 10, n. 5.   ¹⁰) =θάνατος, cf. § 35, n. 3.   ¹¹) =σωθικά,
see preceding n.   ¹²) = χέρια, v. notes 7 and 8.   ¹³) =ποδάρια.
¹⁴) =χειλάκια.
    ¹) The dialect of Karpathos is, like that of Cyprus (No. 8), closely
akin to that of Calymnos.   ²) v. § 18, n. 3.   ³) From μιὰν λ., cf.
§ 34, n. 4.   ⁴) =πῶς.   ⁵) =νιώτερε, cf. § 36 n.   ⁶) § ἀπάν(ω).
⁷) =βουνό, cf. § 22 n.   ⁸) § 22 n.   ⁹) =ἐγώ.   ¹⁰) =σίδερα.   ¹¹) βαροῦν
(see notes 7 and 3).
    ¹) § 10, n. 5.   ²) § 26.

„Ἴντα κλωσσᾷς, γεναῖκα μου, κάτασπρη περιστέρα;
Νὰ κάμῃς θέλεις ὄμορφα κάτασπρα περιστέρκα;
Κρῖμα χάννεις[3]) τοὺς κόπους σου καὶ λύπες ἐννὰ[4]) φέρῃς·
Ἒν[5]) ἀθθυμᾶσαι τί 'παθες στὴν ἄλλην τὴν κλωσσιάν σου;
Τρικὰ καὶ μόνα ἔκαμες, τά 'χασες καὶ τὰ τρία·
Ἄρκον γεράκιν πῆρεν το τὸ ἕνα πεινασμένον,
Καὶ τ' ἄλλα τά 'βραν κυνηοὶ[5]) στὸν ποταμὸν νὰ πίννουν[3])
Καὶ μὲ τὰ δίχτυα τά 'πιασαν, τί ξέρεις ἂν τὰ φάαν;
Σήκου, σήκου καὶ μὲν[6]) κλωσσᾷς, νὰ μὲ μοῦ φέρῃς πόνους,
Γιατί ποῖος ξέρει ὕστερις καὶ τοῦτ' ἴντα θὰ γίνουν.“

9. Chios.

O lolós, o frénimos ts o đrakos[1]).

Nal[2]) lolló[2]) ts[3]) éna[2]) frénimos íxam polla[4]) ᵘúđga[5]), tse mịa méra inniksen[6]) o frénimos tas pórtes, námbum mésa ta ᵛúđga, ts inniksen dz o lollós tim bórtan du, námbi ts etsinú kaénav[7]) vúđim[7]) mésa. imben[8]) dz etsinú énav vúđim mésa, efonazzén du: „énav vúđin ímbem[8]) mestin avlím mu.“ léἰ: „éx'e to“, túpen o frénimos. ipịasen dzínos[7]): „inda to káo[9]) to úđi[10])?“ ipịasen dz isfaksén do, ts epíen ókso ts íđen enađ[7]) đéndron dz ekúnene[11]), ts iléén du: „þi[12]) ts esí kriás?“ túlee. ekúnem bga[13]) tsíno ts iđotsén[14]) du kriás. iléén du: „en éx'is tóra na me peróis[15]), é?“ íkamnem bga tsíno[16]), ekúnene, paénni paratsí, pánda[17]) tu na skođrallúi[18]). „þi ts esí kriás?“ ekúnen dz etsíno ts íđotsén du. paénni paratsí, pánda tu enal lalás[19]). „þi ts esí kriás?“ ekúnem bga ts etsínos, pu to kúnen o aἰéras, íđotsén du ts etsinú.

Ts apéἰ pìen ts ípen tađerfú tu: „pᵃó[20]), lli[21]), na mazzókso ta paráđga[22]) mu.“ paénni tse léi tis el'ás: „plerosé me đa.“

---

[3]) Double consonants, cf. § 36 n.   [4]) § 20, n. 2.   [5]) § 22 n.
[6]) v. § 6, n. 3.
[1]) The phonetic transcription of the editor, Pernot, is partly altered to correspond with the system of transcription adopted in this book.   [2]) =ένας, § 29 n.   [3]) § 17.   [4]) The double consonants are pronounced, v. § 36 n.   [5]) § 10, n. 5.   [6]) =άνοιξεν.   [7]) § 34, n. 4.   [8]) § 208.   [9]) v. § 33, n. 4.   [10]) § 22 n.   [11]) § 245, n. 3.
[12]) =θές (θέλεις), cf. also n. 2.   [13]) =πιά, v. notes 5 and 7.   [14]) =ἔδωκεν.
[15]) § 29 n.   [16]) "Ici, la conteuse remue la tête de bas en haut, pour marquer la réponse négative" (Pernot's note).   [17]) =ἀπαντᾷ.
[18]) Really =κορυδαλάκι "lark" (Pernot).   [19]) A bird, but which bird is not known.   [20]) πά(γ)ω.   [21]) =λέει (unaccented).
[22]) § 70, n. 2.

ekúnen etsíni, ífien dzínos. epíen is tol lalá, lī[21]): „plerosé me ᵈa.“
ekúnem bᵷa ts etsínos, févgi[23]), ᵃpánta tu ena skoðrallúi tse léⁱ tu:
„éla me pleróis[24].“ tripónni tsíno meston díχo, vgálli[23]) tsínos tis
pétres na tóvri tse vríssi[25]) enaχ⁷) χárkọma, ts ítọi⁷) iɇmáto ɤrósa.
tse paénni, lɇⁱ taᵈerfú tu: „ọ́nde, lɇⁱ, na pa[26]) páromen da ɤrósa.“
pira ðɡo ɤaᵈárus ts epían dz efortósan dus. ts ípen du lollú o
frénimos: „sam baénil[27]), léi, a[28]) su leún[29]) i aþþrópi ῾inda n[30])
dúa[31])’, tse na tol léⁱs ῾kaᵛallínes i[30])’.“ opu ið ði[32]) áþþropon,
o lollós túleen: „mba, þaríte pos iɵ[30]) gavallínes, ɤrósa i.“

Íppⁱᵏ′ạasen⁵) o frénimos ts iᵛalén dom mésa s éna sendúi[33])
ts ileén du: „émba mésa, tse a vréksi, a kái⁹), léi, χalázzi.“ íppⁱᵏ′ạasen
o frénimos ts íriksen ao páno[33]) sto sendúi kliþári ts iᵛalen tas
órniþes ao páno ts ettróane[34]). kámam bⁱᵍa i órniþes tráka tráka
tráka ao páno, eþárem[11]) bos ípefte χalázzi. íppⁱᵏ′ạasen o frénimos
ts iriχtén du lukánika mesto sendúine[35]) ts avká[23]). san epíen o
vasilén²) na ton erotísi: „póte távrete ta ɤrósa?“ ípen o lollós:
„san ívreχen o þeós avká tse lukánika.“ ts ípem bⁱᵍa o vasilés[36]):
„etúol[37]), léi, el[38]) lollóse[39])“. ífiem bⁱᵍa tsínose[39]).

Ístilen o frénimos tol lolló. „áme, léi, napís tu ᵛasilé[36]), na
tu píl[40]), léi, a páro tiɵ górin du“. leén du pⁱᵏ′ạa o lollós tu
frénimu, léi: „mme⁴) þí se, léi, na se pári?“ — lɇ́: „þéli me.“
ípen du o ᵛasilés tu lollú: „an éχ′i, léi, pⁱᵏ′óttera sto vasil’ó mu,
tom péro[41]).“ iχ′em bⁱᵍ′óttera sto ᵛasil’ón du, epírem din diɵ górin
du. ípen i kóri tu: „an in éχo[42]), léi, tu ðráku taloái[33]).“ — léi:
„tína þa stílome²)? toɵ gostandím mas.“ stéllun don toɵ gostandí,
tse paénni na to ppⁱᵏ′ạási taloái, ts efónaksen taloái: „ɇ̄ ðráko, pérum
me!“ tréχ′i káto o ðrákos, en eþóreɵ[11]) gani[43]). ikámen o lollós
mian drípam mestiɵ goprián ts eχónnutom mesa ts en don eþóren.
paénni páli na kọdrísi taloái, ts efónaksem báli taloái: „ɇ̄ dráko,
pérum me.“ píeɵ gáto o ðrákos ọχọnús, en íeɵ gani, eχónnuton
ọ kostandís mestin dripa, ts en don eþóren o ðrákos. paénni páli

---

²³) = § 26.   ²⁴) = ἔλα, νὰ μὲ πλερώσῃς.   ²⁵) § 17 n.   ²⁶) = πὰ
(νὰ), cf. p. 197, footnote.   ²⁷) παγαίνεις.   ²⁸) = θά.   ²⁹) § 9 n.
³⁰) = εἶναι.   ³¹) § 145 n.   ³²) = ὅπου εἶν(αι) ’δῇ “ wherever he sees.”
³³) § 16, n. 1.   ³⁴) § 36 n.   ³⁵) § 34, n. 4.   ³⁶) § 71, n. 3.
³⁷) = ἐτοῦτος (cf. note 31).   ³⁸) = ἔν (εἶναι).   ³⁹) § 146, n. 1.   ⁴⁰) νὰ
τοῦ ’πῇς.   ⁴¹) = παίρνω.   ⁴²) = ἂν εἶν(αι) ἔχω, as well as ἂν εἶχα.
⁴³) § 153, n. 4.

na to koḍrísi, óti pu píen o ḍrákos apáno, ts efónaksem báli taloáin: „é̃ *ḍráko, pérum me!*" *o ḍrákos en írkutom b$_i^g$a káto makári, en do pistergen*[44]) *pos to koḍrúsa. epíren do o kostandís ts ífie. ísteri, san epíen etsi, páli tu léune:* „*áme, léi, na tu pári*[2]) *tse to paplomãn du.*" — „*ma índa loí*[45]), *léi, a tu to páro to paplomán du, pu éχ'i kuḍunái*[35])*?*" *paénni tsínos. ípp$_i^{k'}$asen ts emázzoksen o kostandís enas*[2]) *sakulláin*[35]) *gorgús*[46]) *ts enas sakullái psíllus (margóllos*[23]), *more: lolló*[2]) *tse margóllos) ts enas sakullái psíres, tría mázzokse. ts apéi ríχti ta ólla apáno sto ḍráko, tse káuton*[47]) *na vgáli*[23]) *ta*[2]) *psíres ạo páno tu, ts epíren du to páploma tse fév$_g^{k'}$i*[23]).

Tse san epíen etsi, tu léum bali: „*as iχamen tse to ḍrákon ton íḍịo*" (*vre kako χron náχu*[48]), *toꝛ gamméno toꝛ gostandinóm mas pu ton etimorúsa!*). — „*m índa lloí*[45]), *léi, a tof féro?*" *léi:* „*kalá kalá*". *paénni o kostandís páli ts ípen du ḍráku:* „*éla, léi, na péksomen na ꙗelásome.*" *i^{v}allén don dol lolló mesto sendúin o ḍrákos, i^{v}allen dz o lollós to ḍrákom mésa. tse p$_i^{k'}$ánni tse karfónni to o lollós to ḍráko tse sikónni to sendúin tse péri tse to ḍráko. lollós more o átimos, ma ítom margóllos.*

ífia ts eo[49]) *apetsi*
m enaꝛ góssino[50]) *fatsí.*

10. From Northern Lesbos.

The dialect of Lesbos, like that of Velvendos (No. 11), shows in a characteristic fashion the peculiarities of the Northern Greek dialects, on which *cf.* § 7, n. 1, also § 37 n. Because of these peculiarities along with the palatalising of the κ (§ 17) the dialect presents a rather strange complexion [1]).

Ἰ[2]) βασλὲς[3]) ἔχ' τσιρατέλ'.

Μν'ὰ φουρὰ ἦδαν ἕνας βασλὲς τσ' εἰχι στοὺ τσιφάλ' ἕνα τσιρατέλ'[4]) τσὶ τοὺ εἰχι πουλὺ ἀκρυφά. Ὅποιουν βιρβέρ ἔπιρνι.

---

[44]) §§ 23 n. and 26.   [45]) =*ἴντα λογῆς* "how?"   [46]) =*κοριούς, cf.* note 5.   [47]) =(*ἐ*)*κάθουνταν.*   [48]) =*κακὸ χρόνο νά 'χουν,* a curse, "to the devil with."   [49]) =*ἐγώ.*   [50]) =*κόσκινο, cf.* note 25.

[1]) The beginning in phonetic transcription runs: *i vaslés eχ' tsiratél'. Mɩ́na furá ídan énaz vaslés ts íχ'i stu tsifál' éna tsiratél', tsi tu íχ'i pulí akrifá. Ópjun birbér épirni na tu guréps, tun ékani tibíχ' na mi tu lej óχu. Tora ul' i birbérdis ḍen ib*urúsan *na tu vastáχin akrifá; jaftó ts ésfaxi.*   [2]) § 55, n. 3.   [3]) § 71, n. 3.   [4]) § 95, A. 3 n.

νὰ τοῦ *g*ουρέψ ⁵), τοὺν ἔκανι τι*b*ίχ, νὰ μὴ τοῦ λέ*j* ὄξου. Τώρα
οὖλ' οἱ *b*ιρ*b*έρδις δὲν ἰ*b*ουρούσαν ⁵) νὰ τοῦ βαστάξιν ⁶) ἀκρυφά·
j' ἀφτὸ τσ ἔσφαξι.

Πίσου πίσου πῆρι ἕνα *b*ιρ*b*έρ, τσὶ σὰ *d*οὺ ἀποκούριψι, τ εἶπι,
νὰ μὴ τοῦ πῆ σὶ κανέναν, ποὺς ἔχ' τσέρατου, *j*ατί θὰ πάρ τοὺ
τσιφάλ' τ. ᾿Ι *b*ιρ*b*έρς δὲν ἰ*b*όρσι νὰ βαστάξ, πῆγι, ἔστσυψι μέσ'
ἕνα πγά*d* τσὶ φώναξι μ' οὖλ' τ *g*αρ*d*ιά ⁵) τ: „ἰ βασλὲς ἔχ' τσιρατέλ'.‟
Τώρα τοῦ πγά*d* ξιράθτσι, φύτρουσι μέσα μν᾿ὰ καλαμν᾿ά. Μιγάλ'νι
ἡ καλαμνιά. Πέρνα μν᾿ά μέρα ἕνας *dž*ουβάν'ς ⁷), ἔκουψι *d g*αλαμν᾿ὰ
τσ' ἔκανι μν᾿ὰ τσα*b*ούνα τσὶ τν ἔπιζι. Ἡ τσα*b*ούνα ἥλιγι: „*b*ί!
ἰ βασλὲς ἔχ' τσιρατέλ'.‟ Τοὺ ἥξαν, τοὺ εἶπαν τ βασλέ. ᾿Ι βασλὲς
φουνάζ τοὺ *dž*ουβάν', λέ*j*: „ποὺ τν ηὗρις;‟ — „Μέσ' στοὺ πγά*d*.‟
λέ*j* ἰ *dž*ουβάν'ς. Ἔστλι ἰ βασλές, φώναξι τσὶ τοὺ *b*ιρ*b*έρ, λέ*j*:
„ποὺ τοὺν εἶπις αὐτὸ τοὺ λόγου;‟ — „Ἄμ δὲν ἰβάσταξα,‟ λέ*j* ἰ
*b*ιρ*b*έρς, „τσὶ πῆγα τσὶ τοὺ εἶπα μέσ' τοὺ πγά*d*.‟ — Τότις ἰ βασλὲς
τς ἀφῆτσι τσὶ πά*j*καν.

11. From Velvendos in Macedonia.

Cf. the preliminary note to No. 10.—*i̯* sometimes stands for γι̯ (ι̯ά=γιά),
j for ι̯ ¹).

Οἱ τρεῖς οὐρμήνις.

Μνιὰ φουρὰ κ' ἕναν κιρὸ ἦταν ἕνας πατέρας σὰν καλὴ
ὥρα ... Αὐτὸς οὐ πατέρας εἶχιν μούγκι ἕνα πιδί. Τί ἥλιγιν κι
αὐτός; „Αὐτὸ τοὺ πιδί, οὐ Θιὸς νὰ μὶ τοὺ χαρίσ¹, δὰ²) τοὺ κά-
μου νὰ ζήσι̯ ἄρχουντας, νὰ τοὺ γλέπ' ἢ³) κόσμους κὶ νὰ τοὺ χαίριτι, κανένας νὰ μὴν τοὺ λέη 'παρέκ¹ στάς'.‟ Ἀχίρσιν ἀποὺ τότι
κὶ δώθι νὰ ὀλέβ¹ μὶ τοὺ παραπάν. Δλιὰ τ¹ μέρα, ὀλιὰ τοὺ βρά*d*¹,
ὅλου ὀλιά. Πιρνάει μνιὰ χρουνιά, *dj*ὸ χρουνές, τρεῖς κι ἀκόμα
παραπάν, κι ἀκόμα δὲν εἶχιν ἀπουλάψ¹ δίπ-τίπουτας. Μιρουδούλ¹
μιρουφάει, ὅλου ἔτσ¹ πάϊνιν ἡ ὀλιὰ τ. Τί νὰ κάμ¹, τί νὰ σώσ¹
τώρ' αὐτός! Τοὺ νῆμα⁴) τ, ὅσουμ πάϊνιν, κόντιβιν, κὶ παράδις
ἀκόμα δὲν εἶχιν. „Θέ μ, Παναέ μ!‟ γουνάτσιν κ' εἶπιν „μακρύ

---

⁵) § 15, n. 2. ⁶) § 7, n. 2. ⁷) =τσοπάνης.

¹) The beginning in phonetic transcription runs: *Mn'a furá
ḱ énaɔ giró ítan énas patéras saɔ galí óra. Aftós u patéras i̯χ'in mûɔgi
éna pidí. Tí ili̯in ḱ aftós? aftó tu pidí, u þjos na mí tu χarís¹, δa tu
kámu na zisi̯ árχundas, na tu ʒlep i̯ kósmus ḱi na tu χ'ériti, kanénas
na min du lei̯ "pareḱ¹ stás."* ²) § 20, n. 2. ³) § 56, n. 3.
⁴) =μνῆμα.

20

'ν' τοὺ χέρ σ, κάμι τοὺ θᾶμα σ", κὶ πάλι δούλιβιν, δούλιβιν, σὰ λτσ'τής⁵). Ἔ! νὰ μὴν τὰ μακραίνουμι, σήμιρα μνιὰ πιντάρα, ἕνα δεκάρ' ταχειά, ἕνα 'κουσάρ' ν ἄλλ', ἔφκειασιν καμπόσις παράδις. Ἀμὰ ὅσου νὰ τς φκειάσ', εἶδιν κ' ἔπαθιν. Τώρα θέλτς ἀπ' τὰ βάσανα, θέλτς ἀπ' ν τυράννια, θέλτς ἀπ' τὰ γηράματα (δὲν ἦταν κὶ μικρὸς μαθέ, ἦταν ἰξηντάρς) ἀρρώσ'τσιμ βαρειά. Κ' ἦρθιν ἡ ὥρα νὰ πιθάν'. Γιόμουσιν τοὺ σ'πίτι ἀπού γναῖκις, ἄντρ'⁶), μκρὰ πιδjά . . . . ἀλλ' ἔκλιγαν, ἀλλ' παρηγουρούσαν! Ποῦ αὐτός; ἀλλοῦ κὶ σι ἄλλουν κόσμουν. Ἀλά· ἰκεῖ ποῦ κόντιβιν ἡ ὥρα, ξαναδjανώθκιν κα-ψίχα⁷), ἄγξιν⁸) μνιὰ φουρὰ τὰ μάτ'χ'α κὶ Ζήτσιν τοὺ πιδί. Τοὺν τό 'δουκαν· τοὺ παίρν' κουντὰ κὶ τοὺ λέει στοὺ 'φτί⁹)· „πιδί μ, γρόσ'κια¹⁰) πουλλὰ δὲ θὰ σι ἀφήκου, ἔτσ' θέλ'τσιν οὐ Θιός· κ' ἰγὼ κ' ἡ σ'χουριμέν' ἡ μάννα σ δούλιψάμι, δούλιψάμι, τόσου ἦταν ἡ μοῖρα μας. Αὐτὰ ποῦ δὰ σὶ πῶ τώρα νὰ τὰ φλάξ, κι ὅλου κιρδιμένους δὰ βγῆς· μὶ τοὺν τρανύτιρό σ κουκκιὰ νὰ μὴ σ'πέρς¹¹), τὴ γναῖκα σ κρυφὸ νὰ μὴ μ' 'πῆς, πουτές, καμνιὰ φουρά, ψυχουπαίδ' νὰ μὴμ πάρς." Τά 'πιν αὐτά, βάσταξιν ἀκόμα κα-ψίχα κὶ σ'χουρέθκιν. Τοὺ πιδὶ· παντρεύκιν, ἡ ὀλιά τ πάϊνιν καλὰ κὶ φύλαγιν τὰ λόια dᵗ babâ τ. Νὰ ἰδοῦμι τώρα τί λέει κι οὐ κατὴς τς νύχτας (Πχιός¹²); — Ἡ γναῖκα. Ψι ψι ψι τοὺ βράδ' στοὺ στρῶμα brὲ ὄτ' νὰ σὶ 'πῆ, πχιάσ'¹²) τουν αὐτόν, βάλ' τουν νὰ πλύσ' σαπούνι¹³), κόψ' τουν, κρέμασ' τουν· σὰ δὲν τοὺ φκειάϊς¹⁴), ἰγὼ τί νὰ εἶμι). Ἡ γναῖκα τ ἦταν ἀπού τρανὸ σ'πίτ'. Μέσ' 'ς πατρικό τς σέβινιν κ' ἔβγινιν οὐ βασ'λιὰς πᾶσα ὥρα, στοὺ θκό τς, dίπ. Ἔ! οἱ γναῖκις τ' ἀσ'ταίνουντι¹¹) κάτ' τέθκια¹²). Βάσταξιν μνιά, βάσταξιν δjό, δὲν τοὺν ἔκαμιν τοὺν ἄντρα τς παράπουνου, ἀμὰ σὰν πέρασιν καμπόσους κιρός, „ἔ, καημένι ἄντρα," τοὺν λέει, „τώρα κάθισι κὶ συλλουιέσι κὶ σὺ τί σ' εἶπιν οὐ babâς σ. Ἄϊδι νὰ πχιάσουμι κ' ἰμεῖς φιλίις μὶ τοὺ βασ'λιά." Ἔ, τί εἶπιν κι αὐτός; „δὲ γλέπου τί ζμὶ βγῆκιν ὡς τώρα ἀπ' τὰ λόια τ πατέρα μ!"

Μνιὰν κὶ δjό, μωρὲ γιέ μου, πχιάσ'καν¹⁵) φίλ' κὶ τού 'χαν κουλουκύθ' μὶ τοὺ βασ'λιά· φκειάν' κὶ τοὺ δούλου τ ψυχουπαίδ'. „Ἄϊδι νὰ ἰδοῦμι," εἶπιν τώρα, „ἀκόμα ἕνα δὰ φκιάσου, νὰ ἰδοῦμι ποῦ δὰ βγῆ." Ἰκεῖ ποῦ ἦταν στοὺ παλάτ' μνιὰ μέρα, εἶδιν τοὺ

---

⁵) =ληστής; cf. also § 7, n. 2.　　⁶) =ἄντροι (for ἄντρες), cf. § 66.
⁷) =κάτι ψίχα "a little."　　⁸) ἄνοιξεν.　　⁹) =αὐτί.　　¹⁰) =γρόσια,
v. § 10, n. 5.　　¹¹) § 7, n. 2,　　¹²) § 10, n. 5.　　¹³) =βάλ'
τον φυλακή "lock him up!"　　¹⁴) =φκειάσῃς, v. § 29 n.
¹⁵) πιάστηκαν.

πλί, ποῦ οὐ βασ'λιὰς χάνουνταν ιάτι αὐτό. Καλύτιρα νὰ τοὺν ἔπιρνις τοὺ κιφάλ', πέρι τοὺ πλί. Τ' ἀρπάχν', τοὺ κρύβ' στοὺν κόρφου τ κὶ „φιβγᾶσ'τι¹⁶), πουδαράκια μ." Πιρνάει ἀπ' τοὺ παζάρ', ἀγουράζ' ἕνα ἄλλου πλὶ σφαγμένου, τοὺ μαδάει σὶ μνιὰ κρυψάνα κὶ τοὺ πααίν' τὴ γναῖκα τ. „Νά, μουρὴ γναῖκα, αὐτὸ εἶνι τοὺ πλὶ d βασ'λιά, φκειάσ' ἀτου ὅπους ξέρς νὰ τοὺ φάμι τοὺ βράδ'. Ἀμά ... νὰ μὴ δεῖξ πουθινά, χάθκαμι." Ποῦ αὐτός! τοὺ πλὶ d βασ'λιά, ποῦ τού 'χιν στοὺν κόρφου, πααίν' κὶ τοὺ κρύβ' σὶ μνιὰ μιριὰ κρυφὰ 'π' τὴ γναῖκα τ. „Ἄ! νὰ ἰδοῦμι," λέ, „τώρα, δὰ τοὺ βαστάξ' ἡ γναῖκα μ τοὺ κρυφό;"

Ν¹⁷) ἴδjα τ' μέρα φουνές, κακό, τιλιάλ'δις παρατιλιάλ'δις· τί; „ἔκλιψαν d βασ'λιὰ τοὺ πλί· ὅπχιους μαρτυρήσ' τοὺν κλέφτ', δὰ πάρ' μιγάλου ἔπινους." ... Ν ἄλλ' τ' μέρα κάθουνταν ἡ γναῖκα τ μὶ τοὺ κέν'μα¹⁸) στοὺ κατέφλιου ἀπ' ν οὐξόπουρτα¹⁹) μι ἄλλις γειτόντσσις κὶ κιντοῦσιν ... Νὰ κ' ἕνας τιλιάλτς κὶ τιλιαλοῦσιν πάλι ιὰ d βασ'λιὰ τοὺ πλί. „Ἔ!" λέει αὐτή, „δὰ τοὺ βροῦν κὶ καλά! δὲν τό 'φαγάμι κὶ καλὰ ἰμεῖς ἰψές;!" Αὐτὸς οὐ λόγους ἀπὸ χείλ σὶ χείλ' κὶ ζd βασ'λιὰ τοὺ 'φτί²⁰). Τοὺν τσακών τοὺν καλὸ τοὺ νοικοκύρ' κὶ „ἄρουν ἄρουν"²¹) τοὺν πὰν ιὰ κρέμασμα. Πῆγιν αὐτός. Ποῦ νά.'γλιπις ἰκεῖ πούπουλου! μήλου νά 'ρχνις, καταῆς δὲν ἔπιφτιν! Σὰν τοὺν ἀνέβασαν ψ'λὰ νὰ τοὺν κριμάσν, γύρσιν μνιὰ φουρὰ κὶ λέει τοὺ βασ'λιά. (ἦταν κι αὐτὸς ἰκεῖ)· „βασ'λιά μ, νὰ μὶ σ'χουρέῖς²²), τό 'καμα, δὲν ξιγένιτι. Ἄς εἶνι." Ὑσ'τιρα ἔκαμιν κὶ d' διαθήκ'· „Ἀφήνου τρεῖς χλιάδις γρόσ'κια, χίλια δὰ πάρ' ἡ γναῖκα μ, χίλια οὐ παραγιόζουμ κὶ χίλια ἰκείνους ποῦ δὰ τραβήξ' τοὺ σ'κνὶ νὰ μὶ κριμάσ'." Ἀπ' ὅσουν κόσμουν ἦταν ἰκεῖ, κανέναν δὲν τοὺν ἄφνιν ἡ καρδjὰ νὰ τραβήξ' τοὺ σ'κνί. Ἦταν καλὸς κὶ τοὺν ἀλ'πούνταν. Οὐ παραγιός, τί εἶπιν μὶ τοὺ νοῦ τ; „Χίλια μι ἀφήνει αὐτός," λέ, „κὶ χίλια 'π' τοὺ σ'κνί γένουντι δjὸ χλιάδις· ἰγὼ δὰ τοὺ τραβήξου." — Ἀρὰ δὲν τοὺν ἀλ'πᾶσι;" τοὺν λέει οὐ βασ'λιάς. „Τίπουτας!" Ἄς εἶνι, τσάκουσιν τοὺ σ'κνί. Τότις οὐ παραπατέρας τ ξαναγύρσιν ἀκόμα μνιὰ φουρὰ κὰ τοὺ βασ'λιὰ κὶ τοὺν λέει· „βασ'λιά μ, τοὺ πλί σ ζῆ, τό 'χου κρυμμένου." Κὶ τοὺν εἶπιν ὅλα τὰ τριχούμινα. Νὰ μὴν τὰ μακραίνουμι, κρέμασαν ἀντὶς αὐτὸν τοὺν παραγιό τ, αὐτὸν τοὺν ἔδουκαν ἄλλ' μνιὰ γναῖκα κι οὐ βασ'λιὰς τοὺν ἀγάπσιν ἄκομα πλέτι-

---

¹⁶) =φευγᾶστε, v. § 218, n. 2.   ¹⁷) =τὴν.   ¹⁸) =κέντημα.   ¹⁹) ἀπό in place of gen., cf. § 161, 6, n. 1.   ²⁰) =στοῦ βασιλιὰ τὸ αὐτί.   ²¹) =ἄρον ἄρον from the ecclesiastical language, lit. "crucify him," and then by an erroneous conception "as quickly as possible, without delay."   ²²) v. n. 14.

ρου²³). Μὰ σὰν πῶς τοὺ λέ᾽ ἠ³) λόγους; „σὰν τοὺ πάθ᾽ ἡ γριά, μανταλώνιτι,“ ἔτσ᾽ κι αὐτὸς ἀποὺ τότις κὶ δώθι μὶ τοὺ βασ᾽λιὰ δὲν παρακουνούσ᾽τζιν, τὴ γναῖκα τ πουτὲς καμνιὰ φουρὰ κρυφὸ δὲ ν²⁴) ἤλιγιν κὶ παραγιὸν ξανὰ δὲν πῆριν. ῎Ετσι τοὺ βρῆκιν καλύτιρα ὅπους τοὺν εἶπιν οὐ πατέρας τ. Κὶ ζοῦσιν κι αὐτὸς καλὰ κ᾽ ἰμεῖς καλύτερα.

12. From Saránda Klisiés in Thrace.

This dialect only faintly reflects the Northern Greek characteristics
(see Nos. 10 and 11).

Παραμύθι τῆς προγονῆς.

῎Ηδαν ἔνας ἄδρας ¹) καὶ μνιὰ γυναῖκα χηργιοὶ καὶ οἱ δγυὸ καὶ πάρκαν²). Καὶ ὁ ἄδρας εἶχε ἔνα κορίτσ καὶ ἡ γυναῖκα εἶχε τὸ δικό δης³) τὸ κορίτσ. Εἶχαν κι ἀγελάδα κι ὅλο τὶ ἀδροῦ δης τὸ κορίτσ ἔστελνε νὰ πάγ᾽ τὴν ἀγελάδα στὴν ἀγέλ. Μνιὰ μέρα τὸ βρίσκει κεῖ ἔνας παππούς καὶ τὸ γεῖπε⁴)· „ἔλα, κορίτσ μου, νὰ μὲ ψειρίσ᾽ς“. Αὐτὸ κάται⁵) καὶ τὸ βσειρίζ¹). Καὶ τὸ ρωτᾷ ὁ παππούς· „τί μὲ γηῦρες⁴), κορίτσ μου;“ — „Μαργαριταρένια κόνιδα, τὸν λέγ᾽, σὲ γηῦρα⁴) καὶ μαλαματένια ψεῖρα.“ Εἶχε κεῖ πέρα κοδὰ¹) δύο γιόλες, καὶ τὸ λέγ᾽ τὸ κορτσόπλο ὁ παππούς· „πὰν κεῖ καὶ βῆκα¹) σὲ κείν τὴ γιόλα.“ Κ᾽ ἔγ᾽νε τὸ κορίτσ ὁλόχρυσο, γιὼς βῆκε. Καὶ τὸ φκήσκε⁶) κιόλα, ὅδε γελᾷ, νὰ πέφνα⁷) τριαδάφλλα ἀμάραντα πὲ τὸ στόμα τ, κι ὅδε κλαίγ᾽, νὰ τρέχνα⁷) πὲ τὰ μάτια τ δάκρυα μαργαριτάρια. Πῆγε αὐτὸ στὸ σπίτ, τὸ χάσκει ἡ μητρυιγιὰ αὐτὸ ὁλόχρυσο, τὸ λέγ᾽· „μωρή, πῶς γίν᾽κες, λέγ᾽, ἔτσ;“ — „Μὲ γηῦρε, λέγ᾽, ἔνας παππούς στὴν ἀγέλ καὶ μὲ γεῖπε καὶ τὸ βσείρσα κ᾽ ὕστερα μὲ γεῖπε νὰ βήκω⁸) μέσ στὴ γιόλα μέσα κ᾽ ἔγ᾽να χουσό⁹).“ — Τὴν ἄλλ τὴ μέρα στέλνει καὶ τὸ δικό δης στὴν ἀγέλ ἡ μητρυιγιά. Τὸ βρίσκει πάλ ὁ παππούς κ᾽ ἐκεῖνο καὶ τὸ λέγ᾽· „ἔλα, κορίτσ μου, καὶ ψείρσέ μ.“ Τὸ βσείρσε κ᾽ ἐκεῖνο. Τὸ ρωτᾷ· „τούλγη ψεῖρα μὲ γηῦρες;“ — „Γαδουρίσια κόνδα, βουβαλίσια ψεῖρα“. Τὸ λέγ᾽ καὶ κεῖνο· „πὰν λούθτσε¹⁰) σὲ κείννα¹¹) τὴ γιόλα.“ Πηγαίν, λούγεται αὐτό, γίν᾽ται¹²) σὰ βουτέκ μαῦρο. Πλών καὶ στὴν ἄλλ τὴ γιόλα τὸ χέρ δου καὶ γίν᾽ται μόν τὸ δαχτυλόπλο τ χρυσό. Πηγαίν στὸ σπίτ δους καὶ ξυπάζ᾽ται¹²) ἡ μάννα τ

---

²³) § 118, n. 1. ²⁴) =τὴν.
¹) § 15, n. 2. ²) =πάρθηκαν. ³) § 142 n. ⁴) § 23.
⁵) =κάθεται. ⁶) =εὐκήστηκε. ⁷) § 213, n. 5. ⁸) § 221, n. 3.
⁹) § 31, n. 1. ¹⁰) § 222, n. 4. ¹¹) § 144, n. 1. ¹²) § 219 n.

πὲ τὴ μαυρίλα τ καὶ τὸ ρωτᾷ· „γιατί, μωρή, ἔγ'νες μαύρη σὰ
ϐουτέκ;" Κ' ἐκεῖνο τὰ γεῖπε ὅπως ἔγ'ναν. Κούσκε[13]) ποῦ ἔγ'νε ἡ
προγονὴ χουσή[9]), τό 'μαθαν ὁ κόσμος. Πέρασε π' ἔξω καὶ τὶ[14])
βασιλὲ[15]) ὁ γιός, τὸ γεῖδε καὶ κεῖνος, ποῦ γέλασε κ' ἔπεσε ἕνα
τριαδάφλλο πὲ τὸ στόμα τ. Τὸ ἀγάπσε καὶ τὸ γύρεψε νὰ τὸ πάρ.
Ἀρραβωνιάζδαι[16]) καὶ φκειάν τὶς ἑτοιμασίες γιὰ τὴ χαρά. Τότες
ἡ μητρυιγιὰ ζούλεψε, γιατί ἡ προγονή ᴅης νὰ πάρ τὶ βασιλὲ τὸ
γιὸ καὶ ὄχ' τὸ δικό ᴅης τὸ κορίτσ. Πιάν καὶ βγάζ τὰ μάτια τῆς
προγονῆς καὶ τὴ στέλνει σ' ἕνα ἄθρωπο στὸ βουνὸ νὰ τὴ χάσ.
Κεῖ τὸ βρίσκει τὸ χρυσὸ τὸ κορίτσ πὰ σ' ἕνα δέδρο ἕνας παππούς
καὶ τὸ παίρνει σπίτ ᴅου στὴ ϐάϐω τ. Ἡ ϐάϐω πὲ τὴ χαρά ᴅης
δὲ ϐρομάζωνε τὰ χείλια ᴅης. Ἄς ἦᴅαν καὶ τυφλό, ἦᴅαν ἀμμὰ
χρυσὸ καὶ ὄμορφο. Ἡ μητρυιγιὰ πὲ τ' ἄλλ[17]) τὸ μέρος νεϐάζ τὴ
θεγατέρα ᴅης μέσ τ' ἁμάξ καὶ γούλ πὲ τὸ ψίκ διάϐ'καν στὶ βασιλὲ
τὴ ϐολιτεία. Σὰ ϐῆγαν κεῖ, ρωτᾷ τὶ βασιλὲ ὁ γιός· „γιατί ἔν μαύρη
ἡ νύφ;" Λέγ' ἡ μάννα ᴅης· „κεῖνο[18]), τὴν ἔβαλαμ μέσα στ' ἁμάξ
τὸ κλεισμένο καὶ μαύρισε πὲ τὸ κλείσιμο, καὶ μὸν τὸ δαχτυλόπλό
ᴅης, ποῦ ἦᴅαν π' ἔξω, πόμνε[19]) χρυσό." Γίν'ται ἡ χαρά. Φυλάγ'
τὶ βασιλὲ ὁ γιὸς νὰ γελάσ ἡ γυναῖκα τ καὶ νὰ πάρ τὸ ἀμάραντο
τὸ τριαδάφλλο· αὐτὴ κατσούφα[20]), μὴ ᴅύχ καὶ[21]) πιαστῇ ἡ ψευτιά
ᴅης, καμνιὰ φορὰ δὲ γελοῦσε ϐροστά τ. — Ὁ παππούς πάλ καὶ
ἡ ϐάϐω θαμάζδανα[22]) πὲ τὴ θεϊκὴ τὴ χάρ, ποῦ τὶς κατήβ'κε.
Ἔκλαιγε, ἔκλαιγε τὸ κορίτσ τὴ ᴅύχ ᴅου καὶ ὁ παππούς μάζωνε τὰ
μαργαριτάρια καὶ τὰ πουλιοῦσε[23]) καὶ πλούταινε. Πὲ τὰ πολλὰ τὰ
καλά, ποῦ τὸ εἶχαν τὸ κορίτσ, γύρσε μνιὰ μέρα ἡ καρδιά τ καὶ
γέλασε. Τόμτι γέλασε τὸ κορίτσ, πέφ[24]) τὸ τριαδάφλλο πὲ τὸ
στόμα τ. Τὸν δίν τὸ παππού τὸ τριαδάφλλο καὶ τὸν λέγ'· „νὰ
πὰς ὄξω πὲ τὸ παλάτ καὶ νὰ πουλῇς ἕνα τριαδάφλλο ἕνα μάτ."
Τ' ἀκούγ' ἡ μητρυιγιὰ πὲ μέσ πὲ τὸ παλάτ, τὸ ρωτᾷ· „πόσο τὸ
πουλεῖς αὐτὸ τὸ τριαδάφλλο;" Αὐτὸς λέγ'· „γιὰ ἕνα μάτ." —
„Στέκα, λέγ', ἐγὼ ἔχω ἕνα μάτ."

Πηγαίν καὶ τὸ φέρνει τὸ ἕν[25]) τὸ μάτ τῆς προγονῆς. Ὁ
παππούς πὲ μνιὰ χαρὰ τὸ πηγαίν στὸ σπίτ τὸ μάτ, καὶ γούλ.
μαζί, ἡ ϐάϐω, ὁ παππούς, τὸ κορίτσ πὲ τὰ κλάματα πέφνα καὶ
παρακαλοῦνα[7]) τὸ Θεγό, νὰ κολλήσ τὸ μάτ. Καὶ ποῦ κυττάζ,
κόλσε τὸ μάτ στὸ ᴅόπο τ. Πὲ κεῖθε πάλ ἡ μητρυιγιά, ἅμα ὁ

13) =ἀκούστηκἐ.   14) § 55, n. 3.   15) § 71, n. 3.   16) =ἀρ-
ραβωνιάζουνται.   17) § 156, n. 3.   18) § 146, n. 3.   19) =ἀπόμεινε.
20) = "she remained grave."   21) § 280, n. 2.   22) § 220, n. 1.
23) § 245, n. 3.   24) πέφτει.   25) § 128, n. 1.

γα*b*ρός *d*ης, τὶ βασιλὲ ὁ γιός, πῆγε στὸ παλάτ, τὸ *b*ροσπατεῖ καὶ τὸν λέγ'· „εἶδες σήμερα, πῶς γίν'κε καὶ γέλασε τὸ κορίτσ μου καὶ ἔπεσε αὐτόνα τὸ τρια*d*άφλλο πὲ τὸ στόμα τ;" καὶ τῆς τὸ ἔδωκε. Παργορήθκε πγιὰ κι̱ αὐτός· „σὰ *b*άγ', λέγ', τὸ χούσωμά⁹) *d*ης, πόμναν *b*άρεμ τὰ τρια*d*άφλλα".

Πὲ κεῖθε τὶ παππού τὸ κορίτσ πὲ τὴ χαρά τ, ποῦ ἀρχίνεψε πάλ νὰ κυττάζ, γέλασε κ' ἔπεσε καὶ ἄλλο τρια*d*άφλλο. Λήγορα ὁ παππούς τὸ πηγαίν π' ὄξω πὲ τὸ παλάτ καὶ τὸ πουλεῖ πάλ γιὰ ἕνα μάτ ὁ παππούς. Πάλ παρεκάλεσαν τὸ Θεγὸ καὶ κόλλσε καὶ τ' ἄλλ τὸ μάτ τὶ κοριτσιού. Χαρούμενο τώρα πγιὰ τὸ κορίτσ τὶ παππού γούλ μέρα γελούσε καὶ ἄλλα τόσα τρια*d*άφλλα ἔπεφτάνα. Ὁ παππούς δὲ *b*ήγαινε πγιὰ νὰ τὰ πουλῆ στὸ παλάτ, μόν τὰ μοίραζε στοὺς φίλ *d*ου. Περνᾷ στ' αὐτὶ τὶ βασιλέ, ποῦ ἔχ' ἕνας τέτοιο κορίτσ, λόγυρίζ λογκαιλόγερα τὸ σπίτ πὲ στράτεμα καὶ *b*αίν καὶ τὸ παίρνει πὲ μέσα τὸ κορίτσ. Ἴσα τὸ πηγαίν στὸ παλάτ, καὶ κεῖ γούλα πγιὰ τὰ εἶπε τὸ κορίτσ, ὅτι ἔπαθε πὲ τὴ μητρυιγιά. Τότε τὶ βασιλὲ ὁ γιὸς παίρνει τέσσαρα ἄλογα, στὰ δγυ̱ὸ δήν²⁶) τὴ μάννα τ καὶ στὰ δγυ̱ὸ τὴ θεγατέρα, τό 'ν²⁵) τὸ ποδάρ στό 'ν τ' ἄλογο καὶ τ' ἄλλ τὸ ποδάρ στ' ἄλλ τ' ἄλογο καὶ τά 'δωκε πὲ μνιὰ καμπτσικιὰ τ' ἄλογα, κ' ἔφευγαν σὰ *g*απνὸς τ' ἄλογα στὰ χωράφια καὶ τὴ *g*σέσκισαν τὴ στρί̱γλα. Καὶ γύστερα φκει̱άν βασίλισσα τὸ χρυσὸ τὸ κορίτσ κ' ἔζησαν καλόκαρδοι πολλὰ χρόνια.

13. From Pontus (on the Black Sea).

a) Τὸ λεοντάριν καὶ ἄρθωπον¹).

Ἕνας πάρδος ἐξέβεν²) σὸ³) κυνήγιν. Ἀπέσ' σ' ὄρος ἐπέντεσεν⁴) ἔναλ λεοντάρ. Ἄμον ντ' εἶδεν ἄτεν⁵) τὸ λεοντάρ, λέ̣ς ἀτός ἀτον⁵)· „ἀ*b*οῦτος⁶) ἐμᾶς ὁμοιάζ καὶ ἀς ἐμέτερον⁷) τὴμ φυλὴν ἔν, καὶ ντὸ μικρὸς ἔν!" Ἀλλομίαν ἐκοῦξεν καὶ ὀρωτᾷ τον· „ἐσὺ γιατί εἶσαι ἀτόσον μικρός;" Εἶπεν ἄτον καὶ ὁ πάρδον⁸)· „ἐγὼ σ' ἀρθωπίων τὰ χέρι̱α ἐτράνηνα, καὶ τὰ μωρά τουν εἷς ἀπ' ἀδὰ ἐντοῦννεμ με, ἄλλος ἐσκώννεμ με ἀς ὠτίν, γιαὸ τ' ἐκεῖνο ἐπελύστα⁹) μικρός." Εἶπεν καὶ τὸ λεοντάρ· „μῶρε, ἀτεῖν' τόσοιοι¹⁰) ἀρθώπ' εἶν' κ' ἐγὼ 'κ' ἐργωνίζ ἄτς; Εἶα ἄϊτε, ἀς ἐντρανοῦμ ἄτς." Ἐσκώθαν, πάγνε, ὁ πάρδον ἀπ' ἔμπρ καὶ τὸ λεοντάρ ἀπ' ὀπίσ'. Σ'

²⁶) = δένει (?).
¹) Here also § 7, n. 1 is to be compared.　　²) v. § 208.　　³) § 55, n. 2.　　⁴) § 6, n. 2.　　⁵) § 136, n. 3.　　⁶) § 145 n.　　⁷) § 143, n. 3.　　⁸) § 62, n. 1.　　⁹) From ἀπολύω = ἀφήνω; cf., further, § 208.　　¹⁰) § 151, n. 2.

έναν ὁρμάν ἀπέσ' καμπόσοι Λαζοὶ ἐσκίζναν ξύλα. Ἀτεῖν' ὅταν
τὸ πιρόν ἄλλο 'κὶ δουλέβ', σὸ σκίσμαν χτυποῦν πασσάλ καὶ
ἀνοίγνε τὴν ἀραγμάδαν. Ἄμον ντὸ ἔκσαν ¹¹) τὶ λεονταρὶ ¹²) τὴν
κιουρτιτήν, ἐκεῖν' ἔφυγαν μὲ τὰ κόντσια σὸν κῶλον. Ὁ πάρδον
λέϳ' σὸ λεοντάρ ἀς τ' ἐσίμωσαν· „ἐλέπς; ἀτεῖν' οἱ ἀρθώπ' μετ'
έναν ¹³) ἀξιναρέαν πόσον κατηβάζνε τὸ ξύλον;" Εἶπεν καὶ τὸ
λεοντάρ· „ἀτὸ πάλ ντὸ ¹⁴) ἕν; ἐγὼ μὲ τὰ χέρια μ σύρω κὶ ἀπο-
τσιχαλίζ' ἀτο." Ἀτότες ἐξέβεν ἀπάν' σὸ τιζκιάχ, ἐσέγκεν ¹⁵) τὰ
χέρια τ σὸ σκίσμαν καὶ εἴστια ἔσυρνεν ν' ἀποτσιχαλίζῃ ἀτο· τὸ
πασσάλ ἐλάγκεψεν, καὶ τὰ χέρια τ ἐκλειδώθαν ἀπέσ'. Ἐκλώσταν
οἱ Λαζοί, ἐπέραν ¹⁶) κάθα εἷς ἀπ' ἕνα ζωγρίν, ἔρθαν ἀπάν' ἀτ'
καὶ στρώνν ἀτον τὸ ξύλον. „Ἄδεφλε," εἶπεν τὸ λεοντάρ τὸν πάρδον, „ἀβουτεῖν', ἄμον ντ' ὁμοιάζ', ἀς ἐσὲν μικρὸν θὰ ἰφτειάγνε
με." Εἶπεν καὶ ὁ πάρδον· „Σὸ χέρν ἄτουν ἔν, ἄμον ντὸ θέλνε,
ἐφτειάγνε." Ἀτὸς ἐπέλεκεν ¹⁷) κ' ἐδέβεν πλάν, καὶ τὸ λεοντάρ οἱ
ἀρθώπ' ἐντώκαν, ἐντώκαν κ' ἐσκότωσαν.

b) From the vicinity of Samsun (Ἀμισός).
Ἡ κάτα καὶ ὁ πεντικόν.

Ἕναν ἡμέραν εἷς ¹) γοτσαμάνενα κάτα πιάν εἴναν ¹) πεντικόν
καὶ λέ ἀτον· „ὀγὼ ἄρτουκ ἐγέρασα, σὰ σουμὰ χὰ ²) πώγω ³) σὸν
ἂν ⁴) τάφον, ἀθερρῶ, ὅλἄ ⁵) τὰ πεντικάρἄ ⁵) πα ἀπ' ἕναν δύο φο-
ρὰς ἐφοόρτζ' ⁶) ἀτα. Ὀγὼ ἄρτουκ μετ' ὅλἄ τὰ χαϊβάνἄ ⁵) χαλα-
σεύω· δἄβα ⁵), πὲ ὅλἄ τὰ πεντικάρα, ἂς ἔρχουνταν καὶ μετ' ἐεῖνα
πα χαλασεύω." Ὁ πεντικὸν πάει καὶ λέ ἀτα σ' ἄλλα τὰ πεντικάρἄ. Τ' ἄλλα τὰ πεντικάρα ἄμον τ' ἔκσαν ἀτα, ἐχάραν καὶ
ἐχαζουρλαέφταν νὰ πάνε. Ἀτότε ἕναν τρανὸν πεντικάρ ἔρται ⁷)
καὶ λέ ἀτα· „ἐλάτε, μὴ πάτε, τσίγκι ἀδὰ ἕναν τουζάh ἔν." Κανεὶς 'κ' ἔκσεν ἀ ⁸) καὶ ὅλἄ 'πήγαν. Ἡ γοτσαμάνενα ἡ κάτα μάχ-
σᾳς ⁹) ἔνοιξεν ἕναν τρυπὶν κ' ἐκάτζεν σὴν ὀτὰν ἀπέσ. Ἔρθαν ὅλἄ
τὰ πεντικάρα κ' ἐσειραλαέφταν σ' ἕναν σειράν. Ἀτότε ἐσκώθεν ἡ
κάτα, ὁροκλώϊστεν ὀλίγον καὶ μετ' ἕναν δύο λόγια ἄμον βασιετᾶ
ἔρθεν σὸ τρυπὶν κεικὰ καὶ λέει· „γιά, ἐλάτε, ἂς τεροῦμε, ποῖος

---

¹¹) =ἤκουσαν.   ¹²) v. § 95, n. 3.   ¹³) § 128, 1 n.   ¹⁴) § 152,
n. 2.   ¹⁵) § 203, 5.   ¹⁶) =ἐπῆραν.   ¹⁷) Aorist of ἀπολύω, cf.
§ 202.

¹) § 128 n.   ²) § 20, n. 2.   ³) =πάγω.   ⁴) § 11, n. 3.
⁵) § 6, n. 6 ; ὅλἄ, § 156 n.   ⁶) =ἐφοβέρισα.   ⁷) ἔρχεται.   ⁸) § 136, n. 3.
⁹) ə is a sort of e-vowel representing an indeterminate sound (cf. Germ.
unstressed ĕ in lebĕ, etc.).

ἀποπέσ' ἐσουν¹⁰), σιτᾶ ἔστέκεν τὶ σακκὶ¹¹) τὸ στόμαν, ἐτρύπεσεν τὸν κῶλον ἀχτε¹²) καὶ ἔκϭεν¹³) τὸ πρίντς;" Καὶ ἕνα δύο ἄλλα ἀεῖκα ἄμον τὸ εἶπεν, κ' ὕστερα ἐσκάλωσεν νὰ φουρκίζ' καὶ τρώει ἀτα.

The above in Phonetic Transcription:

Énan iméran iz ꝫoḉamánena káta pián inan bendikón ke lé aton: „oꝫó ártuk ejérasa, sa sumá χa róꝫo son an dáfon, aꝑeró, ólä ta pendikárä pa ap énan ꝺío forás efoórdz ata. Oꝫó ártuk met ólä ta χaịvánä χalasévo; ꝺáva, pe ólä ta pendikárä, as érχundan ḱe met eína pa χalasévo.“ O pendikóm baị ke lé ata sála ta pendikárä. Tála ta pendikárä ámon d éksan atà, eχáran ḱe eχazurlaéftan na páne. Atóte énan dranóm bendikár érte ke lé ata: „eláte, mi páte, ḉinki¹⁴) aꝺá énan duzáh¹⁵) en.“ Kanis k éksen a ḱe ólä píꝫan. I ꝫoḉamánena i káta máχsəs éniksen énan dripín k ekáꝺzen sin otán apès. Érꝑan ólä ta pendikárä k' esiralaéftan sénan sirán. Atóte eskóꝑen i káta, orokloïsten ulíꝫon ḱe met énan ꝺio lóịa ámon vasjétá érꝑen so tripín kikà ke leị: „ja eláte, as terúme, pios apopés esun, sitá ésteken ti saki to stóman, etripesen toᴚ gólon axtè ḱe ékšen to prints?“ Ḱe éna ꝺio ála aïka ámon do ípen, k' ístera eskálosen na furkíz ḱe tróị ata.

c) From the vicinity of Tiréboli.

The fable was related to me by an aged priest from the village of Ezreíl (in the neighbourhood of Tiréboli). The narrator spoke very indistinctly, hence the phonetic reproduction is imperfect.

Ἀλεπὸν καὶ ἄρκον.

Ἀλεπὸν¹) καὶ ἄρκον¹) ἔνταν²) συντρόφ καὶ πήγανε ν' ἀράβουν καὶ νὰ τρώνε. Ἔβρεν ἄρκον σὸ³) τουσάκ ἀπὰν ἕναν κομμάτ κρέας, ἐπῆεν τὸ κρέας νὰ τρώη ἀτο· ἔχωσεν τὸ στόμα τ νὰ τρώη τὸ κρέας· τὸ κρέας τὰ⁴) ἔτρωιεν ἀτὸ, ἐπιάστεν ἀσὸ⁵) σεῖλος⁶)· ἐλάγκεψεν ἀδά, ἐλάγκεψεν ἀκεῖ, 'κ ἐπόρεσεν νὰ γλύτωνεν ἀσὸ τουσάκ. Ὕστερις ἀλεπὸν ἔκαμεν ἀλεπέϭα⁷)· ἔθεκεν τὸ κιφάλν ἀτ σὴν γῆν ἀπάν· ἐξέβεν⁸) ἡ ψή⁹) ἀτου ψεματικά.

¹⁰) § 135, n. 1.   ¹¹) § 95, n. 3.   ¹²) § 142 n.   ¹³) § 37 n.
¹⁴) Not *ćiᴚgi*!   ¹⁵) *h* is strongly aspirated.
¹) § 62, n. 1.   ²) = ἐγίνουνταν; for the vocalism of the piece,
v. § 7, n. 1.   ³) § 55, n. 2.   ⁴) = ποῦ (conjunction), *cf.* § 150, n. 1.
⁵) = ἀς (*i.e.* ἀπό) with art.   ⁶) § 21.   ⁷) *i.e.* "he laid him dead."
⁸) § 208.   ⁹) § 37 n.

Ὕστερις ἔρθεν ὁ σάπις τουσαλί, ἐντράνησεν, ἀλεπὸν ἐψόφησεν. Ἐξέγκεν[10]) ἀσὸ τουσὰκ τὸν ἀλεπὸν καὶ ἔθεκεν ἁπλωμένον ἐκεκά· ἔφυγε ἀλεπόν. Ὁ ἄνθρωπος ἐκεῖνος ἐγούλεψεν τὸ τουσάκ ἄτου κ' ἐδέβεν[8]) πλὰν σὸ σπίτιν ἄτ. Ὁ ἀλεπὸν ἔβρεν τὸν ἄρκον καὶ εἶπεν τὸν ἄρκον· „ντὸ λάσκεσαι;" — Ὁ ἄρκον λέει· „ντὸ νὰ φτάω; τιδὲν 'κ' ἔβρα." — „Ἐκεῖ κάτ σὸ μέρος εἶναι ἕναν τουσάκ κ' ἔσει[6]) ἕνα κουμμάτ κρέας." — Ἐπῆγεν και ἄρκον νὰ εὑρήκ[11]) τὸ κρέας καὶ νὰ τρώει ἄτο. Ἐπιάστεν ἄρκον σὸ τουσάκ. Ὁ ἀλεπὸν ἔρθεν, ἐκρύφτεν νὰ τερῇ τ' ἄρκονος[12]) τὸ σεῖρ· ἄρκον 'κ' ἐβλέπ ἄτον. Λαγκεύ ἄρκον ἐκεῖ, λαγκεύ ἀδά νὰ γλυτών, 'κ' ἐπόρεσεν. Ἀλεπὸν κρυφὰ λέει· „Ἄετς πα ποῖκα[13]) κ' ἐγλύτωσα, ξανεποῖκα κ' ἐγλύτωσα." Ἔρθεν τουσαλιοῦ ὁ σάαπις, νὰ τερῇ κανέναν τσαναβάρ, ἂν ἐντῶκεν[13]) σὸ τουσάκ, νὰ παίρ ἄτο. Εἶδεν τὸν ἄρκον, κεῖται[14]) ἁπλωμένος ἐκεάν. Λέει ὁ σαάπις σὸν ἄρκον· „ἐσὺ πάλ ἅμαν[15]) τὸν ἀλεπὸν θὰ φτὰς νὰ ψοφᾷς." Δέκεν[16]) τὸ ξινάρ σὸ κιφάλν ἄτ καὶ σκότωσεν ἄτονε.

14. Cappadocia.

a) From Fertek.

I copied down the piece in Samsun from the lips of a petty officer of Fertek origin. The *tenues* were mostly pronounced with aspiration (κ' for κ, etc.).

Ἕνα κ'αλὸ[1]) κ'ύριο[2]) ἄτρωπος[3]) ἔννε[4]) βαρὺ ἀστενάρ, τσιρούρτισε[5]) τὸ ναῖκα τ — καὶ ναῖκα[6]) τ' ἀκ'όμ ἦτ'ον τελίγαγνε[7]) — καὶ εἶπεν *to*· „σεβgίλι μου, τρανᾷς το, ἦλτε τὸ σαχάτ'ι μ, ἔσεται[8]) χωρὶς καὶ χωρὶς νὰ σ' ἀφήσω καὶ νὰ π'άγω· ἀκ'όμ τελίγαγλ'[7]) εἶσαι, καὶ ἂν κρέβῃς νὰ χατῶ[3]) ραχάτ, νὰ μὲ πκῇς[9]) ἕνα κ'αλό· χωρὶς ἄλλο νὰ παντρευτῇς, ξεύρω το· πολὺ σὲ γιαλβαρτῶ, τὸ κομσού μ μὴ τὸ π'άρῃς. Ὀγὼ μετ' ἐκεῖνο γαυγὰλ εἶμαι[10])· ἄντον μὲ καντίῃς, τότε νὰ τ'ὸ π'άρῃς *d'* ἔναι[11]), νὰ μὴ χατῶ μεραγλə́ς.

Καὶ τὸ ναῖκα ἔ*d*εκε[12]) κασəλə́κ καὶ εἶπε· „*h*ίτσ τ' ἀσὸν[13]) τὸ χάτσιμο σ ὀγὼ μανὶ μ' ἴνω[14])· ραχάτ ραχάτ χάτ[15]), ἂς σὲ 'πῶ τὸ

[10]) § 203, 5. [11]) § 214, n. 5. [12]) § 62, n. 1. [13]) § 202, n. 2. [14]) P. 130, footnote 1. [15]) = *ἅμον* (*σάν*). [16]) § 182, n. 2.

[1]) *καλός.* [2]) *κύριος.* [3]) § 20, n. 1. [4]) Pronounced with double *ν*, = *ἔγινε.* [5]) "Addressed" (?). [6]) = *καὶ ἡ ναῖκα.* [7]) "young." [8]) = *ἔρχεται.* [9]) § 214, n. 5. [10]) Pronounced with *one* stress *γαυγαλεῖμαι* "I contend," from an adj. *γαυγάλ* (Turk.) and *εἶμαι.* [11]) = *δὲν εἶναι.* [12]) = *ἔδωκε.* [13]) § 143, n. 3. [14]) = *νὰ μὴ γίνω.* [15]) "dies," *cf.* § 222, n. 4.

ὀρτάτατ¹⁶), ζάτ᷇ ἐκ῾εῖνο ὀγὼ νὰ τὸ π῾άρω *d'* ἔναι, τσούγκι ὀγὼ ἀπὸ τρία μῆνες ὄμπρο σ' ἕνα π῾αϭκὰ ἄτρωπο ἔᵭωκα¹¹) τσοάπ¹⁷) τον.

b) From Pharasa.

Account of travelling Adventures.

Φοντὲς παγαίεγκαμεν¹), ζάλσαμ²) τὴν στράτα, ξίλσαμ στὰ ρουσία τζαὶ³) τζοὶ⁴) κάτζοι τζαὶ στὰ παγάνια πέσω, βράδυνε· στὴ σκοτεινία τζὸ πόρκαμ¹) νά 'βρωμ τοῦ χωρίον τὴν στράτα. Φοντὲς νεγκώγκαμ¹) ἐδὼ τζ' ἀτζεῖ, ἔβγαν⁵) γνέντα μας πέντε κλέφτοι⁶) τζ' εἶπαν μας· „μὴ σαλεύητε, νὰ⁷) σᾶς δώκωμεν⁸) τζαὶ νὰ σᾶς κρούσωμεν." ΤΖ ἐμεῖς εἴπαμτι⁹) τζαὶ στεκόμαστε, στέρο μαργαώσαμε, δώκαμε¹⁰) πενεντάο¹¹) τζαὶ χάσαμε τζοὶ κλέφτοι. Σάμο ἔφυγαν, κούλθσαμ¹²) τὴν στράτα, ξίλσαμ σ' ἄν¹³) παλὸ ὀρένι, πνώσαμ ἀτζεῖ. Φοντὲς πνώγκαμεν¹) σκοτεινὰ σὼς τὴν ἐβίτζα τζὸ πόρκαμ νὰ πνώσωμεν τζοὶ⁴) κρότοι τζαὶ στὰ στριγγέματα, ἤλεγὲστι¹⁴) τζαὶ κιάζει¹⁵), νά 'ρχουνται τζοὶ⁴) τιέσοι τζαὶ στὰ πηγάδια ποπέσ¹⁶), στ' ἄλλα τοὶ μέρη¹⁷) στοῦ φιδιοῦ¹⁸) τζαὶ στοῦ ἀποῦ¹⁹) τζαὶ στοῦ λύτζοι²⁰) τὰ τζυρίγματα φοβήθαμ²¹) πολὺ κακά. Φοντὲς ἤμαστε στὰ τζέσᵭ ἀπέσ²²), ἄλσεν²³) τὸ λαχτόρι πὸ μακρά, σάμ' ἄλσεν τὸ λαχτόρι, ἔβγ'²⁴) τζ' ὁ φεγγοῦσκος· τζὶπ μᾶς²⁵) σκώθαμ ἀφορὰ²⁶) τάρνα²⁶), ἔβγαμ στ' ἐτζεῖνο στὸ κάγιν τὸ χάνιν πιπέσ²⁷), εὐξώθαμ²⁸) τὸ Θεγό, τοῦ²⁹) μᾶς ἔβγαλ ἀροί³⁰)· σάμ' ἔβγαμεν στὴ στράτα, κατζέφκαμ³¹) πενεντάο τζ' ἤλεγαμ „τάρνα τάρνα, χιϊτᾶτε ἀγκούτι³²)", τζαὶ τὴν ἐβίτζα ἐφτάσαμε στὸ χωρίον.

---

¹⁶) =ὀρθότητα "truth."   ¹⁷) *i.e.* "I gave answer"="I consented."

¹) Imperf. of παγαίνω, *cf.* § 214, n. 6.   ²) =ζαλίσαμε, *cf.* § 38, n. 1.
³) § 17.   ⁴) =στσοὶ (*i.e.* στοὺς).   ⁵) =ἐβγῆκαν.   ⁶) § 69.   ⁷) As a sign of the future.   ⁸) More correctly ντώκωμεν, from the aorist cited in § 202, n. 2.   ⁹) =εἴπαμε.   ¹⁰) =ντώκαμε, *v.* note 8.   ¹¹) § 141 n.
¹²) § 38, n. 1.   ¹³) § 56 n.   ¹⁴) =ἐλέγατε.   ¹⁵) =φαίνεται (?).
¹⁴⁻¹⁶ (ὁ θόρυϐος) "ἐφαίνετο ὡς νὰ προήρχετο ἐκ τῶν τοίχων τοῦ ἐρειπίου καὶ τῶν φρεάτων" (translation of the editor).   ¹⁷) "On the other side."
¹⁸) =φιδιῶ(ν).   ¹⁹) Gen. pl. of ἀπός "fox" (in Pontic ἀλεπός, more commonly ἀλωποῦ, etc., *cf.* § 32 n.).   ²⁰) § 62, n. 1.   ²¹) § 208.
²²) "ἐν τοιαύτῃ ἀγωνίᾳ."   ²³) Aor. of ἀλῶ.   ²⁴) =ἔβγε, *i.e.* ἐβγῆκε.
²⁵) "παρευθὺς δὲ" (editor).   ²⁶) "ὅσον τὸ δυνατὸν ταχύτερον."
²⁷) ἐξῆλθομεν τοῦ ἀπαισίου ἐκείνου κτιρίου."   ²⁸) "we praised" (aor.).
²⁹) § 150, n. 1.   ³⁰) § 108, n. 4.   ³¹) § 214, n. 6.   ³²) I am not acquaint with this word; something like "however, nevertheless."

15. Zaconian.

The Zaconians live on the east slope of Parnon, between St. Andreas and Lenídi. Lenídi, Prasto, Sítena, and Castanitza are the chief places of the country inhabited by them. The Zaconian dialect is noteworthy as the descendant of the *ancient Laconian* patois.

> Puládzj éma[1])éχa[2]) tho[3]) kuiδí[4])
> Dze meruté[5]) nj[6]) éma éχa[7]),
> Tajiχa[8]) nj éma záχaŕi,
> Po[i]kíχa[9]) nj éma mósko.
> Dze apó to mósko tom bersú[10])
> Dze apó ta[11]) niroiδía[12])
> Eskandaliste[13]) to kuiδí
> Dz' efindze[14]) mi[15]) t' aiδóni.
> Dz' aféngi[16]) nj éki[17]) dziniŕú[18])
> Me to kuiδí thu χére[19]):
> „Éa[4]), puli, thon[3]) dópo ndi[20]),
> Éa tho ka[i]kidzie[21]),
> Na átsu[22]) ta kuδúnja ndi,
> Na válu áva[23]) dzinúrdza[24])."

Cf. with this another version from Ladá in Taygetos[1]):

> Πουλάκι εἶχα στὸ κλουδί,
> Μὰ τὴν ἁγιὰ Παρασκευή,
> Καὶ τό 'χα μερωμένο,
> Πουλὶ ζωγραφιζμένο.
> Ἀπὸ τὸ μόσκο τὸν πολὺ
> Μοῦ σκανταλίστη τὸ κλουδὶ
> Καὶ μοῦ 'φυγε τ' ἀηδόνι.

[1]) =ἤμουν.   [2]) =a. Gk. (participle), and so *éma éχa*, a circumlocution for εἶχα.   [3]) *v.* § 35, n. 3.   [4]) § 32.   [5]) =μερωτό(ν), particip. from ἡμερώνω "tame."   [6]) *ni*=αὐτό(ν) "him, it."   [7]) *Cf.* n. 2, and on the construction, § 227, n. 2.   [8]) From *tayíχu*=ταγίζω.   [9]) From *po[i]kíχu*=ποτίζω, *cf.* § 16, n. 2; on the constr. *v.* n. 2.   [10]) περισσό(ν).   [11]) =τὴ(ν).   [12]) =μυρωδία (μυρουδιά).   [13]) ἐσκανταλίστηκε (*cf.* § 208).   [14]) =ἔφυγε.   [15]) μοῦ.   [16]) § 16, n. 2.   [17]) ἦταν.   [18]) =a. Gk. κυνηγῶν, *cf.* n. 2. The ṇ is to be pronounced cerebral, *i.e.* with the tongue tip bent upwards.   [19]) =στὸ χέρι.   [20]) σοῦ.   [21]) *v.* § 16, n. 2.   [22]) =νὰ ἀλλάξω, *cf.* § 32; ξ from *ts*, similarly as in Bova from *dz*, *cf.* § 35, n. 2.   [23]) =ἄλλα.   [24]) =καινούργια.

[1]) For the pronunciation of σ and ζ, *cf.* § 28.

Ποιὸς τὸ εἶδε, ποιὸς τὸ σ̌ώνει;
Κι ὁ κυνηγός, ποῦ τ' ἄκουσε,
Πολὺ κακὸ τοῦ φάνη ·
Νέλα, πουλί, σ̌τὴν κλίνη σ̌ου,
Νέλα σ̌τὴν κάμαρή σ̌ου ·
Ποῦ νὰ κοπῇ ἡ ζωή σ̌ου;

MODERN GREEK WRITING ALPHABET.

α	*A a*	ι	*I ι*	ϱ	*P ρ*
β	*B b*	κ	*K κ*	ςϛ	*Σ Σ σ ς*
γ	*Γ γ*	λ	*Λ λ*	τ	*T τ*
δ	*Δ δ*	μ	*M μ*	υ	*Υ υ*
ε	*E ε*	ν	*N ν*	φ	*Φ φ*
ζ	*Z ζ*	ξ	*Ξ ξ*	χ	*X χ*
η	*H η*	ο	*O ο*	ψ	*Ψ ψ*
ϑ	*Θ δ*	π	*Π π*	ω	*Ω ω*

Ὅτι δὰ κάμῃς κι ὅτι δὰ πῇς,
Τί δὰ συνέβη πρῶτα νὰ στοχασθῇς.

Ὁ χρόνος εἰς τὴν ὥρα του χίλια
φλουριὰ ἀξίζει.

313

SUBSTANTIVES AND VERBS.

SUBSTANTIVES.—Where the gender is easily deducible from the termination according to the rules of grammar it is not given; only in the less common usages in which the ending (-os, -ι [-ν], a) cannot in itself decide it, the gender is given, *i.e.* in the case of feminines (f.) in -ι (-ν), neuters (neut.) in -os, -a, -as.—VERBS with irregularities of stem-formation or conjugation are marked by spaced type and an asterisk *. To these verbs the irregular forms that occur are cited, usually the active and passive aorist or the perfect participle passive. Contracted verbs which follow the second class are clearly distinguished by the addition of (-έω). Compare also what is said about the Glossary in Foreword, p. xix.

LIST OF ABBREVIATIONS.

acc.	= accusative.	*m.*	= masculine.
adj.	= adjective.	*metaph.*	= metaphorical.
adv.	= adverb.	*mid.*	= middle.
a. Gk.	= ancient Greek.	*n.*	= note.
aor.	= aorist.	*neg.*	= negative, negation.
Cap.	= Cappadocia.	*neut.*	= neuter.
cf.	= *confer,* compare.	*nom.*	= nominative.
compar.	= comparative.	*part.*	= participle.
conj.	= conjunction.	*pass.*	= passive.
Cyp.	= Cyprus.	*pf.*	= perfect.
dim.	= diminutive.	*pl.*	= plural.
eccl.	= ecclesiastical (language).	*prep.*	= preposition.
f.	= feminine.	*pres.*	= present.
gen.	= genitive.	*Sar. K.*	= Saranda Klisiés.
id.	= same as preceding word.	*subst.*	= substantive.
imper.	= imperative.	*Ter. d' O.*	= Terra d' Otranto.
indecl.	= indeclinable.	*tr.*	= transitive.
indic.	= indicative.	*v.*	= *vide,* see.
interj.	= interjection.	*Velv.*	= Velvendos.
intr.	= intransitive.	*voc.*	= vocative.
lit.	= literary language.	*w.*	= with.

GLOSSARY.

Ἄ (1)=ἄν. (2)=θά, § 20, n. 2. (3)= αὐτό, § 136, n. 2.

ἀμά (*Velv.*), *interj.* now then! come on!

ἀβγαταίνω, ἀβγατίζω, ἀβγατῶ increase, multiply.

ἀβδέλλα (βδέλλα) leech.

ἀβοκάτος advocate.

ἀβοῦτος this, *v.* § 145 *n.*

ἀβροντάω thunder, hurl down with great noise.

ἄβυσσο abyss, *f.* (§ 87).

ἀγαθός good, kind.

ἀγάλια ἀγάλια, *adv.* little by little, slowly.

ἄγαλμα, *neut.* monument.

ἀγάπη love, beloved, sweetheart.

ἀγαπητικός beloved, lover; in love; *f. v.* § 111.

ἀγαπῶ (ἀαπῶ, § 22) love.

ἀγᾶς aga.

ἀγγαρεμένος put to compulsory labour.

ἀγγελικός angelic.

ἀγγελοκαμωμένος like an angel (of angelic form).

ἄγγελος (ἄντζελος, § 17) angel; ἀγγελάκι, *dim.*

ἀγγίζω (ἄγγιξα) touch.

ἀγγλοσαξονικός Anglo-Saxon.

ἀγελάδα cow.

ἀγέλαστος without laughter.

ἀγέλη herd.

ἀγενής, *adj.* lowly born.

ἀγέρας, ἀγέρι=ἀέρας.

ἅγιος holy (ἅγι, *indecl.* § 63); τὰ ἅγια the holy vessels in the church.

ἀγκάθι thorn; ἀγκαθάκι, *dim.*

ἀγκαλά although.

ἀγκάλη arm.

ἀγκαλιά arm.

ἀγκαλιάζω, ἀγκαλιάζομαι embrace.

ἀγκίστρι (ἀντζίστρι, § 17) hook.

ἀγνάντια, *adv.* against, face to face; ἀ. ’s, *prep.* opposite to, compared with.

ἁγνός venerable, chaste, pure.

ἀγνώριστος unknown.

ἄγονος unfruitful.

ἀγορά market.

ἀγοράζω buy.

ἀγραδυνιά (*Naxos*) evening.

ἄγριος fierce, strong.

ἀγροικῶ (γροικῶ) hear.

ἀγρυπνῶ (-έω) be awake.

ἀγύρικος, *adj.* unreturning.

ἀγῶνας the war of freedom (of the Greeks).

ἀγωνίζομαι struggle, fight.

ἀγώρι, *neut.* boy, son; ἀγωράκι, *dim.*

ἀδά (*Pontos*)=ἐδώ.

ἄδεια permission.

ἀδειανός empty, empty-handed.

ἄδειος empty.

ἀδέλφι=ἀδέρφι.

ἀδελφικός brotherly.

ἀδερφή sister; *pl.* § 90.

ἀδέρφι (ἀδρέφι, § 37, *n.* 1) brother; ἀδερφάκι, *dim.*

ἀδερφός (ἀερφός, § 22 *n.*)=*id.* (*voc.* ἄδεφλε, *v.* § 62).

ᾅδης Hades, underworld.

ἀδιάντροπος insolent.

ἀδιαφορία indifference.

ἄδικος unjust.

ἀδικῶ injure, vex.

ἀδίκως, *adv. to* ἄδικος (*lit.*).

ἀδιόρθωτος incorrigible, uncorrected.

ἄδολος pure.

ἀδράχνω seize, grasp.

315

ἁδρύς raw, rude.

ἀδυναμία weakness, impotence.

ἀεῖκος (§ 148, *n.* 1)=τέτοιος.

ἀέρας (ἀγέρας) air, wind ; ἀεράκι, *dim.* breath of air.

ἀεροκοπανιστής swaggerer.

ἀερολόγος tattler, idle talker.

ἀετός eagle.

ἄ^ετς (*Pontus*), *adv.* thus, so.

ἀηδόνι nightingale ; ἀηδονάκι, *dim.*

ἀθανασία immortality.

ἀθάνατος immortal.

ἀθερρῶ (*Pontus*)=θαρρῶ.

ἀθθυμοῦμαι (*Cyp.*) remember.

ἀθός=ἄνθος.

ἄθρωπος=ἄνθρωπος.

αἲ, *v.* ἒ.

αἰθέρας ether.

αἰθέριος etherial.

αἰθερόπλαστος made of ether.

αἷμα (γαῖμα), *neut.* blood.

ἄϊ(ν)τε, *interj.* come now ! away !

αἴσθημα, *neut.* feeling, sense.

αἰστάνομαι (αἰστάνθηκα) perceive, feel.

αἰσχύλειος of Aeschylus, Aeschylean.

ἄϊτός=ἀετός.

αἰώνιος eternal.

ἀκαμάτης (§ 114) lazy.

ἄκαρπος unfruitful.

ἀκαρτερῶ=καρτερῶ.

ἀκεῖ (*Pontus*) there.

ἀκέριος unhurt, intact, pure.

ἀκλουθῶ follow.

ἀκοή hearing.

ἀκόλαστος luxurious, wanton.

ἀκολουθῶ, *v.* ἀκλουθῶ.

ἀκόμα, ἀκόμη (*in dialect* ἀκόμαν, ἀκόμ, κόμ) still, more ; *in formation of compar. v.* § 119, *n.* 3.

ἀκουή=ἀκοή.

ἀκουμπῶ᾽(ἀκουμπίζω, ἀκουμπισμένος) rely upon, lean against.

ἄκουρος unshorn (of sheep).

ἀκούω (*v.* § 251, 1 ; ἀκούγω, § 23 ; ἀκούστηκα) hear.

ἄκρα extremity, end, highest point.

ἀκρανοίγω open a little.

ἄκρη=ἄκρα ; ἡ ἄκρη τῆς ἐρημιᾶς

extreme solitariness ; ἀπ᾽ ἄκρη σ᾽ ἄκρη from one end to the other.

ἀκρίβεια dearness ; στὴν ἀ. at the highest price.

ἀκριβής exact, accurate.

ἀκριβός dear (expensive), dear (favourite), niggardly.

ἀκρογιαλιά beach, shore.

ἀκροθαλασσιά seashore.

ἀκρυφά, *adv.* secretly ; ἔχω ἀ. I keep secret.

ἀκτή (*lit.*) bank, shore.

ἀκτῖνα=ἀχτῖνα.

ἀλά=*French* à la . . .

ἅλας, *neut.* (§ 105) salt.

ἀλάτι=*id.*

ἀλαφρός=ἐλαφρος.

ἀλέθω grind.

ἀλείφω, ἀλείβω anoint.

ἀλεπέσα (*Pontus*) female fox.

ἀλεπός (*Pontus*) fox.

ἀλεποῦ=ἀλωποῦ.

ἀλεύρι flour, meal.

ἀλήθεια (ἀλήθκια, § 10, *n.* 5) truth ; also *adv.* truly, really.

ἀληθεύω to become true.

ἀληθινός true ; στ᾽ ἀληθινά in truth, really.

ἀλησμόνητος never to be forgotten.

ἀλησμονῶ (*elimonízo Ter. d᾽ O.*) forget.

ἄλικος scarlet red.

ἀλκυών (*lit.*) kingfisher.

ἀλλά but.

ἀλλαγή change.

ἀλλάζω (ἄλλαξα) alter, change ; *mid.* change one's clothes (put on a better suit).

ἀλλιῶς, ἀλλιώτικα, *adv.* otherwise, else.

ἀλλοί, ἀλλοιά, *interj.* alas !

ἀλλοίμονο=*id.*

ἀλλομίαν once more, then, again (*Pontus*).

ἀλλοπιστῶ change one's faith.

ἄλλος (ἄδδο, ἄρος, § 31, *n.* 2) another ; *v.* § 156, *further sub.* τόσος.

ἄλλοτε, *adv.* once, formerly.

ἀλλοῦ, *adv.* elsewhere.

ἄλογο (ἄογο, § 32) horse ; *dim*. ἀλοάϊ (*Chios*).

ἀλοιφή ointment.

ἀλουποῦ, *v*. ἀλωποῦ.

ἀλόχτερας cock.

ἀλυσίδα chain.

ἅλυσο, *f*. (§ 87) chain.

ἀλῶ (*Cap*.) to cry (of animals), crow.

ἀλώνι threshing-floor.

ἀλωποῦ (ἀλεποῦ, ἀλουποῦ) fox (*cf*. § 88).

ἅλωσι, *f*. capture, conquest.

ἄμ, ἀμά = ἀμέ.

ἅμα, *w*. *aor*. *indic*. or *subj*. as soon as (§ 273).

ἀμάθεια ignorance.

ἀμαθής, ἄμαθος (§ 115) ignorant.

ἀμαλαγιά fresh grass.

ἄμαν (*Pontus*), *w*. *acc*. as, like.

ἄμαξα, ἀμάξι waggon.

ἀμάραντος imperishable.

ἁμαρτάνω (ἁμάρτησα, ἁμαρτημένος) to sin.

ἁμαρτιά sin.

ἁμαρτωλός sinful.

ἀμέ (ἀμά, also ἀμμέ, ἀμμά) but, still, yet.

ἄμε (ἄμμε, *Karpathos*), *v*. πηγαίνω.

ἀμέργω (§ 31, *n*. 1) to milk.

ἀμέσως, *adv*. immediately.

ἀμέτρητος innumerable, immeasurable.

ἀμίλητος speechless, silent.

ἀμιρᾶς general, Amir.

ἀμμάτι = μάτι.

ἄμμο(ς), *f*. (§ 87) sand.

ἄμοιρος unfortunate, unhappy.

ἀμολύνω defile, profane.

ἄμον (*Pontus*) = σάν (1) as, like ; (2) since, than (ἄμον [ν]τὸ, τ').

ἀμπέλι vineyard.

ἀμπελοχώραφα, *pl*. vineyards and fields (§ 41, a).

ἀμπώθω push.

ἀμύριστος without smell, odourless.

ἀμφιβολία doubt.

ἄν, *conj*. if, whether ; ἂν καί although, *v*. § 277 f.

* ἀναβαίνω (ἀνέβηκα, θ' ἀνεβῶ, aor.

21

imper. ἀνέβα ἀνεβᾶτε ἀνεβῆτε) ascend, go up ; (*of dough*) to rise.

ἀναβρύζω bubble up.

ἀναγαλλιάζω shout.

ἀναγέρνω (ἀνάγειρα) search for.

ἀνάγκη necessity ; ἔχω ἀ. I need, must.

ἀναγνώθω read.

ἀναγνωρισμένος acknowledged.

ἀναγνωσματάριον (*lit*.) reader, reading-book.

ἀναδεξιμιά godchild.

ἀνάδιος = ἀνάντιος.

ἀνάθεμα, *neut*. curse ; πάγει στ' ἀ. he is going to the devil.

ἀναθεματίζω to curse.

ἀναισθησία insensibility.

ἀνακατώνω mingle.

ἀνακλαδίζομαι shrug the shoulders.

ἀνάκουστος unheard (of).

ἀνάλογος similar, corresponding.

ἀναμένω expect.

ἀνάμεσα, *adv*. in the midst ; ἀνάμεσα 's in the midst (middle) of ; *cf*. also § 141.

ἀνάμεσο, *cf*. *id*. ; ἀνάμεσό τους among one another.

ἀναμεταξύ, *adv*. between, among ; *cf*. also § 141.

ἀνάντια = ἀγνάντια.

ἀνάντιος (ἀνάδιος, § 16, *n*. 3) opposite, opposed to.

ἀναπνοή breath.

ἀναποδιά perverseness, contradiction, caprice.

ἀναρχία anarchy.

ἀναρχικός anarchical.

ἀνάσα the breath.

ἀνασαίνω (ἀνάσανα) breathe.

ἀνασέρνω drag up, draw upwards.

ἀνάσκελα (τ' ἀ.), *adv*. on one's back, supine.

ἀνασκώνω lift up, raise.

ἀναστενάζω sigh, groan.

ἀναστήνω set up again, revive.

ἀναστυλώνω place upon a column, raise high.

ἀνατέλλω rise (of the sun).

ἀνατινάζω shake up, toss.

ἀνατολή rising (of the sun).

ἀνατριχίλα horror, shuddering.

ἀναφέρ(ν)ω quote, cite.

ἀνάφτω light, kindle.

(ἀ)ναχόρταγος insatiable.

ἀναχωρῶ depart.

ἀνδρεῖος (§ 10) brave.

ἀνεβάζω cause to ascend, lead up.

* ἀνεβαίνω=ἀναβαίνω.

ἀνεβοκατεβαίνω go up and down (cf. § 175, n. 2).

ἀνεζητῶ seek, long earnestly for.

ἀνέλπιστος hopeless.

ἀνεμόμυλος windmill.

ἄνεμος wind.

ἀνεπαμένος tranquil.

ἀνεπηρέαστος (lit.) uninfluenced.

ἀνέφαλο cloud.

ἀνήθικος immoral.

ἀνήμερος wild.

ἀνήμπορος unable, weak, sick.

ἀνθηφόρος flowering, bearing flowers.

ἀνθίζω bloom.

ἀνθισμένος blooming.

ἀνθόπλεκτος woven of flowers.

ἄνθος (ἀθός), neut. flower ; pl. § 84.

ἀνθότοπος flower-garden.

ἀνθρωπίζω make like men, civilise.

ἄ(ν)θρωπος (ἄρθωπος, § 31, n. 1 ; ἄθθρωπος, § 36 n.; gen. pl. § 62) man (homo).

ἀνθρωπότη humanity.

ἀνθῶ=ἀνθίζω.

ἀνίδεος without an idea of, ignorant.

ἀνίσως perhaps.

ἀνόητος unreasonable.

ἀνοιγοκλείω open and shut, wink.

ἀνοιγοσφαλίζω open and close.

ἀνοίγω (ἀννοίγω) open, tr. and intr.

ἀνοιξάτικος of the spring-time, spring-like.

ἄνοιξι, f. spring.

ἀνοιχτός (ἀνοικτός) open.

ἀντάμα, adv. together ; ἀ. μέ together with.

ἀνταμώνω come upon, meet, mid. happen.

ἀνταρούλα, dim. of ἀντάρα storm.

ἄντερα, neut. (pl.) intestines.

ἀντίκρυ(ς), ἀντικρύς, adv. opposite, over against.

ἀντικρύζω meet, face.

ἀντιλαλιά echo.

ἀντίλαλος echo, counterpart.

ἀντιλαλῶ (μέ) to echo, resound.

ἀντίο adieu.

ἀντιποιητικός unpoetic, prosaic.

ἀντιπρόσωπος deputy, representative.

ἀντίς, w. acc. (v. § 165) instead of, in place of.

ἀντιφέγγω reflect rays of light.

ἄντον if, when.

ἄντρας man (vir), cf. § 67.

ἀντρειός manly, brave.

ἀντρόγυνο man and wife, married couple.

ἀνωκάτω, adv. up and down, topsy-turvy.

ἀνωφέλευτος useless.

ἀξάδερφος cousin.

* ἀξαίνω, v. αὐξαίνω.

ἄξαφνα (ἔξαφνα), adv. suddenly.

ἀξία worth, honour, fame.

ἀξίζω to cost, be worth.

ἀξιναρέα (Pontus) stroke of an axe.

ἀξίνη axe.

ἄξιος worthy ; εἶμαι ἄ. am capable.

ἀξιοσπούδαστος worthy of effort.

ἄογο=ἄλογο.

ἀοῦτος, v. ἀβοῦτος.

ἀπ'=ἀπό.

ἀπάν=ἀπάνω.

ἀπάνου=ἀπάνω.

ἀπαντῶ answer ; also meet with, face.

ἀπάνω (ἀπάνου) over, above ; ἀ 's (also 's—ἀ.), ἀπάν' ἀπό upon, on (cf. § 171) ; ἀοπάνω=ἀπὸ 'πάνω above, from above, away from ; ἀ. κάτω, about, almost.

ἀπάνωθεν above, from above.

ἀπαρατήρητος unobserved.

ἀπαρνοῦμαι deny.

ἀπάτη deceit.

ἀπάτητος untrodden.

ἀπατός self (§ 157); employed also to form the reflexive, § 140, n. 1.

ἀπέ=ἀπό; also used independently, hereof.

*ἀπεθαίνω, v. πεθαίνω.

ἀπέï (*Chios*) hereupon.

ἄπειρος innumerable.

ἀπέκει (ἀπεκεῖ) beyond, v. § 172.

ἀπέκεινα, adv. from there, from that point.

ἀπέκειο, thereupon, then.

ἀπελπίζομαι to despair of.

ἀπελπισμός despair.

ἀπερνῶ pass, pass by.

ἀπέσ' (*Pontus*) within ; ἀ. 's in.

ἀπετσεῖ=ἀπεκεῖ.

ἀπηλογοῦμαι speak.

ἀπιθώνω put down, place.

ἀπλά(γ)ï side.

ἁπλός (*lit.* ἁπλοῦς) simple, single.

ἁπλώνω spread, extend.

ἀπό (ἀπ', ἀφ', ἀπέ, ἀπού, also πέ), *prep.* from, of ; *cf.* § 161.

*ἀποθαίνω (ἀποθνήσκω), v. πεθαίνω.

ἀποθανατωμένος dead.

ἀποθήκη barn, store, magazine.

ἀποθυμῶ desire.

ἀποκάτω ἀπό underneath, under.

ἀποκοιμίζω lull to sleep.

ἀποκοιμοῦμαι fall asleep.

ἀποκουρεύω shear, clip.

ἀποκρίνομαι (ἀποκρίθηκα) to answer.

ἀπόλλυμαι (*lit.*) perish.

ἀπολύ(ν)ω, ἀπολῶ(-άω), ἀπολνῶ(ἀπόλυσα ; ἐπελύστα, p. 139) release.

ἀπομένω, ἀπομνήσκω to remain, be left, v. μένω.

ἀπομονή patience.

ἀπομονωμένος left alone, isolated.

ἀπόξενος strange, gone astray.

ἀποπάνω=ἀπάνω.

ἀποπέσ' (*Pontus*) in, among.

ἀποπλανήμενος misled, seduced.

ἀπόστολος apostle.

ἀποστότε (Naxos), adv. then, thereupon.

ἀποστροφή abhorrence.

ἀποταχειά (τ' ἀ.), adv. in the afternoon.

ἀποτσιχαλίζω (*Pontus*) split.

ἀποτυχαίνω (v. τυχαίνω) to be unfortunate.

ἀπού=ἀπό, *Velv.*

[ἀπο(υ)λαύω, *defective*], aor. ἀπόλαψα (*Velv.*) enjoy.

ἀπόφασι, f. resolution.

ἀποφασίζω conclude, decide ; give up (a patient).

ἀποχαιρετισμός farewell, bidding adieu.

ἀποχτῶ acquire, attain.

ἀποχωρίζω separate.

ἀπόψε, adv. this evening.

ἄπρεπος unfitting, unbecoming.

'Απρίλις April.

ἀπροσεξία inattention, inadvertence.

ἀπρόσεχτος (ἀπρόσεκτος) careless, unmindful.

ἀρὰ δέν (*Velv.*), interrog. particle= Lat. nonne.

ἀραγμάδα (*Pontus*) opening, fissure.

ἀραγμένος, v. ἀράζω.

ἀράδα row, position ; μὲ τὴν ἀ. in turns, in succession.

ἀραδιάζω arrange (in succession).

ἀράζω (ἄραξα) to land.

ἀραιά, adv. scantily, thinly.

'Αράπης negro, Moor.

ἀραχνιασμένος full of cobwebs.

'Αρβανίτης Albanian.

ἀργά, adv. late.

ἄργανο musical instrument.

ἀργοσαλεύω move slowly.

ἀργῶ (-έω) delay, tarry long.

ἀρδινιάζομαι set about a thing, prepare to.

ἀρέζω, ἀρέσω (ἀρέσκω, ἀρέγω, ἄρεσα, ἄρεξα, ἀρεσμένος) please.

ἀρετή virtue.

ἄρθωπος (*Pontus*)=ἄνθρωπος.

ἀρίς (ἀρύς, v. § 110 n.) thin.

ἀριστοκρατικός aristocratic.

ἀριστούργημα masterpiece.

ἀρίφνητος innumerable.

ἀρκή=ἀρχή.

ἄρκλα trunk, chest.

ἄρκος (*Cyp.*)=ἄγριος.

ἄρκος (*Pontus*) bear.

ἀρκούδα female bear.

ἀρμαμέδο fleet.

ἄρματα, *pl.* weapons.

'Αρματωλός Armatolian.

ἀρμέγω, ἀμέργω (§ 31, *n.* 1) to milk.

ἀρμενίζω fluctuate, hover ; sail.

ἀρμηνεύω to counsel.

ἀρμονία harmony.

ἀρνοῦμαι deny.

ἀρός (*Cap.*) sound, alive.

ἁρπάζω, ἁρπάχνω (ἁρπῶ, ἅρπαξα) seize, rob.

ἀρραβωνιάζομαι to betroth, be betrothed.

ἀρρεβωνιαστικός betrothed, fiancé ; *f.* § 111.

ἄρρητος unspeakable.

ἀρριβάρω (ἀρριβάρισα) arrive.

ἀρρωστημένος sick.

ἀρρώστια sickness.

ἀρρωστῶ to be sick.

ἀρσενικός male.

ἄρτουκ (*Pontus*), *adv.* now, already.

ἀρτυσιά food, repast.

ἀρφανός orphan.

ἀρχαϊκός archaic, ancient.

ἀρχαῖος old, ancient.

ἀρχεύω begin.

ἀρχή (ἀρκή, § 18, *n.* 3), beginning.

ἀρχηγός leader, chief.

ἀρχίζω, ἀρχινεύω, ἀρχινίζω, ἀρχινῶ, ἀρχιρῶ (ἀχιρῶ, *Velv.*) to begin.

ἀρχοδιά=ἀρχοντιά.

ἄρχοντας (ἄρχος, § 65, *n.* 1) governor ; *pl.* princes, gentry, aristocracy.

ἀρχοντιά (ἀρχοδιά, § 16, *n.* 3) nobility, the noblemen.

ἀρχοντόσπιτο house of a nobleman.

ἄρχος=ἄρχοντας.

ἀρωτῶ, (ἐ)ρωτῶ ask.

ἄς, (1) *v.* § 194 ; (2) ἄς=ἀπό (*Pontus*, *v.* § 168, 3), ἄς τό after, afterwards.

ἀσβέστης chalk.

ἄσε, *v.* ἀφήνω.

ἀσημένιος of silver.

ἄσημος=ἄσκημος.

ἄσκεπος unprotected, uncovered.

ἀσκέρι army, retinue.

ἄσκημος (ἄσχημος, ἄσημος, § 28 *n.*) ugly.

ἀσκί (*akhó Zac.*, § 35, *n.* 3) bag.

ἀσόν thine, *v.* § 143, *n.* 3.

ἀσπαλίζω=σφαλνῶ.

ἄσπλα(γ)χνος unmerciful.

ἄσπρο small coin.

ἄσπρος white.

ἀσπρούλις (§ 113, *n.* 2) a little white, whitish.

ἀσ'ταίνουμι (*Velv.*)=αἰστάνομαι.

ἀστάχυ=στάχυ.

ἀστεῖος witty.

ἀστενάρ (*Pontus*) sick.

ἀστενικός weakly, feeble.

ἀστέρας, star.

ἀστέρι=*id.*

ἀστήθι breast, *v.* § 100.

ástos (*Bova*)=αὐτός.

ἀστράφτει it lightens.

ἄστρο star ; *pl.* § 100, *n.* 1.

ἀστροπελέκι (flash of) lightning.

ἀσύγκριτος incomparable.

ἀσυλλόγιστος thoughtless.

ἀσύστατος unsubstantial, groundless.

ἀσφάκα oleander.

ἄσχημος, *v.* ἄσκημος.

ἀτέλειωτος endless, unceasing ; unfinished.

ἀτζεῖ (*Cap.*), *adv.* there.

ἄτθησι (§ 35,*n.* 3), *f.* flowering, bloom.

ἄτι, *neut.* stallion, horse.

ἀτίμητος invaluable.

ἄτιμος infamous fellow, scoundrel.

ἀτμόπλοιο steamer.

ἀτομισμός individualism.

ἀτός=αὐτός ; *cf.* § 136, *n.* 3.

ἀτόσον (*Pontus*)=τόσον.

ἀτότε(s) (*Pontus*)=τότες.

ἄτρωπος=ἄνθρωπος.

ἀττικός Attic.

ἀτύπωτος unprinted.

ἀτύχημα misfortune.

αὐγαταίνω, αὐγατῶ, *v.* ἀβγαταίνω.

αὐγερινός morning star.

αὐγή dawn.

αὐγό (αὐκόν, § 26) egg.

αὐγούλα, *dim.* of αὐγή.

αὐθέντης (*lit.*) master, lord.
αὐκό=αὐγό.
αὐλή court.
*αὐξαίνω, ἀξαίνω (ἄξησα, ἀξήθηκα) increase.
αὔριο, *adv.* in the morning.
αὐτί ear.
αὐτός he, this; self; for the different forms, *v.* §§ 136, 144.
αὐτοῦ (αὐτουνοῦ), *adv.* there, in that place; *v.* also § 139, *n.* 1.
αὐτόχθων (*lit.*) autochthon, native.
ἀφ᾿=ἀπό.
ἀφάγανος insatiable.
ἀφανίζω cause to disappear, annihilate.
ἄφαντος invisible; γίνομαι ἄ. disappear.
ἄφεγγος without light, dark.
ἀφέντης (*pl.* § 76) Mr., lord, Monsieur, father; *dim.* ἀφεντάκις.
ἀφεντικός master, lordship.
ἀφέντρα mistress, lady.
ἀφηκροῦμαι hear.
*ἀφήνω (ἀφίνω, ἀφῆκα ἄφηκα [ἐφέκα, Pontus] ἄφησα, *imper.* ἄφ[η]σε ἄσε, ἀφέθηκα ἀφήθηκα, ἀφημένος) let, allow.
ἀφίλητος unkissed.
ἄφοβος fearless.
ἀφορμή occasion, cause.
ἀφοῦ since, then, after, *v.* § 273.
ἀφράτος fresh.
ἀφρίζω to foam, ἀφρισμένος foaming.
ἀφροντισιά carelessness, indifference.
ἀφρός foam.
ἄφσε, *v.* ἀφήνω.
ἀχάμνια weakness.
ἀχαμνοκυνηγάρις effeminate huntsman.
ἀχαμνοπιάνω seize lightly.
ἀχαμνόπιασμα gentle seizure.
ἀχαμνός weak.
ἀχείλι (§ 100) lip.
ἄχιουρα, *pl.* straw.
ἀχιρῶ, *v.* ἀρχίζω.
ἀχνάρι footprint.
ἀχνός pale, wan.
ἀχόρταστος insatiable, greedy.

ἀχρεῖος common, bad; τὰ ἔχω ἀχρεῖα μὲ κανένα I fare ill with one.
ἀχταπόδι polypus.
ἀχτέ (Pontus), *v.* §§ 136, *n.* 3, 142 *n.*
ἀχτῖνα beam, ray.
ἀχύρä, *pl.* (Pontus) *v.* § 6, *n.* 6.
ἀχώριστος inseparable.
ἀψηλός (Ter. d᾿ O.) high, lofty.
ἄψογος blameless.
ἄψυχος lifeless.

Βαγγέλιο gospel.
βαγένι cask.
βάγια wet-nurse.
*βάζω=βάλλω.
βαθειά, *adv.* deeply.
βαθειά, τὰ the depths.
βαθμηδόν, *adv.* (*lit.*) gradually, by steps.
βαθμός degree, step.
βάθος, *neut.* depth.
βαθουλαίνω (ἐβαθούλανα) hollow, scoop out.
βαθύς deep.
βαίνω (Aegina)=βάλλω.
βαλιδέ mother of Sultan.
*βάλλω (βάζω, βάνω, βέλνω, ἔβαλα, ἐβάλθηκα) put, place, lay.
βαραίνω be heavy, weigh.
βάρβαρος barbarian.
βαρειακούω to be hard of hearing.
βαρειόμοιρος ill-fated, unfortunate.
βαρειοῦμαι, βαρειέμαι (ἐβαρέθηκα) to be weary of.
βαρέλα cask.
βαριστίζω grow tired of.
βαρκάρις boatman.
βαρκούλα small bark.
βαρμένος=βαλμένος (from βάλλω).
βαρόνος baron.
βαρναναστενάζω sigh heavily.
βαρύς (varío, varéo, § 110 *n.*) heavy, oppressive; βαρύ, *adv.*
βαρῶ (-έω), βαρίσκω, βαρέσκω, βαρένω (ἐβάρεσα ἐβάρισα, βαρισμένος) strike, hit; β. κανένα σαγίτες to hit one with arrows; *v.* also βαρειοῦμαι.
βάσανο(s) agony, grief (*cf.* § 100, *n.* 1).

βασιέτ(ι), neut. (Pontus) last counsel, deliberation.

βασιλεία kingdom.

βασίλειο,βασιλειόkingdom; palace (?).

βασιλεύω sink (of the sun).

βασιλιάς, βασιλέας (βασιλές) king; cf. § 55 (voc. βασιλεῦ in Rigas is a. Gk.).

βασιλικό basilicum (favourite ornamental plant).

βασιλικός kingly, royal.

βασίλισσα queen.

βασιλόπαιδο king's, royal, child.

βασιλοπούλα king's daughter, princess.

βασιλόπουλο king's son, prince.

βάσκαμα, neut. the evil eye.

βασλές = βασιλέ(α)ς.

βαστάζω, βαστῶ (ἐβάσταξα) endure, bear, wait.

βάτο(s), neut. prickly bush, bramble.

βαφτίζω baptize.

βάφτισμα baptism.

βαφτιστικός baptismal, of baptism ; β. ὄνομα Christian name.

βάφω to dye ; β. μαῦρα wear black.

βγαγγέλιο (§ 23 n.)=βαγγέλιο.

*β γ ά ζ ω=βγάλλω.

*β γ α ί ν ω (aor. ἐβγῆκα [ἐξέβα, § 208], ἔβγα, imper. ἔβγα) go out.

*β γ ά λ λ ω (v. βάλλω) take out, bring out, send forth ; βγ. περίπατο take for a walk ; (of flowers) intr. shoot forth ; βγ. τὸ ψωμί μου to earn my bread ; βγ. τὴν ὕστερη ἀναπνοή draw the last breath.

βγάλσιμο (§ 104) dislocation.

βγάνω=βγάλλω.

βδέλλα—ἀβδέλλα.

βέβαιος sure, certain ; βέβαια, adv. surely.

βεζίρης vizier.

βελάζω bleat, low.

βελανιδιά oak.

βέλνω=βάλλω.

βελόνι needle.

βελονιά stitch.

βελουδένιος of velvet, velvety.

βελοῦδο velvet.

Βενετζάνος Venetian.

βέργα twig, applied also to a slender girl.

βεργί twig, rod ; bird's perch.

βεργολυγερός slender as a twig.

βεργούλα, dim. of βέργα.

βετούλι kid.

βῆμα, neut. step, pace.

βήχ(ν)ω cough.

βί, interj. (Lesbos).

βιά : μετὰ βιᾶς with difficulty ; cf. § 162, 4, n. 2.

βιβλίο book.

βιβλιοθήκη library.

βιγλίζω keep watch, wait for.

βιός (βίος), neut. fortune, property, means.

βλάμης, Vlamis, brother in a feud.

βλασταίνω (ἐβλάστησα) sprout, shoot.

βλαχοπούλα shepherdess.

βλαχόπουλο young shepherd.

βλάχος shepherd.

* βλέπω (εἶδα [ἔδια Syra, ἔδα Ios], θὰ [ἰ]δῶ διῶ, imper. [ἰ]δές δέ[σ]τε, ἰδώθηκα or διώθηκα) see, look.

βλογιά small-pox.

βογγίζω sigh, groan, roar.

βογγῶ=id.

βόδι=βούδι.

βοήθεια help.

βοηθῶ to help.

βόϊδι=βούδι.

βοΐζω howl, growl.

βολά blow, stroke ; time (enumeration, etc., Fr. fois).

βολεῖ (ἐβόλεσε) it is possible.

βολετός possible.

βόλι bullet, a throw, stroke.

βόλιτα, Fr. fois, time.

βοριάς north wind.

βόρτα=βόλιτα, v. § 31.

βοσκοπούλα shepherdess.

* βόσκω, βοσκίζω, βοσκάω (ἐβόσκισα, ἐβοσκήθηκα, βοσκισμένος) feed, graze.

βοτάνι medicinal herb, remedy.

βουβαλίσιος of a buffalo.

βουγγίζω (ἐβούγγιξα)=βογγίζω.

βούδι (βόδι, βόϊδι) ox.

βουκέντρι (φκέντρ, § 37 n.) ox-goad.

βούλα signet-ring, signet.

βουλευτής deputy; pl. § 76.

βουλιάζω (ἐβούλιαξα, βουλιασμένος) dip in, sink, collapse.

βουλώνω to seal; δὲ βουλώνω μάτι I don't close an eye.

βουνί mountain, hill.

βουνίσιος mountainous.

βουνό = βουνί.

βουρκόλακας vampire, werewolf (a ghost).

βουρκώνω to soil, spatter; βουρκωμένος also clouded.

βούτυρο butter.

βουτῶ to dive, dip.

βραδειά evening.

βράδυ, neut. evening; τὸ β. (Thera βραδύ) in the evening.

βραδυάζει, βραδύνει evening is coming on.

βραδύς, adv. in the evening.

βράζω to boil.

βρακί trousers, breeches.

βράχος rock.

βρέ, βρέ = μωρέ.

βρεμένος, v. εὑρίσκω.

βρέσκω = εὑρίσκω.

* βρέχω (ἐβράχηκα ἐβρέχτηκα) wet, dip; (cause to) rain.

βρίζω (ἔβρισα ἔβριξα) scold.

*βρίσκω (βρίστω, βρίχνω) = εὑρίσκω.

βροντῶ to thunder.

βροχερός rainy.

βροχή rain.

βρόχι (usually pl.) snare.

βρύσι, f. fountain.

βρῶμα, neut. rubbish, stench, dirt.

* βυζαίνω, βυζάνω (ἐβύζαξα or -σα, ἐβυζάχτηκα, βυζασμένος and βυζαγμένος) suckle, suck.

βυθός depth, abyss.

βωμός altar.

b, see μπ and also π, when not found under b.

bάρεμ, adv. at least.

bουτέκ(ι) small buffalo.

Γαδουρίσιος belonging to an ass, asinine.

γά(ϊ)δαρος ass.

γαῖμα, neut. = αἷμα.

γαϊτάνι ribbon, tape.

γάλα, neut. (§ 103, n. 2) milk.

γαλανομάτης (f. -α) blue-eyed.

γαλανός blue.

γάμος wedding.

γαμπᾶς kind of cloak.

γαμπρός son-in-law, bridegroom.

γαπῶ = ἀγαπῶ.

γαρουφαλιά carnation stalk.

γαρούφαλο carnation pink.

γάστρα stem of a flower, flower-pot.

γάτα cat.

γαυριασμένος haughty, proud.

γγόνι = ἐγγόνι.

* γδέρνω (γτέρνω, § 26, ἔγδειρα or ἔγδαρα, ἐγδάρθηκα, γδαρμένος) flay.

γδί = γουδί.

γδύνω put off; pillage, denude.

γδύσιμο (§ 104) undressing, putting off (clothes).

γειά health; γειά σου good-day (morning) to you, or good-bye; σ' ἀφήνω γ. I take my leave of you.

γείτονας neighbour.

γειτονιά (γειτονία) neighbourhood.

γειτόνισσα female neighbour.

γέλοια (ἔλοια, § 22), pl. laughter.

* γελῶ (ἐγέλασα, ἐγελάστηκα) to laugh.

γέμα, neut. eating, meal.

γεματίζω, γιοματίζω to dine.

γεμάτος, γιομάτος (w. acc.) filled, full.

γεμίζω, γιομίζω (w. double acc.) to fill; also to be filled, be full.

γεναῖκα = γυναῖκα.

γένεια, pl. beard.

γενιά race, lineage.

γενικός common, general.

γενναῖος noble.

Γεννάρις January.

γεννῶ beget, give birth to; (of birds) lay (eggs).

γένομαι = γίνομαι.

γεράκι(ν) hawk.

γεράματα, pl. old age, age.

γέρημος = ἔρημος.

* γ έ ρ ν ω (ἔγειρα, γε[ι]ρμένος) to bend.

* γ ε ρ ν ῶ (ἐγέρασα) grow old.

γέροντας old man, old age.

γεροντοκόριτσο old maid.

γέρος (cf. § 63) = γέροντας.

γερός sound, strong.

γεύομαι taste, eat.

γεφύρι, γιοφύρι bridge.

γή = ἤ.

γῆ(s), f. earth, v. § 85 n.

γιά (γιατά, γιαό) : (1) w. acc. on account of, for, v. § 163 ; γιὰ νά in order that ; (2) = γιατί ; why ? (3) w. imper. now ! come !

γιαγιά grandmother.

γιαίνω (ἔγιανα, γιαμένος) heal, cure.

γιαλβαρτῶ (Cap.) request.

γιαλός (sea) shore.

γιάντα (γιάδα), v. ἴντα.

γιαούρτι whey-cheese.

γιαρᾶς = wound.

γιατά = γιά.

γιατί (always w. acute) : (1) why ? (2) for, because ; (3) ιάτι (Velv.) on account of.

γιατρεύω to heal.

γιατρικός medical ; neut. medicine.

γιατρός physician.

γίδιος = ἴδιος.

* γ ί ν ο μ α ι, γένομαι (pres. part. γενάμενος, ἔγινα ἔγενα ἐγένηκα ἐγίνηκα, θὰ γένω γίνω γενῶ, γινω-μένος or γεννημένος) become, take place, be ; γίνεται νὰ it is possible that ; τί νὰ γίνῃ ; what can be done ?

γιόμα (γέμα), neut. meal, dinner ; dinner-time, afternoon.

γιοματίζω = γεματίζω.

γιομάτος = γεμάτος.

γιομίζω = γεμίζω.

γιομώνω be full.

γιορτή feast.

γιός (υίός, lit.) son.

γιούδι little son.

γιοφύρι = γεφύρι.

γιωργός peasant.

γιώς (Sar. K.) when (temporal conj.).

γκαλερία gallery.

γκαρδιακός cordial, hearty.

γκιαούρις unbeliever, giaour.

γκρεμειέμαι collapse.

γκρεμίζω cast down, destroy ; mid. to sink (intr.), collapse.

γλεδίζω to have a drinking-bout, celebrate, amuse oneself.

γλεντοκόπημα, neut. gluttony, debauch.

γλέπω = βλέπω.

γλήγορα (γρήγορα), adv. quickly.

γληγοροσύνη speed, swiftness.

γλιστρῶ slide.

γλύκα sweetness.

γλυκοκελαϊδῶ warble sweetly.

γλυκολαλῶ speak sweetly.

γλυκομουρμουρίζω murmur lovingly, sweetly.

γλυκοπαιγνιδάκι sweet sport, caressing.

γλυκόπνοος sweetly blowing.

γλυκός (γλυκύς) sweet, v. § 110 n. ; τὰ γλυκά sweets.

γλυκοφιλῶ kiss sweetly, lovingly.

γλυκύς = γλυκός.

γλυτώνω rescue, release ; escape, become free.

γλῶσσα tongue, language.

γλωσσικός relating to the tongue, linguistic.

γλωσσοῦ gossip (f.).

γνέθω spin.

γνέντα (Cap.), prep. against, opposite.

γνώμη meaning, opinion.

γνωρίζω recognise, know ; mid. be acquainted, know each other.

γνῶσι, f. understanding.

γνωστικός clever, sly.

γνωστός known.

γομάρι ass.

γόνα (γόνατο, v. § 103, n. 2), neut. knee.

γονατίζω kneel down, fall at one's feet.

γονιοί, pl. parents, v. § 72 (γονεῖς lit.).

γοργά, adv. quickly.

γοτ̇σαμάνος (*Pontus*) old.
γουδί (γδί) a mortar.
γουλεύω set (a trap).
γούμενος (ἡγούμενος) abbot.
γουρούνι pig.
γράμμα, *neut.* letter.
γραμματική grammar.
γραμματισμένος learned.
γραμμή line, row.
γραφή writing, a letter.
γραφόμενο written work.
γράφω (γράφτω, ἐγράφτηκα ἐγράφηκα) write.
γράψιμο (*verbal noun*) (hand)writing.
γρήγορα=γλήγορα.
γριά old woman.
γροικῶ=ἀγροικῶ.
γρόσι piastre.
γρουσάρος corsair, pirate.
γυαλί glass, mirror.
γυαλίζω to shine ; *mid.* be reflected.
γυαλιστερός shining, fresh.
γυμνάζω to practise.
γυμνός naked.
γυμνώνω strip, uncover.
γυναῖκα (γεναῖκα *Cyp.*) wife, woman.
γυναικολάτρης honouring women, gallant.
γυρέματα, *pl.* searching (verbal noun).
γυρεύω search ; seek ; request, demand.
γυρίζω turn about, turn round ; *tr.* and *intr.* twist, turn.
γυρνῶ (ἐγύρισα) turn round ; γ. πίσω turn back.
γῦρος circuit, a walk round.
γύρω, *adv.* round about ; γ. 's, *prep.* around (§ 171).
'γώ=ἐγώ.
γωνιά corner, angle.

g, see γκ or κ.
ᴊιόλα pond, lake.

Δά (strengthening particle with demonstrative pronouns and verbs, *cf.* § 147 *n.*) exactly, forsooth.
δᾶβαίνω (*Pontus*)=διαβαίνω.

δάγκαμα, *neut.* a bite.
*δαγκάνω (ἐδάγκασα, δαγκάστηκα, δαγκασμένος, also δαγκαμένος) to bite.
δάκνω=*id.*
δάκρυ(ον) tear
δακρύζω weep.
δακρυσμένος red with weeping.
δαμαστής tamer, subduer.
δανείζω lend.
δασκαλεύω censure, teach one his lesson.
δασκαλικός of a schoolmaster.
δάσκαλος teacher, schoolmaster.
δάσος (δάσο), *neut.* forest.
δαυλί torch.
δαῦτος=αὐτός.
δαχτυλίδι finger-ring.
δαχτυλιδόμεσος of a slender figure.
δάχτυλο finger.
δαχτυλόπουλο small finger.
δέ=δέν.
δεβαίνω, *v.* διαβαίνω.
δεῖγμα proof.
δειλινό afternoon, evening.
δειλός timid, shy.
δεῖνας, ὁ such and such a one, Mr. So-and-so, *v.* § 157 ; ὁ δ. καὶ ὁ τάδες this one and that one.
δεῖπνο repast, dinner.
δειπνῶ to lunch, dine.
δείχνω, δείχτω show.
δεκάξι sixteen.
δεκαπέντε fifteen.
δεκάρα, δεκάρι a 10 lepta piece.
δεκαριά ten in number, half a score.
δεκάρικο containing ten (*e.g.* lepta), *v.* § 133.
δεκοχτώ eighteen.
δελτάριο(ν) postcard.
δεμάτι bundle.
δέν (δέ) not.
δεντρί tree, *dim.* δεντράκι.
δέντρο=*id.*
δένω bind.
δεξίς (*cf.* § 110 *n.*) on the right (hand) ; δεξί right hand.
δερνοχτυπῶ to whip.

*δέρνω (ἔδειρα ἔδαρα, ἐδάρθηκα) to whip, beat.

δές, v. βλέπω.

δέσποινα blessed Virgin (eccl.).

δεσπότης bishop, pl. § 76 ; δέσποτα, voc. in addressing a priest (eccl.) Reverend.

δευτέρα Monday.

δεύτερος the second.

δεφτέρι account-book.

δέχομαι receive, accept.

δηλονότι, adv. that is to say, viz.

δημιουργῶ create.

δημοκράτης democrat.

δημοκράτικος democratic.

δημοσιογραφικός journalistic.

δημοτικός relating to the populace, popular ; δ. δάσκαλος national school-teacher ; ἡ δημοτική the vernacular.

διά = γιά.

διαβάζω read.

*διαβαίνω (δἄβαίνω, § 6, n. 6 ; διάβ[η]κα, ἐδέβεν ἐδιάη[κ]α, etc., § 208) pass through, traverse, cf. ἀναβαίνω.

διαβάτης traveller.

διάβολος (διάολος, § 22) devil.

διαθήκη testament, will.

διάκος deacon.

διακοσαριά a company of two hundred.

διακόσιοι two hundred.

διαλαλῶ announce.

διαλέγω select, choose ; pluck (flowers).

διαλεχτός selected, distinguished.

διάολος = διάβολος.

διαοντρεύ(γ)ω (Syra) tease, poke fun at.

διασκεδάζω entertain, converse.

διατριβή dissertation.

διάφανος transparent.

διάφορο(ς), neut. (v. § 100, n. 1) interest, gain.

δίγνωμος fickle.

*δίδω, δίνω, δώνω (ἔδωκα ἔδωσα, θὰ δώσω or δώκω, imper. δό[ς] δῶσε δώστε, ἐδόθηκα, δο[σ]μένος) give.

διήγημα, neut. narrative ; dim. διηγηματάκι.

διηγηματογραφία story-writing.

δι(η)γοῦμαι relate, narrate.

δικαίωμα, neut. justice.

δικαστής judge ; pl. § 76.

δίκιος (δίκηος) right, just ; ἔχω δίκιο I am right.

δίκοπος double-edged.

δικός (ἐδικός) : (1) own, one's own, v. § 143 ; (2) a relative, friend.

δίνω = δίδω.

διορθώνω (διορδώνω, Maina) correct, improve.

διορία boundary.

διότι because, v. § 276, n. 1.

δίπλα (ἀπὸ δίπλα), adv. close by, next ; δ. 's, prep. beside (§ 171).

διπλός double.

δισεκατομμύριον billion.

δίσεφτος unsanitary.

δίτσεμα (Ios), neut. right, justice.

δίψα thirst.

διψῶ, διψάζω (ἐδίψασα, διψασμένος) to thirst.

δίχτυ, neut. net.

δίχως (μὲ δίχως), w. acc. without (§ 167); δίχως νά without (with verbs).

δἰῶ, δἰῆς (= ἴδω), v. βλέπω.

διώχνω, διώχτω hunt.

δοκιμάζω put to the test, try.

δόλιος unfortunate, perfidious.

δόλος guile, craft.

δομέστικος courtier, servant at court.

δόντι tooth.

δόξα glory.

δοξάζω make celebrated, praise.

δοξασμένος celebrated, praised.

δόσιμο giving (verbal noun).

δούλα maid, servant-girl.

δουλειά work, task.

δουλευτής workman, day-labourer ; pl. § 76.

δουλεύω to work, serve.

δοῦλος servant, slave.

δραγο(υ)μάνος dragoman, interpreter.

δράκος a figure very common in fable; a violent, powerful monster.

δρᾶμα, neut. drama.

δραματικός dramatic.

δράμι a unit of weight, v. p. 84
  footnote.

δραχμή drachme (coin=cir. 1 franc).

δρεπάνι sickle.

δρόμος way, street ; παίρνω δρόμο
  to take a road.

δροσάτος fresh.

δροσερός fresh.

δροσ(ι)ά (δρόσος, neut.) dew.

δροσίζω refresh.

δροσόπνοος fresh smelling.

δρόσος, neut.=δροσιά.

δροσούλα, dim. of δρόσος.

δρῦς, m. (§ 86, n. 2) oak.

ὐνάρα, δυάρι a 2 lepta piece.

δύναμαι (lit.)=δύνομαι.

δύναμι, f. might, strength.

δυναμώνω to strengthen.

δυνατός able, possible, strong, loud.

δύνομαι can, am able.

δυό two ; κ' οἱ ꝺυό both ; οἱ δυό μας
  both of us.

δυόσμος jasmine.

δύσι, f. sunset, west.

δυσκολεύω render difficult.

δυσκολία difficulty.

δυστυχία misfortune.

δυστυχισμένος unfortunate.

δύστυχος=id.

δώ=ἐδώ.

δώδεκα twelve.

δωδεκάδα a company of twelve,
  retinue.

δωδεκαριά dozen.

δώθε (Velv. δώθι) hence, from there ;
  ἀπὸ τότις κὶ δ. (Velv.), since then,
  from then.

δῶμα, neut. room.

δώνω=δίδω.

d, see also ντ or τ.

dαβατζής friend.

ῬΕ (αἰ) interj. good ! well !

ἑαυτό(ν) sign of reflexive, v. § 140.

ἔβγα, v. βγαίνω.

ἑβδομάδα (ἐβτομάδα, § 26) week.

ἐβίτζα (Cap.) morning.

ἐβλέπω=βλέπω.

ἔβρα, v. εὑρίσκω.

ἐγγίζω (ἀγγίζω) touch.

ἔγγονος (ἔγγονας, § 66 n.) ἐγγόνι
  (γγόνι) grandchild.

ἐγγυτής surety, bail.

ἐγιώ(νη)=ἐγώ.

ἐγκάρδιος hearty.

ἔγνοια=ἔννοια.

ἐγώ (ὀγώ) I, v. § 134.

ἔδια (Syra), v. βλέπω.

ἐδικός=δικός.

ἐδώ, δώ (ἀδά, Pontus) here, ἐδὼ πέρα
  here ; ἀπ' ἐδὼ ἀπό on this side
  (§ 172) ; ἐδὼ καὶ δέκα χρόνια ten
  years ago.

ἐεῖνος (Pontus)=ἐκεῖνος.

ἐθνικός national.

ἔθνος nation, people.

εἶδα, v. βλέπω.

εἰδεμή(ς) else, otherwise.

εἶδος, neut. species, sort.

εἰδωλολάτρης idolater.

εἰκόνα image.

εἰκονοστάσιο(ν) place where the
  saints' images stand in a church
  or house, sanctuary.

εἰκοσάρα, εἰκοσάρι a 20 lepta piece.

εἰκοσαριά a number of twenty, score.

εἴκοσι twenty.

εἰκοσιπενταριά a company of twenty-
  five.

εἰκοσιπεντάρικο consisting of twenty-
  five pieces.

εἶμαι I am, v. § 224, 2.

εἱμαρμένη (lit.) fate, destiny, fatum.

εἰμή unless, except.

εἶπα, v. λέγω.

εἷς (Pontus)=ἕνας.

εἰς, 's, εἰσέ, σέ, prep. in, into, to ; v.
  § 160.

εἰσέβηκεν, v. σεβαίνω.

εἴστια (Pontus), adv. hereupon, then,
  next.

εἶχα, v. ἔχω.

ἐκάνω (§ 182, n. 2)=κάνω.

ἑκατό(ν) hundred.

ἑκατοστάρι that which consists of a
  hundred.

ἑκατοστύ, f. (about) a hundred.

ἐκδότης editor, publisher.

ἐκεάν (*Pontus*) above there.

ἐκεῖ (ἐτσεῖ, § 17), *adv.* there ; ἐκεῖ κάτ (*Pontus*), *id.* ; ἐκεῖ πέρα beyond, on that side.

ἐκεῖθε(ν), *adv.* whence, yonder, beyond.

ἐκεῖνος (ἐκειός) that, *v.* § 146.

ἐκεκά (*Pontus*), *adv.* there.

ἐκκλησ(ι)ά church.

ἐκλαμπρότης, *pl.* -τητες (*lit.*) Excellence (*title*).

ἔλα (ἐλâ[σ]τε) come (*sing.* and *pl. imper.*)

ἐλαία=ἐλιά.

ἐλαφρός (ἐλαφρύς) light.

ἐλεημοσύνη alms.

ἐλεοῦσα, *v.* § 234, *n.* 2.

ἐλέπω=βλέπω.

ἐλευθερία liberty.

ἐλεύτερος (ἐλεύθερος) free.

ἐλευτερώνω liberate.

ἐλεῶ (*w. acc.*) give alms to.

ἐλιά (ἐλαία, § 10, *n.* 1) olive-tree.

Ἕλληνας a Greek ; *also* a giant of former days.

ἑλληνίδα Greek woman.

ἑλληνικός Greek (*adj.*).

ἐλπίδα (ἐρπίδα) hope.

ἐλπίζω (ἐρπίζω) to hope.

ἐμᾶς, *v.* ἐγώ.

ἔμασα, *aor.* of μαζώνω.

ἐμαυτό used to form reflexive pron., § 140.

ἐμεῖς, ἐμέ(να), *v.* ἐγώ.

ἐμέτερος (*Pontus*), *v.* § 143, *n.* 3.

ἐμετικός emetic (*adj.*).

ἔμμετρος metrical.

ἐμορφιά beauty.

ἔμορφος beautiful.

ἐμός (τ᾽ ἐμόν) my, mine, *v.* § 143, *n.* 3.

ἔμπα(s), *v.* μπαίνω.

ἐμπάζω (μπάζω) put, place, bring in.

ἐμπῆκα, *v.* μπαίνω.

ἐμπιστεμένος entrusted, trusted.

ἐμποδίζω hinder.

ἔμπορος (ἔμπορας, § 66 *n.*) merchant.

ἐμπορῶ, *v.* μπορῶ.

ἐμπρός forward ; ἐμπρὸς ᾽s, *prep.* (§ 171) before, against ; ἐμπρὸς ᾽s quite forward, in front; *Pontus* ἔμπρ᾽.

ἔν=(1) εἶναι, *v.* § 224, *n.* 2 ; (2) δέν (*Cyp.*).

ἔναι=εἶναι.

ἔνας, μιά, ἔνα a, one (*numeral and indef. art. v.* § 128); ὁ ἔνας τὸν ἄλλο one another, each other, *v.* § 141.

ἔνδυμα (*lit.*) garment.

ἐνενηντἀεννέα ninety-nine.

ἐνέργεια energy, activity.

ἐνθουσιάζομαι (*lit.*) to be enthusiastic.

ἔνι=εἶναι.

ἐννά (*Cyp.*)=θενά, θά.

ἐννιά nine.

ἔννοια (ἔγνοια) care, worry.

ἐνόσῳ in so far as, so long as.

ἐνταυτῷ at the same time, likewise.

ἔντεκα eleven.

ἐντρανῶ (*Pontus*) regard, see.

ἐντρέπομαι (ἐντράπηκα) be ashamed of.

ἐντροπή shame.

ἐντύπωσι, *f.* impression.

ἐντώκα, *v.* ντούννω.

ἐνῷ during, while.

ἐξαίσιος distinguished.

ἔξαφνα=ἄξαφνα.

ἔξε (ἔξι) six.

ἐξέβα, *v.* βγαίνω.

ἐξέγκα (*Pontus*), *v.* φέρνω.

ἐξελληνίζω Hellenise ; render into ancient Greek style.

ἐξετάζω (ξετάζω, ξητῶ) prove, try.

ἐξηγῶ explain.

ἐξήντα sixty ; ἐξήντα δυό to denote an indefinitely larger number.

ἐξηντάρις man sixty years of age.

ἐξῆς : στὸ ἐξῆς for the future (*Aegina*).

ἔξοδα, *pl.* expenses, cost.

ἐξοδεύω spend (money).

ἐξομολόγησι, *f.* confession.

ἐξόριστος exiled.

ἔξω, adv. out, outside ; also except, with exception of.

ἐξωτερικός externally.

ἐξωτικός exotic.

ἔπαινος praise.

ἐπανάστασι insurrection, revolution.

ἐπάνω, adv. above ; ἐπάνω 's upon.

ἐπειδή(ς) because, since.

ἔπειτα, adv. then, afterwards.

ἐπικρίνω judge, criticise.

ἐπιπόνου in the phrase παίρνω ἐπιπόνου to take (lay) to heart (Aegina).

ἐπίσημος official.

ἐπιστήμη knowledge, science.

ἐπίσω = ὀπίσω.

ἐπιτροπή committee.

ἐπιτυχαίνω (v. τυχαίνω) succeed, attain.

ἐποχή epoch, age.

ἐπροχτές, adv. day before yesterday.

ἐρασιτέχνης dilettante, amateur.

ἐργασία activity.

ἐργάτης workman.

ἔργο work.

ἐργωνίζω (Pontus) = γνωρίζω.

ἐρημιά loneliness, solitude.

ἐρημικός lonely.

ἔρημος lonely, forsaken.

ἐρήμωσι, f. isolation.

ἑρμηνεύω explain, comment upon.

ἔρμος = ἔρημος.

ἐρπίδα = ἐλπίδα.

ἐρπίζω = ἐλπίζω.

*ἔρχομαι (Pontus ἔρται = ἔρχεται, ἔρκουμαι, § 18, n. 3 ; ἦλθα ἦρθα ἦρτα ἦρχα, Pontus ἔρθα ἦλτα, θὰ ἔρθω, θὰ 'ρθῶ, θά 'ρχω, imper. ἔλα ἐλᾶ- [σ]τε, ἐρχωμένος, pres. part. ἐρχάμενος) come ; μ' ἔρχεται νά it occurs to me (to do something).

ἔρωτας (ἔρως, lit.) love ; god of love, Amor.

ἐρωτεμένος in love.

ἐρωτεύομαι fall in love with.

ἐρώτησι, f. question.

ἐρωτικός pertaining to love.

ἐρωτῶ (-άω, -άγω) ask, question.

ἐσέγκα, v. φέρνω.

ἐσεῖς, ἐσένα, v. ἐσύ.

ἔσεται (Pontus) = ἔρχεται.

ἐσήμερα = σήμερα.

ἐσούν (Pontus), v. ἐσύ.

ἐσούνη = ἐσύ.

ἐσταυρωμένος (lit.) crucified.

ἔστωσαν, v. § 224, 2, n. 4.

ἐσύ thou, v. § 135.

ἐσωτερικός esoteric.

ἑτοιμάζω prepare.

ἑτοιμασία preparation, equipment.

ἕτοιμος ready.

ἔτος, neut. year.

ἐτότες = τότες.

ἐτοῦτος = τοῦτος.

ἐτσεῖνος = ἐκεῖνος.

ἔτσι, adv. thus, so.

ettáno, v. αὐτός.

εὐγένεια nobility ; ἡ εὐγενεία σου, v. § 139.

εὐγενής (lit., cf. § 115) noble, nobleman.

εὐγενικός noble, gallant.

εὐεργετικός benevolent.

εὐθύς = εὐτύς.

εὐκαιρέζω to have time, leisure.

εὐκαιρία opportunity.

εὐκαρίστησι, f. contentment, pleasure ; ἔχω εὐκ, I am pleased to, like to.

εὐκαριστῶ thank, satisfy.

εὔκολος easy.

εὐκοῦμαι (εὐχοῦμαι) bless, wish well.

εὐλάβεια piety.

εὐλαβής pious.

εὐλογῶ praise, bless.

εὐνοῦχος eunuch.

*εὑρίσκω (βρίσκω, βρίστω, εὑρήκω, ηὗρα, Pontus εὗρα, εὕρηκα [ἐ]βρῆκα, θὰ εὕρω θὰ βρῶ, imper. [ἐ]βρέ[s], εὑρέθηκα) find.

εὐσπλαχνικός merciful.

εὐτός = αὐτός.

εὐτοῦ, cf. § 139, n. 1.

εὐτύς, adv. immediately.

εὐτυχισμένος happy, fortunate.

εὐχαριστημένος satisfied, contented.

εὐχαριστῶ, v. εὐκαριστῶ.

εὐχή blessing, prayer.

εὔχομαι = εὐκοῦμαι.

ἐφέτο(ς), *adv.* of this year.
ἐφημερίδα newspaper.
ἐφτά seven.
ἐχτές, *adv.* yesterday.
ἐχτρός enemy.
ἔχω (§ 224,1) have; τρεῖς χρόνους εἴχαμε νὰ γελάσωμε we have not laughed for three years, *v.* p. 101 *footnote*; ἔχει, *w. acc.* there is (are), *il y a*; εἶχε δὲν εἶχε whether or not, at any rate.
ἐψές (ψές) yesterday (evening).
ἐώ = ἐγώ.

Ζαλίζω perplex, confuse; ζ. τὴν στράτα miss the way.
ζαλίκι burden (especially of wood).
ζαλισμένος gone astray, perplexed.
ζάτǝ, *adv.* of course, really.
ζάχαρι, *f.* sugar.
ζέσι, *f.* heat.
ζεσταίνω (ἐζέστανα, ἐζεστάθηκα) to make warm, heat.
ζέστη heat, warmth; εἶναι ζ. it is warm.
ζεστός warm, hot.
ζευγάρι pair, couple.
ζεῦ(γ)λα yoke.
ζεύ(γ)ω (ἔζεψα) to yoke.
ζεύκι, *neut.* (Naxǝs) pleasure banquet.
ζηλευτός enviable.
ζηλεύω (ζουλεύω) to envy, be jealous of.
ζηλιάρης (ζουλιάρις) envious, jealous.
ζῆλος, *neut.* envy, jealousy.
ζηλότυπος jealous.
ζήτημα controversy.
ζήτησις, *f.* (*lit.*) search, seeking.
ζητιανεύω to beg.
ζητιάνος beggar; begging (*f.* § 111).
ζητῶ (-έω, -άω) request, ask.
ζιαφέτι feast, banquet.
ζίφω press, squeeze.
ζουλεύω = ζηλεύω.
ζούλια jealousy.
ζουλιάρις = ζηλιάρις.
ζουμί broth, sauce, soup.
ζουναριά girdle.
ζόφος (*lit.*) darkness.

ζυγός yoke.
ζῶ (ζιῶ) live, *v.* § 250; (ἔτσι) νὰ ζήσῃς have the goodness to, I beg of you.
ζωγραφιά image, painting.
ζωγραφίζω paint, draw.
ζωγρίν (Pontus), *neut.* stick, cudgel.
ζωή life.
ζωηρός living, alive.
ζωντανεύω become alive.
ζωντανός living, alive.
ζώνω (ἐζώστηκα) gird.
ζῶο animal, beast.

ʒ, see ζ (*cf.* § 28) or γ (§ 27).

Ἤ (γή) or; ἤ—ἤ either—or.
ἡγεμονικός princely.
ἡγούμενος abbot.
ἡδονή pleasure.
ἠθογραφία history of morals.
ἥλιος (νήλιος, § 34, *n.* 3) sun.
ἥμαρτο excuse! pardon! *v.* § 204.
ἡμέρα day.
ἥμισυ (§ 131) half.
ἤμουν(α), etc. *v.* εἶμαι.
ἤμπα, *v.* § 161.
ἠμπορῶ, *v.* μπορῶ.
ἦρες, *pl.* weeds.
ἦρθα (ἦρτα), *v.* ἔρχομαι.
ἥρωας hero.
ἥσυχος calm.
ηὗρα, *v.* εὑρίσκω.
ἠχολογῶ (-άω) echo, resound.
ἦχος sound, echo.

Θά, *v.* § 224, 3, *n.* 2.
θάβω, θάφτω (aor. pass. ἐθάφτηκα ἐτάφηκα) bury.
θάλασσα sea.
θᾶμα, *neut.* wonder, miracle.
θαμάζω (θαυμάζω), θαμάζομαι wonder, admire.
θαματουργῶ (-έω) to perform wonders.
θαμπώνω to blind, dazzle.
θάν, θανά = θά.
θανατικό disease, plague.
θάνατος death.
θανή death; burial.

θαρρετά, adv. courageously, boldly.
θαρρεύω to be courageous, confident.
θάρρος, neut. courage ; pl. § 85.
θαρρῶ (-έω) believe, think.
θαφτό grave.
θάφτω, v. θάβω.
θάψιμο, neut. (§ 104) burying, burial.
θέατρο(ν) theatre ; ἀνεβάζω στὸ θ. put upon the stage, give a performance of.
θεγατέρα, v. θυγατέρα.
θεγός, v. θεός.
θεϊκός godly.
θεῖος godly, divine (χάριτι θείᾳ, a. Gk. by the grace of God).
θειός (Thera) uncle.
θέλησι, f. the will.
θέλω (telό, § 20, n. 1) to will, wish, v. § 224, 3 ; θέλτς—θέλτς (Velv.) whether—or ; for its use in forming the future, v. § 226.
θέμα, neut. task.
θεμελιώνω lay foundation, found, build ; to have a firm foundation.
θεν(ν)ά=θανά, θά.
θεός, θιός (θεγός, τεό, § 29 n.) God ; θεῷ δόξα God be praised, thank God (eccl.).
θεριστής reaper.
θερμός warm (metaph.).
θέρος, neut. summer.
θερί (θεριό) animal.
θεσσαλικός Thessalian.
θέτω (θέχτω, θήκω, τέκνω ; ἔθεσα ἔθηκα, Pontus ἔθεκα, imper. θές θέστε, ἐτέθηκα, θεσμένος) to place, put.
θεώρατος gigantic.
θεωρία theory.
θήκω=θέτω.
θηλυκός (silikό, § 20, n. 1) female, feminine.
θηρίο(ν)=θερί.
θησαυρός treasure.
θιαμάζω=θαμάζω.
θιός=θεός.
θκός=δικός.
θλιβερός (χλιβερός, § 20) sad, perplexed.

θλιμμένος (χλιμμένος), afflicted.
θλῖψι (χλῖψι), f. affliction.
θολώνω afflict, torment.
θρέφω (ἐθράφηκα ἐτράφηκα) nourish.
θρῆνος, neut. (§ 99, n. 1) dirge.
θυγατέρα, θεγατέρα (Ios τυατέρα) daughter.
θυμάρι thyme.
θύμησι, f. remembrance.
θυμιάζω perfume with incense.
θυμιατό incense.
θυμίζω remember.
θυμός wrath ; μὲ θυμό wrathfully.
θυμοῦμαι remember (w. acc.).
θυμώνω enrage ; to be enraged (μέ with a person).
θύρα door.
θωριά look, glance.
θωρῶ (-έω) see, look.

Ἰγώ, Velv.=ἐγώ.
ἰδανικό ideal.
ἰδέα thought, idea.
ἰδικός, v. δικός.
ἴδιος, ὁ same, self, cf. § 157 ; ἴδιος ὁ exactly like.
ἰδιότητα identity.
ἴδρος perspiration.
ἱδρώνω to sweat.
ἱδρῶτας (ἱδρώς, lit.) sweat.
ἴδω, ἰδῶ, v. βλέπω.
ἱερός holy.
ἱκανός ready, able.
ἱλαροτραγικός tragi-comic.
ἴντα (ἰντά) what ? v. § 152, n. 2.
ἴνω, v. γίνομαι.
ἴσια (ἴσια ἴσια, ἴσα ἴσα), adv. just, precisely ; immediately, at the same moment ; ἴσ(ι)α μέ, prep. to, as far as (§ 173).
ἴσιος equal, live, straight.
ἴσκιος shade, shadow.
ἰσόβαρος of equal weight.
ἱστορία history, narrative.
ἱστορικός historical.
ἴσως, adv. perhaps.
ἰφτειάγνω (Pontus)=φκειάνω.
ἰψές (Velv.)=ἐψές.

Κ'=καί, *Pontus* and *Cap.* also='κί.

κά (*Velv.*)=*v.* κατά.

καβαλλάρις (καβελλάρις) rider, horseman ; *pl.* § 75, *n.* 2.

καβαλλικεύω ride (upon : *w. acc.*).

καβαλλίνα horse-dung.

καβάνα=καμπάνα.

κάβουρας (κάουρας, § 22 *n.*) crab, crayfish ; *pl.* § 66 *n.*

κάβω=καίω.

καγκανένας=κανένας.

κάδι, *neut.* tub, cask.

καένας=κανένας.

καζαντίζω gain, earn money.

καημένος, *v.* καίω.

καημός longing, desire, pain.

κάθα είς (*Pontus*)=καθείς.

καθαρεύουσα literary (pure) language.

καθαρίζω purify ; become pure.

καθάριος, καθαρός pure.

καθαυτό, *adv.* properly, in particular.

κάθε (κάθα) each (*adj.*) ; καθείς, καθένας, κάθετις (κάθα είς) every one (*subst.*), *v.* § 155.

καθημερνός daily.

καθίζω (έκατσα εκάτσα beside εκάθισα) sit, sit down ; καθίζω πίσω remain behind.

καθόλου, *adv.* generally, by all means (*w. neg.* by no means, not at all).

κάθομαι (*pres. partc.* καθούμενος) sit, dwell.

καθρέφτης (καθρέπτης) looking-glass.

καθρεφτίζω to reflect, mirror.

καθώς (also ώς καθώς) like, just as, as ; as soon as, when, *v.* § 273.

καί (κ', κι, τσαί, τσί) and, *v.* § 261.

καινός (*lit.*) new.

καινούργιος new, newly made.

καιρός (τσαιρός, § 17) time, weather ; από κ. σέ κ. from time to time ; μέ καιρούς with time, in course of time.

* κ α ί ω (καίγω, § 23, έκαψα, εκάηκα εκαύτηκα, καμένος, καημένος poor, unfortunate, *v.* § 210, I. 1) burn, burn down (καίομαι, *intr.*).

κάκιωμα, *neut.* sickness, pain, suffering.

κακογραμμένος ill-fated, destined to disaster.

κακομοίρης unfortunate.

κακομοιριά misfortune.

κακόμοιρος unfortunate.

κακός bad, ill, *compar.* § 117 f. ; τό κακό (τό) μάτι the evil eye ; τοῦ κάκου in vain ; τό κακό evil, harm.

κακοσήμαδος foreboding evil.

κακούδης ugly, *f.* § 114 *n.*

κακουσά scald-head, scurf.

κακοφαίνεται (κακοφάνηκε) to be sorry, vexed.

κακόφωνος discordant, out of tune.

καλάθι basket.

καλαμιά (καλαμν'ά) reed.

καλησπέρα good evening.

καλιακούδα petrel (water-bird).

κάλλια, καλλιάς, κάλλιο better, *v.* § 118, *n.* 2.

καλλιτέχνημα, *neut.* work of art.

καλλιτεχνικός artistic, of art.

καλλονή beauty.

κάλλος, *neut.* (or τά κάλλη, *pl.*) beauty.

* κ α λ ν ῶ (εκάλεσα, εκαλέστηκα) call.

καλόγερος monk ; καλογεράκι (καλοεράτσι) *dim.*

καλογνωρίζω to be well acquainted with, know well.

καλόγρια nun.

καλοκαίρι summer.

καλοκαιρινός of summer.

καλόκαρδος happy, fortunate.

καλοπερνῶ live well, lead a comfortable life.

καλοπροαίρετος favourably disposed.

καλορίζικος fortunate.

καλός good, *comp. v.* § 117 f. ; καλέ μ' my dear ; πηγαίνω στό καλό I am going to peace, depart this life ; πάαινε στό καλό or simply στό κ. farewell ; καλώς τον he is welcome, καλώς ωρίσατε you are welcome.

καλοστρατῶ have a good voyage.

καλοσύνη goodness, kindness.

καλοτυχίζω congratulate.

καλότυχος happy, fortunate.

καλύβα, καλύβι cottage ; καλυβάκι, καλυβούλα, dim.

καλτερεύω become better.

καλῶ = καλνῶ.

καλῶς, v. καλός ; καλώτατος, v. § 116, n. 3.

κᾶμα, neut. heat, glow.

καμάρα arch, arcade.

κάμαρα (κάμαρη) room, chamber, dwelling.

καμάρι joy, pride ; darling.

καμαριέρα stewardess (on ship).

καμαροφρύδι eyebrow.

καμαρώνω take pride in, praise ; mid. put on airs, be haughty.

κα(μ)μένος, v. καίω.

* κάμνω, κάμω, κάνω (ἔκαμα [subj. κάω, Chios], ἐφτειάστηκα, καμωμένος) do, make ; κάμ(ν)ω καλά I am (doing) well.

καμπάνα bell.

κάμπος field.

κάμποσος (καμπόσος) a good many, pl. several, some, v. § 156.

καμπτσικιά stroke with a whip.

κάμω = κάμνω.

καμώνομαι pretend as if (πῶς).

κάν (κἄν) even, at least ; οὔτε κάν not even.

κανακάρις darling.

κάνας = κανένας.

κανείς, κανένας any body ; nobody ; v. § 153.

κανίστρι basket.

κανονιά shot of a cannon.

καντήλα, καντήλι candlestick.

καντίζω (Cap.) put to rest.

κάνω = κάμνω.

κάουρας = κάβουρας.

κάπα cloak.

καπέλλο hat.

καπετάν(ι)ος captain, chief, leader of Klefts ; indecl. § 63.

καπηλειό retail shop.

καπνός smoke ; φεύγω σὰν καπνός disappear like the wind.

κάποιος any one, pl. some ; v. § 154.

καπότα cloak, overcoat.

κάποτε(s), adv. sometimes, occasionally.

κάπου, adv. anywhere, somewhere.

κάππαρι, f. (§ 86) caper-bush.

κάπως, adv. somehow.

καράβι ship, boat.

καραβοκύρις owner of a ship, captain.

καρδιά heart, ἀπὸ καρδιᾶς from the heart ; καρδούλα, dim.

καρότσα equipage, carriage.

καρπός fruit.

καρποφορῶ (-άω) bear fruit.

καρτερῶ, ἀκαρτερῶ expect, wait for.

κάρτο a quarter, v. § 131.

καρύδι nut, walnut.

καρυοφύλλι clove.

καρφώνω to nail.

κάστανο chestnut.

καστανομάτης chestnut-eyed, brown-eyed.

καστελάνος court officer, attendant.

κάστρο fortress ; pl. § 100, n. 1.

καϑəλδǿκ (Cap.) answer.

κάτ = κάτου, κάτω.

κάτα, f. cat.

κατά (κά, Velv.), prep. w. acc. (§ 164) to, toward (of direction) ; about, at (of time) ; κατὰ πῶς according as ; κατὰ ἐνενηνταεννέα τοῖς ἑκατό = 99 per cent. (lit.).

καταβαίνω = κατεβαίνω.

καταβάνω throw down, subdue.

καταγάλανος deep blue.

καταγῆς (καταῆς), adv. on the ground.

καταγίνομαι to be busy, occupied (with something σέ).

καταδέχομαι receive, deign, condescend.

καταδεχτικός condescending.

καταδικάζω condemn.

καταδρομή persecution, pursuit.

καταζαλίζομαι to be agitated.

καταῆς = καταγῆς.

κατακαίω burn down.

κατακλυσμός inundation, flood.

καταλαβαίνω (v. λαβαίνω, καταλαμβάνω, lit.) comprehend, understand.

κατάμαυρος deep black.

22

καταμόναχος all alone.

καταντῶ become, reduce to a state, be reduced to.

κατανύσσομαι (κατανύχτηκα) to be seized with compunction, become contrite.

καταπατῶ tread down.

καταπιάνομαι begin afresh, undertake.

κατάρα curse, imprecation.

καταρειοῦμαι (καταρήστηκα) to curse.

καταρτίζω arrange, equip.

κατασπαραγμένος torn, rent.

κάτασπρος quite white.

κατασταλάζω drop down, filter.

κατάστιχο index, account-book.

καταστρέφω (καταστράφηκα) destroy.

καταστροφή catastrophe.

κατασφάζω to slaughter.

κατασχένω (κατέσχεσα, κατεσχέθηκα) seize, distrain.

κατατρέχω pursue.

καταφέρνω attain, accomplish, settle ; deal a blow.

καταφρονῶ despise.

καταχθόνιος subterraneous, infernal.

καταχνιά mist, fog.

καταχωνιάζω devour, engulf.

κατάψηλος very high.

κατεβάζω (κατηβάζω) let down, sink ; reduce.

κατεβαίνω (spelling καταιβαίνω, § 3, n. 2 ; [ἐ]κατέβηκα, etc. v. ἀνεβαίνω) come down, descend.

κατεβασιά catarrh.

κατεβασμένος reduced, lowered.

κατέφλοιο threshold.

κατέχω (Crete, Ios) know.

κατζεύω (Cap.) speak, converse upon.

κάτζος (Cap.) gorge, cleft.

κατηβάζω=κατεβάζω.

κάτης tom-cat.

κατής Cadi, judge ; in TEXTS III. 11 metaph. one who wearies with questioning, tormentor.

κατηφρόνια contempt.

κάτι (κάτιτι, κατιντί) anything, something, a little, v. § 153.

κατιφές velvet.

κατοικία dwelling.

κάτοικος inhabitant.

κατοικῶ dwell.

κατόπι, adv. behind, afterwards.

κατορθώνω attain, accomplish.

κάτου=κάτω.

κατσίκι kid, goat.

κατσούφα sullen, peevish person.

κάτσω, v. καθίζω.

κάτω under, below ; adv. κάτω 's underneath, down ; κάτω ἀπό below (§ 172) ; ἡ κάτου γῆ the lower world (of dead).

κατώφλι threshold.

καυγᾶς quarrel.

καυκοῦμαι=καυχοῦμαι.

καύτω (κάφτω)=καίω.

καυχησιάρις boastful.

καυχοῦμαι (καυκοῦμαι, καυκειοῦμαι) to boast.

καφενές coffee-house.

καφές coffee.

καφετζῆς keeper of a coffee-house.

καφτερός burning, hot.

κάφτω, v. καύτω.

κάχτα nut.

κάψι, f. heat.

καψο- prefixed to substantives to give the idea of poor, unhappy ; th·ıs καψονύφη in TEXTS I. a. 23 =ἡ καημένη ἡ νύφη.

κεῖ=ἐκεῖ.

κεῖθε : πὲ κεῖθε thence, from there.

κεικά (Pontus) there.

κεινέτερος (Pontus) theirs (possess. v. § 143, n. 3).

κεῖνος=ἐκεῖνος.

κειός that, yon.

κεῖτομαι (τσείτομαι, § 17, pres. par. κειτούμενος κειτάμενος, ἔπεσα) to lie.

κελαδῶ, κελαϊδῶ, κιλαδῶ sing, warble (of birds).

κέντημα, neut. prick, sting.

κεντρώνω to prick, goad.

κεντῶ to prick, incite.

κερά (τσερά) woman, wife ; mother (Thera) ; pl. § 90.

κεράσι cherry.

κέρατο (§ 105, *n.* 1, τσέρατου *Lesbos*) horn ; τσιρατέλ', *dim.* (*Lesbos*).

*κερδαίνω (ἐκέρδεσα ἐκέρδισα, ἐκερδέθηκα, κερδεμένος κερδημένος κερδισμένος) gain, win.

κερδεύω, κερδίζω=*id.*

κέρδος, *neut.* gain ; *pl.* § 101.

κερί (τσερί, § 17) candle.

*κερνῶ (ἐκέρασα, ἐκεράστηκα) pour in ; treat, regale.

κεροδοσά wax-gift.

κεφάλα large head.

κεφάλαιο chapter (*in book*).

κεφαλᾶς blockhead.

κεφαλή, κεφάλι (κιφάλι, τσεφάλι, τσιφάλ') head.

κῆπος garden.

κηρύττω proclaim, publish.

κι=καί.

κί, 'κί (*Pontus*)=δέν.

κιβούρι grave.

κιλαδῶ=κελαδῶ.

κιλαΐδισμός singing of birds.

κίντυνος (κίδυνος, § 32, *n.* 3) danger.

κινῶ move ; set out, depart.

κιόλα(s), *adv.* on the whole, absolutely ; now, already.

κιουρτιτή (*Pontus*) roaring.

κλαδευτήρι pruning-knife.

κλαδεύω prune, cut off flowers.

κλαδί (κλαρί) twig, branch.

*κλαί(γ)ω (*v.* § 251, 2, ἔκλαψα, ἐκλαύτηκα, κλαμένος) weep.

κλάματα, *pl.* (§ 103) weeping.

κλαρί=κλαδί.

κλασσικός classical, a classic.

κλάψα weeping, lamentation.

κλέβω=κλέφτω.

κλειδί key.

κλειδομανταλωμένος locked and bolted.

κλειδώνω lock in, confine.

κλειδωτός locked, closed.

κλεί(ν)ω (ἐκλείστηκα) shut in.

κλείσιμο (§ 104) locking in.

κλειστός locked.

κλερονόμος heir.

κλέφτης bandit, Kleft ; *pl.* § 76.

κλεφτοπόλεμος bandit (Kleft)-war, war with bandits.

κλεφτόπουλο child of a Kleft, young Kleft.

κλέφτω (κλέβω, κλέφω, ἐκλέφτηκα ἐκλάπηκα) steal, carry off.

κληματσίδα clematis.

κλητῆρας policeman.

κλιθάρι=κριθάρι.

κλίμα, *neut.* climate.

κλίνη bed, couch.

κλίνω to bend.

κλουβί (κλουδί) cage.

κλώθω to spin.

κλώσκουμαι, *aor.* ἐκλώστα (*Pontus*) approach.

κλωσσιά hatching (eggs).

κλωσσῶ to lay eggs.

κλωστή thread.

κόβ(γ)ω=κόφτω.

κοδρίζω depart.

κοιλιά (τσουλία, § 17) belly.

κοιμίζω put to sleep.

κοιμοῦμαι (τσοιμοῦμαι, τσουμοῦμαι, § 17) to sleep.

κοινός common, general.

κοινωνικός sociable.

κόκκαλο bone.

κοκκινίζω to blush.

κοκκινομύτης (§ 114) red-nosed.

κόκκινος (κότσινος) red.

κοκόνα woman, lady.

κόκορος cock.

κολλῶ glue ; fasten to, adhere (also *mid.*).

κολοκύθι gourd ; τὸ ἔχω κολοκύθι μὲ κανένα to be on very friendly terms with a person.

κολυμπῶ (κολυμβῶ) swim, dive.

κομαντρία, *v.* κουμαντρία.

κομμάτι (κομμάτ,, κουμμάτ') a piece ; a little, *un peu* ; κάνω κομμάτια to smash to pieces.

κομματιάζω smash to pieces, tear up.

κομματιαστός dismembered, in pieces.

κομπλιμέντο (κοβλιμέντο) compliment.

κομπόδεμα, *neut.* small parcel; money saved, savings.

κομῥού (*Cap.*) neighbour.

κονάκι dwelling.

κονεύω stop, lodge.

κύνιδα nit, small louse.

κοντά (κοδά) near; κ 's, *prep.* (§ 171) near, close by; κοντά μου near me; κ. τὸ ἕνα μὲ τὸ ἄλλο beside each other.

κόντες a count.

κοντέσσα countess.

κοντεύω to approach; *used by circumlocution for* almost, nearly, *v.* § 125.

κοντοζυγώνω = *id.*

κοντολογῶ sum up, state briefly.

κοντόμυαλος plain, simple.

κοντός near, short; *compar.* § 117.

κοντοστέκομαι come, stand close to.

κόντσια, *pl.* ankles, knuckles; φεύγω μὲ τὰ κ. στὸν κῶλον comic expression for "take to one's heels."

κοπάδι flock.

κοπανίζω bruise, pound; κ. νερά (*metaph.*) lose one's labour; also without νερά to twaddle, gossip.

κοπέλα maid, girl.

κοπιάζω try, take pains; κόπιασε (*aor. imper.*) may I request? please.

κόπος trouble, effort.

κοπριά manure.

κόρακας raven.

κορασιά, κορασίδα maid.

κορδέλα rope, cord.

κόρη girl.

κοριός bug.

κορίτσι girl, maid; κοριτσάκι, κοριτσόπουλο, *dim.*

κορμί body.

κορφή top, summit (of a mountain); *pl.* § 90.

κορφοβούνι top of a mountain.

κόρφος bosom.

κορώνα garland.

κοσκινᾶς sieve-maker.

κόσκινο (*Chios* κόσσινο, *cf.* § 17 *n.*) sieve.

κοσκινοῦ female sieve-maker.

κόσμος world.

κοστίζω to cost.

κοτσύφι blackbird.

κότ(τ)α hen.

κοτ(τ)ός cock.

κουβαλῶ carry a burden; procure, produce.

κουβέντα conversation, talk, gossip.

κουβεντιάζω to gossip.

κουδούνι bell; *dim.* κουδουνά(κ)ι.

κούζω (*Pontus*) to cry, shout, call.

κουκκί (κουτσί) (kidney)-bean.

κουλθῶ (*Cap.*) follow.

κουλλούρι biscuit, roll.

κουμαντάντες commandant.

κουμανταρία commandaria—a brand of Cyprian wine.

κουμάντο commando.

κουμπάνια (κουβάνια) company, society.

κουμπανιάρω accompany; associate with, suit.

κουνέλι rabbit, *metaph.* (hare's foot), coward.

κουντραστάρω (*Syra*) oppose.

κουνῶ move.

κουπί oar.

κουράζω tire (*tr.*).

κούρασμα, *neut.* weariness.

κουρέλι rag.

κουρελιασμένος ragged, tattered.

κουρεύω clip, shear.

κουρνιαχτός dust.

κουρσάρις corsair, pirate.

κουρσεύω (κρουσεύω) practise piracy, be a corsair.

κούρσος, *neut.* (§ 100, *n.* 1) piracy.

κουτουλλῶ strike, butt against.

κουτσί = κουκκί.

κούτσουρο log of wood.

*κόφτω (κόβ[γ]ω, ἐκόπηκα, κομμένος) cut, cut off.

κράζω (ἔκραξα, ἐκράχτηκα) to call, shout.

κρασένιος consisting of wine.

κρασί wine.

κράτο(ς), *neut.* power, might; kingdom, kingdom of Greece.

κρατῶ (-έω, -άω) hold, seize.
κρέας (κριάτο), neut. (§ 105) flesh.
κρεββάτι bed.
κρέβω (Cap.) desire, wish.
κρεμάζω = κρεμνῶ.
κρέμασμα, neut. hanging ; gallows.
*κ ρ ε μ(ν)ῶ, κρεμάζω (ἐκρέμασα, ἐκρεμάστηκα) to hang (tr.).
κρέμομαι (intr.) hang, be suspended.
κρένω, v. κρίνω.
κριάς, κριάτο = κρέας.
κριθάρι (κλιθάρι, § 30, n. 1 ; κθάρι, § 7, n. 1) barley.
κρῖμα, neut. mistake, sin ; "pity that, (what) a pity," κ. 's pity about.
κρίνο, κρίνος lily.
*κ ρ ί ν ω, κρένω (ἔκρινα, κριμένος) to judge ; also say, speak.
κρίσι, f. judgment ; ἔρχομαι στὴ κρίσι appear before court of judgment.
κριτής judge, pl. § 76.
κρότος noise.
κρουσεύω = κουρσεύω.
κρούω (v. § 251, 1, κρουσμένος) strike against, knock ; besiege.
κρύβ(γ)ω (ἐκρύφτηκα, [Pontus ἐκρύφτα], ἐκρουβήθηκα) to hide.
κρύος cold ; τὸ κρύο the cold.
κρυσταλλένιος of crystal ; also an endearing address to a girl.
κρυφά, adv. secretly ; κ. ἀπό without the knowledge of, Lat. clam., v. § 172.
κρυφός secret (adj.) ; τὸ κρυφό a secret.
κρυψάνα hiding-place.
κρυώνω to freeze ; catch cold.
κτίζω, v. χτίζω.
κτυπῶ, v. χτυπῶ.
κυβερνῶ guide, lead, rule.
κυλῶ (ἐκύλισα, ἐκυλίστηκα) to roll.
κῦμα (τσῦμα), neut. wave, billow.
κυνηγάρις huntsman.
κυνήγι the chase.
κυνηγός huntsman.
κυνηγῶ chase, follow, pursue.
κυπαρίσσι cypress.
κυρά woman, lady, Mrs.

κυράνα (TEXTS I. a. 11) lady, mistress, mother.
κυρία wife, Mrs.
κυριακή (τσ́υρατσ́ή, Maina) Sunday.
κυριελέησο the Kyrieleison (eccl.).
κύριος, κύρις (κύρ, § 63) lord, Mr.
κυρτός bent, curved, crooked.
κυττάζω, κυττῶ (ἐκύτταξα and ἐκύτ-τασα) see, consider.
κῶλος backside (podex) ; (Pontus) bottom (of a bag).
κωμῳδία comedy.

*Λαβαίν ω (ἔλαβα) receive, acquire.
λάβρα, v. λαύρα.
λαβώνω to wound.
λαγκάδι ravine, valley.
λαγκεύω (Pontus) to jump, jump out.
λαγός hare.
λαγύνι bottle, pitcher.
λαγωνικό greyhound.
λαθαίνω (ἔλαθα) escape notice, be concealed.
λάθος, neut. (§ 99) mistake.
λαϊκός layman.
λαιμαργῶ be a glutton.
λαιμός neck.
λάκκος pit.
λαλῶ (-έω) speak.
λαμπάδα lamp, candlestick.
λαμπαδιάζω to shine, light.
λαμπηδόνα beauty - of - the - night (flower).
λαμπιρός = λαμπρός.
λαμπρά (λαμπρή) Easter.
λαμπράδα brightness.
λαμπρός brilliant, shining.
λαμπροφάνταστος imaginative, visionary.
λαμπροφωτισμένος brilliantly lighted.
λαμπρύνω radiate, shed light.
λάμπω to light, shine.
λαός people, folk.
λάσκομαι (Pontus) seek aimlessly.
λασπερός dirty.
λατρεία adoration, worship.
λαύρα heat, fervour ; longing.

λαφρός (ἐλαφρός, ἀλαφρός) light, easy.

λάχ (Pontus), v. § 224, 3, n. 3.

*λαχαίνω (ἔλαχα, λαχεμένος) obtain by lot; μὴ λάχῃ καὶ περάσῃ (Folk-song) let him not by chance pass by (cf. § 280, n. 2).

λάχανα, pl. vegetables.

λαχταρίζω languish, feel longing; in Zante (TEXTS I. a. 20) to cause longing.

λαχταρῶ = id.

λαχτόρι cock.

λεβάντες Levant, Orient; east wind.

λεβέντης active young man, young fellow.

*λέ(γ)ω (v. § 252, 3, pres. particip. pass. λεγάμενος, εἶπα [Ios ἔπα], θὰ [εἰ]πῶ [εἴπω], imper. [εἰ]πέ[s] [εἰ]πέ[σ]τε πῆτε, ἐλέχτηκα and εἰπώθηκα) to say, tell; δὲ θὰ εἰπῇ μ' αὐτό that does not mean; λ. ὄξω to blab; λεγόμενος (lit.) so-called, aforesaid.

λεημοσύνη alms.

λεϊμόνι lemon.

λείπω fail, be wanting, absent.

λειτουργῶ to hold divine service; serve.

λέλε μου, in addressing a person— my good fellow, my dear.

λέξι(s), f. word.

λεοντάρι = λιοντάρι.

λέπρα leprosy.

λεύκα white poplar.

λευκός white.

λευτεριά liberty.

λεφτόκαρο hazel-nut.

λεχοῦσα woman in confinement.

λήγορα = γλήγορα.

λήθη oblivion.

λησμονῶ (ἀλησμονῶ) forget.

λία, from (ὀ)λίγος.

λιανοτρέμουλος gently trembling.

λιβάνι incense.

λιβανιά consecration through in-cense.

λιγάκι a little.

λιγνός slim.

λίγος = ὀλίγος.

λιθάρι (lisári, § 20, n. 1) stone.

λιθαρίζω play with stones.

λίθος stone.

λικοντῶ detain, prevent; mid. (Ios) stay for, wait.

λιμέρι (λημέρι) camp (of an army, or of bandits).

λιμεριάζω encamp.

λίμνη lake.

λιοντάρι (λεοντάρι) lion.

λο(γ)αριάζω reckon, value.

λόγγος forest.

λο(γ)ή manner (Chios); λογῆς in the expressions τί λογῆς of what sort? κάθε λογῆς of every kind; λ. λ. of different kinds, of every description.

λογιάζω consider, think upon.

λογικό understanding, reason; ἔρχο-μαι στὰ λο(γ)ικά μου I become con-scious of, learn of.

λογικός logical.

λόγιος learned.

λογκαιλόγερα (Sar. K.), adv. from all around.

λογογράφος novelist, literateur.

λόγος (λόος) word, speech, literary account; pl. § 96; τοῦ λόγου σου, etc., as circumlocution for the personal pron., v. § 139.

λογοτεχνικός literary.

λόγυρα = ὀλόγυρα.

λογυρίζω surround.

λοϊκά, v. λογικό.

λοιπό(ν), τὸ λοιπό(ν) therefore, so.

λόος = λόγος.

λόρδος lord.

λοστρόμος chief steward (on a ship).

λούζω (λούγω), λούνω, λούω bathe, wash (mid. intr. bathe oneself).

λουκάνικο sausage.

λουλλούδζι = λουλούδι.

λουλούδι flower; λουλουδάκι, dim.

λουλουδίζω to bloom.

λούλουδο = λουλούδι.

λούνω, λούω = λούζω.

λουτρό bath.

λυγερή pliable, slender—designation of a young girl.

λυγμός sobbing.

λύκος (pl. λύτζοι, Cap.) wolf.

λύνω loosen, set free.

λύπη grief, distress.

λυπημένος grieved.

λυπητερός lamentable.

λυποῦμαι to sorrow, be troubled.

λυράκι (Naxos) small lyre (a musical instrument with three strings).

λυσσαλέος furious, rabid.

λυτρώνω loose, liberate.

λυώνω (λόνω, § 6, n. 6) dissolve, melt.

λωλός foolish, stupid.

Μά (ἀμά, ἀμή, ἀμέ) but.

μαγείρισσα female cook.

μαγερειό cooking, kitchen.

μαγερεύω to cook.

μάγερος (μάγερας, § 66) cook.

μαγεύω bewitch.

μαγιά spell, magic.

μάγισσα sorceress.

μάγουλο cheek ; dim. μαγουλάκι.

μαδῶ pluck (e.g. poultry).

μαζεύω collect.

μαζί, adv. at the same time, together ; μ. μέ (§ 173) (together) with ; μαζί μου with me.

μαζώνω (ἐμάζωξα, ἔμασα [properly from ὁμάζω] ἐμαζώχτηκα) collect, mid. assemble.

*μαθαίνω (ἔμαθα, μαθημένος) learn, teach.

μαθέ(ς), parenthetic word—that is to say, forsooth, indeed, v. § 259.

μάθησι, f. education, culture.

μαθητής pupil ; pl. § 76.

μαϊμοῦ monkey.

Μάϊς May.

μακάρι, particle, if only, would that, v. §§ 193, 195, nevertheless, in spite of.

μακαρίτης blessed, late (dead).

μακελάρις butcher.

μακρά=μακρειά.

μακραίνω (ἐμάκρηνα) be prolix.

μακρειά, adv. wide, far ; away ! begone ! μ. ἀπό far from.

μακρολαίμης (§ 114) long-necked.

μακρυνός distant, far, wide.

μακρύς (μακρός, v. § 110) far, distant.

μαλακός soft.

μαλακώνω make soft, mollify.

μάλαμα, neut. gold.

μαλαματένιος golden.

μάλιστα by all means, of course ; quite, very.

μαλλί hair ; dim. μαλλάκι.

μαλλιάζω be troubled.

μαλλιαρός hairy, with long hair,— to denote the younger writers who take a decided stand for a popular reform of the literary language.

μαλώνω to quarrel, scold.

μαμμή midwife ; pl. § 90.

μανάβης fruit and vegetable dealer, greengrocer.

μανθάνω (a. Gk.)=μαθαίνω.

μανια(σ)μένος raving, rabid.

μάννα mother, pl. § 90.

μαννούλα little mother.

μανταλώνω to bolt, bar.

μαντήλι handkerchief, cravat.

μαντολίνο mandoline.

μαντρί fold, pen.

μαράζι care, anxiety.

*μαραίνω (ἐμάρανα, ἐμαράθηκα) cause to wither ; mid. wither.

μαργαριταρένιος consisting of pearl.

μαργαριτάρι pearl.

μαργώνω (Cap.) to fight.

μαρινέρος sailor.

μαριόλικος, μαριόλος knavish, artful.

μαρμαρένιος of marble.

μάρμαρο marble.

μαρμαροβούνι hill of marble, marble quarry.

Μάρτις March.

μάρτυρας witness.

μαρτυρῶ acknowledge, confess ; inform.

μᾶς, v. ἐγώ.

μασσῶ chew.

μάστορας, μάστορης (§ 69) master, master-workman.

⟨θὰ⟩ μάσω, v. μαζώνω.

ματαβγαίνω come out again.

ματαγυρίζω return again.

ματαιοδοξία passion for fame, ambition.

μάτι (ὀμμάτι, pl. μάθια, v. § 16, n. 3) eye ; μάτια μου endearing term of address—my eye, my treasure ; ματάκι, dim.

ματιά glance, look.

ματώνω make bloody ; ματωμένος bloody.

μαυρίζω turn black.

μαυρίλα blackness, black colour, dark clouds.

μαυρομάτης (§ 113) black-eyed.

μαῦρος black ; unlucky.

μαυροφρύδης with black eyebrows.

μαχαίρι knife, sword.

μάχη battle.

μαχμουτιές a Turkish coin (mahmūdi = cir. 9d.).

μάχσϑς (Pontus), adv. intentionally, with a fixed purpose.

μέ : (1) prep. w. acc. (§ 162) with ; μὲ μιᾶς at once, with one stroke, suddenly ; (2)=μή (Cyp.) ; (3) μμέ (Chios)=μά.

μεγαλαίνω make great, magnify ; become great.

μεγαλοδύναμος of great power, mighty.

μεγαλόπνοος long-breathed, elevated, lofty.

μεγάλος great ; neut. also μέγα, v. § 180, n. 2.

μεγαλόστομος with a loud voice, stentorian.

μεγαλόσωμος with a large body, huge.

μεγαλότεχνος highly artistic.

μεγαλοφάνταστος very imaginative.

μεγαλόφωνος with a loud voice.

μεγαλώνω (ἐμεγάλωξα, p. 139) become great.

μεθαύριο, adv. day after to-morrow.

μέθη drunkenness.

μέθοδο, f. (§ 87) method.

μεθῶ (μεθύζω, p. 138, μεθυσμένος) to be inebriated.

μείνω, v. μένω.

μελανωτής (τοῦ χαρτιοῦ) ink-boy, printer's devil.

μέλει : τί μὲ μέλει what does it matter to me ?

μελετῶ intend ; study.

μέλι honey.

μέλισσα bee.

μελίσσι=id.

μέλλεται νά . . . be about to, on the point of.

μελλούμενο the future.

μελωμένος honey-sweet.

μέν (Cyp.) = μή(ν).

μενεξές violet.

μένω (μείνω, § 204 ; μνέσκω, μνήσκω, ἔμεινα) remain, dwell.

μέρα (ἡμέρα) day.

μεραγλός (Cap.) vexed, peevish.

μεράδι (small) part ; χίλια μεράδια ὀμορφύτερη a thousand times more fair.

μεριά side, region, place.

μερικοί some, several.

μεροδούλι—μεροφάγι, proverbial expression—daily work, da‘ly fare, i.e. living from hand to mouth.

μεροκάματο a day's work.

μερόνυχτα, adv. day and night.

μέρος, neut. part ; side ; region, locality.

μεροφά(γ)ι, v. μεροδούλι.

μερτικό portion.

μερώνω to tame.

μέσ’, μέσα, adv. inside, within, in ; μέσ(α)(’s), prep. (§ 171) in the midst of, into ; ἡ μέσα κάμαρα the middle room.

μεσάνυχτα, pl. midnight.

μέση middle ; μέσ’ στὴ μ. τοῦ χωριοῦ in the midst of the village.

μεσημέρι midday, noon.

μέσο means, measure ; also at, in, by (w. gen.), v. § 171, n. 4.

μεσοχώρι village in the middle, e.g. of a plain or of a district.

μεστός full, exuberant.

μέστωμα development, maturity.

μετά=μέ with.

μετανοιώνω repent.

μεταξύ between, among, v. ἀναμεταξύ.

μεταξωτός of silk.

μετατοπίζω transpose, disfigure, pervert.

μεταφιλῶ (-έω) kiss a second time, kiss repeatedly.

μεταφράζω translate.

μεταφραστής translator.

μεταχειρίζομαι to use.

μετερίζι ambush.

μετοχή participle, participation.

μέτρο (μέτρος, § 100, n. 1) measure.

μετρῶ to measure, count.

μέτωπο forehead.

μεφιστοφελικός Mephistophelian.

μή (μήν, § 34, n. 2, μέ[ν] Cyp.) no, not (prohibitive); in order not; v. § 284.

μηδέ not even, neither (also in affirmative sentences); μηδὲ τίποτα nothing at all, absolutely nothing; μηδέ—μηδέ neither—nor (cf. § 285).

μηλιά (μηλέ, § 81, n. 2; μηλέα, § 10, n. 1; μπλιά, § 37 n.) apple-tree.

μῆλο apple.

μήν=μή; also as an interrogative particle (v. § 255).

μήνα interrogative particle, v. § 255.

μῆνας mouth.

μήνυμα, neut. information, message.

μηνῶ (ἐμήνυσα) announce, proclaim.

μήπως lest perhaps; possible if—to introduce a question, v. § 255.

μήτε not even, neither; μ.—μ. neither—nor (even in affirmative sentence), v. § 285.

μητέρα mother.

μητρικός motherly.

μητρυγιά stepmother.

μιά (μνιά, v. § 30; μία, § 10, n. 1), f. of ἕνας.

μιαουρίζω to mew.

μικροδουλειά trifle, bagatelle.

μικρός small.

μικρούτσικος quite small.

μίλημα, neut. speaking, conversation; proclamation, order.

μιλιά conversation, speech, gossip.

μιλλιούνι million.

μιλῶ (ὁμιλῶ) speak.

μιμοῦμαι imitate.

μιναρές minaret.

μισανοίγω to open half-way.

μισεύω start off, depart, journey.

μισομετανοιώνω to half regret.

μισοξυπνῶ to half awake.

μισός half; μισύ, v. § 131; τὸ μισό the half.

μισοτελειωμένος half-completed.

μισῶ to hate.

μνέσκω=μένω.

μνῆμα, neut. tomb.

μνήσκω=μένω.

μνιά (μν'ά)=μιά.

μόδος, neut. manner, mode.

μοιάζω, ὁμ(ν)οιάζω (ἔμοιασα ἔμοιαξα) be like, resemble (μέ).

μοῖρα fate; goddess of fate, fairy.

μοιράζω divide.

μοιραίνω (ἐμοίρανα) determine the destiny. The goddesses of fate (Μοῖρες), according to the popular superstition of modern Greece, come to newborn children in order to determine their life-destinies.

μοιριολογῶ sing dirges, lament.

μοιρολόγι dirge.

μοιρολο(γ)ῶ=μοιριολογῶ.

μόλις, adv. just now, hardly; as soon as (§ 273, 2).

μολογῶ confess.

μολονότι (μ' ὅλο[ν ὅ]ποῦ) although (§ 278, 2).

μοναδικός peculiar, unique.

μονάκριβος dear, only.

μοναξιά loneliness.

μοναστήρι cloister; -άκι, dim.

μονάχα (μοναχά), adv. alone, only.

μοναχός, μονάχος alone.

μόν(ε), μόνο(ν), μόνον, μούνε, adv. alone, only, but; μόνο ποῦ (πῶς), v. § 282, 2.

μονοπάτι path.

μόνος alone; μόνος του, etc. self, § 157; μονός simple, single.

μόνου = μόνο.

μορφή form.

μορφιά beauty; μιὰ μ. adverbial, very gracefully.

μόσκος (μόσχος) musk.

μοσχοβολῶ, μοσχομυρίζω smell sweet.

μούγκι, μούνε = μόνε.

μοῦλος mule, metaph. bastard.

μουρή = μωρέ.

μουρμουρίζω to murmur.

μουρμούρισμα, neut. murmuring.

μοῦρο mulberry.

μουρτάτης unbeliever, renegade.

μουσική (μουσιτσή) music.

μουσικόλαλος speaking like music.

μουστάκι moustache.

μουστρί ladle.

μπᾶ, particle used in warding off or refusing.

μπάζω bring in.

* μ π α ί ν ω (ἐμπῆκα [bῆκα, ἤμπα], θὰ μπῶ θὰ ἔμπω [θὰ bήκω, Sar. K.], imper. ἔμπα[s] ἐμπᾶ[σ]τε) enter, go in.

μπαλωματής cobbler.

μπαλώνω cobble, mend.

μπαμπᾶς (babâs, Velv.) father, papa.

μπάμπω (bábω) grandmother, aged woman.

μπάντα (Ios πάda) side ; μιὰ μπ. once more ; τὸ καράβι μὲ τὴ μπάντα the boat rides on the side, capsizes.

μπάρκα bark, small boat.

μπαρόνος baron.

μπαρούτη powder.

μπάτος sole.

μπέης Bey.

μπέμπω (§ 15, n. 3) = πέμπω.

μπερδεύομαι become entangled in.

μπιραρία (§ 10) beer-house.

μπιρμπέρις (birbέρς) barber.

μπιστικός, μπιστός (§ 15, n. 3) true, faithful.

μπλέκω implicate, meddle in (μέ).

μποζιατίζω (Cal.) = μπογιατίζω to paint, colour.

μπολιάζω to graft, inoculate (also metaph.).

* μ π ο ρ ῶ (bορῶ, bουρῶ, πορῶ), ἐμπορῶ, ἠμπορῶ (ἐμπόρεσα) can, be able.

μπόσικος empty, of no use, in vain.

μποτίλια bottle.

μπουλουκμπασῆς leader of a company, general.

μπουμπούκι bud.

μπουταλᾶς blockhead.

μπρός, adv. in front, forward ; μπρὸς 's (μπροστὰ 's) prep. (§ 171) before, in front of, over against (§ 171).

μπροστά = id.

μυαλό (usually pl.) brains, understanding.

μυγδαλιά almond-tree.

μυθιστορικός romantic, romance.

μυῖγα gnat.

μυλόρδος, i.e. My lord, in addressing an Englishman.

μύλος mill.

μυλωνᾶς miller.

μυρίζω to smell.

μυρμήγκι ant.

μυρωδάτος fragrant, sweet-smelling.

μυρωδιά fragrance.

μυστήριο secret.

μυστικός secret (adj.) ; neut. a secret.

μυστρί ladle, trowel.

μύτη nose.

μωρ', μωρέ (μῶρε, Pontus), μωρή (μωϊρή), μουρή, βρέ, interj. halloa ! look !

μωρό small child, suckling, baby.

Νά (1) behold ! there ! also in pl. form νάτε, v. § 170, n. 2. ; (2) (also νάν, § 34, n. 2) particle, in order that, to, v. § 262.

ναί, ναίσκε yes.

ναῖκα (Pontus) woman.

νανά, (interj. word used in lullaby.

ναννάρισμα, neut. lullaby.

ναστενάζω = ἀναστενάζω.

νάτε, v. νά (1).

ναύτης marine, sailor.

ναχόρταγος = ἀναχόρταγος.

νεβάζω = ἀνεβάζω.

νεγκώσκω (Cap.) go, go around.

νέκρα stiffness of death, stillness of death.

νεκρανάστασι, f. resurrection of the dead.

νεκρικός pertaining to the dead.

νεκρός dead.

νέλα = ἔλα.

νενέ mother.

νέος (§ 10) new ; *also* young, a youth, young man ; νέα young maiden.

νεοτυπωμένος newly printed.

Νεράϊδες female creatures in the folk-mythology, elves, nereids.

νερό water.

νευρικός nervous.

νευρώδης nervous ; energetic, emphatic.

νέφαλο cloud.

νέφτι naphtha, turpentine, injected behind into draught or riding animals to make them go faster.

νή—νή (§ 34, *n.* 3) either—or.

νήλιος = ἥλιος.

νησί island.

νησιώτικος belonging to the islands, insular.

νηστικός sober, hungry.

νιάτα, *pl.* youth

νίβω (νίβγω, § 23 *n*). wash, bathe ; *mid.* bathe oneself.

νικῶ conquer, gain victory.

νιός (νέος) young ; young man.

νιότη youth.

νοικιάζω (νοιτσάζω) to hire, rent.

νοικοκύρις owner or master of a house.

νοικοκυρίτσα lady of a house, mistress.

νοιξάτικος, *v.* ἀνοιξάτικος.

νοιτσάζω, *v.* νοικιάζω.

νοιώθω perceive, notice, feel.

νομίζω think, believe.

νόμος law.

νοσοκομεῖο hospital.

νοστιμάδα pleasant taste ; grace, jest.

νοστιμίζω be amiable, graceful.

νόστιμος tasteful ; expensive, pleasant ; charming, amiable.

νουρά = οὐρά.

νοῦς (§ 63, *n.* 2) mind, understanding ; ἔρχεται στὸ νοῦ μου it occurs to me ; χάνω τὸ νοῦ μου lose one's reason.

ντά = ἴντα.

νταβάνι cover, ceiling.

ντάμα lady (in cards).

ντεβλέτι government.

ντελή (*v.* § 74, *n.* 2) brave.

ντένω get entangled in.

ντερβένι narrow pass, defile.

ντζαμί = τζαμί.

ντό (*Pontus*) = τί, *v.* § 152, *n.* 2.

ντουζίνα dozen.

ντουλάπι closet, cupboard.

ντούννω, *aor.* ἐντῶκα, § 202, *n.* 2 (*Pontus*) beat ; fall into (a snare).

ντουφέκι = τουφέκι.

ντρανῶ (*Pontus*) see.

ντρέπομαι (ἐντράπηκα) be ashamed.

ντροπή shame, disgrace.

ντύνω put on ; *mid.* dress.

ντύσιμο (§ 104) dressing.

νύπνος = ὕπνος.

νυστάζω (ἐνύσταξα) be sleepy, nod.

νύφη (νύφφη, § 36 *n.*) bride, daughter-in-law, young wife (*pl.* § 90).

νύχτα (*nífta*, § 14, *n.* 2) night ; *gen.* § 84.

νυχτιά night (season).

νυχτοπούλι night-owl.

νυχτορεύω spend the night ; work through the night.

νῶμος = ὦμος.

νωρίς, *adv.* early.

νωρίτερα, *adv.* earlier.

Ξάγναντος against, opposite.

ξαδερφοπούλα cousin (*f.*).

ξαθός (ξαθθός, § 36 *n.*) blond, fair.

ξαίνω (ἔξανα) card wool.

ξανά again, once more, *v.* § 159, 2.

ξαναβλασταίνω (*v.* βλασταίνω) shoot up (again).

ξαναβλέπω see again.

ξαναγεννοῦμαι be born again.

ξαναγυρίζω turn back again, turn around again.

ξαναδιανώνομαι come to consciousness again, come to oneself
again.

ξαναζωντανεμένος resuscitated.

ξανακοιμοῦμαι fall asleep again.

ξανακτυπῶ = ξαναχτυπῶ.

ξαναλαβαίνω (v. λαβαίνω) receive
again.

ξαναλέγω say once more, repeat.

ξανάνθισμα, neut. blossoming.

ξανανιώνω renew (again).

ξαναπερνῶ go past once more.

ξαναφαίνομαι appear once more.

ξαναφιλῶ kiss a second time.

ξαναχτυπῶ strike another time.

ξανεποῖκα (Pontus), v. φτάω.

ξανθούλα, dim. from ξα(ν)θός, term
applied to a young girl.

ξανοίγω look at, discern.

ξαντικρύζω meet.

ξάπλα, adv. outstretched, length-
wise.

ξαπλώνω stretch out, spread.

ξαποστάζω to take rest.

ξαρχινῶ begin.

ξαστεριά starry heaven, unclouded
heaven.

ξαφνίζω frighten, surprise.

ξάφνω, adv. suddenly.

ξεγίνεται it changes; δὲν ξ. it cannot
be changed, helped.

ξεγλυτώνω to finish a work, be freed
from work.

ξέγνοιαστος heedless.

ξεγορεύομαι confess.

ξεγυμνωμένος uncovered, stripped.

ξεθάφτω excavate.

ξεθυμαίνω (ἐξεθύμανα) give vent to
wrath; subside.

ξελογιάζω seduce, dishonour.

ξεμολογῶ = ξομολογῶ.

ξεμπαρκάρω (ἐξεμπαρκάρισα) disembark.

ξεμπερδεύω find a way out of a
difficult position, extricate
oneself.

ξενιτειά abroad, foreign land.

ξενιτεύομαι go abroad, emigrate.

ξενοδουλεύω to work for strangers.

ξένος strange, peculiar, the stranger,
foreigner; τὰ ξένα foreign land.

ξένω = ξύνω.

ξεπαγιασμένος numbed with cold.

ξεπαίρνομαι (v. παίρνω) fly into a
passion, be puffed up.

ξεπερνῶ excel, surpass.

ξεπεσμένος decayed, dilapidated.

*ξεραίνω (ἐξέρανα, ἐξεράθηκα) to
dry

ξεριζώνω pluck out by the roots;
δὲν ξεριζώνει it cannot be ex-
terminated.

*ξερνῶ (ἐξέρασα, ξερασμένος) to
vomit.

ξεροβήχω to have a dry cough.

ξερόβραχος barren rock.

ξερός (ξηρός) dry.

ξέρω, v. ξεύρω.

ξεσκίζω (ξεσκῶ) split, tear asunder.

ξεσπαθώνω draw the sword.

ξεσπάω break forth, give vent.

ξεσταυρώνω take down from the
cross.

ξεστομίζω speak out, divulge.

ξετάζω = ἐξετάζω.

ξετελεύω completely finish.

*ξεύρω, ξέρω, ἠξεύρω, ἠξέρω (ξές,
§ 252, 3, n. 1; ἔμαθα) know.

ξεφεύγω (ἐξέφυγα) escape.

ξεφτερουγιάζω flee away from.

ξεφυτρώνω shoot up, flourish.

ξεφωνίζω cry aloud.

*ξεχάνω (ξεχάννω, p. 135, n. 2),
ξεχνῶ (ἐξέχασα, ξεχα[σ]μένος)
forget.

ξεχωρίζω separate; differentiate,
pick out; separate from a person.

ξεχωριστός separated, peculiar, distinguished.

ξεψυχῶ breathe one's last.

ξημέρωμα (or pl. τὰ ξημερώματα) day-
break.

ξημερώνει day breaks.

ξηραίνω, v. ξεραίνω.

ξηρός = ξερός.

ξητῶ = ἐξετάζω.

ξιλῶ (Cap., aor. ξίλσα) fall, degenerate to.

ξινάρ(ι) axe.
ξόβεργο lime-twig (to catch birds).
ξοδεύω, ξοδιάζω spend (money).
ξομολογῶ (ξεμολογῶ) hear one's confession, shrive (w. acc.).
ξορίζω to exile.
ξουρίζω=ξυρίζω.
ξύλινος of wood.
ξύλο wood.
ξυνός sharp, acid.
ξύνω, ξένω, ξύζω, ξῶ (ἐξύστηκα) scrape, scratch.
ξυπάζομαι be astonished.
ξυπνῶ wake up.
ξυπόλυτος barefooted.
ξυρίζω (ξουρίζω) to shave.
ξύσιμο (§ 104) scraping.
ξῶ=ξύνω.
ξώρας, adv. late.
ξωτικό ghost.

Ὁ, ἡ, τὸ the, v. § 55.
Ὀβριός Jew.
ὄγιος, rel., for composition of which, v. § 150, n. 2.
ὀγώ=ἐγώ.
ὄθε whence.
οἶνος (lit.) wine.
ὀκά a liquid measure (about a quart); pl. § 90.
ὀλάνοιχτος standing wide open.
ὀλη`μερίς, adv. the whole day long.
ὀλίγος (λίγος) few; μὲ ὀλίγα, σὲ λίγο soon, in a short time.
ὀλόγυρα (λόγυρα), adv. all around; ὁ. ἀπό, prep. round about (§ 171).
ὀλόδροσος quite fresh.
ὀλοένα, adv. without interruption, continuously.
ὀλόκληρος (ὀλόκερος, § 31, n. 1) quite, whole.
ὀλομόναχος quite alone.
ὀλόμορφος very fair.
ὀλόρτος quite erect.
ὅλος (οὖλος, Sar. K. γούλος) whole, all; v. § 156.
ὀλούθε, adv. from, on all sides, everywhere.
ὀλόφλογος flaming brightly.

ὀλόφωτος shining bright.
ὀλόχρυσος all of gold.
ὀλόχυτος at one cast, of one mould.
ὀμιλῶ=μιλῶ.
ὀμμάτι=μάτι.
ὀμ(ν)οιάζω, v. μοιάζω.
ὀμόθρησκος one of same religion.
ὅμοιος (ὅμνοιος) similar.
ὀμορφιά (μορφιά) beauty.
ὄμορφος (ἔμορφος) beautiful; compar. § 117.
ὀμότεχνος colleague in art.
ὀμόφυλος of the same race.
ὄμπρο (Pontus), w. ἀπό before of time (§ 174).
ὀμπρός=ἐμπρός.
ὀμώνω swear.
ὅμως nevertheless.
ὀνειρεύομαι to dream.
ὄνειρο dream; pl. § 94.
ὄνομα (ὄνομαν, § 34, n. 4), neut. name; γιὰ ὄνομα τοῦ θεοῦ! for God's sake!
ὀνομάζω to name.
ὄντα=ὄντας.
ὀντᾶς (ὀτᾶς, Pontus) room, chamber.
ὄντας, ὄντε(ς), ὄντεν, ὄταν(ε) if, when, as often as, § 272.
ὄντε (Chios) halloa, indeed!
ὄξον, ὄξω (ἔξω), ἀπ' ὄξω outside, without; ὄξω ἀπό outside, on the outside, v. § 172.
ὀξώπορτα outside-door, street-door.
ὀπίσω (ὀπίσ', Pontus) backwards, behind; cf. also πίσω.
ὅπλο weapon.
ὅποιος (ὅποιος κι ἄν) who, whoever, v. § 150.
ὁποῖος, ὁ who, which, v. § 149 n.
ὅπου, ὁποῦ where; rel. who, that, v. § 149; so that (consec.), v. § 279; ὅπου κι ἄν wherever.
ὅπως how, as; ὅπως κι ἄν however.
ὅρασι(ς), f. vision, sight.
ὄργανο organ, instrument.
ὀργασμός desire, passion.
ὀργισμένος angry, furious.
ὀργώνω put under cultivation.
ὀρδινιάζω to order.

ὀρένι (*Cap.*) a ruin, dilapidated house.

ὀρθάνοιχτος wide open.

ὀρθός (ὀρτός, § 18, *n.* 3) straight, correct ; steep.

ὀρίζω to command, prescribe (*w.* acc.) ; νὰ σ᾽ ὀρίσω is it agreeable ? if it please you ; καλῶς ὀρίστε welcome.

ὀρισμός order, disposition.

ὀρκίζω to swear (*tr.*) ; ὀρκίζομαι swear.

ὅρκος oath, swearing.

ὀρμάν (*Pontus*) = ρουμάνι.

ὀρμήνεια (*Velv.*) counsel, advice.

ὀρμητικός rushing, impetuous.

ὄρνιθα, ὀρνίθι hen.

ὀροκλωΐσκουμαι, *aor.* ὀροκλωΐστα (*Pontus*) go slowly to and fro.

ὄρος, *neut.* mountain.

ὀρπί(δ)α hope.

ὀρτάτατ (*Cap.*) truth.

ὀρτός = ὀρθός.

ὀρφάνια state of being orphan, orphanhood.

ὀρφανός orphaned, *neut.* orphan.

ὀρωτῶ (*Pontus*) = ἐρωτῶ.

ὄσκε, *v.* ὄχι.

ὄσο as long as ; ὄσο νά or ὄσο ποῦ until (§ 275) ; ὄσο γιά as for, as far as concerns ; ὄσο, ὄσα (ὄσο κι ἄν) however much ; ὄσο—(ἄλλο) τόσο the more—the more.

ὄσος as great as (§ 150) ; ὄσοι (all) who.

ὀσπίτι = σπίτι.

ὄτα, ὄταν(ε) = ὄντας ; ἀπ᾽ ὄτα since.

ὀτᾶς = ὀντᾶς.

ὄτι (1) that (§ 267, *n.* 2) ; (2) as soon as, when, *also* ὄτιπου, ὄτι νά (*v.* § 273) ; (3) ὄτι, ὄτι κι ἄν whatever ; that which, all that.

οὐ (*Velv.*) = ὀ.

οὐδέ—οὐδέ neither—nor.

οὖλος = ὄλος.

οὐρά (νουρά, § 34, *n.* 3) tail.

οὐράνιος heavenly.

οὐρανός heaven.

οὐσία being, essence ; taste, good

taste ; πάνω στὴν οὐ. in the prime of life.

οὔτε—οὔτε neither—nor ; οὔτε κάν not even, nor.

ὀχ, *prep.* out of, from, of (*v.* § 168, 2).

ὄχι, ὄχισκε, ὄσκε no.

ὀχονοῦς, *adv.* immediately.

ὄχτος slope, base of a mountain.

ὀχτρός = ἐχτρός.

ὀχτώ eight.

ὄψι, *f.* countenance.

Πά : (1) (*Pontus*) *enclitic* = πάλι ; (2) ἀπὸ πά (*Maina*) from there ; (3) πά ᾽ς upon (§ 171) ; (4) *from* πάγω, *v.* § 252, 1.

πα(γ)αίνω, πααίνω = πηγαίνω.

παγάνι (*Cap.*) ravine.

πά(γ)ω, *v.* πηγαίνω.

παγωμένος icy, frozen.

παγωτιά, *pl.* freezing, ice.

παδά, *adv.* hither, here.

πάδα = μπάντα.

παζάρι (μπαζάρι) market, bazaar.

* π α θ α ί ν ω (ἔπαθα, παθωμένος) endure, suffer.

πάθος, *neut.* suffering, passion ; *pl.* § 100.

παιγνίδι (παιχνίδι) sport, game with music.

παιγνιδίζω to play.

παιδί child ; *dim.* παιδάκι ; ἀπὸ παιδί from a child (childhood).

παιδιάτικος pertaining to children, childlike.

παιδόπουλο small child.

παίζω (ἔπαιξα, ἐπαίχτηκα) to play ; παίζω κανονιές to shoot off cannon.

παινῶ (ἐπαίνεσα) to praise.

* π α ί ρ ν ω *also* παίρω (ἐπῆρα ἔπηρα, θὰ πάρω, Pontus θὰ παίρω, ἐπάρθηκα) take, fetch ; π. τὰ βουνά go over the mountains, go away, get lost ; π. ἐπιπόνου take to heart (*Aegina*)

παιχνίδι = παιγνίδι.

πάλ = πάλε.

παλαιοβέτουλο the old, *i.e.* mean, kid
(*cf.* § 41, a).

παλαιός = παλιός.

παλάμη (palm of) hand.

παλάτι palace.

πάλε, πάλι (πάλ), *adv.* again, yet.

παλεθύρι = παραθύρι.

παλεύω wrestle.

παλιογυναῖκα ugly (old) woman.

παλιόπαιδο street-boy, dirty fellow.

παλιός (παλαιός) old, ancient.

παλληκάρι young fellow, youthful
warrior, hero, *pallicar*; παλληκαρούδι, *dim.*

παλληκαρίσιος like, pertaining to a
pallicar.

παλμός palpitation of heart.

παλός (*Cap.*) = παλιός.

παναγύρι = πανηγύρι.

παναέ, *voc.* (παναέ μ', *Velv.*) *exclamation,* great heavens !

πανέκλαμπρος most illustrious.

πανηγύρι (παναγύρι) festival (holy
day).

πανηγυρίζω celebrate, solemnise.

πανί, cloth.

πάντα, *adv.* always ; γιὰ π. for
ever.

παντέρα banner.

παντέχω expect, suppose, believe.

παντοδύναμις almighty (*Provelengios*).

παντοῦ, *adv.* everywhere.

παντοχή expectation, patience.

παντρεύω marry ; *mid.* get married.

παντῶ, *v.* ἀπαντῶ.

πάντων, *v.* τέλος π.

πάνω = πάγω, πηγαίνω.

πάνω, *adv.* above, over; π. 's upon,
on (§ 171) ; τό 'να καὶ πάνω and
one more into the bargain.

πανώριος very fair.

παξιμάδι biscuit, *zwieback.*

παπαδιά clergyman's wife.

παπᾶς priest, clergyman ; *indecl., v.*
§ 64.

παπατρέχας (§ 73) superficial person.

πάπια duck.

πάπλωμα, *neut.* covering, counter-
pane.

παπλωματᾶς manufacturer, retailer
of quilts.

παπουτζῆς cobbler.

παπούτζι shoe, boot.

παππούς grandfather ; old man.

παρά than *after the compar.,* except,
but, *cf.* § 158 *n.*

παραβαίνω transgress (a command-
ment).

παραβολή parable.

παραγγελία commission, order.

παραγγέλνω (παράγγειλα παράγγελα)
to order.

παραγιός adopted son.

παράγω produce.

παραγωγή production.

παράδεισο(s) *f.* (§ 87) or *m.* paradise.

παραδίδω to surrender.

παράδοσι, *f.* transmission, tradition ;
education.

παραζάλη confusion, bother.

παραθύρι (παλεθύρι) window.

παραιτῶ abandon, resign.

παρακαλῶ (*v.* καλνῶ) request.

παρακάνω exaggerate, overdo.

παρακάτω, *adv.* lower down.

παρακεῖ (παρατσεῖ), *adv.* farther on,
forward, more.

παρακλητικός entreating.

παρακουνουστίζω (*Velv.*) inform (a
person μέ).

παρακούω hear wrongly, hear, disobey.

παράλυτος paralytic.

παραμονεύω wait for, waylay.

παραμονή evening before a festival
(of the church).

παραμύθι fable, tale.

παρανιός very young.

παράνω, *adv.* farther above, up ; beyond, over.

παραξενεύ(γ)ομαι to wonder, be
astonished.

παράξενος striking, odd.

παραπάνω higher up, over, more ;
μὲ τὸ π. in excess.

παραπατέρας adoptive father.

παραπέρα, *adv.* farther away, beyond
(ἀπό than).

παραπονεμένος lamentable, sad.

παραπόνεσι, f. trouble, lamentation.

παράπονο lamentation.

παραπονοῦμαι lament, bewail.

παρᾶς (Velv. f., pl. also παράδια) a coin, Para ; money.

παρασκευή Friday.

παρατεντώνω extend, spread (tr.), mid. intr.

παρατήρησι, f. observation, watchfulness.

παρατιλιάλις, v. τιλιάλις.

παραχώρησι, f. concession.

παργορῶ, v. παρηγορῶ.

πάρδος (Pontus) tom-cat.

παρέκει, adv. farther over, a little farther on ; on the side, out of the way ; π. ἀπό beyond (§ 172).

παρεμπρός, adv. in front, forward, farther.

παρηγοριά consolation.

παρηγορῶ (παρηγόρεσα) console ; mid. to become contented.

παρθένα virgin.

παρθενιά virginity.

παρισιάζω, παρουσιάζω present, show, put forward ; mid. appear, be present.

παρώ, indecl. (v. p. 47 footnote, § 234, 3, n. 2) present.

πᾶσα, πασαένας each, every one, v. § 155, n. 1.

πασᾶς pasha.

παΐκά (Cap.) another.

πασκίζω try, attempt.

πασσάλι pole, peg, wedge.

πάσσο pace, step.

παστρικός clean, neat ; f. § 111.

πασχαλιά Easter.

πασχάλια, pl. Easter-money for the priest.

πασχίζω = πασκίζω.

πατέρας father ; pl. § 73.

πατρίδα fatherland.

πατρικός fatherly, paternal ; neut. father's house or family.

πατρίς (lit.) = πατρίδα.

πατριωτισμός patriotism.

πατσά a blow.

πατῶ to step, tread.

πάτωμα, neut. storey, floor.

πατωσιά (Syra) = id.

παύω cause to cease, stop, cease.

πάχνη hoar-frost, frost.

παχύς (παχειός, cf. § 54 n.) thick, fat.

πγάδ = πηγάδι.

πέ = ἀπό.

πεγάδ(ι) = πηγάδι.

πεζογράφημα, neut. prose.

πεζογράφος prose writer.

πεζός (lit.) on foot ; in prose, prosaic.

πεθαίνω, v. ποθαίνω.

πεθαμμένος dead.

πεθερ(ι)ά mother-in-law.

πεθερός father-in-law.

πείθω persuade, convince.

*πεινῶ (πεινάζω, ἐπείνασα, πείνασμένος) to hunger.

πειότερος, v. πολύς.

πειράζω (ἐπείραξα, ἐπειράχτηκα) torment, tease ; δὲν πειράζει it does not matter.

πέλα(γ)ο sea.

πελιστέρι = περιστέρι.

πέμπω (ἔπεψα, πεμπάτος, v. § 212 n.) send.

πενεντάο (Cap., v. § 141 n.), adv. mutually, promiscuously, against each other.

πενήντα fifty.

πενηντάρα a company of fifty.

πενηντάρικος containing fifty pieces, cf. § 133.

πένητας poor.

πέννα pen.

πεντακόσιοι five hundred.

πεντάρα (πεντάρι) a 5 lepta piece.

πέντε five.

πεντικάρι, πεντικός mouse.

πέρα, adv. beyond, above, over on the other side ; ἐδὼ πέρα here, in this case ; ἀπὸ—καὶ πέρα beyond (§ 172).

περβατῶ = περπατῶ.

περβόλι = περιβόλι.

πέρδικα (περτίκιν, § 26) partridge.

περδικούλα, dim. to id.

περηφάνεια pride, arrogance.
περηφανεύυμαι be proud.
περήφανος proud.
πέρι (*Velv.*)=παρά after compar.
περιβολάρικος cultivated in a garden.
περ(ι)βολάρις gardener.
περιβόλι (περβόλι) garden.
περιγέλασμα, *neut.* laughter.
περιγελῶ laugh at, deride.
περικαλῶ (περκαλῶ) request, ask.
περιλαβαίνω (*v.* λαβαίνω) embrace.
περιμένω expect, wait.
περιοδικό periodical, journal.
περιορίζομαι limit, restrict oneself (to σέ).
περίπατος a walk ; βγαίνω περίπατο go walking.
περιπατῶ go, walk, step.
περιπλανώμενος wandering around.
περισσεύω to have abundance.
περίσσιος, περισσός (περίσσος, περσός) (very) much, enough.
περιστέρα, περιστέρι (πελιστέρι) dove.
περιττοσύλλαβος (*gram. term*) non-parisyllabic.
περιφρόνησι, *f.* contempt.
περιχύνω pour around ; ἱδρὼς μὲ περιχύνεται the perspiration runs off me.
*π ε ρ ν ῶ (ἐπέρασα, περασμένος) go past, go over ; advance, outstrip ; περνᾷ στ᾽ αὐτὶ κανενός it reaches somebody's ear.
περπάτημα, *neut.* step, walk.
περπατησιά walking, gait.
περπατῶ, περβατῶ (-έω) go for a walk, to step, advance.
περσός=περισσός.
πέρυσι, *adv.* of last year.
πεσκέσι (πεστσέσι) gift.
πέσω (*Cap.*) within, inside ; *with* σ(έ) within (of motion).
πεταλούδα butterfly.
πετειοῦμαι, *pres. particip.* πετούμενος πετάμενος) fly, hasten.
πέτρα stone, rock.
πετριά stone's throw, cast.

23

πέτρινος of stone.
πετρότοπος stony ground.
πέτσα rope, halter.
πετσί leather.
πετούμενο (*v. foll. word*) bird.
*π ε τ ῶ (*v.* also πετειοῦμαι, ἐπέταξα -σα, ἐπετάχτηκα) fly, fly up, throw away.
*π έ φ τ ω (ἔπεσα, πεσμένος) fall ; πέφτω τοῦ θανάτου fall dead.
πηγάδι (πεγάδι, §. 6, *n.* 2) fountain, spring.
*π η γ α ί ν ω (πηαίνω, πηαίνω, πηαίννω p. 135, *n.* 2), παγαίνω (*Maina*, παϊζαίνω) πάγω (*v.* § 252, 1), also πάνω (ἐπῆ[γ]α [ἐπάγηισα, πά(γ)ηκα, § 202, I. 6, *n.* 2], θὰ πάγω, *imper.* νὰ πᾶς or ἄμε, § 218, *n.* 3, πηγαιμένος παγωμένος, *pres. part.* πηγαινάμενος) go.
πηγή source, fountain.
πηδῶ to leap.
πήζω (ἔπηξα, πη[γ]μένος) curdle.
πήρπυρο *perpyr* (a coin).
πηττίτσα cake, pastry.
πῆχυ, *f.* (§ 86, *n.* 2) cubit.
πηχῶ (-άω) heap up, wall up.
πιά=πιό.
*π ι ά ν ω (ἔπιασα, ἐπιάστηκα) catch, seize ; overtake ; πιάνομαι be caught, get involved ; πιάνετ᾽ ἡ ἀναπνοή breathing ceases.
πιγωρός strongly developed, powerful.
πιθανός probable.
πιθυμιά desire, appetite.
πιθώνω to place, put down.
πικαρϊμένος (*Syra*) embittered, irritated, annoyed.
πίκρα bitterness, sorrow.
*π ι κ ρ α ί ν ω (ἐπίκρανα, πικραμένος) embitter, cause sorrow ; *mid.* to be sorrowful, vexed.
πικρός bitter.
*π ί ν ω (πίννω, *Cyp.* ; ἤπια, θὰ πιῶ, *imper.* πιέ[s] πιέτε, ἐπιώθηκα) to drink.
πιό, πιά (πλιό πλιά, *v.* § 32; πλέο, § 10, *n.* 1) more, in the formation of

the *compar. v.* § 119 ; *also* already, now.

πιότ(τ)ερα, *adv.* more, rather.

πιπερίζω taste of pepper.

πιπέσ᾽ (*Cap.*) within, inside.

πιρόν(ι) (*Pontus*)=πριόνι.

πιστεύ(γ)ω (*pistéo*, § 23 *n.*) believe.

πίστι(s), *f.* faith.

πιστολιά pistol-shot.

πιστός true, faithful.

πίσω (πίσου), *adv.* behind ; πίσου πίσου (*Lesbos*) in the course of time ; πίσω ᾽s, *prep.* behind, π. ἀπό behind ; *v.* also ὀπίσω.

πιωμένος drunken, from πίνω.

πλάγι side.

πλαγιάζω go to sleep.

πλάθω to fashion, form.

πκῶ, *v.* φτάνω.

πλάκα slab (*e.g.* of a tomb).

πλακώνω strike down, hurl to the ground, strike.

πλάν (*Pontus*), *adv.* away, far behind.

πλανῶ (-άω -έω, ἐπλάνεσα, ἐπλανέθηκα) lead astray, cause to wander ; *mid.* lose one's way.

πλάσι, *f.* creation.

πλάσμα, *neut.* creature.

πλάστης creator, inventor.

πλατάνι (πλατανιά, πλάτανος) plane-tree.

platéguo, *v.* § 23 *n.*

πλατύς (πλατειός, § 110 *n.*) broad, wide.

πλειότερος, *v.* πολύς.

πλέκω (πλέκνω) weave.

πλένω=πλύνω.

πλέο(ν)=πλιό.

πλερώνω (πληρώνω) pay ; *mid.* receive pay.

πλέτιρου, *v.* πολύς.

πλευρό side.

πλέω (πλέγω, ἔπλεξα) swim, travel.

πληγή wound.

πλῆθος, *neut.* multitude, company ; *pl.* the people.

πλήν but.

πληρώνω=πλερώνω.

πλησιάζω approach.

πλιό(ν), πλιά=πιό.

πλοῖο boat.

πλουμίζω adorn.

πλουμιστός adorned.

πλούσιος (πλούσος, § 10, *n.* 4) rich.

πλουταίνω (πλουτυνίσκω, § 199, I. 4, ἐπλούτηνα) grow wealthy.

πλοῦτος, *m.* and *neut.* (*v.* § 100, *n.* 1) wealth, riches.

πλύνω, πλένω, πλυνίσκω, § 199, I. 4 (ἔπλυνα ἔπλυσα, ἐπλύθηκα) wash.

πλώνω=ἁπλώνω.

πνεῦμα, *neut.* spirit.

πνευματικός spiritual ; *m.* father-confessor.

πνέω to blow.

πνίγω (ἐπνίχτηκα ἐπνίγηκα) suffocate, strangle, drown, cause to drown ; *mid.* drown (*intr.*).

πνοή breath, breathing.

πνώνω (*Cap.*) to sleep.

πό=ἀπό.

ποδάρι, πόδι (*róda*, *Ter. d' O.*) foot ; *dim.* ποδαράκι.

ποδιά seam of a garment, apron.

*ποθαίνω, πεθαίνω, ἀποθαίνω, ἀπεθαίνω, ἀποθνήσκω (ἀπόθανα [ἀ]πέθανα ἐπέθανα, πεθαμμένος) die.

πόθος longing, desire.

ποΐδά=ποδιά.

ποίημα, *neut.* poem.

ποίησι, *f.* poetry.

ποιητής poet ; *pl.* § 76.

ποιητικός poetic.

ποῖκα (ἐποῖκα), *v.* φτάνω.

ποιός (ποῖος, πσός, etc. § 10, *n.* 5) who? which? *v.* § 151.

ποιότητα quality.

ποκάμισο shirt.

ποκάτω, *adv.*=ἀποκάτω.

ποκρίνομαι to answer.

πολεμικός warlike.

πολέμιος enemy.

πολεμιστήριον war-song.

πόλεμος war, struggle.

πολεμῶ to fight, struggle ; endeavour.

πολησμονῶ=ἀπολησμονῶ.

πόλι, *f.* city, especially Constantinople.
πολιτεία state, city.
πολίτης citizen.
πολιτισμένος civilised.
πολυθεΐα polytheism.
πολυθόρυβος rioter.
πολύς much, many, *v.* § 112 ; *adv.*
πολύ, πολλά ; *compar.* § 118.
πολυσυνηθίζω to be well accustomed to.
πολύτροπος adroit.
πολυχρονεμένος a person to whom one wishes many years.
'πομένω = ἀπομένω.
πονεμένος feeling pain, vexed.
πονέντες (*Crete*) west.
πονηριά wickedness, baseness.
πονηρός wicked, cunning.
πόνος pain, grief.
ποντίκι mouse.
πονῶ (-έω, ἐπόνεσα, πονεμένος) suffer, feel pain ; have a longing, πονεῖ it pains.
ποπές (*Cap.*), *adv.* within, from within (§ 174).
πόρτα gate.
πορφύρα purple.
πορφυρογέννητος born in purple.
πορῶ, *v.* μπορῶ.
πόσος so great, so much.
ποτάμι river.
ποταμός = *id.*
πότε when ? ὡς π. until when ? how long ? πότε—πότε now—then ; κάποτε καὶ πότε sometimes.
ποτέ(s) at any time, ever ; never (*with neg. v.* § 126).
ποτίζω (*v. double acc.*) make to drink, water.
πότισμα, *neut.* watering.
ποῦ, *adv.* (1) where ? (2) (also ὁποῦ) who, which, *usual relat. particle, v.* § 149 ; (3) (also ὁποῦ or ποῦ νά) that, so that (§§ 267, 279) ; ὡς ποῦ νά until (§ 275), σὰν ποῦ = σάν as, just as (§ 281) ; ποῦ 'ν' of TEXTS I. a. 20 = ποῦ εἶναι (+a redundant εἶναι).

πούβετις, *adv.* anywhere.
πουγγί purse.
ποῦθε(ν), *adv.* whence.
πουθενά, *adv.* anywhere, *with neg.* nowhere.
πουλητής vendor ; *pl.* § 76.
πουλί (πουλλί) bird ; *dim.* πουλάκι.
πουλύ = πολύ.
πουλῶ sell.
πούπετα, πούπετις = πούβετις.
πούπουλου, *neut.* (*Velv.*) populace.
πουρνάρι (πρινάρι) evergreen (holly) oak.
πουρνό in the morning.
ποῦς = πῶς.
πρᾶ(γ)μα, *neut.* thing ; *dim.* πρα(γ)-ματάκι.
πραγματειά, *v.* πραμάτεια.
πραγματικός actual, real.
πράζω (πράσσω, ἔπραξα) do, act.
πραμάτεια, πραγματειά wares ; business ; ἀνοίγω πρ. (*Naxos*) open a business.
πραματεύομαι carry on business with, deal.
πραματευτάδικο business.
πραματευτής business-man, merchant ; *pl.* § 76.
πρᾶξι, *f.* action.
πρασινάδα the green (of meadows, etc.).
πράσινος green.
πρέπει (ἐπρέπισε) it is fitting, necessary, one must.
πρεπός (§ 115) proper, becoming.
πρεπούμενο propriety, decorum (from πρέπει).
πρέσβυς (*lit.*) ambassador.
* π ρ ή σ κ ω, πρήζω (ἔπρηξα, πρησμένος) swell, rise.
πρίγκηπας (*lit.* πρίγκηψ) prince.
πριγκηπόπουλο son of a prince.
πρικός (πρικύς, § 111) bitter.
πρί(ν) before, previously ; πρὶ (νά) before (§ 274).
πρινάρι = πουρνάρι.
πρίντς, *neut.* (*Pontus*) rice.
πριόνι (*Pontus* πιρόν) saw.
πριτά before (§ 274).

πρίτς away, begone !

πριχοῦ νά before (§ 274).

πρόαλλος : τὶς πρόαλλες during the past days, recently.

προβάλλω propose, come forward.

πρόβατο sheep.

προγονή step-daughter.

προδίδω betray.

προεστός (§ 65, n. 1) president.

προζύμι leaven, yeast.

προικίζω furnish with dowry, fit out.

προκομμένος capable, diligent.

προκόφτω come forward, progress.

προμαζώνω : δὲν προμαζώνει τὰ χείλια της (Sar. K.) she does not close her lips.

προξενιά wooing, betrothal (of a fiancée).

προξενῶ (-έω) cause, procure.

προπέρυσι, adv. two years ago.

πρός, prep. at, toward, on, v. § 168, 1.

προσέχω (ἐπρόσεξα) attend ; be on one's guard ; observe, guard against a person (acc.).

πρόσκαιρος lasting for a season, temporary.

προσκαλῶ call, invite.

προσκυνῶ honour ; greet respectfully ; also as a greeting, Your humble servant, I take my leave, offer my respects.

προσμένω await.

προσοχή attention.

προσπάθεια effort.

προσπατῶ go to, meet.

προστάζω (v. τάζω) to order.

πρόστυχος ordinary, common.

προσφέρω offer, present.

πρόσωπο face ; person, pl. § 94.

προτοῦ (νά) before (§ 274) previously.

πρότυπο(ν) model, pattern.

προφέρω utter, give an opinion.

προφητεία prophecy.

προφήτης prophet.

προφτάνω overtake.

προχτές, adv. day before yesterday.

πρωΐ, τὸ early in the morning.

πρῶτα, adv. at the first, early.

πρωτόβγαλτος presented for the first time, débutant.

πρωτομάστορας first or chief architect, contractor.

πρωτόπαπας chief priest ; archpriest (an eccles. dignity).

πρῶτος first, compar. § 117 ; πρῶτο(ν) at first, in first place.

πρωτοφανέρωτος appearing for the first time.

πρωτοχρονιά New Year.

πρωτοχρονιάτικος relating to the New Year.

πσός = ποιός.

πτερούγα = φτερούγα.

πτωχός = φτωχός.

πυργοφύλαχτος protected by a tower, secure.

'πῶ, 'πῇς, etc. from λέγω.

πώγω (Pontus) = πάγω, πηγαίνω.

πωλῶ = πουλῶ.

πωρικό fruit.

πωρνό, v. πουρνό.

πῶς, adv. (1) how ? (2) that (§ 267) ; εἰδεμὴ πῶς else.

Ρ

Ράβ(γ)ω = ράφτω.

ραβδί stick, staff.

ραγίζω, ραγίζομαι break (intr.).

ραζακί species of white grape.

ρακί, brandy, gin.

ράπυ, f. (§ 86, n. 2) rape, turnip.

ράτσα race, splendid family ; metaph. personal prowess, strength.

ράφτης tailor ; pl. § 76.

ράφτρ(ι)α tailoress.

ράφτω (ράβ[γ]ω) sew.

ραχάτ = ρεχάτι.

ράχι, f. ridge (of a mountain).

ραχούλα (small) ridge of a mountain, hillock.

ράψιμο (§ 104) sewing.

ρεῖτενίζομαι (Maina) get into difficulty.

ρέμα (ρεῦμα), neut. river, stream.

ρεματιά brook.

ρετσίνη resin.

ρεῦμα, v. ρέμα.

ρεχάτι (ραχάτ) rest, stillness; ραχάτ ραχάτ very tranquil.
ρέω flow, cf. also § 252, 3, n. 1.
ρήγας king.
ρημάζω render lonely (ρημαγμένος isolated).
ρημιά (ἐρημιά) desert.
ριβάρω (ἀρριβάρω) arrive (Syra).
ρίζα root, foot of a mountain.
ριζί=id.
ριζικό destiny.
ριζοβολῶ take root.
ρίφτω, ρίχνω, ρίχτω (ριμμένος ριχμένος) throw, cast away; ρ. τουφέκι discharge, fire a gun.
ροβολῶ descend.
ροδάκινο peach.
ρόδινος rosy.
ροδίτης species of grape (rose-coloured).
ρόδο rose.
ρολό(γ)ι watch, clock.
ρούγα strect.
ρουζέτα rosette, ornament; metaph. jewel, treasure.
ρουμάνι (ὀρμάνι) forest.
ρουσί or ρουχί (Cap.) mountain.
ρουτίνα routine.
ροῦχο, usually pl. clothes.
ρο(υ)φῶ (ἐρούφηξα, § 201, II. c. n.) sip, suck up.
ρύζι rice.
ρυθμίζω throw into rhythm, arrange, harmonise.
ρυθμός rhythm.
ρύνω pour in.
ρυπαρός dirty.
ρωμαίικος mod. Greek, " Romaic."
ρωμιοσύνη peculiarity of the Ρωμιός (the popular designation of the Greeks); (modern) Greekdom.
ρωτῶ=ἐρωτῶ, ἀρωτῶ.

Σ' (σέ)=εἰς.
σά=σάν.
σάαπις, v. σάπις.
σάβανο pall, shroud.
σαβανωμένος wrapped in a winding sheet.

σαγίτα, σαῖτα (σαῖτθα, § 35, n. 3) arrow; σαΐτίτσα, dim.
σαγιτεύω shoot, hit with an arrow.
σαϊτανᾶς Satan.
σακκί bag, sack; σακκούλι, σακουλά(κ)ι, dim.
σαλεύω move, stir.
σαλιβάρι bridle.
σάλι(o) saliva.
σαλμᾶς kind of musket with a short barrel.
σαμάρι pack saddle.
σάμο (Cap.) conj. then, when, after.
σάν (ὡσάν), σά as, just like; if, whereas, as soon as (§ 272); σὰν νά like, as, just as, σὰν ποῦ according as (§ 281).
σαπίζω (ἐσάπισα ἐσαπήθηκα) rot, decay.
σάπις (σάαπις) lord, owner.
σαπούνι soap.
σαράγι castle, palace.
σάρακας (wood-)worm.
σαρακώνω corrode, gnaw.
σαράντα forty.
σαρπάρω τὴν ἄγκουρα weigh anchor.
σάτο a corn measure.
σαχάτι hour.
*σβήνω, σβῶ (ἔσβησα, ἐσβήστηκα, σβη[σ]μένος) extinguish, exterminate; also intr. be extinguished, die away.
σβηστός extinguished.
σγουρά, pl. ringlets.
σγουρομάλλης (§ 113) with ringlets of hair.
σγουροτρίβομαι grate, rub on (a person).
σέ (σέ)=εἰς.
σεβαίνω (εἰσέβηκα) go in, enter; cf. ἀνεβαίνω.
σέβας (§ 105 n.), neut. reverence.
σεβγίλι (Pontus) darling.
σεβντᾶς love.
σέδια sedan-chair.
σείρ (Pontus), neut. condition.
σειρά row, order.
σειραλαεύκουμαι to be arranged in a row.

σείω (σείζω) shake.

σελήνη (*lit.*) moon.

σέλλα saddle.

σεμνός venerable.

σεντόνι linen (towel).

σεντού(κ)ι(ν) chest, box.

σερβίρω (ἐσερβίρισα, σερβιρισμένος) serve, wait upon (*w. acc.*).

σεργιανίζω go for a walk.

σερνικός male.

*σ έ ρ ν ω (*sérro* in Bova, ἔσυρα, ἐσύρθηκα) drag, draw out, tow ; also *intr.* go, depart ; σύρε on ! ahead !

σέτερος your, *v.* § 143, *n.* 3.

σεφέρι war.

σήκω (σήκου) arise, get up ; *v.* § 222, *n.* 3.

σηκώνω (σκών[ν]ω) lift, elevate ; *mid.* rise, stand up.

σημαδεύω denote.

σημαία banner.

σημαίνω denote ; σ. τὴν καμπάνα ring the bell.

σημαντικός designating, significant.

σήμαντρο a kind of bell.

σημειώνω observe, note, denote, announce.

σήμερα, *adv.* to-day.

σημερ(ι)νός, of to-day.

σιάζώ (σιάνω) arrange ; *mid.* prepare, direct.

σιγά, *adv.* gently ; σιγὰ σιγά slowly, gradually.

σιγαλά, *adv.* gently.

σίδερο iron.

σιμά 's, *prep.* near to, at (§ 171) ; σιμὰ νά about to, on the point of (§ 273).

σιμώνω (συμώνω) approach.

σινάπι, *f.* mustard.

σίντα (Texts I. a. 24. 45) if, when.

σιόρ(ι) (*indecl.*, § 74, *n.* 2) Mr., sir.

σιργιάνι a walk.

σιτᾶ (*Pontus*) while, during, when.

σιτάρι (στάρι) wheat.

σιχαίνομαι (ἐσιχάθηκα) feel an aversion for.

σιχασιάρις fastidious, having an aversion for.

σιωπηλός taciturn.

σκάβω = σκάφτω.

σκάζω (σκῶ, ἔσκασα) burst asunder.

σκάλα stairs, ladder.

σκαλίζω chisel, carve (in stone).

σκαλώνω (*Pontus*) set about, begin to.

σκαμνί stool, bench.

σκαμπαβία a kind of boat.

σκανταλίζομαι to be alarmed.

σκαρί keel, boat.

σκάφτω (σκάβ[γ]ω, σκάφω) excavate, dig out.

σκεδιάζω take the measure of, survey.

σκέδιο, *neut.* (σκέδιος, *neut. v.* § 100, *n.* 1), measure, measuring.

σκέλος, *neut.* thigh, limb ; *pl.* § 100.

σκεπάζω (στσεπάζω) to cover.

σκέπασμα, *neut.* cover(ing).

σκέπη (σκεπή) cover, lid.

σκέφτομαι (ἐσκέφτηκα) consider, reflect upon.

σκέψι, *f.* reflection.

σκηνή stage, scene.

σκιάζομαι (ἐσκιάστηκα ἐσκιάχτηκα) be afraid of.

σκίζω (σκίζνω *Pontus*, στσίζω) split.

σκίσμα (σκίσμαν), *neut.* fissure, crevice.

σκλαβιά slavery.

σκλάβος slave.

σκληρός hard.

σκοδραλλούι (*Chios*) a kind of bird, lark (?).

σκοινί (σχοινί) rope, cable.

σκολειό school.

σκόλη holiday.

σκολνῶ (σκολῶ, ἐσκόλασα) cease, rest.

σκοντάφτω (σκοντάφνω) stumble.

σκοπός aim, goal.

σκορπίζω strew, scatter ; also *intr.* spread.

σκόρφα (σκρόφα) sow.

σκοτάδι darkness, obscurity.

σκοτεινία darkness.

σκοτεινιασμένος darkened, obscured.

σκοτεινός dark.

σκότος, *neut.* darkness.
σκοτούρα torment.
σκοτώνω slay.
σκούζω (ἔσκουξα) cry, lament.
σκουλήκι worm.
σκουντάφτω stumble.
σκουντῶ (ἐσκούντηξα) knock against.
σκούπρα, *pl.* sweepings, dust.
σκουριάζω rust ; be stupefied.
σκύβω=σκύφτω.
σκνθρωπός gloomy, peevish, angry.
σκύλα bitch.
σκυλί dog.
σκύλος (ὀτσούλος, § 6, *n.* 4 ; § 17 ; ὄύλος, § 28 *n.*)=*id.*
σκυφτός bent, stooping.
σκύφτω, σκύβω (στσύβγω ὀτσούβω, § 6, *n.* 4, and § 17) bend, bow.
σκῶ=σκάζω.
σκωλήκι=σκουλήκι.
σκών(ν)ω=σηκώνω.
σμίγω associate, unite with.
σοβαρός serious.
σοκάκι (σοκάτσι) lane.
σολδί soldo, sou.
σουβλί roasting-spit ; stake ; βάζω στὸ σ. impale, crucify (as capital punishment).
σουβλίζω impale.
σοῦκο=σῦκο.
σουμά : σὰ σουμά (*Pontus*) these days, recently.
σουπιά sepia, cuttle-fish.
σουσάμι (§ 6) sesame.
σοφολογιώτατος the man of great wisdom (*ironical*).
σοφός wise.
σπάζω=σφάζω.
σπαθί sword ; πῆγε ἀπὸ κακὸ σπ. στὸ σεφέρι he went in an evil hour to the war ; σπαθάκι, *dim.*
σπάραζω jerk, wriggle.
σπάρτης sower.
σπέρα evening.
*σπέρνω (σπείρω, ἔσπειρα [σ'πέρς, § 7, *n.* 2], ἐσπάρθηκα) sow.
σπετσαρία apothecary shop.
σπηλιά, σπήλιο (σπελὄν, *Pontus*, § 6, *n.* 6) cavern.

σπίθα spark.
σπίτι(ν) (σ'πίτ', § 7, *n.* 2 ; ὀσπίτι) house.
σπιτικό family, household.
σπιτοπαράθυρο window of a house.
σπλάχνα, *pl.* bowels.
σπλαχνίζομαι to pity (*acc.*).
σπλαχνικός merciful.
σπόρος seed.
σπουδάζω (ἐσπούδαξα -σα) study.
σπουδαῖος (*lit.*) eager, serious.
σπρώχνω push, jostle.
σπυρί small grain (pimple).
στάζω (ἔσταξα) to drop.
σταθερός fixed, firm, unalterable.
σταίνω=στήνω.
σταλαματιά drop.
σταματῶ remain standing, stop, hinder.
στάμνα pitcher ; σταμνάκι, *dim.*
σταμνί pitcher.
στανικῶς, *adv.* by violence, unwillingly.
στάρι=σιτάρι.
στάσου (North. Gk. στάσ) stop ! (from στέκω).
σταυροπόδης (§ 114) with legs crossed.
σταυρός cross ; κάνω τὸ σταυρό μου cross myself.
σταυροφορία crusade.
σταυροφόρος crusader.
σταυρώνω cross(the hands in prayer).
σταφίδα raisin.
στάφνη rule, guide.
στάφυλι grape, cluster.
στάχτη ashes.
στάχυ (ἀστάχυ), *neut.* ear (of plant).
στεῖρα barren (of females).
* στέκω, στέκομαι (*imper.* στέκα στεκᾶτε, ἐστάθηκα, *pres. part.* τὰ στεκάμενα the things that stay, goods) stand. This verb also serves for the defective forms of εἶμαι, *v.* § 224, 2.
στελέττο dagger, stiletto.
*στέλνω, στέλλω (στέρνω, § 31 ; στείλω, § 204 ; ἔστειλα, ἐστάλθηκα) send.
στενάζω (ἐστέναξα ἐστένασα) to sigh.

στενός narrow ; τὰ στενά narrow pass, defile.

στενοχώρια perplexity, difficulty.

στενοχωρειέμαι be in perplexity.

στένω = στήνω.

στερεύω rob, deprive.

στερνός later, latter.

στέρο (Cap.), adv. after, thereupon.

στεφάνι, στέφανο(s) garland.

στεφανώνω crown with garlands ; to garland a pair of lovers, i.e. betroth ; pass. (w. acc.) also wed (Aegina).

στήθι, στῆθος, neut. (v. § 100) breast (also pl.), dim. στηθάκι.

* στήνω, στένω (Zac. thénu, § 35, n. 3, ἔστησα ἔστεσα, ἐστήθηκα, στημένος στεμένος) set up, erect ; στένω πόλεμο carry on war.

στι(γ)μή moment.

στιχηρός in verses.

στιχοπλέχτης versifier.

στίχος verse.

στοιχειό spirit, ghost.

στοιχειώνω make a ghost of, become a spirit.

στολίδι ornament.

στολίζω adorn.

στόμα, neut. mouth.

στομάχι stomach.

στουππί oakum.

στοχάζομαι think of, meditate.

στοχαστικός meditative.

στραβοπάτημα, neut. false step.

στραβοπατῶ make a false step.

στραβός steep ; crooked, false.

στράτα street, way, journey.

στράτεμα, neut. army.

στρατιώτης (στραθιώτης, § 16, n. 2) soldier.

* στρέφω (ἐστράφηκα) turn ; turn back.

στρίγγεμα (Cap.), neut. noise.

στρίγλα (στρίγλα) witch.

στρίφω twist.

στρῶμα, neut. couch, bed, covering.

στρώνω spread ; make a bed.

στύλος pillar.

σύ = ἐσύ.

σύβασι (§ 33, n. 3) agreement, compact.

συγγενεύω be related.

συγγενής (§ 115) related.

συγγραφέας writer, author.

συγκινῶ move (metaph.).

σύγνεφο, v. σύννεφο.

συγυρίζω arrange ; mid. prepare, begin.

σύγχρονος contemporary.

συγχωρητός pardonable, to be forgiven (eccl.).

συ(γ)χωρῶ (συχώρεσα, συχωρέθηκα) forgive, pardon ; ὁ συχωρεμένος "one whom may God forgive," i.e., dead, late, συχωρέθηκε also = ἀπέθανε (Velv.).

συδέω (§ 33, n. 3) bind together.

συδζενής = συγγενής.

σῦκο (σοῦκο, § 6, n. 4) fig.

συκώτι liver.

συλλο(γ)ή consideration, reflection.

συλλογίζομαι, συλλογοῦμαι think, meditate, consider.

συλλογισμός reasoning, consideration.

συλλογοῦμαι (-ειέμαι) = συλλογίζομαι

συμβαίνει, συνέβη(κε) it is fitting, proper (v. § 207 n.).

συμβιβασμός (lit.) agreement, compromise.

συμβιβαστικός conciliatory, mediating.

συμβούλιο (lit.) counsel.

σύμβουλος (lit.) counsellor.

συμπληρώνω complete, fulfil.

συμπολίτης fellow-citizen.

συμπονῶ (-έω, συμπόνεσα, συμπονέθηκα) to pity.

σύμφωνος (lit.) according with, harmonising ; σύμφωνο μέ in agreement with, according to.

συμώνω, v. σιμώνω.

συνάγω, συνάζω (ἐσύναξα) collect.

συνδρομή (lit.) co-operation.

συνείδησι, f. conscience.

συνεπνίγω suffocate, choke.

συννεφιάζω to cloud.

σύννεφο (σύγνεφο) cloud.

σύνορα, *pl.* boundaries.

συντάχτης redactor, editor.

συντετά, *adv.* together, in common.

συντρίβω break to pieces, lay in ruins.

συντρίμμια, *pl.* ruins.

συντροφιά escort, company.

σύντροφος companion.

συρτάρι drawer.

συφορά (*lit.* συμφορά) misfortune, accident.

συφωνῶ agree, unite.

συχνά, *adv.* frequently.

συχωρῶ, *v.* συγχωρῶ.

σφαγή slaughter, massacre.

σφάζω (σπάζω, § 18, *n.* 4 ; ἔσφαξα, ἐσφάγηκα ἐσφάχτηκα) to slaughter.

σφαλίζω, σφαλνῶ (ἀσπαλίζω, § 18, *n.* 4 ; ἐσφάλιξα or -σα, ἐσφαλίστηκα ἐσφαλίχτηκα) close, lock.

σφαλιχτός shut, locked.

σφάλλω (ἤσφαλα) be deceived, err.

* σ φ α λ ν ῶ, *v.* σφαλίζω.

σφῆκα (§ 84) wasp.

σφίγγω (σπίγγω, ἔσφιξα) press, tie together, squeeze.

σφιχτός fixed.

σφουγγάρι sponge.

σφουγγίζω (ἐσφούγγιξα -σα) dry off, sponge.

σφυρίζω (ἐσφύριξα) whistle, hiss.

σχεδόν, *adv.* almost

σχέσι, *f.* relation, respect.

σχῆμα, *neut.* shape.

σχίζω, *v.* σκίζω.

σχοινί, *v.* σκοινί.

σχολαστικός pedant, pedantic.

σῶμα, *neut.* body.

σώνω (σώζω, *cf.* § 224, 3, *n.* 3) save ; complete, finish, attain ; suffice.

σώπα (§ 10, *n.* 4) hush ! be still !

σωπάζω, σωπαίνω (ἐσώπασα) to be silent.

σωριάζω heap up ; bury.

σωρός mound (tomb) ; heap, μὲ τὸ σ. in heaps.

σώς (*Cap.*), *prep.* until.

σωστός correct, right ; μὲ τὰ σωστά (μου) rightly (*adv.*).

σωτηρία deliverance.

σωτικά (σω[τ]θικά, *according to* § 36 *n.*), *pl.* intestines.

Ταγάρι travelling-bag.

τα(γ)ίζω nourish.

τάδες, *v.* δεῖνα.

τάζω (τάσσω, ἔταξα) promise, vow.

ταίρι pair, mate.

ταιριάζω unite, pair ; apply ; *mid.* fit, match.

ταμπακίζω smoke tobacco, *or* snuff.

ταμπούρι dike, embankment.

ταμπουρώνομαι fortify one's position, entrench.

ταξείδι journey.

τάξιμο (§ 104) a vow, promise ; command.

ταπεινός humble.

ταπεινοσύνη humility.

ταράζω (ταράσσω) perplex.

τάρνα (*Cap.*), *adv.* quickly.

τάρταρα, *pl.* Tartarus, lower world.

τάσι cup, dish.

τάφος tomb.

τάχα, *adv.* perhaps, perchance ; τάχα νά seemingly as if, forsooth to.

τάχατις, *adv.* perhaps.

ταχειά (*Velv.*) to-morrow.

ταχτικός regular.

ταχυτερνή (*Naxos*) morning.

ταχυτέρου, *adv.* (*Naxos*) later ; *v.* § 123, *n.* 2.

τεῖχος, *neut.* wall.

τέκνω = θέτω.

τέλεια, *adv.* completely.

τελειώνω finish.

τελευταῖος (*lit.*) last.

τέλος, *neut.* end ; τέλος πάντων (πάντα) finally, lastly.

τεμπέλης lazy.

τενεκές tin.

τενεκετζῆς tinsmith.

τέρατο, *neut.* (§ 105, *n.* 1) miracle.

τερῶ (*Pontus*) = τηρῶ.

τεσόν thine, *v.* § 143, *n.* 3.

τέσσερις (§ 128) four.

τέταρτος fourth ; *neut.* a fourth, quarter.

τέτοιος such, v. § 148.

τετράγωνο square.

τετράδη Wednesday.

τετρακόσισοι four hundred.

τετράστιχο strophe (verse of four lines).

τέχνη art.

τεχνικός artistic, ingenious, technical.

τεχνίτης artist.

τζαί=καί.

τζαμί (ντζαμί) mosque.

τζύριγμα, neut. whistling, hissing.

τηγάνι frying-pan.

τηρῶ (τερῶ, Pontus) watch.

τί (1) what? which? (2) why? wherefore? (3) for (§ 258). τί always retains its acute accent. (4) also a form of the article, v. § 55, n. 3.

τιβίχ, neut. order, κάνω τ. (Lesbos) to order.

τιδέν (Pontus)=τίποτα.

τιζκιάχ' (Pontus) frame on which are laid large logs of wood to split.

τιλιάλις (τιλιάλτς, Velv.) herald, auctioneer; τιλιάλιδις παρατιλιάλιδις auctioneer above auctioneer.

τιλιαλῶ (Velv.) cry out, proclaim.

τιμή (1) honour; (2) price, value.

τίμιος honest, honourable.

τιμῶ to honour.

τιμωρῶ punish, chastise.

τινάζω (τινάγω) shake.

τινάς anybody, v. § 153, n. 3.

τίποτα(s), τίποτε(s), τίποτις, τίβοτσι anything; w. neg. nothing, v. § 153.

τιποτένιος null, of no value.

τίποτες, τίποτις=τίποτε.

τίς who? v. § 152 and τί.

τίτλος title.

τοιμάζομαι get ready, prepare.

τοῖχος wall.

τόκος interest; βάλλω στὸν τόκον put out to interest.

τόλμη daring, enterprise.

τολμηρός daring bold.

τολμῶ venture, dare.

τόμτι, temporal particle (Sar. K.) when.

τόντις, adv. really, truly.

τονώνω strengthen (of medicine).

τόπος locality, home, region, land; position; place.

τός (§ 136 f.) he.

τόσοιος (Pontus)=ποιός.

τόσος so great, so small, so much; ἄλλος τόσος as much again; τόσο so very; ὡς τόσο yet, nevertheless, meanwhile; v. also ὅσος.

τότε(s) (τόα v. § 22 n.), adv. then, at that time; ἀπὸ τότε since then.

τοῦ (Cap.)=ποῦ (Rel.).

τουζάη, neut. (Pontus) craft, cunning.

τουλάχιστο, adv. at least.

τούλγος (§ 152, n. 3) what kind of.

τουλούπα clew, coil.

τούμπανο timbal.

túndo, v. τοῦτος.

τοῦνος, v. αὐτός.

τοῦος (Chios)=τοῦτος.

τουρκεύω turn Turk.

túrtea (Otr.) here, hither.

τουσάκ, τουσάη (Pontus), neut. snare.

τοῦτος (§ 145) this.

τουφέκι musket, gun.

τραβησιά blow, stroke.

*τραβῶ (also written τραυῶ, ἐτράβηξα, ἐτραβήχτηκα) draw, drag; lift to strike; intr. (also mid.) retire, depart, go.

τραγανός gristly.

τραγούδι song; dim. τραγουδάκι.

τραγουδιστής singer, poet.

τραγουδῶ sing.

τράκα τράκα tramp, tramp (onomatopoeic word).

τρακόσιοι=τριακόσιοι.

τραναίνω (ἐτράνηνα) become great, grow up.

τρανός clear; great; compar. § 117.

τρανταφύλλι rose.

τρανταφυλλιά rose-tree.

τραντάφυλλο rose.

τρανῶ (Pontus) see.

τράπεζα altar-table.

τραπέζι table.

τράτα net.

τρανῶ, v. τραβῶ.

τράφος (§ 68, n. 2) tomb.

τραχύς rough.

τρεῖς, τρία (τριά τρικά, § 10, n. 5) three.

τρέλλα madness.

τρελλαίνω (ἐτρέλλανα, ἐτρελλάθηκα) be crazy.

τρελλός crazed ; τρελλούτσικος somewhat crazy (a little off).

τρέμω (without aor.) tremble.

τρέξιμο (§ 104) running, race.

*τρέχω (τρέχνω, pres. part. τρεχούμενος τρεχάμενος, imper. τρέχα τρεχᾶτε, perf. part. τρεχάτος) run, flow (w. acc.) ; τὰ τρεχούμενα course, current events.

τριάδα trinity, v. § 133, n. 2.

τριακόσιοι (τρακόσιοι) three hundred.

τριάντα thirty.

τριανταριά company (number) of thirty.

τριαντάρις thirty years of age.

τριανταφύλλι ⎫
τριανταφυλλιά ⎬ v. τριαντα
τριαντάφυλλο ⎭ φυλλο

τρίβ(γ)ω (ἐτρίβηκα, ἐτρίφτηκα) rub, grind.

τρίβων(as)=a. Gk. τρίβων shabby mantle, philosopher's garb.

τριγυρίζω surround.

τριγύρω, τριγύρου, adv. all around ; τ. 's, prep. (§ 171) around, round about.

τριλογία trilogy.

τρίσβαθος thrice deep, very deep.

τρισχαριτωμένος exceedingly graceful.

τρίτος third, neut. a third ; τρίτη Tuesday.

τρομάζω (ἐτρόμαξα) fear, be afraid.

τρομάρα fear, consternation.

τρομαρισμένος, τρομασμένος astounded, frightened

τρόπος manner ; μὲ κανέναν τρόπο in every way, by all means.

τρυγητής reaper ; name applied by

the ordinary folk to the month of September.

τρύπα, τρυπί hole.

τρύπιος bored, punctured.

τρυπῶ perforate, pierce.

τρυπών(ν)ω penetrate into, insert.

τρυφερός tender.

*τρώ(γ)ω (v. § 252, 2, ἔφαγα, ἐφαγώθηκα, φαγωμένος) eat ; gnaw.

τσ, v. also under κ.

τσ (τσῆ, etc.) from the article or conj. pron. (§§ 55, 136, 142).

τσαβούνα flute.

τσαί=καί.

τσάι tea.

τσακίζω break (in pieces).

τσακώνω (Velv.) seize, grasp.

τσαμί=τζαμί.

τσάν=κιάν.

τσ'αναβάρ, neut. (Pontus) animal.

τσεκουριά blow with an axe.

τσερνῶ, v. κερνῶ.

τσηγαρίζω roast ; torment.

τσίγκι, τσούγκι (Pontus) for, because.

τσιμπίδα spark.

τσιμπλιάρις deep-eyed.

τσιμπῶ prick, bite, pinch.

τσιούπρα (Epirus) maiden.

τσίπ (Pontus), adv. very.

τσιριμόνιες, pl. ceremonies ; κάνω τσ. be very formal, make much ado.

τσιροφλίζω burn up.

τσίχ, interj. (Naxos) not at all, not the slightest.

τσ'οάπ (Cap.), neut. answer.

τσοπάνης (dζουβάν's) shepherd.

τσούγκι, v. τσίγκι.

τσωπάζω be silent.

τνατέρα=θυγατέρα.

τυλίγω envelope.

τύπος type, form of language.

τύπωμα, neut. printing.

τυπώνω print.

τυράννια torment, sorrow.

τυραννικός tyrannical.

τύραννος tyrant.

τυρί cheese.

τυφλός blind; ἔτσι στὰ τυφλά blindly, at random.

*τυχαίνω (ἔτυχα) happen, be accidental; μὴν τύχῃ καί, v. § 280, n. 2.

τύχη luck.

τυχόν(ε), adv. perhaps.

τῷόντι (lit.) in reality, really.

τώρα, adv. now.

Ὑβρίζω=βρίζω.

ὑγειά health; also as a greeting like γειά.

ὑγρός damp, moist.

υἱός=γιός.

ὕμνος hymn.

ὑναῖκα=γυναῖκα.

ὕπαρξι, f. existence.

ὑπάρχω be present, exist.

ὑπερσυντελικός (gram. term) pluperfect.

ὑπηρετῶ (-έω) serve, wait on.

ὑπναροῦ, f. the sleeper, sleepy-head.

ὕπνος (νύπνος, § 34, n. 3) sleep; soporific.

ὑποκάτω ἀπό, v. ἀποκάτω.

ὑπομονή patience.

ὑπόσκομαι (ὑπόσχομαι, ὑποσχέθηκα) to promise.

ὑρίζω=γυρίζω.

ὕστερα, adv. afterward, then; ὕ. ἀπό, prep. after (§ 172).

ὕστερι(s)=id.

ὑστερνός last, additional.

ὕστερος last.

ὑστερῶ deprive.

ὑστερώτερα, adv. afterwards, later.

ὑψηλός high.

ὑψωμός exaltation, elevation.

ὑψώνω elevate, erect.

Φαγᾶς eater, gourmand.

φαγί eating, repasu.

φαγοῦ, f. from φαγᾶς.

(θὰ) φά(γ)ω (§ 252, 1), v. τρώγω.

φαητό food, repast.

φαίνομαι (ἐφάνηκα, imper. φανοῦ φάνου) appear, manifest oneself, make appearance.

φαινόμενο appearance, phenomenon.

φακῆ (φατσῆ) lentil.

φακιόλι turban.

φαμιλικός pertaining to a family; φαμιλικὸν ὄνομα family name.

φανερός manifest, apparent; φῶς φανερά, adv. clear as the sun.

φανερώνω (φανερώννω, § 199, i. 6, n. 2) reveal; mid. appear; give to know.

φανός lighthouse, lamp, light.

φαντάζομαι (φαντάζω) imagine, fancy.

φαντασία imagination, fancy.

φάντασμα, neut. ghost.

φαρδύς wide, broad.

φαρμακερός poisonous.

φαρμάκι poison.

φάρμακο medicine, drug.

φαρμακωμένος poisoned, unwholesome.

φαρμακώνω to poison.

φεγγάρι (φεγάρι, Ios) moon; dim. φεγγαράκι.

φεγγοβολή giving light (gerund).

φεγγοβολῶ give light.

φεγγοῦσκος moon.

φέγγω (ἔφεξα) shine, be bright.

φελῶ (-έω, φέλεσα) assist, be useful.

*φέρνω, φέρω (ἔφερα [ἐσέγκα ἐξέγκα, § 203, 5, n.] ἐφέρθηκα) bring, carry; mid. conduct oneself.

φέρσιμο (§ 104), neut. conduct.

φέσι fez.

φέτο(ς)=ἐφέτος.

*φεύγω (φεύω, φύγνω, imper. φεύγα[s] φευγᾶ[σ]τε, ἔφυ[γ]α, perf. part. φευγάτος) flee; depart.

φήμη glory.

φθάνω, v. φτάνω.

φιδές (§ 77) kind of vermicelli.

φίδι snake.

φιλάργυρος avaricious.

φιλενέω receive friendly, entertain, wait on.

φίλημα, neut. kiss.

φιλί kiss.

φιλία friendship.

φιλοδοξῶ love glory, be ambitious.

φιλολογία literature.

φιλολογικός literary ; τὰ φιλολογικά literature.

φιλονεικία quarrelsomeness, ambition.

φιλοπατρία love of native land.

φίλος dear ; m. friend.

φιλοσοφία philosophy.

φιλόσοφος philosopher.

φιλῶ (-έω) to kiss.

φκαριστημένος = εὐχαριστημένος.

φκαριστῶ = εὐκαριστῶ.

*φκειάνω, φτειάνω (ἔφκειασα, ἐφκειάστηκα) make.

φκυάρι shovel.

φλέβα vein.

φλεβάρις February.

φλόγα flame.

φλογέρα shepherd's flute.

φλογερός flaming, glowing.

φλουρένιος consisting of (gold) ducats.

φλουρί, φλωρί florin.

φλυαρία gossip.

φοβέρα threat.

φοβερίζω frighten.

φοβερός terrible, fearful.

φοβοῦμαι (φοοῦμαι, § 22 n.) fear, be afraid.

φονιάς (φονές, § 71, n. 3) murderer.

φονικό murder.

φοντές (Cap.) then, when (temporal).

φοορίζω (Pontus) = φοβερίζω terrify.

φορά (φουρά) time, Fr. fois ; καμιὰ φ. sometimes ; πολλὲς φορές frequently ; στὴ(ν) φορά at once.

φορέζω put on, wear (a garment).

φόρεμα, neut. clothing, garment.

φορεσιά = id.

φορτώνω to burden, load ; mid. take on a burden, carry a load (w. acc.).

*φορῶ (-έω, ἐφόρεσα, ἐφορέθηκα) carry, yield ; wear a garment, (aor.) put on.

φουκαριστῶ = εὐκαριστῶ.

φουμίζω make celebrated.

φουντωτός luxuriant, bushy.

φουρκίζω hang, kill.

φούχτα fist ; also what would fill the hand, a handful ; μὲ τὲς φούχτες with full hands.

φουχτιά handful.

φράγκικος Frank, European.

φράζω (ἔφραξα) enclose.

φρένιμος = φρόνιμος.

φρόνησι, f. reason, cleverness.

φρόνιμος reasonable, sensible.

φροντίδα care.

φροντίζω care (for one γιά).

φροντιστικός full of care.

φρύδι eyebrow.

φταίξιμο (§ 104) guilt, fault.

φταί(γ)ω (cf. § 251, 2, φταίχω ἔφταιξα) to be at fault.

*φτάνω (ἔφτασα and ἔφταξα, φτασμένος) arrive, reach ; comprehend (TEXTS II. a. 22) ; φτάνει it is enough.

φταρμίζομαι sneeze.

φτάω, ἐποίκα, θὰ πκῶ (Pontus) make, do (§ 202, n. 2, and § 214, n. 5).

φτειάνω, v. φκειάνω.

φτέρα, φτέρη fern.

φτερό wing ; κάνω φτερά flee away from, make off.

φτερούγα wing.

φτερωτός winged.

'φτί = αὐτί.

φτονῶ to envy.

φτύνω (φτῶ) expectorate.

φτωχαίνω (ἐφτώχηνα) be poor.

φτώχεια poverty.

φτωχικός poor, miserable.

φτωχός poor.

φτωχούλις (§ 113, n. 2) miserable, poor.

φυγή flight.

φυλά(γ)ω watch, guard against, observe, lie in wait for ; mid. be on guard against.

φύλακας (§ 65) watchman.

φυλακή prison, imprisonment.

φυλαχτό amulet, protection.

φυλή race, tribe.

φυλλανθῶ put forth foliage, bloom.

φύλλο leaf.

φυλλοκάρδι valve of the heart.

φυρνῶ, φυρῶ (ἐφύρασα) decrease (tr. and intr.) ; lose.

φυσικός natural.

φυσιοκρατικός physiocratic.
φύσι(ς), f. nature.
φυσῶ (ἐφύσηξα) to blow.
φυτεύω to plant.
φυτό plant.
φυτρώνω grow.
φωλιά nest.
φωλιάζω have a nest, dwell.
φωνάζω (ἐφώναξι) call, call to, shout.
φωνή voice, cry ; pl. screaming.
φῶς, neut. light.
φωστήρας light, light of eyes, eye.
φωτεινός clear, bright.
φωτερός shining.
φωτιά light, fire.

Χά (Pontus) = θά.
χα(δ)εμένος, v. χαϊδεύω.
χαζουρλαεύκουμαι (Pontus) prepare, begin.
χαϊβάν(ι) (Pontus), neut. animal.
χαϊδεύω, χαδεύω caress.
χαιρέτισμα, neut. greeting, salutation.
χαιρετῶ, χαιρετίζω to salute, greet.
χαίρομαι, χαίρω (ἐχάρηκα, imper. χαροῦ χάρου) rejoice.
χαλάζι hail ; κάνει, πέφτει χ. it hails.
χαλαρός loose ; unrestricted.
χαλασεύω (Pontus) beg pardon.
χαλεύω demand ; desire.
χαλίτσι (Maina) pebble, stone.
χαλκῆ brass gate.
χαλκιάς smith.
χάλκωμα, neut. brass, metal ; bronze vessel.
*χαλνῶ, χαλῶ (ἐχάλασα, ἐχαλάστηκα) destroy, exterminate, perish.
χάμαι (χαμαί) = χάμω.
χαμάλης (§ 74) porter.
χαμηλολογιάζω meditate, reflect with bowed head.
χαμηλός humble, downcast (of eyes).
χαμηλώνω cause to sink, cast down (the eyes) ; (intr.) sink.
χαμόγελο laughter.
χαμογελῶ laugh.
χαμός destruction, loss.
χάμω (χάμου, χάμαι) adv. upon the ground, Lat. humi.

χάνι(ν) inn, khan.
χάνω (χάννω, § 199, I. 6, n. 2, ἔχασα, ἐχάθηκα, Pontus ἐχάτα) lose ; destroy, annihilate, defeat (enemy) ; mid. perish, be undone ; also to be bent upon, very eager for (Velv.) ; νὰ χαθῇς ἀπ' ἐδώ go and be hanged !
χαρά joy ; festival, wedding ; χαρά σας joy be with you.
χαραυγή dawn.
χάρι, f. grace (also personified—the ancient Graces) ; kindness, gratitude ; χάριτι θείᾳ (lit.) thank God ! by God's grace.
χαρίζω present, make a gift.
χάρισμα, neut. gift.
χαριτωμένος graceful, charming.
χάρκωμα, v. χάλκωμα.
χαροκαημένος overtaken by Death (Charon).
Χάροντας, Χάρος Charon, god of death.
χαροτεντωμένος stiff in death.
χαρούμενος (from χαίρομαι) happy, joyful.
χαρτί (χαρκί, § 16, n. 2) paper.
χαρωπός joyful, happy.
χάσκας (§ 73) gaper.
χάσκω (ἐχάσκισα) open the mouth wide, gape ; (Sar. K.) see.
χασμουρειέμαι yawn.
χατζῆς pilgrim ; indecl. § 64.
χάτσιμο (Pontus) death.
χάφτω gulp down, swallow.
χάχας (§ 73) laugher.
χειλᾶς thick-lipped.
χείλι, neut. (pl. τὰ χείλια and τὰ χείλη, v. § 100) lip ; dim. χειλάκι (σειλάτσι, Cal.).
χειμῶνας winter.
χειρότερος (χερότερος) worse (§ 118).
χελιδόνι swallow ; dim. χελιδονάκι.
χελιδόνισμα, neut. swallow-song.
χελώνα turtle.
χέρι hand (χεῖρας, acc. pl., lit. form) ; dim. χεράκι.
χερότερος = χειρότερος.
χῆνα goose.

χήρα widow, *pl.* § 90; widowhood (TEXTS I. a. 9).

χηργιός widowed.

χθές=χτές.

χïτῶ (*Cap.*) run, go.

χιλιάδα thousand.

χιλιάρικος containing a thousand units.

χιλιεκατομμύριο(ν) milliard.

χίλιοι thousand; χίλια δυό, *v.* § 133, *n.* 3.

χιλιοπατημένος trodden of thousands, oft-trodden.

χιλιοπλούμπιστος decked with a thousand ornaments, very beautiful.

χιλιοτρύπητος pierced a thousand times.

χιονάτος ice-cold.

χιονερός with much snow.

χιόνι (also *pl.*) snow.

χιονίζει it snows, is snowing.

χιονισμένος snow-white.

χλιβερός=θλιβερός.

χλιμμένος=θλιμμένος.

χλιός tepid, lukewarm.

χλίψι=θλίψι.

χλωμός pale.

χλωρός green.

χνάρι=ἀχνάρι.

χνουδάτος with downy hair, soft; (of a rock) covered with a soft mantle of plants.

χνοῦδο down, fluff.

χοῖρος pig.

χολή gall, bile.

χολιάζω be angry, enraged; to be troubled.

χοντραίνω (ἐχόντρηνα) thicken, grow hard.

χοντροκοπιά roughness, vulgarity.

χοντρός (χονδρός) coarse, rough; *compar.* § 117.

χορεύτρ(ι)α dancer (*f.*).

χορεύ(γ)ω to dance.

χορός dance; στρώνω τὸ χορό lead the dance, dance.

* χορτάζω, χορταίνω (ἐχόρτασα) satiate.

χορτάρι grass, weed.

χόρτο grass.

χουμῶ rush upon.

χούσωμα (*Sar. K.*)=χρύσωμα.

χρειάζομαι (*pres. part.* χρειαζούμενος) to need, use (*w. acc.*); χρειάζεται it is necessary.

χρέος, *neut.* debt, duty.

χρήματα, *pl.* money, riches.

χριστιανικός Christian.

χριστιανός a Christian.

χρόνος year, *pl.* § 96; τοῦ χρόνου next year, in a year; μὲ χρόνους with the years, in the course of years; κακὸ χρόν(ο) νά 'χη to the devil with him.

χρουστῶ=χρωστῶ.

χρυσοβεργῆς (figure in fable) prince with the golden rod.

χρυσολάτρης slave of Mammon.

χρυσομάλλης golden-haired; *f. v.* § 114 *n.*

χρυσοπλεμένος woven with gold.

χρυσός golden.

χρυσοφωτισμένος illuminated with gold.

χρυσόφωτος shining like gold.

χρυσοψάλιδο golden shears.

χρύσωμα, *neut.* gilding (with gold).

χρῶμα, *neut.* colour.

χρωστῶ (χρουστῶ) owe.

χταπόδι=ἀχταπόδι.

χτενίζω to comb.

χτές (ἐχτές), *adv.* yesterday.

χτίζω build, found.

χτικιάζω to be *or* to make consumptive.

χτικιάρις consumptive.

χτίστης mason; *pl.* § 76.

χτυπῶ beat, knock; χτ. στὰ μάτια strike, come to notice of.

χυδαῖος dirty.

χυμός sap.

χύνω pour (out); let fall; χύνεται (of the sun) sets (TEXTS II. a. 22).

χῶμα, *neut.* ground, earth.

χωνεύω digest.

χώνω pierce, insert.

χώρα land, larger village, centre of
χωρατᾶς joke.   [a district, city.
χωρατεύω to joke.
χωράφι acre, field.
χώρια νά without (§ 282, 1).
χωριάτης peasant, boor ; pl. § 76.
χωρίζω separate.
χωριό (χωρίον, χωρκόν, § 10, n. 5)
  village.
χωρίς (also χώρ[ι]s) without (§ 167) ;
  χ. ἄλλο, χωρὶς καὶ χωρίς at all
  events, at any rate ; χ. νά without
  (with verbs, § 282, 1).
χωρισμός division, separation.
χωρῶ (ἐχώρεσα) hold, contain (of
  space).

hίτ͜ς (Pontus) by no means, absolutely not.

Ψάθα heap of straw.
ψαλίδι shears.
*ψάλλω, ψέλνω (ἔψαλα, ἐψάλθηκα
  ἐψάρθηκα) sing.
ψαλμῳδία singing of psalms.
ψάλτης singer, poet ; pl. § 76.
ψαρᾶς fisherman.
ψαρεύ(γ)ω to fish.
ψάρι fish ; dim. ψαράκι.
ψαροῦ fisherwoman.
ψάχνω (ψάχω) try, ferret out,
ψεῖρα louse.   [rummage.
ψειρίζω to louse, pick off lice.
ψέλνω=ψάλλω.
ψέμα (ψόμα), neut. lie, falsehood.
ψεματικός apparent, seeming.
*ψένω, ψήνω (ἔψησα) boil, roast.
ψέro (Otr.)=ξέρω.
ψές=ἐψές.
ψευδός lying, false.
ψεύτης liar.
ψευτιά lie.
ψεύτικος false, counterfeited.
ψευτογγάστρωμα, neut. apparent
  pregnancy.
ψευτογγαστρωμένο : κάνω τὸ ψ. become pregnant, get in the family
  way.
ψευτογραμματική pseudo - grammar,
  debased grammar.

ψευτομάθησι, f. false culture.
ψευτοσοφία conceited wisdom.
ψεύτρα liar (f.).
ψή=ψυχή.
ψηλός high.
ψῆλος, neut. (§ 100, n. 1)ₓ height.
ψήνω=ψένω.
ψηφίζω, ψηφῶ observe, esteem.
ψίκι nuptial procession.
ψιλός thin, fine.
ψίχα crumb, bit ; little piece.
ψόμα, neut.=ψέμα.
ψοφῶ (ψοφισμένος) perish, die.
ψύλλος flea.
ψυχή (ψή, Pontus, v. § 37 n.) soul.
ψυχοπαίδι adopted son.
ψυχούλα, dim. to ψυχή.
ψυχρός cold.
ψωμᾶς baker.
ψωμί bread ; βγάζω τὸ ψ. μου earn
  my bread ; dim. ψωμάκι.
ψωμοῦ female baker.

'Ωιδή ode.
ὠϊμέ, interj. ah !
ὦμος (νῶμος) shoulder.
ὥρα hour, time, o'clock ; τί ὥρα
  what o'clock is it ? ὡς στὴν ὥρα
  up to the present time ; ὥρα καλή
  formula of salutation or blessing,
  like ἡ ὥρα νὰ σ' εὕρῃ wish thee
  every happiness, good luck.
ὡραῖος, ὥριος beautiful.
ὡριοστάλαχτος dropping beautifully,
  trickling.
ὡς (1) prep. until, till (§ 166) ; ὡς
  πότε until when ? how long ? ὡς
  τόσο in the meanwhile, nevertheless ; (2) ὡς ποῦ νά, conj. until,
  as long as (§ 275) ; (3) as, as for
  example, thus also ; (4) ὡς καθώς
  when, while (temporal, § 273).
ὡσάν=σάν.
ὥστε νά until (§ 275).
ὠτίν (Pontus), neut. ear.
ὠφελεῖ (cf. φελῶ) it is useful, ad-
  vantageous.
ὤχ, interj. ah !
ὠχρός pale.

APPENDIX.

BIBLIOGRAPHY.

NOTICE should be taken of the works cited in the Foreword to the first German edition, which are not again given in this list. For a sketch of the progress made in modern Greek philology, compare the helps also cited in the same Foreword. My notices in the *Anz. der Indogerm. Forsch.* (vols. i. vi. ix. xiv. xv.) reach to the year 1902. Cf. also the reviews and items of information in the *Byzant. Zeitschr.*, edited by Krumbacher, i. and ff. (Leipzig, 1892 ff.) and E. Schwyzer, "Über die neugriech. Studien," in *Jahrb. d. Vereins schweizer. Gymnasiallehrer*, 1908.

GRAMMARS.

Those from the 16th–18th century (*cf.* the Foreword, p. xvii, on Simon Portius) are given in

Girolamo Germano, Grammaire et vocabulaire du Grec vulgaire publiés d'après l'édition de 1622 par H. Pernot. Paris, 1907.

To which are to be added :

Grammatica linguae graecae vulgaris . . . per Patrem Romanum Nicephori Thessalonicensem Macedonem. Ed. par J. Boyens. Liège, 1908. (A Grammar of the 17th century.)

Κανέλλου Σπανοῦ γραμματικὴ τῆς κοινῆς τῶν Ἑλλήνων γλώσσης . . νῦν πρῶτον ἐκδιδ. ὑπὸ Ἰ. Βασιλικοῦ. Triest, 1908. (A Grammar of the year 1749.)

Recent Grammars are :

H. Pernot, Grammaire grecque moderne. Paris, 1897.

W. Barth, Neugriech. Unterrichtsbriefe. Two parts. Leipzig, n.d.

K. Petraris, Lehrbuch der neugriech. Volks- und Umgangssprache. Heidelberg, 1903.

M. Φιλήντας, Γραμματικὴ τῆς ρωμαϊκῆς γλώσσης. αʹ. Φωνολογία. Athens, 1902 (2nd ed. 1907).

MANUALS.

J. K. Mitsotakis, Neugriech. Sprachführer. Konversationswörter-
buch. Leipzig, 1892.

A. N. Jannaris, Wie spricht man in Athen? 2nd ed. Leipzig, 1893.

M. and H. Pernot, Manuel de conversation français-grec moderne.
Paris, 1899.

LEXICA, Loan-words.

Sophocles, A Greek Lexicon of the Roman and Byzantine Periods.
New York, 1888.

Du Cange, Glossarium ad scriptores mediae at infimae latinitatis.
Lugduni, 1688.

A. da Somavera, Tesoro della lingua greca-volgare ed italiana.
Paris (Venice), 1709.

Ἀ. Κοραῆς, Ἄτακτα. 5 vols. Paris, 1828–1835.

Ἀ. Βλάχος, Λεξικὸν ἑλληνογαλλικόν. Athens, 1897.

Ἀ. Ἡπίτης, Λεξικὸν ἑλληνογαλλικὸν τῆς λαλουμένης γλώσσης.
Athens, 1908 (13 numbers, up to ζύμωσις).

R. A. Rhousopoulos, Wörterbuch der neugriech. u. deutschen
Sprache. Leipzig, 1900.

A. Jannarakis, Deutsch-neugriechisches Handwörterbuch. Hanover,
1883.

K. Dieterich, Taschenwörterbuch der neugriech. Umgangs- und
Schriftsprache. Deutsch-Neugriechisch. Berlin, 1909.

A. Buturas, Ein Kapitel der histor. Grammatik der griech. Sprache.
Über die gegenseitigen Beziehungen der griechischen und der
fremden Sprachen. Leipzig, 1910.

G. Meyer, Neugriech. Studien. II. Die slav., alb. u. rumän. Lehnwörter. III. Die lat. Lehnwörter. IV. Die roman. Lehnwörter.
S.-Ber. d. Wiener Akad., vols. 130, 5. 132, 3. 6 (1894 f.).

M. Triandaphyllidis, Die Lehnwörter der mittelgriech. Vulgär-
literatur. Strassburg, 1909.

HISTORY OF LITERATURE, TEXTS.

K. Krumbacher, Geschichte der byzant. Literatur. 2nd ed. Munich,
1897.

K. Dieterich, Geschichte der byzantin. u. neugriech. Literatur.
Leipzig, 1902.

A. Thumb, Die neugriech. Literatur. Die Kultur der Gegenwart,
i. 9 (1908), 246 ff.

K. Παλαμᾶς, Γράμματα. 2 vols. Athens, 1904.

J. Mitsotakis, Chrestomathie der neugriech. Schrift- und Umgangssprache. Stuttgart, 1895.

H. Pernot and Legrand, Chrestomathie grecque moderne. Paris, 1899.

E. Brighenti, Crestomazia neoellenica. Milan, 1908.

Δ. Π. Ταγκόπουλος, Νέα λαϊκὴ ἀνθολογία. Athens, 1899.

Texts of the Folk-literature.

Ζωγράφειος Ἀγὼν ἤτοι Μνημεῖα τῆς ἑλληνικῆς ἀρχαιότητος ζῶντα ἐν τῷ νῦν ἑλληνικῷ λαῷ, i. Constantinople, 1891.

Λαογραφία. Δελτίον τῆς ἑλληνικῆς λαογραφικῆς ἑταιρείας, i., ii. 1. Athens, 1909, 1910.

C. Fauriel, Chants populaires de la Grèce moderne. 2 vols. Paris, 1824–1825.

A. Passow, Popularia Carmina Graeciae recentioris. Leipzig, 1860.

É. Legrand, Recueil de chansons populaires grecques. Paris, 1874.

Jean Pio, Νεοελληνικὰ παραμύθια. Contes populaires grecs. Copenhagen, 1879.

Ν. Γ. Πολίτης, Μελέται ἐπὶ τοῦ βίου καὶ τῆς γλώσσης τοῦ ἑλληνικοῦ λαοῦ. Παροιμίαι. Vols. i.–iv. Athens, 1899–1902. Παραδόσεις [Legends]. Vols. i., ii. Athens, 1904.

LINGUISTIC PROBLEM.

Ψυχάρης, Τὸ ταξίδι μου. Athens, 1888. 2nd ed. 1905.

Ψυχάρης, Ῥόδα καὶ μῆλα. 5 vols. Athens, 1902–1909.

Φ. Δ. Φωτιάδης, Τὸ γλωσσικὸν ζήτημα κ' ἡ ἐκπαιδευτική μας ἀναγέννησις. Athens, 1902.

K. Krumbacher, Das Problem der neugriech. Schriftsprache. Munich, 1903.

Γ. Ν. Χατζιδάκις, Ἀπάντησις εἰς τὰ τοῦ κ. Κρουμβάχερ. Athens, 1905.

K. Brugmann, Schrift- und Volkssprache und die Sprachfrage der heutigen Griechen. Deutsche Revue, 1906, 211 ff.

A. Thumb, Zur neugriech. Sprachfrage. N. Jahrb. für das klass. Altertum. xvii. (1906) 704 ff.

G. N. Hatzidakis, La question de la langue écrite néogrecque. Athens, 1907.

Ν. Γ. Χατζιδάκις, Ἀκαδημεϊκὰ ἀναγνώσματα περὶ τοῦ γραπτοῦ ἡμῶν λόγου. Ἐπετηρὶς τοῦ Πανεπιστημίου, 1910, p. 25 ff.

M. Τριανταφυλλίδης, Ξενηλασία ἢ ἰσοτέλεια; Μελέτη περὶ τῶν ξένων λέξεων τῆς νέας ἑλληνικῆς, i. 1, 2. Athens, 1905, 1907.

DIALECTS, *Patois.*

Tozer, The Greek-speaking Population of Southern Italy. Journ. of Hell. Stud. x. (1890) 11 ff.

D. Comparetti, Saggi dei dialetti greci dell' Italia meridionale. Pisa, 1866.

G. Morosi, Studi sui dialetti greci della Terra d' Otranto. Lecce, 1870.

G. Morosi, I dialetti romaici del mandamento di Bova. Archivio glottol. ital., iv. (1874) 1 ff.

Pellegrini, Il dialetto greco-calabro di Bova. Turin, 1880.

A. Pellegrini, Nuovi saggi romaici di Terra d' Otranto. Turin, 1895.

Παπαζαφειρόπουλος, Περισυναγωγὴ γλωσσικῆς ὕλης. Patras, 1887 (Peloponnesus).

A. Thumb, Μελέτη περὶ τῆς σημερινῆς ἐν Αἰγίνῃ λαλουμένης διαλέκτου. Ἀθηνᾶ, iii. (1891) 95 ff.

Chalkiopulos, De sonorum affectionibus quae percipiuntur in dialecto neolocrica. Curtius' Studien, v. (1872) 339 ff.

Π. Ἀραβαντινός, Ἠπειρωτικὸν γλωσσάριον. Athens, 1909.

Ἀ. Τζαρτζάνος, Περὶ τῆς συγχρόνου θεσσαλικῆς διαλέκτου. Athens, 1909.

E. Μπουντώνας, Μελέτη περὶ τοῦ γλωσσικοῦ ἰδιώματος Βελβεντοῦ. Ἀρχεῖα τῆς νεωτέρας ἕλλην. γλώσσης, i. 2 (Athens, 1892).

Στ. Ψάλτης, Θρακικὰ ἢ μελέτη περὶ τοῦ γλωσσικοῦ ἰδιώματος τῆς πόλεως Σαράντα Ἐκκλησιῶν. Athens, 1905.

P. Kretschmer, Der heutige lesbische Dialekt. Vienna, 1905.

H. Pernot, Phonétique des parlers de Chios. Paris, 1907.

Πασπάτης, Χιακὸν γλωσσάριον. Athens, 1880.

Β. Φάβης, Γλωσσικαὶ ἐπιστάσεις ἀναφερόμεναι εἰς τὸ Σκύριον ἰδίωμα. Τεσσερακονταετηρὶς Κόντου (Athens, 1909), 242 ff.

A. Thumb, Beiträge zur neugriech. Dialektkunde. Der Dialekt von Amorgos. Indog. Forsch. ii. (1892) 65 ff., vii. (1896) 1 ff.

K. Dieterich, Sprache und Volksüberlieferungen der südlichen Sporaden. Vienna, 1908.

G. N. Hatzidakis, Ikarisches. Indog. Forsch. ii. (1893) 371 ff.

M. Beaudouin, Étude du dialecte chypriote moderne et médiéval. Paris, 1883.

Ἀ. Σακελλάριος Τὰ Κυπριακά. 2nd ed. 2 vols. Athens, 1890, 1891.

R. M. Dawkins, Modern Greek in Asia Minor. Journ. of Hell. Studies, xxx. (1910) 109 ff. (Summary—especially on dialect of Silli in Cappadocia.)

D. E. Oeconomides, Lautlehre des Pontischen. Leipzig, 1908 (important for material).

Π. Καρολίδης, Γλωσσάριον συγκριτικὸν ἑλληνοκαππαδοκικῶν λέξεων. Smyrna, 1885.

P. de Lagarde, Neugriechisches aus Kleinasien. Abh. d. Gött. Ges. d. Wiss., 1886 (Cappadocia).

H. Grégoire, Notes sur le dialecte de Farasha. Bull. de corr. hell. 33 (1909), 148 ff.

M. 'I. Μουσαῖος, Βατταρισμοὶ ἤτοι λεξιλόγιον τῆς Λειβησιανῆς διαλέκτου. Athens, 1884.

A. Thumb, Die ethnographische Stellung der Zakonen. Indog. Forsch. iv. (1894) 195 ff.

Deville, Étude du dialecte tzaconien. Paris, 1866.

M. Deffner, Zakonische Grammatik, i. Berlin, 1881. On which cf. the criticism of Hatzidakis, in Gött. gel. Anz., 1882, 347 ff.

HISTORY OF THE MODERN GREEK LANGUAGE.

Investigations on Special Questions of Grammar.

G. Meyer, Über die linguistische Stellung des modernen Griechisch. Essays u. Studien, i. (1885) 91 ff.

G. N. Hatzidakis, Einleitung in die neugriech. Grammatik. Leipzig, 1892.

Γ. Ν. Χατζιδάκις, Γλωσσολογικαὶ μελέται. Athens, 1901.

Γ. Ν. Χατζιδάκις, Μεσαιωνικὰ καὶ νέα Ἑλληνικά, i., ii. Athens, 1905, 1907.

Γ. Ν. Χατζιδάκις, Περὶ τῆς ἑνότητος τῆς ἑλληνικῆς γλώσσης. Ἐπετηρὶς τοῦ Ἐθν. Πανεπιστημίου, 1909, 47 ff.

K. Dieterich, Untersuchungen zur Geschichte der griechischen Sprache. Leipzig, 1898.

A. Thumb, Die griechische Sprache im Zeitalter des Hellenismus. Strassburg, 1901.

A. Thumb, Prinzipienfragen der Κοινή-Forschung. N. Jahrb. f. d. klass. Altertum. xvii. (1906) 246 ff.

J. Psichari, Essai sur le grec de la Septante. Rev. des Études juives, 1908, 161 ff.

D. C. Hesseling, De Koine en de oude dialekten van Griekenland. Versl. der Kon. Akad. Amsterdam, 1906, 133 ff.

K. Krumbacher, Beiträge zu einer Geschichte der griech. Sprache. Kuhns Zschr. f. vgl. Sprachf. xxvii. (1885) 481 ff.

J. Psichari, Études de philologie néogrecque. Paris, 1892. (A collection of works of the editor and his students.)

J. Psichari, Essais de grammaire historique néo-grecque. 2 vols. Paris, 1886, 1889.

G. Meyer, Zur neugriech. Grammatik. Analecta Graeciensia (Graz, 1893), 1 ff.

K. Foy, Lautsystem der griech. Vulgärsprache. Leipzig, 1879.

K. Dieterich, Akzent- und Bedeutungsverschiebung im Mittel- und Neugriechischen. Indog. Forsch. xvi. (1904) 1 ff.

K. Krumbacher, Ein irrationaler Spirant im Griechischen. S.-Ber. d. Münchener Akad, 1886, 359 ff.

J. Psichari, Essai de grammaire historique sur le changement de λ en ρ devant consonnes. Mém. orientaux (Paris, 1905), 291 ff.

H. Pernot, La dissimilation du σ intervocalique dans les dialectes néogrecs. Rev. des Études grecques, xviii. (1905) 153 ff.

G. Meyer, Analogiebildungen der neugriech. Deklination. Bezzenbergers Beitr. i. (1877) 227 ff.

Σ. Μενάρδος, Ἡ γενικὴ κατὰ Κυπρίους. Ἀθηνᾶ, viii. (1896) 435 ff.

Ἀ. Τζαρτζάνος, Μικρὰ συμβολὴ εἰς τὴν κλίσιν τοῦ ὀνόματος ἐν τῇ νέᾳ ἑλληνικῇ. Τεσσερακονταετηρὶς Κόντου (Athens, 1909), 217 ff. (Use of the Genitive in Thessalian.)

G. N. Hatzidakis, Zum Gebrauch der medialen Verbalformen. Indog. Forsch. xxv. (1909) 357 ff.

M. Deffner, Die Infinitive in den pontischen Dialekten. Monatsber. d. Berl. Akad., 1877, 191 ff.

K. Dieterich, Die präpositionalen Präfixe in der griech. Sprachentwicklung, i. ἀπό. Indog. Forsch. xxiv. (1909) 87 ff.

N. Dossios, Beiträge zur neugriech. Wortbildungslehre. Zürich, 1879.

G. N. Hatzidakis, Zur Wortbildungslehre des Mittel- und Neugriechischen. Byz. Zschr. ii. (1893) 235 ff.

Γ. N. Χατζιδάκις, Συμβολὴ εἰς τὴν παραγωγὴν τάξεως τινὸς λέξεων. Ἐπιστημονικὴ Ἐπετηρὶς τοῦ Ἐθν. Πανεπιστημίου, 1905–1906, p. 46 ff. (on the composition of substantives).

E. Schwyzer, Altgriechische Syntax und neugriechische. N. Jahrb. f. d. klass. Alt. 21 (1908), 498 ff.